UNIVERSITY REPRESENTATION
IN ENGLAND, 1604–1690

UNIVERSITY REPRESENTATION IN ENGLAND

1604–1690

MILLICENT BARTON REX

Preface by
Robert Livingston Schuyler

*Études présentées
à la Commission internationale
pour l'histoire
des Assemblées d'états
Volume XV*

George Allen & Unwin Ltd
RUSKIN HOUSE MUSEUM STREET LONDON

*Printed in Great Britain
in 10 pt Times Roman
by Jarrold and Sons Limited
Norwich*

TO MY MOTHER

PREFACE

Although university representation in the House of Commons was a part of the English parliamentary system for nearly three centuries and a half, it has not hitherto received thoroughgoing, or in any sense adequate, historical treatment. Now, happily, it has found its historian. Discretion warns against speaking of any contribution to our knowledge of the past as definitive, yet one is tempted to apply this adjective to the present work. To do this would not imply that Dr. Rex presents as finalities the conclusions to which judicious study of laboriously amassed evidence has led her. On the contrary, scholarly caution in the expression of opinion characterizes her writing throughout. But it would be ill gleaning after her in the field she has harvested with such care and devotion and with a knowledge of English history in general that has enabled her to see her subject in its historical context.

The author deals with her theme in much detail. This, however, is not owing to inability or disinclination on her part to take broad views. It is, rather, because she believes that historical truth emerges only from detailed investigation. She has a healthy distrust of the sweeping generalization that despises particulars and disdains illustrations. She would agree, I think, with that great medievalist, who was also a great master of detail, Thomas Frederick Tout, when he said, "To imagine the past correctly, we must picture it in its minutest details, because it is only by studying it in such a fashion that we can rightly obtain a sound conception of bygone society." The history of history is haunted by the ghosts of once confident generalities which have perished in the light of increasing factual knowledge.

In all detailed historical writing there is a danger that the author will lack perspective in the presentation of materials and that the reader will be overwhelmed by masses of uninterpreted facts—the danger that has given rise to the cliché about the trees and the forest. And the trees are often thick along the trail Miss Rex has blazed. But she is a considerate guide, and from time to time she leads us to outlooks whence we can discern with unobstructed vision the contours of the terrain we have traversed. Such are the three chapters of retrospect in which she surveys and reviews her subject as it developed during the early Stuart period, the age of the Puritan Revolution, and the generation from the Restoration through the Glorious Revolution, respectively. These are stock-taking chapters in which trends and characteristics are considered and conclusions presented.

7

The present study is, of course, only the first part of the entire history of university representation in England, for university representation lasted till 1948. It is to be hoped that Miss Rex will be able in the near future to carry the story to the end. The broad and solid foundation has been laid, and it may be safely predicted that in what remains to be done she will continue to show the thoroughness of research, the curiosity that is never satisfied with superficial explanations, the historical mindedness, and the clear and cogent style that characterize this first volume.

ROBERT LIVINGSTON SCHUYLER

ACKNOWLEDGMENTS

First and foremost I am indebted to Professor Robert L. Schuyler of Columbia University for his efforts in guiding this study through its various stages. His interest, advice, and encouragement have been of the utmost value at all times. I also want to thank Professor John Bartlett Brebner of Columbia for reading two drafts of the manuscript and giving advice and suggestions. To Professor Helen Cam of Harvard I am most grateful for the pains taken by her in reading parts of the manuscript and in making helpful suggestions and corrections. Professor Caroline Robbins of Bryn Mawr also gave assistance on numerous points and in particular was most generous in giving me the opportunity to examine a photostat copy of the privately owned Salway MS., otherwise inaccessible. The basic research covering the career of Sir Isaac Newton and the history of university representation in the eighteenth century was done in the seminar of Professor Charles Wolsey Cole, now President of Amherst, who also offered encouragement and suggestions in regard to the project as a whole. Professor J. E. Neale of the University of London, Professor Conyers Read of the University of Pennsylvania, Professor David Harris Willson of the University of Minnesota, Professor Walter Notestein of Yale and Professor Juan Beneyto of the University of Madrid, have all been most kind in answering specific inquiries. For information on the practice of university representation in America, I am indebted to Professor Samuel Eliot Morison of Harvard and Dr. Ray O. Hummel of the Virginia State Library. My attention was called to the practice of university representation in Spain by Professor Garrett Mattingly of Columbia. Other useful items of information have been contributed by Professor William A. Aiken of Lehigh University, Professor Douglas R. Lacey of the Naval Academy at Annapolis, Professor Howard V. Jones of the University of New Hampshire and Professor Antonio Marongiu of the University of Pisa. In addition, Professor Ernst Correll of the American University in Washington deserves my gratitude for the original encouragement he offered in the early stages of my work for the doctorate.

In a work such as the present study—made up as it is, a mosaic of assorted facts gathered from all manner of sources—it would not be surprising to discover that some errors still persist in spite of the most careful checking. For any such errors, I myself am responsible.

For facilitating my research and for giving permission to have photostats and microfilms made, the Archivists and the Librarians of the

9

University of Oxford and the University of Cambridge should receive my especial thanks, and I am also grateful for services rendered by the British Museum, the British Federation of University Women, and the Institute of Historical Research of the University of London. Likewise, the resources and the staffs of the New York Public Library, the Folger Library, the Library of Congress, and the Libraries of Columbia University have all been important in the gathering of information for this study. In particular, I must thank Miss Ruth Anna Fisher of the Manuscripts Division of the Library of Congress for her deciphering of a manuscript letter, as also Dr. Irene Rosenzweig of the Madeira School, Greenway, Virginia, for assistance in translating some of the more difficult Latin passages. The efforts of the research assistants in England and in the United States who have done some of the initial spadework for me at different times—Miss Margery Hollings of Charlbury, Oxfordshire, the late Miss Lucy Drucker of London, and Miss Rose Vickers of Washington, D.C.—must also not go unregarded.

Finally, I wish to express my appreciation of the grant of the Vassie James Hill Fellowship of the American Association of University Women for the year 1945-6, which enabled me to get a good start on the fundamental research for this study.

FOREWORD

Students of the British Constitution have somehow overlooked the existence of university representation as a political phenomenon, in spite of the fact that it functioned as a recognized part of the governmental structure of England for three hundred and forty-four years— from 1604 until 1948. In all this time—except for two cursory chapters in the Porritts' *Unreformed House of Commons* (Vol. I, Ch. 5; Vol. II, Ch. 49)—not a page, and scarcely even a paragraph, so far as I know, has been devoted to the subject until very recently. This neglect is not so surprising as it might at first seem, for on the whole, university representation has not had any notably significant influence upon British politics, even though the university seats have been occupied from time to time by many celebrated personages.

In the past few years, however, several writers have shown an interest in the subject. For example, an article by Michael Maclagan, Dean of Trinity College, entitled "The University Franchise", appeared in the special number of the Oxford University graduates' magazine, *Oxford*, for 1949 (pp. 13–36). Before this, there was a series of articles by T. Lloyd Humberstone in *Parliamentary Affairs* (Vol. I (1947–8), nos. 1, 2, 4) and a chapter (Ch. XII) in *The British General Election of 1945*, by R. B. McCallum and Alison Readman (1947). Most recent of all is Mr. Humberstone's fuller treatment of the subject, *University Representation*, advertised as "A Controversial Question expertly analysed" (1951).

As this caption suggests, latter-day interest in university representation seems to have been aroused by the proposals of the British Labour Party to abolish the university franchise, as inconsistent with modern democratic theory. These proposals, of course, were at last carried through in the summer of 1948, with the result that—at the present writing at least—the whole story of university representation seems finally to have passed into the realm of history.

The institution was first established in England by a royal grant of King James I. From the beginning, it was an institution peculiar to England, and in the form in which it was found there, it remained unique among the representational systems of the world, except in the few places where it was introduced in conscious imitation of the English model. Such places were Ireland, Scotland, India, and colonial Virginia —and possibly Spain and Sicily. In Ireland, Trinity College at Dublin received the right to elect members to the Irish Parliament in 1613—

11

almost as early as the privilege was given to Oxford and Cambridge —and this right of representation was carried over to the Parliament at Westminster after the Act of Union in 1800. When the Free State was created in 1922, the National University and Trinity College each sent members to the Dáil Eireann, while the University of Belfast, which had been given one seat in 1918, was still represented at Westminster. The Free State, however, unlike the rest of the British Isles, did not permit university electors to have a plural vote. A further change was introduced in the Irish constitution of 1937, when the university seats were transferred from the Dáil to the Seanad, and this is the only place in the whole world where university representation still survives today.

In India, proposals for university representation were made in the House of Commons as early as 1892 by Lord Curzon, then Under Secretary of State for India. Under the India Councils Act of 1909, the universities were among the special constituencies permitted to send representatives to the legislative council. In further development of the idea, the Government of India Act of 1919 and the Constitution of 1935 both provided for university seats in most of the provincial legislatures. The new constitution of independent republican India has abolished university representation in its original form, although the upper house of the new Parliament is to have specially appointed members chosen by the President from the world of science and letters. This is similar to the practice that obtained in Prussia and in Italy in the nineteenth century where members from the Prussian universities and the Italian Royal Academy were appointed by the Crown to the House of Peers and the Senate, respectively.

In India, where the composition of the legislature was not based primarily upon purely territorial units, but upon the existence of many varying communal groups, university representation was not an anomaly. This may also be said of the university seats in the present Irish Seanad, since other vocational interests are represented there as well. But in Virginia, as in England itself, no such scheme of government was involved, and the system was ill adapted to the existing conditions. In fact, in the beginning it was almost impossible to put the system into operation at all, since in 1693, when William and Mary College was founded, the electoral body consisted of only two professors. Controversy arose, and it was not until 1718 that a member for the college began to sit regularly in the House of Burgesses. The most distinguished of these William and Mary members was undoubtedly George Wythe, the famous law professor, under whom so many notable Virginians of the Revolutionary period were trained. Wythe represented the college in 1758–61. But by this time the experiment had nearly run its course. In 1776, when a new constitution for Virginia was drawn up, the William and Mary seat was abolished, and university representation in America came to an end. Harvard College, curiously enough, although founded some sixty years earlier than William and Mary, was never granted the privilege of having members in the General Court of Massachusetts, and, except for Dartmouth in New Hampshire (where the question was raised but no action was taken), the idea of university representation seems never to have migrated to any of the other British colonies in North America. As for the Scottish universities, they did not receive the privilege until 1868, and were deprived of it, along with the universities of England and Northern Ireland, by the Labour Party's legislation of 1948.

The question of the origins of university representation in Spain is an obscure one. There was apparently no such system involved in the earlier Cortes of the Iberian Peninsula, but after 1812, and in the Constitution of 1876 (in the Senate), the universities were allowed parliamentary seats. Whether the English influence so prominent in Spain in the nineteenth century and in the closing years of the eighteenth is accountable for this trend, is impossible to say. It seems likely, but the undeveloped state of modern Spanish history makes the matter difficult of determination. In Sicily, also, in 1812 and 1846, the abortive introduction of university representation was probably patterned on the British model.

The corporate character of university representation might lead one to suppose that the practice originated in the Middle Ages. Such a supposition would appear all the more reasonable because of the great authority possessed by the medieval universities. But, except in a very limited sense, this was not the case. In the first place, this theory does not allow for the fact that medieval representation was a duty rather than a right, and that the medieval universities were not, like the shires and boroughs, sources of revenue from which taxes were to be levied by consent. In the second place, the few instances of university representation that did appear in the Middle Ages were insufficient to provide a strong enough precedent to lead to continuous practice. Edward I and Philip the Fair (and very occasionally other French kings) are known to have summoned men from the university communities to come to Parliament, but this was done chiefly for the purpose of obtaining legal advice for the Crown, and seems to have had no influence upon later developments. On the contrary, it was not the memory of medieval practice, but the breakdown of the medieval Church and the first stirrings of modern parliamentary consciousness that seems to have precipitated the demand for university seats in England. Thus, the "twelfth-century renaissance" and the Renaissance proper—the age of Roger Bacon and that of Erasmus—both antedated the university franchise. The reasons for the first grant of representation will be discussed in detail in Chapter I. For the present, it is enough to repeat that representation was obtained by Letters Patent from King James I, and that it lasted without serious challenge—or so it would seem—until 1931, when the Labour Party made its first proposal to abolish the university seats.

As an example of functional representation, the university franchise—at least in the period covered by this study—was not particularly successful. During much of the seventeenth century, it served largely as a means of securing a number of safe seats for the Crown. Even when the university members in Parliament were called upon to act on behalf of university interests, the interests involved—often clerical concerns of limited scope—and the number of occasions when action was called for, were scarcely such as to justify the institution of university seats. Moreover, the argument that the House of Commons contained so many members who were university men that there was no need for special representatives to safeguard university interests was as valid then as in the twentieth century. Indeed, Anthony Wood and John Ayliffe, contemporary historians, regarded university representation not merely as superfluous, but as actually detrimental, since the presence of special burgesses tended to make other loyal sons less zealous in coming to the defence of their respective universities.

Another aspect of university representation that has been much debated in modern times is the question of the contribution to be made to public affairs by the trained mind. This aspect did not interest the seventeenth century. If it had, the argument could have been advanced, then as now, that the large number of university men serving for other constituencies was a sufficient guarantee that the university-trained mind would be brought to bear upon the matters dealt with by Parliament. Interest still attaches, however, to the question, how did the universities' chosen representatives acquit themselves? For this reason, one of the objects of this study has been to present the university members in action, not merely as university representatives, but also as members of Parliament in a broader sense, taking part in the great affairs of the time. Many of them were leading figures in politics; others were lesser lights, but nevertheless much engrossed in public concerns. Indeed, in the case of many members, it would be impossible to tell from the parliamentary records that they had any university interests at all. Perhaps such members had little time remaining from their general activities to spare for the needs of their constituencies, or perhaps there was really little call for any special services. At any rate, an attempt has been made here to portray the university members in all their parliamentary capacities—general as well as special—and in their obscurity or in their celebrity, as the case may be.

Another matter of interest in connection with the history of university representation is the subject of elections and election procedures. The election procedures of the universities were somewhat different from those of the boroughs and counties, and the details of various election campaigns will be presented here for the light they cast upon university procedures in particular, as well as upon the general political history of the century. Some attempt will also be made at intervals to sum up the characteristics of the university members of each period, in order to assess the nature and calibre of the personnel as a whole.

This study has been planned as an introductory volume to a further investigation of university representation. Material has already been collected in part for the eighteenth century and for the more recent years of our own time. Some of the results of research in this last field appeared in an article in the *Journal of Politics* for May 1946—"The University Constituencies in the Recent British Election"—an election which we now regard as the last election in which university representation was to have any place in the political life of the United Kingdom.

For this introductory volume, the year 1690 has been taken as a closing point, partly because the Glorious Revolution has long been a traditional landmark in English history, and partly because, in the history of university representation in particular, some slight changes in university politics seem to be discernible with the new political alignments of the Revolution Settlement.

MILLICENT BARTON REX

WASHINGTON, D.C.

NOTES ON CHRONOLOGY

The rendering of dates in English History before the adoption of the Gregorian Calendar always presents something of a problem. It will be remembered that in the Old Style the year began on 25 March, instead of 1 January, and that in the seventeenth century the difference in time amounted to ten days. Thus, in the Old Style, William and Mary were made sovereigns on 13 February 1688, while, according to modern chronology, this date would be 23 February 1689. Some of the seventeenth-century documents themselves use both systems, as 13/23 February 1688/9. This was especially true of writers who had lived abroad and were familiar with the Gregorian system.

In the present work, the Old Style is used consistently in citing the *day* of an event, but the *year* is indicated by the double form—1688/9—whenever any event falls in the period between 1 January and 25 March. For most readers, it is the year only that is significant, and for this reason an adjustment of the ten-day differential seems unnecessary, since readers who are concerned with strict accuracy can easily make their own adjustments, once they are informed that the Old Style system is maintained throughout.

One problem that still persists, however, in dealing with chronology, is the fact that the authors of secondary works, as well as editors of seventeenth-century writings, frequently fail to indicate which calendar they have adhered to. This is particularly true of the historical writers of the early nineteenth century. It is difficult, and at times probably impossible, to avoid errors, when such works are depended upon. For this reason, no attempt has been made to check on every date mentioned in this work, in cases where the date has no particular significance for the history of university representation and is only cited as a fact in general history or biography.

ABBREVIATIONS

A.O.	Wood's *Athenae Oxonienses.*
The *"Annals"*	Wood's *History and Antiquities of the University of Oxford* (ed. Gutch).
B.B.	*Biographia Britannica.*
Cat.	*Catalogue of the Harleian Manuscripts*
C.J.	*Journal of the House of Commons.*
C.S.	Camden Society.
C.S.P.	*Calendar of State Papers.*
Cal. Clar. S.P.	*Calendar of Clarendon State Papers* (Ogle and Bliss, Firth)
Clar. S.P.	*Clarendon State Papers* (Scrope and Monkhouse).
D.N.B.	*Dictionary of National Biography.*
E.H.R.	*English Historical Review.*
Fasti	Wood's *Athenae Oxonienses,* Vol. V.
G.E.C.	G. E. Cokayne (*Baronetage* and *Peerage*).
G.M.	*Gentleman's Magazine.*
H.M.C.	*Historical Manuscripts Commission Reports.*
Life and Times	*Life and Times of Anthony Wood.*
L.J.	*Journal of the House of Lords.*
Old P.H.	*The Parliamentary or Constitutional History of England.*
O.R.	*Official Return of Members of Parliament* (1878). Vol. I.
Oxfordshire	W. R. Williams, *Parliamentary History of the County of Oxford, 1213–1899.*
P.H.	*Parliamentary History* (ed. Cobbett).
Th. S.P.	*Thurloe State Papers* (ed. Birch).

CONTENTS

Preface   *Page* 7

Acknowledgments   9

Foreword   11

Note on Chronology   16

Abbreviations   17

I. *The Origins of University Representation*   21

II. *The First University Burgesses*   40

III. *Electoral Procedures in University Representation*   56

IV. *The Period of Royal Influence, 1621–1640*   97

V. *Retrospect, 1604–1640*   129

VI. *The University Representatives in the Long Parliament*   143

VII. *Decline and Revival, 1653–1660*   183

VIII. *Retrospect, 1640–1660*   211

IX. *The University Members in the Cavalier Parliament*   231

X. *The First Exclusion Parliament*   261

XI. *The Later Exclusion Parliaments, 1679–1681*   276

XII. *University Representation through Absolutism and Revolution, 1685–1690*   296

XIII. *Retrospect, 1660–1690*   326

XIV. *Conclusion*   349

Appendices   351
     I. Sir Edward Coke's Letter to the University of Cambridge
     II. James I's Letters Patent to Cambridge University (*De Burgensibus*)
     III. Cambridge Letters, 1620/1
     IV. An Account of the Election at Oxford, 1625/6
     V. Sir Robert Naunton's Absence from Parliament
     VI. Letter concerning the Candidacy of Edward Montague
     VII. The Method of Voting in the Oxford Election of 1673/4
     VIII. University Representatives, 1604–89

Glossary   373

Note on Sources   374

Bibliography   381

Index   393

Studies presented to the International Commission for the History of Representive and Parliamentary Institutions   407

CONTENTS

	Page
Preface	7
Acknowledgments	9
Foreword	11
Note on Chronology	15
Abbreviations	17
I. The Origins of University Representation	21
II. The First University Burgesses	40
III. Electoral Procedures in University Representation	56
IV. The Period of Royal Influence, 1627-1640	87
V. Interregnum, 1640-1660	127
VI. The University Representatives in the Long Parliament	143
VII. Decline and Revival, 1604-1690	183
VIII. Retrospect, 1640-1690	217
IX. The University Members in the Cavalier Parliament	231
X. The First Exclusion Parliament	261
XI. The Later Exclusion Parliaments, 1679-1681	279
XII. University Representation through Absolutism and Revolution, 1685-1690	296
XIII. Retrospect, 1640-1690	336
XIV. Conclusion	349
Appendices	351

I. An Edward III's Patent to the Chancellor of Cambridge
II. Letter of Patent from to Chancellor, University City, Burgesses
III. Oxford and Exeter Mayor
IV. An Account of the election at Oxford, 1679
V. Sir Robert Napier's Account from Sir Walter
VI. Constituencies Independent of University Members
VII. The Member for Exeter in the Oxford Election 1680(?)
VIII. University Representation, 1603-83

Glossary	357
Note on Sources	374
Bibliography	381
Index	401

Studies prepared for the International Commission for the History of Representative and Parliamentary Institutions

CHAPTER I

THE ORIGINS OF UNIVERSITY REPRESENTATION

King James I has sometimes been credited by historians with being the founder of university representation in England.[1] Careful examination of this claim, however, seems to indicate that the King had little or nothing to do with the matter beyond the actual granting of the Letters Patent that established the university seats. His interest in learning, of course, might have been a factor, in so far as it would have made him favourable to university representation, once the idea was suggested to him. Likewise, there might have been an additional argument for the universities' cause in the belief that they would offer strong support for the Crown's prerogatives and the Established Church. But so far as any direct initiative is concerned, there is no evidence—at least in any of the more obvious sources of information—that the King had any part in the original proposals for representation.

His interest in learning, on the other hand, and his recognition of the universities as institutions of learning, are common knowledge. So also, his zeal for religious conformity. The most striking example of his genuine personal concern for learning is perhaps the remark attributed to him upon the occasion of his visit to Oxford in 1605, when, after a prolonged stay in the library that may have been a little irksome to his retinue, he left at last, announcing that if he had not been born a king, he would have preferred to be a 'University-man''. [2] Besides this personal interest in the universities, he had also a very lively sense of their importance as agencies of propaganda and defenders of throne and Church, for in the early years of his reign, he insisted that university orthodoxy be maintained by demanding that all candidates for degrees —bachelors of arts no less than doctors of divinity—subscribe to the doctrines of the Anglican Church. These doctrines were presented in a form called his "three darling Articles", which comprised acceptance of the King's supremacy over the Church, the Thirty-nine Articles, and the Prayer Book. This requirement served substantially to check the Calvinistic trend that had never quite died out in the universities since the days of Leicester and Cartwright. James was also inclined to favour the universities financially, in granting them church livings confiscated from recusants.[3] But nowhere, either in his own writings or in the chronicles of any gossiping contemporary pen, is there anything that would suggest that he ever at any time planned to give the universities representation in Parliament. Nor would it seem that there was anything in his past experience that might have put such an idea in his mind. His own university of St. Andrews had no seats in the Scottish Parliament—in fact, the Scottish universities never had any seats at all until 1868—and his old tutor, the famous George Buchanan, though full of plans for the reform of the Scottish universities, seems not to have included university representation in his projected schemes.[4]

The idea of university parliamentary representation in fact seems to have stemmed from the English universities themselves in the middle years of Elizabeth's reign, long before the accession of James I. At that time it was an innovation, for never before in medieval England, in Scotland, or on the Continent, had such a system been in operation in any regular way. It is true that on several remote and isolated occasions there had been university representatives called to Parliament from the universities, both in England and France, but this practice was not continued, and on the occasions when it was introduced (notably under Edward I and Philip the Fair) it appears to have been done more for the King's benefit—to give him legal advice—than for the advantage of the universities.[5] There was also university representation of a sort in the church councils of the fifteenth century, but it is hard to find any traceable connection here with membership in the English House of Commons.[6] The exact and specific circumstances that first led to the sixteenth-century desire for university seats is probably not possible of determination.[7] A careful search among promising sixteenth-century records has brought very little specific information to light. But it is comparatively easy to point out certain general conditions that might have had a bearing on the origin of the demand.

One such condition was the breakdown of ecclesiastical supremacy, and another, the rise of the House of Commons. Both of these were, in some degree, characteristic of Elizabethan England, although, in the case of the House of Commons, the trend was not realized until the time of the Stuarts. But, even in Elizabeth's reign, the right of parliamentary representation was coming to be appreciated by men and communities, as never before. Under such circumstances, it is not surprising that the universities, deprived of the support of the universal Church, and dependent solely upon the Crown for the defence of their privileges, should seek additional security through representation in the House of Commons.

The idea of such representation may have been suggested to the universities by their close association with the borough corporations of Oxford and Cambridge. This association had never been a happy one. Privileges encroached upon, and powers exercised concurrently, had led to conflict and tumult for more than three hundred years. On the whole, the universities had come off best, but now, under the new order of things, they may have had some misgivings. V. A. Huber, the German historian of the English universities, writing in the mid-nineteenth century, is responsible for the suggestion that one cause of the demand for university representation may have been the fact that the universities felt the loss of ecclesiastical support, but he did not go as far as to indicate the boroughs as a special cause of concern. This was left to Sir Charles Mallet, in his *History of the University of Oxford*, who connected the loss of ecclesiastical status with the quarrels between the universities and the towns by remarking, "The citizens were quick to note the decline of clerical privilege." But Mallet, also, did not connect this special circumstance with the desire for representation. He was probably basing his observation merely upon a statement by Thomas Fuller, the seventeenth-century historian of Cambridge, who wrote, in reference to the reign of Edward VI:

> The townsmen of Cambridge began now to hope their time come to cast off the yoke (as they counted it) of the University, as if on the alteration of religion, the ancient privileges of scholars should be abolished under the notion of superstition . . . therefore they began their pranks. [8]

Huber may have also had this passage in mind when he made the comment upon the origin of university representation noted above, but, as the record stands, neither historian, Mallet nor Huber, went so far as specifically to combine both factors, ecclesiastical and borough, into one cause leading to a demand for university seats. Mallet, in fact, did not investigate the problem of the origins of university representation at all.

Quite a different approach to the problem of origins was made by J. Bass Mullinger in his *History of the University of Cambridge*. Ignoring all other circumstances, he stressed what he believed to be the fact that at least one of the university's attempts to gain representation stemmed from the desire of the Puritan faction to have a political base from which to resist ecclesiastical restraints exercised by the powers above. [9] This objective, if it existed, was never attained, for, as we have seen, the grant of representation was speedily followed by the imposition of James's "three darling Articles", which ensured that the universities would thereafter be predominantly Anglican. But the Puritan elements in the universities before the accession of James may well have hoped for a different result, once their interests were represented in a Parliament that was tending to become increasingly Puritan in its sympathies.

At this point a reminder as to the universities' position during the

Tudor era may not be out of place. In the time of Henry VII and Henry VIII, the universities enjoyed a period of great prosperity. These were the years of the English Renaissance, of Erasmus, Colet, and More; of the founding of the Lady Margaret and the Regius Professorships; of the patronage and leadership of Wolsey and Fisher. Then with the rift between King and Papacy, there followed an era of uncertainty. The dissolution of monasteries made the universities begin to fear for their own financial and corporate security, and the rapid succession of religious changes from Henry to Elizabeth jeopardized the status of individual masters and students. Headships of colleges, fellowships, degrees, professorships, were gained or lost as each party won ascendancy. The names of the Chancellors themselves ring out the changes of the century—Fisher, Cromwell, Somerset, Northumberland, Gardiner, Pole, Leicester, Cecil, Essex. Among these, it is striking to note that five were executed for treason.[10]

There were also the Marian exiles and the Marian martyrs—both closely connected with the universities—and in Elizabeth's reign, Thomas Cartwright and Edmund Campion, the one an ejected professor, the other, a former proctor. With all these events in succession, the universities had good reason to realize that they were living through perilous times.

Besides the political and religious turmoil, there were also other sources of stress and strain for the universities. New statutes for their government were given out from time to time by various royal hands, and cancelled and revised and given out again. There was a real need for many of these changes, since the old medieval regulations were no longer suitable for the new world, where learning was growing more secular; where Greek was challenging Latin; and where canon law was going out, and the doctrines and practices of the Reformation were replacing those of the universal Church. But also at the same time, there was much less of medieval democracy and more of Tudor absolutism in the new statutes, and they were not always received without protest.

Then, too, as noted above, the old bitterness between town and gown flared up from time to time, as, in the course of events, either side saw an opportunity to attack the other. With every new set of statutes, with every new Chancellor or Sovereign, with every new charter and bill that touched on town or university rights, old quarrels were likely to be reopened, and the battles of the Middle Ages fought over again. In the face of all this confusion, it is no wonder that the universities sought whatever security they could hope for in gaining representation in the House of Commons.

The first record of such action dates from the year 1566 when a petition for parliamentary representation was drawn up by the University of Cambridge.[11] Oxford followed four years later with a similar request, asking, according to Anthony Wood, the classic historian of the university, that leave might be obtained

> to choose against every Session of Parliament, two Burgesses of their Body to sit therein, and to be aiding and assisting to the University if need required.[12]

Wood's account of this move is given in close proximity to his remarks on the incorporation of the brewers of the City of Oxford, and it may not appear too far-fetched to suggest that there could have been some connection between the two events, when it is remembered that the university's right to regulate the sale of food and drink was one of the perennial causes of contention between the university and the city.[13] However, there were also other circumstances that may have led to the emergence of the demand for university seats, for Cambridge also was again petitioning at this time—at least, so it is surmised by Cooper in his *Annals of Cambridge*.[14]

Most notably the question of new charters of incorporation was in the air. Indeed this question may have been raised as far back as 1566, at the time of Cambridge's first petition. At least, in 1567, a conference had been held on the subject of uniting under one charter the two Cambridge corporations of town and university. Such a proposal must have been rejected with abhorrence on both sides, but the fact that it was seriously discussed at all, makes possible the assumption that from this time on the University of Cambridge, at least, was set to thinking earnestly about its status.[15] Moreover, the attempt to unite the university and the town suggests again that discord between them was a current problem of some concern. As it turned out, when the actual act of incorporation for the two universities was passed, the borough corporations were left separate, the universities were confirmed in all their privileges, and the disputes continued.

This act of incorporation occurred in 1571, one year after the agitation at Oxford described by Anthony Wood, and the Cambridge petition for parliamentary seats predicated by Cooper. But Cambridge had another source of anxiety at this time as well as the matter of its new charter. This was the question of its new statutes, much disliked and vigorously protested against, with argument and petition. Moreover, for both universities, religious conformity was an issue much to the fore. A reformation of ecclesiastical laws by the church authorities was under way without parliamentary sanction, while at the same time Elizabeth's recent excommunication had made the views of Roman

Catholics suspect, and Cartwright's ejection had disconcerted the Puritans.

All these circumstances combined may have resulted in a document that is attributed by the *Calendar of State Papers* to the year 1572. This document from Cambridge, entitled "Remembrances for the University addressed to Lord Burley", asks, among other things, for two burgesses, in terms that show the university to be clearly on the defensive:

> We also desire that the Universities may have two burgesses in Parliament which Mr. Speaker and others think requisite, as they will not always have such as your Lordship to assist them; not having any burgess in the House who can so aptly answer objections against the Universities as they that remain in them, and best know their present state.[16]

The source from which these "objections" might come—whether from the boroughs, the Crown, or the ecclesiastical authorities—is not intimated here, but one source of support for the universities' cause is named directly—"Mr. Speaker". If the *Calendar of State Papers* is correct in placing this document in 1572, then "Mr. Speaker" was Sir Robert Bell, member for Lynn, and later Chief Baron of the Exchequer. According to the *Dictionary of National Biography* and the sketches in the university registers, there is nothing to suggest that Bell had anything to do with university representation. He had, however, once been a Cambridge man and was later a Visitor for the University of Oxford, and he was much interested in the question of representation in general. This being so, when weighing the issue of non-resident burgesses for other constituencies, he may well have recommended resident burgesses for the universities.[17] On the other hand, if the document belongs to the previous year, 1571, there would also be good reason to associate the Speaker then in the chair with the idea of university representation, for the Speaker in 1571 was Sir Christopher Wray, who was largely responsible for the bill of incorporation for the University of Cambridge passed in that year.[18] Thus both Speakers were interested in the universities, and both were men of vigorous personality capable of promoting an innovation of this sort. Either one, therefore, may be the first individual person we can identify as an advocate of the idea of university representation.

What share Lord Burleigh may have had in the matter is at present impossible to say. As Chancellor of Cambridge and the Queen's principal adviser, he was appealed to in petitions, but there is nothing to show that he was at all interested in this particular cause, however much he was ready to trouble himself with other university business. His concern for the universities, and especially for Cambridge, was genuine, as is shown by the innumerable items listed in the *Calendar of State Papers*, the *Catalogue of the Lansdowne Manuscripts*, and the *Salisbury Manuscripts* (*Historical Manuscripts Commission, Appendix to the 9th Report*). Indeed, in the face of serious crises, such as those arising over Mary Queen of Scots and the Spanish Armada, it is no less than amazing to find Burleigh patiently listening to the university's pleas, and painstakingly struggling to settle controversies on relatively insignificant matters, such as court jurisdiction, forestalling, illegal arrest, the profits of the Stourbridge Fair, wine licences, and the restraint of plays and shows. Nevertheless, with all this devoted attention to university affairs, there is not one inkling, in all the mass of Burleigh correspondence and memoranda, of any idea that the universities might be granted seats in Parliament.[19]

The petition of 1572 was followed some ten years later by a series of other petitions. What precipitated these later petitions is not clear, but again in the 1580's, as in the early 1570's, religious unrest was widespread. The Jesuit activities, the arrest of Campion, the position of Mary Stuart, aroused a new wave of antagonism towards the Catholics, while Puritanism was strengthened in the universities by Walsingham's Divinity Lecture at Oxford and by the foundation of Emmanuel College at Cambridge.

The first of the new set of petitions dates from the year 1584. At Cambridge, according to J. Bass Mullinger, the university historian, it was the Puritan movement that was responsible for the petition. There, so Mullinger held, the rank and file of the younger masters wished to establish contact with the pro-Puritan House of Commons in order to protect themselves from the Anglican policies of the ecclesiastical authorities—in particular, perhaps, from Whitgift, who had just been appointed Archbishop of Canterbury—although Mullinger does not mention any names, and in fact does not give any specific evidence for his theory. Even if this is the explanation for Cambridge's action, the petition at Oxford would have to be explained somewhat differently, for there the Puritan faction already had control of the vice-chancellorship—at least in 1571 and 1572—in the person of Lawrence Humphrey, a noted Nonconformist.[20] In any case, whatever the cause, "there was great suit made" on the part of both universities, according to Anthony Wood, with appeals from Oxford directed to the Lord Chancellor (Sir Thomas Bromley, who also later became deputy Chancellor of the University in 1585, while Leicester was in the Low Countries); to the Lord Treasurer (Burleigh); to the university's Chancellor (Leicester); and to Sir Francis Knollys (member of Parliament for Oxfordshire, 1572–96, a courtier and a relative of the Queen). All of these men, for the sake of either past or present association with one or other of the two universities might have had reason to hear the universities' cause willingly, but there is no evidence that any of them took any initiative or was especially active in the matter before or after the petition, or at any time.[21]

After 1584 other motives than religious ones seem best to explain the universities' desire for parliamentary seats. The first indication of this may possibly be detected in a communication addressed to Lord Burleigh from Cambridge in 1586/7. This memorandum—"Remembrances", as it was called, petitioned for justices of the peace for the university (a request, incidentally, that had been made and supposedly granted some thirty-four years before) and went on to ask further:

> To have ij burgesses in Parlyment expedient for the necessary defence of the libertes of the Universitie, lest any thing through untru . . . or ignorance of some thinges might be enacted or pretermitted to the hinderance of the Universitie.
> The request hurtfull to none, verie beneficiall to them to grant it till ther be occasions given to the contrary.[22]

The tenor of this application, like that of 1572, emphasized the universities' need of protection—but not necessarily protection against the Church. Rather, since the request appeared in combination with a petition for justices of the peace, it seems easier to believe that the hostile forces that they feared were none other than their "insolent and malicious" neighbours, the corporation of the Town of Cambridge.[23]

There were two other petitions after this one—in 1588 and 1597—but Anthony Wood reports no details about either. The Porritts mention another petition, but they give no source for their statement, and make no comment upon it. Perhaps they refer to a document to be found in the Appendix of Gilbert Burnet's *History of the Reformation of the Church of England*, which petitions for seats in the House of Commons both for the universities and the lower clergy. Here again is found a connection between the demand for representation and the cross-currents of ecclesiastical pressure, although the towns are only mentioned incidentally, as similar to the counties in the possession of the privilege of representation. Part of the petition reads:

> Though the clergy and the universities be not the worst members of this commonwealth, yet in that respect [that is, as regards representation] they are of all other in Worst condition; for in that assembly every shire hath their knights, and every incorporate town their burgesses, only the clergy and the universities are excluded.

The wisdom and justice of this realm both intend, that no subject should be bound to that law whereunto he himself (after a sort) hath not yielded his consent; but the clergy and the universities may now be concluded [bound] by law without their consent, without their just defence; without their privity.

This petition according to the notes in Burnet's volume, was addressed first to Elizabeth, and then later presented to James I. There is no date given, but the paper must have been drawn up during the early months of James's reign, since by the time of the summoning of his first Parliament in March 1603/4, the question of university representation was no longer an issue.[24]

It is at this point that we come upon Sir Edward Coke, who suddenly stands forth as the real patron and founder of university representation —at least according to his own account, given in two letters, one addressed to Oxford and the other to Cambridge. These letters were written to inform the universities of their new privilege of representation, and to advise them concerning its exercise. The wording of the two letters is almost identical. That directed to Cambridge is reproduced in its entirety in Appendix I below, but liberal quotations from it are cited in the following paragraphs.

In view of Coke's known tendency to take liberties with the facts, the evidence of these letters should probably be accepted with caution, yet since no other sources of information on the origin of university representation appear to exist, Coke's account must assume considerable prominence. In this account we find Coke himself presented as the central figure in the story—the original initiator and moving force of the whole project, as appears from the following excerpt:

I thought good, [he wrote] out of the great duty and service I owe to our University (being one of the famous eyes of the Commonwealth) to confer with Mr. Dr. Neville Deane of Canterbury, and Sir Edward Stanhope (two worthy members thereof) that a sute were made at this time (when his Majestie, exceeding all his progenitors in learning and knowledge, so favoureth and respecteth the Universities, when our most worthie and affectionate Chancellor my Lord Cecill his Majestie's principall Secretary is so propense to further anything that may honour or profitt our University) for the obteyning of two Burgesses . . . which with all alacrity the good Deane and Sir Edward Stanhope apprehended, our Chancellor was moved, who instantly and effectually moved his Majestie, who most Princely and graciously graunted and signed yt. The booke being ready drawne and provided.

This excerpt was from his letter to Cambridge, his own Alma Mater. The letter to Oxford is substantially the same, except for the names of the personages who collaborated in the undertaking. These personages naturally were Oxford men—Sir Daniel Dunne, Dean of the Arches, who later became one of the first two burgesses elected by the university, and Lord Buckhurst, the university Chancellor, Earl of Dorset and Lord Treasurer of England.[25]

There are several points to be commented on here. One is, that some colour is given to Coke's claim to be the guiding spirit of the project by the mere fact that in these letters he particularly urged the universities to thank the personages whom he named as having contributed to the securing of the university seats—the King; the Lord Chancellor of the Realm (Sir Thomas Edgerton, recently made Lord Ellesmere); the two university Chancellors, Robert Cecil and Buckhurst; and the individual members of the two universities who had assisted in the measure—Dr. Neville, Sir Edward Stanhope, and Sir Daniel Dunne. If these personages had been as active as Coke himself, it would seem that such a reminder would have been unnecessary—although here, perhaps, some allowance may be made for Coke's general officiousness. However, there is no positive evidence in any of the accounts of the lives of these men to suggest that they had any concern for the cause of university representation. This is true even for Stanhope and Neville, who both had close university associations.[26] As regards the King himself, it was noted at the beginning of this chapter, that his contribution appears to have consisted only in a general benevolence towards the universities, and a probable willingness to comply with the proposal when the idea of representation was broached.[27] And in this connection it may be noticed that Coke in his letter said that "the book" (i.e. the Letters Patent) was ready "drawne and provided" for his Majesty to sign, indicating that someone—presumably Coke himself—had made it as easy as possible for the King to give his royal consent, with the least likelihood of postponement or reconsideration.

It is also to be noted in favour of Coke's position as guiding spirit of the move—though this is not remarked by any of the writers on this subject—that the phrasing used by Coke in the latter half of his letters is in part almost word for word that of the official Letters Patent. Such repetition would be all the more likely if the official draft had been prepared by Coke himself. At the very least, it would suggest that Coke had given the subject such close attention that the official words had become his own.

This official grant of Letters Patent is known as *De Burgensibus*. There are three versions of it, one for each of the two English universities, and one for Trinity College, the new university that had been founded in Dublin under Elizabeth. This last grant of representation made in 1613, is somewhat longer than the others, but in parts is a verbatim copy of the earlier grants.[28] The grants for Oxford and Cambridge were dated 12 March 1603—that is, in the year 1604, New Style. Many writers, in mentioning this event—even historians of the universities—fail to take the change of calendar into account, and do not note that the Letters Patent were issued only some seven days before the opening of James's first Parliament, and not in the March of the year before. 12 March 1603, in fact—that is, 1602/3—would have been before the death of Queen Elizabeth.[29]

Why it should be Coke who took such a prominent part in securing burgesses for the universities, is not entirely clear. There are, however, some general factors in his experience and in the nature of the times that help to explain his action. In the first place, he was an old Cambridge man, and had always had a high regard for the universities as "our most worthy Athens, the splendour of our Kingdome, the very eies and soules of our Kingdome".[30] In the second place, as Attorney-General, within the last six or seven years, he had handled at least one dispute involving the University and the Town of Cambridge, and thus had had his attention drawn to some of the university's problems.[31] And in the third place, there was, as he explained in his letters to the two universities, a particular difficulty regarding the universities that he had observed in former Parliaments, "and specially when I was Speaker"—that is, in 1592/3. This was that the rules and regulations established in the universities and their various colleges were of the greatest complexity, so that it was not possible, as he said, "for any one generall Lawe to fitt every particular Colledge especially when your private Statutes and Ordynances be not knowne". This circumstance made it difficult for Parliament to frame legislation for the universities without running counter to some already existing regulations. To have burgesses in Parliament ready to forestall such conflicts seemed to Coke —as it may have also seemed to that earlier Speaker, Sir Robert Bell, who is also alleged to have supported such a proposal—a necessary means of protection for the universities.

It is interesting to note that the Parliaments of the mid-century, during the drastic legislation of the Civil War and the Interregnum, encountered this very difficulty, and although the objectionable regulatory legislation was passed in spite of whatever protests the current university members may have made, it was, nevertheless, not enforced because of obstructions raised on the grounds of conflicting obligation. Considerable study has been made of the university policies of this later period; but for the time of Coke's speakership, there is nothing indicated in D'Ewes's *Journal of All the Parliaments* to show how the question of contradictory authority might have then come to Coke's attention. When Bell was Speaker, however, there were several university bills to the fore, both in the year before his speakership, and in the later sessions when he was in the chair, and although the connection is by no means obvious, there may have been something then in the course of debate on these bills that led Bell to think that special university spokesmen in the Commons would be desirable.[32]

The reasons for granting university representation given by Coke in his letters are substantially the same as those given in the Letters Patent of the King. There is the same recognition of the problem presented by the existence of the many ancient and complicated regulations, and the same emphasis upon the universities' need of protection. However, this last objective, in Coke's letters, is only implied, while in De Burgensibus it is expressly stated. The burgesses, so the grant read, were to report from time to time "to that supreme High Court of Parliament the true state of the University and its Colleges", so that no statute or act would "prejudice or injure them, generally or severally", without due opportunity for the university cause to be heard. In the petition on behalf of the clergy and the universities that had been projected shortly before the granting of De Burgensibus, there had been likewise a similar theme of protection from parliamentary action. The clergy and the universities, it was there urged, needed representation in order that "the many motions made so prejudicial to the state of being of the clergy and the universities" might be "utterly silenced or soon repressed" by the "sober and sufficient answers" of the clerical burgesses.[33]

All this emphasis upon the universities' relation to Parliament was something new in political history and in university history alike. In earlier times the regulation of university concerns had been chiefly a matter of royal or royal-ecclesiastical authority. But now, with their demands for representation, the universities were turning their attention away from the university Chancellor, from the Sovereign and their other great patrons of the Court, to the arena of Parliament. This shift is regarded by Huber in his study of the English universities as "one of the earliest symptoms of its [that is, of Parliament's] extending powers".[34]

Whether the universities themselves and their friends at this early date had any such clear idea as this of the change that was taking place in political relationships is doubtful. Whatever their conception of Parliament's power, they at least never sought a confirmation by statute of the privilege of representation, either at the time of the grant or later after the Glorious Revolution, when their other general rights and privileges were secured by new statutes of incorporation. The universities' failure to press for such confirmation is probably explained by the fact that the traditional mode of enfranchising boroughs was by royal authority, and that therefore they continued to regard the original Letters Patent as sufficient, even though the power of Parliament in other fields had been enlarged.

Coke himself made no direct observations on the question of Parliament's power. All that he noted was that many bills—"especially now of later time"—were being offered on university matters. But in any case he would have been aware that representation was now being prized for its own sake, if merely as a mark of a community's prestige, and for this reason, if for no other, the universities would have deemed themselves worthy of parliamentary seats. Moreover, whether they recognized the full significance of the situation or not, it was Parliament that they were fearful of, and it was in the House of Commons that they wished to assert their claims. The burgesses they asked for were to sit there so as "to be aiding and assisting ... if need required"; to "aptly answer objections against the Universities"; to be "expedient for the necessary defence of the libertes ... lest any thing ... be enacted ... to the hinderance of the Universitie". No pretence is made that the granting of the franchise will be beneficial to Parliament, to the King, or to the country as a whole. All that is claimed is that university representation would be "hurtfull to none".[35] This original line of argument in defence of the university franchise is, then, quite different from that of modern times, which has been based upon the supposition, not that the universities need protection, but that they have a contribution to make to public life.

In spite of all this emphasis on protection, there was no unfriendly legislation pending in any of the years when the petitions for representation were issued, so far as can be ascertained. But it is evident from repeated appeals for aid throughout this whole period, that the universities were in an anxious state. For Cambridge, this anxiety was apparently at one of its peaks in 1598, when the death of Burleigh had left the university forlorn, and it was looking hopefully towards Essex (then in high favour) as Burleigh's successor. Writing to the Vice-Chancellor, Archbishop Whitgift gave his approval of this choice, as an advantage to be secured in view of "how fewe frends the University now hath and the endeavours to infringe and break the liberties by some in place and authority". There is no hint given as to who those were "in place and authority" that were to be feared, but, since most of the court circle seem to have been well enough disposed towards the universities, it would appear that the Archbishop could rather have had in mind the town government of Cambridge and whatever supporters the town may have had in the courts of law or in the Commons. Such a supposition is made possible by the fact that of late years the conflicts between the university and the town had been increasingly sharp, and that they continued to become even more acute thereafter, during the first part of the chancellorship of Robert Cecil. If this was the trend, it would not be surprising that by 1604 at Cambridge, at least, the desire for university seats would have grown correspondingly stronger.[36]

There is, moreover, added evidence that protection, especially against the boroughs, was one of the chief motivating forces behind the drive for university representation at the time of the grant of *De Burgensibus*. This evidence is to be found in a document of which there are at least two copies, one in the Bodleian Library and the other in the Cottonian Collection. The Bodleian copy is entitled "A Demurre about the Burgesses of the Parliament for bothe the Universities", and is further labelled, "Drawen up by Sir Edw. Cooke, esq it is Reported". The document was written after the election of the new burgesses, and seems to be designed as an aid to them in defending their rights to seats, should those rights be "oppugned"—as was apparently expected. There is no record in the *Commons' Journal*, however, of any such challenge, and there is no specific indication in the "Demurre" from what direction the challenge was expected to come. Nevertheless, significantly enough, towards the end of the document there is mention made of the towns, and how

> ... commonly, the Townes are against the Universities, and ever readie to oppugne their libties: and there fore it is necessary for them [the universities] to have some, to enforme them [that is, the House of Commons], lest prejudicial action be taken against the Universities.

The rest of the argument stresses the allegedly greater antiquity of the universities over the towns; the "divers and many worthy men" from the universities, "who are well able to serve this high court"; the right of the King to grant the privilege of representation; and the need of the universities to have a voice in the Commons because of their property interests, and because of the complexity of their statutes and regulations —in this last returning again to the argument set forth at length in Coke's two letters.[37]

Besides the "Demurre", there is another piece of contemporary evidence of somewhat later date that also describes university representation as a protective measure. This is a work attributed to Sir John Glanville which treats of the electoral procedures of the English Parliament. Writing in the mid-century or earlier, and—according to report, at least—himself once elected a university member, Glanville described the practice of university representation as a means of providing representatives "to serve for those Students, who, though useful members of the community, were neither concerned in the landed nor the trading interests; and to protect in the Legislature the Rights of the Republic of Letters".[38] A present-day political scientist might not be willing to concede that "the Republic of Letters" was so completely divorced from the "landed interest" of the seventeenth century as Glanville implied, but here at least is a contemporary statement of the purpose and function of university representation, as it appeared in the abstract, to a political scholar of the time, and here we may note that, in setting the universities in a category separate from the "trading interest", Glanville was probably not unaware of the town and gown controversies that had plagued the universities for centuries.

One of Glanville's contemporaries, Sir Bulstrode Whitelocke—a man who also had close connections with the universities and who was also a student of the English constitution—seems to have held a different view of university representation from any that has so far been presented. In his study of the King's writ for summoning Parliament, there is no suggestion that the universities were given seats to protect themselves from hostile legislation, inspired perhaps by the boroughs, their enemies. On the contrary, the implication is that it was the Crown that would benefit from the system. In speaking of the enfranchisement of new boroughs, Whitelocke wrote:

> . . . these grants may be usefull to the crowne, being made to those places which have dependence on it, and are well affected to it. Such were the graunts to the two universities.[39]

As it happened, Whitelocke's interpretation was correct in the light of what actually developed in regard to university representation. Writing well along in the seventeenth century (1662?), as one who had been a member of the Parliamentarian party, he was probably more conscious of the Crown's monopoly of the university seats than was the royalist Glanville. But in 1604 it may be doubted whether such a monopoly was foreseen either by James I or by Sir Edward Coke, although from the vantage-point of later knowledge one might on first thought be inclined to believe that this indeed was the basic purpose of the grant from the beginning. Such a theory, however, does not seem very tenable, even considering Whitelocke's comment, in view of the fact that in all the documents of 1604 and before, the emphasis is put entirely on protection for the universities, and on protection in particular from the borough corporations.

When all is said, there is still much that remains obscure about the origins of university representation. Without further evidence, all conclusions must be somewhat speculative. The question of how much religious dissatisfaction had to do with the matter is particularly indefinite. The main points that seem to emerge with some clearness are that Sir Edward Coke, not James I, was the moving force in the establishment of the system, that the idea originated long before the privilege was actually granted, and that the underlying purpose was protection against unfavourable legislation. Whether or not the manœuvres of the borough governments had anything to do with the matter, is less certain, although it seems likely that such was the case.

As for protection, this end was probably obtained—at least in part—although it may be questioned whether there was ever so great a need for representation as Coke and the early petitioners thought. Anthony Wood, in fact, went so far as to declare not only that university representation was not necessary, but even that it was detrimental. Noting that at the time the privilege was granted, "it was accounted a great favor to the Universities, as to the prosecuting their affairs in Parliament", he went on to say:

> . . . yet since not, as it hath been observed by many.
> For whereas before, most of those members that had been Students in the Universities would stand up as occasion offered in behalf of their respective Mothers, now none will do that office, because it is incumbent on two, who commonly are found negligent by following their own affairs, or else not able as to their parts and understanding to undergo what their places require.[40]

A similar analysis of the results of university representation, couched in even more forcible language, with vague references to specific cases, was made by John Ayliffe in his *Antient and Present State of the University of Oxford*, published in 1714.[41] How far these estimates were correct, we will perhaps be able to consider in later chapters of this study. For the present, it will be enough to note that other historians of the universities have not so much disapproved of university representation as they have ignored it. This has been true from the time of the editor of *Notitiae Oxonienses* in 1675, who failed to include the burgesses in his list of university dignitaries—as did Ayliffe himself—down to the report of Lord Curzon in 1909, who in the course of discussing university reform, did not even mention in passing this peculiar university privilege. Most surprising of all such omissions is the failure of Andrew Clark, in his great editorial monument, *The Register of the University of Oxford*, to take any notice of the university representatives when listing the university officials and describing university procedures in regard to their elections, duties, and qualifications for office.[42]

NOTES FOR CHAPTER I

1. For example, even W. H. Hutton in his section on the universities in H. D. Traill, ed., *Social England* (New York, 1904), IV, 90; and Sir Charles Mallet, in his *History of the University of Oxford*, II, 238–9, give the impression that the initiative in granting representation came from James I. See also D. L. Keir, *The Constitutional History of Modern Britain*, p. 416, n. 3, in relation to Trinity College, Dublin.

2. James's visit to the library at Oxford is described in John B. Nichols, ed., *The Progresses of King James the First*, I, 554, n. 1. V. A. Huber, however, the German historian of the English universities, in his *English Universities*, II, pt. i, 2, does not rate James I's interest in the universities very highly: "the pedantic vanity of James I made that Royal Smatterer look upon the Universities as playthings for his hours of idleness".

3. For the "three darling Articles", see George Dyer, *Privileges*, I, 234, 347, 349, 459, 460; J. Bass Mullinger, *History of Cambridge*, II, 487–9. For the grant of church livings, see John Griffiths, *Enactments*, pp. 40–1; Dyer, I, 135; Mallet, II, 238, 239. There is some evidence, however, that the real motive force behind these grants, at least for Cambridge, was not the King, but Sir Edward Coke. James Heywood and Thomas Wright, *Cambridge University Transactions*, II, 206–7. See also Mullinger, II, 449–51, 461.

4. For Buchanan's work on university reform, see P. Hume Brown, ed., *The Vernacular Writings of George Buchanan* (Scottish Text Society), Edinburgh, 1892.

5. John Ayliffe, *Antient and Present State of the University of Oxford*, II, App. lxxxviii–ix; E. Lousse, *La Société d'Ancien Régime. Organisation et représentation corporatives*, p. 137, and esp. n. 3, p. 138.

6. In all these early cases there is also the question of whether the delegates were elected or appointed. C. H. Cooper, *Annals of Cambridge*, II, 69, states that the university delegates of 1300–1 were elected, but the extant documents do not make this point clear. (Ayliffe, *loc. cit.*) Election, however, would be good medieval corporative practice.

7. The only accounts that attempt to deal with the origins of university representation are Cooper, III, 3–4; Huber, II, pt. i, 1–4, 421; Mullinger, II, 459–60; Edward and Annie G. Porritt, *The Unreformed House of Commons*, I, 99–100; and T. Lloyd Humberstone's article in *Parliamentary Affairs*, I (1947–8), no. 1, and his subsequent book, *University Representation*, Ch. I–III, inc. Of all the accounts, Humberstone's is the most complete, though by no means definitive.

8. See Huber, II, pt. i, 3; Mallet, II, 108; Thomas Fuller, *A History of Cambridge*, pp. 240–1. For the idea that the universities needed representation to defend themselves against the boroughs, see also below, pp. 34–5.

9. Mullinger, II, 306. See below, p. 27.

10. Mallet, II, 115n.

11. Humberstone, *op. cit.*, p. 16.

12. Anthony Wood, *Annals*, ed. Gutch (1796), II, pt. i, 169.

13. See also the petition of 1597. *Ibid.*, p. 264.

14. Cooper, II, 269.

15. Dyer, I, 49; *Calendar of State Papers, Domestic, Edward VI–James I*, I (1547–80), 403. (This last item is attributed to the year 1570.) For the attitude of the town on this proposal, see Cooper, II, 292.

16. *C.S.P., Dom., Edw. VI.–Jas. I.*, VII (Addenda 1566–79), 439–40.

17. For Bell, see *D.N.B.* The debate in the House of Commons on non-resident burgesses, as reported by Sir Simonds D'Ewes, *Journal of All the Parliaments*, pp. 168–71, contains no reference to the idea of university representation.

18. *D.N.B.*

19. Burleigh's interest in the affairs of Cambridge may be studied most conveniently in the selections printed in Cooper, II, 146–592, *passim*, many of them being taken from the various volumes by John Strype.

20. For Mullinger's views, see II, 235. For Humphrey, see *D.N.B.*

21. For the petition of 1584, see Wood, Gutch, II, pt. i, 223. Biographies of Bromley, etc., may be found in the *D.N.B.*

22. In citing his reference for this item, Cooper gives Lansdowne MS., LI, f. 144, apparently an error for LI, f. 54. For the earlier petitions for justices of the peace, see Cooper, II, 63, 66. For the petition of 1586/7 for justices and burgesses, see *ibid.*, p. 435.

23. These were Vice-Chancellor Jegon's words in 1601. *C.S.P., Dom., Edw. VI– Jas. I*, VI (1601–3), 51.

24. For the petitions of 1588, etc., see Wood, Gutch, II, pt. i, 223, 264, and Porritt, I, 99; and Gilbert Burnet, *The History of the Reformation*, ed. Pocock, V, 175.

25. The extract is taken from Coke's letter to Cambridge. See Appendix I below. Coke's letter to Oxford is printed in Humberstone, pp. 21–3.

26. Stanhope was a devoted Trinity man and a later benefactor; Neville was Master of Trinity College and a former Vice-Chancellor, who had been active in the defence of the university in its quarrels with the town. For both men, see *D.N.B.*, and for Neville and the town, see Cooper, II, 559–64. If either Neville or Stanhope had been eager to urge university representation upon the King, they would each have had ample opportunity to do so before this—Stanhope, when the King was his guest *en route* to claim the throne; Neville, when he was sent to Scotland to convey the greetings of the English clergy at the time of James's accession. *Historical Manuscripts Commission, Appendix to 9th Report, Salisbury MSS.*, xv, 52. Humberstone, p. 19, lays emphasis on Robert Cecil as instrumental in obtaining the grant of parliamentary seats, but there seems to be no grounds for this assumption other than the statements made in Coke's letter.

27. Mullinger, as usual preoccupied with religious dissent, attributes the King's willingness to grant seats to the universities to their recent declarations against the Millenary Petition. Mullinger, II, 448, 459–60.

28. The Cambridge version of *De Burgensibus* is given below in Appendix II. The Oxford version, printed in translation in Humberstone, p. 25–8, is considerably longer. The Trinity College version, still longer, is in Denis C. Heron, *History of the University of Dublin*, p. 305.

29. For example, the date 1603 is cited without qualification by Cooper, III, 3; Huber, II, pt. ii, 421; Mallet, II, 238–9; Keir, p. 416, n. 3; Benjamin D. Walsh, *Historical Account of the University of Cambridge*, p. 54; Frederic A. Ogg, *European Governments and Politics* (2nd ed., New York: Macmillan, 1947), p. 144. And even by the Porritts, I, 99, and Humberstone, p. 75. On p. 88, however, Humberstone has the correct date, 1604. Dyer, I, 52, has 1602, but this must be a misprint.

30. Quoted in J. J. Smith, *A Cambridge Portfolio*, p. 223. A similar expression is in Appendix I, below, p. 351.

31. For Coke as Attorney-General, involved in university disputes, see Cooper, II, 580–1; *H.M.C., Salisbury*, IX, pp. 434–5; *C.S.P., Dom., Edward VI–Jas. I*, VI (1601–3 and Addenda), 31.

32. For Coke's letter, see below, Appendix I. For the relation between Parliament and the universities during the Civil War and Interregnum, see below, Ch. VI, pp. 166–73, p. 180, nn. 101, 102, p. 181, n. 125. For university legislation in the time of Sir Robert Bell, see *Journal of the House of Commons*, I, 91, 92, 93, 110, 111, 112.

33. Burnet, V, 175.

34. Huber, II, pt. i, 3.

35. See above, pp. 25, 26, 28, 29.

36. Whitgift's letter is in Cooper, II, 592. For the disputes with the town at this time, see Mullinger, II, 441–4. See also Coke's part in these events, n. 31, above. For an earlier complaint from Cambridge regarding the town in 1572, the year of one of the petitions, see *C.S.P., Dom., Edw. VI–Jas. I*, I (1547–80), 442.

37. The "Demurre" is printed by Humberstone, pp. 30–3. The manuscript copies are Wood MS. F 27, ff. 177–8, and Cottonian MS., Faustina C, VII, ff. 183a–6a.

38. [Sir John Glanville], *Laws concerning the Election of Members of Parliament*, p. 11. For Glanville as a possible university member, see below, Ch. VI, p. 164; Ch. VII, p. 205, n. 27.

39. Sir Bulstrode Whitelocke, *Notes upon the King's Writt*, I, 501.

40. Wood, Gutch, II, pt. i, 282. Huber differs completely from Wood on this point, but he does not give his sources. He states that at first the parliamentary franchise was not valued, but that later it was seen to be important as the House of Commons became more powerful. Huber, II, pt. i, 3.

41. *Ancient and Present State*, I, 202–3. See Ch. XIII, p. 338.

42. *Notitiae Oxonienses* (Oxford, 1675), pp. 10, 17; Ayliffe, I, 278–311; Lord Curzon, *Principles and Methods of University Reform* (Oxford, 1909); Andrew Clark, *The Register of the University of Oxford*, vols. II–IV (Oxford Historical Series, vols. X–XIV).

CHAPTER II

THE FIRST UNIVERSITY BURGESSES

Within eleven days after the granting of *De Burgensibus* four university burgesses had been elected and duly presented in the House of Commons. They were Sir Daniel Dunne and Sir Thomas Crompton from Oxford, and Dr. Henry Mountlowe and Dr. Nicholas Steward from Cambridge—all of them doctors of the civil law, two of them recently knighted, and all but one of them already established as minor personages in the administration of public affairs.[1] The choice of these men, with this particular set of qualifications, set a pattern for the traditional character of university burgesses for years to come. The burgesses of the future, like these first four members, were to be drawn largely from the country gentry; they were likely to be fellows of their colleges, and to hold degrees in the civil law; they tended to be members of the Inns of Court and office-holders under the Crown—men with judicial or diplomatic experience.[2]

The policy of choosing doctors of the civil law for university representatives stems from the advice of Sir Edward Coke given in the same letters in which he had notified the universities of their new privilege:

> That at the first Eleccion you make choice of some that are not of the Convocation House, for I have known the like to have bredd a question. And it is good, that the begynning and first season be cleere and without scruple. In respect whereof if you elect for this tyme some Professor of the Civil Lawe or any other that is not of Convocacion House, it is the surest way.[3]

This advice must have fallen upon willing ears, for it came at a time when the civil lawyers of the universities were much agitated over what they regarded as the declining state of their profession. In fact, only six to ten days before the date of Coke's letters, meetings to protest against the plight of the "civilians" had been held at both Cambridge and Oxford, and letters on the subject had been sent to various personages. The letter sent by Cambridge to the university Chancellor, Secretary Cecil, complained on behalf of the civil lawyers that the common law was "too potent for them", and asked for "room in the state for the exercise of their profession".[4] Room for a few of them, at least, was now made available through the creation of the four new university seats, and though these seats were not always occupied exclusively by civil lawyers, the civil lawyers were always well represented among university members.

40

If Coke had not spoken so strongly against the election of clergymen, it is possible that clerical burgesses, instead of lawyers, might have become traditional for the universities. The Clerical Disabilities Act of 1642 was still in the future, and although a clergyman had been disabled to sit in the Commons during Coke's speakership,[5] and the issue had been raised more than once in Elizabeth's reign, the question was still unsettled. As recently as 1601, in fact, the seat for Morpeth had been occupied by Sir Christopher Parkins, Dean of Carlisle, who occupied the same seat again in 1611.[6] This being the situation, it would have been only natural—as Gilbert Burnet's *History of the Reformation* seems to assume—for the universities to have sent doctors of divinity to represent them instead of doctors of the civil law. The universities were largely made up of clergymen, and most of their administrators were in holy orders. But Coke's stand at the start forestalled such a development, and by the time one of the universities got around to sending a clerical burgess—from Oxford in 1654—the law of 1642 was on the statute book, and the burgess was readily disqualified.[7]

In the first university election of 1604, the civil lawyers chosen, as it turned out, were all trained also in the common law. Moreover, with one exception—Dr. Henry Mountlowe—they were all men of experience and achievement, with many other qualifications for public service besides the D.C.L. degree. Only one of the four—Sir Daniel Dunne—has found his way into the *Dictionary of National Biography*, but the names of Crompton and Steward are scattered, along with Dunne's, throughout the administrative and judicial records of the realm for some twenty years before they entered Parliament as university burgesses. And even then, while they were attending sessions of Parliament as faithful university members, they were at the same time deeply involved in other matters. Sir Daniel Dunne, for example, as Dean of the Arches, was an authority on marriage law, and in addition, he was active in maritime questions, such as fishing controversies and charges of piracy. From 1608 on, he served regularly on the Admiralty Court.[8]

Though both less prominent than Dunne, Sir Thomas Crompton and Dr. Steward were similarly employed in Church and State. Steward had held an important church post as far back as 1574, when he was *Custos Spiritualis* of the diocese of Norwich at the death of the Bishop, and in 1590 was listed among "nine of the learnedest civilians" who were appointed to consider the problems of oaths in ecclesiastical courts. Crompton, also—Dunne's colleague from Oxford—was made Advocate General for Ecclesiastical Causes in 1603, and attended the Hampton Court Conference as a "Doctor of the Arches", along with Dunne and

Steward.[9] In secular administration, likewise, Steward and Crompton were familiar figures. In 1599, Steward had been made "Counsellor for the Queen's cause" (assistant to Attorney-General Coke), while Sir Thomas Crompton—referred to as "a man of great learning in the civil law"—was "King's Advocate-General of Foreign Causes" in 1603. In this capacity, in the years that followed he was busy with piracy causes and shipping disputes.[10]

There was, as it happened, a fifth university burgess in this first Parliament of King James, Dr. William Byrd—later Sir William—who succeeded to Crompton's Oxford seat, upon the latter's death in 1608.[11] Though references to Byrd are more infrequent than those to Crompton, Steward, or Dunne, it appears that he was a man of similar qualifications and interests, active in legal and ecclesiastical matters.[12] This leaves only Henry Mountlowe, of all the five university burgesses of this first Parliament, who did not participate in public affairs. From the little that can be learned about him, it seems that he was entirely occupied with his work as Professor of Law in Sir Thomas Gresham's new college in London, and never entered government service except for the years he sat in the Commons on behalf of the University of Cambridge.[13]

The careers of these first university members have been touched on in some detail in order to emphasize the extent to which most of them were involved in affairs of State. As university representatives, however, it is also important to consider what connections such men still had with their universities, and how far they may be looked upon as real representatives of the university mind and experience.

Their connections, in every instance, were rather closer than was the case with many later university burgesses of the century who were also royal officials. The men of 1604 and 1608 were all, at least, bona-fide graduates, the possessors of duly earned degrees—although none of them, at the time of his parliamentary service, was a university officer or a resident fellow. Besides their doctorates in the civil law, all five had also been either bachelors or masters. Mountlowe and Crompton held arts degrees, both B.A. and M.A., and Dunne, Byrd, and Steward, were bachelors of law before they became doctors. Dunne, in addition to his Oxford degrees, had been given a courtesy degree by Cambridge. Crompton's degrees had been obtained with some difficulty, because he had been suspected of "backwardness in religion". After a delay of some five years or more, he had finally come around to conformity, and declared himself wholeheartedly in favour of the Queen's Establishment, admitting that in the past he had not been "so well settled" as he should have been, and that his attitude at that time quite properly gave "some cause for suspicion". With this declaration, it appears that the degrees due to him were granted, and he entered soon thereafter upon a successful career among the "learnedest civilians".[14]

Besides the mere fact of their degrees, at least four of these men also had other ties to bind them to their universities. Mountlowe in particular, the most strictly academic of the five, had been scrutator, proctor, and public orator at Cambridge; and in 1599 had been proposed by the Queen to be Head of Clare College, although he was not elected. Dunne had been Principal of New Inn Hall at the time of receiving his doctorate in 1580; while Byrd had been acting Vice-Chancellor in 1591, and was considered for an office in All Souls, probably in the year following—it is not clear whether he obtained the place or not. Steward's only special connection with the university was by virtue of his legal services. All of these men, except Steward—and possibly Crompton—had been fellows of their colleges, and it is likely that Crompton also was a fellow, since he seems to have lingered on at Oxford in some capacity in the extended interval between the receipt of his master's degree and the date of his disputed D.C.L. These connections show that the first university burgesses, though not currently in residence, were men whose interests in the past had been closely bound up with their respective universities.[15]

For two of the university members elected in 1604, it was no new experience to find themselves in Parliament. Dunne and Crompton had both served in the Commons previously, Dunne in 1601, and Crompton in 1601 and 1597. But, on the whole—whether experienced in Parliament or not—the first university representatives were not particularly distinguished in the Parliament of 1604–10. Their names appear on numerous committees, and occasionally a speech by one of them is recorded in the *Journal* of the House—as, for example, one of the first speeches of the session made on the opening day by Sir Thomas Crompton on a matter of procedure—but compared with some later university members and with prominent members from other constituencies, their part is small. Even Dunne, the most conspicuous, was a distinctly minor figure.[16]

It must be remembered, however, in estimating committee service—in later Parliaments as well as in this first one—that the university members would sometimes be comprised under certain general groups of men who were called to committee work under such descriptions as "all the Civilians", "all the Lawyers of the House", "the King's Learned Counsel", etc. This means that the committee service of the university burgesses was often considerably more extensive than would seem from an estimate based solely upon the appearance of their personal names on committee lists.

Henry Mountlowe's name appears most infrequently. This is not surprising, for Mountlowe was without experience of any kind in public affairs, and a direct correlation can generally be traced between the extra-parliamentary interests of the members and the committees they served on. Thus, Sir Daniel Dunne, with his judicial and diplomatic background was appointed to committees on the Union with Scotland, the circulation of Popish books, church attendance, excommunications, marriage, foreign trade, and legal procedures, showing that his talents and experience were well recognized by the House. He was also frequently appointed to conference committees, when consultations were to be held with the Lords (nine times, as contrasted with Steward and Crompton's twice, and Mountlowe's once) and, in addition, was also named one of the commissioners appointed in May 1604 to act upon the Union with Scotland.[17]

The main business of the university members, of course, was supposed to be the defence of university interests. Among these, the related topics of education and religion in general were included, so that it is not surprising to find "the burgesses of both Universities" placed on the committee that was to consider "the Providing of a learned and godly Ministry"—although in so far as this may have been a Puritan bill, the university members would not have been in sympathy with it.[18]

There were two main issues that most concerned the universities in this first Parliament. Both of them were matters of vested interests and property rights. One was the question of pluralities of benefice, and the other, the residence of married men in colleges. The abolition of pluralities was being advocated for the purpose of securing better religious leadership in the parishes. It was largely a Puritan move, but this alone probably does not explain the universities' firm opposition to it. The accumulation of good livings was the mainstay of most university fellows and professors. Whitgift, indeed, when the issue of leases of tithes had been raised in the reign of Elizabeth, had declared that the universities could not survive without this subsidy, and he would probably have put forth the same argument in connection with plural benefices. Both Sir Thomas Crompton and Sir Daniel Dunne, even when members for other constituencies, had opposed a previous bill for abolition of pluralities, on the ground that without pluralities there would be no rewards for the more deserving clergy. When the pluralities bill was brought in in 1604, all the burgesses of the universities were placed on the committee. Their action this time is not recorded, but we may be reasonably certain that they did their best to defeat the measure, and as it dragged on through many years unsettled, it would seem that their efforts were at least partly successful.[19]

The law forbidding married men and their families to live in college buildings within the university precincts reflects an attitude surviving from the medieval tradition. The bill first appeared in June 1604, but, strangely enough, no university members were named in connection with it at that time. Upon its reappearance in January 1605/6, however, three of the four university members were appointed to the committee. About a month later, as an incident in the course of debate, a minor university crisis was produced, through the naming of Cambridge before Oxford in the wording of the bill. This occasioned, according to the *Journal*, a "great Dispute, and much Time spent in the House". In the end, however, tradition prevailed, for when it came to the question, "whether Cambridge or Oxford, first", it was, in the *Journal's* words, "Resolved with much Odds, that Oxford".[20] This victory cannot be entirely ascribed to the superior efforts of Oxford's burgesses, for on this, as on other such occasions in later years—for the issue was perennial—all the Cambridge and Oxford men in the House doubtless rallied to their respective universities, regardless of the arguments of the four burgesses, and since Oxford men were likely to be the more numerous, the Oxonians would naturally come out victorious.[21]

There were also other questions, more practical in character, in which the university members interested themselves—an exchange of land involving Trinity College, Cambridge; some business matters concerning Oriel, All Souls, and Corpus; a bill on housing directed against the subdividing of tenements and the establishments of "Victuallers" in the neighbourhood of the universities; the suppression of "tippling houses"; enclosures in Cambridgeshire and the Isle of Ely; a bill for highway repair; and a proposal for the draining of the Fens. In the latter question, the University of Cambridge was always concerned because of the interference that was offered by the drainage projects to navigation and the shipping of "sea coals".[22] All four of the university burgesses were assigned to the committee on the Trinity College land transaction, but Sir Daniel Dunne may have taken a larger part than either of the Cambridge members, since a fragment of his speech on the subject is preserved in the *Journal*. On the matter of the highway bill, also, the Cambridge representatives seem to have been somewhat inert, for there is no record of their intervention in the debate when the suggestion was made that Cambridge's name be added to that of Oxford, so as to share in the benefit of the improved roads.[23]

The issues that have thus far been mentioned as the concerns of the first university burgesses were quite typical of the issues that were to occupy their successors throughout the century—religion, property rights, precedence in the naming of the universities. But there is a second aspect of university representation that must also be considered, and it is in connection with this that the question now arises, what contribution in this, their initial term, did the first university members make to the larger issues of their day? When we examine this question, it becomes clear that here, too, the part played by the first burgesses foreshadows the part their successors were to play in the later Parliaments of the century.

It is especially interesting to consider this matter in connection with the Parliament of 1604, since this Parliament was the first in which the House of Commons began to assume that initiative so characteristic of its position in later years. To look for anything like clear-cut party lines in this period, is, of course, unhistorical, but from the little evidence that is offered in regard to the stand taken by the university representatives, it seems that they range themselves where one would expect to find them—on the side of the King and the Church as against the new trends of parliamentary independence and ecclesiastical reform. It is probably significant that not one of the four university members was appointed to the committee that drew up the famous Apology of June 1604, which pointed out to the King that the English House of Commons was possessed of ancient rights and privileges that it would be well for him to recognize.[24] After all, the members for the universities—with the exception of Mountlowe—were officers of the Crown, and their thinking over a period of time had naturally been geared to ideas of administrative, judicial, and ecclesiastical authority. Even their status as doctors of the civil law would have tended to prejudice them in favour of the royal supremacy.

In the case of Sir Daniel Dunne and Sir Thomas Crompton, this is made clear by a note in the *Salisbury Manuscripts* where a number of items are listed for discussion "this afternoon" (apparently the opening day of Parliament, 23 March 1603/4) by "all the Privy Councillors being Members of the House", who were to report on the "causes offered this day" in the Commons. Among those to be present were Dunne and Crompton, thus already recognized as adherents of the Court party, such as it was at that time. Neither Dunne nor Crompton was a Privy Councillor proper, but the scarcity of Privy Councillors in this Commons was so great that Secretary Cecil was forced to seek support for his policies from lesser personages in the royal employ.[25]

With the background of this note, we may be reasonably certain that when Sir Daniel and Sir Thomas were appointed to the committee on grievances at the beginning of the session, they were less eager to "confirm unto the Subjects of the Realm their ancient Liberties and Privileges" than to safeguard the prerogative from attack.[26] At least, most of the allusions to their activities offered by the *Journal's* record, lead to this view. One of the less obscure of the references occurs in a debate on the reform of the ecclesiastical courts. The King had proposed a conference between the House of Commons and the Convocation of the Church, and the House had rejected the proposal as without precedent. In the course of a speech in defence of the courts, Sir Thomas announced that he had already conferred on the matter with some of the bishops. This admission aroused great indignation, as a procedure entirely contrary to the recent pronouncement of the House. For a time Sir Thomas was threatened with a charge of contempt, for having consulted the bishops without authority. However, the incident passed off upon further explanations, although the impression conveyed of Crompton is that of a member who was out of sympathy with the objectives of the majority of the Commons, and lacking in respect for the traditions of secrecy and independence that were so prized at this time by those who were pressing for an enlargement of parliamentary powers.[27]

The debates on the ecclesiastical courts and related subjects also brought Sir Daniel Dunne to the notice of the *Journal*, and here he, like Crompton, also appears in the role of defender of the Establishment. One of the issues on which he spoke was that of the "silenced ministers" —those clergymen who had been deprived of their cures under the rigidly orthodox policies of Archbishop Bancroft. Here the notes of Dunne's speech seem to show him endeavouring to limit the action of the House to a "Petition of Mercy, and not to justify the Ministers: urging their wrong". Another question was that of the *ex officio* oath, which was objected to as involving self-incrimination by defendants. The gist of Dunne's speech, so far as can be ascertained from the fragmentary record, was that the grievances complained of were "no fit grievances to be presented".[28] A similar stand against reform is shown by his remarks on the commutation of royal feudal dues. The *Journal's* notes are, as usual, incoherent:

> Temerarium majestatem principis finibus includere.—Whether Regalia may pass by Contract.—Less prejudicial.—More prejudicial.—To hold, or not to hold.—The King's Plenty, his Bounty, ours.—Never Prince gave more Honours, Dignities.[29]

This may have been very well for Sir Daniel Dunne and the universities, who had all received some of these honours, but to the more restless spirits of the House, the argument may not have been so convincing.

For the other three university members—Steward, Mountlowe, and Byrd, there are no such significant speeches on record as for Dunne and Crompton. But the committees that they served on are some guide to their interests, and when we find them examining bills on excommunication, tithes, marriage, and the new church canons,[30] the presumption is strongly in favour of their supporting the side of the Church and the King, in the light of the stand taken by Dunne and Crompton, and by most of the university members in the following Parliaments. For this tendency to become apologists and defenders was a trend that grew more and more marked in the history of university representation in the years to come. It was a trend, in fact, which ultimately resulted in a general conservatism of outlook that continued throughout the eighteenth and nineteenth centuries, and in the twentieth century contributed in no small degree to the final abolition of the university franchise.

By 1610 this political position had become clearly recognized by the House of Commons. At least, it was in this session for the first time that a university representative was called upon to defend his constituents for their political views. Certain personages in both Oxford and Cambridge were reported to have made critical remarks in public against the Commons, and the House was quick to show its resentment. In retaliation, it threatened, in drawing up a tax bill, to remove the exemption from contributing to subsidies that had long been the universities' acknowledged privilege. This time it was the quiet Dr. Mountlowe who spoke—not the members who were royal officials— and he—with others, not university representatives—was able to calm the Commons' wrath "touching the Words of Scandal", and the punishment was averted. From the financial point of view, this was certainly a major service to the universities, and the most striking direct use of university representation to be found in this period.[31]

About six months later, this first Parliament in which university members participated was dissolved. To the next Parliament—the so-called "Addled Parliament"—meeting in April 1614, only one of the original burgesses was returned—Sir Daniel Dunne, now Oxford's senior burgess. His former colleague, Sir Thomas Crompton, as noted above, had died in 1608, and Dr. William Byrd, Crompton's successor, seems not to have tried for the seat again in 1614. Instead, Oxford sent Sir John Bennett, a legal officer of the Crown, already prominent in administrative and judicial posts, and a very active member in previous Parliaments, where he had sat for the Archbishop of York's pocket borough, Ripon.[32]

The election of 1614 is notable in the history of university representation for two reasons. In the first place, because it was the first election in which contests for the university seats assumed enough importance for electioneering to develop, and secondly, because it produced the first of the only two disputed parliamentary elections that ever arose in the course of university history. So far as any clear evidence goes, there had been no contests in the election of 1603/4. The procedures followed, and the reasons for the choice of the first burgesses, are both alike undetermined. Only one fact seems to emerge—that Sir Daniel Dunne very probably won his seat because he had contributed to winning the universities their franchise by his "inwarde and harty solicitations"— to use Coke's phrase.[33] But by 1614, political campaigning had begun in real earnest. At Oxford, this is suggested by the existence of one electioneering letter, the first of a long series of such letters written to influence university elections for Parliament. This letter was written by Lord Ellesmere, Chancellor of Oxford and Chancellor of the Realm, to urge the re-election of Sir Daniel Dunne, especially on the grounds of the university's due gratitude to one who had first worked to secure its enfranchisement. Ellesmere was moved to write the letter because he had heard a rumour that Dunne was to be passed over in favour of someone else. There is no clue as to who this other person was. Perhaps it was Sir John Bennett, who at that time was very popular and prominent at Oxford because of his administration of the bequest of Sir Thomas Bodley. With Bennett the university's choice—if so he was —and Dunne, the Chancellor's choice, as appears in this letter— Dr. Byrd would have stood little chance to hold his seat, and may have, for this reason, been disinclined to enter the contest. At any rate, according to the Oxford Archives, Byrd's name did not appear in the poll, and Bennett and Dunne were duly elected.[34]

At Cambridge, there was much more ado—in fact, a stormy and controversial conflict, distinguished by fraud and disorder. The details will be described in the next chapter.[35] For the present it is enough to name the two new Cambridge members, Sir Francis Bacon and Sir Miles Sandys,[36] and to indicate their contributions to the activities of the new Parliament. In passing, it is also interesting to note that both Bacon and Sandys, perhaps because of the known uncertainty of the outcome at Cambridge, had been also standing for other boroughs, but that each of them, on being presented with a choice, selected Cambridge. This may indicate that already the university seats were being looked upon as a special honour.[37]

It appears particularly fitting that the greatest intellectual of his day should occupy a university seat. With Bacon's election, for a moment, indeed, it would seem that the ideal university member is about to step upon the stage—that it was for such men as he that the university seats had been created. But this expectation is not borne out by Bacon's actual performance. For Bacon in Parliament was not Bacon the essayist, nor Bacon the scientist, nor Bacon the author of the

4

New Atlantis, but rather Bacon the Attorney-General—a King's man, playing the King's game against a confused and exasperated Commons. It is not to be denied that he played this part with a largeness of vision and a willingness to make concessions that the lesser men who later occupied his seat and played his role showed no inkling of, and if he had had his way between King and Commons, he might have laid the foundations of a more secure State and one that would have been strong enough to weather the storms of the seventeenth century more successfully than either Stuart monarchy or parliamentarian republic. But this was impossible, for with all Bacon's rationality and balance, and apparent sympathy with some of the Commons' grievances, he was not the free agent that so great an intellect should have been.[38]

The Commons were quick to sense this, and quick to challenge his right to sit, on the ground that as Attorney-General he would have a divided allegiance. This question had been raised twice before, in 1576 and 1606, but it was not until the Parliament of 1614 that the issue was settled, when the House laid down a rule that in the future no Attorney-General could be a member of the Commons. Out of their respect for Bacon as an individual, however, and because of the confidence his bearing inspired, they made an exception for the current session, and allowed his election to stand.[39] Bacon justified their respect and his own status as a man of intellect by his fair handling of the question of impositions. Even when dissension had advanced to a critical stage, he still retained the confidence of the House, as is shown by his being chosen head of one of the delegations that was to present the Commons' case to the Lords. As Bacon himself noted, in the words of the *Journal*, "Trust in his person discharged their Suspicion of his Place", and this, considering the times, was for him a real triumph.[40]

The Parliament of 1614 was not a Parliament that was much concerned with university matters, and in the one or two issues that were of this nature, there is nothing in any of the records to show that Bacon or any other university member acted as the special representative of university interests. There was little time for the consideration of such matters as college leases, or disputes over precedence in naming Oxford and Cambridge.[41] Serious constitutional issues were to the fore, feeling was high, and the life of the Parliament was correspondingly short and bitter—"factious and turbulent", as Bacon had forecast it.[42] The legality of "undertaking" and of impositions without consent of Parliament occupied the centre of the stage, and it is in the light of these considerations that we must examine the actions of the university members.

They are found present at the very opening of the session, performing their usual share of committee work. The important Committee of Privilege included three of the four university representatives—all, that is, except Bacon—as did the committee that was appointed to search for precedents on the question of seating the Attorney-General. Two other constitutional committees at the beginning of the session—one on "undertakers", and another on general grievances—contain the names of Bennett and Sandys in one case, and of all four members in the other.[43] Bennett was appointed along with Bacon to take part in a conference with the Lords on the subject of the Princess Elizabeth's marriage, and later for another conference on the subject of impositions. On this last occasion, Sir John vainly tried to get himself excused, on the ground that he had no understanding of the matter—an excuse that rings a little false in view of his reputation for ability.[44] That he was an unqualified supporter of the Crown, is indicated by a letter he wrote to Sir Dudley Carleton, then ambassador to the Low Countries, describing the opening days of this Parliament in terms that show sympathy for the King and disapproval of the critical spirit of the Commons. Except for one speech, however, and for what he may have accomplished in his committee work, where he doubtless served as a brake in the King's interest, Bennett was not particularly prominent in a Parliament where the most active members belonged to the opposition.[45] This was even more true of his colleague, Sir Daniel Dunne.

Even Bacon, who started out as a leader, became more and more silent and inactive towards the end of the session, probably because he was aware of the difficulty of his position. It was a position often to be occupied in the future by other university members who were, like Bacon, at the same time royal officers and spokesmen for the Crown. In attempting to guide an exasperated and disorderly Commons against its will, Bacon, however, never took the extreme stand that some of his successors did. Instead, he met the Commons half-way—in words, at least. For example, according to the disjointed minutes of the *Journal*, the gist of one of his speeches was: "Liketh the House's feeling of their own Power, yet proceeding with Moderation, speaking sharply, but concluding mercifully." After this he went on to admit freely that "we live not in Plato, his Commonwealth, but in Times wherein Abuses have got the upper Hand".[46] A Privy Councillor of this moderation and tact was not to be found again among the university representatives of the century, unless, perhaps, in Sir William Temple in 1679.

Nothing has so far been said about Sir Miles Sandys, the fourth of the university burgesses in this Parliament. He is barely mentioned in the *Journal*, and information about him elsewhere is equally scattered and meagre. But a certain amount of interest is attached to him, as the storm centre of Cambridge's disputed election—of which more will be told in the next chapter—and as the twin brother of Sir Edwin Sandys, the leading figure and the moving force in this obstreperous Parliament. It is quite possible that Sir Miles shared his brother's political views, and that these views may have had some bearing upon his disputed election. But quite apart from this connection, it would not be surprising to find that Sandys, as a country gentleman not dependent on the Crown, held different notions from those held by his university colleagues. If so, he would occupy a unique place in the history of university representation, as the first of the university burgesses to depart from the royalist tradition. But this is only a surmise, and cannot be established by known facts.[47]

The "Addled Parliament" of 1614 lasted only two months. Its significance for university representation rests not on any legislation that was introduced, but rather in the distinctive character of one—and perhaps two—of the university members chosen—Bacon, as the first of the university Privy Councillors, and one of the three great intellects of the century to occupy a university seat, and Sandys, as possibly the first of the university members to belong to the "Country party". In general, the actual conduct of all the university members, both in regard to their action and to their lack of action, was in keeping with the pattern for university representation that was taking shape in these first years, and maintained with notable consistency throughout the century. One element only was lacking as yet, which was to become conspicuous in the next decade—the full force of royal intervention and influence.

NOTES FOR CHAPTER II

1. For the returns of the university elections of 1603/4, see the *Official Return of Members of Parliament*, I, 445, and Harold Hulme, "Corrections and Additions to the Official Return, 1603/4", *Bulletin of the Institute of Historical Research*, I (1927–8), 99, 102. The Oxford election was held 16 March. No date is given for the election at Cambridge.

   Dunne and Crompton were among those knighted at Whitehall just before the coronation of James I. Wm. A. Shaw, *The Knights of England*, II, 114. For other biographical references to these four burgesses, see below, nn. 8–10, 13–15, inc.

2. For a discussion of the general character of the university burgesses of the seventeenth century, see below, Ch. V, VIII, XIII.

3. See Appendix I, below. One occasion that "bredd a question" was the case of Alexander Nowell in 1553. *D.N.B.* and *C.J.*, I, 27. See also below, nn. 5–7, inc.

4. For Oxford and the civil law, see Wood, Gutch, II, pt. i, 281–2. For the Cambridge letter, see *H.M.C., Salisbury*, XVI, 38–9. See also below, Ch. VII, pp. 190, 191.

5. The only evidence for this is Coke's statement in the Parliament of 1620/1. *C.J.*, ı, 513. He did not specify here who the clergyman was or what constituency he was elected for—perhaps Morpeth.

6. Parkins had previously sat for Ripon in 1597. See *D.N.B.* Thanks are due to Professor Howard V. Jones of the University of New Hampshire for calling my attention to the Parkins case.

7. For a discussion of the question of clerical burgesses in general, see Gilbert Burnet, *History of the Reformation*, ıı, 103–7; John Hatsell, *Precedents*, ıı, 12–17. Remarks in the Parliament of 1614 seem to imply that it had long been a recognized policy to exclude clergymen from the Commons. *C.J.*, ı, 460. Hatsell does not note this item in his *Precedents*, but he refers to a later case in 1620/1 (the time of Coke's remarks cited in n. 5, above), when a clergyman attempting to claim his seat was rejected. This shows that the issue was not entirely dead, even at so late a date. For Oxford's clerical burgess of 1654, see below, Ch. VII, pp. 188–9.

8. For Sir Daniel Dunne's career, see *D.N.B.*; John and J. A. Venn, *Alumni Cantabrigienses*, ıı, 75; Joseph Foster, *Alumni Oxonienses*, ı, 433. As an expert in church law, he defended the procedures of the ecclesiastical courts at the Hampton Court Conference, and was later one of the lawyers to pronounce on the Essex marriage case. Numerous references to his ecclesiastical and legal activities may be found in the volumes of *H.M.C.*, *Salisbury*; in John Strype, *John Whitgift*; and in *The Somers Tracts*, vol. ıı.

9. For Steward's ecclesiastical concerns, see Strype, *Whitgift*, ıı, 32–3, and Strype, *Matthew Parker*, ıı, 362, 398–9, 433. For Crompton's ecclesiastical concerns, see *C.S.P.*, *Dom.*, *Edw. VI–Jas. I*, vııı (1603–10), 14, and Strype, *Whitgift*, ıı, 496. For Steward, Dunne, and Crompton, at the Hampton Court Conference, see William Barlow, "Sum and Substance", *The Phoenix*, ı, 171.

10. For the administrative and judicial activities of Steward and Crompton, see *H.M.C.*, *Salisbury*, ıx, 354; xvı, 168, 244, 245; xvııı, 406; *H.M.C.*, *Cowper*, ı, 55, 60; *C.S.P.*, *Dom.*, *Edw. VII–Jas. I*, vııı (1603–10), 11, 444; xıı (Addenda 1508–1625), 509.

11. There is no record of Byrd's election in the *Official Return*. He is mentioned in Hulme, *op. cit.*, p. 102, but with no date of election. W. R. Williams, *The Parliamentary History of the County of Oxford*, p. 144, gives the date as 21 October 1609, but in the Archives of the university (Oxford University Archives, K22, ff. 40, 40d) it is recorded as 21 October 1608.

12. For Byrd's employment in the public service, see *H.M.C.*, *Buccleugh*, ı, 130, and *C.S.P.*, *Dom.*, *Edw. VI–Jas. I*, ıx (1611–18), 447, 489, 511. See also Shaw, ıı, 161.

13. Good accounts of the careers of all the first university members except Dunne are largely lacking. For Mountlowe, see Venn, ııı, 225; John Ward, *Lives of the Gresham Professors*, pp. 237–8; for Steward, Venn, ıv, 161; for Byrd and Crompton, respectively, see Foster, ı, 127, 354. Information about all these men is scattered and uncertain. The uncertainty springs from the fact that all five names are spelt in a variety of ways, Steward being sometimes "Stewart" and sometimes "Styward", while Byrd appears as "Bird", "Byrde", and "Burd", and Crompton as "Crumpton", and possibly even as "Compton". Dunne is sometimes "Dun" and sometimes "Donne". Mountlowe is the most distorted of all, the form varying from "Mowtlow" to "Mouctlow", but the name itself is more unusual than the others, and so more easily distinguished even in misspelled forms. A further difficulty arises when first names are omitted, and the matter is made still worse by the fact that there appears to have been another William Byrd, and another Thomas Crompton at this same period—perhaps even two other Thomas Cromptons, one of whom was made *Sir* Thomas four years after Oxford's Sir Thomas was knighted. One of these Cromptons seems to have been a secretary to the rebel Earl of Essex. There was also a Thomas Compton, some ten years

after the death of Sir Thomas Crompton, D.C.L., who married the mother of the Duke of Buckingham. References to all these persons are scattered in bewildering confusion through the *Calendar of State Papers*, the *Salisbury MSS.*, and Strype's *Whitgift*.

14. For Crompton's difficulties with his degrees, see Wood, Gutch, II, pt. i, 235–6; Clark, *Register*, II, pt. i, 38, 116, 157.

15. For the university connections of the first burgesses, see, in addition to the references cited in the preceding notes: Wood, Gutch, II, pt. i, 247; Strype, *Whitgift*, III, 299; Clark, II, pt. i, 120; *C.S.P., Dom., Edw. VI–Jas. I*, VI (1601–3, with Addenda, 1547–65), 295–6; *H.M.C., Salisbury*, XIV, 113. The only reference to Crompton as a fellow is found in Geo. C. Brodrick, *Memorials of Merton*, p. 68.

16. For Crompton's speech, see *C.J.*, I, 151. For speeches by Crompton and other university members, not specially cited below, see *ibid.*, pp. 179, 233 (Steward); 179, 304, 376 (Dunne); S. R. Gardiner, *History of England*, II, 77 n.

17. References to Dunne's committee service in the *Commons' Journal* are too numerous to be cited except in special connections. For his appointment as Commissioner for the Union of Scotland, and a speech on the subject, see *C.J.*, I, 208, 376.

18. For the committee on "godly Ministry" and for the fact that Dunne and Crompton spoke on this subject, see *ibid.*, pp. 231, 234.

19. For Whitgift's stand on tithes, see Mullinger, II, 450–1. See also Godfrey Davies on the necessity of pluralities (*The Early Stuarts*, p. 67). For Dunne's and Crompton's speeches against the earlier bill, see Hayward Townshend, *Historical Collections*, p. 219; Strype, *Whitgift*, II, 444. For the university burgesses on the committee on pluralities, see *C.J.*, I, 231–2, 258, 277, 347, 375, 396, 397.

20. *C.J.*, I, 275. Thomas Birch, *The Court and Times of James I*, I, 61–2, seems to be in error in placing this debate in February 1606/7 instead of 1605/6. For the university members on the committee for the bill forbidding married men in residence, see *C.J.*, I, 260.

21. This presumption is based upon the outcome of the vote in 1605/6, the fact that a hasty survey of the university men in the Long Parliament shows that Cambridge was outnumbered by Oxford in 1640, and the fact that the total electoral vote in later years was always larger at Oxford. See Ch. VIII, pp. 226–7; Ch. XIII, p. 341.

22. For the draining of the Fens, see *C.J.*, I, 207, 277, 414. It is possible that in one of these references only the burgesses of the Town of Cambridge were intended, although in later Parliaments the university burgesses were also commonly assigned to study such matters.

23. For the Trinity College land transactions, see *ibid.*, pp., 226, 234. For the bills on the various colleges, see *ibid.*, pp. 278, 286, 287, 364. For the housing bill, see *ibid.*, pp. 351, 374. For the highway bill, see *ibid.*, p. 239.

24. *Ibid.*, p. 243.

25. *H.M.C., Salisbury*, XVI, 42–3. For the scarcity of Privy Councillors in the Commons, see David Harris Willson, "The Earl of Salisbury and the 'Court' Party in Parliament, 1604–10", in *American Historical Review*, XXXVI (1931), 279–82.

26. *Ibid.*, I, 161.

27. *Ibid.*, p. 173.

28. *Ibid.*, pp. 286, 304. Besides making speeches on the ecclesiastical courts, Dunne and Crompton, as representatives of the existing system, were named to many committees on the subject of these courts. *Ibid.*, pp. 240, 291, 296, 326, 329.

29. *Ibid.*, pp. 280–1.

30. *Ibid*, pp. 205, 232, 234, 329, 424.

31. *Ibid.*, pp. 449, 450, 453. See also Sir Dudley Carleton's letter of July 1610, quoted in Fuller, *Cambridge*, pp. 300–1, n. 32; and in Cooper, III, 39–40. This letter of

Carleton's is part of an extended correspondence, largely with John Chamberlain, which provides invaluable information upon the politics of the early seventeenth century. Scattered items are to be found in various printed sources, including the *C.S.P.*, and Thomas Birch's *James I* and *Charles I*. See below, p. 51, and n. 42; Ch. IV, p. 125, n. 44.

32. For Bennett's career see *D.N.B.*; Foster, I, 106; Venn, I, 133. See also below, Ch. IV, pp. 99, 101.

33. See above, Ch. I, p. 30.

34. There is no entry in the *Official Return* for Oxford University in 1614. It is possible this absence is an indication of something controversial about the returns, even though there is no record of a contest in the Archives (Oxford University Archives, K22, ff. 139–40d). For Ellesmere's letter, see Tanner MS., 74, f. 34r.

35. See below, Ch. III, pp. 58–9, 63–5.

36. *O.R.*, p. 448. Humberstone, p. 78, incorrectly cites the date of this election as 1615.

37. For further discussion of the idea that the university seats were regarded as especially desirable, see below, Ch. VIII, p. 225; XIII, pp. 344–5. Sandys's other seat was Shaftesbury (*O.R.*, p. 448); Bacon's were Ipswich and St. Albans (*D.N.B.*; *D.N.B.*, *Errata*, p. 12).

38. For an account of Bacon in the Parliament of 1614, see James Spedding, *Letters and Life of Francis Bacon*, XI, pt. v, Ch. I, 13–30, Ch. II; David Harris Willson, *The Privy Councillors in the House of Commons*, pp. 132–5; Gardiner, *History*, II, 250–1.

39. *C.J.*, I, 456, 460; *C.S.P., Dom., Edw. VI–Jas. I*, IX (1611–18), 231. For Spedding's view of this affair, see *Bacon*, IX, pt. v, 31–3. For a contemporary account by Sir John Bennett, member for Oxford, see Add. MS., 34,179, f. 29a. For a discussion of the disabling of Attorneys-General, see Hatsell, II, 26–9.

40. Spedding, XI, pt. v, 53–4; *C.J.*, I, 481, 486–7. That Bacon himself valued the confidence of the House is shown by a letter he had written to the King in 1612. Spedding, XI, pt. iv, 280.

41. It was in this Parliament, however, in one of the perennial debates on pluralities, that the solution of the dispute over precedence was proposed by the use of the expression, "both the Universities". *C.J.*, I, 482. But this suggestion was not made by a university burgess, and the expression never became customary in this period.

42. Bacon's prediction is quoted in Willson, *op. cit.*, p. 143. A similar picture of the Parliament of 1614 is given in a letter to Sir Dudley Carleton, ambassador to the Low Countries: "Many sat there who were more fit to have been among roaring boys." Quoted in John Forster, *Sir John Eliot*, I, 241.

43. *C.J.*, I, 456, 457, 464.

44. *Ibid.*, pp. 465, 474, 481–2.

45. For Bennett's letter to Carleton, see Add. MS., 34,179, ff. 29a–30b. For Bennett's one speech, see *C.J.*, I, 479.

46. *C.J.*, I, 477.

47. The fullest accounts of Sir Miles Sandys are in Chas. H. and Thompson Cooper, *Athenae Cantabrigienses*, II, 352; Venn, IV, 19; G. E. Cokayne, *Complete Baronetage*, I, 88–9; E. P. Hunt, *Register of Merchant Taylor's School, 1561–1934* (London, 1936), vol. II. The last two accounts completely ignore Sandys's university education. The fact that there are other persons by the same name makes the search for information about Sandys difficult.

CHAPTER III

ELECTORAL PROCEDURES IN UNIVERSITY REPRESENTATION

The nature of the general government of the universities is more or less satisfactorily described in the university histories, and in such special studies of the statutes and practices as those by Gibson, Peacock, Wall, Walsh, and Griffiths. But in all these works—with the exception of one short section in Wall—no attention whatever is paid to the procedures followed in the elections of the university parliamentary burgesses.[1] The subject therefore is somewhat elusive, for the sources from which information must be drawn are none too accessible. The Porritts, in their study of the unreformed House of Commons, dismiss the matter very summarily with the remark, "The *Journals* of the House . . . may be searched in vain for information as to election usages in university constituencies."[2] It is true that if one consults the *Journal* only, very little is revealed upon the subject. From other sources, however, bits and pieces of information can be gathered and put together so as to present at least a partial picture of the proceedings that went on in connection with a university parliamentary election. For example, there are the minutes of several specific elections as recorded in the Oxford University Archives—Cambridge seems to have no such minutes of its Senate meetings—and there are a number of elections described at length in Anthony Wood's *Annals* and in his *Life and Times*. There are also two first-hand accounts of disputed elections written by the Vice-Chancellors involved, and a petition regarding one of these elections. Besides these major sources, there are a number of useful passages in various contemporary letters, diaries, and manuscripts. Then, too, the statutes of the universities governing the choice of other officials—especially the election of Chancellor—may also be taken as tentative guides in reconstructing procedures in the election of members of Parliament. Here however, much caution must be used, as usages varied considerably.

When the universities set about to put their new parliamentary franchise into effect, there were two patterns they could base their procedures upon—the method of election used in other parliamentary constituencies, and the methods of election already existing in the universities for their own officials. The grant of *De Burgensibus* itself seems to point to the first pattern, for, although it did not specifically provide for any method of election to be followed, it was couched in the terms of the usual parliamentary writs, and laid no limitations upon the choice to be made, save that it should be confined to "the more discreet and sufficient men" of the constituency, and that they should be sent at the constituency's expense in the same way ("eisdem Modo et Forma") as the representatives from the other cities, towns, etc.[3] The grant was made specifically to the "Chancellor, Masters, and Scholars" of the university, and the Sheriff's rescripts and the indentures for the elections were also so inscribed. This would suggest a free and un-trammelled election by the whole university body—though the meaning intended by the word "scholars" may present something of a puzzle, as will be seen later when the composition of the electorate is further examined.[4]

The idea of such a free and untrammelled election, however, ran counter to two powerful influences that were operating at this time. One was the tendency within the universities for the Vice-Chancellors and Heads of colleges to monopolize all possible agencies of control; the other was the interference of the Sovereign from outside—especially in the case of Charles I, who took the view that the university con-stituencies were royal pocket boroughs. The result was that when the King—or the university Chancellor on his behalf—failed to name one or more candidates, the Vice-Chancellor, in his smaller sphere, might push forward candidates of his own. In either case, whether such nominations were made by upper university circles or from outside, the electorate was likely to be deprived of the free choice of members that was implied in the terms of the Letters Patent.

The reader may need to be reminded here that the governmental pattern of the universities consisted on the one hand of a Chancellor, a Vice-Chancellor, several other officials, and an executive and judicial council made up of Heads of colleges; and on the other, of a governing body, known at Oxford as Convocation, and at Cambridge, as the Senate. The officials, including the Chancellor (though not the council), were all elected by the governing body. This body had more freedom of choice in some elections than in others. Considerable revision of the statutes of both universities had taken place in the sixteenth and seven-teenth centuries. Cambridge received a complete new set of statutes under Queen Elizabeth, but Oxford's statutes were merely revised from time to time until the chancellorship of Archbishop Laud, when an entirely new university code was established in 1636. The trend of these new statutes and revisions was definitely towards a general curtailment of university freedom. Under these circumstances, it is not surprising that a similar tendency appeared in regard to the new parliamentary franchise.

On first thought, it might be expected that appropriate legislation would have been passed at each university immediately after the grant of the parliamentary franchise, so as to set forth exactly what the electoral procedure in choosing representatives should be But no such statutes were laid down at either university, then or at a later date, and the method of election was thus left undefined. Under such circumstances the procedures of the first election of 1603/4 would have tended to set a precedent, but there is no evidence as to what those procedures were, and no clear indication indeed that there was any consideration of the question at that time. In fact, the span was so short between the grant of the franchise and the first employment of it—only four days at Oxford, and very likely the same at Cambridge[5]—that there was probably little opportunity for deliberation. Whatever method was used, it is conceivable that the idea of an alternative was largely overlooked in the excitement of using the new privilege.

In 1613/14, however, the issue was brought squarely forward at Cambridge by the Vice-Chancellor and Heads. Their object in doing this was to control the choice of burgesses so as to put two of their own number into the university seats. To bring this about more easily, they issued a decree, De modo eligendi Burgenses, in which they proclaimed that the method of election to be used would be that used for the choice of Vice-Chancellor. Now there were two election systems in use at Cambridge—that used for the election of Chancellor, and that used for the election of the Vice-Chancellor. The first method still preserved the ancient medieval tradition of complete freedom of choice, and best corresponded to the instructions laid down in King James's Letters Patent and in the writs for parliamentary election issued by the Chancery for the borough constituencies. This method of election, because of its similarity to the procedures used—or supposedly used—by the boroughs, came to be spoken of as the "borough system", or election more burgensium, in order to distinguish it from the more circumscribed system used in choosing the Vice-Chancellor. In the latter system, the Senate was offered a choice only between two candidates, both selected beforehand by the Heads of the colleges.[6] Obviously this procedure would better suit such a purpose as the Vice-Chancellor and Heads had in mind in 1613/14, and therefore this was the method which they proclaimed as legal in De modo eligendi. Their excuse for this proclamation was that there had been disceptationes at the time of the previous election—that is, when burgesses were first granted "by the indulgence, etc." of King James. If there were such disputes in 1603/4— and this decree is the only evidence for their existence—it is not unlikely that in retrospect they were exaggerated to serve the purposes of 1613/14.

De modo eligendi, however, went farther in trying to confuse the voters. The decree itself was supposedly based upon the right of the Vice-Chancellor and Heads to interpret anything in the university statutes which might seem obscure. The university franchise, however, was not part of the statutes, but a separate authority given in Letters Patent from the King, so that, strictly speaking, such an interpretation by the Heads was legally questionable. This aspect of the matter, notwithstanding, was very cleverly ignored and the emphasis was put entirely upon minor elements of timing and procedure so as to make it appear that the Heads were only bent upon full observance of all legal requirements. Apparently they hoped in this way to lead the electors to forget that there was any alternative system of election that might be just as properly used as the one decreed in this document.[7]

But the rank and file of the electors were not so easily misled. They wished to choose their burgesses by the system used for the election of the Chancellor and to be able to nominate their candidates as well as to elect them—or so we may judge by the events of the election day itself, which will be described in some detail later in this chapter.[8]

For the moment, we must follow the fate of *De modo eligendi*. Somehow an appeal must have been addressed to the university Chancellor, the Earl of Northampton, and for some reason he was readily enlisted in the electors' cause—possibly out of personal antagonism to the Vice-Chancellor and Heads, some of whom had opposed his own election two years before. Without this as a motive, it is difficult to understand how a Chancellor would have come to take the side of the rank and file of the voters. Such action was otherwise never known in the history of university representation throughout the seventeenth century. Whatever the Earl's motives, the result was that *De modo eligendi* was withdrawn after he wrote three letters to the Vice-Chancellor and insisted that parliamentary elections should be conducted *more burgensium*. His argument here was that the university should "follow the expresse words" of the charter and of the writ, and no system of their own.[9] It may be noted here, however, in reference to freedom of election, that the Letters Patent did not include the words "freely and indifferently", which were customarily part of the phraseology of the parliamentary writs, and that it may be on this ground that it seemed legal for the Heads to introduce a more restricted system of voting in the university elections. No notice of this difference in wording is taken, however, by any of the writers on this question, either in the seventeenth or eighteenth centuries, or in modern works.

In the election of 1614, then, the rank and file had their way. But this was not the end of the matter. The Cambridge Heads seem to have raised the issue again in February 1620/1. This time the election was conducted according to their wishes. Its legality, to be sure, was brought into question, but an appeal was taken to the King, who confirmed the method laid down in *De modo eligendi* as in harmony with *De Burgensibus*, and desirable in elections "for prevention of such faction and disorder as have heretofore happened herein".[10] How long this decree remained in force is not clear, but the university must have shaken it off before many years, for by 1640—and even perhaps as early as 1627/8— there was a degree of competition for the university seats that would have been impossible under the system of election prescribed in the King's ruling in 1620/1.

At Oxford the controversy about establishing electoral procedures for choosing members of Parliament seems to have taken a different form. Moreover, in general, there is less information available about procedures at Oxford than there is about procedures at Cambridge. Occasionally, mention is made at Oxford of conducting an election according to the "form of the statute", but just what statute this was, is not made clear—whether a general parliamentary statute regarding the conduct of elections, or one of the university's own regulations— probably the former. So far as is known, Oxford in the seventeenth century had no statutes governing parliamentary elections, with the exception of a section in the Laudian Code of 1636 that made provision for the method of counting votes at the time of the poll. In regard to the nomination of candidates, this code had nothing to say beyond its general pronouncement on elections—"which we wish to be free, according to the ancient custom, by the greater part of all those voting".[11]

The liberality of this electoral policy is somewhat surprising, in view of Laud's dictatorial nature. It is much to be wondered at that he did not seize the opportunity offered by the rewriting of the statutes to bring the election of parliamentary burgesses more under his control. It may be that he was a little less keenly aware of the possibilities available to him because of the fact that the code was written during the Personal Rule when Parliament and its elections presented no particular problem. Or perhaps he was already well satisfied with the results that had been obtained in the 1620's under the existing system. Certainly, both at Cambridge and at Oxford, all through the century, even when elections were *more burgensium*, influence and pressure were highly effective in filling the university seats with members more or less acceptable to the governing powers.

So far, little has been said of the nature of the bodies in which the right of election of members of Parliament was vested—the Oxford Convocation and the Cambridge Senate. In each university these bodies consisted of two main groups of electors, the regents and the non-regents.[12] Both groups were composed of masters of arts. "Regents" meant those masters who had a share in the "ruling" of the university through the delivery of lectures, the conduct of disputations, and the granting of degrees. These duties were supposedly required of all masters for a stated time—one, three, or five years—after receiving their degrees, although in practice this requirement was little enforced as the seventeenth century advanced. Correspondingly, masters from whom these services were no longer legally due were "Non-Regents", and were probably in most cases, non-residents, also.[13]

The Letters Patent, *De Burgensibus*, in granting the franchise, bestowed it upon the "Chancellor, Masters, and Scholars" of each university. This was the customary legal description of a university as a corporate body, and it was by this expression, "and by none other name or names", that each university had been recognized in the Elizabethan Statute of Incorporation.[14] In analysing this phrase, as applied to university representation, it is relatively easy to identify the persons included in the first two terms, but the third term presents some difficulty. "Masters" would include all persons holding that degree—and the Vice-Chancellor, the Heads of colleges, and the university officers would also qualify on this count—but how far did the term "scholars" extend?

One of the most satisfactory interpretations of the problem is that the expression "scholars", in formal documents of this sort, is a relic of the Middle Ages, when the scholars, as undergraduates, did actually have a share in the governing of the university. As time went on, however, this governing group of masters and scholars was gradually replaced by the more regular guild of masters, and the original participation of the scholars was forgotten.[15] This being the case, it is easy to conceive that when the university franchise was granted, the right to elect university burgesses could be considered a natural extension of the masters' right to elect all university officials, and the word "scholars" in the Letters Patent could be regarded as a mere traditional redundancy, a statement of a purely vicarious privilege, exercised by the masters alone for the whole body of scholars.[16]

There is another possible interpretation, however, that gives a more concrete meaning to the term "scholars", when used in reference to the university electorate. That is, that only certain specific scholars were included—to be precise, the bachelors. Although in arts the bachelor's degree was regarded as a mere part-way stage towards the master's degree, holders of the bachelor's degrees in other faculties—especially the bachelor's degree in divinity, to which some teaching duty was attached—were possibly thought worthy of a share in governing the university and electing parliamentary burgesses. This speculation is strengthened by the fact that mention of bachelors of divinity is to be found in several contemporary references to parliamentary elections. Such mention, nevertheless, is extremely rare.[17]

There remains the question of the doctors. They are seldom mentioned specifically as parliamentary electors, although a casual allusion to them occurs as early as 1625/6 (in the Vice-Chancellor's account of the Oxford election of that year), along with the bachelors of divinity. In *De Burgensibus* the doctors were not named as a separate group, but here, as in almost all official documents, they seem to have been always comprehended under the term "masters". The fact that they are sometimes mentioned separately springs from the circumstance that in the Middle Ages, at least at Oxford, they had originally met as a separate assembly, and voted as a unit. In the seventeenth century, in both universities, they still voted first, before the masters' votes were taken.[18]

From all this we gather that the main qualification for voting in university parliamentary elections was the possession of the doctorate, the master's degree, or the possession of an advanced baccalaureate, especially in divinity. As to social rank, nothing appears to have been done—at least in the seventeenth century—to prevent bishops and peers from voting, if they were otherwise qualified—although it would seem just as inconsistent for bishops and peers to vote for university burgesses as for them to vote for other members of the House of Commons.[19] Requirements of age or residence also mattered little. Age, indeed, presents no great problem, if it is agreed that only the masters were privileged to vote, for an analysis of the ages at which the university burgesses themselves received their M.A.'s would suggest that the voting age of the "young masters" of the seventeenth century seldom dropped below twenty-one and never below nineteen.

As to the question of residence or non-residence, although this was sometimes a bitter issue in connection with the choice of the proctors (the chief disciplinary officers of the university), it was never raised but once in connection with the election of parliamentary burgesses. On this one occasion—at the time of the Restoration—the one protest against the non-residents seems to have been made in vain.[20] In fact, in many parliamentary elections, great efforts were customarily made by interested persons to have non-resident masters return to the universities at election time so as to register their votes.[21]

The question of the qualifications required of candidates for the university seats must now be considered. Here residence—a matter of little consequence as regards the electors—occasionally became a serious issue. The original documents—Coke's letters, *De Burgensibus*, and several of the sixteenth-century petitions—all stressed the fact that the burgesses were to be *de se ipsis*, "of their own body". This was also the traditional wording of the royal writs issued for parliamentary elections. Part of the argument for university representation, indeed, had been that such burgesses would be—in the words of one of the early petitions— "they that remain in them [that is, in the universities] and best know their present state".[22] But, just as the towns had been electing non-resident burgesses for a century or more, so now also, in the case of the universities, non-resident burgesses became generally acceptable. Even at the very beginning of university representation, in the first election of 1603/4, there was no attempt made, so far as is known, to insist that the burgesses should be *de se ipsis*, in the sense of their being actually resident in the university halls. The civil lawyers chosen at that time, as pointed out in Chapter II, were all men of affairs, attached to the Inns of Court or Doctors' Commons, and active in the service of King or Church through the length and breadth of the land. They could never have been regarded as members of the university body in a narrow territorial sense—though some of them had, indeed, once been fellows or Heads of colleges, and all of them held degrees of some description.

By the election of 1614, however, the issue of non-residence was brought forward at Cambridge. This was the election already mentioned in connection with the attempt of the Cambridge college Heads to secure control of the university seats by changing the electoral system.[23] When the Heads failed in this first manœuvre, they concentrated on the question of non-residence. Neither of the representatives elected by free vote on the day of the poll was a *bona-fide* resident, or "gremial", as the expression went, while, on the contrary, both the opposing candidates were closely attached to the university—Dr. Clement Corbet, as current Vice-Chancellor and Head of Trinity Hall, and Dr. Barnaby Gooch, as Master of Magdalene and a former Vice-Chancellor. The university electorate had been all for the two outsiders, Sir Francis Bacon, the Attorney-General, and Sir Miles Sandys, a local country gentleman from the Isle of Ely. The Heads, however, were determined that Sandys, at least, should be set aside for Dr. Gooch, who stood third in the poll. Accordingly, the deputy Vice-Chancellor, Dr. John Duport, who was presiding, pronounced Sandys disqualified on grounds of non-residence, and Dr. Gooch elected instead.

This was not well received. The electors showed overwhelming enthusiasm for Sandys when they saw his seat imperilled, and there was great disorder and confusion in the Senate House. As a result of the hubbub that followed, there was uncertainty about the legality of the certificate of the election return. From the deputy Vice-Chancellor's account, it appears that Sandys (perhaps, as we have seen above, with the collusion of the university Chancellor, who may have had reasons for opposing Dr. Gooch) had secured the collaboration of the Sheriff, who accepted a somewhat dubious certificate of election for Sandys, at the same time refusing to provide the Heads with the proper papers for reporting the return of Gooch.[24] Nevertheless, the Heads stubbornly entered Gooch's name on the university rolls as burgess for 1614, and there it still stands in Tanner's *Register* today. However, it was Sandys, not Gooch, whose name appeared on the committee lists of the *Commons' Journal* in 1614, and whose name is recorded in the *Official Return* as Cambridge's second member in this Parliament.[25]

These conflicting records seem to show that the matter was never cleared up properly, perhaps because the Parliament was so short. The *Official Return* states that Sandys chose Cambridge in preference to another seat, but also notes that there was no return for Sandys from Cambridge, and that an order for a new writ for the university was issued 17 April. There is no such order mentioned in the *Commons' Journal* for 17 April, or for any other date, and no indication in the Cambridge University Archives of any other election than the one in which Gooch is named as burgess. There is likewise no statement in the *Journal* regarding Sandys's choice of seat. As we noted in Chapter II above, Sandys was present in the House, and taking part in committee work long before 17 April—indeed from the very opening day of Parliament. But there is nothing to indicate whether he was acting at this point on behalf of Cambridge, or for his other seat. As long as he was entitled to sit for Shaftesbury as well as for the university, there would be no question of his being excluded in any case. On 18 April there was a debate and a decision rendered on the election for the County of Cambridge which was also in dispute at this time. It may be, of course, that the university's election was settled at the same time even though nothing is said of it in the *Journal*.[26] Thus, the question of electing non-resident university burgesses remained open, until custom and precedent came to establish it as legal.

Sir Miles Sandys's celebrated colleague, Sir Francis Bacon, was also open to attack on grounds of non-residence, but the Heads did not raise this challenge against him. He stood at the top of the poll, and perhaps they never really expected to capture both seats, or perhaps, in the last analysis, they did not have sufficient temerity to exasperate the electorate further, or to put obstacles in the way of the King's Attorney-General. Whatever their reasons, they justified their acceptance of Bacon by the announcement that since he was master of arts and counsel to the university—a position he had held for a number of years—he might thereby "seeme after a sort to live and breath among us". As far as this first qualification went, Sir Miles Sandys was better equipped than Bacon, for Bacon's degree was only an honorary one—Bacon had once been a student, but had earned no degree, while Sandys held a *bona-fide* M.A., had once been a fellow of Queens' College, and was the son of a former Vice-Chancellor. If the case had ever come before a Committee of Privilege, Sandys would have had good grounds on which to claim his seat.

The Heads were probably aware of this. At least the document in which the deputy Vice-Chancellor, Dr. Duport, described the whole episode has a distinctly apologetic tone, as if he were trying to exonerate himself for his part in the affair. This air of uneasiness may suggest that the document was written for submission to some authority which had called him, as the presiding officer, to account for his conduct—perhaps the university Chancellor, or the King, if not a Committee of Privilege.[27]

From this time on, the issue of non-residence was never seriously raised against any candidate, although preference was frequently expressed for a burgess who was a "gremial", rather than an outsider.[28] This preference, however, was seldom gratified, particularly in the decade of the 1620's. Dr. Gooch, it is true, finally got his seat in the election of 1620/1, but with the exception of Gooch, all the burgesses up to 1625/6 were men whose primary interests centred in the royal palace, the law courts, or the council table, rather than in the colleges and schools. In 1625/6 appeared the one other lone "gremial" of this period, Dr. Thomas Eden, Master of Trinity Hall, who, when once elected, sat continuously from 1625/6 until his death in 1644.

A curious variation on this theme of non-residence is provided by the case of Sir Robert Naunton, elected by Cambridge in 1620/1. Naunton at this time, although Secretary of State, was in the royal disfavour, and feared that the King would disapprove of his accepting a seat in Parliament. In his endeavour to convince the King of his entire submission to the royal will, Naunton went so far as to disclaim membership in the university: "Yet do I not hold myself bound to admit of their choice that elected me, being now none of that body."[29] Naunton was here taking a position exactly opposite to the line of thinking that would have been followed in justification of Sir Miles Sandys's claim in 1614, for Naunton, like Sandys, was a genuine degree-holder, had formerly held university office, and had been a fellow long resident in the university. This is the only occasion in the history of university representation in the seventeenth century in which a university parliamentary candidate tried to disqualify himself on the grounds that he was no longer resident in a university.

Closely connected with the question of residence as a requirement for university representatives was the matter of degree-holding. As time went on, men began to serve as burgesses who were not only not residents, but not even masters of arts—and more surprising still, men who had never attended any university at all. It would seem inconsistent for such persons to be accepted as candidates, when they would not be eligible as electors, were it not comparable to the corresponding action of the boroughs in electing non-resident members who were not necessarily local voters. In the university constituencies, the practice of putting up candidates who were not university men was never a common one, but it did occur from time to time, more especially in the revolutionary years of the Interregnum.[30]

Generally, in cases where the candidate could not qualify in any other way as a member of the university body, the fiction of his being *de se ipsis* was kept up by the grant of courtesy degrees—"naturalization", as it was sometimes called—degrees by "creation", given voluntarily by the university, or if at the royal request, by "mandate". There was also the practice of "incorporation", whereby a student or graduate of one university was admitted to commensurate standing—*ad eundem gradum*—in the sister institution.[31]

A distinction between the privileges granted by "mandate" degrees and purely honorary degrees was introduced in a comment made by Isaac Newton in 1687, during the controversy over the granting of a degree by Cambridge to the protégé of James II, Father Alban Francis. "Mandate" degrees, according to Newton, gave the holders all the rights of a university graduate, including the right to vote for burgesses, while honorary degrees, such as those given to visiting foreign celebrities, did not carry this right. In mentioning honorary degrees, Newton did not use the term "created", and perhaps did not intend to include in this second category those holders of honorary degrees who were not visiting foreigners, but English subjects and former students of the university.[32]

Such was the status of Sir Francis Bacon, the first university burgess who was not a regular degree-holder. He had received a "created" M.A. some years before he became a candidate for the university seat, but in 1614 this degree alone seems to have been held scarcely sufficient grounds to qualify him as burgess, for the deputy Vice-Chancellor, in justifying his election, also emphasized the fact that Bacon was at the same time official counsel to the university. This emphasis on the office of counsel, however, as we noted above, was probably introduced in order to present Bacon's claims in a stronger light than those of

Sir Miles Sandys. After Bacon's time, both "created" degrees and regular degrees were routinely accepted as suitable evidence of membership in the university body.

There were other disqualifications for university burgess that were maintained more consistently than those connected with residence and degree-holding. These other disqualifications had both been laid down by Coke in his original letter of advice. One was that the Vice-Chancellor should never be eligible for a university seat, and the other, that no clergyman should be chosen. The first was certainly sound good sense, in view of the great powers already exercised by the Vice-Chancellor while in office. On only two occasions throughout the entire seventeenth century was this rule set aside, and on both these occasions the Vice-Chancellor-candidate failed to obtain his seat. The first occasion was the Cambridge election of 1614, just described, when one of the two Heads running for Parliament, was Dr. Corbet, the Vice-Chancellor, who came out at the foot of the poll. The other occasion was in 1654, when the Vice-Chancellor, Dr. John Owen, was elected at Oxford. By Coke's standards, Owen was doubly disqualified, for he was not only Vice-Chancellor, but a clergyman, just recently created D.D. On this second count, he was undoubtedly ineligible under the Clerical Disabilities Act of 1642, and accordingly the House refused to seat him. This is the only instance in the history of university representation when a clergyman was chosen for Parliament.[33]

The remainder of this chapter will be largely devoted to the details surrounding the actual process of voting in university parliamentary elections. One of the first matters to consider is the fixing of the day of the poll. At Cambridge the election was called within fourteen days after the Sheriff had delivered the rescript. In 1603/4 it must have been held sooner, for only a week intervened between the date of Coke's letter and the official opening of Parliament. The Letters Patent had mentioned no time limit, but the fourteen-day period came to be observed at Cambridge apparently because this was the interval set by the university statutes in connection with the election of the Chancellor. It was perhaps first observed in 1614, when a more or less unnecessary emphasis was laid upon it by the Heads in their decree, *De modo eligendi*. It was still insisted upon in the royal letter of 1621, but sometime between that date and the end of the eighteenth century, a new interval had been established—eight days, with at least four days' notice of the election. By the twentieth century, the eight days had been reduced to six. In seventeenth-century Oxford there was apparently less emphasis upon this matter, for no mention of any specified interval has come to light. According to the Laudian Statutes of 1636, the election of the Chancellor was to be held "as soon as conveniently possible", and this may have been the policy also adopted at that time for the choice of parliamentary burgesses. Later, as at Cambridge, the eight-day and the six-day interval was observed in accordance with parliamentary statutes.[34]

The universities received their rescripts for the election from the Sheriff and returned their indentures to him, in accordance with the practice followed by the boroughs. In the first election of 1603/4, however, the writs seem to have been delivered directly to the universities along with the Letters Patent, and Sir Edward Coke, in his instructions, specified that the Vice-Chancellor after the election should "certifie the same to the Sheriffe, and he shall retorne them", or else that the returns might be sent to Coke himself under the Vice-Chancellor's seal, and he would in turn deliver them to the Chancery. The universities did not choose to take advantage of this special privilege, but returned their results in the customary manner to the Sheriff. This became a precedent for their later practice. There is, however, a puzzling remark on this subject entered in Pym's parliamentary diary in the course of a debate in the Parliament of 1620/1. Here it is noted that "to the Universitie of Oxford and the Cinque Ports the Summons was browght but not by way of the Sherriffe". Despite this statement, the Oxford Archives offer no evidence of any other method of procedure than the usual one[35].

In two cases, at least, the question of the proper certification of the indenture arose. One was in the disputed election at Cambridge in 1614, and the other at Oxford in 1625/6. Certification was made by the signature of the Vice-Chancellor as returning officer, with the university seal affixed, and the names of the two proctors and several of the electors subscribed. Just who these electors were, or how they were selected, does not appear. Possibly they could have been members of the "Caput" or Council. In the minutes of the Oxford election of 1673/4, these persons were merely described as "about six Doctors and as many Masters". In 1614 the Sandys party at Cambridge had got possession of the proper form for certification, and had it signed by a more or less unauthorized assemblage of electors who had stolen the ballots and adjourned to King's College *en masse*—"in great heapes", to use the words of the deputy Vice-Chancellor, who went on to explain how he himself could

> . . . obtain by noe meanes possible either the Shreiffe [*sic*] or his Depute to come to him & joyn to certify (as by Lawe he is bound) . . . Soe . . . he [the Vice-Chancellor] was inforced to certifie in such manner as he could not in such as he would.

At Oxford in 1625/6, the Vice-Chancellor was accused of certifying to a return rejected by the Convocation, and not using the university seal. In both cases, the irregular certification was the result of an attempt on the part of the Vice-Chancellor to substitute a candidate of his own choice for the candidate preferred by the electorate.[36]

To carry out a parliamentary election, the Vice-Chancellor summoned the university body to meet—in a Convocation, as it was called at Oxford; in the Senate, at Cambridge. In the seventeenth century, there was a fixed place of assembly in both universities. At Cambridge, the Senate met in the "new Chapel", over the Divinity Schools, now part of the Library. By the eighteenth century, there was a separate building for the Senate, the Senate House. At Oxford, Convocation was held in the crypt of St. Mary's Church from the fourteenth century until 1638, when Archbishop Laud's additions to the Bodleian Library provided the university with a special Convocation House.[37]

A very definite picture of the seating arrangement in an Oxford Convocation is preserved for us in the Laudian Statutes of 1636. This is also identical with the seating plan prescribed in an earlier ruling of the fourteenth century. In the absence of the Chancellor, who was seldom present, the Vice-Chancellor, or his deputy, presided. On either side of him, sat the doctors of divinity, and on either side of them, the doctors of the civil law on the left, and the doctors of medicine on the right. The two proctors occupied places just below the Vice-Chancellor, while the masters regent and non-regent filled the rest of the hall.* There seems to have been no particular order of seniority among the masters, except that a superior place would be given to any master who was at the same time the Head of a college. At Cambridge, the regents and non-regents sat separately. Otherwise, the arrangement was apparently very similar to that of Oxford, although no such detailed description has come to light as is found in the Oxford statutes.[38] In both universities, the masters seem to have occupied actual seats of some sort, or at least assigned places, as there are several references to orders requiring them to "keepe their seates", and not rise and stand about irregularly, or run from one seat to another, exchanging views or influencing votes.[39]

After the university body had assembled, the first step towards the

*DIAGRAM OF SEATING ARRANGEMENTS IN
CONVOCATION

D.C.L.   D.D.   Chancellor   D.D.   M.D.
                          or
                    Vice-Chancellor
                   Proctor   Proctor
              Masters Regent and Non-Regent

election was the announcement by the Vice-Chancellor of the purpose of the meeting, and the reading of the Sheriff's rescript by the senior proctor. In some accounts of elections, as noted earlier, there is also mention made of the reading of a statute. In 1614, at Cambridge, it seems to have been the old parliamentary statute forbidding the election of non-residents—which would have then suited the purposes of the Heads very well, in barring Sir Miles Sandys from standing for the university seat. In the Oxford indenture of 1673/4—and perhaps in all writs and indentures—there is also a reference to some statute, but this reference is even more vague. On the other hand, Wall, writing in 1798, specifically mentions the reading of "the statute against bribery, etc.", which he identifies as 2 George II, c. 24. From all this, we can probably assume that the statutes read in the university assemblies were the general regulations that were in operation at the time in regard to all parliamentary elections.[40]

The nomination of candidates then followed. The Vice-Chancellor usually suggested one or more names, often with the reading of "letters commendatory" from the King or the university Chancellor. Most frequently these nominations were accepted without further question, whether out of satisfaction, indifference, or submission, and the voting followed promptly. Under such circumstances, there would be an uncontested election, and no poll recorded. Nominations of this sort were practically equivalent to appointments, and the actual process of election was merely a matter of form.

While most of the university elections for burgesses were of this type, there were times, as we have already seen, when real competition was introduced. It is not clear in such cases just how candidates other than those suggested by the Vice-Chancellor had their names brought before the Convocation. There are several instances of nominations made from the floor, merely by shouting the name of the candidate. In the tumultuous Oxford election of 1625/6, the nomination of Sir Francis Stewart, the electorate's favourite, was made in this way, much against the Vice-Chancellor's will, and in the midst of great disorder. Another example of nominations from the floor, made with some attendant confusion, is described by Anthony Wood in his account of the election of 1678/9:

> After the writts had been read, was a strange noise made in Convocation house; some cried out *Hennage Finch*, others *Lamphire*, another *Edisbury*.

In more orderly Convocations, it may be that the names were put forward in some other way. For example, an entry in the Oxford Archives for the nineteenth century in reference to parliamentary elections notes that the Vice-Chancellor asked the Convocation for nominations and that the Heads of colleges gave in names. In any case, in most elections, there seems to have been no resistance on the part of the Vice-Chancellor when candidates other than those named by himself or by the Chancellor were entered in the contest.[41]

In the ordinary course of events, the names of the most likely candidates became known in the university before the day of the poll, and in such cases, as we shall see shortly, lively pre-election campaigns took place over an extended period. It was customary, however, for candidates who became convinced that they had no chance to win, or who were persuaded that their candidacy was undiplomatic, and offensive to "those above", to "desist", and withdraw their names before the Senate assembled—sometimes, it would seem, in the very meeting itself. There was a strong sentiment to the effect that a candidate once proposed must not be defeated, and unanimity in the final vote was prized.[42]

This introduces the subject of electioneering. In university elections, other than for burgesses and Chancellors, electioneering was frowned upon, as leading to "faction" and "tumult", and, in Oxford at least, in 1574 in the elections of proctors, it was expressly forbidden under the name of "conspiracy", and heavily penalized. Similarly, almost a hundred years later, at Cambridge, a royal letter of Charles II reprimanded the university for its conduct during elections, and forbade the electors to "goe about from Coll. to Coll. or elsewhere, by gathering hands & subscriptions to make partys & factions".[43]

How far this attitude of disapproval originally extended to campaigns for parliamentary burgesses is not clear. Unanimity was frequently urged as an ideal, but, in the early stages of an election, electioneering on behalf of different candidates came to be an important part of the process of filling the university seats. This was especially true of the mid-century and thereafter. For the earlier period, there is less evidence available, although, if we may judge by the activity that went on in connection with the elections for Chancellor (which were, as may be remembered, the pattern for the election of burgesses—at least, at Cambridge) it is probable that some lively campaigns took place, although no records have survived.

In 1626, for example, when the Duke of Buckingham was being pushed by the Heads to be Chancellor of Cambridge at the King's request, there was much dissatisfaction among the rank and file of the university: "We of the body murmur", wrote the Rev. Joseph Mead, one of the discontented fellows.

> We run one to another to complaine; we say, the heads [that is, the Heads of colleges] in this election have no more to do than any of us, wherefore we advise what to do and whom to set up.

Despite much opposition, in the end, the Duke won, though only by three votes.[44]

The election of Buckingham was probably more hotly contested than most—perhaps than any—of the elections for university burgesses, for Buckingham was a controversial figure of great importance, and the chancellorship was held for life, and not merely for the space of one Parliament. Moreover, the Chancellor's authority in university affairs was so great that the choice of a Chancellor could affect the welfare of every member of the university more profoundly than any election of a university burgess. Nevertheless, this picture of an election campaign in full swing as presented in connection with Buckingham's election may serve to show that the techniques of electioneering were well known and practised in the universities in the earlier part of the seventeenth century, and it is therefore to be presumed that they were also used in the elections of the university representatives.

Certainly, the election of 1614 at Cambridge could not have been what it was without previous agitation and organization, both on the part of the Vice-Chancellor's party, and on that of Sir Miles Sandys. So also with the case of Sir Francis Stewart at Oxford in 1625/6—although, as will appear below, Stewart's followers did not seem to be so well organized then as they should have been. Previous planning must also have gone into the candidacy of some of the various members in the elections of the 1620's who were pushed forward under the royal aegis, with "letters commendatory", both public and private—to say nothing of the more obvious manœuvres of the election campaigns of the latter part of the century.

As will be seen in the chapters that follow, the forms that electioneering took were all the usual ones: letters—both to the university at large, and to private friends or personages therein; personal visits on behalf of oneself, or of one's favourite candidate; threats, rumours, promises, "treating". "Treating" is first mentioned in university elections at Oxford in 1660, when the son of Speaker Lenthall of the Long Parliament entertained his father's prospective supporters handsomely at the local tavern. In spite of this outlay, Lenthall lost in the poll, and the winning candidates—two university "gremials"—after the election was over, treated their voters more modestly to "bisket and wine". The most extreme case of this kind of bribery seems to have occurred in the by-election of 1673/4 at Oxford, when Thomas Thynne, a "pretty gentle-man" of good family connections, kept a table for the university masters at a local tavern for a whole week before the election. Treating at Cambridge never seems to have reached these proportions, although there are a few references to the practice.[45]

One other difference between the electioneering usages at the two universities which prevailed for a time at least, was in the matter of personal appearance at the university on the part of the candidates. This was forbidden at Oxford—at least in the eighteenth century—according to Thomas Oldfield's *History of Boroughs* (1792). After noting the university's deep-seated Toryism (also as of the eighteenth century) Oldfield wrote:

> So little are they however to be influenced in the choice of their representatives, that they do not suffer any canvas to be made, nor either of the candidates to be, at the time of the election, within ten miles of the jurisdiction of the university.

When these stringent regulations were first established does not appear—perhaps not in the seventeenth century, for there are several instances of personal appearance at Oxford mentioned by Wood and other contemporary writers. There were also other campaigns, such as that of William Lenthall in 1660, in which the candidate's cause was advanced by relatives or members of his college. At Cambridge no trace of any restriction on personal canvass has been found. There a personal appearance not only was accepted, but even seems to have been considered necessary to a candidate's success.[46]

After the period of electioneering and the placing of names in nomination in the Convocation, the voting took place. This might be by ayes and noes—that is, *placet* and *non-placet*—or by acclamation, if there was no contest. In other cases, where there was room for controversy, the "scrutiny" by written votes was resorted to, for in a voice vote the will of the assembly could be easily misinterpreted to suit the Vice-Chancellor's purpose, as was done in the case of Sir Francis Stewart in 1625/6—and also, according to Anthony Wood and William Prynne, at the time of the election of Archbishop Laud as Chancellor of Oxford in 1630.[47]

The "scrutiny", as a method of voting, had long been used in university elections. It was conducted with some degree of privacy, by allowing the voters to present written slips to the election officials (at Cambridge), or to add their names to a written list (at Oxford), thus indicating their choice of candidates (or their *placets* and *non-placets* for a piece of legislation). The election officials were sometimes the proctors, sometimes the scrutators, according to the nature of the business going on, but they always included the Vice-Chancellor, as presiding officer. The medieval university statutes had endeavoured to insure that the votes should be kept secret, for the scrutators were sworn to secrecy, and in the sixteenth century additional statutes at Oxford stressed this point. In these later statutes, the scrutators' oath regarding an election for proctors involved a promise not to reveal "the vote, votes, or comparative size of the votes", or the individual decisions of the voters, "by word, nod, sign, or in any way whatsoever to anyone whatsoever, either before or after the announcement of those who are elected".[48]

At Cambridge also, before the Elizabethan Statutes of 1570, there was a similar rule in regard to secret voting, but the new statutes abolished this system, and introduced instead the "open scrutiny", for all elections except those for Chancellor, to the great disgust of the electorate. A long and bitter complaint appears in Cooper's *Annals*, where the scrutators are accused of altering the votes, and the Vice-Chancellor is charged with intimidation. According to this complaint, when some gave "their voices simplie and freely", the Vice-Chancellor (Dr. Whitgift) became angered "and called for pen and ynke to rite their names, thinking that with so terrifying of them, they would for feare give as he would have them".[49]

In elections for parliamentary burgesses at Cambridge, however, a species of secret voting seems to have been practised from the very first, through the use of the ballot. Some of these ballots for the elections in 1656 and from 1660 on are still preserved in the University Registry. There are no ballots left from the early elections—only the results are recorded. Nevertheless, ballots are mentioned by Dr. Duport as in use in 1614, and this is the first parliamentary election at either university of which there is any detailed account. At this time, Duport confessed that he had intended to put the ballots for Sandys in his pocket, and then later reported that the ballots for both Bacon and Sandys had been made off with by the rebellious faction. Likewise, in a note on the election of 1620/1, reference is made to seven or eight "suffrages" that were found to be stolen from the Registrary's collection.[50] From these examples, it will be seen that the use of the ballot did not secure either an honest election or complete privacy for the voter, but in most cases, the system probably worked more satisfactorily than on these two occasions, and tended in general to make for order and accuracy.

Even when there was no tampering with the count, however, the ballot as used here was not completely secret, for the name of the elector was inscribed on each paper along with the name of the candidate. The formula for this inscription is given by Wall in his eighteenth-century account of parliamentary elections at Cambridge. It ran as follows: "A. B. (the name of the elector) *eligit* C. D. (the name of the candidate) *in burgensem huius academiae in parliamento*." The inscribed ballots were delivered—presumably by each voter on his own behalf—to the election officials. By Wall's time—and possibly before, although there is no indication of this in the seventeenth century—there was also a teller to check the votes on behalf of each candidate. Any ballots that were dubious were laid aside until the poll was finished, although what was done to decide their final validity is not made clear.[51]

There is no summary discussion of procedures in use at Oxford similar to this of Wall's for Cambridge. Information about the actual process of voting must therefore be gathered from various sources. According to the document printed in Appendix IV below, a mere open *viva voce* vote seems to have been used in the beginning, but in 1620/1 a scrutiny was introduced, and in 1625/6, a scrutiny was demanded. Thereafter some sort of written system appears to have been followed, although not by means of ballots.

The disputed Oxford election of 1625/6, already alluded to several times above, involved this question of electoral method, and seems to have established the scrutiny as an accepted procedure. This election is also important because it was, so far as the records go, the only university election to be sent to the floor of the House of Commons for settlement throughout the whole century. It is true that the Cambridge election of 1614 was, as we have seen, the first university election in which the outcome was disputed, but there is no evidence that any decision in regard to it was ever made by the Commons, or indeed that the dispute was ever officially settled at all. All that we know is that Sir Miles Sandys took his seat, and kept it. The dispute at Oxford in 1625/6, on the other hand, may be followed through to a conclusion. Anthony Wood gives a detailed account of the affair,[52] and there are also echoes of the controversy in the *Commons' Journal*, and in the records of Convocation. The chief source, however—on which Wood seems to have depended largely—is the document printed below in Appendix IV. This is the petition that was presented to the Commons by the disgruntled electors, and the Vice-Chancellor's answer to the charges in the petition.

In this altercation, as in the disputed election at Cambridge, the controversy was between the Vice-Chancellor and the voting members of the university, rather than immediately between the two candidates and their parties. The Oxford voters, probably affected by the general discontent that had seized the country at this time, in opposition to the policies of the Duke of Buckingham, grew bold enough to reject Sir Thomas Edmondes, the Treasurer of the King's Household and a member of the Privy Council, when he stood for re-election as Oxford's burgess, and instead declared for a candidate of their own, Sir Francis Stewart. This was an unexpected assertion of independence, and a source of dismay to the Vice-Chancellor, Dr. John Prideaux, who was acting in the Court's interest. The Convocation had been opened as usual by the Vice-Chancellor, with the reading of "2 letters from noble personages" on Edmondes's behalf. The university records disclose that the "personages" were the Earl of Pembroke, the university Chancellor, and George Abbott, the Archbishop of Canterbury, both of whom had recommended Edmondes in the previous election.[53] Prideaux then made a little speech, "wherein he among other things spoke these words, 'Facilius est multos annos irritare quam unum reconciliare'" or, as it is given in other versions, "It is easier to irritate the magnates than it is to reconcile them" ("irritare magnates quam reconciliare"). This was taken as an attempt at intimidation. He, himself, however, claimed that what he had said was: "It is easier to irritate many friends than to reconcile one", although this observation does not seem so much to the point as the other versions.[54] As to what happened next, accounts differ, but the Vice-Chancellor appears to have proceeded much too hastily at this juncture—probably because he scented opposition and was bent on checking it. He pronounced Edmondes elected on the grounds that there were only a few "Nons" against him, and that those who opposed him had failed to nominate their candidate in time to hold a "scrutiny".

A vivid picture of the confusion of the scene is obtained from the petition and answer printed in Appendix IV. As a glance at this document will show, the charges are listed in one column, and the answers in another, in a series of point by point rebuttals. Considerable information about the methods of voting is conveyed in the course of this argument. For example, when the petitioners claimed they had answered "Sir Francis Steward", after they had been asked whom they would have for burgess, the Vice-Chancellor replied:

> Most false for they generally cried Edmonds & placet Not above 5 or 6 then crying Non, others held their peace & being willed by ye Vice-chancellour to name anyone whom they pleased against Sr Tho. Edmonds & to divide themselves yt their number might appeare, they would not . . . coming indeed as some have since confessed, to oppose Sir Tho. Edmonds but having not agreed wn ye Election was first proposed whom to name.

Again the petitioners claimed that upon their demand for a scrutiny, the Vice-Chancellor ordered a division, and when "a greater part by much went on Sr. Franc. Stuart's part or side", the Vice-Chancellor simply ignored the fact and pronounced the Convocation closed. In another Convocation a few days later, the Vice-Chancellor returned to the subject, and tried to get the Convocation to agree that they had chosen Sir Thomas Edmondes, but again they refused, saying that they could not elect freely but by a "suffrage", presumably that is, a separately counted vote, in a scrutiny. To this the Vice-Chancellor rejoined that they would not listen to him when he read the statement of what he considered to be the proper election of Edmondes—"Strange! How denied they yt, wn they would not heare wt it was?"—and to the claims that all the Convocation were against him, he repeatedly asserted that there were only one or two—"alwaies a few vocall men", "some few . . . who keepe a greater noise than ye rest". As far as the scrutiny was concerned, he insisted "ye election was past & there was nothing to be observed but a few men keeping up a stirre for they knew not wt". From the charge that he had not used the proper university seal in endorsing the indenture, he excused himself on the ground that he thought the "manuall seale", used in letters to the King, etc., equally legal. As a final complaint, the petitioners objected that some of their number had been persecuted for their stand by the Vice-Chancellor, and even imprisoned. Prideaux's reply here was that these persons had been convicted in open court of breaking university rules about wandering the streets at night and sitting "in a Taverne drinking sack at sermon time on Sunday", and were committed to prison for these offences, and not for their political activities.

Despite the Vice-Chancellor's defence, the House of Commons was not satisfied that the election had been properly conducted. A new writ was ordered, and after a by-election, Sir Francis Stewart finally obtained his seat. The Vice-Chancellor's dignity was saved by allowing the penalties against the unruly masters to stand, but the university right of free election was vindicated.[55] From now on, the scrutiny and the division became part of the voting system at Oxford. When the Laudian Statutes were issued in 1636, there were provisions for various methods of voting—some general, in relation to all university elections; some specifically indicated for choosing parliamentary burgesses. The general provisions stated that elections were to be free, and decided by majority vote, and voters were to register their votes, according to the nature of the business, "either by a scrutiny in writing or *viva voce* in the ear of the proctor or, finally, by going aside to another part of the house". For parliamentary elections in particular, the special provision was made that the choice should be indicated *viva voce*, or by moving in accordance with the opinion to be expressed ("aut pedibus eundo in sententiam").[56] This last provision, as also the previous one—"going to another part of the house" ("per secessionem in alteram partem domus") —seems to suggest something like a parliamentary division. There is further evidence of this in the petition about the disputed election of 1625/6, and in Wood's description of the Convocation of 1678/9. From some of the records in the University Archives it would appear that in such cases the votes were recorded as the members of the Convocation filed past the election officials one by one—*vocatim, sigillitim, viritim*, as it is variously described. The votes seem to have been taken while the electors were either leaving the hall, or else re-entering it, after having been dismissed for the purpose of conducting the scrutiny. It is not clear whether the actual voting was accomplished by each voter's writing his vote with his own hand or by "pricking" (as the old expression went) a name on a list, or whether each voter merely indicated his vote verbally to an official for entry on an official list. Both methods are suggested in the report of the parliamentary investigation of the disputed election of 1625/6 in the *Commons' Journal*, where, in reference to Oxford, mention is made of "their manner of Scrutiny being by their Names in Writing or in aurem of the Proctor".[57] In later years—for example, in the election of Thomas Thynne in 1673/4—special tellers were appointed for each candidate (generally members of his college), to ensure further accuracy in the count. In the Thynne election also it is clear that the votes were recorded in some detail rather than as a mere tally, for there were three contestants for the one vacant seat, and the count was kept on three separate pages, and arranged so that "if anyone's right of election should be called in doubt", the record "could be recalled for examination". This proviso suggests that the list included each elector's name along with the candidate he voted for.[58]

If this was the usual method of recording the votes at Oxford, then the Oxford system with its official list, like the use of signed ballots at Cambridge, would provide for only a degree of privacy—that is, privacy as far as one's fellow voters were concerned, not complete secrecy in the modern sense. Moreover, it is obvious that the amount of privacy of any sort that was offered would depend entirely upon the discretion and fair-mindedness of the election officials. This being the case, it is interesting to note that there are no particular complaints in the seventeenth century on this score, as there are in later periods. However this may have been, the fact still remains that the votes would be known to the presiding officials and this in itself must at times have been a deterrent to the making of a free choice.

In considering the use of ballots and election lists, the question arises, what became of these records after the polls were completed. For the whole seventeenth century, there are no lists preserved in the Archives at Oxford, and at Cambridge there are no ballots before 1660, except for the one year 1656. The presumption is that after a certain time both the Oxford lists and the earlier ballots at Cambridge were officially destroyed. Indeed, after 1636, this should have been the legally required procedure at Oxford, for the Laudian Code distinctly made mention of "the lists on which the votes of each person had been inscribed being completely destroyed and burned" ("schedulis ... quibus Singulorum vota inscripta penitus abolitis et igni traditis"). There is one vague Cambridge reference about total scores of the losing candidates being "suppressed", but no specific statement as to the treatment of the individual ballots themselves. Whatever was done at either university, the results of each election remain recorded only in the barest form. At Oxford this consists of the final returns, with the names of the burgesses-elect, or, if there was a contest, the names of the defeated candidates as well, with the number of votes received by each of the contestants. These items are found in the minutes of each Convocation in which a parliamentary election took place. At Cambridge there are no minutes. For the period up to 1660, there is only a simple list of burgesses-elect. After that there are the ballots, and, in a "Book of Representatives", a more or less complete list of all contestants and the number of their votes, after the manner of the Oxford entries. In the records of both universities, where no figures are given and there were only two candidates in the field, we may generally assume that the name given first is that of the burgess who received the greater number of votes. But there are occasional exceptions to this practice.[59]

In the eighteenth century there is much more certainty about the returns, for a different system seems to have been followed in both universities. Cambridge had lists, such as those used at Oxford, and both universities preserved these lists intact in the records. What the lists were like, is shown by certain printed polls that were circulated in the eighteenth century for both universities at different times. These polls gave the names of the voters arranged by colleges, the persons for whom they voted, and the total scores. Similar lists for the eighteenth-century elections are still preserved in manuscript in the Cambridge Registry. Their circulation in print was probably illegal, and the result of breach of faith or outright theft, for the privilege of the private vote continued to be maintained in theory, and according to the Porritts, was still regarded as a practice peculiar to the university constituencies at the time of the agitation for the reform of Parliament.[60]

In this connection it is interesting to note that however much the universities were ahead of the rest of the country in this respect in the seventeenth and eighteenth centuries, they had lagged behind in the twentieth, for in 1945 they were still voting for parliamentary burgesses on signed "voting papers", where each voter's choice could be noted by all the university tellers—and was, indeed, frequently gossiped over, to judge from remarks made on the subject by Sir William Beveridge and others, who were complaining of the fact in the House of Commons some weeks before the election of that year.[61] Nevertheless, in the seventeenth century, the university system of voting was undoubtedly preferable to most of the other methods in practice at that time—such as a show of hands, acclamation, the voice vote—and the existence of the private vote and the frequent use of the official scrutiny may perhaps account in part for the degree of university independence that was shown in the university constituencies throughout the century.

Although there is some uncertainty, as we have just seen, as to exactly how the votes were recorded in a university scrutiny, there is less doubt about another aspect of the procedure, that is, the order of voting. This would perhaps not have been important in parliamentary elections at Oxford, where the voice vote and the division were the accepted methods, but at Cambridge where the ballot was used, seniority and rank could easily be given due consideration. The first to vote were the Chancellor (if present), the Vice-Chancellor, and the two proctors (or at least one of them—Wall says that at Cambridge in the election of Chancellor the senior proctor voted last, and this may also have been true in parliamentary elections). These officials were the presiding officers and received the votes of the other voters. The doctors came up next, probably one by one, according to seniority. After them the masters voted, perhaps in reverse order of seniority. Noblemen, regardless of academic rank, seem to have voted with the doctors, before the masters. Towards the conclusion of the voting at fifteen-minute intervals, the bedell made three turns around the hall, gathering in stray voters with the cry, "non ad variandum sed ad suffragandum", or, as it is given in Wall, "ad scrutinium, cessatum est a scrutinio". After this the polls were held open for some time longer, and then closed.[62]

From such descriptions of the process of voting as have just been given, it would seem that the time devoted to elections in the seventeenth century was comparatively limited. Meetings of the Senate at Cambridge were generally held at nine a.m., although in Dr. Duport's account of the election of 1614 the hour named was eight, and later in the century at least two elections (1656 and 1688/9) are known to have taken place in the afternoon.[63] At Oxford, according to the Laudian Statutes, Convocation could be called at the Vice-Chancellor's discretion, and here, too, there were afternoon elections at least twice, in 1640 and in 1661. In any case, the business must have been completed in a half-day, unless unusual complications developed—as at Oxford in 1678/9, when it took five hours to complete the poll. For the election of proctors, however, two days were allowed by the Oxford statutes of 1574. Ultimately for burgesses also, a longer period came to be customary, as more and more non-residents voted. In 1826, the poll was kept open for four days, and in 1945, for five.[64]

There was a fixed procedure for the announcement of the returns, once the votes were counted. At Oxford, the Vice-Chancellor, and at Cambridge, the senior proctor, read the names of the contestants and the number of the votes each received. A plurality was all that was necessary for election. In parliamentary elections in both universities, names of the contestants appear to have been read to the assembly in the order of the number of votes obtained, beginning with the candidate with the smallest number. In 1614 at Cambridge this order of reading was reversed—the winners, Bacon and Sandys, being announced first, and the losers, Gooch and Corbet, last. This was done, the deputy Vice-Chancellor admitted, for the express purpose of confusing the electors and contributing to the success of the Heads' plan to oust Sandys. In explaining this action, Duport made it clear that the regular usage in reporting the returns of both Chancellor and burgesses was otherwise. This statement is confirmed by later practice. A memorandum of the results of the election for the Short Parliament among the Baker Manuscripts at Cambridge has the names listed with the lowest scores first, and Adam Wall, writing in the eighteenth century, also makes this point. Similarly, the first lists that are available for Oxford, and many of the lists available thereafter, follow the same pattern. At Cambridge, at least one deviation from the practice (after 1614) seems to have occurred in 1660—in an election in which there was also much competition, as will appear in a later chapter.

The precise form in which the final results of an election were proclaimed at Cambridge is included in Dr. Duport's account. Approximately the same words are repeated in their Latin version by Wall as in use one hundred and eighty-four years later, although here they are attributed to the senior proctor. Dr. Duport's version reads:

> I, John Duport, deputy Vice Chancellor . . . doe choose & pronounce to be choosen by the greater part of the Regents & non-regents for the Burgesses of the universitie against the next Parlament the Hobl. Knight Sir Francis Bacon . . . & also the Rt. Woll. Barnabie Gotch. . . .

When this announcement was made, the indenture was prepared by the official known as the register, and, as described earlier in this chapter, was signed with the consent of the Senate by the Vice-Chancellor, the proctors, and several others, sealed with their individual seals, and with the university seal. The meeting was then dissolved, and the indenture and rescript delivered by the register to the Sheriff or his deputy.[65]

One matter that is made clear by the several accounts of Convocations

held for the purpose of electing parliamentary burgesses is that there
was apparently meant to be some little opportunity for discussion
between the time of the Vice-Chancellor's opening speech with its
letters of recommendation, and the actual moment of voting, although,
in cases where the Vice-Chancellor was eager to rush through his
nominees, he allowed as little time as he decently could, so as to prevent
the raising of too many questions. Such, for example, seems to have
been the procedure at Oxford in 1625/6. But from reading the accounts
of election meetings in general, the impression is gained that, besides
the mere naming of the candidates, and sometimes a considerable
amount of rebellious murmuring and shouting from the floor, there
were usually opportunities for questions to be asked, and protests made,
in an orderly fashion. In Dr. Duport's account, it is stated how masters
could come up to the Vice-Chancellor in small groups—"not above 2 or
3 . . . together"—to "move for justice or direction in any thing". This
done "discrietlie & modestly", when they had been answered, they
were to return to their places. In this particular meeting, two masters
did speak out, one "with an audible voice", and he "did petire jus et
justitiam of the Vicecanr. & that 1mo 2⁰ 3⁰ & Instanter, instantius,
instantissime". One suspects, however, in this particular case, that he
had been primed with his petition by the Vice-Chancellor himself, since
the motion made was against the election of a non-resident, and thus
against the interests of Sir Miles Sandys. However, others rose to press
Sandys's case and bring out further letters in his favour from the university's Chancellor. The Vice-Chancellor, however, perceiving that
"matters would grow hott with much talk", tried to pass off objections
as best he could, and hurry on to the voting. At Oxford, also, in 1625/6
there seems to have been some remarks from the floor—"alwaies a few
vocall men", as the Vice-Chancellor noted in his report of the proceedings.[66]

As the accounts of these two elections prove, comment from the floor
was not always of an orderly nature. Indeed, in reading on the subject
of election procedure in general in the universities, the impression is
formed that an astonishing amount of disorder prevailed. The modern
reader, unacquainted with the long history of disorder in the universities, dating back to the Middle Ages, would find himself in agreement with King Charles I, when the latter wrote to Oxford in 1628, at
the time when a great uproar was going on over the election of proctors:
"We could hardly be induced to believe that in such a Body of Schollers
there could be found such strange and violent humors." But readers
of Wood will be familiar with frequent mention of electoral "tumults",
and the earlier documents of the sixteenth century, as well as those of

the seventeenth, abound in references to "Laughinges, hemminges, his-
singes and clamorous speeches", "Stamping and hissing", "Promisce et
confuse vociferabantur", shouts of names of candidates ("A Sandys, a
Sandys"), or of "placet" or "non-placet", "ad scrutinium", "you do us
wronge!", "Lett the suffrages be read!" and other "unseemly speeches",
and "bold and irreverent language".[67] Most of this unruly behaviour
seems to have been owing to resentment against the illegal attempts of
Vice-Chancellors to push through legislation or elections against the
will of the voters, as in the two disputed elections of 1614 and 1625/6,
so often referred to above. Dr. Duport, for example, from past experience, had anticipated disorder from the first moment of his chairman-
ship, and his fears were speedily justified. The members of the assembly
as he had feared, became "very troublesome", "mutinous & violent",
and they "continually cried upon & shouted" at him "with the greatest
extremitie", so as either to prevent him from speaking at all, "or else
to putt him out". In fact, he wrote, the "noyse and shout" which they
made was so great it was "herd a great way of". The Vice-Chancellor of
Oxford in 1625/6 also complained that business could not be transacted
because of noise and tumult.[68]

It was apparently in apprehension of a similar situation that a later
Vice-Chancellor at Cambridge wrote of the electorate of 1678/9: "I
could almost kneele to them that they would return to some Sobriety."
Unruliness of this sort must have antedated the university statutes of
Elizabeth's reign, for the prevalence of disorder was the excuse then
given for the changes introduced at that time. Lord Burleigh and Archbishop Whitgift and the Heads of the sixteenth century felt that new and
stricter rules were necessary to "bridle the untamed affections of the
younger Regents". It has been suggested by Mullinger that these stricter
rules were aimed not alone at the youthful spirits of the young Regents,
but possibly also, as we have noted before, at their growing sympathy
with the Puritan doctrines of Cartwright.[69] Whatever the intention of
the new rules, they only brought forward more occasions for resentment,
and the disorders continued. In discussing the tumults of the parliamentary election of 1625/6 at Oxford and other elections of later years,
Wood constantly returned to the theme of Burleigh and Whitgift. Such
irregular performances, according to his view, were to be attributed to
"dissolute Juniors, or such as we call Blackpot men, who carry all before
them in elections". This was also the idea of Dr. Prideaux in 1625/6,
in regard to "some of ye cheif sticklers in this petition", who, he
intimated, were "idle, drunken, swearing & irreligious companions wch
. . . corrupt others by their examples". Archbishop Laud, when university Chancellor, was particularly incensed at the "Juniors'" conduct,

and made every effort to bring them into conformity, with only partial success; still later in the century—more than one hundred years after Burleigh and Whitgift thought they had arranged things to their satisfaction—we find a royal letter to Cambridge from Charles II still censuring that university for its failure to preserve "decency, quietness & gravity in the transactions of the Senate House".[70]

In any discussion of election disorders in the universities, the question of the age of the voters must be considered, since it was the younger regents, the "Juniors", upon whom the blame for disorder was generally placed. As a qualification for voting, the question of age has already been dismissed in the earlier pages of this chapter as relatively unimportant, but as a cause for disorder it has more bearing. In Burleigh and Whitgift's time the regents are said to "come to that place with fewer years than in times past they did". Whatever the facts of the sixteenth century as compared to the Middle Ages, the age level of the seventeenth century, if the statistics of the university representatives themselves are any guide, was not excessively low. Some of them entered the university at thirteen or fifteen, thus possibly becoming regent masters before they were twenty. Few, however, won this status before the age of twenty-two. Nevertheless, in a full Convocation there was at all times probably a sufficient number of "Young Masters", in addition to the bachelors, to account for some of the turbulence of the proceedings. Theoretically, in parliamentary elections, there should have been something of sedateness added by the presence of the older non-regents, but it is probable that in actual practice they were generally in a minority. The non-regents, in fact, had been somewhat pushed aside, despite their supposed superior maturity and responsibility, by the changes in the statutes under Elizabeth and Laud, which left the universities more and more under the control of the Heads on the one hand and the "Juniors" on the other. The result may have been to intensify the tendency for university government to alternate between the two extremes of rebellion and suppression.

However this may be, the conduct of the electors in both of the universities was at times undoubtedly reprehensible. One form of disorder that must have been particularly disconcerting, in addition to the shouting, was the tendency of the members of Convocation not to keep their places "quiet & peaceable", as they were told to do, but, instead, to run, as Dr. Duport wrote, "in heapes in the Regent house from one seat to another", or, according to Charles II's royal letter, to go to and fro "from one side to another, from one classe to another, to bespeake" one another for votes. In addition, when the presiding officer attempted to speak, or to make his way to and from the chair, attended by the bedells, the members of the assembly would come forward and press about him so fiercely that all dignity was lost and violence to his person seemed to be threatened. Such an occasion is described by Wood, where the Vice-Chancellor "was so thrust upon and thronged . . . that no Bedell could come to him".[71]

But the "dissolute Juniors" sometimes went even farther than this Besides the mere impediment of business by tactics of obstruction, they engaged in positive action. They made speeches without the presiding officer's consent, they refused to disband when he declared the meeting dissolved, they stayed in session in the Senate House, carrying on business without his authority, they even refused to admit newly elected officials to the hall. Worse things occasionally occurred. For example, in the parliamentary elections at Cambridge in 1614 and 1620/1 the ballots were stolen, as also in the "factious and tumultuary" election of proctors at Oxford in 1628. Moreover, it was in the latter election that the senior scrutator was so crowded upon by the clamorous masters that, in Wood's words, he "gave a great shreake . . . and fell down dead to the great astonishment of all those present". (Fortunately, however, he had only fainted, and was later revived.)[72]

Incredibly enough, all this sort of "base, riotous business", as Archbishop Laud called it, continued to go on, despite the repeated efforts of successive Chancellors and Vice-Chancellors to suppress it. Even Laud was not successful, though when roused by affronts offered to a retiring proctor, he was outraged, and wrote to the Vice-Chancellor in 1638, that "the whipping of a few boys" was too lax a punishment, and urged that the Vice-Chancellor locate the ringleader and "banish him the University". The next year Laud recommended prison, and asked to have the offenders' names given to him. Imprisonment as a penalty was not an innovation, for it had been resorted to before, notably in the case of the ringleader in the election of burgesses at Oxford in 1625/6. But it seems not to have been particularly effective in the long run. At least in 1669, after the uproar over the election of an esquire bedell at Cambridge, we find King Charles II suggesting what may have been a more stringent penalty, and one more respected by the young masters— suspension from university office and from degrees ("omni Gradu suscepto et suscipiendo") at the pleasure of the Vice-Chancellor and Heads. This penalty was to be laid down for any form of irregularity, from electioneering outside the Senate House (presumably this part would not apply to parliamentary elections) to using rebellious language to the Vice-Chancellor.[73] How far this threat was successful as a deterrent is not clear, nor whether the penalties suggested were ever actually imposed. For parliamentary burgesses, at least, the elections tended with some exceptions to grow more orderly as the seventeenth century wore on. The explanation in this case may be, not that disorders were more severely penalized, but possibly that the universities were gaining more real freedom of choice, and so were less in need of public expression of dissatisfaction than in the earlier years of their representation.

Considering the frequency of the election disorders in the universities, it is probably surprising that there were not more cases of disputed elections. In all the history of university representation, there are only the two instances which we have already discussed, in 1614 and 1625/6. The pages of the *Commons' Journal* during the seventeenth century are filled with innumerable disputes submitted from other constituencies, most of them to be decided on the basis of misconduct in elections, some of them genuine problems involving the determination of what the correct electoral procedure for a specific constituency should be. Of this latter type, there were thirty-four cases from "South Britain" between 1624 and 1689, according to the *Candidate's Guide, or the Elector's Rights decided*, a work published in 1735. Oxford's controversy of 1625/6 is not listed here, probably because the dispute was not essentially over the legality of having either a scrutiny or voting *viva voce*, but rather over the Vice-Chancellor's misconduct as presiding officer. Very likely, as the Porritts point out, one reason why there were so few election disputes submitted to Parliament by the universities is that in the universities the right to a vote was easily established by reference to the university records, and thus one of the most common sources of controverted elections was eliminated.[74]

This chapter has been largely devoted to describing the details of the process of electing the university members. There are other aspects of university representation that are also of interest to the student of constitutional history—the question of the popularity of the university seats, the size of the electorate, the varying degrees of freedom of choice that prevailed in specific elections, and so on. Some of these matters will be discussed in later chapters of this study.[75] Two of them will be touched on here—the question of the double vote, so much debated in the 1930's and 1940's, and the matter of payment of "parliamentary wages".

As to the first, what evidence there is seems to indicate that the situation was about the same as it was during the first half of the twentieth century—that is, a university M.A. might vote both for a university burgess and for a member of Parliament for another constituency, if he was otherwise qualified to vote in that constituency. Two entries for 1624 in the *Commons' Journal* on the subject of scholars and fellows voting in Cambridgeshire elections laid down the rule that such persons might vote in the county elections only if they were *bona-fide* freeholders.

An echo of this is found in the financial accounts of the Vice-Chancellor of the university for this date which reads: "A journey to London about scholars' voices in electing Knights of the shire. And to Serjeant Bing for pleading our right."[76]

Whether the "scholars" ever tried to have "voices" in the town governments as well as in the counties is not clear. No evidence for such a move has come to light, and the antagonism that existed between the corporations and the universities would probably stand in the way of a relationship of this sort. Indeed, according to L. H. D. Buxton and Strickland Gibson's *Oxford University Ceremonies*, such a privilege was never obtained at Oxford until 1885.[77] There were always, of course, a few members of Convocation, like Anthony Wood, or Dr. Thomas Sclater at Cambridge, who, as residents and property owners in the towns, might have also qualified as borough electors, or have been made honorary freemen. This last status indeed was conferred on Dr. Sclater in 1670.[78] But without extensive research it would be impossible to form any notion of the amount of influence such persons could bring to bear on the corporations—or, conversely, from the point of view of borough interests, on the universities.

It is hard to see in what other way than by direct participation in the Convocation or Senate the corporations or their citizens could interfere very much in university elections. Certainly, if the original purpose of the grant of university representation was in part to off-set the influence of the borough members in Parliament, as seems probable, then the universities would be unlikely to tolerate any kind of interference, direct or indirect, on the part of the corporations. On the other hand, there is some slight evidence that what influence there was ran in the other direction. That is, the universities from time to time were able to bring a certain amount of pressure to bear upon the corporations through influencing the votes of the various tradesmen and servants who were closely bound to the universities by economic ties, or who partook of special status as "privileged persons", subject to the university courts, by virtue of these ties.[79]

If town influence was not very important in parliamentary elections in the universities, the same is probably less true of county interests. Between county and university there was no long-standing history of hostility, as between town and gown; and among the county gentry and clergy there possibly may have been a much larger proportion of degree-holders who were entitled to a double vote than among the citizens of the borough.[80] At least the university returns seem sometimes to suggest a closer relationship. For example, according to Mullinger, the choice of the two sons of Cromwell as parliamentary burgesses for Cambridge was the result, not of the Protector's authority or the support of the town, but rather because of the family's popularity in the shire. There are also other county names upon the university lists, as burgesses or as candidates—Sandys and Steward for Cambridge, Fiennes and Lenthall for Oxford. Then, too, a preference for a "neere neighbor" as parliament man was openly expressed in a campaigning letter of 1660 at Cambridge, urging the candidacy of Edward Montague, the patron of Pepys, and when Montague in the end did not stand for the seat, another member of the same family was elected.[81] Nevertheless, in these choices the double vote in itself does not appear as a factor, and the universities' liking for county candidates may be simply the result of political principles held in common.

There still remains the question of the payment of "parliamentary wages". James I's Letters Patent specifically prescribed that the university burgesses should be at the charge (*ad onera*) of the Chancellors, masters, and scholars "just as in the case of the other towns, etc." But already, in Elizabeth's time and before, the towns were ceasing to pay their burgesses, and during the seventeenth century such payments became less and less customary. It is not clear to what extent the university burgesses were paid, although occasionally they were provided with money for extraordinary expenses, such as when they waited on the King with addresses or petitions. The Porritts suggest that the extensive influence of the Crown in university matters in the first part of the century probably would have led to the early abandonment of parliamentary wages on the part of the universities.[82]

For whatever reason, the only actual example of payment is in the case of Henry Mountlowe, member for Cambridge in James I's first Parliament. Mountlowe received five shillings a day from the university. He was perhaps the only burgess who really needed the money, for he had less outside employment than his colleague, Dr. Steward, who was engaged in so much of the government's legal business. The payments made to Mountlowe are in the Vice-Chancellor's accounts, and they amount to £15 each for the sessions of 1604 and 1605, and £20 "for part of his wages for attendance at Parliament" in 1606. From this time on, the university fell into arrears until 1614, when a full settlement was made for the sum of £60. This was four years after Mountlowe had ceased to sit. There are no other references to parliamentary wages in this section of the Vice-Chancellor's accounts which go through 1657.[83]

The subject was raised at Oxford, however, in the campaign of 1627, when the Chancellor made the proud boast on behalf of the candidate he was pushing, Sir Henry Marten, that the latter would be no expense to the university as a burgess, since he was already kept in London by necessity because of his position as Admiralty Judge. After this, the question ceased to be an issue until the early part of 1677, when a bill was introduced in Parliament for the abolition of parliamentary wages. During the debate on this bill, Thomas Crouch, member for the University of Cambridge since 1660, noted that he had never received any wages from his constituency, nor did he expect any, but he did not say how long it had been the custom in university circles to allow the payments to lapse. During the Long Parliament, the members of all constituencies were voted a subsidy of £4 a week for their services, but none of the university members appears to have accepted this payment. Probably as a result of his remarks in the House, Thomas Crouch issued a formal release later in 1677, freeing the university of all obligations for wages or fees that might be claimed in the future by him or his executors. This is the last reference to the subject of parliamentary wages that has come to light in connection with the history of university representation.[84]

It appears, instead, that as the years went on, the university burgesses were expected to pay out money in the university's behalf, rather than themselves to receive payment. In the Vice-Chancellor's accounts of the early seventeenth century, mentioned above, it is the university that pays for the expenses of the election—that is, the fees of the Sheriff, the bedell, the proctors, etc.[85] But in the time of Adam Wall, about one hundred and fifty years later, these expenses were at the charge of the parliamentary burgesses, not to speak of additional prizes they were expected to dispense as well.[86] This change is symptomatic of the change in attitude towards the nature of service in Parliament that came over England in the seventeenth and eighteenth centuries.

In final comment upon the electoral system of the universities, the point must be made that, despite all the controversy, undue influence, and outright dishonesty that sometimes accompanied their elections, the universities possessed two or three characteristics that set them apart from the great majority of the constituencies of the time. The first has been already discussed at length—the existence of a secret, or semi-secret, method of voting. A second distinguishing feature was that there was no property qualification for voting or sitting in Parliament. Throughout three centuries, the sole test of a university elector's right to vote was his membership in the Senate or Convocation, whether or not he was a forty-shilling freeholder or a ten-pound householder. Similarly, Queen Anne's Property Qualification Act of 1711 contained a special exemption from the property requirements for members of Parliament for the benefit of university burgesses.[87] In many, probably most cases, the absence of such property qualifications may have meant little in determining the outcome of elections in university constituencies, in view of the circumstance that there was such a close relationship between the universities and the country gentry. Nevertheless, the fact that there was such a complete separation in theory between economic status and the right to vote and serve in Parliament remains one of the peculiar features of university representation.

There is a third aspect of university political practice that is also worthy of emphasis. This also pertains to property interests of a kind. That is, in theory and in legal status, the universities were no one's pocket boroughs. In practice, it is true, the universities were sometimes treated as such, by King and Protector and university Chancellor, but not for long, and sometimes not even once without rebuff. And even when royal influence and political intrigue were at their height, there was always the lively possibility that some degree of university independence might assert itself. In practice, this happened often enough to maintain the precedent of freedom, so that, as time went on, and the pocket borough system gained ground, the universities remained among the surviving constituencies where the legal right to a free election was still preserved.[88]

But that the universities were destined to preserve this freedom, was far from apparent in the third decade of the seventeenth century, when they entered upon one of the periods in the history of university representation when their independence was most seriously threatened.

NOTES FOR CHAPTER III

1. Adam Wall, *Different Ceremonies of the University of Cambridge*, pp. 153–5. The only other place where parliamentary elections are treated as part of the general electoral system of the universities is in Tit. X, Sec. 6, in the Oxford statutes of 1636. John Griffiths, *Statutes of the University of Oxford*, p. 134.
2. Porritt, i, 102.
3. For the text of *De Burgensibus*, see below, Appendix II. For the usual wording of the writs for parliamentary elections, see *C.J.*, i, 140, and Whitelocke, *Notes upon the King's Writt*, vols. i–ii, *passim*.
4. See below, pp. 61–2.
5. Coke's letter was written on 12 March, and Oxford's election took place on the 16th. The date of the Cambridge election is not recorded.
6. For the two systems of election at Cambridge, see Dyer, i, 181–2. George Peacock, *Observations on the Statutes*, p. 132. The expression, *more burgensium* is Peacock's. Humberstone, p. 14, suggests that this system of election corresponds most closely to that of the freeman boroughs, where the electors were ostensibly members of a guild—in this case the guild of scholars.
7. For the decree *De modo eligendi*, see Dyer, i, 275, 292–3. The decree is dated 23 March 1613 (1613/14), ten days before the date of the election, which was 2 April 1614. For discussions of the attempt to change the method of election,

see Cooper, III, 61; v, 349; Mullinger (1884), II, 463–4; Mullinger (1888), pp. 140–1; Walsh, pp. 54–5.

8. See below, pp. 63–5.

9. For details of the Earl of Northampton's election in 1612, see Cooper, III, 47–52; Heywood and Wright, I, 238–49; Mullinger, II, 464. For his letter to the Vice-Chancellor in 1614, see Cooper, v, 349.

A somewhat similar situation, so far as the alignment of the university Chancellor and the electorate was concerned, may be seen again at Cambridge in 1678/9, but in this case, the nomination of the candidate not preferred by the Heads and liked by the voters seems to have originated with the Chancellor himself, and not with the university body. See below, Ch. X, pp. 261–5.

10. The letter from the Cambridge Registrary in regard to the election of 1620/1, and King James's pronouncement in favour of election according to the system used for Vice-Chancellor are both given below in Appendix III. This item was apparently neglected by Mullinger, Cooper, and Walsh, in their respective studies of the *De modo eligendi* controversy, cited above in n. 7.

11. Griffiths, *Statutes*, pp. 129, 134. For parliamentary statutes, see below, p. 70.

12. The Convocation and the Senate are not to be confused with the lesser assemblies of the universities, known respectively as the "Congregation" and the "House of Regents". These bodies consisted only of regents, and had the sole right of electing certain university officials and passing certain kinds of legislation.

13. Some account of the distinctions between regents and non-regents may be found in Clark, II, pt. i, 90–101; Mullinger, I, 358, 362; Walsh, pp. 58–60. At Oxford they seem to have been called also "Junior" and "Senior" masters. The period of regency at Oxford in the sixteenth and early seventeenth centuries was one year. At Cambridge it had been enlarged from three years to five years in the sixteenth century, in spite of the fact that this move ran directly counter to the increasing tendency to require less and less service from the newly graduated masters. Ultimately, the distinction between regents and non-regents disappeared. Peacock, p. 143.

14. For the text of *De Burgensibus*, see Appendix II. For the text of the Statute of Incorporation (13 Eliz., c. 29), see Griffiths, *Enactments*, pp. 27 ff. A curious variation in the expression appears in the statute that confirmed James I's grants of advowsons in 1606. Here the grant is made to the "Chancellor and Schollers", with no reference to masters at all, except in so far as "Schollers" is taken to be synonymous with masters. *Ibid.*, pp. 40–1.

15. Hastings Rashdall, *The Universities of Europe in the Middle Ages*, II, pt. ii, 364, 367. Mallet follows Rashdall in describing the masters regent as "its [the university's] only members strictly speaking", I, 176.

16. Sir Bulstrode Whitelocke seems to suggest some such view in commenting on the parliamentary franchise in his *Notes upon the King's Writt*, I, 501. Unfortunately, his remarks were introduced only incidentally, in the course of an attempt to indicate various constituencies that were distinguished by the fact that the right of election was limited to "a special number of inhabitants", and he is not sufficiently explicit. His statement runs: "Such were the graunts to the two universities, restraining the elections to certain persons of those bodies, and not allowing all the scholars' voices in those elections."

17. For the teaching duties of bachelors of divinity, see Mullinger, I, 363. For references to bachelors of divinity in parliamentary elections, see below, Appendix IV, and Ch. VII, p. 188. Also the letter of the Rev. Joseph Mead cited in William Laud, *Works*, ed. Bliss, v, 4. For another example of special mention of bachelors, see the King's letter in 1535 to the "Chancellor, Vice-Chancellor, Doctors, Masters, Bachelors, and all other students and scholars" referred to in Mullinger, I, 629. It is probably also significant in this connection that the bachelors of divinity and others in the higher faculties are ranked above the masters in the Laudian Code from the point of view of the number of years required to qualify

for the degree. Mallet, II, 324–5. This longer residence would doubtless entitle them to vote for parliamentary burgesses, and probably with the doctors rather than with the masters.

18. The earliest specific reference to the doctors as parliamentary electors so far discovered is in Browne Willis, *Notitia Parliamentaria*, I, 153; III, 40, published in 1715–50. They are casually alluded to, however, as early as 1625/6, in the Vice-Chancellor's account of the Oxford election of that year. See below, p. 188 and Appendix IV. For the status of doctors at Oxford in the Middle Ages, see Rashdall, II, pt. ii, 387, n. 3.

19. Porritt, I, 103, assumes that peers and bishops did not vote for university burgesses. But the parliamentary resolution against peers' voting for members of the Commons was not passed until 1699, according to Mark Thomson, *Constitutional History of England, 1642–1801*, p. 186, and "noblemen"—perhaps only noblemen's sons, of course—are sometimes mentioned. See below, p. 80.

20. For the complaints against non-resident voters at Oxford in the case of elections for proctors—as "discontinuers from the University", "Old Masters", "strangers", "country Ministers", "Curates", "Schoolmasters and others that had been honoured with the Degree of Master"—see Clark, II, pt. i, 244–6; Gibson, *Statuta Antiqua*, pp. 329, 331, 451–2; Wood, Gutch, II, pt. i, 257–8, 359–61. Samuel Pepys participated as a non-resident in such an election at Cambridge in 1662. Samuel Pepys, *Diary*, ed. Henry B. Wheatley, II, 192.

The lone protest against non-resident voters in parliamentary elections was made at Cambridge in 1660 on the day of the poll by one of the current candidates for a seat in the Convention, Thomas Crouch, himself a resident master, and perhaps for that reason understandably partial to resident voters, to whom he was better known than to non-residents. Cambridge University Registry, 50: Book of Petitions, No. 3.

21. The chaplains of interested nobles and churchmen, for example, and the local parsons, were often sent by their patrons back to their universities to add a vote to a dubious majority. Porritt, I, 103; see also below, Ch. XI, p. 279. By the twentieth century the right of non-residents to vote was exercised by the use of "voting papers", sent out by mail to all graduates who were British citizens.

22. See above, Ch. I, p. 26.

23. See above, pp. 58–60.

24. For the deputy Vice-Chancellor's account of the election of 1614, see Cooper, V, 348–51, and Mullinger's comment, II, 464.

25. J. R. Tanner, *Historical Register*, p. 30; *O.R.*, p. 448.

26. For Sandys in the Parliament of 1614, see above, Ch. II, pp. 51–2. For the entry on the Cambridgeshire dispute, see *C.J.*, I, 468. In Willis, *Notitia*, I, 153, there is another perplexing item that may also have some relation to the university election of 1614. Here Gooch is listed as chosen as a burgess for Cambridge University in the first year of King James. Hulme, perhaps following Willis's lead, listed Gooch in "Corrections and Additions", *Bulletin of the Institute of Historical Research*, I, 99, as elected to this Parliament in a by-election, although he was puzzled by the entry, since he could discover no cause for such a by-election at Cambridge. Perhaps Willis's error arose from miscopying a date on some stray document he had come across that related to the election of 1614 rather than that of 1603/4. There is no shred of evidence that Gooch ever sat in any Parliament before 1620/1. His name is not found in the *Commons' Journal* for the Parliament of 1604–10, and he was, in fact, during part of this time, in the Fleet Prison on account of some legal difficulties arising in connection with the finances of his college. See Mullinger, II, 465.

27. See n. 24 above, and the biographical references for Sandys and Bacon given in Ch. II, p. 55, nn. 37, 38; p. 55, n. 47.

28. On the preference for "gremials", see below, Ch. VII, p. 193; Ch. VIII, pp. 213–14; Ch. XI, p. 278; Ch. XII, p. 302; Ch. XIII, pp. 328–30.

29. Godfrey Goodman, *The Court of King James the First*, ed. Brewer, II, 226. For further details on Naunton's relationship to the university seat, see Ch. IV, pp. 97–108, *passim*, and Appendix V, below.

30. The Porritts' statement on this point is much too sweeping (I, 103). For burgesses with no university connections, see below, Ch. VIII, p. 213; Ch. XIII, p. 331.

31. For a detailed discussion of the degrees held by university representatives of the seventeenth century, see below, Ch. V, p. 136; Ch. VIII, pp. 212–13; Ch. XIII, pp. 330–2. For an explanation of the practice of granting degrees by "creation", "mandate" and "incorporation", see Clark, II, pt. i, 233–4, 345–6; Heywood and Wright, I, 171, 173, 211, 213; Mullinger, II, 232; John and J. A. Venn, *Matriculations and Degrees, 1544–1659*, Introduction, pp. xxiii–xxvi.

32. *Biographia Britannica*, ed. 1747–66, V, 3230 n.

33. For Coke's disqualification for candidates, see Ch. II, pp. 40–1, and Appendix I, item 5. For Owen as a university member, see below, Ch. VII, pp. 188–9.

34. For the fourteen-day period at Cambridge in 1614 and 1621, see Dyer, I, 292, and Appendix III, below. For the eight-day period, see Wall, p. 153. For the twentieth century, see Tanner, *Register*, p. 30. For the interval at Oxford for the election of Chancellor, see Griffiths, *Statutes*, p. 163.

35. For Coke's directions on the delivery of the election returns, see below, Appendix I, item 6. For reference to documents returned to the Sheriff from Oxford in 1603/4, see Reginald Lane Poole, *History of the University Archives*, Appendix I, pp. 34–5. For the return of indentures at Cambridge, see Dyer, I, 292, and Wall, p. 154. For characteristic procedures at Oxford, and samples of documents, see Oxford University Archives, N23, p. 3839, f. 215r and 250v–1a, and Tb28, p. 3839, f. 54. For the remark in Pym's diary, see Wallace Notestein, Frances Helen Relf, and Hartley Simpson, *Commons' Debates, 1621*, IV, 182.

36. Duport's account of the irregularities in certification in 1614, is in Cooper, V, 351. For the Oxford items on certification, see Appendices IV and VII, below. See also Ch. X, p. 270, where the Convocation in 1678/9 refused to agree to the signing and sealing of the indenture.

37. For maps and comments on the meeting-place of the Senate at Cambridge, see Thomas D. Atkinson, *Cambridge Described and Illustrated*, pp. 270, 273, 274, 279–80. For the Oxford Convocation, see Christopher Hobhouse, *Oxford as it Was and as it Is Today*, pp. 6, 13, 46, 47, and also Laud, V, pt. i, 143 n., for the new Convocation House of 1638. Anthony Wood, *Fasti*, II, 56, says that the Convocation in 1643 was meeting in the North Chapel of St. Mary's Church. This was probably because the Convocation House was being used by the "Anti-Parliament" that was called in January 1643/4.

38. For the seating arrangements at Oxford, see Gibson, pp. 187–8, and p. xxv, n.; Griffiths, *Statutes*, p. 139. For a description of a meeting of the Cambridge Senate in 1657, see Robert W. Ramsey, *Richard Cromwell*, pp. 22–4, and J. J. Smith, *A Cambridge Portfolio*, p. 421.

39. For reference to seats at Oxford, see Falconer B. Madan, *Oxford Books*, II, 141. For seats at Cambridge, see Cooper, V, 349; Dyer, I, 363.

40. For mention of the statute against non-residents in 1614, see Cooper, V, 349. See also Ayliffe, II, 158. For mention of a statute in the indenture of 1673/4, see Appendix VII, below. For mention of parliamentary statutes in the general writs, see Whitelocke, *King's Writt*, I, 400–2. For the statute against bribery, see Wall, p. 153.

41. For nominations at Oxford in 1625/6 and 1678/9, see below, p. 76, Appendix IV, and *Life and Times*, II, 442–3; III, 326. For nineteenth-century notes on nomination, the reading of the statutes, the interval of election, etc., see Oxford University Archives: Victorian Papers relating to Parliamentary Elections. The word "nomination", incidentally, is used in its modern American sense, meaning *named as a candidate*, in almost all the sources relating to university representation, from the beginning of the seventeenth century.

42. For examples of desisting before the poll, see below, Ch. VI, pp. 146, 147; Ch. IX, pp. 232, 233–4, 244; Ch. X, pp. 264, 267, 268; Ch. XI, p. 280. For expressions of opinion in favour of unanimity and against risking a defeat, see below, Ch. VIII, p. 225; Ch. IX, p. 233; Ch. XII, pp. 301–2.

43. The statute for the election of proctors for Oxford in 1574 provided the severe penalty of loss of the right to vote and hold office for anyone who tried to persuade another to nominate or vote for any person as proctor. Moreover, an oath was required of all voters, stating that they had not tried to influence anyone's vote "neither by a price, nor an entreaty, nor a promise, nor by any other method, directly or indirectly", and requiring them to give names of any whom they know to have exerted such influence. Gibson, pp. 400, 401. The disorderly election that called forth the royal letter at Cambridge in 1669 was for esquire bedell. See Dyer, I, 362. For the promising of votes in parliamentary elections, see, for example, below, Ch. VIII, pp. 224–5; Ch. IX, pp. 232–3; Ch. X, p. 262; Ch. XII, pp. 296–7; and C.S.P., Dom., Chas. I, I (1625–6), 530.

44. The details of Buckingham's election at Cambridge are given in the letters of the Rev. Joseph Mead, fellow of Christ's College. Heywood and Wright, I, 338–9. For the figures of the vote, see Parliamentary History, ed. Wm. Cobbett, II, 165, Henry Mountlowe was the only university burgess, past, current, or future, who is recorded as voting for the Duke. See Cooper, III, 186.

45. See below, Ch. VII, p. 201; Ch. IX, p. 244; Ch. X, p. 262; Ch. XIII, p. 344. The impression that the custom of treating was less common at Cambridge may merely be the result of a dearth of information. At Oxford, Anthony Wood was quick to report the activities of the "pot companions" in every election.

46. For the Lenthall canvass, see Ch. VII, pp. 200–1. For the ten-mile limit, see Thomas H. B. Oldfield, History of Boroughs, II, 387. For personal canvass, see below, Ch. VI, p. 147; Ch. IX, p. 244; Ch. X, pp. 263, 264, 269, 270; Ch. XI, pp. 279, 280–1; Ch. XIII, p. 344.

47. For the election of 1625/6, see below, pp. 75–7, and Appendix IV. For Laud's election as Chancellor, see Laud, V, pt. i, 4 n.; Wood, Gutch, II, pt. i, 368.

48. Gibson, pp. 399, 401.

49. Cooper, II, 299.

50. Ibid., V, 348–51; see also below, Appendix III.

51. Wall, p. 154. Another form of semi-private voting seems to have been sometimes used at Cambridge besides the ballot—though not necessarily in parliamentary elections. A note in Smith, Cambridge Portfolio, p. 421, describes the votes as being taken by officials "going down the line" of regents and non-regents, somewhat after the fashion in use at Oxford. See pp. 77–8 of this chapter.

52. Wood, Gutch, II, pt. ii, 357.

53. Oxford University Archives, N23, p. 3639, ff. 214, 215r.

54. The first version is Wood's, the others from the petition given in Appendix IV. Willson, Privy Councillors, p. 76, has still another version of the speech—invitare magnatus.

55. For a more detailed account of the settlement of this dispute, see Ch. IV, pp. 107, 108–9.

56. Griffiths, Statutes, pp. 128–9, 134.

57. C.J., I, 837. According to L. H. D. Buxton and Strickland Gibson, Oxford University Ceremonies, p. 53, the first method of taking the votes superseded the second from 1400 on.

58. The account given here of the Oxford scrutiny is taken largely from the Convocation minutes of the election of Thomas Thynne in 1673/4. See Appendix VII, below. A slightly different version, without the special tellers, dates from 1627. Oxford University Archives, N23, p. 3839, f. 252r. For other accounts of divisions, see below, Ch. X, pp. 269–70; Ch. XI, p. 288. This latter division was the result of a mere prank.

59. Two examples of such exceptions are found in the Oxford returns for 1678/9 and 1679 where the court candidates, Finch and Jenkins, respectively, are named first, Griffiths, *Statutes*, p. 136. At Cambridge the ballots of the early years were preserved for a time at least, to judge from Appendix III, No. 2, below.

60. Porritt, I, 103. For two of the printed polls, see *The Poll for the Election of Two Representatives in Parliament for the University of Cambridge, 1780*, and *The True Copy of the Poll for Members of Parliament for the University of Oxford, March 21, 1721/2*. See also notice of two other polls (1710 and 1727) in Cooper, IV, 194, and H. R. Luard, *Index to Catalogue of Manuscripts in the Library of the University of Cambridge*, V, 129, respectively.

61. *Parliamentary Debates*, 408 (1945), 1552–3.

62. The description of the order of voting given here is based upon provisions in the Oxford and Cambridge statutes for the election of Chancellor (Dyer, I, 181–2; Griffiths, *Statutes*, pp. 135–6), and Wall's account of Cambridge procedures, pp. 153–4. Reference to the calls of the bedell and the voting of noblemen are also found in Dr. Duport's report (Cooper, V, 349), Peacock, App. lxi–lxii, and a manuscript in the Cambridge University Library (Cambridge University Library MS., Mm 457, pt. 2, no. 21, f. 302). According to Rashdall, II, pt. ii, 367, n. 3, this order of voting, as also the traditional query of the presiding officer in conducting other kinds of business, "Placet-ne vobis, domini doctores? Placet ne vobis, magistri?", is a survival from a time when the faculties each voted as a separate unit.

63. In 1627, however, according to a note in the Baker MSS., a great stress was laid upon the statutory hour of nine, as if a choice of burgesses made at any other time might not stand the test of legality. Cambridge University Library MS., Mm 457, pt. 2, no. 21, f. 302. See also Cooper, V, 348; Dyer, I, 181–2; J. E. Foster, ed., *Diary of Alderman Newton*, Cambridge Antiquarian Society, no. 23 (1890), pp. 97–8, and below, Ch. VII, p. 189.

64. For the Oxford regulations regarding the time of meeting, see Griffiths, *Statutes*, pp. 85, 128. For afternoon elections, see Ch. IV, p. 121; Ch. XII, p. 303. For the two-day election of proctors and for the poll of 1826, see respectively, Clark, II, pt. i, 245, and Porritt, I, 102. For the five-hour election of 1678/9, see below, Ch. X, p. 269.

65. Information about the reading of the election returns at Oxford is drawn from the Convocation minutes in the Archives cited in various previous notes, and from Griffiths, *Statutes*, p. 136. The data regarding Cambridge is taken from Cooper, V, 350–1; Wall, pp. 154–5; Cambridge University Library MS., Mm 457, pt. 2, no. 21, f. 303. For the return, see also above, pp. 68–9, and below, Ch. VIII, pp. 227–8.

66. Cooper, V, 348, 349; Appendix IV, below. One way in which the Vice-Chancellor could prevent discussion was to postpone the poll, if he foresaw difficulties. See below, Ch. X, p. 269.

67. For the King's remarks, see Wood, Gutch, II, pt. i, 362. For descriptions of disorderly assemblies, see Cooper, II, 527–8; Dyer, I, 362–3; Laud, V, pt. i, 195, 231–2; Appendix IV, below.

68. Cooper, V, 348–9; Tanner MS., 39:171; Appendix IV, below.

69. Ch. X, p. 265, below; Cooper, II, 179. For Mullinger on the Puritan influence, see II, 222–30, and above, Ch. I, p. 27.

70. Wood, Gutch, II, pt. i, 357; Appendix IV, below. See the reference to the "Juniors" in the elections of 1678/9 and 1685, and the youthful pranks of 1680/1 in Ch. X, pp. 269–70; also Ch. XI, p. 288; Ch. XII, p. 298. For the royal letter of Charles II, see Dyer, I, 363.

71. Cooper, V, 349–51; Wood, Gutch, II, pt. i, 363. Laud, as university Chancellor, in a letter ordering the re-election of the Vice-Chancellor in 1639, goes into considerable detail about this form of disorder. (*Works*, V, pt. i, 231.) See also the uproar over the taxor's election in 1597 in Cooper, II, 527–8.

72. A change in the method of electing proctors resulted from this affair, and thus removed one of the most common occasions for election tumults, but disorders in general still continued from time to time. Wood's account is found in Gutch, II, pt. i, 361–6.

73. For the imposition of penalties for disorders, see Dyer, I, 368; Laud, V, pt. i, 195, 196; and above, p. 77.

74. Porritt, I, 102.

75. See especially Ch. V, Ch. VIII, Ch. XIII.

76. *C.J.*, I, 714, 798. For the Vice-Chancellor's accounts, see Harleian MS., 7046, f. 84 (78). There is a similar ruling about university personnel voting in Cambridgeshire elections given in *The Candidate's Guide*, p. 13, under date of 28 May 1724. It would seem that this must be a misprint for 1624, as the day and month correspond to the 1624 decision. Porritt, I, 24, says that Cambridge students voted in the shire elections in 1679.

77. L. H. D. Buxton and Strickland Gibson, *Oxford University Ceremonies*, p. 66. Participation in the privileges of the City of Oxford was definitely prohibited by the Laudian Statutes. This prohibition would seem to include participation in the borough parliamentary elections.

78. Foster, *Alderman Newton*, p. 57.

79. See below, Ch. X, p. 263; Ch. XII, p. 300; Ch. XIII, pp. 341–2. See also the unsuccessful efforts of the royalist poet, John Cleveland, to prevent the election of Oliver Cromwell as member for the Town of Cambridge in 1640, and the role of Exeter College in the Oxford county election of 1754, where the mere proximity of the college to the polling booth allowed of considerable university influence over the outcome. Mullinger, III, 147; R. J. Robson, *The Oxfordshire Election of 1754, passim.*

80. This is only a supposition, and may not be correct. In fact, the evidence based upon a sampling derived from a check of the town and county M.P.s of the period 1604–90 does not entirely support such a conclusion. At Cambridge three of the borough members, and five of the knights of the shire could have voted in the Senate, but not one of the Oxford members from either county or city was qualified to have a vote in Convocation (although from twenty-five to fifty per cent of them had spent some time at a university).

81. Mullinger, II, 515 n.; Appendix VI, below.

82. For payments for extraordinary expenses to John Owen, 1653, and to Sir Thomas Clarges, 1689/90, see *Life and Times*, IV, 61, 82. For the Porritts' comment, see I, 101.

83. For Mountlowe's payments in the Vice-Chancellor's accounts, see Harleian MS., 7046, ff. 82–4 (74–7), *passim.*

84. For these references to "parliamentary wages", see Oxford University Archives, N23, p. 3839, f. 251 v.; Anchitell Grey, *Debates*, IV, 237–8; *C.J.*, IV, 161; Thomson, p. 80; Cambridge University Registry, 50: 22; and below, Ch. IX, p. 252.

85. Harleian MS., 7046, f. 84 (78). For example, the writ for Nathaniel Bacon's election cost the university £2.25.

86. Wall, p. 349.

87. Lionel L. Shadwell, *Enactments in Parliament*, I, 337.

88. For examples of the compromise by which the universities were able to maintain their freedom of choice, even under considerable pressure, see below, Ch. V, p. 130; Ch. VII, pp. 193, 199; Ch. VIII, pp. 214–15; Ch. IX, p. 234. See also Oldfield's remarks on university freedom in the eighteenth century, *supra*, p. 73.

CHAPTER IV

THE PERIOD OF ROYAL INFLUENCE, 1621–1640

When the stormy Parliament of 1614 was dissolved, no other Parliament was summoned for seven years, and when the next House was elected, only one of the former university members, Sir John Bennett, stood for his old seat. New stars, instead, were rising on the university horizon. At Oxford, there was Sir Clement Edmondes, Clerk of the Council since 1609, and at Cambridge, Sir Robert Naunton, his Majesty's new Secretary of State. These were joined by that former aspirant, Dr. Barnaby Gooch, now at last secure in the seat he had tried to wrest from Sir Miles Sandys in the election of 1614.[1]

With the new Parliament of 1620/1, a new trend appeared in university politics, a trend which had already shown itself in the previous period, but which now became intensified—the increasing use by the King and his advisers of university representation as a means of introducing members into the Commons who would advance the purpose of the court party. The result of this policy was that the university seats in the 1620's and on through the Short Parliament of 1640 came to be the special province of the King's chief spokesmen, the Privy Councillors.[2] This point is very clear when the facts are reduced to statistical form. From 1621 up to the spring of 1640, there were fifteen university burgesses in all, and of these, seven were of the Privy Council, and five of these seven were Secretaries of State.[3] Besides these Privy Councillors, there were four other university members who held crown appointments. This leaves only four others who were more or less free agents—in this first election, for example, only Barnaby Gooch.

The most extreme example of the subjection of a university member to the royal will is the case of Sir Robert Naunton, Gooch's colleague in 1620/1. Naunton's entire attention was directed towards the King, and what should be his Majesty's pleasure. At no time did he seem to regard himself as having any obligation to the university in connection with his seat. Indeed, when first elected, even the basic question of whether or not the seat should be accepted was submitted to the King. This was done in a letter to Naunton's patron, the Duke of Buckingham. The problem was presented in somewhat awkward language:

> Though I have not yet refused to serve, because I should so have made myself incapable to answer the obligation I have to do his Majesty service

there when he shall be pleased to accept thereof. Yet do I not hold myself
bound to admit of their choice that elected me . . . till I shall receive
assurance of his Majesty's gracious approbation.[4]

Naunton, to be sure, was at this moment situated in peculiar circumstances, such as no other university burgess-elect ever found himself in.
He was confined to his own house by royal order, having come under the
King's displeasure because of some words spoken to the French envoy
in favour of a French marriage for the Prince of Wales instead of a
Spanish one. He was thus unable to claim his seat in Parliament without the King's permission.[5] On the other hand, if he failed to attend,
as the session wore on, the House might take it as an offence, and
subject him to parliamentary discipline. Of this possibility he wrote
dramatically:

> They shall send me to what prison they will, yes, and pull me in pieces,
> too, before I will be fetched out of my house with my own consent, till my
> sovereign dear master shall enlarge me, who hath confined me hither.

Despite the fervour of this protestation, the King remained unmoved.
He did not "enlarge" Naunton for parliamentary service, and throughout the whole session, Naunton never appeared on the floor of the House.
No crisis was produced, however. Naunton's absence aroused comment,
but the matter was never brought to an issue. Nevertheless this meant
that because of the King's caprice Cambridge was deprived of half of its
representation. Moreover—and what is still more astonishing—in spite
of the royal interdict, Naunton was re-elected by the university in
1623/4, and the situation was repeated throughout the next Parliament.[6]
The whole episode is one of the most striking illustrations of the way
in which the King's will in this period ran counter both to the privileges
of Parliament and to the rights of the university constituency.

But royal influence alone, exercised directly in positive or negative
form, was not the only type of outside interference suffered by the
universities. Pressure was also brought to bear, sometimes on behalf
of the King, sometimes for their own purposes, by the King's ministers
and favourites, and by various university Chancellors. There were, for
example, at least three occasions where the Chancellor's personal secretary was put forward as a candidate. Two of these attempts failed, but
the third succeeded in 1640—though not, in this case, with detriment
to the university's real interests.[7]

In the face of all this, the universities did not relinquish their right of
free election without resistance. Oxford, in particular, ignored the
recommendations of its Chancellor more than once, and in 1625/6, as
we have already seen in Chapter III, took a disputed election to the

floor of the House. Cambridge, also, "murmured", as the Reverend Joseph Mead noted, but here the university was less successful on the whole in making its protests felt. The reason for Cambridge's apparently greater docility may be that it was really less free in its opportunity for expression. It was noted in Chapter III that in 1620/1, as in 1614, the Heads at Cambridge attempted to introduce a more restricted system of voting into parliamentary elections, in which the nomination of candidates was taken out of the hands of the electorate. Probably in an attempt to challenge this action, the choice of Naunton and Gooch in 1620/1 was called into question more than a month after the poll, but the opposition was downed by a letter from the King ratifying the action taken by the Heads. If this situation prevailed throughout the subsequent elections, it would explain the inability of Cambridge to assert itself as vigorously as Oxford.[8]

The subjection of the universities in this period is further demonstrated by the fact that both universities ultimately had to stomach the two royal favourites, Buckingham and Laud, as university Chancellors, though in each case the conduct of the election was not above suspicion of fraud and intimidation.[9]

When we turn from the question of outside interference with elections to study the actions of the university members after they were seated, we find the same influences at work. The most active of the university members were generally those who were Privy Councillors, and their chief interest in the proceedings of the House was to get the King's business carried through, and to protect the prerogative from the growing onslaughts of criticism.[10] The university burgesses were less successful in accomplishing these aims in the Parliament of 1620/1 than they were later. There were several reasons for this. The most obvious was the absence and disgrace of two of the four members—Sir Robert Naunton, one of the Secretaries of State, and Sir John Bennett, Judge of the Prerogative Court of Canterbury. The cause of Naunton's absence has already been explained. As for Bennett, we shall see presently that he was the central figure in one of the several impeachment proceedings for which this Parliament was famous, and that he ultimately lost his seat by being expelled from the House. For the present, we need only note that the absence of Bennett and Naunton meant that, of the university burgesses in high favour, only Sir Clement Edmondes was left to speak on the King's behalf.

But Edmondes, to judge from the parliamentary records, was not a vigorous speaker. He does not stand forth with any of the prominence that might have been expected in the case of one who had been Clerk of the Council for so many years, and who was shortly to be a candidate for appointment as Secretary of State. In committee work, he was sufficiently occupied with matters concerning trade and the City of London—he had been Remembrancer there—but in the debates he figured only once, in the early weeks of the session, when he "spoke for the King's wants"—a move very characteristic of a Privy Councillor.[11] Beyond this, any service he may have rendered, either to King or university, seems to have gone unnoticed.

His colleague from Oxford, after the expulsion of Sir John Bennett, was Sir John Danvers, a member of a prominent Oxfordshire family, and brother to the Earl of Danby. Danvers, for some reason, became immensely popular with the university, and was re-elected to his seat for every Parliament but one from 1621 through the Short Parliament of 1640. His popularity is not easy to explain, except through the circumstances of his family's local standing, and his brother's benefactions to the university—in 1622 the Earl gave Oxford land for botanical gardens with an endowment for maintenance. As far as Danvers himself is concerned, as a burgess his contribution to the university's welfare or prestige seems to have been slight, for in Parliament he was always a silent and inactive member. Moreover, in the end, his conduct in the Civil War must have shocked his old constituents very deeply, when he turned first Parliamentarian, and then Regicide.[12]

But in 1621 he was still a Gentleman of the Privy Chamber to the Prince of Wales, and made no stir in the political world on one side or the other. He missed all the first session of the Parliament, for he was not elected to Bennett's seat until 29 May, and in the second session, his name is not found in the Journal until 20 November, and then on a minor committee affecting the Prince's property interests.[13] He took no part in the debates on privileges and grievances that led up to the Great Protestation.

The man Danvers replaced, however—Sir John Bennett—had been in the centre of the spotlight in the early weeks of the Parliament. At first he had been happily at work engaged in the prosecution of some recusants.[14] Then the great blow fell, and he was accused of extortion practised in the settlement of wills coming under his jurisdiction as Judge of the Prerogative Court of Canterbury. Of all the excitements of this Parliament, only the impeachment of Bacon created greater uproar. The Commons fastened the more fiercely upon Sir John's misdemeanours since the issue gave an opportunity for action denied them in connection with other grievances. Debate waxed fast and furious.[15]

Sir John's fellow university burgesses said nothing in his behalf. His guilt was too apparent to admit defence. "His cause was put into the balance and corruption was the heavier", so one account put it. One speaker declared that Bennett was proved to be "the most dishonest man that ever hee heard of"; and still another proclaimed that Bennett's acts were "the basest bryberyes that ever were". Sir George Calvert, Secretary of State, and destined later to be, like Bennett, a member for Oxford, urged that Bennett be sent to the Tower while the case was being discussed, for fear he should escape to the Continent and avoid punishment. Others, though inclined to be charitable, were no less severe in their final judgments. Sir Edward Coke declared, "I love Sir John Bennett, but I hate bribery." Bennett's two best friends, Sir Dudley Digges and Sir Edwin Sandys, did what they could to present his case in the best light possible, but in the end they must have joined in the vote of expulsion, since it was unanimous, with the exception of one vote, that of Bennett's son-in-law.[16]

Though present when the case was opened, Sir John, during this debate, kept to his own house, claiming he was ill and could not attend Parliament to answer for his conduct. This was suspected to be a subterfuge, as also his communications promising further explanations and asking for more time to examine the charges. The House finally proceeded to impeach him in his absence, "whereas he had time for defence & did not, & he also has not answered six points sent him by order of this house"; and it ordered the Sheriffs of London and Middlesex to have him in safe-keeping until such time as the Lords were ready to try him. In the meantime, he was to "bee put out & continue noe longer a Member of the said house"; and a warrant for a new writ was to be issued for the University of Oxford to choose his successor—who was, as we know, Sir John Danvers.[17]

When Bennett's case came before the Lords, there, too, considerable indignation was displayed, and a demand was made for "great Bayll" —£40,000.[18] However, when Bennett finally appeared before them, some mercy was shown him because of his illness and his large family—ten children and forty grandchildren—and also because—as a private letter of 2 June 1621 likewise reported, he had been proved in the end somewhat less guilty than at first had been expected.[19] His plea that he had only done what others had done was probably true, in view of the corruption of the times, but the fact that he had appropriated funds willed to charities, including some of the Bodleian bequest to Oxford, made his offence particularly unacceptable. His case was ultimately taken over by the Star Chamber, and a fine of £20,000, deprivation of all office, and imprisonment at the King's pleasure was the sentence rendered. He spent two years in the Fleet and died some two years afterwards.[20]

The scandal of Sir John Bennett was Oxford's most notable contribution to the Parliament of 1620/1. But Cambridge, as we have already seen, also had a burgess under a cloud, although Sir Robert Naunton's eclipse, in contrast to Bennett's, was without reproach, for Naunton had incurred his disgrace by a mere indiscretion, not by repeated and wholesale acts of dishonesty. Moreover, it was felt by many Englishmen that the indiscretion itself deserved praise rather than punishment, since it was an attempt to prevent the hated Spanish marriage. For this reason the Commons were all the more irked by Naunton's absence, and were inclined to order him to take his seat, when the question of absent members was discussed at the opening of Parliament on 6 February. Sir Samuel Sandys had to remind them that Naunton was absent only because of the King's restraint, and that such restraint was not within "the priviledge of this Howse".[21]

This argument was apparently brought forward at Naunton's own request, since in the letter to the Duke of Buckingham, from which an extract has been quoted earlier in this chapter, Naunton had told the Duke that he had "entreated" some of his friends to oppose any motion that might be made to force him to disobey the King's orders for his seclusion.[22] Sir Samuel Sandys was successful in carrying out this request and the matter was dropped. Likewise, in the next Parliament, although the circumstances were similar, and Naunton anticipated further difficulties, the Commons took no further notice of his peculiar status.

The result was that Cambridge's only acting burgess in the Parliament of 1620/1 was Dr. Barnaby Gooch, who, though new to the great world of politics, proved to be the only university representative in this House to play any sort of respectably prominent part. In the index to Notestein, Relf, and Simpson's *Commons' Debates, 1621,* there is a long list of references to Gooch's various speeches and activities. Among these, he appears as a university representative most notably when contesting the claims of Oxford to be mentioned before Cambridge in the usual proviso exempting the universities from the subsidy. This was one of those perennial controversies over precedence that involved so many university burgesses from time to time. In the end, Oxford won out, despite Gooch's efforts,[23] and he was likewise defeated in his attempts to get certain financial claims of his college (Magdalene) recognized by an act of Parliament. There seems to have been no other university issues at stake, unless perhaps the draining of the Fens.[24]

Gooch's knowledge of the law was recognized in a number of appointments to committees involving legal questions. Perhaps the most important general issue of the session with which he had to do was Floyd's case, when he served on the committee that was appointed to consider a conference with the Lords.[25] Though a free agent, in that he had no known relations with the Court, he was nevertheless partial to the Court party—to judge by his speech at the end of the first session in favour of adjournment, and against further discussion of grievances.[26]

In the next Parliament—that of 1623/4—both Gooch and Naunton were again returned for Cambridge, while Oxford dutifully presented the King with two right-hand men to serve him—Sir George Calvert, Secretary of State since 1617, and Sir Isaac Wake, Ambassador to Savoy.[27] These royal university burgesses from Oxford did not contribute much to the Crown's control of the Commons, however, for Calvert, though a fairly skilful manager for the King's interests, was somewhat irregular in attendance, especially towards the end of the session, when he was ill for a time,[28] and Sir Isaac Wake departed on a mission abroad before the Parliament was over. Sir Robert Naunton was apparently also absent, still under orders to keep to his house. All this meant that Barnaby Gooch again was left as the only university member who was regularly in his seat throughout the session.

Naunton's enforced absence seems to have been something of a surprise. Naunton had been told by the Lord Keeper, Archbishop Williams, that the King expected to use his services in this Parliament although he was no longer Secretary of State, and that accordingly the university had been asked to choose him burgess again for this express purpose. In view of the fact that the Spanish influence was now removed from the Court, it would seem that there was no further reason for Naunton's seclusion. But even after Naunton had learned that the university had re-elected him, no word was received from the King. Naunton was then forced to write to Buckingham, urging the Duke to persuade the King to permit him to go free at once, lest it be thought that any subsequent liberation would come as a result of parliamentary pressure, and not as an act of the King's free will.[29] In spite of this appeal to the royal vanity, the King seems to have remained obdurate. There was no parliamentary pressure for Naunton's release, and another Parliament appears to have come to a close without Cambridge's favourite representative's ever having entered the House. His name, at least, is not found anywhere in the *Commons' Journal*.[30]

Fortunately, the university could still count upon the indefatigable Gooch to represent its interests—although he was unsuccessful in his efforts to preserve for the universities certain court rights which he felt were impaired by a bill regarding informers in infringements of penal laws. It was on this point that he made his one recorded speech. Otherwise, his activity is only attested by his service on a number of committees on various subjects.[31]

The exertions of Sir Isaac Wake of Oxford, on the other hand, were more conspicuous and all directed to one purpose—the interests of the Crown's new foreign policy. It will be remembered that in this Parliament Buckingham and Prince Charles were trying to reverse the trend that had been followed since 1618 when the alliance with Spain was first undertaken, and to make a shift from the Spanish alliance into one with the Protestant nations, which might be used as a vantage-point for making war on the former ally. This sudden reversal was bewildering to the Commons, and it was Sir Isaac Wake's business to assist in their adjustment to the new plans. His skill in doing this had already won him "much reputation", according to young Dudley Carleton's letter to his father on 4 March, but Wake's success was not complete for some weeks. By the 20 March, Carleton reported again:

> Sir Isaac Wake attends Parliament closely, his employment being at stake on what passes, there, where matters go on uncertainly, the King's speeches needing interpretations, and the Houses being so wary and suspicious as though dealing with enemies.[32]

By late April, however, the air had cleared, and Wake prepared to depart on his mission, lingering only long enough, as he said, "to see if all goes well between the king and his people", and being able to comment with satisfaction on 29 April that the King's letter had been well received in the House. By 13 May, he was reported *en route* for Italy.[33] This left Oxford's representation to the preoccupied Calvert, whose hands were full of the King's business, and whose mind was now full of his own religious dilemma. The session, however, soon came to a close (29 May 1624), and by the time the next Parliament was summoned, new burgesses—with the exception of Sir Robert Naunton, who was held over for the third time in his old seat—had come once more to the fore.

Naunton's popularity with the University of Cambridge is somewhat difficult to account for. It seems unlikely that it could have stemmed entirely from his position as Secretary of State and Privy Councillor, for he was out of favour with James I during all these years, and the royal influence, if exerted at all (as suggested in the correspondence at the time of Naunton's second election) was probably not over enthusiastic. Indeed, after 1623/4 Naunton was more out of favour than ever for he had even lost his post as Secretary. Moreover, as far as the university was concerned, in this second Parliament, as in the first, he was completely useless, since he seems not to have been released from the King's order of seclusion until August, after the Parliament had been dissolved. Thus he came far short of the university's expectations, as set forth in the fulsome letter sent him upon the occasion of his first election in 1620/1, when they hailed him as their "stronghold of wisdom and eloquence", the protector of their "privileges, foundations, edifices, establishments, the whole equipment of the Muses", all of which was now entrusted to him as their burgess.[34]

In the wake of such anticipations, the university must have been disappointed at Naunton's insufficiency, but nevertheless, again in 1625 they remained stubbornly faithful to him. They were probably unaware of the indifference to their claims that he had expressed in his letter to Buckingham at the time of his first election,[35] and they may have felt some old-time respect and indulgence towards him, as one who had once been Cambridge's public orator, and who now was a man of scholarly interests and abilities, caught in the current of difficult times, a victim of the late King's caprice, and something of a Protestant champion because of his stand on the Spanish treaty.[36]

With this new Parliament of 1625—the first of Charles I's reign—the high tide of royal influence was reached. Two other Privy Councillors besides Naunton were chosen by the universities—by Cambridge, Sir Albertus Morton, and by Oxford, Sir Thomas Edmondes. The first was at the same time Ambassador to France and to the Low Countries, and Secretary of State in Calvert's place; the second was Treasurer of the King's Household. Then, in addition to these three Councillors, there was Oxford's favourite burgess re-elected, Sir John Danvers, still presumably close to the throne as the King's former Gentleman of the Privy Chamber.[37]

In this election there had been a great deal of preliminary activity everywhere, and probably the universities also had had their share, though there is very little evidence to be found upon the subject. At Oxford, a letter from the Chancellor, the Earl of Pembroke, was delivered on behalf of the new candidate, Sir Thomas Edmondes,[38] but Danvers received no such assistance—perhaps he needed none. Edmondes also must have stood well with the university, even without the Chancellor's recommendation, if the remark he made in the Parliament of 1620/1 during the debate on precedence was remembered. At that time, he had joined issue on behalf of Oxford by quoting James I to the effect that "Cambridge was worthye but to be but a handmaide to Oxford."[39] At any rate, however acceptable Edmondes may have been, the choice of burgesses at Oxford seems to have caused no particular stir.

At Cambridge, on the contrary, the Reverend Joseph Mead wrote in his usual discontented tone:

> We are here very busy about our burgesses afore the writ be come. I doubt the heads and body will not agree: the heads would prick whome we should choose, saying Rey [that is, the King?] made such an order, but the body think themselves free, and will go nigh to choose, as I hear, some which they [the Heads] prick not, as Sir Simeon Steward.

It seems more than likely that the candidacy objected to here was that of Morton, then high in the favour of both Buckingham and the King. The candidate suggested by Mead, Sir Simeon Steward, was a former Cambridge scholar, a county personage, and perhaps a relative of Cambridge's first burgess, Nicholas Steward.[40] His political views are not ascertainable, but his following must have been sufficient to lend some uncertainty to the outcome of the election, for Sir Albertus Morton, in spite of having the support of the Heads, took care to make his position secure by standing also for a seat for his home county of Kent.[41] He need not have taken this precaution, however, for the "busie Faction", as it was called,[42] was unable to arouse sufficient opposition at Cambridge, and when the time came to choose, both Morton and Naunton were elected without competition.[43] Morton was also chosen for the Kent seat, and it was said that this was really the seat of his preference, but it does not appear that he ever actually relinquished his Cambridge place in favour of Kent.[44] As it turned out, whether he sat for Kent or Cambridge did not matter, for Morton, like Naunton in 1621 and 1624, never appeared in this Parliament at all. He was away on official business during the entire term, engaged in negotiations in France and the Netherlands, and before the next Parliament was summoned, he was dead.[45] The other university burgesses are scarcely mentioned in the scanty records of this Parliament, although each one spoke at least once—Sir Robert Naunton and Sir Thomas Edmondes in defence of the King's need of supply, Sir John Danvers, on a matter of procedure.[46] Danvers was also fairly active in committee work, and served in his special character of university representative, when he and Sir Thomas Edmondes were deputed by Parliament to convey a protest to the Vice-Chancellor of the university against the preaching of a certain High Church divine who had been appointed by the Vice-Chancellor as official preacher during the summer of 1625 when Parliament was in session at the university because of the prevalence of the plague in London.[47] But in comparison with the important part played in this Parliament by Sir Francis Seymour, Sir Robert Phelips, and Sir John Eliot, the university members cut a very modest figure.

This is all the more surprising in view of the fact that it seems that there were a number of university issues under consideration at this time, which should have called for action on the part of the university burgesses. A letter from the Rev. Joseph Mead mentions bills "against the universities" relating to pluralities and benefices, and an entry in S. R. Gardiner's *Commons' Debates, 1625*, also shows that some kind of general university reform was being proposed.[48] There is no indication that the university representatives took any action on these subjects, but for some reason—perhaps because of the general pressure of business rather than on account of concerted opposition—the bills were never passed.

The next Parliament was summoned for 6 February 1625/6. This was the occasion of the famous disputed election at Oxford, already discussed in detail in the previous chapter. As noted there, the Convocation was opened by the reading of two letters of recommendation on behalf of Sir Thomas Edmondes, one from the Earl of Pembroke, the university Chancellor, and the other from George Abbot, the Archbishop of Canterbury, both of whom had recommended Edmondes in the previous election. The candidate preferred by the opposition was Sir Francis Stewart, a son of the Earl of Moray, and therefore a cousin to the King. This relationship, however, as will be seen later, did not prevent Stewart from taking a stand against the Duke of Buckingham during the latter's impeachment. Possibly the rank and file of the university voters were aware of Stewart's attitude at the time they made such a demonstration in his favour.[49] Otherwise it is hard to account for his popularity, and their determination to reject Sir Thomas Edmondes. The other candidate preferred by the voters was, as usual, Sir John Danvers.

In staging this revolt against a Privy Councillor, Oxford seems to have been caught up in the general spirit of resistance that was rising everywhere in the country—a spirit that ultimately produced what Sir Bulstrode Whitelocke called a "great, warm, and ruffling parliament".[50] Cambridge, however, contributed very little to the revolt, for the most prominent burgess from Cambridge in the next two Parliaments was a crown agent *par excellence*, Sir John Coke, Secretary of State. From this time on until the Personal Rule, Coke was the King's chief mouthpiece in the House. Naunton by now was no longer a court favourite, and he was not named at Cambridge when the burgesses were chosen. Nevertheless, he was still well thought of in other circles as is shown by a letter written by a former Cambridge man, Dr. John Winthrop of Suffolk, later Governor of Massachusetts, in which the latter attempted to advance Naunton's chances of election as a knight for that shire.[51]

This possibly means that Winthrop was aware that Naunton was un-likely to hold his old seat at Cambridge—partly perhaps because his candidacy there was an obstruction to the advancement of other plans regarding the disposal of the university seats. In any case, the outcome was that Naunton was successful in Suffolk, and the *Vanum Parlia-mentum*[52] of 1625 had seen his last appearance in the House as a uni-versity representative.

Whether it was Naunton's possible candidacy or the general temper of the country, something at least must have put the Cambridge elec-tion in doubt, for Naunton's successor, Sir John Coke, despite the royal favour, had apparently been far from certain of success in gaining the university's seat. The evidence for this is a letter from Sir George Chud-leigh written 1 February, offering Coke a blank burgess-ship for East Looe, for use in case he failed of election in either of the two consti-tuencies he was then standing for, St. Germains and Cambridge, the latter seat being, Chudleigh noted, "in some competition".[53] Coke, however, managed in the end to secure Cambridge, although he lost at St. Germains through the influence of Sir John Eliot.[54] At Cambridge he had as colleague a university figure, Dr. Thomas Eden, Master of Trinity Hall, a "civilian" who was active from this time on in various matters of royal administration.[55] That there was something dubious about the Cambridge election is suggested by the fact that the return is missing, and that the Venetian agent in England later reported that there had been a plan afoot to oust "the Secretary Cuch" from his parliamentary seat, for illegal election, just as Sir Thomas Edmondes had been ousted from his place as Oxford's representative in this same Parliament.[56] Whatever the difficulty was, it would seem that the choice of these two men—Coke and Eden—the one an instrument of the Court, the other a resident of the university, represented some sort of compromise between the university's independence and its role as docile supporter of the Crown. If so, this proved a relatively lasting com-promise, for the same two members were returned for the Parliament of 1627/8.

University affairs and university members were alike more prominent in this second Parliament of Charles I than perhaps in any Parliament heretofore. In the first place, there was the disputed election at Oxford, which was brought by petition before the Committee of Privilege, and mentioned several times in the *Commons' Journal*. Early in the session, on 1 March, the Committee reported, after hearing some witnesses, that they also wished to hear the evidence of the Vice-Chancellor himself "in those Things which shall be demanded of him, concerning the said election, but not as a Delinquent". Sir John Danvers (here spelled

"Davers"), as Oxford's only accredited representative, engaged to notify the Vice-Chancellor and bring him in to the Committee.[57] Of this event, the Reverend Mr. Mead wrote—we may imagine with a certain amount of satisfaction, in view of his earlier and later comments on royal interference at Cambridge:

> Dr. Prideaux, Vice-Chancellor of Oxford, is sent for by the Parliament . . . about the misguiding of the election of Sir Thomas Edmondes; and his adversaries of the body of the university are said to be very stout and resolute.

Then Mead added—whether with complacence or with envy at Oxford's audacity—"Our vice-chancellor had never this honour."[58]

The parliamentary Committee of Privilege decided, as we have already seen, against the Vice-Chancellor and in favour of a free election, and Sir Francis Stewart was duly elected—or perhaps re-elected—six days after the Committee's decision, 23 March. At least this is the date given in the *Official Return* and the Oxford Archives,[59] although it was not until 4 April that Stewart notified the House that he had been re-elected, and as late as 19 April that the fact of his re-election was referred to the Committee of Privilege. After this, however, no further action on the matter is recorded in the *Journal*.[60] The whole episode presents an interesting example of mutual support rendered each other by the Commons and the university in opposition to the Court—an alignment of a kind that is seldom encountered in the history of university politics.

Regardless of his status, Sir Francis Stewart had been present in the House from the beginning, taking no insignificant part in the important business that was afoot.[61] The fact that his right to sit was not challenged may be owing to the circumstance that he had been elected for Liskeard as well as for the university,[62] so that, until the university case was settled, presumably he still held an option on both seats. The position of his rival, Sir Thomas Edmondes, is not so clear. As "Mr. Treasurer", Edmondes appears in the earlier pages of the *Journal*—only, it would appear, by virtue of his Oxford credentials, for after 4 April, when Sir Francis gave the House notice of his re-election by the university, Edmondes's name no longer is to be found upon the committee lists.[63]

Stewart's part in this Parliament is especially interesting in view of his background, for, on the surface of things, he might be expected rather to have been a member of the Court party than to have supported the insurgents. Of royal blood by an illegitimate line, the son of the first Earl of Moray, and first cousin of James I, he had been treated with great favour by that monarch, raised to be a Knight of the Bath, naturalized by Act of Parliament in 1623/4, mentioned for an earldom, and entrusted with important posts in the navy.[64] At the time that he entered the House in 1625/6 he had been serving as Vice-Admiral under Buckingham in the war against Spain. But it is possible that his relations with Charles were not so cordial as they had been with James, and it is certain that Stewart was dissatisfied with the way the navy was being handled in the summer of 1625. It is possible, too, that his frequent association with the Duke of Buckingham in the earlier Spanish marriage ventures, as well as his recent naval experience, had all combined to render him disillusioned with the Duke as a governmental influence. At any rate, he early took a stand on the side of the Duke's accusers. On the very day that the Committee of Privilege made its first report upon the Oxford election, Sir Francis was giving evidence in the House upon the matter of some bags of gold and silver that he had removed from a prize ship which he had captured, and turned over to the Duke. This was the famous case of the *St. Peter*, which ultimately figured in one of the charges in the Duke's impeachment.[65]

The Duke's reaction to this stand of Sir Francis's is described in one of the Reverend Mr. Mead's letters, where a conversation is reported that supposedly occurred one day as the Duke and Sir Francis were leaving Parliament. Mead gave this conversation in dialogue form:

Duke: "Sir Francis, though you have not spared me this parliament time, yet have I spared you."

Sir Francis: "My lord, concerning the first I have been very silent in your affairs; but for the last you deserve no thanks; where have you spared me?"

Duke: "When all passages shall be examined, you will not be found so clear from pillaging as your flourishes persuade the world."

Sir Francis: "My lord, you had best begin with me by times, for tomorrow in the morning, I mean to fall upon you."[66]

There is no record in the *Journal* of such an attack on Sir Francis against the Duke—for the report he made on the delivery of the bags from the *St. Peter* had been delivered six weeks earlier—and indeed the next information we have on Sir Francis's action in Parliament reveals him defending the Duke from the charge of having had the late King James poisoned.[67] This was one of the more extreme charges brought by the Duke's enemies, and Sir Francis's moderation on this point makes his firmness on the other charges all the more noticeable. That he was more than firm on the other points is indicated by the fact that, later in the session, he served on the committee that was to consider how to urge the Duke's commitment, and at this time was in constant danger of being committed himself, along with the other opponents of the royal favourite. The Earl of Pembroke, Oxford's Chancellor, at one stage of the proceedings, interceded with the King on Sir Francis's behalf, but the Duke still held a warrant in reserve to use against him, and Sir Francis was forbidden to attend the Court as a sign of the King's displeasure.[68] Nevertheless he himself openly took the part of others who had already suffered, in making a stand in favour of Sir Dudley Digges, when the latter was imprisoned, and by his support of Lord Digby, the Earl of Bristol's son, in the same circumstances. On this last occasion, Joseph Mead reported, Sir Francis, "out of his noble courtesy, went in a coach and brought him [Digby] to his lodgings".[69] From all these accounts of Sir Francis Stewart in the Parliament of 1625/6, it would appear that rebellious Oxford knew what it was about, when it was so insistent upon its choice of a representative in the university election.

In contrast to the dashing Sir Francis, Oxford's other member, Sir John Danvers, played his usual unobtrusive role, although he seems to have taken a larger part in committee work than he did in the two earlier Parliaments.[70] The crowning crisis of this "great, warm, and ruffling parliament" was, of course, the impeachment of Buckingham, but—with the exception of Sir Francis Stewart—none of the university members appears to have been active on either side of the question. There is no record of a poll for the Duke's impeachment. However, according to the Reverend Mr. Mead—and also the diary in the *Lonsdale MSS.*—both Cambridge burgesses voted in favour of it,[71] although this is almost impossible to believe in the case of Sir John Coke, one of the most faithful of royal henchmen, and a particular protégé of Buckingham's.

What made the Duke's impeachment a university as well as a parliamentary crisis is the fact that in the face of all the charges against him, the Cambridge Heads persisted in forcing him upon the university as Chancellor. We have seen in the previous chapter that this was only accomplished with great difficulty and under extreme pressure, and that the election did not represent the will of the university voters.[72] Nevertheless Joseph Mead was quite right when, in reporting these events, he foresaw that the election would have repercussions in the Commons: "what will the parliament say to us?" he wrote. "Did not our burgesses condemn the duke in their charge given up to the Lords?"[73]

The Commons indeed were infuriated, and Dr. Eden, on whom the burden of Cambridge's defence seems to have fallen, did what he could to pacify them, asking the House, according to Mead:

. . . not to have so hard a concept of the Universitie till they had more information, when perhaps they should find that which was done not to be an act of rebellion, but of loyaltie and obedience.

This was about all he could dare to say, under the circumstances, but his efforts were in vain, and his speech, as Mead said, was "much distasted".[74]

The House hastened to show its displeasure in its own way. A Committee of the Whole decided on a statement that

> . . . this house has just cause of complaint on the election of the duke of Buckingham to be Chancellor of the University of Cambridge: and do think fit, that a letter should be written to the corporation of that university, to signify that dislike; and to require them to send some of their body . . . to inform and give account . . . of the manner of their proceeding in the said election.

This plan was approved in spite of Dr. Eden's protest.[75] It was, in fact, the same general procedure that had been followed when Parliament had called Oxford's Vice-Chancellor to account earlier in the session; but with this difference: that in the case of Oxford, the position in dispute was within the jurisdiction of the House, as pertaining to its own membership, whereas the chancellorship of Cambridge was a matter legally beyond its authority. The King promptly reminded the House of this fact in a sharp letter in which he forbade them to proceed, pointing out that, since all corporations drew their powers by charter from the Crown, the question of the election of the Chancellor did not concern the House.

The Commons, however, were not disposed to yield, and returned a message to the King, explaining that the university officials were not to come to the House "as delinquents", but only to give information. This communication also stressed the fact that the universities' own burgesses had joined in the accusations against the Duke: "their burgesses being amongst us, and for them so accusing him, he ought not to have been elected". But the King—and later his Chancellor of the Exchequer—still objected on the ground that the Duke was as yet only under accusation, not actually proved guilty. The Commons finally desisted, and the matter was dropped.[76]

Dr. Eden, in addition to his efforts in the debate on the Duke's election, seems to have made another attempt to defend his university from adverse criticism in the Commons. This time the charge was Arminianism. There is no record of this argument beyond a fragmentary extract from one of Mead's letters, but from this it would appear that, whatever the general opinion of the House, Eden's opponent, at least, remained unconvinced.[77]

In all these university issues, it was Eden rather than his colleague, Sir John Coke, who appeared as Cambridge's representative. Sir John, apparently, was at all times too much occupied with the King's business to spare any attention for his constituency, and in no way throughout his entire parliamentary career did he ever figure in the House as a real representative of the university, although letters of gratitude in the Library of Cambridge seem to indicate that at some time or other he did the university great service in connection with the university press.[78] But, in Parliament or out, his willing but somewhat inadequate shoulders were already loaded down with the weight of all the necessities of State on behalf of his royal master. His position in this respect will be described more adequately later on, in connection with events of Charles's third Parliament.

This Parliament was called for the spring of 1627/8, almost two years after the dissolution of the Parliament that had undertaken the impeachment of Buckingham. By this time, the Duke, as Chancellor, had gained full control of Cambridge, and seems to have been involved in pulling some rather devious strings in connection with the new election of burgesses.[79] What he had in mind is not clear—indeed it is not even certain whether the project under way was the Duke's own idea or that of his secretary. But something in any case was afoot.

The university—or at least the "busie faction"—was, as usual, inclined to be intractable. Joseph Mead wrote to his friend Stuteville on 1 March 1627/8: "We have not yet chosen burgesses.... We of the university are indifferent for any the duke will signifie."[80] Whom the Duke would signify, on the other hand, was just what his secretary, one Robert Mason, wanted to know, according to a letter written by Mason about this same time to Edward Nicholas, then also a secretary to Buckingham. In this letter Mason said that he wished to be informed of the Duke's will, before he, Mason, should come up to London "about the Burgesship". Four days later, Mason again wrote more specifically, pointing out that the university "earnestly desire his Grace would declare himself for the election of their burgesses", and noting that the university had "importuned him [that is, Mason] not to stir till they hear good news from the Duke". The implication of this letter is that Mason himself was to be one of the candidates—at least, without this assumption, the letter is very difficult to understand. Mason went on to say that he was sending a dispensation "ready for the King's hand", so that he might be enabled to take a degree. This procedure would not have been really necessary in Mason's case, for he was already a Cambridge man—a master of arts and fellow of St. John's—but it would appear that, as the Duke's secretary, some special attention was to be shown him by the grant of a mandate degree in civil law. Mason, however, was not entirely dependent upon the favour of the King and the Duke for recognition at Cambridge. He seemed also to have the support

8

of some influential circles within the university, for in his letter he warned his master that if the latter at this time should "cross the intention of the University", he would "disenable" Mason thereafter "to do him the service it is necessary his secretary should do".[81]

Whatever the situation—and it is by no means clear—Mason's plans seem to have come to naught, for, as it turned out, neither Mason nor any other new candidate appeared at the poll on 11 March, and the two previous members, Sir John Coke and Dr. Thomas Eden, were unanimously returned to their seats.[82] Perhaps the Duke decided not to press his secretary's cause; perhaps he was lukewarm to the idea in the first place; perhaps he feared to throw in jeopardy the chances of a more important factotum, his own naval administrator and the King's chief spokesman, Coke. Indeed, it is a fact that there seems again to have been some doubt about Coke's status, though whether because of Mason's manœuvres, or because of the opposition of the "busie faction", is not clear. This is suggested by an apologetic letter that the university wrote to Coke some weeks after the Mason correspondence. The subject of the letter was mainly the misdemeanours of those old enemies of the university, the Town of Cambridge and the London Stationers, but it opened on a somewhat timid note, with reference to the recent election: "We humbly crave our late choice of you to be a burgess of our university may not prejudice her in your thoughts, yourself one of her chief masters."[83] There is no evidence to show that a similar reluctance had arisen in regard to the choice of Eden. Possibly Eden, as the university's own man, was more secure than Coke, so that the real issue rested between the two court candidates. The whole matter must be left in considerable obscurity. All that can be stated with certainty is that the election of 1627/8 at Cambridge was not without its undercurrent of influence and electioneering.

The same was true of the election at Oxford. Here the part played by the university Chancellor, the Earl of Pembroke, was more pronounced. He conducted himself, however, with the utmost diplomacy. His first letter of recommendation to the university was couched in carefully conciliatory tones. He knew, he said, that Oxford did not lack candidates among their own immediate numbers, but nevertheless he would recommend to the university Sir Henry Marten, whom they already knew and valued. His letter in Marten's favour was to be regarded as only in the nature of a vote cast for him by Pembroke as a mere member of Convocation acting in conjunction with the other members. In concluding his arguments on behalf of Marten, the Chancellor added another item of special interest to the historian of university representation. This was the point that Marten's burgess-ship would cost the university nothing, as his circumstances (presumably as Admiralty Judge) demanded that he live in London regardless of his status as a member of Parliament. This is one of the rare allusions to be found in university politics to the old custom of "parliamentary wages".[84]

The university was probably not averse to Marten in any case. He was a man of great ability and long experience in public life, a former fellow of New College, a doctor of the civil law, and—as was to be proved by his action in the Parliament that was just opening—a person of independence and keen judgment.[85] The Chancellor, indeed, seems to have rightly counted on Marten's popularity with the university, and to have decided to turn it to his own advantage. For he followed up his first letter with a second, this time assuming that Marten was already settled upon as burgess, and that he therefore, the Chancellor, might now be allowed to name a second candidate of his own choice—that is, his secretary, Michael Oldisworth. This left the university with three candidates to choose from, for Sir John Danvers also announced his willingness to serve in his old seat. A "scrutiny" was resorted to—the second, so far, in Oxford's parliamentary history—and the result was that Marten and Danvers were chosen burgesses for the Parliament of 1627/8.[86]

The events of this election are interesting for their demonstration of three things. The first is the acknowledged right of the Chancellor to propose one university burgess, but only one. The second is the readiness of the university to ignore the Chancellor's request when they felt that he had overstepped his prerogative—a stand that is reminiscent of their action against Pembroke's candidate in 1625/6, Sir Thomas Edmondes. The third is their unaccountable loyalty to Sir John Danvers, which has been discussed before. Another point worth noting in surveying the circumstances of this election is the character of the man they rejected, Michael Oldisworth, whose political views did not harmonize, or so one might think, with the position of one who was a Chancellor's secretary. For Oldisworth was inclined to the Country party, was a friend of Sir John Eliot, and later, when secretary to Pembroke's brother (who was a later successor as Chancellor of the university), was supposed to be largely responsible for the latter's co-operation with Parliament in the 1640's. Oldisworth as university burgess in 1628 might have made an even stronger stand against the Court than either Sir Henry Marten or Sir John Danvers—both of whom were now drifting into the opposition—but perhaps the university was not ready for such a candidate as yet. It seems more likely, however, that the real explanation for Oldisworth's failure to win in this election is to be found partly in the resentment aroused by the Chancellor's attempt to dictate and partly in the affection that was felt for Danvers, and not in any alarm felt over the radical character of Oldisworth's politics.[87]

Of all the four burgesses elected by the universities to the Parliament that met in March 1627/8, Sir John Coke was by far the most prominent. Indeed, his part in the proceedings of the Commons at this time was so great that it has been described in more or less detail by every writer on this period from Forster and Gardiner to David Harris Willson.[88] All agree in pointing out Coke's failures as a parliamentarian—his tactlessness, his lack of imagination, his slowness, and his pedantry. Clarendon and Eliot in Coke's own century[89]—as Willson in modern times—all found Coke lacking in every important quality except industry and honesty—having the qualities indeed of a good administrator rather than those of a successful parliamentary leader and a maker of policy. And yet it was Coke, who, on the floor of the House, had to ward off the Commons' demands, to coax them into granting subsidies, or to overawe them with the might of majesty, as the occasion might require.[90] Moreover, outside of Parliament, he had to accommodate himself to the political uncertainties of the King and the Duke, and the vagaries of their foreign policy—now trying to man and equip the navy (though without funds); now arresting recusants, or ignoring them, as the King's needs might demand. Indeed, reading the *Calendar of State Papers*, the records of the Privy Council, the *Cowper MSS.*, and other such correspondence, one cannot help but come to an understanding of the impatience felt by Privy Councillors and men of administration, like Coke, in the face of the strange new intransigeance that was developing in the Commons. With Coke especially, the busiest and most badgered of them all—even more than with Calvert, Wake, Edmondes or Naunton—this contrast in purpose is perhaps most marked. Immersed in the practical needs of the moment, in the face of pending military action, trade problems, religious intrigues, treaties, it is hardly to be wondered at that abstract theories of parliamentary privilege, and Parliament's obstinate reiteration of its grievances, seemed to Coke and men like himself mere petty annoyances unworthy of serious attention.

Coke's part as impatient mover of supply, supply, and more supply, had commenced in 1625 before he was a member for Cambridge, and although he was somewhat in the background during his first term as university representative in 1625/6, he was then clearly beginning to use his new seat as a vantage-point from which to plead the King's cause. As Secretary of State, he could now speak with an authority he had not previously possessed as a mere private member. In the Parliament of 1627/8-9, his responsibility in this role grew greater and greater, as the important issues of the Petition of Right and tonnage and poundage came to be inescapable.

During the debates on the Petition, for example, Coke's part was chiefly to hold back the tide as best he could. On 12 April 1628, he warned the House that it was pressing "not only upon the abuses of power but on power itself". On the 28th he reminded them of the King's moderation—how patient he had been to "endure dispute so long", how, indeed, "he hath shewed himself the best of kings".[91]

And so it went on until he departed for Portsmouth to resume his naval duties, in preparation for the attack on La Rochelle. Here he stayed, somewhat miserably, lodged uncomfortably and unable to remedy the inadequacies of the fleet without sufficient money, piteously asking the Duke for release in letter after letter addressed to deaf ears,[92] all through the final stages of the Petition of Right, and on through the summer, until he finally returned to London in October, where he remained ready to attend the next session of the Parliament.

When the second session opened in early 1629, Sir John, again in his usual role urging supply, implied that the King had "commanded" tonnage and poundage. The House was quick to pounce upon such an affront to their ancient rights, and Coke was quickly forced to apologize for his slip of the tongue, just as, the year before, he had had to explain away his tactless inclusion of the Duke of Buckingham's name when as Secretary he was presenting the King's thanks for Parliament's grant of supply.[93] Not long after the tonnage and poundage error, another blunder followed. In an attempt to win the House away from their animus against the King's government, Coke introduced a diversion in the form of a Jesuit plot that reputedly had been recently discovered and suppressed—the well-known Clerkenwell affair. This strategy, however, proved to be a boomerang, for, once the House had looked into the business, the result was only to add one more grievance to the list. The real truth of the story involved a matter of pardons for recusants, granted directly at the King's command, the revelation of which was an utter outrage to all but the most High Church Protestants.[94] As things thus went on from bad to worse, Coke threatened a dissolution as he had in the last session,[95] and on 2 March the dissolution finally came.

Sir John's parliamentary career has been given in some detail, not because it has anything primarily to do with university representation but because it illustrates in perfect form the position of the university member as Privy Councillor in the period of royal influence. As a matter of fact, however, in these very sessions when Cambridge's burgess was so wholeheartedly the King's man, the tide had begun to turn as regards the other university members. This was in sharp contrast to the situation in the previous Parliaments, when all four of the university seats were occupied by unqualified court stalwarts. But now it was Coke alone who was fighting the royal battles.

Oxford's perennial member, Sir John Danvers, was still strangely silent for a future Regicide, although by now he was probably becoming aligned with the reform party—to judge by a bill he was sponsoring to prevent bribery in the courts.[96] Dr. Eden, Coke's colleague from Cambridge, took no part in the debates of the session, either against the King or for him, but from what is known of Eden's stand later on, it seems unlikely that he would have followed Coke's lead in this Parliament in defending the Crown's growing absolutism.[97] About Sir Henry Marten's stand, on the contrary, there is less doubt. He was the first of all the university members of the period to take an active part in pushing the Commons' interest, going even farther than his predecessor, Sir Francis Stewart. This is all the more surprising when it is remembered that he had long held crown offices, and had frequently been summoned to the council table. But his inside knowledge of the way affairs were being conducted seems to have strengthened his determination to institute a change.

He was a man, as Sir John Eliot described him, of "great years, great knowledge, great experience, and great abilities of nature to support them".[98] He had entered the House of Commons from another constituency for the first time in 1625, after a long life of judicial service.[99] In these positions, and especially as Admiralty Judge, he had worked, first with the Duke of Buckingham, and then against him, as the Duke's policies became more and more to his distaste.[100] In the *St. Peter* case, which later became part of the charges against the Duke, Sir Henry had sat at the council table and advised against the seizure as firmly as he dared. When he entered Parliament in 1625, he began to take a stand with the opposition, and in the next Parliament, he was clearly on the side of Sir John Eliot and John Selden, being a witness in regard to the *St. Peter* during the preliminaries of Buckingham's impeachment, and later serving on the impeachment committee itself.[101]

Now, in the Parliament of 1627/8–9, as burgess for Oxford, Marten had no small share in pushing the Petition of Right to its conclusion. In particular, his speech against the Lords' Addition to the Petition was instrumental in getting modifications rejected that would have completely destroyed the Petition's value as a statement of fundamental liberties. This speech has been praised as a "masterpiece of tact and firmness",[102] and it includes among other things a declaration in regard to sovereign power that must have been distasteful to the Court party in Marten's emphasis on the fact that all sovereign power is committed to the King for the good of the people—"ad salutatem & pro bono populi regi comissa".[103]

Nevertheless, Sir Henry was always less insistent in his opposition than Sir John Eliot. It was said of him that he had a "moderate and middle way; so in managing of affairs of Parliament, he had a healing method".[104] For example, he was not in favour of naming the Duke directly in the Remonstrance of 1628, and he urged moderation both at the opening of the session of 1628/9, and in the course of the bitter debates of the preceding year. One of his speeches, indeed, had quite the ring of the Privy Councillor:

> Take heed of too much repetition and overbeating of grievances; it is dangerous, and may make a further separation. . . . Let us do as poets in a tragedy, that sometimes have comical passages.[105]

There might have been some wisdom in this, but the House was in no mood for "comical passages", and paid no more heed to this advice than if it had come from Sir John Coke. Later, as the Parliament drew to a close and the tonnage and poundage issue sharpened, Marten apparently despaired of an accommodation and took no stand on either side. Perhaps this was all noted by the King. At least his Majesty seems to have taken Marten's opposition in not too bad part, for Marten never lost any of his judicial offices, but on the contrary, continued to exercise all his old powers during the period of Personal Rule, while Sir John Eliot and John Selden were captives in the Tower. Nevertheless it is an unusual situation in this decade of royal influence to find a university member in active resistance to the Crown—no matter to what a limited degree.

In the midst of all the critical events of this Parliament, there arose several questions that more directly concerned university interests. On these occasions the university burgesses laid aside their general character as members of Parliament engaged in great affairs of state, and became the special representatives of the universities. This happened when they were appointed to consider such matters as a bill for the "better Continuance of Peace and Unity in Church and Commonwealth"; an act against corruption in securing places in colleges and halls; a question regarding a printer that probably involved the rights of the university presses; and an inquiry into religious conformity as enforced by the universities.[106] This last was a move apparently arising out of the drive against recusancy which agitated the House in the early part of 1629.

In all these matters, the burgesses of both universities were assigned to the committees concerned, and in regard to the conformity issue, they were specifically directed to present an inquiry to the universities for a detailed report on the enforcement of conformity since the days of Elizabeth. The universities, indeed, seem to have been distinctly under a cloud during this discussion, to judge from the somewhat ominous order that was issued by the House to the effect that the universities were to be required to present their titles of incorporation to the Speaker.[107] Whatever this might have meant, no more is heard of it in the *Journal*, and although no defence of the universities is recorded, it is possible that if anything was threatening, their representatives were able to ward off action until the hostility of the House—if it was hostility—was forgotten in the midst of larger issues. For this Parliament was, of course, the famous Parliament that closed with the Speaker held in the chair by force while Sir John Eliot finished his last speech on tonnage and poundage. None of the current university burgesses figured in this exciting scene, so far as the record goes, but a previous Oxford burgess, Sir Thomas Edmondes, is characteristically mentioned as among those most active in trying to free the Speaker, until prevented by an overpowering number of younger members.[108]

With the close of this Parliament the history of university representation comes to a pause. During the eleven years of Personal Rule, the university members returned to their usual routines and are partly lost sight of, though traces of their activities may be found here and there. Sir Henry Marten and Dr. Eden, for example, continued to be busy with their judicial duties, while Sir John Coke, still Secretary of State, functioned much more happily without the interference of a Parliament.

Two of the former university members were connected with the new statutes for Oxford which were introduced in 1636 by Archbishop Laud, now Chancellor of the university. Sir Henry Marten served on the commission to draw up the statutes and Sir John Coke made the speech of presentation—with suitable royalist sentiments scattered generously throughout.[109] Dr. Eden, on the contrary, instead of co-operating with Laud on the latter's projected regulation of Cambridge, was searching old precedents in order to find a means of escaping the Archbishop's authority.[110] In Sir John Danvers, also, the rebel spirit appeared for the first time in full clearness, when in 1639 he was among those gentlemen who refused to give money to the King for the Bishops' Wars, and was therefore cited before the Privy Council.[111]

So the years went on until the Short Parliament assembled in April 1640. This time, instead of Coke (who had retired as Secretary the year before) there was another royal Secretary in a university seat—Sir

Francis Windebanke, elected for Oxford along with Sir John Danvers.[112]
The juxtaposition of these names suggests again the usual compromise
between court candidate and university favourite. That Windebanke
owed his place to pressure politics—ultimately to the influence of the
King and Archbishop Laud—is indicated by a letter written by his son,
then a student at New College:

> This afternoon the whole university are assembled to elect our burgesses.
> I intend on Wednesday to acquaint my father with the proceedings. I hear
> already that the vice-chancellor has given order to the masters of arts to
> name my father burgess in the first place before Sir John Danvers.[113]

The elections throughout the country, so the elder Windebanke reported
on 27 March, were very "tumultuary",[114] but that at Oxford, where
Windebanke's own candidacy was concerned, seems to have gone off
quietly. Archbishop Laud, contemplating what was perhaps his own
handiwork, was able to write complacently that "Sir Francis Windebanke and Sir John Danvers were on Monday March 9th sworn
burgesses of the parliament for the university, with an unanimous consent of the whole house", that is, the house of Convocation.[115]

Dr. Eden, now getting to be as popular at Cambridge as Sir John
Danvers at Oxford, was back in the Commons for a third time as
Cambridge's representative. With him came a new figure, Henry Lucas,
secretary to the Earl of Holland, the university's Chancellor. There had
been a third candidate, Sir John Lambe, Dean of the Arches, as successor
to Sir Henry Marten, and a strong prerogative man, a supporter of
Laud, a member of the Court of High Commission, and recently made
Chancellor to the Queen. But, in spite of this backing—or more likely
because of it—when the choice was made—probably between Lucas
and Lambe—Lambe "did loose it", as Dr. John Worthington succinctly
reported in his *Diary*. This outcome was characteristic of an election
where, as one royalist nobleman wrote, "such as have Dependence upon
the Court, are in divers places refused; and the most Refractorie Persons
chosen".[116]

How "refractorie" Lucas was at this time, it is impossible to determine, for Lucas is one of the more elusive of the university members
so far as the details of his life and thoughts are concerned. However,
in view of his later stand, and in view of the position taken by his
patron, Lord Holland, it is unlikely that he would have had much
sympathy with the ultra-Royalists of the Short Parliament.[117] The
probability is that, of all four university burgesses, only Windebanke
was left on the side of the Court, as Coke was in 1627/8—a sharp
contrast to the full royalist phalanx presented by the universities in
1623/4, and clearly symptomatic of the times ahead.

If Windebanke got no support from his brother burgesses of the universities, he likewise got little support from the Commons as a whole. He was, as Clarendon said, "a bashful speaker", but, with the Commons in their present mood, even a man of compelling eloquence would have found his part difficult. An interesting insight into Windebanke's thinking may be obtained from a letter written by him after the Parliament had been in session about two months. Here Windebanke complained of the Commons' bad behaviour, and then contrasted it with that of the King, who, according to the Secretary,

> . . . has omitted nothing on his part whereby a better intelligence might have been settled between him and the people. As the case now is, his Majesty must resort to other counsels and ways for the preservation of the monarchy, which if they become more burdensome to them they may thank themselves.[118]

With this point of view, Windebanke was not likely to effect a meeting of minds with the Commons. The Commons, indeed, were prepared to dislike him on all grounds—as an instrument of Archbishop Laud, as one suspected of special sympathy for the Catholics, and as a reckless and overbearing upholder of the prerogative. And on these counts they were not far wrong in their estimate.

It is interesting to note that, in the opening days of the Parliament, Windebanke was kept busy running back and forward to the House of Lords with messages about a fast, while the Commons themselves fell to work on grievances with undiminished vigour. It is true that negotiations for a fast were generally put into the hands of a Privy Council man—as Coke in the 1620's and Roe later in the Long Parliament—but in Windebanke's case, such action seems particularly futile, since during this time he never gained any real control of the trend of business as a whole. He did serve on some of the more critical committees of the session,[119] but his appointment to these may have been merely a matter of routine deference to his position as Secretary of State. In the *Journal*, at least, there is no record of his having taken any consistent steps to check the House's course of action.

The parliamentary records of the other university representatives are also rather inconclusive. Dr. Eden served on a number of committees; Sir John Danvers, on only one, the important Committee of Privilege.[120] Lucas was either not present, or, as was frequently the case with him in later sessions of Parliament, merely silent and inactive. The Parliament was too short for any university business to be introduced, and with its dissolution in May 1640, the period of royal influence in university representation comes to an end.

NOTES FOR CHAPTER IV

1. *O.R.*, pp. 450, 452. Gooch had also been elected for Truro, but he chose Cambridge. *C.J.*, I, 511.

2. Willson, *Privy Councillors*, pp. 73–6, 99, comments on this alignment.

3. This estimate includes Sir Clement Edmondes who died before taking office. The number of Secretaries of State who were university members in this period might also be enlarged to six, to include Sir Isaac Wake, elected by Oxford in 1623/4, who was in line for the office, but died before his appointment was actually made.

4. Naunton's letter is printed in Goodman, II, 226–7, although under the wrong date (1622 instead of 1620/1). There is also a letter here from Naunton to the King, defending himself from the charge of Puritanism. For Naunton's career, see *D.N.B.*; Thomas Fuller, *Worthies of England*, pt. 2, 64; David Lloyd, *State Worthies*, ed. 1665, pp. 569–72; Venn, III, 231.

5. S. R. Gardiner, *History*, III, 391; Stowe MS., 176, f. 445. Florence M. Grier Evans, *The Principal Secretary of State*, p. 78, gives a different reason for Naunton's absence.

6. See below, pp. 102, 103, 104–5, and Appendix V.

7. See below, pp. 113–15, 121; Ch. VI, p. 147.

8. See above, Ch. III, pp. 59–60, and Appendix III, below.

9. For the election of Buckingham, see Thomas Birch, *The Court and Times of Charles I*, I, 107–9; Heywood and Wright, II, 338–42. For Laud, see Birch, II, 74. See also above, Ch. III, pp. 71–2, 73.

10. For a general account of the university members who were Privy Councillors, see Evans, pp. 83–9, 349; Willson, pp. 60–4.

11. For Sir Clement Edmondes's career, see the *D.N.B.*; *A.O.*, II, 322–3; Foster, II, 445; Fuller, pt. 3, 6; Lloyd, pp. 547–8. For his committee service in the Parliament of 1621, see Wallace Notestein, Frances Helen Relf, and Hartley Simpson, III, 415 n.; and *C.J.*, I, 521, 537, 572. For his speech, see *ibid.*, 813; Birch, *Jas. I*, II, 223.

12. For Sir John Danvers's career, and also for the Earl of Danby's gift of botanical gardens to Oxford, see their respective biographies in the *D.N.B.* For other references on Danvers, see John Aubrey, *Brief Lives*, ed. Clark, I, 195–6; John E. Bailey, *Life of Thomas Fuller*, pp. 416–31, *passim*, pp. 450, 545; Foster, I, 372; Mark Noble, *English Regicides*, pp. 164–7.

13. *C.J.*, I, 652.

14. Notestein, Relf, and Simpson, III, 3, 41, 49.

15. The debates over Sir John Bennett's guilt are found in *P.H.*, I, 1236, 1241, 1256, 1270–5. This last reference gives the charges against him in detail and his defence. The debates in Notestein, Relf, and Simpson, also contain references to Bennett's case, too numerous to cite here, although some of them are given in the notes below.

16. For comments and action on Sir John Bennett, see Notestein, Relf, and Simpson, II, 302, 314; III, 28, 29, 31, 57; V, 339, 340, 341; VI, 91.

17. *Ibid.*, p. 467.

18. S. R. Gardiner, *Debates in the House of Lords, 1621*, pp. 19, 22–3.

19. *C.S.P., Dom., Edw. VI–Jas. I*, X (1619–23), 260. Bennett's guilt was at first considered so great that Walter Yonge had expected to see him hanged. See *Diary*, ed. George Roberts, C.S., o.s., no. 41, p. 37.

20. Sir John Bennett's case is mentioned with considerable detail in various places; for example, in private correspondence, such as that of Mead and Chamberlain (Birch, *Jas. I*, II, 253, 256, 350; *C.S.P., Dom., Edw. VI–Jas. I*, X (1619–23), 248, 249, 465, 467). See also Gardiner, *History*, IV, 108, 125, 350. For Bennett's career in general, see references in Ch. II, p. 55, n. 32.

21. Notestein, Relf, and Simpson, IV, 18.
22. Goodman, II, 226.
23. Notestein, Relf, and Simpson, III, 158–9; IV, 144–5; V, 34–5 and n., 288. See also Cooper, III, 89–90.
24. For Magdalene College, see Notestein, Relf, and Simpson, V, 139, 370. For the bill on the Fens, see below, Appendix III, No. 2.
25. Gooch was also assigned to Sir John Bennett's case. *C.J.*, I, 583–4, 586. For some of Gooch's general activities, see Notestein, Relf, and Simpson, III, 96, n. 4; IV, 265, 311, n. 9; V, 291, 513; VI, 141; *C.J.*, I, 612, 614, 619, 622, 631.
26. *P.H.*, I, 1277.
27. *O.R.*, pp. 456, 459. For biographies of Calvert and Wake, see the *D.N.B.*, and Foster, I, 332, and IV, 1553, respectively. For Calvert, see *A.O.*, II, 522–3; Fuller, pp. 901–2; Lloyd, pp. 526–8; and a discussion of his career as a Privy Councillor in Lewis W. Wilhelm, *Sir George Calvert*, pp. 99–105. For Wake, see also *A.O.*, II, 539–41; Aubrey, II, 272–3; Fuller, p. 286; Lloyd, pp. 674–6.
28. Judging from the committee lists and the speeches by Calvert reported in the *Commons' Journal*, Calvert's attendance was somewhat better than Willson, p. 65, suggests. However, his name does appear more infrequently towards the end of the session, and a letter of his to Secretary Conway on 20 May makes definite reference to the fact of his absence from the House. *C.S.P., Dom., Edw. VI–Jas. I*, XI (1623–5, with Addenda, 1603–25), 250, 251.
29. *Ibid.*, p. 148. A fuller version of this letter is given in Willson, p. 62.
30. For a discussion of the question of Naunton's absences, see below, Appendix V.
31. For Gooch's action on the "Act for the Ease of the Subject, concerning Information upon Penal Laws", see Cooper, III, 162, and *C.J.*, I, 449, 674, 719. Sir Edward Coke, usually the champion of academic privilege, differed with Gooch upon this issue. For Gooch's committee service, see *ibid.*, 672, 673, 680, 717, 731, 736, 762.
32. *C.S.P., Dom., Edw. VI–Jas. I*, XI (1623–5, with Addenda, 1603–25), 179, 193. For Wake's efforts, see *C.J.*, I, 676, 726, 727–8, 729, 734, 750.
33. *C.S.P., Dom., Edw. VI–Jas. I*, XI (1623–5, with Addenda, 1603–25), 207, 224, 227, 244; *C.S.P., Venetian*, XVIII (1623–5), 292, 293.
34. Heywood and Wright, II, 302–3. Cambridge University Registry: Grace Book (1589–1620), p. 304. These expectations were apparently based on services that Naunton had already rendered the university.
35. *Supra*, pp. 97–8. Naunton's insistence that he owed no obligation to the university to serve as their burgess was based upon the fact that he was "no longer of their body". This probably refers to his relinquishing of his fellowship at Trinity Hall in 1616, but the statement seems to imply that membership in the university depended upon the matter of residence—a point of view precisely opposite to that brought forward in 1614 in favour of the election of Sir Miles Sandys. See Ch. III, pp. 63–6, 66–7.
36. See below, p. 107, n. 51, for an expression of the esteem in which Naunton was held at the time of the next election in 1625/6.
37. *O.R.*, pp. 462, 465.
38. Oxford University Archives, N23, p. 3839, f. 203. Edmondes's career is briefly sketched in the *D.N.B.* See also Lloyd, pp. 734–5; *B.B.*, III, 829–32; and Willson, p. 92.
39. Notestein, Relf, and Simpson, IV, 35.
40. Birch, *Chas. I*, I, 5. For Sir Simeon Steward, see *D.N.B.*; Venn, IV, 162.
41. Morton's candidacy in Kent was pushed by Lord Westmoreland and the Earl of Montgomery, both of Buckingham's party. Stowe MS., 743, ff. 60, 64; *The Gentleman's Magazine*, LXVIII (1798), pt. i, 116–17.
42. The phrase is Lloyd's. *State Worthies*, p. 761.
43. "For no man else did stand." Cambridge University Library MS., Mm 457, pt. 2, no. 21, f. 303.

44. John Chamberlain, in writing to Sir Dudley Carleton, ambassador at The Hague, 6 May 1625, six days after the election, implied that Sir Albertus had already chosen Kent. Willson, p. 73, seems to have repeated this error, if it is one. At least there is no record in the *Commons' Journal* of Morton's having made any official choice for Kent, and both the *Official Return*, p. 462, and the Cambridge *Register* have Morton listed as Cambridge's representative. It is true that the *Return* has no indication of the issuance of a new writ, as would be the case in the usual course of things if Morton had declined Kent, but this, like the want of a record in the *Journal*, is probably owing to the short duration of the Parliament and the absence of Morton during the session.

It is interesting, in this connection, however, to note that Chamberlain in this letter said that if he had been Secretary Morton he would have "esteemed as much the choice of the Universitie of Cambridge . . . as this higher title in shew with the expense of two or three hundred pounds they say at least". This case of Morton's is one of the rare instances where a university seat was not rated higher than one from a county or town. It is also to be noted that even Chamberlain, who would have preferred the Cambridge seat, put the emphasis in its favour, not in terms of prestige, but of expense. See below, Ch. V, pp. 140–1; Ch. VIII, pp. 225–6. Chamberlain's letter is quoted in Birch, *Chas. I*, I, 18–19, and probably with more accuracy, in Willson, p. 73.

45. Willson, pp. 66, 94; Gardiner, *History*, v, 335. For a general account of Morton's career, see *D.N.B.*; Venn, III, 217; *G.M.*, LXVIII (1798), pt. i, 20–3, 115–18.

46. S. R. Gardiner, *Commons' Debates, 1625*, pp. 77, 80, 107, 135; *C.J.*, I, 813 (Edmondes); Forster, *Eliot*, I, 360, 406–7. Forster also mentions (p. 441) other speeches of Edmondes, adding the suggestion that both Edmondes and Naunton at this period were not unwilling to see the Duke of Buckingham discomfited, in the hope, perhaps, that the latter's loss of prestige might advance their own interests as royal advisers. Forster likewise points out (p. 335) that Sir John Eliot believed that Edmondes was shielding the Lord Keeper, Archbishop Williams, by making a speech designed to divert attention from action he had taken regarding the pardon of Jesuits. Since Williams and the Duke were beginning to drift apart at this time, there may be some reason to think that the university members in this Parliament were acting a more complicated part than merely their usual role of straightforward supporters of the Crown.

47. For Danvers on committees, see *C.J.*, I, 800, 807, 809. For the protest to the Vice-Chancellor, see *ibid.*, p. 810, and Forster, *Eliot*, I, 343. This occurred at the time of the Montagu-Killison affair, and the unpopular divine was a follower of Montagu.

48. Birch, *Chas. I*, I, 39; Gardiner, *Commons' Debates, 1625*, p. 29. See also item of 26 January 1625/6 in *C.S.P., Dom., Chas. I*, I (1625, 1626), 236, 248. One of these bills may possibly be related to the bill against simony which was assigned to a committee that did include the Oxford burgesses. *C.J.*, I, 809.

49. This is Willson's view, pp. 184–5. For the previous account of this election, see above, Ch. III, pp. 75–7.

50. Sir Bulstrode Whitelocke, *Memorials*, ed. 1853, I, 18.

51. Tanner MS., 72, f. 69v. It is indicative of the times that this letter recognizes that Naunton's position as Privy Councillor would be against him in an election. In opposition to this argument was urged "consideration of what he hathe formerly suffered for this Commonwealth", probably a reference to his fall from royal favour during the period of Spanish ascendancy. Because of this, he might be presented to a nationalistic and Protestant-minded constituency as something of a hero. Winthrop, as a future governor of Puritan Massachusetts, would take kindly to such a view. For Winthrop's influence in Suffolk, and association with Naunton in the Court of Wards, see *D.N.B.*

52. This was Wood's name for the Parliament of 1625. Wood, Gutch, II, pt. ii, 355.

53. *H.M.C., Cowper*, I, 249, 252–3, 257. Except for Naunton, nothing is known of

any other potential candidate at Cambridge. It is odd that Mead, usually so communicative and so interested in the "busie faction", had nothing to say of this "competition" for the university seats.

54. Willson, p. 78.
55. For Eden's career, see n. 117, below.
56. *O.R.*, p. 470; *C.S.P.*, *Ven.*, XIX (1625–6), 380–1.
57. *C.J.*, I, 821.
58. Birch, *Chas. I*, I, 84–5. Chamberlain, in writing to Carleton, also refers to the incident. *C.S.P.*, *Dom.*, *Chas. I*, I (1625, 1626), 273.
59. *O.R.*, p. 468; Oxford University Archives, N23, p. 3839, ff. 217 d–18 d.
60. *C.J.*, I, 843, 846.
61. *Ibid.*, pp. 820, 827, 832, 836.
62. *O.R.*, p. 468. Liskeard was apparently obtained through the efforts of the Earl of Pembroke's vice-warden of the Stanneries in Cornwall, perhaps as an attempt on the part of Oxford's Chancellor to divert Sir Francis from his claims to Edmondes's university seat. *C.S.P.*, *Dom.*, *Chas. I*, I (1625, 1626), 1; *Notes and Queries*, 4th ser., X, 325. Sir Francis was considered one of Pembroke's friends (Willson, pp. 201–2), but Edmondes was Pembroke's candidate at Oxford, and Pembroke, formerly at odds with the Court, had come to terms with Buckingham by this time. C. H. Firth, *The House of Lords*, pp. 42–3.
63. For "Mr. Treasurer's" activity in the earlier weeks of the Parliament, see *C.J.*, I, 816–24, *passim*, 832, 836. He and Sir Francis Stewart were appointed to the same committee (to consider the war at sea) on 13 March.
64. There is no adequate biographical sketch of Sir Francis Stewart. Aubrey, II, 239–40, has a few details, and also Clark, II, pt. i, 238; pt. iii, 261. See also Foster, IV, 1422; *Fasti*, I, 369; Firth, *The House of Lords*, p. 12. There are many scattered references to him throughout the *C.S.P.*; *H.M.C.*, *Cowper*, and the collections of Birch and Nichols.
65. *C.J.*, I, 827.
66. Birch, *Chas. I*, I, 95.
67. *H.M.C.*, *Lonsdale*, p. 9.
68. *C.J.*, I, 858; *C.S.P.*, *Ven.*, XIX (1625–6), 415. Birch, *Chas. I*, I, 97–105.
69. Birch, *Chas. I*, I, 97, 105, 116; *H.M.C.*, *Lonsdale*, p. 25.
70. *C.J.*, I, 818, 819, 821, 833, 836, 838.
71. Birch, *Chas. I*, I, 109. Also, Heywood and Wright, II, 339; *H.M.C.*, *Lonsdale*, p. 32.
72. *Supra*, Ch. III, pp. 71–2.
73. Birch, *Chas. I*, I, 109.
74. Heywood and Wright, II, 344–5.
75. *C.J.*, I, 866–7. Dr. Eden and Cambridge's former burgess, Sir Robert Naunton, served on the committee considering Cambridge's case.
76. Besides the accounts noted above, other sources of information on the reaction of the House to the Duke's election are: *P.H.*, II, 164–6; *H.M.C.*, *Lonsdale*, pp. 31–2; *C.S.P.*, *Dom.*, *Chas. I*, I (1625, 1626), 346; Fuller, *Cambridge*, pp. 311–12, n.
77. Mead's letter is in Heywood and Wright, II, 344.
78. The letters to Coke about the Printers, etc., are in the Cambridge University Library: Add. MSS., 22, ff. 62 r, 67 v, 69 r, 69 v. They bear no date, but may belong with the letters on the same subject in *H.M.C.*, *Cowper*, I, 249, 341, dated January and March 1625/6. Or else with the letter cited below in n. 83 which was written shortly after the confirmation of the Cambridge University charter concerning printing. For the charter, see *C.S.P.*, *Dom.*, *Chas. I*, II (1627–8), 493, 546. For Coke's activities on behalf of the Court, see *C.J.*, I, 823, 826–7, 832, 836, 843, 844.
79. The Venetian agent had foreseen the year before that one of the bad results of the Duke's election, from the point of view of the Commons, would be that

"in parliament he could control the votes of the University". *C.S.P., Ven.,* XIX (1625–6), 439.

80. Heywood and Wright, II, 364. The words quoted are followed by others which are not very clear: "and it may be as wise in this extreme as others be in the contrary".

81. Mason's letters are in the *C.S.P., Dom., Chas. I,* III (1628–9), 5, 9. For his career, see *D.N.B.*; Foster, III, 983; Venn, III, 157. (He is to be distinguished from another Robert Mason who was a contemporary, but of the opposition party.) Although he did not become burgess, he received a doctorate in law from the university in 1628 by royal mandate, probably by the very dispensation mentioned in the letter quoted here.

82. "For every man gave with Sir John Cooke and Dr. Eden." Cambridge University Library MS., Mm 457, pt. 2, no. 21, f. 302; *O.R.,* p. 474.

83. *H.M.C., Cowper,* I, 341.

84. Oxford University Archives, N23, p. 3839, f. 250 v. For the question of "parliamentary wages," see *supra,* Ch. III, pp. 88–9.

85. For Sir Henry Marten's career, see *D.N.B.*; Lloyd, pp. 695–6.

86. Oxford University Archives, N23, p. 3839, ff. 251v–2r.

87. For Oldisworth, see the *D.N.B.* In the Civil War he was a witness against Laud, and a member of the Board of Visitors for Oxford. His inclination towards the Country party in earlier years is not so surprising when it is remembered that Pembroke himself at times opposed the Court. See *supra,* n. 62, and below, Ch. VI, p. 182, n. 136.

88. Forster, *Eliot,* II, 133–4, 167, 188, 408, 439, 494; Gardiner, *History,* V, 311, 370; Willson, pp. 95–6. See also Coke in the *D.N.B.*

89. For Eliot's opinion of Coke, see Forster, *Eliot,* I, 222–3; II, 301. For the Earl of Clarendon's opinion, see *History of the Rebellion,* ed. W. D. Macray, I, 80–1. Lloyd, as a retrospective Royalist, is more sympathetic, pp. 716–19.

90. For a general view of Coke as leader of the Court party, see also Evans, pp. 85–6. Coke's parliamentary career may be followed in *P.H.,* II, 273–9, 342–8, 453–7; *C.J.,* I, 872–97; 920–32; Notestein and Relf, ed., *Commons' Debates for 1629,* pp. 8, 12, 108, 110, 111, 112–18; Birch, *Chas. I,* I, 337–54, *passim.*

91. *P.H.,* II, 278, 332–3, 342, 348; *C.J.,* I, 897.

92. *C.S.P., Dom., Chas. I,* III (1628–9), 116, 149–50, 154, 177, 182, 212, 264.

93. *P.H.,* II, 456–7; Notestein and Relf, pp. 31, 33; Forster, *Eliot,* II, 44.

94. *P.H.,* II, 471–5, 482; Forster, *Eliot,* II, 423–5. There are also scattered references throughout Notestein and Relf, and in the *Camden Miscellany,* C.S., o.s., no. 55.

95. Foster, II, 435.

96. Harleian MS., 6799:93, f. 335. The bill appears to be that mentioned in *C.J.,* I, 920, 922.

97. Eden's activity in this session was limited to committee service, where his legal and ecclesiastical knowledge could be called upon to advantage. *C.J.,* I, 885, 887, 903, 914.

98. Quoted in Forster, *Eliot,* I, 335.

99. Marten had succeeded Sir Daniel Dunne, Oxford's first burgess, as Judge of the Admiralty and Dean of the Arches. In addition, he had become Judge of the Prerogative Court of Canterbury at the death of Sir William Byrd.

100. Marten was said to have complained that the Duke's idea of Admiralty justice was that every ship seized should be automatically declared a prize of war, regardless of the evidence. Forster, *Eliot,* II, 304.

101. *Ibid.,* I, 507–9; *C.J.,* I, 823, 826–7, 858.

102. See *D.N.B.* under Marten.

103. For Marten on the Lords' Addition, see *C.J.,* I, 903; *P.H.,* II, 366–71; *Journal of the House of Lords,* III, 818–20. For his continuous service in furtherance of the Petition of Right, see *C.J.,* I, 887, 897, 903, 905, 908, 910, 916, 918.

104. Lloyd, p. 696.

105. *P.H.*, II, 255–6. For his stand on the Remonstrance, see *ibid.*, p. 419.
106. *C.J.*, I, 879, 901, 903, 927, 928, 932.
107. *Ibid.*, pp. 903, 928, 929, 930. See also Wood, Gutch, II, pt. i, 364–5.
108. *P.H.*, II, 490; Notestein and Relf, p. 104.
109. Laud, V, pt. i, 126–32; Wood, Gutch, II, pt. ii, 403.
110. The correspondence regarding Cambridge's claims to freedom from Visitation by the Archbishop has been published in a number of places. See *H.M.C., App. 5th Rep.*, p. 313; Laud, V, pt. ii, 556–7, 562; Heywood and Wright, II, 408–17.
111. *C.S.P., Dom., Chas. I*, XVI (1640), 120, 155. Danvers's reluctance to give the King money, however, may have sprung from his own financial difficulties, rather than from political principle.
112. *O.R.*, p. 480. For Windebanke's career, see *D.N.B.*; Foster, IV, 657; Evans, pp. 93–108.
113. *C.S.P., Dom., Chas. I*, XV (1639–40), 531. In spite of these orders regarding Windebanke, the university seems to have chosen Danvers at the top of the poll.
114. *Calendar of Clarendon State Papers*, ed. Ogle and Bliss, I, 196.
115. Laud, IV, 263. Curiously enough, there is no letter of recommendation for Windebanke in the Oxford University Archives—from Laud or anyone else.
116. *O.R.*, p. 482; John Worthington, *Diary*, I, 7 (Chetham Society, vol. XIII); Arthur Collins, *The Sidney Papers*, II, 641. Sir Henry Spelman was also a potential candidate in this election. See Add. MS., 34,601, ff. 3–36, and below, Ch. VI, pp. 146–8. For Lambe's candidacy and career, see *D.N.B.*; *Fasti*, II, 58; Mullinger, III, 123–31.
117. For a discussion of the political views of Eden and Lucas, see below, Ch. VI, pp. 149–51, 157–8. For Eden's career, see *D.N.B.*; Lloyd, *Memoires*, pp. 593–4; Venn, II, 84; Ward, pp. 240–3. For Lucas's career, see *D.N.B.*; Isaac Barrow, *Oratorical Preface*; Venn, III, 113.
118. *C.S.P., Dom., Chas. I*, XVI (1640), 127.
119. For the fast, *C.J.*, I, 4, 6, 8, 9. For Windebanke's committee service, see *ibid.*, pp. 4, 7–10, *passim*, 12, 19.
120. *Ibid.*, pp. 4, 8, 9, 17.

CHAPTER V

RETROSPECT, 1604-1640

After the first thirty-six years of university representation, we reach a point from which we can look back with profit upon the institution as a whole, taking stock of the part it played in the general history of the period, observing any changes that may have appeared in the course of its development, and summing up the characteristics of the individual representatives.

In this period, as throughout the seventeenth century, university representation is seen to have performed two functions. The first— the function for which it was designed—was that of allowing the universities a voice on the floor of the House where university interests could be presented and defended. The university issues, however, that were advanced in these first years of representation were none of them critical or essential. In fact, some of them appear to have been merely matters of vested interest or academic prestige, such as the abolition of pluralities of benefice, and the question of precedence in naming Oxford before Cambridge. University issues, even such as they were, were also not very numerous. Some estimate of the nature and quantity of such legislation may be obtained by an examination of the statutes listed in Lionel L. Shadwell's *Enactments in Parliament concerning the Universities.* Here we find that thirteen laws affecting the universities were passed in the reign of James I and only four in the reign of Charles I (not including the ordinances of the Long Parliament).[1] Of course, in drawing conclusions from these figures, it must be remembered that Shadwell lists only the statutes that were actually passed. Many other bills were projected—or even seriously considered—that ultimately failed of passage, owing to general circumstances or to the opposition of the university burgesses and other friends of the universities. It may be noted in this connection also that in all kinds of issues, university interests were defended quite as often by members of Parliament from other constituencies as by the university members themselves. This is partly explained by the fact that there were always a goodly number of members in the House who had once attended one or other of the universities. According to the estimate made by Harold Hulme in his examination of the personnel of the House of Commons from 1604 to 1629, over one-half of the 825 members whose characteristics he studied belonged in this category. A count of the members serving in the Long Parliament reveals an even larger proportion—something like three-quarters of the membership.[2] In both periods, of course, those who actually held degrees were much fewer in number. But among those who did hold degrees, there were often men who had much closer ties to their universities than the burgesses who currently were occupying the university seats. All these circumstances together—the number and character of the issues and the action of the other university men in the House—seem to minimize the importance of representation to university welfare—at least as representation actually operated in the first decades of the seventeenth century.

In abstract theory, however, there would still remain some justification for the institution if it could be shown that any sizeable number of the resident masters and doctors of the universities had no opportunity to vote for parliamentary members elsewhere. In such a case, it would seem that the constituents of the "Republic of Letters"—in Sir John Glanville's phrase[3]—should not be deprived of some voice in public affairs, especially at a time when Parliament was becoming of greater and greater governmental importance and major transfers of political power were taking place.

But whatever value this kind of university representation might have would of necessity depend upon the degree of freedom that was involved in the exercise of the franchise. As it happened, we have seen in Chapter IV that the universities were allowed less and less freedom of choice throughout this period, and that it was only when the most strenuous efforts were made, as at Cambridge in 1614 and at Oxford in 1625/6 and 1627/8, that the university bodies were able to maintain their independence. The fact that a tacit compromise had been established which allowed the Chancellor or other outside influence to name one candidate, while reserving the other to the university—as in the case of Eden and Coke, Danvers and Windebanke, Danvers and Marten[4]—shows that the universities had not been entirely defeated, but that there was such a compromise at all, shows also that the ideal of university representation as a political form had been by no means completely fulfilled.

This was because a second function of university representation had come to be recognized—the function of providing "safe seats" for the King's official family, as illustrated by the burgess-ships of Naunton and Coke, Morton and Wake, Calvert and the two Edmondes. This function was now regarded in some quarters as superior to the original purpose of the grant. Some of these officials, to be sure, were persons of genuine university interests and affiliations, but their importance in the House of Commons stemmed from their crown posts rather than from their university connections. Whether this situation was a benefit to the universities or not, one result of it, at least, was that the institution of university representation was brought into close relation with the great events of the day.

Since this was the case, it becomes of interest to inquire what kind of men of affairs such university representatives made on this larger stage. At the outset, it must be admitted that most of these men were not statesmen of distinction. Even Bacon was not at his best in his short term as university burgess, although he belongs, of course, in a very different category from that of the other court figures. They were mostly men of some capability—diligent and responsible, but lacking in brilliance and vision. Of them all, Sir George Calvert was perhaps the most able. Equal to Sir Robert Naunton or Sir John Coke in industry and honesty, he was a more skilful parliamentary leader than either, with greater political sense and greater flexibility of mind. A near-contemporary—a Royalist, to be sure—described him as follows:

> He was the only Statesman that being engaged to a decryed party, yet managed his business with that huge respect for all sides, that all who knew him applauded him: and none that had anything to do with him, complained of him.

Calvert's efficiency in administrative matters was as notable as his parliamentary skill. It was said that he was appointed Secretary of State partly for the purpose of assisting Sir Robert Naunton, who found his task in that post somewhat beyond his powers.[5]

Naunton, indeed, in some ways seems to have been out of place in public life. He suffered from a lack of knowledge of the law, and from a rather cramped personality, which prevented his having much influence upon others. He was greatly admired by the moderate Anglicans and Puritans for his staunch Protestantism, and his later conduct in the administration of the Court of Wards was so scrupulous that it aroused the animosity of the other officials, more greedy for the rewards of corruption. But as a statesman in the broader sense, he must be rated rather low, and we can be certain from his career in earlier and later Parliaments, that he would have cut no figure in the House, had he been permitted to be present during those two terms when he was prevented from serving as university burgess. Much the same may be said of Sir John Coke. Though somewhat more prone to speak in Parliament than Naunton, he had no greater political genius. Faithful and hard-working, and probably with considerable executive ability as routine administrator of the navy, Coke in the House as burgess for the University of Cambridge was only—to use Gardiner's words—"a mere tool ready to do or say anything he was bidden to by Buckingham and the

King". Even so, he was of a higher calibre than Sir Francis Winde-banke, the last crown official among the university representatives of this period, whom even the royalist biographer David Lloyd found it hard to portray in favourable colours.[6]

Among the other court supporters, there were two or three who were especially well thought of by their contemporaries, or near-contemporaries. Sir Isaac Wake, while member for Oxford in 1623/4, was admired for his "excellent elocution" in explaining the reasons for the breaking of the Spanish Marriage treaty, and Sir Clement Edmondes and Sir Thomas Edmondes were each highly praised, the one by David Lloyd and Anthony Wood, and the other by David Lloyd and Sir Dudley Carleton.[7] Nevertheless, when all is said that can be said in favour of the university members who were attached to the court circle in this period, they still remain—with the exception of Bacon—third-or fourth-rate figures, both as individuals and as political leaders.

The same evaluation must be made of those university burgesses who can be classed as members of the opposition. Except for Sir Henry Marten, none was outstanding. The only other representative who was at all prominent in the Country party was Sir Francis Stewart, whose part in the impeachment of Buckingham attracts attention largely because it seems surprising to find one so closely tied to the throne in blood and official position standing out so strenuously against crown policy. The other burgesses who ultimately became the real university Parliamentarians of the future—Danvers, the Regicide; Eden and Lucas, the signers of the Covenant—were at this stage for the most part silent and ineffective. It must be conceded then that the university burgesses of the first part of the century were not men of first rank in statesmanship, when measured either against the best of the Country party, such as Sir John Eliot or John Selden, or against such supporters of the Crown as Salisbury or Wentworth.

One of the reasons that a more favourable impression of the political competence of the university members is not obtained is that so many of those who held major offices did not attend Parliament regularly. Sir Albertus Morton, for example, was out of England during the entire session of Charles I's first Parliament; Naunton, it appears, was in seclusion during two whole Parliaments—from 1620/1 to 1624; while Sir Isaac Wake—primarily an ambassador, and thus bound to be abroad—left before the session of 1624 was over. Sir John Coke did the same, both in 1626 and in 1628, although on each occasion a parliamentary crisis was impending, and Coke was the Court's chief spokesman in the House. Illness appears to have been the reason for his absence during the impeachment of Buckingham, but during the debates on the Petition of Right it seems odd to find Coke with the navy at Portsmouth instead of in his parliamentary seat. The conclusion seems to be that, in spite of all the pressure put upon the universities to elect court candidates, the King did not care whether they took any part in the activities of the House or not, so long as the university seats were safely out of the hands of the opposition. If this was so, perhaps it sprang from that basic underestimation of the importance of Parliament in the constitutional life of England that lay behind the thinking of the Stuarts and their divine-right supporters.[8]

Turning from a consideration of the university burgesses in their relation to public affairs, we may now find it of interest to inquire what sort of men they were in their private capacities, particularly as regards their intellectual interests, since, being university representatives, they might be expected to possess some special tastes and talents of this sort. Here again, their record is a little disappointing. The fact that the great Bacon is included in their company does not entirely compensate for the rather mediocre level of achievement characteristic of the other university members of this period.

Nevertheless they were not completely lacking in interests proper to men of their condition.[9] Sir Francis Stewart, for example, according to Aubrey, was a "learned gentleman, and one of the club of the Mermayd", a friend of Raleigh and of Ben Jonson, who dedicated his play, *The Silent Woman*, to Oxford's member, the "truly noble by all titles, Sir Francis Stewart".[10] Sir John Coke took an interest in the poetry of Lord Brooke; and Sir John Danvers, besides architecture and Italian gardens, had literary tastes that brought him close to the poets, John Donne and George Herbert, to the church historian, Thomas Fuller, and to Sir Francis Bacon.[11]

Sir Isaac Wake had considerable reputation as a linguist and as a writer on serious subjects. When public orator at Oxford, he had early won attention by his address to the King, *Rex Platonicus*, delivered in 1605 upon James's first visit. A passage from this oration is said to have led to the writing of *Macbeth*. Later, Wake produced other works, such as funeral orations (one on Sir Thomas Bodley) and treatises on foreign affairs. Wake also, like Danvers, was interested in horticulture, and, according to a report in Aubrey, was the first man to plant "firres" in England.[12] Sir Clement Edmondes was placed by his contemporaries among the ranks of the learned, chiefly perhaps because of his translation of Caesar's *Commentaries* and the studies of military strategy that he published. Ben Jonson, for example, wrote two epigrams addressed to Edmondes, on the subject of the latter's work on Caesar, praising Edmondes's "learned hand and true Prometheus art", and declared that

Edmondes's skill had such an effect that it ". . . not only doth restore His [Caesar's] life, but makes that he can dye no more".[13] Sir Robert Naunton wrote biographical sketches of the famous figures of Queen Elizabeth's days, a work known as *Fragmenta Regalia*, still an important source of information for the period. The legal minded among the university burgesses seem not to have sought literary expression, except in the case of William Byrd, who appears to be the author of some manuscripts in the Harleian Collection on matrimony and on the origins of the shires.[14]

Another kind of evidence that indicates interest in intellectual matters on the part of university burgesses consists of gifts and bequests made to their universities and colleges. Such benefactors were Thomas Eden, who left manuscripts from his collection; Henry Lucas, who gave a library of mathematical works and the princely gift of the Lucasian Chair which still exists at Cambridge; as well as Sir Henry Marten and Sir Miles Sandys, who are credited with lesser unspecified donations.[15]

If the record of the early university representatives in intellectual matters, as in political life, seems on the whole unimpressive, either in achievements accomplished by themselves or in the appreciation and support of such achievements in others, the comment at least may be made that this record is probably neither better nor worse than the record of any other comparable set of seventeenth-century gentlemen. Nevertheless, when compared with the levels reached by later university burgesses, it must be admitted that the burgesses of the early period seem to be notably lacking in intellectual and literary distinction.

In the process of assessing the intellectual interests of these representatives, it again becomes apparent how few of them were primarily academic figures. Only three, indeed, out of the twenty-two members who served from 1604 through the Short Parliament, were actually engaged in academic work at the time of their election. These were Dr. Gooch of Cambridge (rather voluble in the House), and Dr. Mountlowe and Dr. Eden, also of Cambridge (relatively silent).[16] Oxford presented several persons noted for their learning—Marten, Crompton, Wake, Sir Clement Edmondes, Dunne, Sir Francis Stewart —but not one of these was a true university figure. This paucity of "gremials" is somewhat surprising. Sir Edward Coke, it would seem, had not expected such an outcome in 1603/4, when he cautioned the universities not to elect a clergyman, but to choose some professors of the civil law—presumably persons currently resident, and active in university affairs. But, regardless of what Coke had intended, university representation as it worked out seldom resulted in the sending of either serious scholars or university celebrities to Westminster. The preponderance of crown officers among the university members probably helps to account for this fact.

Among the burgesses who were not resident in the universities at the time of their election, there were many, however, who had had close ties of association with the university world in the past. At least eleven of these non-resident burgesses had been fellows of some college, and six of them—Byrd, Dunne, Naunton, Wake, Bennett, and Sandys—had held university office. Some of them, sadly enough, still seemed to partake of the university mind in its more limited aspects. Such, perhaps, was Sir John Coke, whom Clarendon described as a man "of very narrow education and narrower nature, having continued long in the university of Cambridge where he had gotten Latin learning enough" though he was still "unadorned with parts of vigour and quickness". Sir John Eliot's judgment of Coke was also similar: "Thus his conversation being with books, and that to teach not studie them, men and business were subjects which he knew not, and his expressions were more proper for a schoole than for a state and councell."[17] This was Naunton's difficulty also. "The could rhetoric of the schooles", said Eliot, in characterizing Naunton, was not the same as "that moving eloquence wch does affect a Parliament".[18] Sir Robert, indeed, according to Lloyd, had found "his temper agreeable with the University", and may have been happier there than in the great world of affairs, where he showed himself "close, retyred, and reserved".[19] This being the case, it is rather surprising to note that it was Naunton, alone among all the university representatives of the century, who scorned membership in the university body, when he, inconveniently, was elected parliament man.[20] Sir Clement Edmondes, unlike Naunton, seems to have escaped the taint of the objectionably academic. Just as hard-working, he was described as "wise but not presumptive, exact, but not pendantic".[21]

There were other university representatives, however, who—far from being too limited by academic narrowness—were but remotely related to the universities they sat for. The most extreme case—and the only one in this period—was that of Sir Thomas Edmondes, who, according to Sir Edward Coke, had never attended either university.[22] Others, like Calvert, Bacon, Windebanke, and Stewart, had left their universities long ago, without ever having kept up any very close connection with them. Sir John Danvers would also belong in this group, were it not that through his local residence in Oxfordshire and his brother's benefactions, he had a kind of special relationship to the university, not similar to that of any other burgess of this period.

One aspect of the burgesses' relations to their universities that may be readily studied is the matter of degrees. Of the twenty-two members who occupied the university seats between the accession of James I and the close of the Short Parliament, only two were without degrees of any sort. These were Sir John Danvers and Sir Thomas Edmondes.[23] Of the rest, Sir Francis Windebanke alone held only a B.A. All the other representatives had either earned a master's degree or better, or had received one by "mandate" or "creation". Most of the members had obtained one or more of their degrees in the usual way, even when additional degrees had been bestowed upon them gratuitously. The degrees were evenly divided as to faculties—ten men for their final awards held master's degrees in arts and nine held doctorates in the civil law. These last were Dunne, Crompton, Byrd, Bennett, and Marten from Oxford, and Mountlowe, Steward, Gooch, and Eden from Cambridge.[24] Thus the tradition established by Sir Edward Coke of choosing men with legal training was well maintained. A number of the burgesses had also spent some time in the Inns of Court. Those from Oxford were Dunne, Crompton, Calvert, Danvers, Marten, Wake, and Windebanke; from Cambridge, Bacon, Gooch, Morton, Eden, and Steward. Thus Oxford had a slight preponderance in the common law, although there was little difference between the two universities as regards the number of doctor's degrees. As to "incorporated" degrees, the proportion was the same. Bennett and Dunne of Oxford had been incorporated at Cambridge as M.A. and D.C.L., respectively, while Naunton and Gooch of Cambridge had received equivalent degrees at Oxford.

While there was little difference between the two universities in the matter of the degrees held by their burgesses, there was a greater divergence in regard to the number of burgesses employed in the King's service. There were seventeen of these in all—eleven from Oxford, and only six from Cambridge. The major offices of Secretary of State and Privy Councillor were evenly divided, with the two Edmondes, Calvert, and Windebanke on one side, and Bacon, Naunton, Morton, and Sir John Coke on the other. Oxford definitely exceeded Cambridge in legal and judicial appointments, but the only two burgesses who could be classed as country gentlemen without occupation were also evenly divided—Danvers and Sandys. Burgesses who had been former fellows were also equal in number. However, the burgesses who were still members of the academic world were, interestingly enough, all from Cambridge: Gooch, Head of Magdalene College; Eden, Master of Trinity Hall; Mountlowe, Professor in Gresham College. Possibly Lucas, as secretary to the university Chancellor, might also be included in this group.

No noticeable trend seems to be discoverable, either as to the colleges represented among the university members of this period, or as to the geographical localities associated with the members. In regard to the first consideration, it is not surprising that the civil law colleges, like All Souls at Oxford, and Trinity Hall at Cambridge, should show the only preponderance that is observable. As to the second consideration, insufficient data in some cases, and rapid change of residence in others, make conclusions of any sort difficult, and when information is available, the geographical distribution is so diversified that it proves little beyond the fact that, as might be expected, the Cambridge representatives tended to come from Cambridgeshire and the eastern counties, and the Oxford members from Oxfordshire and the west, and that few representatives from either university came from the north. This inconclusive situation regarding the distribution of the members as to colleges and shires prevails throughout the century, and for this reason no further attempt to comment upon it will be made in later chapters of this study.

There is one differentiation between the representatives of the two universities, however, that is very striking. Every single one of the twelve Oxford burgesses was a knight,[25] whereas only five of the ten Cambridge members were of that rank. This makes a total of seventeen out of the twenty-two members from both universities, who were knights. Cambridge had the only baronet—Sir Miles Sandys—and Oxford the only Knight of the Bath—Sir Francis Stewart. Each university could boast of one representative ennobled, Bacon from Cambridge, and Calvert from Oxford. Fifteen out of the total twenty-two burgesses of the period can be definitely classified as belonging to the gentry, and at least seven of these had distinguished or noble family connections. Among the Cambridge members there were Bacon, nephew of Lord Burleigh and son of Sir Nicholas Bacon, Lord Keeper; Sandys, son of Archbishop Sandys; Coke, related to Fulke Grenville, Lord Brooke; and Morton, nephew of Sir Henry Wotton. From Oxford came Danvers, the brother of the Earl of Danby; Windebanke, grandson of Sir Thomas, prominent in Elizabeth's reign; while Sir Francis Stewart, as the King's cousin, introduced an illegitimate strain of royalty. In the case of some of the rest, the picture is not so clear. Facts about the family background are lacking for Dunne and Lucas, and this in itself suggests an absence of distinction, although Lucas is said to have alluded to a patrimony lost in childhood. Crompton and Calvert are entered on the university records as "pleb", but Clark explains that this may have been merely a way of avoiding the payment of higher fees.[26] The lower social ranks are more clearly represented by Sir Henry

Marten and Sir Clement Edmondes. Marten was the son of a copy-holder—though a wealthy one—while Sir Clement Edmondes was of yeoman origin, with a brother in London who was a draper. Sir Thomas Edmondes—no relative, despite Wood's efforts to prove him son of Sir Clement—provides the only purely urban note—his father was a customs official in Cornwall, later Mayor of Fowey, but the family further back belonged to the gentry.

This survey of the social status of the various burgesses is somewhat inexact, but, such as it is, it seems to show that the university members shared in that general upgrading of social status that is usually said to be a characteristic of the Tudor and Stuart periods. Curiously enough, this analysis does not reveal so much difference between the social circumstances of the burgesses of the two universities as, at first sight, the disproportionately large number of knights among the Oxford representatives would lead one to assume. The balance is about even as regards classification by family status into greater and lesser gentry, while, if anything, the weight of obscurity and plebeian origin is heavier on the Oxford side, despite the larger number of individual knighthoods.

When it comes to a study of the ages at which men became university members, lack of information about the early lives of some of these men again interferes with any secure conclusion about age trends. The ages of six out of the twenty-two are still unknown, while the figures given for some of the others are at least dubious. To judge from what facts there are, however, it would seem that Oxford's representatives were generally men in their forties when first elected to Parliament by the universities, while Cambridge's burgesses were in their fifties. Representatives in their sixties were sent by both universities. Sir Henry Marten of Oxford, one of the most active of all the members, was the oldest, being at the time of his election "full of years", as Sir John Eliot described him, at sixty-six. The youngest was Sir John Danvers, who was thirty-three when he was chosen in 1621 to replace Sir John Bennett, then serving his second term for Oxford at sixty-eight. This was not, however, Danvers's first experience in the Commons, for he had been member for other constituencies in two previous Parliaments. Similarly, about half of the other university burgesses of this period had also had parliamentary experience before they occupied the university seats. It is no surprise to discover that this was the case, or that the age-level of the members was relatively high, when it is remembered that the universities at this time were choosing a preponderance of crown officers, or else trying to set up against such candidates men of comparable ability and experience.

Many of the conclusions drawn from the statistics analysed in this chapter will be found true of university representatives in general all through the seventeenth century—for example, the preponderance of the gentry and officials of State and men of affairs; the varying degrees of relationship to the universities; and—to some extent—the nature and scope of the intellectual interests of the members. Many of these conclusions are likewise noticeably similar to the conclusions regarding such points as rank, education, age, origins, occupations, and economic interests drawn by J. E. Neale in his *Elizabethan House of Commons* and by Harold Hulme in his analysis of the total personnel of the House of Commons in the years 1604–26.[27] The inference here seems to be, as already suggested, that the members chosen by the universities were not very different from the other parliament men of the period.

Not all of the characteristics of the university representatives, however, remain constant throughout the century. Such considerations in particular as age, political affiliation, and parliamentary experience vary with the times, and in general reflect similar changes in the character of the total membership of the House. For despite the usual tendency of university representation to express the basic conservatism of the universities, the choice of candidates was nevertheless affected—in later Parliaments as in the Parliaments of the 1620's—by the general trends that beset English politics in this most political of centuries.

For instance, it was in accordance with the royalist temper of the early Stuart period that the court candidates should have so little difficulty in obtaining university seats. At the same time, there was a strong enough spirit of opposition in the universities to produce a number of contested elections, or near-contested elections. Out of a possible nineteen seats—eight regular elections in both universtities and three by-elections (all three at Oxford)—there were eight cases where opposition is known to have existed, and there were quite possibly others of which no record survives.[28] Some of this opposition never materialized in the final vote, but in two of these eight cases—in 1614 and in 1625/6—the contests were severe enough to result in disorders at the polls and to cause the official returns to be called into question.

It is not easy to explain why the only two disputed elections in the whole history of university representation should have happened in this period and not at a later time when university representation was a fully established tradition. Perhaps the very newness of the universities' privilege may partly account for the determination of the electorate to make its views prevail. Later, under the Commonwealth and Protectorate, the pressure for conformity was too strong to allow of any such independence, and still later, in the Restoration, there was perhaps not enough open domination on the part of the ruling powers to produce a correspondingly open resistance. But in the reigns of the first two Stuarts there was probably just a sufficient combination of freedom and compulsion to engender rebellion, without there being sufficient authority to suppress it.

Whatever the explanation is, it is interesting to note that the disputed elections were equally divided between the two universities, and that Oxford was just as effective in its general objection to domination as Cambridge.[29] This observation may be surprising to those who always think of Oxford as the more conservative and the more royalist of the two universities. But this latter estimate is based upon Oxford's eighteenth- and nineteenth-century tradition. Such a judgment will not hold true for Oxford in the 1620's. Under the early Stuarts, both universities were restless—witness Cambridge's dissatisfaction as portrayed in the letters of the informative Mr. Mead—but it was Oxford that was bold enough to reject, not a mere college Head like Barnaby Gooch, but Sir Thomas Edmondes, Treasurer of the King's Household and a member of the Privy Council. And this action was taken in favour of a candidate whose stand was to forecast the storm to come—Sir Francis Stewart, soon to be reproached by the Duke of Buckingham and threatened with "seclusion" for his part in the Duke's impeachment.

Besides the disputed elections, this period is distinguished by two other developments, unusual in the history of university representation. One of these is the Chancellor's apparent support of the rank and file in their rebellion in 1614.[30] The other has to do with the honour that was generally thought to be conferred by the occupation of a university seat. When Bacon, Sandys, and Gooch expressed their preference for Cambridge over the other constituencies that had elected them, and Sir Francis Stewart held out for Oxford instead of Liskeard, they were all acting in accordance with what in later years became the customary practice of university burgesses-elect.[31] But such was not the stand taken by Sir Robert Naunton or Sir Albertus Morton, one of whom was ready to disclaim his right to represent the university body, while the other allegedly expressed a preference for another seat. In no other period were the university burgess-ships regarded so lightly. This attitude may be in part accounted for by the newness of the institution of university representation; in part, by the special circumstances of each burgess-elect. John Chamberlain, on the contrary, in writing to Sir Dudley Carleton, gave an early expression to one of the more practical reasons for preferring a university seat, when he said that he would not have agreed with Morton in preferring Kent, because the expense of winning a county seat was so much greater.[32] This aspect of university representation was not lost sight of in later years when the price of pocket boroughs mounted higher.

NOTES FOR CHAPTER V

1. Shadwell, I, xvii.
2. Hulme, *Personnel of the House of Commons, 1604–29*, p. 2. See also J. E. Neale, *The Elizabethan House of Commons*, pp. 303–6.
3. *Supra*, Ch. I, p. 35.
4. *Supra*, Ch. IV, pp. 108, 114–16, 121.
5. Lloyd, *State Worthies*, p. 528; *A.O.*, II, 523. For modern estimates of Calvert, see Evans, pp. 80–1; Gardiner, *History*, III, 195–6; Willson, *Privy Councillors*, pp. 87–9.
6. For Windebanke, see Evans, pp. 93–108; Lloyd, *Memoires*, pp. 62–8. For estimates of Naunton and Coke, see respectively, Gardiner, *History*, III, 101 ("a quiet second-rate man"), and v, 370; Willson, pp. 93, and 95–6. Compare Forster on Coke, *Eliot*, I, 222–3. See also below, p. 135.
7. For Wake, see *A.O.*, II, 539; Fuller, *Worthies*, pt. 1, 286. For Sir Clement Edmondes, *A.O.*, II, 322; and Lloyd, *State Worthies*, pp. 547–8. For Sir Thomas Edmondes, *ibid.*, pp. 734–5, and Birch, *Jas. I*, II, 52. Willson, p. 92, thinks well enough of Sir Thomas to express surprise that he did not make more of an impression on his times than he did, considering his abilities.
8. An interesting contrast to the attitude displayed towards the absence of Morton and Naunton in the seventeenth century is the reaction of the Scottish Universities in 1946 to the absence of Sir John Boyd-Orr when serving the United Nations as head of the Food and Agricultural Organization. Pressure was brought upon Boyd-Orr to resign, and a new university representative was elected in his place. *Glasgow Herald*, July 5, 8, 9, 12, 1946. For ambassadors disqualified as members of Parliament as early as 1606, see Hatsell, II, 22–4.
9. Unless otherwise indicated, the statements made about the intellectual and artistic interests of the university burgesses of the period are based upon data to be found in the biographical sketches of the members in the *D.N.B.*, or other references of the sort cited in earlier chapters.
10. Aubrey, II, 239–40; *Fasti*, I, 369.
11. For Bacon's consultation of Danvers while writing his *Henry VII*, see Aubrey, I, 70.
12. *Ibid.*, II, 272; *A.O.*, II, 539–41.
13. *A.O.*, II, 322–3; Lloyd, p. 547; Jonson, *Epigrams*, Facsimile Text Society, pp. 804–5 (CX, CXI); Fuller, pt. 3, 6.
14. The treatises by Byrd are listed in *The Catalogue of the Harleian Manuscripts*, ed. Wanley, I, 427; II, 4. A work entitled *Epistola Dedicatoria*, probably by Sir Thomas Crompton, is listed in F. M. Madan, *The Early Oxford Press*, p. 177.
15. Some of the benefactions are mentioned in Francis Blomefield, *Collectanea Cantabrigiensis*, pp. 107, 154.
16. Mountlowe, perhaps, should not be counted as a resident member of the university community, since at the time of his election he was a professor in Gresham College, London, and not at Cambridge. He is included here, however, because his main concern was with the academic world rather than with a country estate or a crown office.
17. Clarendon's estimate of Coke is in *History of the Rebellion*, ed. Macray, I, 80–1. For Eliot's comment, see Forster, *Eliot*, I, 301.

18. Forster, *Eliot*, I, 406–7.
19. Lloyd, pp. 570–1. The statement quoted, however, does not seem to agree with another of Lloyd's remarks to the effect that Naunton was "more inclined to publick accomplishments than to private studies".
20. *Supra*, Ch. III, pp. 65–6; Ch. IV, p. 124, n. 35.
21. Lloyd, p. 548.
22. Willson, p. 210. This statement appears to be borne out by the fact that there is no entry for Sir Thomas Edmondes in Foster, *A.O.*, or Venn.
23. For the question of university members without degrees, see *supra*, Ch. III, pp. 66–7.
24. Of these master's degrees, four were "created" or issued in response to *Literae Regis*—those of Calvert, Bacon, Lucas, and Stewart. Of the doctorates, two also were "created"—Mountlowe's and Eden's.
25. William Byrd, however, was not knighted until after his term as university burgess was over. Shaw, I, 108.
26. Clark, II, pt. i, xxv.
27. Neale, Ch. XV; Hulme, *loc. cit.*
28. The elections in this period that might be called contested or near-contested are as follows:

    1614   Gooch *v.* Sandys at Cambridge, and a movement against Dunne at Oxford.

    1625   Someone (probably Sir Simeon Steward) against Morton at Cambridge.

    1625/6   Stewart *v.* Edmondes at Oxford, and a movement against Coke at Cambridge.

    1627/8   Danvers *v.* Oldisworth at Oxford, and Robert Mason against either Coke or Eden at Cambridge.

    1640   Lucas *v.* Lambe at Cambridge.

    There was also some irregularity at Cambridge in 1620/1. See *supra*, Ch. III, pp. 63–4; Ch. IV, pp. 99 (See also Appendix III, No. 2), 106, 107, 108, 113–16, 121.
29. For one explanation of Cambridge's apparent docility, see *supra*, Ch. III, pp. 58–60; Ch. IV, p. 99.
30. *Supra*, Ch. III, pp. 59, 64, 91, n. 9. See also the position of the Duke of Monmouth in 1678/9. Ch. X, pp. 261–5.
31. See below, Ch. VIII, pp. 225–6.
32. *Supra*, Ch. IV, p. 125, n. 44.

CHAPTER VI

THE UNIVERSITY REPRESENTATIVES IN THE LONG PARLIAMENT

With the Long Parliament a new era in the history of university representation emerged. For the first time since the granting of the franchise, the Crown's interests were disregarded, and men were elected as burgesses whose interests and efforts, with one exception, were more closely related to the interests of the constituencies which sent them than to the policies of the Court. This was particularly true of the Cambridge delegation, Dr. Thomas Eden and Henry Lucas. Both were re-elected from the Short Parliament, one being the Master of Trinity Hall, and the other, secretary to the university's Chancellor. At Oxford, the connection was less clear, for Oxford had returned an entirely new slate of burgesses—John Selden, the great student of legal history, and Sir Thomas Roe, once ambassador to the Great Mogul and to the Sultan, now engaged in the diplomacy of the Thirty Years War. Neither of these two men had any present contact with the university, but Selden, by virtue of his all-inclusive zeal for learning, might be considered a truer representative of a scholarly community than many a *bona-fide* resident. With Roe, however, there was a real divergence of interests. Roe's concerns had been those of a man of affairs, a diplomat, and a courtier, and his only connection with the university during all the years since his student days had been through the gift of some manuscripts which he had sent home from Turkey.

However, though Roe, in the course of his career, had drifted farther away from university interests than the other burgesses, he was now, in the current crisis, like them in his willingness to further the cause of reform. For in this, also, the university representatives of the mid-century differed from their predecessors—not one of them was an exponent of divine right. And this is all the more extraordinary when it is remembered that the constituencies themselves—once the excitement of their elections had subsided—soon again became wholeheartedly and unqualifiedly Royalist.

The period of the Long Parliament, indeed, saw the university member at his best—in the character of non-partisan reformer. Here for the first time in the history of university representation—for almost the only time, in fact—we catch a glimpse of that balanced judgment, that thoughtful approach, which—according to modern standards, at least

—might be felt to be the chief contribution of the university mind to public affairs. With Eden and Lucas, the evidence for the existence of this quality is less conclusive, but in John Selden's whole parliamentary career, and in Sir Thomas Roe's private letters, the tendency to weigh and balance, to take into consideration all aspects of a situation, to respect the varying claims involved, is revealed repeatedly.

Selden, indeed, appears as the ideal university member of his century —and perhaps of the whole history of university representation—for he combined eminence in the world of scholarship with activity and responsibility in the world of affairs, and in spite of all his preoccupation with the public concerns of the kingdom, he never ceased to defend the legitimate interests of learning and of the universities, when these were threatened. Only Isaac Newton, as representative for Cambridge during the crisis of 1689, approached him as an equal, and Newton never held the position in public life that Selden so long occupied.

THE UNIVERSITY ELECTIONS

In both universities the elections for the Long Parliament were vigorously contested. At Oxford, the chief interest centred in the candidacy of Secretary Windebanke, who wished to keep the seat he had won for the Short Parliament. It is not clear why Windebanke found this so difficult, unless the reason is to be sought in some changed attitude of Archbishop Laud, the university Chancellor. Laud had been a strong supporter of Windebanke in earlier days, and had been largely responsible for his appointment as Secretary of State, but at this time he may have chosen to throw his influence elsewhere. At least, one of Selden's seventeenth-century biographers asserts that Selden had Laud's backing for the Oxford seat, though whether as Windebanke's colleague or in place of Windebanke, is not clear. This assertion is not very convincing without further evidence, however, for although it is true that Laud and Selden had met on somewhat friendly ground in connection with Selden's *Mare Clausum*, and Laud is supposed to have boasted that he could win Selden over to the Court, it would appear more probable on the surface of things that if Laud shifted his support at all, and only one candidate was concerned, that candidate would be Sir Thomas Roe rather than Selden.[1]

Roe and his wife had been personal acquaintances of Laud for many years, and Roe, from his posts abroad, had kept up a correspondence with the Archbishop, reporting on his negotiations, urging Laud's influence on behalf of his projects, and even complaining of the King's failure to recognize his ambassadorial efforts, hinting very delicately that he would welcome Laud's assistance in advancement to a higher office. But twice when the secretaryship fell vacant, Laud supported another man for the place, one of these men being Windebanke. When the Short Parliament was called, however, Laud, in his concern for the King's interest, expressed the wish that Roe could serve, but Roe was detained abroad, and could not be considered.[2] In the light of this long association between Roe and the Archbishop, it seems not unlikely that Laud at last decided to push Roe forward as a candidate at Oxford —although, by this time, ironically enough, Roe and he no longer held the same views on the King's prerogative. Probably if Laud had known what Roe's views on the royal policies had come to be, he might not have been so eager for Roe's presence. At all events, one curious circumstance bearing on this whole question of whom Laud supported in 1640, is the fact that in the Oxford Archives there is no letter of recommendation from the Chancellor for Roe or for Selden—or even for Windebanke.

Some light on other influences at work is given, however, in a private letter written by Secretary Windebanke's nephew, Dr. Thomas Read, at Oxford, just after the poll. This letter presents a contrast to the one written so complacently by Windebanke's son on the same subject at the time of the April election.[3] Here we gather that one of the criticisms made of Windebanke was his lack of leadership in the Short Parliament. It also appears that there were two factions working against him within the university, the Puritan party and another group—that behind Roe and Selden—which was supported by a "higher power". Read's letter was written to his brother Robert, who was Windebanke's secretary. It ran as follows:

> Though for my own part, I know my uncle's wisdom to be such that the University should not have suffered through his silence in the last Parliament, yet I have not the power of other men's opinions who are guided only by their own perverseness. Most of our Doctors and the principal men of the University were well inclined towards him, but I am informed that some higher power was directly or indirectly interested in the election of bothe the last [i.e. the members-elect, Roe and Selden]. However, I am glad the Puritan faction prevailed not.[4]

The problem of identifying the "higher power" presents some difficulty. The name of Archbishop Laud first comes to mind, but another interpretation is possible, based on a clue given in a note of Windebanke's written 9 October, and calendared as follows: "The Lord Chamberlain threatening Secretary Windebank. Sec. Windebank likely to miss Oxford."[5] This suggests that the opposition was coming from Philip Herbert, the fourth Earl of Pembroke, brother of Oxford's former

Chancellor. Pembroke was making his influence felt behind the elections in as many constituencies as possible in this campaign, and in every case against the Court. At Oxford, this would mean against Windebanke, but whether on behalf of Roe and Selden, or for the Puritan party, does not appear. If Roe and Selden were indeed being supported by Archbishop Laud, then Pembroke would probably have been against them, for Laud had been his successful rival for the chancellorship in 1630, and Pembroke's religious preferences were Calvinist. On the other hand, although as a Calvinist sympathizer, he should have backed the Puritan faction, the middle ground reformist views of Selden and Roe, if not associated with Laud, might have satisfied him.[6]

That at this time there was a Puritan party of some strength at Oxford is also recognized by Anthony Wood in his account of this same election.[7] Its candidate was Sir Nathaniel Brent, Warden of Merton (Wood's own college), and later Judge of the Prerogative Court of Canterbury. His two chief supporters were two college Heads, Dr. John Prideaux of Exeter, and Dr. Paul Hood of Lincoln. All three— Brent, Prideaux, and Hood, were active opponents of Laud and his policies. Sir Nathaniel, in fact, later became a pillar of the reform group in the university, and one of the most influential personages there throughout the Civil War. It will be noted that by this time the reform spirit of the day had spread beyond the rank and file into more influential quarters. This was rather different from the situation in 1625/6 and 1627/8, the other occasions upon which Oxford had shown itself in a rebellious mood. In 1640 the leaders of protest were all Heads of Houses, and it is significant to note that the Dr. Prideaux now backing a Puritan for parliament and described as early as 1631 as "ye cheife encourager of younge factious men" was the same Dr. Prideaux who had tried to prevent the election of Sir Francis Stewart back in 1625/6.[8]

Under the pressure of all this opposition, Windebanke withdrew his name before the time of the poll, and was provided with a Cornish seat instead.[9] The Puritan party, on the contrary, continued to press the claims of their candidate almost to the end. The contest really ran between Brent and Selden, for Sir Thomas Roe stood at the top of the list, as unanimous choice, whereas, according to Wood, Selden was only chosen "by the better part". The opposing party, "being outvied with votes, sate down in peace", which seems to mean that they "desisted", for the Archives give no figures of a poll, and Brent's name is not mentioned.[10]

At Cambridge, also, there was considerable election activity, but here the court candidates were not so clearly identifiable as in the case of Windebanke, and here the Puritan party seems to have been in a measure triumphant, for Dr. Eden and Henry Lucas—whose anti-Court attitudes have already been noted—were re-elected at Cambridge, though not unanimously, as they had been for the Short Parliament.[11] Their opponents were Henry Hopkins, the Warden of the Fleet, and the celebrated "antiquary" and benefactor of the university, Sir Henry Spelman, each of whom polled only half as many votes as the winning candidates.[12] Spelman's adherents claimed that he would have had a much larger poll, had it not been for the electioneering tactics of Eden's chief manager, Mr. [Charles?] Eden of Trinity Hall, possibly Dr. Eden's brother, who circulated a report around the university that Spelman had declined the honour.[13] In fact, according to Abraham Wheelocke—Professor of Arabic and Anglo-Saxon, and one of Spelman's scholarly correspondents and great admirers—many of the Heads and "prime men" of the university had been thinking of Spelman as a candidate even at the time of the last election, and were now so enthusiastic over his candidacy that they only gave up at the last moment on the very floor of the Senate House, when they finally found they "could not shake off the former Burgesses".

Wheelocke hastened to assure Sir Henry, however, that he had the hearts of the university, if not their votes, and explained at length the difficulties which had been encountered by Spelman's followers. It was not only the false report put out by the Eden faction—and Wheelocke sent as enclosures several statements signed by indignant electors explaining how they had been tricked—but also the pressure brought upon the Vice-Chancellor (who had himself started the "visiting" for Spelman) by Dr. Eden in person—who pointed out "in plaine tearmes" that if Sir Henry should be named, he (Eden) could not be—and by two other Heads of colleges, who were alarmed over the possible effect of Spelman's candidacy upon the chances of Henry Lucas, the Chancellor's secretary. As a result, the Vice-Chancellor was "beaten of his course" and "everyway perplexed". And on top of all this, came word from the Bishop of Ely (who was, significantly enough, the patron of Dr. Eden, the chancellor of that diocese) announcing that Sir Henry Spelman would be above any such minor honour as a mere university burgess-ship.[14]

Spelman himself had no such lofty notions, but on the contrary, was frankly gratified that "soe many worthie men of ye Universitie" had been, as he wrote, in thanking Wheelocke, "pleased to cast their thoughts on me (not dreaming of it)", and he assured them that, if elected, he would indeed have done all he could for the Church, the kingdom, "and her my ever honoured and deare Mother, your famous Universitie".[15] What this protestation would have meant in terms of politics, is hard to say. In earlier years Spelman's historical researches had not been entirely pleasing to the Court, but the fact that he was set up by the Heads of colleges in opposition to Lucas and Eden, and the fact that Abraham Wheelocke's letters laid so much stress on Spelman as a defender of the Church, suggest that in this campaign Spelman perhaps, along with Hopkins, was the candidate of the more conservative elements of the university, though probably not himself an extreme Royalist.[16] If Spelman had won the seat, and lived to serve his term, Cambridge would indeed have contributed another Selden to the House, as far as scholarship and a sincere interest in learning were concerned, though it is unlikely that Spelman could have equalled Selden as a political figure, however independent and judicious his attitude, for he lacked the latter's long political experience.

THE UNIVERSITY BURGESSES IN ACTION

When the new university members assembled at Westminster on 3 November, two of them—Sir Thomas Roe and John Selden—were immediately plunged full into the activities of the House. Roe, as Privy Councillor, appeared on the first day with the royal officials who administered the oath of office, and soon thereafter became the Commons' chief messenger to the House of Lords. At the start, his service in this capacity, like Windebanke's in the preceding Parliament, related to the usual routine preparations for the public fast, but soon thereafter Roe was engaged in the really serious business of the treaty with the Scots, which was to put an end to the Bishops' Wars. This was a suitable employment for one with Roe's long experience in diplomacy, and if, as seems likely, he displayed in this new post the same energy and thoroughness that he had always shown in his old office of ambassador, his contribution to the committee work of the Long Parliament in these early weeks must have been considerable. This supposition is borne out by the fact that it was Roe who time and again was selected as reporter for the various committees and conferences with the Lords on this subject. Besides his part in the Scots' treaty, Roe was noted in this session for his speech on foreign trade, the arguments of which, according to David Lloyd's complimentary passage, would hold good as long as Britain was an island.[17]

After 17 February 1640/1, Roe's name ceases to appear on the committee lists of the *Journal*. D'Ewes notes that he was ill for some weeks at this time.[18] By 17 April, he was once again named on a committee, but a week later he informed the House that he had been appointed a delegate to the Diet at Ratisbon for the settlement of affairs in Germany, and asked the Commons' permission to be absent and yet to "continue a Member of this House, notwithstanding his Employment as his Majesty's Ambassador in Germanie".[19] The leave was granted, and shortly thereafter, Roe set sail. No one could foresee at this time that this would be Roe's last appearance in Parliament, and that, though technically he remained Oxford's burgess until well on into the Civil War, it would only be by virtue of a continuous extension of this leave. For after two years of service abroad, Roe returned to England only to spend two more years in illness and retirement until his death in November 1644, without ever resuming his parliamentary duties in the House of Commons.[20]

Compared to Sir Thomas Roe, Dr. Eden of Cambridge, in the early days of the Long Parliament, played a relatively insignificant part. In the opening weeks, according to D'Ewes, Eden was moderately prominent as a speaker and a maker of motions during the debate on the new church canons, which had been introduced by Archbishop Laud in the preceding June, and which were arousing much animosity in the House.[21] Eden himself at first was under something of a cloud, as one who had been a legal agent of church administration during the Personal Rule— chancellor of Ely and a member of the High Commission—and probably for this reason his name is conspicuously absent from the committee lists of the first six months of the Parliament. Indeed, he was even under impeachment along with some other officials (Sir Henry Marten, Oxford's former burgess, being one, and Sir Nathaniel Brent, recent candidate at Oxford, another), and ordered to make reparation to Dr. John Bastwick for his share in Bastwick's condemnation.[22]

But after June 1641, Eden seems to have gained the confidence of the House. His name begins to appear with more frequency upon the pages of the *Journal*, and he was entrusted with increasingly important duties. His work falls into two main categories, both of them suitable for one with his legal training and experience—church matters, such as the suppression of Papists, and the abolition of pluralities, and—in later years—questions of maritime law.[23] He was at least three times on the committee appointed to collect funds for the parliamentarian treasury— although in this connection some recurrence of suspicion of his loyalty may once again have arisen, since his authority was at one time revoked for a short interval.[24] However, by the end of his parliamentary career, he had the esteem of the House to such an extent that he was made a member of the committee appointed to manage the Admiralty.[25] His concerns in regard to his constituency of Cambridge were comparatively minor throughout his career, but, such as they were, they will be touched on later.

When Dr. Eden died in 1645—less than a year after Sir Thomas Roe —the universities were each left with only one burgess. Of these two— Selden and Lucas—Henry Lucas of Cambridge was in the end the final survivor and the only one of the original four elected in 1640 to live on through the whole period of the Long Parliament and into the Restoration. Of all these burgesses Lucas was the most obscure. His name is rarely met with even on the committee lists of the *Commons' Journal*, to say nothing of speeches, motions, or reports. There is in fact no evidence even of his presence in the House until the Long Parliament had been in session six months, and the Protestation was presented for the members' attestation on 3 May 1641. Lucas signed this document, and shortly thereafter began to figure in various questions involving the army's financial matters.[26] The explanation of this seems to be that his patron, Lord Holland, the university Chancellor, had been appointed General of the army, and Lucas, as his secretary, appears to have acted as his lordship's chief financial agent in this, as in other matters. Indeed, it may be that the silence of the *Journal* as regards Lucas is owing to the latter's absence with the army in this connection. Leave, at least, was given him to be absent for this purpose on two occasions.[27] His capacity for this employment, however, seems to have been questioned, for Sir William Uvedale, the paymaster-general, in a letter written three days after the granting of Lucas's first leave, described Lucas as "totally ignorant of all business of this nature", and in need of assistance in carrying it on.[28] How long Lucas did carry it on, is not clear—probably only so long as Lord Holland remained general. At any rate, by August of 1642, the tables had turned, and it was Sir William Uvedale whose management of the army finances was in question, and Lucas who appeared as Uvedale's defender in acting as teller for the Noes in a division on a proposal to summon Sir William for interrogation.[29]

During the years 1642–6, Lucas's name turns up at scattered intervals upon the committee lists of the House, most generally on those committees connected with university business. The revolutionary character of the Civil War does not seem to have frightened him away from Parliament, as it did some members, who lost heart in the parliamentarian cause and deserted their seats as the war went on. At least Lucas's name is not found on any of the lists of absent members who were commanded to attend from time to time—although upon a call of the House in 1647 and 1648, he was twice excused from attendance—once upon grounds of illness.[30] However, there was a limit to his compliance with the times. By December 1648, he was among the members excluded and imprisoned as a result of Pride's Purge and he was not listed among those released on 20 December.[31] During the term of the Rump, he apparently never returned to claim his seat, and from this time on, Lucas's name passes from the history of university representation, although it has been perpetuated in an academic way at Cambridge ever since, through his foundation of the Lucasian Chair of Mathematics by bequest at his death in 1663.

When we come to consider the career of John Selden, at last we reach a university member of full stature. Rarely can more than two or three pages of the *Commons' Journal* be turned over during the years 1640 to 1648 without coming upon a reference to Selden. In the first ten months of the Long Parliament he served on at least thirty-seven committees, made at least four reports, and took part in nineteen conferences with the Lords. This rate of activity was maintained pretty consistently throughout the years that followed. Selden's range of action ran the whole gamut of parliamentary business, from regulating the wherrymen of the Thames to abolishing "idolatry", and in all (or almost all) of the most critical issues of the time, he played some part—in the bringing of charges against the Earl of Strafford and Archbishop Laud; the abolition of ship money, forest laws and distraint of knighthood; the destruction of the prerogative courts; the making of peace with the Scots; the attempted arrest of the Five Members; the evaluation of the King's commission of array; the removal of the bishops; and later the consideration of the Nineteen Propositions and other negotiations for peace between the King and Parliament, as they dragged out over the years.[32]

To all of these issues he brought a mind well stored with a knowledge of past societies, laws, and governments, and well trained in the rigours of search and evidence, whether in the wider field of history, or the narrower field of law. He brought, also, into the dark fanaticisms of the seventeenth century a breadth of thought and a freshness of approach that is like the opening of a door on to a spring landscape. "Liberty above all", or "Liberty in all things", as it is variously translated, was the Greek motto he inscribed in all his books, and the spirit of this motto runs through all the fragments of his speeches that survive, just as it runs through his famous *Table Talk*, published many years after his death. But it was a liberty that rested upon reason and balance, for to Selden's sceptical cast of mind, extremes of any kind were suspect. To such a one, the period that was opening in 1640 presented many problems.

Considering Selden's importance as a member of the Long Parliament —both because of the frequency of his service and the continuity of his attendance—and because of the esteem with which he was regarded, it is strange that a more complete record of his parliamentary career has not been preserved. Outside of the innumerable notations in the *Journal*, and some casual mention of his leadership in the letters and diaries of the period, the only other trace of his activity that is to be found is in a few scattered fragments of speeches, printed here and there in so haphazard a fashion that their full meaning is not clear. For this reason the complete story of Selden's part in the proceedings of that day cannot be properly told.[33]

The outline, however, appears to be clear. Always suspicious of the excesses of the prerogative and the Laudian conception of the Church, he stood in the forefront of the reforming party in the early months of the Long Parliament.[34] At the same time, as became one of moderate mind, he always rejected the more radical measures urged by those of his colleagues who were ultimately to take the country into civil war, fanaticism, and dictatorship. Selden's position in regard to Strafford serves as an example of this middle course. Involved as he was in all the major reforms of the session, Selden was naturally placed on the committee appointed to bring in charges for Strafford's impeachment, and he seems to have worked diligently to this purpose.[35] But when it became clear, after Strafford's defence, that the proofs of treason were insufficient and that only a bill of attainder would serve, Selden withdrew from the committee, apparently unwilling to assist in the basic injustice and unreason of this procedure, and ranged himself among those who voted against the attainder. This stand was to the utter outrage of the more extreme Parliamentarians, and in consequence, a list of the names of those who had rejected the attainder was posted in the Old Palace Yard under the heading, "Straffordians, Betrayers of their country." Selden was number 27 on this list.[36]

A similar unwillingness to see true justice jeopardized led Seldon to protest against the removal of Dr. John Cosin, as Vice-Chancellor of Cambridge—the same Vice-Chancellor who was but lately furthering the candidacy of Sir Henry Spelman—for certain High Church actions, by a mere vote of the House, without impeachment proceedings before the Lords.[37] Likewise Selden objected, in terms very similar to those he had used in discussing the charges against Strafford, to the too-sweeping definition of treason applied in the debates on the army plot of 1641: "the conspiracy to bring upp an army to compell the parliment by force is not treason, but if act bee put in execution, 'tis treason".[38] Later, in the same spirit of fairness, he was to protest against one of the charges against Charles I, and also—probably on the same count—to withdraw his support of the charges against Laud. On the other side of the political battle-line, he opposed the prerogative courts, including the Court of Wards, as agencies of tyranny and injustice.[39]

Besides his interest in the application of principles of reason and justice, and besides his efforts to curb the royal power and ministers, Selden took an active part in church matters, especially on the question of the bishops. Here again, in tracing the origins of the secular authority of the clergy and the grounds on which this authority might be justified, Selden's vast store of legal and historical learning was brought into play. He had become convinced that the claims of the bishops had been greatly enlarged throughout the centuries, and that their power, though perhaps of practical value, was not sacrosanct, or, in the phrase of the day, *jure divino*. Holding this view, he was willing to go rather far with the Puritan party in curbing the higher clergy. On the other hand, measured by that touchstone of political opinion, the Remonstrance of November 1641, he was still a moderate, for there is no evidence that he—or indeed any of the university members—adhered to the principles of that document.[40] Moreover, unlike the majority of the Puritans, he did not welcome a mere transference of power from bishops to presbyters and ministers, and resisted this kind of ecclesiastical tyranny as firmly as he had that of the Establishment. Also, unlike the Puritan group with whom he so often found himself working, he did not favour the complete abolition of bishops or the removal of the bishops from the House of Lords—although he accepted these measures when they were finally adopted.

Selden frequently took his more solemn colleagues aback by his turn for repartee. The debate on the status of the bishops provides one much quoted example of this characteristic. An advocate of the abolition of episcopacy had made the point that it was illogical for archbishops, who were admittedly not *jure divino*, and bishops, who were only dubiously *jure divino*, to exercise authority over ministers, who, all agreed, were divinely sanctioned. Selden's reply follows:

> That the Convocation is *jure divino* is a question; that Parliaments are not *jure divino* is out of the question; that religion is *jure divino* there is no question. Now, Mr. Speaker, that the Convocation which is questionable whether *jure divino*, and Parliaments which out of question are not *jure divino*, should meddle with religion which questionless is *jure divino*, I leave to you, Mr. Speaker.

His opponents interposed with the remark that archbishops were not bishops, to which Selden rejoined: "That is no otherwise true than that judges are no lawyers, and aldermen [his opponent being an alderman] no citizens." Aiken, in quoting this passage—perhaps the longest of Selden's surviving speeches—notes, quite rightly, that this after all was "mere dialectical fencing", but it illustrates the nimbleness of Selden's wit, and the lightness with which he carried his learning. No wonder Sir John Coke's son—inheriting perhaps his father's somewhat heavy seriousness—reported that "Mr. Selden puzzled all the House" by his arguments.[41]

Although Selden did not wish to see episcopacy abolished, he was nevertheless quite willing to examine into the past actions of the clergy, and to censure them for misuse of power. Early in the session, in the autumn of 1640, he was on the committee formed to investigate the new church canons made in Convocation the previous June and alleged to be illegal because not consented to by Parliament. Later, however, Selden seems to have withdrawn his support of the investigation at the request of Archbishop Laud, who appealed to him to use his influence to allow the "poor canons" to die a peaceful death. Aiken's view of this is that Selden desisted because of his past association with Laud and their present connection through the university.[42] Selden nevertheless served on the committees that were to prepare the charges against Laud and the other bishops who were under impeachment—although in the case of Laud, at least, he seems to have withdrawn later when the move reached its more extreme stages, probably because he felt there were insufficient grounds for an accusation of treason. In this connection, a gruesome note appears in the *Journal* for January 1644/5, when a committee was appointed to draw up an ordinance to provide that Laud should be executed by beheading only. Selden's name is entered here, probably indicating that he exerted himself in favour of obtaining for the condemned Archbishop the most humane terms possible.[43]

But we must return to Selden's activities in the period before the outbreak of the Civil War. As the months wore on through 1641 and 1642 and Parliament assumed an authority never before exercised by any such body in the past, Selden became employed in new problems, where precedents and former principles of justice were no sure guides. What, for example, was to be used as a substitute for the royal assent, if the King remained in Scotland, out of touch with the course of events in Westminster? Selden was put to work to produce suggestions for a *Custos Regni*. Later came the question of the ordinance of militia and the commission of array. But before wrestling with these, Selden had already served on the committees to consider the King's breach of privilege in the case of the Five Members, and to clear the Five Members of the charges the King had laid against them.[44]

To Selden, the issues of the militia and the array, pushed to the fore as practical necessities of the times, were both illegal; and in taking this characteristically middle ground, he disappointed both sides, each of which had hoped to secure him as a partisan. The royalist camp had never regarded him as a real enemy, despite his leadership in the Long

Parliament's reforms, and they were confident of his support in this crisis.[45] Lord Falkland, the most moderate of the Royalists, and the one most likely to appreciate Selden's point of view, wrote him earnestly on the subject. Selden—perhaps with reluctance—wrote back that he was forced to disagree, that in fact he considered the King's action in summoning troops as definitely unlawful, and that his opinion on this point must stand until he should be genuinely convinced it was incorrect—"which shall, as in all other things change, when I shall be taught the contrary"—so he put it. Nevertheless, he reassured the King, through Falkland, that he also regarded the ordinance of militia as unlawful, and would speak against it in the House, where he hoped his evenly balanced stand would make his argument all the more convincing. In this he was wrong, however, for, as Clarendon said, Selden's views were much too rational for the current temper of the House. The militia ordinance passed despite his logic, and Selden yielded to the will of the majority, and ranged himself on the side of Parliament in the Civil War.[46]

He might have had the Great Seal, if he had chosen to join the King, but when it was offered, he declined it, partly perhaps out of unwillingness to leave London, but also probably because of his political views. In his letter to the Marquis of Hertford on this subject, he gave as his excuse his fears that acceptance would only widen the rift between the Commons and the King, and he protested a loyalty to his Majesty "as great and as hearty as any man's"—but it was loyalty in parliamentary terms, not as understood by the true followers of the Stuart cause.[47] From this time on up to Pride's Purge, Selden moved in more or less conformity with the general trends of parliamentary action. In February 1642/3 he subscribed to the declaration of adherence to the Earl of Essex, and in June 1643 took the Covenant when it was first offered to the members of Parliament.[48] He refused to join Waller's royalist plot in the summer of 1643, and at this time became a lay delegate to the Westminster Assembly and took an active part in the reconstruction of ecclesiastical affairs, though sometimes to the great puzzlement and dismay of the extreme Puritans there.[49]

Selden's biographers give the impression that he lost interest in parliamentary activities as the Civil War progressed, and absented himself from the House over long intervals, but the *Commons' Journal* does not bear this out.[50] There Selden's name appears with its customary regularity on the committee lists from 1642 to 1648, although, of course, it may be true that he spoke less frequently, feeling that the voice of moderation was less and less welcome to his colleagues. His activities were largely concerned with legal and ecclesiastical matters, with the prosecution of various charges and impeachments, and with the consideration and phrasing of the various items involved in the negotiations with the King, the Scots, and the army. During this period came the years of his greatest service to the university, and to the cause of learning in general, a subject that will be discussed in some detail later. Here also belongs one of his characteristic and oft-quoted speeches—on the subject of excommunication as practised by the local clergy, a procedure that was winning approval among the Presbyterians, but which Selden regarded as a door opened to ecclesiastical tyranny. Selden's argument convinced the House, and the proposal to legalize the custom was voted down.[51]

A man of Selden's moderation could scarcely look with satisfaction upon the way things were going in the years 1647 and 1648, though he may have hoped that the efforts of himself and others in the pending negotiations would prevent a further crisis. When Pride's Purge was only three weeks away, he was still at work in a committee set to prepare an act "justifying the proceedings of the Parliament in the late war in declaring all oaths, etc. void".[52] This was his last appearance as Oxford's representative, as far as any records go.

His name, however, is not found upon the list of those "secluded and imprisoned" on 6 December 1648, though David Lloyd, in his account of Selden among the "Sufferers" on behalf of the King, speaks of Selden as "outed that Parliament (to use his own words) by those men that deposed his Majesty". The occasion thus referred to, however, may be, not Pride's Purge, but a further ejection which took place in the following February in the case of those members who had voluntarily absented themselves as a mark of disapproval of the policies of the Rump.[53] Whatever his status, Selden's name never again appears upon a parliamentary committee after November 1648.

Cromwell, like Laud ten years before, would probably have liked to have the moral support of so great an intellect, and one that so long had occupied itself with opposition to the authority of Church and Crown, but Cromwell's party contained too many elements of violence and dogmatism to win Selden's unqualified support. He went along with them, as the times dictated, but without enthusiasm. Cromwell had sensed this attitude the year before, when in January 1647/8 he had tried to have Selden expelled from the House for having refused to countenance the old charge that Charles I had conspired with Buckingham to have King James poisoned. The motion failed, however, by a vote of 80–30,[54] and Cromwell later became so reconciled to Selden that he tried to persuade him to write the answer to *Eikon Basilike*, later undertaken by Milton in *Eikonoclastes*. But Selden refused the task.[55]

It would be of supreme interest to have some record of Selden's thoughts and actions during the last months of the monarchy and the early days of the Commonwealth, and again in 1653 after the expulsion of the Rump, but whatever his views were, they must remain a secret, since he never expressed himself fully in public or in private—so far as any record goes. He seems to have practised his own maxim, as set down in his *Table Talk*: "Wise men say nothing in dangerous times."[56] Some may find this an inglorious policy, and note uncharitably that, in his moderation, Selden all through his life generally found himself, in his final stand, on the side of the superior power, whether King, Parliament, or Protector. Something of this view is found in Clarendon's comment: "How wicked soever the actions were which were every day done, he was confident he had not given his consent to them; but would have hindered them if he could with his own safety, to which he was always enough indulgent."[57] But Mallet, the modern historian of the University of Oxford, has a contrary opinion. Speaking of Selden in the Long Parliament, he writes, "Few men played a franker, saner, more honourable part", and—describing Selden's contributions further— he continued: "No more impressive advocate of precedent and principle raised his voice among those warring counsels. No university member had more care for his constituents, though he remained with the Round-heads at Westminster while his constituency became a camp of Cavaliers."[58] This last aspect of Selden's service—his assistance to the university—will be considered in detail later on.

In discussing Selden, to describe his parliamentary career is to de-scribe at the same time, so far as the sources of information permit, his political views. As to the other university members (with the exception of Sir Thomas Roe, who presents a special case), their views appear to have been somewhat similar to those of Selden, although the evidence is by no means either plentiful or clear.

Eden's position is especially ambiguous. Unlike Selden—who had never received any favour or protection from the Crown and who had been three or four times under the royal displeasure[59]—Eden had held legal and ecclesiastical positions since 1625, and had served on the Court of High Commission during the Personal Rule—an activity for which, as we have already seen, he was repeatedly questioned during the first months of the Long Parliament.[60] Moreover, in the early days of the session, he also appeared, in his character of royal official, as something of an apologist for the Laudian canons, although, to be sure, his defence was perhaps only half-hearted, for he readily came round to the view that they "were all naught and all to be condemned; and hee hoped ther buriall would bee more honorable then ther birth". In line with this evidence of his inclination to the royalist cause, is the fact that he was included by David Lloyd among those who had suffered on behalf of the King.[61] It is difficult, however, to see that Eden underwent any hardship other than that of being deprived of his offices in the course of the ecclesiastical legislation carried out by the Long Parliament. He was seemingly otherwise unmolested, and he did not live long enough to be among those "outed" by Pride's Purge.

In contrast to these insufficient indications of royalist and churchly leanings, is the fact that Eden took the Covenant when it was first offered in June 1643, and that earlier, his name was not on the list of those voting against the attainder of Strafford. It is also possible that he may have been among those who adhered to the Grand Remonstrance in the autumn of 1641, which would be significant as being one of the key tests of political opinion at this period.[62] Notwithstanding these circumstances, it may be going too far to classify him, as R. N. Kershaw does, in his study of the elections to the Long Parliament, as one of the "Puritanical brethren", for Eden, in his will, provided for a bequest to Trinity Hall Chapel which was to ensure a regular supply of candles for the altar.[63] A more likely explanation of his stand is that he took a midway position, between the Royalists and the extreme Parliamentarians, either out of a natural moderation of temperament, or out of opportunism. His conduct in his relations with his college and university seem to point to the first interpretation.[64]

Henry Lucas, unlike Eden, had never had any connection with Church or Crown. He had, to be sure, obtained his master's degree by royal mandate in the "Caroline Creation" of 1636, but this was probably not because of any special favour from the King, but rather because of Lucas's relationship to the Earl of Holland, the university's Chancellor. This relationship may also be thought to be the motivating force in Lucas's political stand as a member of Parliament, since in the early days of the session the Earl was among those peers who opposed the royal power. But later, when Holland twice deserted to the King's side —in 1643, and again in 1645—Lucas remained continuously at Westminster. This would seem to indicate that his adherence to the parliamentarian cause was on his own initiative. That his stand was that of a man of the middle road, however, and not that of an extremist, is suggested by the fact that, in the great crisis of December 1648, he was excluded from the House and imprisoned along with those other members who were unwilling to go so far as the dethronement and execution of the King.[65]

The fourth of the four burgesses elected by the universities in the autumn of 1640—Sir Thomas Roe—was also a man of the middle road, but his position was notably different from that of Lucas, Selden, and Eden. Roe, like the others, never forsook the Parliamentarian party, but, at the same time, he never actually attached himself to it, as did the other three. His aim, indeed, was a true neutrality, adhering to neither side—though with a natural bias in favour of the King, arising on the one hand out of the character of his own past career, and on the other, out of a strong feeling of personal loyalty. In fact, considering all things, it is much to be wondered at that he was not an outright Royalist, instead of a doubting neutral. The occupation of his whole lifetime had led him to think of the King's interest above all things, and to identify the King's interests with that of the nation. As envoy to India, to Turkey, to the Germanies, he had thought, not in terms of legislation, but of administration, not of rights and privileges, but of power. Yet when the Long Parliament opened, he seems to have taken up his new duties with cheerful enthusiasm, to have welcomed the opportunity for reform, and to have believed that his royal master and the Privy Council could be won over to a programme of sweeping change. Roe's religious views were also of a nature to fit in with the new trend of affairs, for, although an ardent Anglican, his interests ran rather to "accommodation" with the other Protestants than to the erection of a separate Laudian Church, conciliatory to Rome.

Roe then seems to have gone along with the Parliament up to the time of his departure for Ratisbon in April 1641. After that, we have no way of knowing how much farther he was willing to go, for there are no letters of his touching the constitutional issues of this period, as there are for the later years, 1642–4. He was at first, it would seem, mainly concerned with affairs at home only in so far as they strengthened or weakened his position as a diplomat. His reports were directed to the King or the Secretary of State in the traditional fashion. As yet the claims of Parliament to oversee foreign relations had not become a serious issue. When the question arose, Roe at first denied Parliament's authority, but later his actions were such that it was surmised, as the Venetian Secretary in the Netherlands expressed it, that he cherished "a strong leaning to the party opposed to his sovereign".[66]

This leaning, however, was far from partisan, for Roe's strongest desire in this crisis was not for the triumph of the parliamentarian cause, but for a workable compromise between the two factions. His dismay at the turn of events was so great, according to the Venetian, that Roe had little desire "to return to the royal Court unless the present aspect of affairs changes", and it was for this reason that he opened negotiations for a trade treaty, so that he might remain longer in the Netherlands, "free", so the Venetian cryptically added, "from the

observation of those who watch his proceedings with remarkable closeness, and who seem more eager than they need to be". Who these
observers were, whether royalist or parliamentarian, is not clear, but
in any case, the remark seems to show that Sir Thomas Roe was already
reaping the uncertain rewards of neutrality. He explained his views to
the Venetian Secretary, saying that if he was compelled to return to
England, "the first thing he would do would be to place himself between
the king and the parliament, to pray God to appease those troubles or
else take away his life, so that he might not feel them".[67]

This statement was unhappily a true forecast of the course of his
career in the two years that followed. When he landed in England in
September 1642, he was jeered as a Royalist by an unfriendly mob in
London, while at the same time he was forbidden by the King to join
the Cavaliers at York. This order of the King was phrased, to be sure,
in such a way as not to suggest that it had been issued out of any disapproval of Roe, but rather because of the uncertainty of the King's
movements and the military situation.[68] And it may be true in this case
that the reason for the Court's attitude was really regard for Roe's
welfare rather than distrust of his neutral views. Nevertheless, there are
several later indications that his presence was not entirely welcome. For
example, it was not until January 1642/3 that he was allowed to show
himself at Court, and then only at his own request: "to see & kiss His
Majestie's handes, and give some account of the Treaty". At this
audience he seems to have been continued in the King's service in
charge of correspondence relating to German affairs, a charge which he
apparently kept for at least ten months, for as late as 27 December 1643,
he was still sending reports.[69]

At first Roe spoke of this situation cheerfully enough, but as time
went on he felt himself more and more neglected by the King, and complaints occasionally escaped him. In writing to Falkland in May 1643,
Roe noted that he was barred from Oxford not by his own wish, but
by "his Maties commands, and the little use I found of my services
there". Shortly before this it is true that he had received a somewhat
lukewarm invitation to join the Court, but it was obviously issued per-
functorily, and very likely in response to Roe's complaints of parliamentarian taxation, and not out of a desire on the King's part for Roe's
services. The King, Falkland wrote, was very sorry that his friends
should be in danger, and he be unable to protect them, and that "if
retiring yourself hither out of their power [that is, Parliament's?] would
stand with your occasions, he assures you you shall be very welcome".
Roe did not accept the invitation, partly because of his ill health, and
partly—and this is significant—because he knew Parliament would

withhold permission.[70] It was clear that the Court was losing interest in Roe. Five months later, in October 1643, he was not invited by the King to attend the conference held at Oxford with the French Ambassador. Roe felt this slight keenly, but he attributed it to personal enemies of his own—"the ill usage & ingratitude of some about the King whom he had obliged". By February 1643/4, he was no longer consulted on foreign affairs at all.[71]

With the Parliament, Sir Thomas's relations were equally ambiguous. He seems never to have presented himself at Westminster after his return in September 1642, but, at the same time, he also never ceased to regard himself as a member of the House, subject to parliamentary authority, and from the seclusion of his estate at Woodford in Essex, had some correspondence with influential members concerning questions of foreign affairs, up until a few months of his death.[72] This hybrid position, in which Roe acted partly as the King's foreign agent, and partly as a member of Parliament, seems to have been tacitly accepted by all concerned.[73]

By April 1643, however, some demand arose for his presence in the House, soon after the issuance of a general call for the return of absent members to their seats. Sir Thomas referred to this incident in the same letter to Lord Falkland at Oxford referred to above:

> Perhaps you may have heard how the jealousys of ye members called me in question, and divers harangued against me: whereupon, by order of the house, I was sent for by the Serjeant's man; but being then in a condition not able to move, sick, and lame, the house was pleased to accept my [excuse?], and since, though carryed in a chayre, I have been advised by my freinds there, who understand the grounds of the suspition against me, to retyre hither among the woods and wild beasts, to avoyde all occasion of scruple of affairs.

The letter further expressed a desire to join the King at Oxford, but noted that to apply to Parliament for leave to make such a visit would "rayse more doubts", and result in a refusal.[74]

In this same letter, as in others, Sir Thomas complained bitterly of the parliamentarian levies. These were exceedingly heavy, yet if he failed to make payment, his remaining resources would be confiscated— and, in fact he seems already not to have escaped penalties of some sort. But he was also fearful lest his submission to Parliament on this score would be frowned on by the Court, and begged for instructions, which he said he would obey, regardless of consequences—"to my shirt though nakedness be an ill companion to my age".[75]

This remark, and the general tenor of the letter as so far quoted, might be regarded as the expression of a wholehearted Royalist, caught by mischance between the battle-lines, were it not that the concluding sections of the letter sounded quite a different note—being the sober advice of an anxious neutral, urging that the only way to achieve peace was by the "Parliamentary way", "the meeting of the King, and his subjects in Parliament wherein all disputes, and breaches may be reconciled, and bound up by votes and lawes, which are the only, and publique security".[76] Such a view was much closer to that of Roe's Oxford colleague, John Selden, than to that of Charles Stuart and the majority of the Cavaliers.

Mediation, indeed—the search for a middle ground of compromise— had been Sir Thomas's aim from the moment of landing in 1642, and he clung to it with persistent earnestness all through the months that followed, though the bitterness of faction deepened, and the gulf between the parties widened. It was his constant theme in all his letters —to the Palatinate family, to his own friends, in reports to Secretary Nicholas, in offers to the King of his own experienced service as mediator.[77] Strangely enough, so far as Parliament is concerned, there appears to be no evidence that Roe attempted to exert any influence upon it for mediation,[78] but this may be because he felt his influence there was less likely to bear fruit than in court circles.[79]

The details of Roe's efforts and plans to bring about a compromise settlement cannot be gone into here, but an examination of his correspondence shows that he was not much in sympathy with the royalist manœuvres. In April 1643, he wrote to Lord Falkland on the latest negotiations:

> It may appear great presumption in me to give any opinion . . . but . . . the passions of a troubled spirit may excuse the errors of well affected zeal. I cannot forbear to inform you that the last message of his Majesty hath utterly discomposed even all those who seriously pursue and grasp after the hopes of accommodation. They pretend to have no ground or subject left to them to continue their endeavors.[80]

Roe realized that his own situation was not such as to make him an ideal mediator, since a mediator, to be successful, as he wrote in another letter, should be able to speak freely, in a way that "no Subject may to his King, nor no Member dare to Parliament".[81] For this reason, he vainly hoped and urged that the States of Holland would take this office upon themselves.[82] But nothing was done, and the situation grew worse.

In January 1643/4 Charles I summoned to Oxford the assembly that came to be known as the "Anti-Parliament". This was a true test of Roe's allegiance, but by now he was too seriously ill to respond, even if he had wished to range himself so decisively among the ranks of the

Cavaliers. He wrote to Secretary Nicholas of his regret that he could not "obey his Majestie's commands", adding, in the words of the summary in *The Catalogue of the Harleian Manuscripts*, that "his Bed hath been all his consolation", and further, that, "If God shall enable him, he shall faithfully serve his Majestie; if too late, he shall die enjoying the peace of a loyall Heart." But, in spite of this protestation, perhaps he was well satisfied that his illness gave him an excuse to avoid a summons with which he was not in full sympathy.

It also gave him a way of escaping the demands of Parliament. Though absent on 22 January 1643/4—the day of the call made to count those members who had deserted to the "Anti-Parliament"— Sir Thomas was respited,[83] and his prolonged absence permitted him to avoid meeting that other test of Parliamentarianism, the Covenant, which had been accepted, perhaps unwillingly, by the other three university members.

After the meeting of the Oxford Anti-Parliament, Sir Thomas's connection with the Court grew less and less, and he ceased to receive instructions for the conduct of his foreign correspondence.[84] Perhaps the Cavalier party had begun to distrust him a little. One letter, at least, written by a Royalist in Vienna in March 1644 expressed some such doubt. Mentioning Sir Thomas Roe, the writer noted, "a great friend of yours as he made us believe here, but I believed him only by discretion, for I think he has more of the Fox than the Roe".[85] Roe, himself, however, never ceased to lament his inability to serve the King, and— in what is possibly his last letter on public affairs—wrote in June 1644 to his great friend, the Queen of Bohemia, with some bitterness that he hoped that those who had neglected his service might never need it; "nor too late, know that those Counsells are safest, or more honest wherein there is no Self-Interest".[86] Thus to Sir Thomas Roe, inclined to the side of the Royalists, the middle road proved to be no easier than it was for his colleague, John Selden, inclined to the side of Parliament.

Sir Thomas maintained his parliamentary status as burgess for the university to the last, and Parliament never deprived him of it. His final act as a member of the House was to apply to the Speaker for a safe-conduct to go to Bath, to "make the last trial of hope upon earth for some ease" of his misery. The request was granted 3 July 1644,[87] but this last trial, sadly enough, was unsuccessful, and Oxford's seat in the House was left vacant by Roe's death in the following November.

Contemporaries and later writers alike have only good to say of Sir Thomas Roe. The estimate given in Wood and in the *Biographia Britannica* in slightly varying forms, may well be quoted here:

His spirit was generous and public; and his heart faithful to his prince. He was a great statesman, as good a commonwealth man, and as sound a Christian as our nation hath had in many ages.[88]

If it were not for Selden's presence on the parliamentary lists, the historian of university representation might be inclined to acclaim Sir Thomas Roe the most distinguished burgess that Oxford sent to Parliament throughout the whole of the seventeenth century. His distinction, however, has no relation to his position as a member of Parliament, much less to his status as a university representative. In this specific capacity, as a matter of fact, he did not figure at all, and it is only by virtue of the richness of his personality and the moderation of his views in time of crisis that he qualifies for any sort of prolonged attention in a history of university representation in the seventeenth century.

An order for a new writ for an election to fill Roe's place was issued for the University of Oxford on 18 November 1646, less than six months after the city and university had fallen into the hands of the parliamentarian forces. In the Oxford Archives, however, there is no mention of any election, and no indication in the *Official Return* or in the *Commons' Journal* of the presence of any new university member.[89] It would appear that Roe's place remained vacant, and that the university went unrepresented for the rest of the term of the Long Parliament—unless, as is barely possible, Serjeant Sir John Glanville, Speaker of the House in 1641/2, was chosen and not allowed to take his seat. At least, two of Glanville's early biographers, both Royalists, make the statement, otherwise unconfirmed, that Glanville, "in one of the Usurping Times of the *Pseudo*-Parliament", was elected member for the University of Oxford. All things considered, however, if Glanville ever was elected, it is more likely that the election took place for some Parliament of the Interregnum than as a "recruiting" measure in 1646.[90] Since Glanville never actually served, such an election, if it occurred, would only be significant as an indication of Oxford's strong royalist sentiment and its unwillingness to bow to parliamentarian supremacy.

There was an election at Cambridge, however, on 27 November 1645, to fill the seat of Dr. Eden who had died the previous July. Nathaniel Bacon, a half-nephew of Sir Francis Bacon, was chosen for the place. There seems to have been some difficulty here also, for an order in the *Commons' Journal*, under date of 29 December, indicates that the Sheriff had been remiss in making this return—perhaps because of the legal difficulty involved in the issuing of writs without the royal authority.[91] By 20 January, however, the matter must have been settled, for Bacon's name appears on a committee list, and by 28 January, he had taken the Covenant.[92]

With Bacon's election, for the first time in university history, an out-and-out Parliamentarian occupied a university seat. For Bacon was no middle-of-the-road reformer, like Selden, no troubled neutral, like Roe. Quite on the contrary, he had been a Puritan and a rebel from the earliest days of the Civil War, and for him this election for Cambridge in 1645 was to usher in a long period of parliamentary service on behalf of the revolutionary cause, not only while sitting for Cambridge in the Long Parliament, but also as member for Ipswich in later Parliaments, and as Admiralty Judge and Master of Requests under the Protectorate.[93]

According to the committee lists of the *Journal*, Bacon was a moderately active member. His committee assignments ran along the lines of his interests and experience: legal questions—he was a Bencher of Gray's Inn; military affairs—he had been connected with the organization of the Eastern Association; and religious matters—as an ardent Puritan and a university member.[94] It is impossible, however, to determine the exact nature of his service in the House, because of the fact that there were two "Mr. Bacons" present.[95] Nevertheless, there are something less than thirty committee lists from January 1645/6 until September 1649 on which the full name, Nathaniel Bacon, appears, and there is good reason to think that he is also the "Mr. Bacon" of many at least—perhaps most—of the other committees.[96] As a member concerned primarily with the universities, his full name is mentioned only once.[97]

As a speaker, his name does not appear in the *Parliamentary History* or in Rushworth's *Historical Collections*, but this is not conclusive, as none of the records are very full for the later years of the Long Parliament. On the other hand, perhaps Bacon had not yet acquired the readiness of expression he subsequently displayed in the pages of Burton's *Diary*. As to the committees to which he was assigned, perhaps the most important were those relating to the propositions for accommodation with the King in 1648.[98] In these discussions, it may be assumed with some confidence that Bacon was among those who presented the views of the more extreme wing of the Parliamentarian party. At least, his book, *Historical Discourses*, published in 1647, reveals him as an opponent of the Crown and the episcopal hierarchy to such a degree that the book was suppressed after the Restoration.[99] Moreover, Bacon alone, of all the university members of the Long Parliament, kept his seat after Pride's Purge and took the Engagement. However, he appears on only three committees between January 1648/9 and the following September, and after that, up to the expulsion of the Rump, his name is entirely missing.[100]

UNIVERSITY INTERESTS IN THE LONG PARLIAMENT

Of all the Parliaments of the seventeenth century, the Long Parliament was the Parliament in which university affairs were most to the fore, the Parliament in which the universities were most under attack. Their very nature and past history made them strongholds of the Established Church, and their ties of loyalty had always attached them to the Crown rather than to the Lords and Commons. For this very reason they were immediately suspect to the more extreme Parliamentarians. As agencies in the formation of ideas, whether through the educative process or through the press and the pulpit, they were influences that a revolutionary assembly could not overlook. Accordingly, regulations for the control of the universities came to be an important part of Parliament's programme. For the first time in any serious way, the university burgesses were called upon to defend their constituencies from hostile—and often potentially destructive—legislation. In the forefront of this defence was John Selden. Compared to him, Dr. Eden and Henry Lucas played minor roles, while Sir Thomas Roe did not figure at all, and Nathaniel Bacon could scarcely be counted on to oppose a programme that must have been in most respects in line with his own thinking.

The issues involving the universities had never been so numerous before. They ranged all the way from questions of exemption from taxation and abolition of the right of Vice-Chancellors to hold court as justices of the peace to the ejecting of officials from university posts for not subscribing to the Solemn League and Covenant. The later stages of university legislation, in particular, involved the creation for each university of a parliamentary Board of Visitors who had extensive power to control students and professors, appointments and ecclesiastical practices, as well as the right to institute alterations in the statutes of college and university. In the case of Cambridge—inclined at first to support the King but soon under the watchful eye of the parliamentarian army—regulation by Visitors was decreed in 1644 and 1645, while for Oxford, because of its possession by the Royalists until June 1646, a similar law was not passed until 1 May 1647. Under the Protectorate further Boards of Visitors were authorized.

All of this regulation was, of course, ultimately subject to Parliament itself, and carried out in co-operation with parliamentary committees appointed for the universities. In the enforcement of the regulations considerable leeway was found for action both for and against certain details of the regulations, and in the course of administration some friction developed between the religious groups, not only between the moderate Anglicans and the Puritans, but especially in later years, between the Presbyterians and Independents. These circumstances produced controversy, and kept the universities in a continuous state of uncertainty as to their rights and privileges.[101]

On the whole, however, modern writers do not believe that the upheaval caused by this parliamentary meddling was so great as it was formerly pictured. That there were in fact some desirable improvements in the way of stricter discipline, more genuine devotion to study and higher standards generally, is admitted even by some of the royalist writers of the period, such as Anthony Wood.[102] If this was really the case, the university members may well have had no valid objection to certain of the reforms. Moreover, there may have been some willingness on their parts to see the Laudian influences removed from the universities' ecclesiastical life, since none of the four members of 1640 was a bigoted High Churchman. In any case, moderation, we may be reasonably sure, would have been the attitude with which at least three of the active university members—Selden, Eden, and Lucas—approached the situation.

As to the exact action taken by the university members on university questions, this is no easy matter to determine, because of the nature of the records. In D'Ewes's *Journal*, there are only a few fragments giving light on this subject;[103] and after January 1641/2, when the Notestein and Coates editions of D'Ewes leave off, there is not much to depend upon besides the committee lists of the *Commons' Journal*, and a few stray comments by contemporaries. Moreover, for this period, unfortunately—unlike the records of the earlier years of the century—no account is kept in the *Journal* of the members who introduced bills, or presented petitions, so we cannot be sure how often university issues were handled by members other than the university burgesses. A standing committee for university matters was established quite early, but in a notation of April 1641, the chairman's is the only name given, and he was not a university member.[104] Later, from time to time, similar committees were revived or reconstituted, and on these committees at least some of the university burgesses were included.

Of the two Cambridge members, Dr. Eden's part in the House on behalf of university interests seems to have been far less than that of his colleague, Lucas. In the opening weeks of the Long Parliament, Eden made two speeches on university matters—one in defence of Dr. Cosin, the Vice-Chancellor, when the latter was under attack for "superstitious innovations".[105] Outside of this, Eden seems to have acted in his capacity of university burgess on only two or three other minor matters—once on the committee for the "Relief" of the

university—probably a matter of taxation—and again, for the defence of
the university from charges of "superstition".[106] His greatest service
appears to have been in connection with the enforcement of the oath
to support the Solemn League and Covenant. In June 1643, after the
Covenant had been presented to the members of Parliament, an order
was issued that the burgesses of Cambridge take the Covenant down to
the university for signing, and that they return with a report on those
who refused to sign.[107] Though Eden had accepted the Covenant
easily enough himself, he was apparently very lenient with those who
did not feel they could adhere to it, and managed somehow to keep the
members of his own college, Trinity Hall, who were "politically . . . a
good deal divided", in Mullinger's phrase, from being ejected for having
failed to subscribe to it properly.[108] It was for this leniency, perhaps,
as well as for his loss of his ecclesiastical posts, that Eden won mention
among Lloyd's "Sufferers" for the King.[109]

Henry Lucas was more largely concerned with university business
than any of the other university members except Selden. About
fifteen of the committees on which his name appears during the years
1640–8 were devoted to university matters. Most of these involved
petitions to be considered, or messages to be delivered or responded to.
For example, it was he, along with Selden, who presented one of the
first university petitions of this period—that against the proposed
abolition of Deans and Chapters in May 1641. In the following October
occurred his only recorded speech—on the bill prohibiting clergymen
from exercising civil power. Here he proposed to exempt the university
Vice-Chancellors so that they might continue to act in their customary
capacities as justices of the peace.[110] A year later he was on the committee for considering the contributions of university plate to be made
in response to Parliament's general levy, and also to examine the matter
of Trinity College's sequestered rents.[111] He was also named to several
of the committees concerned with the regulation of the university,
although there is no way of learning whether or not he took any large
part therein.[112] He would very likely have been named to the Board
of Visitors, although there is no list preserved of the Visitors for Cambridge in the period before the 1650's. With Selden, he was set to
prepare a letter to the Eastern Association in August 1645, warning the
latter that the rights and privileges of the University of Cambridge
should stand unimpeached until otherwise determined by Parliament.
At this same time, Lucas was also concerned with the rights of the
university in its relations with the town.[113]

One of the main problems of Cambridge during this period was to
keep its financial resources intact. University property in the past had

been exempt from taxation, but the Long Parliament, in need of money for the prosecution of the war, and suspicious in any case of the universities' old associations with the endowments of the Established Church, put an end to this privilege. Cambridge, because of its ostensible adherence to the Parliament, suffered in this respect slightly less than did Oxford, the hotbed of Royalism.[114] Perhaps some of the favour received by Cambridge was owing to the efforts of Lucas.[115] There is no direct evidence whatever to support this conjecture, but Isaac Barrow, the first occupant of the Lucasian Chair of Mathematics, would have us believe that this was the case. Addressing the university on the occasion of his installation in 1664, within a year of Lucas's death, he spoke of Lucas's service as follows:

> For in these wicked and unhappy Times when a covetous Barbarity gaped after the Profits of the University, imposing Burthens upon all, and everywhere exacting the most unreasonable Taxes; [he] stoutly defended your Cause and maintained your immunities; he strenuously exerted all his Power, and effected much, what through Advice, what through Persuasion, that the Gown might not be made tributary to the Cloth; that the Fury of Mars might not prey upon the property of Minerva; that the Wealth dedicated to the Nurture of the liberal arts might not be perverted to maintain the worst of Tyrants, and to promote the Enterprizes of wicked men. Thus he at that time made himself your Shield against a dangerous Intolerance that he might afterwards become your Sword against Ignorance.[116]

If even a part of this encomium is deserved, Lucas surely played a much larger part as representative of the university than the grudging notes of the *Journal* and the noncommittal pages of the *Parliamentary History* would indicate.

We now come to John Selden and his services to the cause of learning in time of trouble. This story has been recounted by each one of his biographers, and cannot be told again in full detail here.[117] The pages of the *Commons' Journal* are witness to Selden's constant interest in the affairs of both universities and in the concerns of learning in general. This is especially true of the years after 1644, when Selden's early work on the constitutional reforms was over, and the success of the Puritan party emboldened its more radical members to make over the universities in line with the new scheme of things. Ordinances of various kinds, petitions, provisions in regard to finance, to "godly preaching", the disposal of library collections, appointments, the requirement of oaths—all were assigned to the attention of committees that invariably included "Mr. Selden", and in some cases the issue under consideration was designated as especially consigned to his charge.[118] There are, however, only a few surviving speeches of his that bear directly on university interests.[119] Much of his service may have been performed in a private capacity, when not on the floor of the House, or else in committee meetings, where little or no record of proceedings was preserved.[120]

He is credited, none the less, with a series of achievements, some of which benefited the sister institution quite as much as his own constituency. At Oxford, when, with the condemnation of Archbishop Laud, the endowment of the Arabic Professorship there was in danger, it was Selden who secured its continuance, and later saw that the former professor, the celebrated Edward Pococke, was restored to his chair.[121] On the other hand, in the interests of Cambridge, when Archbishop Bancroft's library was seized, it was Selden who instigated the University of Cambridge to petition the Lords to gain possession of it, and it was Selden who argued the university's case before the Lords and won the library.[122] In 1648, after his own constituency had come once more under the direct authority of Parliament, Selden was appealed to by the Vice-Chancellor to "make interest in the Parliament" for the salaries of the law professors and the lecturer in theology,[123] and before this, soon after the surrender of Oxford, a similar letter describing the university's sad plight, had begged for his support in the face of parliamentary interference with the university's rents. This letter has been often quoted, but it is worth repeating as evidence of the dependence that the university was then putting on its representative's influence.

> I pray [wrote the Vice-Chancellor to Dr. Gerald Langbaine, the antiquary, then in London] let the worthy Mr. Selden, the great honor of our Mother the Universitie know it [that is, the university's need], and desire him to releive his declining undon Mother.[124]

Similarly, when first confronted with the necessity of subscribing to the new oaths—probably the Covenant—Oxford in the autumn of 1646 petitioned that the question be referred to Mr. Selden, that he might explain that their excuses were on genuine legal grounds, and not mere pretences.[125]

Selden had taken little part in the Visitation of Cambridge, begun under the ordinances of 1643/4 and 1645, or the investigations of the Manchester Commission, first initiated in the autumn of 1643;[126] but when Oxford was put under an ordinance of regulation in May 1647, his university activities increased. In the first place, he was busy on the committees that prepared the ordinance,[127] and in February 1646/7 he was named on the parliamentary Committee of Appeal which received protests against the Visitors' actions.[128] His influence here was apparently of great importance in tempering the wind of Puritanism to the scrupulous Anglicans of Oxford.

Selden's indifference to the details of religious dogma, and his ability to take a broader view of political differences than was possible with most men of his time made it easy for him to recognize the merits of all sorts and conditions of men—Cavalier and Puritan, Presbyterian and Independent—and so disposed him to spare worthy scholars, of whatever persuasion, the rigours of strict conformity. The ordinances empowered the Visitors to enforce the Covenant, to oversee discipline and doctrines, and to punish the bearing of arms against the Parliament, or the encouraging of others to do so. But Montagu Burrows notes that at Oxford the Covenant was never pressed with full force, and that the number of ejections from university posts was not very great, considering that Oxford had been with the King from the very beginning of the war. How far this was owing to Selden's influence, is probably impossible to say, but Burrows gives him a large share of credit.[129] There is clear evidence that in a number of cases, at least, Selden was directly responsible for the action taken by the authorities.

One of these cases was that of the Professor of Arabic, Edward Pococke, a scholar of the first rank whose ejection would have undoubtedly been a great loss to the university, but whose "popishly inclined" tendencies had brought him under the Visitors' suspicion. For him, Selden "did plead eagerly", according to Anthony Wood, and succeeded in having him evade the Covenant, and later receive further university appointments.[130] Selden's disgust at the Visitors in regard to these proceedings is noted by Pococke's biographer and by the article on Selden in the *Biographica Britannica*: "He complained greatly of such injustice and wilful baseness, as made him weary of striving against the stream, tho' he said he despaired not of doing Pococke some good."[131] This must have been his state of mind much of the time during the latter stages of his term as university representative.

Lesser lights of the university, as well as Pococke, also received Selden's assistance,[132] and his defence of the university in general at some meetings of the parliamentary Committee of Appeal in 1647 is recorded at length in a note in the *Clarendon State Papers* and also in Wood's *Annals*. Here it is told how the Committee was acting on the ejection of those university officials, including the Vice-Chancellor, who had refused to submit to the Visitors, and how the Committee proceeded without allowing those accused a hearing, and without examining the legal basis of their objections. This action was made all the more irregular because of the fact that the offices thus made vacant were immediately awarded to some of the very members of the Committee who were voting for the ejections. Selden, as one of "the just advocates of our just cause", to use the phrase quoted by Wood, protested with his usual vigorous and intricate logic, which "puzzled them a little", for they could not answer his arguments, but, as the writer of the *Clarendon* note observed, "being resolved that nothing should stop them", they continued with their proceedings. As they went on from one arbitrary act to another, Selden, exasperated, warned them sternly that they "would themselves destroy rather than reforme one of the most famous and learned companies of men that ever was visible in the Christian world", but his words were heard in vain, and the controversy waxed high until, to keep the peace, the meeting had to be adjourned. Finally, at a later session, Selden, "by much disputation and importunity", forced them to give way on one point at least, but later, the commentator says, the meetings were held secretly—"stolen, and very short, though much mischief has been done in them"—the secrecy being, apparently, for the purpose of preventing the university's defenders from knowing what was afoot.[133] One distinct gain, however, from Selden's exertions in these meetings was that the university was ultimately allowed to have counsel in resisting the Visitors, and the famous lawyer, Matthew Hale, later Chief Justice and member for the university, was engaged on their behalf.[134] The time gained by these measures was no doubt in itself of great value in lessening the general confusion in the university caused by too much zeal in the administration of the ordinance. The next year, 1648, when a second ordinance of regulation was passed, the clause that empowered the Visitors to make ejections solely on the ground of refusing the Covenant was kept out of the law, possibly, so Anthony Wood thought, through the influence of Selden, since the clause was in the first draft, and later removed.[135]

A royalist satire in the *Harleian Miscellany* seems to refer to these same controversies. It purports to be a speech by the fourth Earl of Pembroke, the parliamentarian Chancellor of Oxford, telling the Visitors how Selden had obstructed the action of the extremists in their plans for the regulation of the university.

> You know what a coil I had e're [*sic*] I could get hither; Selden did so vex us with his law and his reasons, we could get nothing pass; you saw I was fain to swear him down, and Mr. Rous . . . and other friends voted bravely, else Selden had carried it. S'death, that fellow is but burgess for Oxford, and I am chancellor, and yet he would have the parliament hear his law and reasons against their own chancellor.[136]

What the exact issue was, is not clear, and the implication is that Selden lost out in spite of his efforts, but it serves to confirm other reports as to Selden's zeal on the university's behalf.

That the value of Selden's services was fully recognized by the university is shown by a letter from Dr. Gerald Langbaine, often quoted by Selden's biographers. It was written in March 1647/8, apparently in reference to Selden's part in gaining the university time against the precipitate action of the Visitors and the parliamentary Committee. Acknowledging Selden's "unwearied care and passionate endeavors" for the university's preservation, Langbaine went on: "We know and confess: 'if Pergamum could have been defended by any right hand, it would certainly have been defended by this one of yours (Si Pergama dextra Defendi Poterant, etiam hac defensa fuissent)'." And further: "it must be imputed to your extraordinary providence, that we have stood thus long—By your good acts and prudent manage [sic] our six months have been spun into two years."[137] From Cambridge also Selden had received another tribute, when in 1645, upon the death of Dr. Eden, the fellows of Trinity Hall wished to make him their Head in Eden's place, so that, as they phrased it, they who had been "secure in Eden" might be "happy in Selden". Selden declined the honour, perhaps at Parliament's wish, perhaps entirely according to his own inclinations. But it was some time before the fellows could be persuaded to elect another candidate.[138]

With all his good will towards the universities, Selden may at times have found dealing with them a little trying. At least, the two remarks in his *Table Talk* concerning the subject of "Universities" are far from flattering. One, made upon hearing of a history lecture to be founded in the university, runs as follows: "Would to God, sayes hee, they would direct a Lecture of discretion there, this would doe more good a hundred times." The other comment could be applied to university representatives, as well as to other university men in public life: "Hee that comes from the University to govern the state before hee is acquainted with the men & manners of the place does just as if hee should come into ye presence all dirty with his bootes & rideing Coate & his hatt all dawb'd; they may serve well enough upon the way but when hee comes to Court hee must conforme to the place."[139]

Before leaving the subject of Selden's service to the universities, it may not be amiss to note certain other services of his to the cause of learning in general, which may come properly under the concerns of a university representative, taking that office in its larger sense. Such, for example, was his interest in safeguarding the records of the Tower, and preserving them and other books and manuscripts from destruction by the zealots of Puritanism.[140] Such also was his protection of the learned Archbishop Usher, in the latter's right to attend the Assembly of Divines, to keep possession of his library, and to conduct services in London.[141] When Parliament decided to further the translation and printing of the Septuagint, it was Selden to whom the business was chiefly entrusted,[142] and it was Selden, also, who, on his own initiative, saw that the books and manuscripts in the royal collections were safe-guarded after their seizure by Parliament.[143] In somewhat the same category come his own later bequests of books, manuscripts and sculp-ture to his constituency, the University of Oxford.

With Selden's retirement and the exclusion of Henry Lucas in 1648, the history of university representation in the Long Parliament virtually comes to an end, for Nathaniel Bacon's action in the Rump Parliament was negligible. The same problems, however, confronted the uni-versities in the later Parliaments of the Interregnum, though the occupants of the university seats by that time were all Puritans and Cromwellians.

NOTES FOR CHAPTER VI

1. Laud's backing of Selden is referred to only by Lloyd, *Memoires*, p. 51, who was writing from a royalist point of view. For the reconciliation between them, see Geo. W. Johnson, *John Selden*, p. 226; S. W. Singer, ed., *Table Talk of John Selden*, Introduction, p. xli. See also Laud's remark on "J.S." in 1635/6, *Works*, III, 225.

2. At the time of Windebanke's appointment, Roe wrote to the Princess Palatine: "here is a new secretary brought out of the dark . . . by my Lord of London. . . . These are the encouragements we receive that have labored abroad." Laud again in 1639 failed to push Roe's claims sufficiently upon the retirement of Sir John Coke as Secretary, but this may have been owing to the opposition of the Weston faction, to whom Roe was not acceptable. See Gardiner, *History*, VII, 200. For Laud's concern that Roe might serve in the Short Parlia-ment, see Laud, VII, 537. For Laud's earlier relations with Roe, see *ibid.*, pp. 73–4, 75, 86–8, 458–75, *passim*, 575–99, *passim*.

3. *Supra*, Ch. IV, p. 121.

4. *C.S.P., Dom., Chas. I*, XVII (1640–1), 197.

5. *Ibid.*, p. 151.

6. That Roe was unsure of his success at Oxford seems to be suggested by the fact that he also stood—apparently rather late in the campaign—at New Windsor, where his election was later invalidated for undue notice to the voters. Willson, p. 82. For Pembroke's political views, see *D.N.B.* Pembroke had already been one of Selden's benefactors, and was instrumental in getting him released from prison in 1631. By 1640 Pembroke's influence in the elections for the Long Parliament was apparently so great that Windebanke had at first sought his assistance in getting as many of the King's Ministers elected as possible. *C.S.P., Dom., Chas. I*, XVII (1640–1), 105, 151, 166. See also below, p. 172, for Pem-broke's later relation to the university as Chancellor.

7. Wood, Gutch, II, pt. i, 424.

8. For Brent, see *D.N.B.* For Hood, see Venn, II, 401. For Prideaux, see *D.N.B.*; Thomas Crossfield, *Diary*, p. 56, 128 n.

9. *Cal. Clar. S.P.*, I, 209.

10. If Wood is correct in his account of the election, Singer, Introduction, p. xxviii, and his probable source, David Wilkins, *Vita Seldenis*, p. xxx ("uno ore renuntia-batur"), must be mistaken in stating that Selden was unanimously chosen. On the other hand, the absence of any detailed entries in the Oxford Archives would tend to support Singer's view. Oxford University Archives, R24, ff. 181–2.

R. B. Mowat, in "The Mission of Sir Thomas Roe to Vienna, 1641–42", *English Historical Review*, xxv (1910), 266, is clearly in error in saying that Roe was sitting for Oxford in June 1640, instead of November. *O.R.*, p. 492.

11. *O.R.*, p. 485. For references to Eden and Lucas, see *supra*, Ch. IV, p. 128, n. 117.

12. For Hopkins, see Venn, II, 405. For Spelman, see *D.N.B.*. For the poll, see Cooper, III, 304.

13. The "Mr. Eden" who was Dr. Eden's manager was very probably the Charles Eden in Venn, II, 284, and also the same who voted against the Duke of Buckingham in 1626. Cooper, III, 186. If so, he would very likely represent the more discontented elements in the university.

14. For the letters regarding Spelman's candidacy, see Add. MS., 34,601, ff. 302–3, 305, 308, 309.

15. Spelman's letter is printed in Cooper, III, 304, and in Sir Henry Ellis, *Letters of Eminent Literary Men*, C.S., o.s., no. 23, p. 163.

16. For Spelman's earlier difficulties with James I, see R. L. Schuyler, "The Antiquaries and Sir Henry Spelman", *Proceedings of the American Philosophical Society*, XL (1946), 92. On the other hand, among Spelman's supporters at Cambridge, there was at least one man who was later prominent as a strong royalist divine, Peter Gunning of Clare Hall, later Bishop of Ely. See *D.N.B.* and Add. MS., 34,601, f. 309.

17. Lloyd, *State Worthies*, pp. 807–9. For Roe in the opening days of the session, see *C.J.*, II, 20, 22, 23. For his part in the treaty, see *ibid.*, pp. 27, 30, 31, 32, 33, 45; Sir Simonds D'Ewes, *Journal*, ed. Wallace Notestein, pp. 39–41, 48n., 49, 81. Most of Roe's reports are printed in full in the *Commons' Journal*. Some of his speeches and reports are also printed elsewhere in other contemporary sources, such as Rushworth's *Historical Collections*, Nalson's *Impartial Collection*, Northcote's *Notebook*, etc., and there are also several different manuscript copies and pamphlets in existence—all of which seems to indicate that Roe's role in the Long Parliament attracted at that time a good deal of attention. For a complimentary estimate of Roe as a parliament man, see *A.O.*, III, 112; *B.B.*, v, 3504.

18. D'Ewes, Notestein, p. 362.

19. *C.J.*, II, 123, 127. Roe delivered a petition of some kind to the House on the day he requested leave of absence. It is possible that this petition was one of the several issued by Oxford at this time on behalf of episcopacy, and in defence of the university's endowments. Wood, Gutch, II, pt. ii, 429, 431, 432; Mallet, II, 346.

20. For Sir Thomas Roe's career, see *D.N.B.*; *B.B.*, v, 3501–6; *A.O.*, III, 111–14; William Foster, *The Embassy of Sir Thomas Roe*, I, v–vi. No adequate biography exists of this interesting and important figure. Many of his letters are in the Harleian Collection, MS. 1901. See below, pp. 159–63.

21. D'Ewes, Notestein, pp. 40–1, 125–6, and n. 148, 163.

22. *Ibid.*, pp. 38–9; *C.J.*, II, 53, 90, 93; *C.S.P., Dom., Chas. I*, XVII (1640–1), 479; XVIII (1641–43), 5. See also Tanner MS., 65, f. 4r, listing charges against Eden. His superior, the Bishop of Ely, Matthew Wren, had been a great persecutor of Puritans, and Eden may have had some share in Wren's acts. See Wren in the *D.N.B.*

23. For church matters, see *C.J.*, II, 298, 431, 913; III, 55; D'Ewes, Notestein, p. 59. For maritime questions, see *C.J.*, II, 465, 501, 534, 568, 593, 713; IV, 152; *C.S.P., Dom., Chas. I*, XIX (1644), 144, 306, 380; XX (1644–5), 102, 197, 289.

24. For Eden as collector, see *C.J.*, II, 199, 601–2, 610, 924, 932, 982; III, 53. R. S. Rait and C. H. Firth, *Acts and Ordinances*, I, 633.

25. Rait, I, 669; *C.J.*, IV, 112.

26. *C.J.*, II, 133, 149, 302; III, 186; v, 341.

27. *Ibid.*, II, 189, 245.

28. *C.S.P., Dom., Chas. I*, XVIII (1641–3), 29.

29. *C.J.*, II, 724.

30. *Ibid.*, v, 259, 329, 513.

31. *Ibid.*, VI, 30, 39. Lucas's last committee assignments in the House were in September 1648, but he was appointed a commissioner for the Militia of Cambridgeshire as late as 2 December 1648. Rait, I, 1235. For reference to his exclusion, 9 December, see *P.H.*, II, 601; III, 1249, 1251.

32. As it is impossible to enumerate all the entries in the *Commons' Journal* recording Selden's committee service, citations will only be given in special cases.

33. There are many biographical accounts of Selden. The earliest full account was David Wilkins, *Vita Seldenis* (1725–6) on which most of the subsequent works lean heavily. The fullest accounts in English are those by John Aiken (1812), George W. Johnson (1835), S. W. Singer (Introduction to *Table Talk*, 1897), and Robert Waters (1899). Shorter sketches are: *D.N.B.*; *A.O.*, III, 366–79; Aubrey, II, 219–25; [Pierre] Bayle, *General Dictionary*, IX, 143–50; *B.B.*, VI, pt. i, 3605–24; Lloyd, *Memoires*, pp. 518–21; Anthony Wood, *Life and Times*, I, 424–5. The best accounts of his career in the Long Parliament are in: Aiken, pp. 101–35; *B.B.*, VI, pt. i, 3616–19; Johnson, pp. 226–324, 328–42. Singer, Introduction, pp. xxxviii–lxxvi; Waters, pp. 41–7; Wilkins, pp. xxi–xxii.

34. Aiken, p. 101.

35. *C.J.*, II, 31, 39, 64, 72, 93, 98; D'Ewes, Notestein, p. 63 n.; Rushworth, III, pt. i, 153; Whitelocke, *Memorials*, I, 113.

36. For Selden's stand on Strafford, see the discussion in Aiken, p. 102, Gardiner, *History*, IX, 350; Johnson, pp. 234–5; and items in John Bruce, ed., *The Verney Papers*, p. 58; Rushworth, III, pt. i, 248.

37. D'Ewes, Notestein, p. 271 n. See Cosin's biography in *D.N.B.*

38. Bruce, p. 117. This is perhaps the same incident alluded to by Johnson, p. 268. Sir Edward Verney, in his abbreviated style, noted another similar speech of Selden's made during the deliberations on Strafford. Referring to the definition of a traitor, Selden said: "Hee that levies warr against the King and he that doth intend to kill the King, but the intent to levy warr against the King is not. How can this be treason since it is a bare endeavour?" Bruce, p. 58.

39. See below, pp. 154, 156, for the charge against Laud and the King. For Selden and the royal courts, see Aiken, pp. 134–5; *C.J.*, III, 179, 663, 647; D'Ewes, Notestein, p. 97; Johnson, p. 323; Whitelocke, I, 577.

40. For Eden's attitude towards the Remonstrance, however, see below, p. 158.

41. *C.S.P.*, *Dom.*, *Chas. I*, XVII (1640–1), 450–1; Aiken, p. 106; *H.M.C.*, *Cowper*, II, 274–5. See also accounts of "Mr. Selden's puzzling Queries" in the Westminster Assembly in Thomas Fuller, *Church History*, p. 213; Lloyd, *Memoires*, p. 518; Whitelocke, I, 209; *Harleian Miscellany*, VI, 57–64.

42. *C.J.*, II, 30, 48; Laud, VI, pt. ii, 589; Aiken, p. 105.

43. *C.J.*, II, 18, 168, 252, 257; III, 68, 628, 633; IV, 13, 14. Johnson, p. 270, states that Selden had no part earlier in preparing the articles for Laud's impeachment, but the *B.B.*, VI, pt. i, 3619, and Aiken, pp. 113–14, hold otherwise, perhaps basing their statements upon the committee lists in the *Journal*. There is no mention of Selden, however, on the final committee to consider Laud's trial. *C.J.*, III, 694.

44. *C.J.*, II, 243, 247, 251, 383, 398.

45. *C.S.P.*, *Dom.*, *Chas. I*, XVIII (1641–3), 359.

46. Selden was a teller for the Noes when the ordinance for the militia was passed. *Old P.H.*, XI, 281. His letter on the commission of array is quoted in *B.B.*, VI, pt. i, 3617 n., where his stand on this subject is discussed at length. See also Aiken, p. 120; *C.J.*, ii, 630, 632, 643, 645; and Clarendon, *Rebellion*, I, 205, 206, 265; Johnson, pp. 284–5; Singer, p. xlvii.

47. Clarendon says that Selden's refusal to accept the Seal was not unexpected to those who knew him and his circumstances—his weakening health, his age, his

wealth, his comfortable living quarters. *Rebellion*, I, 445; II, 114. Selden's letter declining the honour is printed in *B.B.*, VI, pt. i, 3618n. See also Aiken, pp. 115–16.

48. *C.J.*, II, 957; III, 118. His name also appears on the list of those taking the Covenant on 30 September of the same year. (*Ibid.*, p. 445.) But this seems a redundant entry, as during the summer Selden had been a member of the Westminster Assembly, and if he had not already subscribed to the Covenant as an M.P., he would have been required to do so later, in order to serve in the Assembly. *B.B.*, VI, pt. i, 3618–19. Both Aiken, p. 130, and Johnson, p. 310, seem to be in error in dating Selden's subscription to the Covenant as late as 1644.

49. For the Assembly, see *C.J.*, III, 119, and also the references in n. 41, above. For Waller's plot, see Whitelocke, I, 203–4.

50. The *D.N.B.* suggests that Selden may have been somewhat withdrawing from his parliamentary activity as early as 4 February 1641/2, when an order was issued for his attendance in the House. There seems to be an error here, also repeated by Singer, p. xlvii. There was no such order issued on 4 February 1641/2. Selden was assigned to a committee on the Scots' treaty on that day. (*C.J.*, II, 412.) The order for Selden to attend on Wednesday next "peremptorily at the farthest", and to continue his service in the House, was issued 4 February, the next year, 1642/3. (*Ibid.*, p. 953.) The issue at stake may have been the declaration of adherence to the Earl of Essex, which Selden complied with two days later. It is possible also that the committee to draft a declaration (subject unspecified) to which Selden was assigned on 9 February, had to do with this same issue. (*Ibid.*, p. 959.)

51. Rushworth, IV, 203; Whitelocke, I, 504–5. Selden's speech on this subject probably arose out of his service on the various committees assigned to study the question of debarring unsuitable persons from the sacrament. *C.J.*, III, 553, 559, 705; IV, 114, 290, 300.

52. *C.J.*, VI, 79.

53. This suggestion was made by Johnson, pp. 337, 342. For the list of those excluded, see *Old P.H.*, XVIII, 470. For Lloyd, see *Memoires*, pp. 520–1.

54. *Clarendon State Papers*, ed. Scrope and Monkhouse, II, App. xliv.

55. Aiken, pp. 145–6; Wilkins, p. xliv. According to Edmund Ludlow, *Memoirs*, I, 358, Selden was also asked to assist in drawing up an instrument of government after the forcible dissolution of the Rump in April 1653.

56. Quoted in Waters, p. 211. Pollock's version (*Table Talk*, p. 92) is: "The wisest way for men in these times is to say nothing." In accordance with this principle, Selden, on his death-bed, ordered his private papers to be burned. D. M. Barratt, "The Library of John Selden", *Bodleian Library Record*, III (1951), p. 131, n. 1.

57. Clarendon, *Life* (1827), I, 35–6.

58. Mallet, II, 350.

59. The nearest that Selden ever came to being in the royal favour was during the Personal Rule, at the time he wrote *Mare Clausum*.

60. For Eden under impeachment, see *supra*, p. 149.

61. D'Ewes, Notestein, pp. 125 and n., 126 and n., 148; Lloyd, *Memoires*, p. 593–4.

62. Eden's adherence to the Covenant is recorded twice in *C.J.*, III, 118, 410. The article in the *D.N.B.* notes the second date only—28 February 1643/4. For the Remonstrance, see H. E. Malden, *Trinity Hall*, p. 137, where no reference is given. The absence of Eden's name from the list of "Straffordians, Betrayers of their Country" (Rushworth, III, pt. i, 248), may possibly be merely the result of a convenient withdrawal from the House upon the day of the vote against the attainder.

63. R. N. Kershaw, "The Elections for the Long Parliament, 1640", in *E.H.R.*, XXXVIII (1923), 503n. For Eden's bequest of candles, see Lloyd, *Memoires*, p. 593.

64. See below, p. 168.
65. For Lucas as one of the excluded members, see *P.H.*, III, 1249; *Old P.H.*, XXI, 374. The Henry Lucas who was committed to Peterhouse by order of a committee of both Houses in the summer of 1648 for raising arms against the Parliament seems to have been a different person, for Cambridge's Henry Lucas was at this time busy with his duties in Parliament. *C.S.P., Dom., Chas. I*, XXII (1648–9), 184, 325. *C.J.*, VI, 30, 39. The *D.N.B.* and Edmund Carter, *The History of the University of Cambridge* [1753], p. 464, state that Lucas later took the Engagement, but no contemporary reference to this fact has come to light. Lucas's name is not on the list of those who submitted to Parliament in October 1649. *Old P.H.*, XIX, 215.
66. *C.S.P., Ven.*, XXVI (1642–3), 27, 151.
67. *Ibid.*, p. 139.
68. *C.S.P., Dom., Chas. I*, XVIII (1641–3), 389, 398, 402.
69. *Catalogue of the Harleian Manuscripts*, ed. Wanley, II, 329 (Harleian MS., 1901: 50b, 51, 52); *C.S.P., Dom., Chas. I*, XVIII (1641–3), 507.
70. Harleian MS., 1901: 74; *C.S.P., Dom., Chas. I*, XVIII (1641–3), 450–1.
71. *Cat.*, II, 329, 341, 343 (Harleian MS., 1901: 11b, 113b, 119). For other examples of Roe's exclusion from the Court, and his reaction, see *Cat.*, II, 329, 341, 342, 343 (Harleian MS., 1901: 50, 113, 116b, 118b, 122b); *C.S.P., Dom., Chas. I*, XVIII (1641–3), 294. For the King's previous disregard of Roe, see *supra*, pp. 144–5.
72. *Cat.*, II, 330, 332, 343 (Harleian MS., 1901: 58b, 66, 120b).
73. For example, in a letter to the Princess Elizabeth of the Palatinate, December 1642, Roe noted that he had "no commerce with the Court, such being his Majestie's pleasure", and went on to add that no notice of him was taken by Parliament either, they being apparently content to "connive" at his "retyrement". *Cat.*, II, 329 (Harleian MS., 1901: 50).
74. *C.J.*, III, 38, 45. Harleian MS., 1901: 74.
75. Harleian MS., 1901: 74. For other complaints about Roe's financial status, see *Cat.*, II, 332, 337 (Harleian MS. 1901: 66, 97).
76. Harleian MS., 1901: 74. In this same letter, Roe stated his neutrality in its negative form: "I am guilty of no offense to the Parliament, but in my absence and disability to serve them, wherein I am as guilty toward [His] Matie." See also Harleian MS., 1901: 87. "I lye at a continuall guard, to protect me from suspition, but I shall preserve my selfe from any guilt: for all my endeavours shall have no end, nor no other can be wholesome for the kingdom, but accommodation."
77. In addition to the letters already cited, and to be cited in other notes below, mention of Roe's plans for mediation is made in the following letters: *Cat.*, II, 329, 330, 333, 334, 335, 340, 341 (Harleian MS., 1901: 49b, 50, 58b, 80, 87, 100b, 114).
78. The only example so far discovered of Roe's attempting to influence Parliament in the direction of compromise is in a letter to Denzil Holles, in May 1644. *Cat.*, II, 343 (Harleian MS., 1901: 120b).
79. Of those at Court, Lord Falkland was closest to Roe in his thinking, and to him Roe especially appealed, though without success. See *Cat.*, II, 331, 332, 333 (Harleian MS., 1901: 62b, 64, 74). The first of these letters is quoted in Gardiner, *Civil War*, I, 118–19.
80. Gardiner, *Civil War*, I, 118–19. Roe's difficulties in persuading the Court to measures of conciliation may be gauged by the reply he received in December 1643 from Secretary Nicholas to one of his numerous proposals that he (Roe) might undertake to bring about a conclusion of the "plus quam Civile & Unnaturall War". Nicholas agreed that Roe might attempt the task, but added discouragingly ". . . the perverse men will not hearken to any moderation . . . If the city of London will in a humble way seek their peace, I am very confident they may have it on as good and gracious terms as may be wished, but

they must totally abandon the rebellious faction." *Cat.*, II, 341 (Harleian MS., 1901: 114); *C.S.P., Dom., Chas. I*, XVIII (1641–3), 18, 503.

81. *Cat.*, II, 329 (Harleian MS., 1901: 49b).

82. The whole of a letter to Philip Burlemachy, the King's financial agent, written 23 May 1643, is devoted to the arguments in favour of intervention by the Dutch. Harleian MS., 1901: 81.

83. For Roe's letter to Nicholas, see *Cat.*, II, 342 (Harleian MS., 1901: 118). For his absence from Westminster, see *C.J.*, III, 374. Rushworth, II, pt. iii, 575, thus appears to be in error in listing Roe among the members of the "Anti-Parliament", even under the heading, "absent on the King's business". The error is repeated in John L. Sanford, *Studies*, p. 502, and *P.H.*, II, 614; III, 220.

84. *Cat.*, II, 342, 343 (Harleian MS., 1901: 116, 119).

85. *C.S.P., Dom., Chas. I*, XIX (1644), 35.

86. *Cat.*, II, 343 (Harleian MS., 1901: 122b).

87. *H.M.C., App. 6th Rep.*, p. 16; *C.J.*, III, 549. The *B.B.*, V, 3505, is in error in dating this permission, 2 July 1642. The *D.N.B.* is also incorrect in giving it as 1643.

88. *A.O.*, III, 113. The version given in the *B.B.*, V, 3505, runs somewhat differently: "He was a great, able, and honest statesman, and as good a Patriot, and as sound a Christian as this Nation hath had in many ages." A similar tribute to Roe had been earlier paid by Ben Jonson, *Epigrams*, Facsimile Text Society, p. 798.

89. *C.J.*, IV, 724. The fact that there is no record of an election in the Oxford Archives is not conclusive, however, since the Oxford records for this period were burned before the surrender of June 1646. F. J. Varley, *Cambridge during the Civil War*, Introduction, p. x.

90. *Fasti*, II, 65; Lloyd, *Memoires*, p. 585. It is possible, of course, that Glanville's election was for the "Anti-Parliament", to fill Selden's seat, since Selden remained at Westminster in 1643/4 and Glanville had followed the King to Oxford. There are no surviving records of the "Anti-Parliament" which would provide confirmation of this supposition. It seems most unlikely that Glanville could have been chosen to fill Roe's place at Westminster, since Glanville throughout the years 1644 and 1645 was in Parliament's bad books for his royalist stand, and in September 1645 had been finally disabled to sit in the House for his original constituency of Bristol, more than a year before the writ for filling Roe's seat was ordered. *C.J.*, III, 8, 9, 536, 567, 587, 720; IV, 143, 285, 648, 661, 662. He was later imprisoned, but was finally pardoned and released in 1648. For further discussion of Glanville as a university member see below, Ch. VII, p. 205, n. 27.

91. *O.R.*, p. 724; *C.J.*, IV, 385. Members elected to fill vacancies in the Long Parliament without the King's writ were known as "Recruiters", and by the strictest constitutional interpretation were not true members at all. See R. N. Kershaw, "The Recruiting of the Long Parliament, 1645–47" in *History*, n.s., VIII (1923–4), 169–72.

92. *C.J.*, IV, 412, 420.

93. Information about Bacon is hard to come by. There are scattered references to him in many records and contemporary sources, but the only biographical sketches of him are in the *D.N.B.* and Venn, I, 65. See also below, n. 99.

94. For Bacon on legal questions, see *C.J.*, IV, 550, 701; V, 83, 87; on military affairs, *ibid.*, IV, 505; V, 597; on religious matters, *ibid.*, IV, 502, 545, 549, 550, 714, 719; V, 10–11, 52, 471; VI, 231, 280.

95. The other Bacon was Francis Bacon, M.P. for Ipswich. Venn, I, 65. The *Journal* at times distinguishes between them, at other times specifies that the two Mr. Bacons are both meant. *C.J.*, IV, 551. But quite as often no Christian name is entered, although sometimes it appears that the clerk intended to go back and insert the proper name, as the entry "Mr. * Bacon" is found on a number of lists.

96. For example, Nathaniel Bacon is probably the Bacon listed in such entries as those relating to the sermon by Dr. Fell and the printing of the Septuagint, both suitable subjects for the attention of a university member. *C.J.*, IV, 695; V, 4.

97. *Ibid.*, pp. 352–3.

98. *Ibid.*, pp. 577, 597, 643. He may also be the same Bacon who worked on the Propositions in 1648. *Ibid.*, IV, 423, 553.

99. This work, nevertheless, was highly regarded by later critics, including the first William Pitt, and it remains one of the classical political treatises of the age. It must be admitted, however, that there is doubt as to the book's authorship, for by some the work is assigned to Selden, and by others to an author unknown. See especially *G.M.*, LXXIV (1804), pt. ii, 807; XCVI (1826), pt. i, 20–4.

100. For the Engagement, see *Old P.H.*, XIX, 215. For Bacon's later committees, see *C.J.*, VI, 231, 280, and possibly, 298. For his position as a "Rumper", see below, Ch. VII, p 208, n. 79.

101. For the universities under Parliament in the Civil War and after, see Mallet, II, 341–91; Mullinger, III, 211–80; Shadwell, IV, App. II; Varley, *The Siege of Oxford* and *Cambridge during the Civil War* (especially Introduction and Ch. IV, V, VI). The *Querela Cantabrigiensis*, long regarded as a contemporary picture of Cambridge, is now known to be an inaccurate account, compiled in Oxford. Varley, *op. cit.*, Introduction, p. ix, and Ch. V. Montagu Burrows, *Register of the Visitors*, gives a detailed report of the proceedings at Oxford, but the records of the Manchester Commission and the Visitors at Cambridge have been lost since the eighteenth century. Varley, *op. cit.*, Introduction, p. x. For Oxford, the standard contemporary account of conditions during the Civil War is, of course, Anthony Wood's *Annals* (Wood, Gutch, II, pt. i, 425; pt. ii, 700), and his *Life and Times*, vol. I. esp. pp. 291–6. (For a comparison of these two records, see below, n. 102.) For contemporary documents covering the period at Cambridge, see Heywood and Wright, II, 460–2.

102. For modern writers on the results of the regulation of the universities, see Burrows, *Register*, pp. xxviii–ix, xxxii, lxxxix–xc; Mullinger, III, 278, 501; Varley, *op. cit.*, pp. 44, 57. Burrows notes significantly (*Register*, pp. lii–liii) that Wood's strictly contemporary account of university conditions in the Civil War, as given in his *Life and Times*, does not reveal so violent an upheaval in university life as his later works, the *Annals* and the *A.O.*, suggest.

103. The longest item relating to the universities in D'Ewes's *Journal*, is a speech by D'Ewes himself and not by a university member, on the perennial subject of the precedence of Cambridge over Oxford. D'Ewes, Notestein, p. 212, and n. 19. Also printed in Cooper, III, 307–8.

104. *C.J.*, II, 126.

105. *Ibid.*, p. 328. For this Cosin case, see *supra*, p. 152.

106. *C.J.*, II, 124; D'Ewes, *Journal*, ed. W. H. Coates, p. 59.

107. *C.J.*, III, 124. For the time being Oxford's burgesses escaped this order, since the university was then still in the hands of the King.

108. Mullinger, III, 293.

109. Lloyd, *Memoires*, pp. 593–4; *B.B.*, VI, pt. i, 3619–20 n. See especially the allusion to Eden's protection in the letter written by the Hall after his death, as quoted in *B.B.*, *loc. cit.*—"secure in Eden". Malden, pp. 137–8, mentions the esteem in which Eden was held by his college, even though the members were largely royalist. See also Edmund Carter, writing in the eighteenth century: "as the Doctor was a Person of a better Character than most that joined with the Parliament 'tis likely enough, that he skreened the Fellows of his College, as not one was ejected; nor can it be imagined they were all in the same way of thinking". Carter, p. 109.

110. Bruce, p. 76; *C.J.*, II, 144; *P.H.*, II, 789–91; D'Ewes, Coates, p. 30; Mullinger, III, 211.

111. *C.J.*, ii, 825; iii, 329.

112. *Ibid.*, p. 338 (The Manchester Commission); iv, 312 ("godly preaching"); iv, 350 (the ordinance for regulation of 1645); iv, 350 (oaths to be taken by university officials, sheriffs, etc.), 678. Lucas was also on the committee conferring with the Lords on where to settle the Oxford students for study during the King's occupation of Oxford. *Ibid.*, iii, 329.

113. *Ibid.*, iv, 229, 241.

114. Questions of taxation and endowments during the Civil War are discussed in the references cited in nn. 101 and 102, *supra*.

115. Opportunities for action on behalf of Cambridge's financial interests may be noted in at least two of the committees on which Lucas served: for "Relief", and for assessments (*C.J.*, iii, 124; vi, 30), and the fact that Lucas had had some previous experience in financial matters, as secretary to Lord Holland and acting paymaster of the army, makes it likely that he would have particularly interested himself in this aspect of the university's problems.

116. Isaac Barrow, pp. xii–xiii.

117. For Selden's efforts on behalf of the universities, learning, and learned men, see: Aiken, pp. 135–42; *B.B.*, vi, pt. i, 3619–22; Johnson, pp. 324–8; Mallet, ii, 375, 382n.; Waters, pp. 50–1, 231–40; Wilkins, pp. xxx–xxxi, xxvii–xliv; Wood, Gutch, ii, pts. i and ii (especially items cited below in notes, nn. 124, 125, 130, 132, 133, 134, 135.

118. For example, *C.J.*, iii, 329, 344, 356; iv, 174, 190, 229, 312, 350, 595, 675, 739; v, 2, 51, 143, 251, 267, 515, 603.

119. For example, his defence of Dr. Cosin of Cambridge, and the latter's right to a fair trial, and also the Vice-Chancellor's right to act as a J.P. *Ibid.*, ii, 159; D'Ewes, Notestein, pp. 146n, 227, 271n.

120. For one of Selden's speeches in committee, see Northcote, pp. 59–60.

121. *C.J.*, v, 603, 612; Leonard Twells, *Dr. Edward Pocock*, i, 100–2.

122. *C.J.*, v, 515; Johnson, p. 325. Two letters of thanks from Cambridge are quoted in *B.B.*, vi, pt. i, 3620n. The library, however, was returned to Lambeth after the Restoration.

123. *H.M.C.*, *App. 5th Rep.*, p. 312.

124. Quoted in Wood, Gutch, ii, pt. i, 487.

125. Wood, Gutch, ii, pt. ii, 528. The petition was referred to a committee that included Selden. *C.J.*, iv, 675. The university fellows complained that the new requirements conflicted with the oaths they had taken when they entered upon their fellowships.

126. Selden had, however, served on committees investigating various matters concerning Cambridge, such as sequestration of property, "godly preaching", and university privileges, as well as on the committees that framed the ordinance of regulation. *C.J.*, iii, 344, 356; iv, 174, 229, 312, 350.

127. *Ibid.*, pp. 595, 739; v, 2, 3, 5, 51, 83, 143, 174, 251, 267; vi, 200.

128. *Ibid.*, v, 83. Shadwell, iv, App. II, 273. On this same committee were also both a past and a future burgess of the university—Sir John Danvers and Nathaniel Fiennes—as well as a future candidate for one of the university's seats—William Lenthall, Speaker of the House.

129. Burrows, *Register*, pp. lxxxix–xc, lxixn.

130. Wood, Gutch, ii, pt. ii, 555, 851. Pococke was also appointed Hebrew Professor and Canon of Christ Church through Selden's influence. *A.O.*, iv, 319; *C.J.*, v, 603; Twells, i, 106–8, 113, 115–16, 121. By 1650, Selden was unable to protect Pococke further. *Ibid.*, pp. 130, 139.

131. *B.B.*, vi, pt. i, 3620–1; Twells, i, 122–3. In Twells the quotation reads "shuffling of business" instead of "wilful baseness".

132. Whitelocke, i, 150. Wood, Gutch, ii, pt. ii, 546–7.

133. For Selden in the parliamentary Committee of Appeal, see Mallet, ii, 375; *Clar. S.P.*, ii, 397–8; Wood, Gutch, ii, pt. i, 533, 534, 544–7.

134. Wood, Gutch, II, pt. i, 537, 540.
135. *C.J.*, v, 538–9; Wood, Gutch, II, pt. ii, 546; Twells, I, 18, 126–7 n.
136. "News from Pembroke and Montgomery or Oxford Manchesterized By Michael Oldisworth and his Lord", *Harleian Miscellany*, VI, 134. The Oldisworth mentioned in the title, interestingly enough, is the same Oldisworth who was proposed to the university as a candidate for burgess by the third Earl of Pembroke in 1627/8. *Supra*, Ch. IV, pp. 115–16.
137. For Langbaine's letter, see Twells, I, 109. Also in John Leland, *De Rebus Britannicis*, ed. Thos. Hearne, v, 282–4, there are a number of letters to Selden, including some on the disposal of prebends and on required tests for "godliness", showing how constantly Selden was appealed to on all matters affecting the university, even, in fact, in 1653, when he had ceased to be a university representative.
138. *H.M.C.*, *App. 2nd Rep.*, p. 22; *B.B.*, VI, pt. i, 3620. That Selden's own university was not completely satisfied with him as a representative, however, seems to be indicated by an incidental remark during the candidacy of Sir Heneage Finch, member for Oxford in 1661. Here the statement was made that because of "Mr. Selden's abuse of the University favour", the university had conceived a prejudice against all lawyers as university representatives. It is hard to see what is meant here, in the light of the information that is available, unless the remark merely represents a cavalier prejudice. *C.S.P., Dom., Chas. II*, I (1660–1), 527.
139. John Selden, *Table Talk*, ed. Sir Frederick Pollock, p. 134.
140. *C.J.*, III, 291, 298; IV, 739; Rait, I, 343; *B.B.*, VI, pt. i, 3619; Singer, p. lx; Johnson, p. 325; *C.S.P., Dom., Commonwealth*, II (1650), 130, 391, 476. Interestingly enough—showing perhaps the suspicion with which learning was regarded by the ruling forces—in one of these orders Selden was instructed to give his opinion of the records surveyed, as to their value "not only to particular men but to the Commonwealth".
141. *C.J.*, v, 29, 327, 393, 416, 423; Aiken, p. 129. See also Selden's famous *bon mot* when Usher's membership in the Westminster Assembly was questioned, and Selden implied that Usher was as much above membership in the Assembly as Inigo Jones would be above membership in the association of mouse-trap makers. *Life and Times*, I, 424–5.
142. *C.J.*, IV, 9, 86, 114, 409, 410, 695; Whitelocke, II, 170–1; IV, 9, 695.
143. *C.J.*, v, 436; Whitelocke, III, 74.

CHAPTER VII

DECLINE AND REVIVAL, 1653–1660

The materials for the history of university representation during the rest of the Interregnum are somewhat limited, in comparison both with the period of the Long Parliament and with the Restoration. Very little has come to light in the form of personal letters or diaries, and the public records are also rather meagre. Perhaps the atmosphere of dictatorship limited free expression and fear of political entanglements discouraged even the preservation of private papers. Whatever the cause, an inside picture of political events in the universities is hard to come by, and the impression is gathered that there was on the whole very little political life going on.

The university members seem also more circumspect in their parliamentary conduct than ever before—at least, the references to them in the debates are disappointing. The *Commons' Journal* still reports committee lists, and Burton's *Diary* carries on the story of the proceedings of Parliament, but no full delineation of any university burgess in action is available until the election of 1658/9. The other chief sources for the period, the *Calendar of State Papers*, the *Clarendon State Papers*, and the *Thurloe State Papers* are likewise not very rewarding, and Cromwell himself has nothing to say on the subject of university representation in any of his published writings.

This part of the Interregnum, consequently, has a very definite and clear-cut character, as far as university representation goes, and that character is negative in its quality. That is—in their contributions to the work of the House, and in the conduct of their parliamentary elections—the university members appear to have been notably inert and passive. The trials through which the universities had passed, and through which they were still passing, probably help to explain this passivity. Even more than this, and related to it, was the supremacy of the dictatorship after 1653.

The influence of the dictatorship is especially apparent in regard to the choice of representatives. While no inside information is at hand about election pressures, it is apparent from the results, that the universities at this time sought to obey the will of the Protector more meekly than ever they had that of Charles I. Hardly a breath of complaint or protest has survived, such as Oxford showed in 1625/6 and 1627/8, or Cambridge, through the letters of Joseph Mead, in 1626 and

1628.[1] In fact, in 1654 and 1656 there were probably not even any opposing candidates in the field. Cromwell's men were chosen almost without a murmur, right down the line.[2] In the case of the Nominated Parliament of 1653, of course, there was no question of an election, but if there had been, Oxford would probably have just as readily chosen the official nominee, Cromwell's personal physician and the chief physician of the army, Dr. Jonathan Goddard, as it did his successors, who were elected in the regular way for the Protectorate Parliaments that followed: Cromwell's favourite Independent preacher, Dr. John Owen; his Commissioner of the Great Seal and chief adviser, Nathaniel Fiennes; and later his former Judge Advocate of the army, Dr. John Mills. Cambridge was no less quick than Oxford to take suggestions from Cromwell's book, choosing first, the Protector's own sons, Henry and Richard, and then, his Secretary of State, John Thurloe, for Richard's Parliament of 1658/9—although by the time of this last campaign, as with that of Dr. Mills above, the elections were again free.

Besides the deadening effect of personal influence on university politics during part of this period, there were other reasons why the history of university representation in the later Interregnum offers so many blank spots. In the first place, the system of representation itself was changed. In the Instrument of Government, the number of seats was reduced from two to one for each university, while in the Nominated Parliament no direct representatives of the university constituencies in themselves were named at all—only members for the counties as a whole. For Oxfordshire, three members were nominated, and for Cambridgeshire, four. However, in each case, one of these county members did actually come from a university body, and so, in a sense, such members may be thought of as representatives of their universities. But their constituencies comprised more than the university communities alone, and the universities had nothing whatever to do with the choice of the members. In the second place, the universities' representation was further limited by the absence of the members. In one of the Parliaments—the Parliament of 1654—the member from Oxford was refused a seat, and the university remained without a representative throughout the rest of the session, while in the next Parliament short vacancies occurred, when both of the universities' members were removed to the new House of Lords.

All these circumstances together, then—the inadequacy of the records, the inaction of the university representatives, the dominance of Cromwell, the vacancies, and the reduced number of seats, combine to make the later Interregnum, as a whole, one of the least important and least interesting periods in the history of university representation. At the very end of the period, however, come some incidents and evidence of decided importance in the revival of freedom of choice in the elections of 1658/9 and 1660.

The parliamentary history of the later Interregnum normally begins with the Nominated Parliament of 1653, but whether the university members who sat in this Parliament belong, strictly speaking, to the history of university representation is somewhat of a question. In the first place, as explained above, they were not elected members, and in the second, they were not even specifically designated to represent the universities, but only their respective shires.[3] Moreover, no information is available as to how or why these members were appointed. Nevertheless, since in each of the two lists of county members (for Oxfordshire and for Cambridgeshire) there was one member from a university community, it is possible to assume that Cromwell in this way was intentionally providing a spokesman for each of the universities. As it happens, even to this very day, the universities themselves seem undecided about the matter. The *Oxford Register* boldly lists Jonathan Goddard as its representative for 1653, while the *Cambridge Register*, on its list of parliamentary burgesses, omits any reference whatever to John Sadler.[4]

The appearance of Jonathan Goddard is a matter of interest, for in being the first medical man to be inscribed on the university lists—even if only as a nominated representative—he started a tradition among university members that became somewhat characteristic, showing evidence of the seventeenth century's new interest in science. During the Protectorate and the Restoration, four other medical men, and Isaac Newton, successfully followed Goddard into university politics. Several other medical men, also, were unsuccessful candidates.[5] In the new scientific age, Goddard, indeed, was well to the fore, being one of the original members of the Royal Society before it was officially recognized, and in 1663, after it had received its charter, one of its first council members.

But his rise to political eminence dated from his acquaintance with Cromwell, which came about when he was called in by chance to prescribe for an illness sometime in the later 1640's. In 1649 he became physician to the army, and was taken on Cromwell's Irish campaign in 1649, as the Lord General's "great confident", so Wood says. Other appointments followed—Warden of Merton College, 1651; member for Oxfordshire in the Nominated Parliament of 1653, as already stated; Visitor for the University of Oxford of 1653, and earlier, one of the commissioners for the university to act in the absence of its Chancellor, Oliver, while the latter was in Scotland; finally, Professor of Physick at Gresham College, London, 1655.[6]

The Nominated Parliament consisted of only 140 members, all hand-picked and faithful to the Commonwealth. They produced no solid accomplishments, and after weeks of fruitless debate, they surrendered the country into the hands of Oliver, as beyond their capacity to deal with. In such a Parliament, Dr. Goddard could not have had the best opportunity to prove his worth, though what ability he had must have set him well above the majority of the members. He was not particularly active, but served on three committees, and twice acted as teller.[7] His real distinction came in being elected to serve on the Council of State, his name being near the top of the poll among those chosen,[8] but this was probably owing to the fact that the House knew him to be a trusted associate of Cromwell, rather than to any other sort of recognition of his worth.

What little is known about his career in the House seems to show that at least in his peculiar capacity of university member, he filled his place with credit. He was on the committee for the advancement of learning.[9] Here—and later in 1654 on the Board of Visitors of the university —as a man of genuine intellectual interests, he seems to have acted as a moderating influence against the sectarian zealots of the time. This was distinctly needed in the Nominated Parliament, because of its unfriendly attitude towards higher learning. The Venetian ambassador, writing in December 1653, shortly after the final closing of the Parliament, noted with disapproval that the Nominated Parliament had been bent on "abolishing what from their antiquity give lustre to England, viz. the universities and colleges of Oxford and Cambridge, where every sort of knowledge and literature may be said to be cultivated with success".[10] Under these circumstances, whatever Goddard might have done to secure the interests of learning, was certainly a contribution worthy of a university representative.

The details of his actions are lost. Probably they were performed more in his character of parliamentary Visitor than as university burgess. Whatever they were, they were remembered with appreciation in later years by various persons of royalist sympathies. Anthony Wood, always quick to condemn when condemnation in his eyes was due, found in Goddard his first patron, and dedicated his first book, a collection of his brother's sermons, to the good doctor. The *Biographia Britannica*, an eighteenth-century biographical dictionary, noted of Goddard that he was "without any distinction of party, having none of that narrowness of mind which was the common failing of the great men of those times", while likewise, Seth Ward, later Bishop of Salisbury, who also dedicated a book to Goddard, wrote of him that he was "deservedly conspicuous in the management of public affairs with the utmost prudence, and the highest reputation for integrity".[11] Thus, we can conclude with a considerable degree of confidence, despite the meagreness of the records, that Dr. Jonathan Goddard followed in the footsteps of John Selden as far as his political moderation went, and that in this, and in his interest in the advancement of learning, he belongs in the best tradition of university representation.

The other university member in the Nominated Parliament was John Sadler, Master of Magdalene College, Cambridge, said to be a relative of Cromwell and much in Oliver's favour. According to Falconer Madan, he had some share in editing Charles I's letters captured after the battle of Naseby. He was a common-law lawyer from Lincoln's Inn, a Master in Chancery, a Master of Requests, and a Judge of the Admiralty.[12] His name is found on a good number of committee lists, including one with Goddard on the advancement of learning, and one on the reform of law, and another on tithes where he acted as reporter. It was probably in this last connection, or in connection with a bill on glebe lands, that he was designated to report an unspecified petition of the Vice-Chancellor of Cambridge to the House on 2 December 1653, towards the close of the session. He was a reporter, all in all, six times; a teller, thrice; and once a chairman of the House in Grand Committee.[13] Like Goddard, Sadler also was chosen to the Council of State, no doubt because of his connections with Cromwell, and was on the second board of parliamentary Visitors for the universities, appointed in 1654.[14] Interestingly enough, his poll for the Council of State was higher than either Henry Cromwell's or Dr. Goddard's.[15]

In the next Parliament—the first Parliament of the Protectorate, summoned for 7 September 1654—the proceedings of the university members were almost as lacking in vigour and interest as those of the nominated members of the year before. This time Cambridge was represented by the Lord Henry Cromwell, the Protector's son. Mullinger thinks that Henry Cromwell, and his brother Richard, who were each members for the university in successive Parliaments, gained their seats quite as much through general family and county connections as through any direct influence exercised by their father.[16] The fact that the electoral return of Henry Cromwell is defaced may, however, indicate some turbulence or irregularity in his election.[17] However this may have been, Henry served his constituency faithfully, at least as far as attendance goes. His name appears on fourteen of the fifteen committees of this Parliament, including the committee on the universities.[18]

But there is no record of any speech of his on any subject whatsoever, even on the one issue of all others that might have called for university action—the unsuccessful proposal to give the universities more seats. This proposal was made because the Nominated Parliament at the end of its term, in drawing up plans for the Instrument of Government, had—as noted before—allowed the universities only one seat each, an evidence of the current distrust of the "nurseries of learning".[19]

Henry Cromwell was also, like Sadler and Goddard, on the board of parliamentary Visitors,[20] and in view of his later liberality in religious matters while Lord Lieutenant of Ireland, it is likely that his influence, as a Visitor, as on other parliamentary committees, was of a moderating nature. But his departure for his new post in Ireland shortly after the dissolution of January 1654/5 cut short his connections both with Parliament and with the university, and brought his career as a university representative quickly to a close.[21]

Henry Cromwell's colleague as university representative was John Owen, D.D., member for Oxford, Dean of Christ Church, and Vice-Chancellor of the university.[22] The most interesting thing about Owen from the point of view of university representation is the fact that—so far as any evidence goes—his election was the only university election during Oliver's Protectorate in which there was any doubt about the outcome. Just how this came about is not clear. It would normally be expected that Owen—once on the Chancellor's commission for governing the university and now for two years Vice-Chancellor, recommended to that office by the Chancellor Oliver himself—would have had no difficulty in gaining an easy victory. But this was not the case. And what is even more curious is that the opposition that Owen met seems to have stemmed largely from the personal resentment of a recent student with whom Owen had had some words on the subject of the former's Anglicanism.[23] The result was that the disgruntled student mustered forces against Owen at the time of his election, and "so managed matters with the doctors, bachelors of divinity, and masters of arts . . . that he [Owen] was very difficultly returned".[24]

This was bad enough for Oliver's favourite preacher and the Vice-Chancellor of the university, but further impediments were to follow. The question of Owen's eligibility as a parliament man was raised, on the grounds that the Clerical Disabilities Act of 1642 closed civil offices of all kinds to clergymen. There is no evidence to show how this challenge arose, nor from what quarter it came, except that, when Owen appeared in the House, the Committee of Privilege seems to have taken his case under consideration. The university sent a petition that they might be heard in defence of their burgess, and if unsuccessful, that a new writ might be issued for another election.[25] According to Anthony Wood, Owen was so eager to sit that he renounced his orders, and declared himself a "mear layman", though only the year before he had been created a doctor of divinity. In spite of all this, his claim was set aside, and he had to return to his deanery and vice-chancellorship.[26] The Parliament was dissolved 22 January 1654/5, and no election to fill Owen's place seems ever to have taken place.[27]

This was perhaps just as well, since this Parliament was so singularly ineffectual that it did not pass a single piece of legislation throughout its whole term of six months.[28] The next Protectorate Parliament, however, has somewhat more to offer towards the history of university representation than either of the two Parliaments preceding. In this House, as noted above, Lord Richard Cromwell succeeded his brother as member for Cambridge University. Here again there are no details at hand about the election. Both the university seats were held by strong Cromwellians, for Richard's colleague from Oxford was the Right Honourable Nathaniel Fiennes, the son of Lord Say and Sele and at this time at the height of his influence with the Protector. Despite their high positions, however, these two candidates may not have been entirely acceptable to their constituents, since the return for Lord Richard is entirely missing, and that for Fiennes is defaced, both circumstances suggesting that there may have been some disorders in connection with the elections.

The surmise that Richard Cromwell's election was not an enthusiastic one is further borne out by an entry in the Cambridge University Registry where he is recorded as having polled only thirty-three votes. No opposing scores are given, and there was apparently no official return for this election. A news note in the *Mercurius Politicus* places the election on August first, and the fact that the election occurred in the afternoon may suggest that the Senate was slow to act, as elections usually began at eight or nine a.m.

> This afternoon we have made choice of the Lord Richard Cromwell to be burgess for our University, and hope that he will accept it. To that end we have drawn up a Letter, to present our desires and services to his Lordship.[29]

As we know, the Lord Richard did "accept" of the Cambridge seat—in fact, although he was chosen for two seats in this election (Southampton and Cambridge University), it was for the university that he preferred to serve when the choice was offered.[30]

Like his brother, he seems at first to have been a faithful attendant, and, as a son of the Protector, was assigned to many committees—sixteen committees in the period between the opening of Parliament,

17 September, and 18 February 1656/7, when he ceased to take part in the affairs of the House—and acted as a teller once.[31] Among these assignments, there were two that concerned the direct interests of the universities—a matter of property rights in which Cambridge was involved, and the perennial question of the status of the civil law.[32] On the former issue, Richard made one of the few speeches that are recorded for him in this Parliament.[33] After 31 December 1656, when he was absent on account of illness,[34] his name drops out of the parliamentary records, except for one or two items, for the rest of the session. Firth says that he retired from the House during the debates on the Humble Petition and Advice, out of a feeling of delicacy, in view of the obvious fact that he was likely to be regarded as his father's successor, if the latter received the Crown.[35]

His letters to his brother Henry in Ireland give some idea of his attitudes at this time. He was vague and allusive about politics in general: "Things that might be whispered ought not to be committed to paper." He did not know whether his father would accept the Crown or not. He knew no news—Henry might be better informed, even though not so close to the scene. He congratulated the latter that he was out of England "oute of the spattering dirte which is thrown about here". He went on to explain his ignorance of affairs as owing to his absence from Parliament—and not, incidentally, for the reason given by Firth, but for one quite contrary. "I know noe news being by reason of some debates in ye House sent out for a rangler."[36] There is no allusion to such an incident in Burton or in the *Journal*. Whatever it was, it was the end of Richard's service as university member, for Parliament adjourned in June 1657, and before it met again the following January, he had been raised to the new Upper House.[37]

During the first days of the new session, however, one of Richard's first acts in the Upper House was to concern himself over the question of the civil law, by forwarding a petition to William Lenthall, now Master of the Rolls, asking him to present a bill on the subject in the Commons. But by this time Richard was representing Oxford rather than Cambridge, for he had been made Chancellor of the sister university in July, while still officially parliament man for Cambridge, and it was at Oxford that the petition concerning the civil law originated. This was his last parliamentary act on behalf of the universities, for the Parliament was dissolved ten days later.[38]

The other university member in this Parliament was Nathaniel Fiennes. Unlike Richard Cromwell, he was exceedingly active and a ready speaker. He was indeed at this time Cromwell's chief spokesman and defender. As Commissioner for the Great Seal, he had a place on

all the committees involving legal matters; as Cromwell's right-hand
man, he spoke often—defending the Protector's policy of excluding
duly elected members; acting as teller for the postponement of protests
against this policy; explaining the war with Spain. As an old parliament man whose revolutionary activities dated back to the first days
of the Long Parliament, he took a prominent part in the debates on the
Humble Petition and Advice, speaking urgently in favour of giving
Cromwell the Crown.[39]

Among all these concerns, university interests were not neglected.
Along with Lord Richard Cromwell, he was assigned to the committee
on the civil law, and for Oxford in particular, he brought in a petition
for the claims of Corpus Christi College to some benefices, and another
regarding lawsuits involving students. Fiennes's service to the university did not begin with his burgess-ship. He had served on the Board
of Visitors of 1654 and earlier on the parliamentary Committee of
Appeal, and had been one of the "just advocates" mentioned by Wood
as defending the university from the worst excesses of Puritan regulation.[40] Curiously enough, however, neither Fiennes nor Cromwell is
recorded as taking any part in two issues on which university members
might have been expected to take a firm stand—the exemption of the
universities from taxation and the question of the confirmation of the new
ordinance for regulation of the universities, about which, according to
Burton, there was "great Debate". In the taxation discussions, in fact,
Fiennes's efforts were spent in defending the Inns of Court rather than
his own constituency.[41] Like Lord Richard Cromwell, Lord Commissioner Fiennes also ceased to be a university burgess by being raised
to the "other house",[42] so that the second Protectorate Parliament
closed in February 1657/8 with both the university seats vacant.

The next Parliament was summoned to meet 27 January 1658/9,
almost a year later, by Richard himself, now Protector. This Parliament stands as a landmark in the history of university representation,
since, for the first time in nearly twenty years, the university candidates
appear to have engaged once more in real contests for their seats. Once
again we can catch a glimpse of electoral activities going on beneath the
surface, and for the first time since the departure of Sir Thomas Roe for
Ratisbon in 1641, we can see four university members all together again
on the floor of the House of Commons. This was because the representation of the kingdom was restored as it was before the Instrument of
Government.[43]

Probably the addition of the extra seats contributed to the revival of
competition in the universities. In each university one seat was ultimately filled—as usual—with a candidate in the Cromwellian tradition

—for Cambridge, John Thurloe, Secretary of State since 1653, and for Oxford, Dr. John Mills, Judge Advocate of the army during the Civil War. On the other hand, these two Cromwellians had each as colleague a burgess who seems to have been much more truly the choice of the university. Curiously enough, and probably indicative of the times, both of these independent burgesses were men whose sympathy with the Protectorate was somewhat dubious, though both had conformed sufficiently to be not unacceptable as candidates. What seems to be happening here is a return to the old system of the 1620's—the compromise between Court and university, allowing each to name one representative. Indeed, an open recognition of this policy is alluded to in one of the letters written from Cambridge during the campaign.[44]

For weeks before Parliament met, Secretary Thurloe was engaged in little else but intervening in various constituencies on behalf of court candidates,[45] but his own election at Cambridge was apparently accomplished without intervention on his part. Some electioneering in his favour, however, was carried on by others, especially through influence exerted by Oliver St. John, Thurloe's old patron, now Chief Justice of the Realm and Chancellor of Cambridge. A letter to St. John from Dr. Benjamin Whichcot, Provost of King's, dated 11 December, expressed satisfaction in regard to "the person your lordship doth propose"— that is, Thurloe—but went on to explain that another candidate had also been put forward by Henry Cromwell—an Irish knight, Sir Anthony Morgan, whose campaign was to be pushed by Sir Francis Russell, one of the magnates of the shire, now a member of the Upper House. This latter personage wrote directly to Thurloe a few days later, explaining that he had intended to propose Thurloe as member for the county, until someone had brought him word that the university had "unanimously resolved to make choyse" of the Secretary for one of their seats.

> This they give out already, and send me word of what they resolve [wrote Sir Francis]. Old Mr. Fairclough was with me, when that message was brought me, and was ready to put pen to paper to write to his friends of the cleargy about you, and to serve you as myself intended.

But first Russell had hastened to write to Thurloe for "Advise and directions", whether to "goe on or desist". As to the Irish knight, "who was very likely to have bin your brother burgesse", Russell now reported that he was to be given one of the new Irish seats instead, while thanks were to be tendered the Vice-Chancellor and university for their "respects towards my Lord Henry and Sir Anthony", in considering the latter for the Cambridge seat.[46]

Five days later the question of Thurloe's candidacy was finally settled, for Dr. Whichcot wrote again to Chancellor Chief Justice St. John to announce that the Irish knight had indeed withdrawn, and that so far as Whichcot could tell—though he could not venture to predict with certainty—all in the university were agreed upon Thurloe. This left the question of the second burgess still undetermined, and for this place, there were two or three competitors, who would run, not against Thurloe, but against each other. For this second place, Whichcot explained, the university preferred to choose a "gremial", that is, a resident, who would know "all our affaires".[47]

Thurloe seems to have had his doubts about the Cambridge seat, in spite of the assurances of Dr. Whichcot, for he had been careful to provide other possibilities for himself elsewhere, both at Tewkesbury and at Huntingdon, and favourable reports from these places were being received at the same time that the manœuvres described above were going on at Cambridge.[48] In fact, the very day that he was elected at Cambridge, he was also chosen at Huntingdon, while he had just written to accept the nomination for Tewkesbury, and was later chosen also at Wisbech. All these precautions proved unnecessary, however, for his election at Cambridge was unanimous,[49] and when Parliament met, he chose the university seat in preference to any other.[50]

The letter that announced Thurloe's success gave an account of what had been done in regard to the university's second seat. It was written by Dr. Ralph Cudworth, famous in university history as one of the "Cambridge Platonists", and a close friend of Thurloe's. At the last minute, a "Mr. Bacon" had been proposed—probably Nathaniel Bacon, once a "Recruiter" for the university in the Long Parliament,[51] since then member for Ipswich, and very active in the Parliaments of the Protectorate. But by this late date, most of the electors had promised their votes, and so he was not chosen—though otherwise, Cudworth wrote, Bacon would have been the university's preference. Instead, as things were, the second burgess was a candidate not known to Thurloe —a local personage, Dr. Thomas Sclater, a physician prominent in the town of Cambridge, a "very ingenious person, of very good abilities, and one"—Thurloe's correspondent went on—who would "readily concurre with such resolutions as tend to the settlement and establishment of the commonwealth, as well as mind the interest of the university". This estimate of his future colleague may have been very welcome to the harassed Secretary, who was already somewhat apprehensive about the success of the new Parliament. He seems to have expressed a wish to meet his "brother burgess" before the opening of Parliament, for about three weeks later a second letter from Cudworth notified the Secretary that Dr. Sclater was about to "waite" upon him according to his invitation. Here again Cudworth recommended the Doctor heartily: "I am persuaded you will be well satisfied in his ingenuity, when you are acquainted with him."[52]

There has been very little written about Dr. Sclater on the whole, considering the fact that he achieved some local prominence in his time.[53] He first appears as a fellow of Trinity College, Cambridge, whence he was ejected during the Civil War. He seems to have gone to Oxford where he received a medical degree in 1649 through the influence of Sir Thomas Widdrington, at that time (or very recently) Commissioner of the Great Seal. This part of Sclater's career suggests that he may have started out as a Royalist, but later have become reconciled to the new régime. This view is borne out by the fact that in 1655 he was empowered to certify as to the "godliness" of various persons, and that in 1657 his name appeared among the lists of good citizens of the Protectorate entrusted with the levying of assessments in the town of Cambridge,[54] and finally that in 1658 he was, as we have just seen, so heartily recommended to Thurloe as a colleague.

For the election manœuvres that may have gone on at Oxford in 1658, no details survive. A news note in the *Mercurius Politicus*, 29 December, ventured the prediction that the university burgesses would be Serjeant Hale and either Dr. Petty—later Sir William Petty, the founder of "Political Arithmetic", then assistant Professor of Physic —or Dr. John Palmer, (M.D.), Warden of All Souls, and according to Anthony Wood, a favourite of Oliver's and a "great Rumper".[55] The *Mercurius'* correspondent proved to be inaccurate as to the second prediction, though correct as to the first.[56] The second place went, instead, to Dr. John Mills, a "civilian", who had been Judge Advocate of the army from 1644 to 1651, and a member of the first Board of Visitors along with Selden and Owen. For a time he had been quite a power at Oxford—he had taken part in carrying out the terms of surrender in 1646, had received a created degree in law and had been appointed a canon of Christ Church. But his preferences were Presbyterian rather than Independent, and his early enthusiasm for Oliver seems to have received a setback. By 1651, he refused to take the Engagement, and was accordingly deprived of his canonship. With the coming of Richard, however, he appears to have been reconciled again to the Protectorate, for he joined with Thurloe in proclaiming Richard's succession.[57]

Oxford's other burgess, Matthew Hale, then Serjeant-at-Law and Justice of the Common Pleas was one of the great legal figures of the century. Like Mills, his sympathy with the Protectorate was only lukewarm, but he conformed successively to each new development, and his legal reputation was so great, and his legal conduct so unimpeachable, that all parties wished to claim him. The revolutionary governments had given him full scope for his powers. Since 1641, he had been allowed to offer himself as defending counsel for all Royalists in difficulties, from Strafford, Laud, and the King himself, down to the rank and file, while at the same time he served Cromwell as a member of the Trade Committee of the Council of State and Chief Justice of the Common Pleas. Hale's doubts as to the constitution of the Protectorate, however, appeared as early as 1654, when he opposed the idea of a "single person", and the fact that he had refused to accept a new appointment as Chief Justice from the hands of Richard Cromwell shortly before his own election as Oxford's representative in 1658/9 indicates that he probably did not stand with Thurloe and Mills among those who were staunch for Richard in this last Parliament of the Protectorate.[58]

Thurloe was the official leader of the Government in this House, and he played somewhat the same part here that Sir John Coke had played when Charles I was losing ground in the last Parliament of the 1620's—except that there is a distinct difference in the calibre of the men themselves. Thurloe's greater intelligence and better sense of the situation shows up clearly, in spite of the fact that he made fewer speeches and put forth less effort to control what he saw was impossible to control. From the very beginning he foresaw trouble. As we have seen above, every attempt was made before the elections to get the proper persons into the House—the Court's "creatures", as Edmund Ludlow called them.[59] Without unity and agreement—so Thurloe had written Henry Cromwell, 14 December 1658—he, Thurloe, could not see how it would be possible "to keep out the common enemye long". By the 21st he was more hopeful, but again by 4 January, he was disturbed at the prospect of a "very troublesome scene". "That which I most feare is disunion among friends. There are distances in affection to this house, What that may be the root of, I am not able to say."[60]

Considering John Thurloe's prominent position as Secretary of State and spokesman for the Protector, his name appears with surprising infrequency upon the records of this Parliament. Perhaps he thought it the part of wisdom not to press the Court's case too strongly, lest he antagonize its opponents still further. At the beginning of the session, he introduced a bill for the recognition of the new Protector. This was passed successfully, although Sir Thomas Clarges (later M.P. for Oxford in the Convention of 1688/9) reported that there was a "tuffe debate" upon its second reading.[61] Some weeks later Thurloe again appeared in his capacity of Secretary of State, explaining the military and diplomatic aspects connected with the Baltic situation and the war with Spain, and the Government's policy thereon.[62] Other issues followed,[63] and finally a crisis in the form of an attack on Thurloe himself. He had already warded off criticism of the Protector's "evil counsellors", and offered to have himself investigated with the others.[64] But in the last week of March a petition was brought in to the effect that the Secretary had exceeded his police powers in 1655 as head of the secret service and had unjustly deported one Rowland Thomas to the Barbadoes. This was the opening gun in the campaign of the Royalists to discredit the Protector's régime, for from the beginning of the session, one of the chief parts of their plan had been to get the House to "fall upon Thurloe", whom they regarded as the chief obstacle to Richard Cromwell's reconciliation with the Stuart monarchy.[65] Thurloe spoke in his own defence, and the case was dropped, but not until there had been, according to *The Clarke Papers*, "some heat and bitterness not fit to be mencioned".[66]

At the same time, Thurloe was accused of having secured, through his letters, the election of more than four-score members of the present Parliament. That exertions of this sort were made seems clear from the comments of Ludlow and the Venetian ambassador, as well as from the correspondence of Clarges and Thurloe himself. On 14 December Thurloe had written to Henry Cromwell, "We do little here but prepare for the next Parliament", though these preparations may not have taken the form of letters commendatory. In any case, Thurloe denied the charge of interference. "I know not of three members thus chosen into this House. If I say not truth, those four score can contradict me. They hear me."[67] This was a bold statement, but the fact that the House was so antagonistic to Thurloe and the Protector suggests that there may have been some truth in Thurloe's declaration. At least whatever efforts had been made, they were certainly not successful in bringing in "above four score" members who could be counted on as supporters.[68]

By 12 April Thurloe was again on the defensive, this time on behalf of one of the Major-Generals who was being disabled from holding military and civil office without a hearing.[69] The next day the Secretary wrote to Henry Cromwell in some bewilderment: "I am not wise enough to understand the present condition of our affaires here. Wee spend much tyme in great matters, but very little progress there in."[70] The royalist letters in the *Clarendon State Papers* supply the clue—which Thurloe seems to have missed at this point, although earlier he had alluded to "underhanded workeinge" to "disaffect the officers of

the army".[71] This concerted effort to create a deadlock and a dissolution was verging on success. Thurloe's last recorded action in this
Parliament was to serve as teller in favour of an Excise Bill on 15 April.[72]
A week later occurred the long-awaited dissolution, but even to the last,
the Secretary stood out against it. Of all the Council of State only he
and Sir Bulstrode Whitelocke supported Richard in the latter's determination to resist dissolution.[73] Their efforts, however, were in vain,
and Thurloe's term as university representative thus came to an end.
Though his conduct throughout the session had had almost no direct
relation to the interests of the university, it was on the whole a creditable
performance—a rather gallant defence of a failing régime, carried on in
a straightforward and intelligent fashion not unworthy of a university
member at his best.[74]

The other university members of this Parliament—Mills and Hale,
and Thurloe's colleague, Dr. Sclater—are passed over almost unnoticed
in the records. Sclater and Hale each served on two committees, Mills
on one.[75] Neither Mills nor Sclater seems to have raised his voice in
any cause, and Serjeant Hale spoke only once, to record his protest at a
reflection on a fellow member.[76] The political views of these members
up to this period have already been discussed. As the session lengthened
and the prospect of a Restoration grew clearer, it is likely that Hale and
Sclater, both of whom had been uncertain Cromwellians, became gladly
reconverted to the royalist cause. Hale, at least, in the next Parliament,
was clearly in favour of a Restoration, but a Restoration with the
Crown's powers limited. By the time of Charles II's return both Hale
and Sclater were sufficiently in favour with the new régime to receive,
respectively, a knighthood and a baronetcy. Hale, in addition, was
immediately put on the commission for the trial of the Regicides and
made Chief Baron of the Exchequer, and ultimately (1672) Chief Justice
of the King's Bench. Dr. Mills, on the other hand, though only
recently restored by Richard, was ousted again from his prebendary at
Christ Church, along with the other Parliamentarians, and like Thurloe,
passed into obscurity with the Restoration.

In this uneasy Parliament, there was no time for university business,
and the university members were seldom called upon to serve in their
functional capacity. One possible example of such service is Sclater's
presence on the committee considering the representation of Durham.
At least on this committee Sclater could have been ready to register
Cambridge's protest against any move to establish a university in that
city. The foundation of such a university had always been one of
Oliver's favourite projects, and it had already been partly realized by
the founding of a college there, so that there was perhaps some ground

for apprehension of a rival on the part of the older universities. At least it was about this time that both universities petitioned against the idea, though there is no indication that Sclater or any of the other university representatives took any action on the subject in Parliament.[77]

As for Thurloe, he was once appealed to by Cambridge, because of his influence with the Protector, to prevent the latter's forcing a mandated fellow into St. John's College.[78] But this did not require any parliamentary action. Indeed, the fact that Thurloe's constituency in this House was a university counted for so little in his career that neither Sir Charles Firth in his article on Thurloe in the *D.N.B.* nor Mrs. Evans in her study of Thurloe among the Secretaries of State make any mention of it. The same omission appears in the biography of Sir Matthew Hale written by Gilbert Burnet, and the sketch of Hale in the eighteenth-century *Biographia Britannica*.

The Parliament that succeeded the last Parliament of the Protectorate was the restored Long Parliament, consisting at first, in May 1659, only of the Rump, but later, in January 1659/60, with the surviving "secluded" members added. It is not possible to determine what part, if any, the university representatives played in these sessions. Three of the original university burgesses of 1640 were dead—Eden, Roe, and Selden—and there is no evidence to show that either Henry Lucas or Nathaniel Bacon ever reclaimed his seat.[79] But with the campaign for the Convention Parliament in 1660—"the healing and blessed parliament", as Anthony Wood called it—once more there was a stir of life running through the university constituencies. Freedom of choice was again restored, even more fully than for the Parliament of 1659/60, and a corresponding bustle of electioneering was under way.

General Monck was the hero of the hour, and therefore the first choice of both universities. But he declined both offers in favour of his native Devon. In spite of his withdrawal, at Cambridge he was elected just the same, the university having perhaps either ignored his protestations, or carried through the election without waiting to hear his views.[80] The Vice-Chancellor wrote to inform him of his election. It was accomplished, he reported, "with great alacrity and unanimity—not ten dissenters", but even in the face of this insistence, Monck adhered to his original intention, and made a declaration in favour of Devon, leaving Cambridge to hold a second election two months later.[81]

In spite of the Vice-Chancellor's report, Monck's poll in the first Cambridge election had not been quite so unanimous, but it was reasonably close to unanimity—341 out of 355, compared to 211 and 157 for the other two candidates.[82] The second on the list, Thomas Crouch, was, like Sclater, a gremial, and, to judge from the lack of information about him, even more obscure than Dr. Sclater.[83] His popularity in the poll perhaps sprang from the fact that he was a university figure pure and simple, an ejected fellow of King's,[84] with no outside interests or contacts, and thus a welcome change from the long line of candidates imposed from without, such as the university had known alike under King and Protector. At least, this seems a reasonable explanation of the fact that in the poll he stood far ahead of the university's own Chancellor, Oliver St. John, Lord Chief Justice. Another explanation, and one not entirely unrelated to the first, may be that Crouch, as one of those ejected in 1650, represented the current upsurge of royalist sentiment, while St. John's former association with the Protector was unlikely to inspire the university's confidence on the very eve of the Restoration.

Though the university poll only gives the names of the three final candidates, Monck, Crouch, and St. John, at least one other aspirant may have been in the offing. Dr. Sclater's biographer in the *Cambridge Antiquarian Society Proceedings* states that Sclater was a candidate for the Convention Parliament, though possibly this means that the constituency Sclater proposed to serve for was the Borough of Cambridge rather than the university.[85] However, if it was the university that he was interested in, it is not improbable that he was involved in the stir of electioneering that arose after the official poll, when it was realized that General Monck was likely to decline the seat. At this time several candidates' claims were advanced. Among them may have been Sclater. Another actually was Edward Montague, later the first Earl of Sandwich, the patron of Samuel Pepys, of whom Pepys wrote: "The University of Cambridge had a mind to choose him for their burgess, which pleased him well, to think that they do look upon him as a thriving man, and said so openly at table."[86] Montague's candidacy is discussed in a letter written by one of his supporters probably soon after the first poll. Here the chief argument given in Montague's favour was the desire of the university to have "one eminent person ioined with Crouch and not two gremialls". The other gremial in addition to Crouch who would be likely to win if General Monck declined the seat was "a young man of 7 years master", the son of Sir John Gore, who apparently had considerable following, sufficient at least "to foile my Lord St. John"—who also seems to have been thinking of offering himself again in Monck's place. Montague's correspondent assured him, however, that Gore himself could be persuaded to retire from the contest, although his party might still persist, and that two-thirds of Crouch's party and Crouch himself, and all of St. John's followers would support Montague, so that his election would be guaranteed and as nearly unanimous as General Monck's had been.[87] In spite of this rosy prospect, Montague's claims were not pushed, either because of his own reluctance to stand, or because the cross currents at Cambridge proved too much for his supporters. Likewise nothing further is heard of young Mr. Gore. The new election did not take place until 22 June, and it was seemingly uncontested. The burgess elected was a cousin of Edward Montague, William Montague, later Sir William and Chief Baron of the Exchequer.[88] Unlike his cousin, William Montague was distinctly royalist in tradition.[89] Thus Cambridge began the new era by a clear-cut break with the old Cromwellian past, returning two representatives, Crouch and Montague, who were both in complete sympathy with the restoration of the monarchy.

At Oxford in 1660 there were likewise a variety of candidates contending for the university's seats. Here also General Monck had been the first choice until he had declined the honour. But Oxford accepted his refusal, and sought other candidates. Monck, in fact, before he had been informed that the university had set its choice upon himself, had recommended William Lenthall, Speaker in the revived Long Parliament, and Master of the Rolls. Lenthall, wrote Monck, according to the letter quoted by Wood, was "a worthy patriot to his country and knowne freind to learning and the University". To press Lenthall's case further, the General sent down in person one of his captains of horse, Lenthall's nephew—"a gentleman of an estate", so Wood described him.[90] A statement from Lenthall accompanied Monck's letter, the gist of which was—according to Wood's summary—that since it had been "the pleasure of his excellency the Lord General to recommend him to the University, he [Lenthall] could not otherwise but write to let them know what honour it would be to him if they chose him". He spoke of opposition being made against him, and reminded them of his service to the university "in the late times",[91] and suggested that if chosen now "in this juncture of affairs," he might "render himself no less usefull in the settlement of this nation than active for their advancement". This latter sentence was doubtless calculated to win over the royalist-minded of Oxford, but according to Wood, Lenthall's real support came not from the Royalists but from the "Presbyterian party and fanatical party of the university with the Vice-Chancellor [who was a Presbyterian]". In order to further Lenthall's cause, so Wood further reported, the Vice-Chancellor, Dr. Paul Hood, called a special Convocation on purpose to read a second letter from Monck on Lenthall's behalf, and circulated "some hundreds of [printed] copies" about the university, so that "the loyall and royall partie might know how earnest the desires of Monck".[92]

After all this, next came Sir John Lenthall, William Lenthall's son, to canvass for his father, entertaining his father's supporters at a dinner of roast-beef and ale at the Mitre Inn, and threatening those who opposed him—though Wood reports the latter circumstance with some caution: "'Twas then said that he did in a manner threaten the Masters that would not give votes to his father."

Despite all this vigour of electioneering, and despite the great General's expressed wish, the university in the final Convocation chose otherwise. A rumour against Lenthall was circulated at the last moment by a member of Christ Church, Henry Stubbs, formerly a Parliamentarian but by this time an ardent Royalist, who was now, according to Wood, "elevated by the change that was to be". This person so "grumbled about among the Masters that 'William Lenthall was a rogue', and that he had 'run away with the mace to the army at Windsor when he was Speaker in 1647'," that Lenthall lost the election, and Dr. Mills, Oxford's burgess for 1658/9, was re-elected along with Dr. Thomas Clayton, Regius Professor of Medicine. This outcome was predicted six days before the election in a letter in the *Calendar of Clarendon State Papers*: "The General's commendation of the Speaker does not take: it is said they will choose Dr. Mills, a civilian, and Dr. Clayton, a physician."[93]

Since Dr. Clayton was Anthony Wood's pet aversion, what Wood reports about him cannot wholly be trusted. Wood's constant charge is that he "sided with all parties", and that he "cringed to the men of the interval", that he was arrogant and extravagant, "a most impudent and rude fellow—the very lol-poop of the University", who sold himself after the Restoration into the wardenship of Merton and a fine estate formerly belonging to one of the Regicides (Sir John Danvers, Oxford's member in the Short Parliament and earlier).[94] Whatever Clayton's character, his election completed the filling of the university seats with persons ready to usher in the new régime, either because, as at Cambridge, they had always been Royalists at heart, or because, as at Oxford, factors of discouragement and opportunism were at work.

In this same election of 1660, there had been one other candidate who was not averse to entering the Oxford lists, but he had not been willing to let his name be put up without assurance of success. This was Matthew Hale, late burgess with Dr. Mills, in Richard's Parliament. "Serjeant Hale"—so wrote the parish clergyman of Hale's home community to a member of Corpus Christi—"will not stand to be chosen a parliament man; but if chosen he will stand, if new oaths and engagements be not laid in his way." The university wrote to find out Hale's inclinations, noting that they had received a report that he would not accept the seat. "This hath somewhat discouraged and distracted the minds of some who are otherwise cordially for you", wrote the Vice-Chancellor. "Wherefore . . . 'tis humbly desired that you would be pleased positively to declare your willingness, if chose, to accept thereof."[95] But Hale remained somewhat coy. He explained in his reply, that if no engagements were required "to prevent the liberty of those that are chosen", he would not refuse to serve, although he was not eager to do so. His difficulty was that since the university had not spoken its mind earlier, he was already half-committed to accept a seat for his own county of Gloucester. If he should retract this acceptance, he would "much disappoint and discontent many", and yet if he should decline the university's offer, he would "seem ungrateful", he said, "especially when my last election seems to make me their debtor forever in the present service".

The rest of his letter reflects a mind in the throes of indecision. He could not ask the university to wait until the Gloucester returns were known—though it is obvious that this was what he really wanted—for he realized that such a request "would be much below that weighty and honourable body of the University and arrogance in me to expect it", especially since the Gloucester poll would not take place for some time to come, and this, he thought, might "give too much advantage, it may be to other's importunities, and leave you too little roome after for your own choice. The sum is," he continued, in a final attempt to speak decisively, "if I am chosen here, I shall look upon myself as equally concerned for the good of the University as if chosen there, and", he added, "the same would be true if the choice were the other way round." Clearly his fundamental preference was for the university seat, and his reluctance to relinquish his chance of obtaining it was revealed in his postscript: "Perchance, if the election be not before Tuesday, I may by conference with some, learn more of the sense and resolution of the country here, and send you word of it."[96] But Oxford was not thus to be trifled with. Its election came off six days before Gloucester's, and, as we have already seen, the university seats were bestowed elsewhere.

The university members of the Convention Parliament were on the whole rather more active than their predecessors had been throughout the Protectorate. The passing of the Cromwellian régime permitted more freedom of action on the floor of the House, just as it permitted more freedom in the conduct of elections, and as a result, the names of the university burgesses are found more frequently in the parliamentary records—on committee lists as tellers, in delivering reports or bills to both Houses, now and then in a brief speech or two. Of the four members, Dr. Clayton was perhaps the most active, although if Cambridge's William Montague is always the "Mr. Montague" encountered on committee after committee, then it was Montague that was the most prominent of the university members. This cannot be well established, however, for there was another Montague in the Convention Parliament, and "William" is cited in only three cases, though there are twelve or more lists, mostly on legal subjects, containing the surname.[97] There is no such doubt about the identity of Thomas Crouch, the other burgess for Cambridge. Leaving Montague aside, Crouch would probably come next to Clayton in activity. Dr. Mills from Oxford, on the other hand, served on only five committees,[98] although he was one of those who took some part in debate, in at least one speech, mentioned below.

In general, the university members were assigned to committees on specialized subjects, such as legal matters or ecclesiastical appointments. This was a return to the tradition established quite naturally in the first Parliament of James I, when the earliest university burgesses had all been trained in the civil law. Among their number now in the Convention Parliament, only one "civilian" remained, John Mills; but William Montague of the Middle Temple possessed knowledge of the other system of law, and, as noted above, it is on the legal committees that "Mr. Montague's" name most often appears. Likewise, the Convention employed the university members, especially Dr. Clayton and Mr. Crouch, on ecclesiastical matters, such as church livings and leases of church property—problems now again much to the fore, with the Restoration close at hand.[99]

It was Dr. Clayton, also, who took part in one of the debates on religion, and who spoke—quite in the old character of a university burgess—in defence of the Established Church, urging the inclusion of the Thirty-nine Articles along with the Old and New Testaments as a basis of doctrine and discipline.[100] Purely university matters also received the attention of the university burgesses in this Parliament—mostly financial problems of leases and livings, although once, in a debate on the post office, the question of the universities' right to have their mail carried as in the past was raised by Dr. Mills, and both Dr. Clayton and Mr. Crouch spoke in support of this proposal.[101] Another university matter occupied the university members—a petition from Oxford—a protest by the "Heads Put in by the Late Power", probably against their ejection from office. Clayton and Crouch both spoke against this petition, Crouch, according to the writer of the Salway Diary, being "excellent" on the subject.[102]

Besides legal questions, ecclesiastical matters, and university interests —their traditional fields of activity—the university members of the Convention were engaged on a number of private bills on various unrelated subjects, and in several concerns of major importance. Among the latter were the committees to consider the public debt and the disbanding of the army, and the granting of a general pardon. Clayton and Crouch were named jointly and separately on several of these committees:[103] "Mr. Montague" was on the committee to consider the attainder of Cromwell;[104] while Dr. Mills at the very opening of the session was assigned to the powerful Committee of Privilege.[105] Outside of Parliament, but within the range of university interests, Dr. Clayton was appointed by the new Chancellor of Oxford, the Earl of Hertford, to the Board of Visitors who were to carry out the parliamentary order mentioned above to investigate the persons then holding university posts with a view to their ejection. Incidentally, Dr. John Mills, Clayton's colleague in the Convention, was one of those soon to suffer under the new Visitors.[106]

Of all the university members who were sitting when the Convention Parliament came to an end in December 1660, only one was to be returned to the same seat in the following April—Thomas Crouch of Cambridge—and as we follow up his career, the history of university representation passes on into the period of the Restoration.

NOTES FOR CHAPTER VII

1. *Supra*, Ch. III, pp. 63–4, 75–7; Ch. IV, pp. 106, 107, 108, 113, 114–16.
2. There was some attempt, however, to prevent the election of Dr. John Owen in 1654. See below, p. 188 and n. 24.
3. Willis, *Notitia*, III, 255, 256.
4. *Historical Register of the University of Oxford* (1900), p. 39; J. R. Tanner, *Historical Register of the University of Cambridge*, p. 30. Cooper, III, 453, n. 7, regards Sadler as entrusted with the university interests of Cambridge, but Williams, *Oxfordshire*, p. 150, makes no mention of the University of Oxford in the Oxfordshire lists of 1653.
5. For the medical burgesses (Clayton, Sclater, Clarges, and Brady), and the medical candidates (Sir William Petty, Dr. John Palmer, and Dr. John Lamphire), see below, pp. 193–4, 201; Ch. X, pp. 266, 267; Ch. XI, p. 278; Ch. XII, pp. 300–1.
6. For Goddard's career, see *D.N.B.*; *A.O.*, III, 1029–30; *B.B.*, IV, 2216; Foster, II, 575; Wm. Munk, *Roll of the Royal College of Physicians*, I, 240; Ward, pp. 270–1. Wood has scattered references to Goddard in the *Annals* and in the *Life and Times*.
7. *C.J.*, VII, 335, 355.
8. *Ibid.*, p. 344.
9. Thomas Burton, *Diary*, I, 111.
10. *C.S.P., Ven.*, XXIX (1653–4), 160. See also *Life and Times*, I, 294–5; Cooper, III, 453–4; *Old P.H.*, XX, 220, 245; C. H. Firth, *Oliver Cromwell*, p. 355; Henry A. Glass, *The Barebone Parliament*, p. 333. There is, however, no indication of an attitude unfriendly to learning in the *Commons' Journal*, in Burton's *Diary*, or in the *Severall Proceedings*.

11. *B.B.*, IV, 2216 and n. For Goddard's cautious attitude towards hasty reform, see Mallet, II, 395.

12. For Sadler's career, see Madan, *Oxford Books*, II, 399, item 1790; Mullinger, III, 384–5; *D.N.B.*; Bayle, IX, 19–21; Glass, pp. 83, 91–2; Mark Noble, *Protectorate House of Cromwell*, II, 523n.; Venn, IV, 3; Worthington, *Diary*, II, pt. ii, 252n. (Chetham Society, XIII).

13. *Severall Proceedings*, IV, 3213–15; *C.S.P., Dom., Commonwealth*, VI (1653–4), 262; *C.J.*, VII, 305, 310, 323, 325, 327, 332, 340, 361.

14. Rait, II, 1027.

15. *C.J.*, VII, 344.

16. Mullinger, II, 515, n. 2.

17. *O.R.*, p. 499.

18. Some of these appointments are noted in *C.J.*, VIII, 380, 390, 406, 407, 419.

19. Burton, I, cx. Even the Agreement of the People had been more generous in allowing the universities their usual two seats each. *Old P.H.*, XVIII, 522.

20. Rait, II, 1027.

21. For Henry Cromwell's career, see *D.N.B.*; Oliver Cromwell, *Memoirs of the Protector*, II, 571–629; Noble, I, pt. iv, 252–85; Venn, I, 422; and a biography by Robert W. Ramsey. That Henry Cromwell was M.P. for Cambridge University is ignored both by Firth in the *D.N.B.* and by Cromwell, *Memoirs*.

22. *O.R.*, p. 501.

23. The student was Robert South, who later became a famous divine and something of a man of letters. See *D.N.B.* Owen had aroused South's antagonism by his objections to South's receiving his degree.

24. *Memoirs of the Life of Dr. Robert South*, I, iv–vi; Andrew Thomson, *John Owen*, pp. 76–8. There seems to be some discrepancy about the date of this incident. If it refers to Owen's election in June 1654, then the degree of South's that Owen had opposed was a B.A., for South did not receive his B.A. until 1654/5. It seems somewhat unlikely, however, that a mere student, not yet even a bachelor, could have had enough influence with the doctors and masters to obstruct the plans of the Vice-Chancellor—unless, of course, there was such antagonism to Owen throughout the university that opposition was easy to stir up. But this seems equally unlikely, in view of the generally recognized mildness and beneficial character of Owen's régime there, which conciliated even strict Anglicans like Anthony Wood. There is one other possible explanation, in view of the fact that none of the sources describing the incident cite a date for the election. That is, that South's opposition was exercised as a master of arts at the time of some other later election, when perhaps Owen had planned to run again. This seems to be the view of the *B.B.*, VI, pt. i, 3763, note C, although such a view may be only the result of a careless reading of South's biography.

25. 21 November 1654. Oxford University Archives, T26, p. 3839, ff. 254–5.

26. *A.O.*, IV, 99; Thomson, pp. 76–7. There is no reference whatsoever to this case in either the *Commons' Journal* or Burton's *Diary*, nor, curiously enough, in Wood's *Life and Times*, usually so full of gossip. The question of Owen's ineligibility to sit may explain the ease with which Robert South was able to muster so much force against Owen's election in the first place.

For Owen's career, see *D.N.B.*; *A.O.*, IV, 97–113; *B.B.*, V, 3291–6; David Bogue and James Bennett, *History of Dissenters*, I, 444–51; Burrows, *Register*, pp. xxxv–xliv; Edmund Calamy, *The Non-Conformists' Memorial*, I, 152–7; Foster, III, 1100; and full-length biographies by Andrew Thomson and William Orme (*Memoirs*, as introduction to *Works*, ed. Thomas Russell, I, 76–150). There are scattered references to Owen in many of the sources of the period, such as *The Clarke Papers*, ed. C. H. Firth, IV, and *The Writings of Oliver Cromwell*, ed. W. C. Abbot.

27. There is no record of any second election in the Oxford University Archives or in the *Official Return*. However, there is a possibility that a new writ was actually

issued, and that it was upon this occasion that Sir John Glanville was chosen by the university, and not as a successor to Sir Thomas Roe in 1645, as suggested above in Ch. VI, p. 164. The year 1654 would certainly fit the time indicated— "in one of the Usurping Times"—and the fact that "Serjeant Glanville" had been recently under consideration for rehabilitation as a lawyer to practise at the bar may lend some colour to this supposition. *C.S.P., Dom., Commonwealth,* VII (1654), 1, 17, 203. Other references to Glanville at this period show that he was at hand, and, by 1658/9 at least, interested in resuming political life. John Evelyn, *Diary,* I, 308; *O.R.,* p. 507. However, if indeed Glanville was elected by Oxford in 1654, the university would still have remained unrepresented, for according to Glanville's biographers, cited in Ch. VI, n. 90, though elected, he was also disabled to sit.

28. *P.H.,* III, 1430.
29. *O.R.,* p. 504, App., p. xlv; Cambridge University Registry, 50; *Mercurius Politicus,* August 1656, p. 7158.
30. *C.J.,* VII, 432.
31. *Ibid.,* pp. 436–7.
32. *Ibid.,* pp. 457, 466; Burton, I, 95. For the civil law, see *C.J.,* VI, 270; VII, 44, 73; *Life and Times,* I, 187, and *supra,* Ch. II, p. 40.
33. For Richard Cromwell's speech on behalf of Cambridge's property rights, see Burton, I, 84. He was also moved to speak on the Naylor case, where he showed considerable fanaticism, in contrast to the moderation of Nathaniel Fiennes, Oxford's member. *Ibid.,* pp. 90, 126.
34. *Ibid.,* p. 284.
35. C. H. Firth, *The Last Years of the Protectorate,* I, 186–7.
36. The letters are quoted in Robert W. Ramsey, *Richard Cromwell,* pp. 18, 822.
37. Materials for Richard Cromwell's life are not numerous. See *D.N.B.*; Foster, I, 354; Noble, I, pt. iii, 202–52; Venn, I, 422–3; and the full-length biography by Ramsey.
38. *C.S.P., Dom., Commonwealth,* XI (1657–8), 272.
39. *C.J.,* VII, 426, 520, 535, 540; Burton, II, 5; Firth, *Last Years of the Protectorate,* I, 171–2. See also *Monarchy Asserted,* a pamphlet possibly written by Fiennes himself.
40. Burton, I, 268, 353–4; *C.J.,* VII, 462, 498; Wood, Gutch, II, pt. ii, 544. Six months before Fiennes's election to Oxford's seat, a laudatory and petitionary letter had been sent by the university to express their appreciation of Fiennes's services. Oxford University Archives, T26, p. 3839, ff. 293–4.
41. Burton, I, 212–13; II, 63–4.
42. For Fiennes's career, see *D.N.B.*; *A.O.,* III, 877–9; Lord Campbell, *Lives of the Lord Chancellors,* II, 69–77; Edward Foss, *Judges of England,* VI, 424–9; Foster, II, 495; Noble, II, 466–7.
43. Burton, III, 335n. David Ogg, *England in the Reign of Chas. II,* I, 2, gives no reason for the change in representation. But see *Old P.H.,* XXI, 246.
44. See below, p. 193, and Ch. VIII, pp. 214–15. The first reference to this practice was made at Oxford in the election of 1627/8. *Supra,* Ch. IV, p. 115.
45. The *Thurloe State Papers* (ed. Thomas Birch), Ludlow's *Memoirs,* and the *Venetian State Papers* alike all bear witness to the frantic efforts being made by the Secretary and the Major-Generals to influence the elections. Ludlow, II, 49; *C.S.P., Ven.,* XXXI (1657–9), 276–7, 282, 284, 285. See below, p. 196.
46. Sir Francis Russell was the father-in-law of Henry Cromwell. See *Fasti,* II, 154; Noble, II, 387–9; Venn, III, 499. Morgan was a great favourite of the Cromwells. See *D.N.B.,* and Sir C. H. Firth, *The Regimental History of Cromwell's Army* (Oxford, 1940), I, 117–18. "Old Mr. Fairclough" was a Puritan clergyman of some note. See *D.N.B.*; Venn, II, 116.
47. Whichcot's letters are printed in Cooper, III, 470–3, and the *Thurloe State Papers,* VII, 574, 587. Russell's letter is in Cooper, III, 470–1. St. John seems to have

forwarded Whichcot's second letter to Thurloe, enclosed with a letter of his own, predicting that Thurloe would be successful at Huntingdon, where St. John's son was also standing. *Th. S.P.*, VII, 582.

48. *Th. S.P.*, VII., 572, 582, 585, 586, 588.

49. Cooper, III, 470–2. According to *Mercurius Politicus*, 31 December 1658, p. 135, and the *Thurloe State Papers*, I, xvii, Thurloe was chosen "by 120 Suffrages", a greater number than the writer had ever known "upon the like occasion". The meaning of this is not quite clear, for if this was "unanimity in the first place", as Cudworth described it (Cooper, III, 472), it would mean that there were only 120 electors at the most, and in this case the total poll was much below the usual figure, which may very well have been the case, considering the nature of the times. Compared to Richard Cromwell's 33 votes, for example, Thurloe's 120 would seem large. Sclater, his colleague, had 84 votes. For a discussion of the size of the electorate, see below, Ch. VIII, pp. 226–7.

50. What finally happened at Tewkesbury is not clear. There is no entry for 1658/9 in the *Official Return*, and Tewkesbury is not mentioned in Burton as one of Thurloe's possible constituencies. *O.R.*, p. 507; Burton, III, 450.

51. *Supra*, Ch. VI, pp. 164–5.

52. Cudworth's first letter is in Cooper, III, 472, and in *Th. S.P.*, VII, 587. The second letter is only in *ibid.*, p. 595.

53. The only references found for Sclater's career are in J. and J. B. Burke, *Extinct Baronetage*, p. 474; *Fasti*, II, 156; Foster, IV, 1324; Venn, IV, 88; and some biographical notes by W. M. Palmer, in the *Proceedings of the Cambridge Antiquarian Society*, XVII, n.s., xi (1912–13), 124–7. See also below, Ch. X, pp. 262–3, 265–6.

54. Palmer, p. 125; Rait, II, 1063. A notation by the Council of State in 1651 refers with some suspicion to a Dr. Sclater who had sent false news in an intercepted letter. *C.S.P., Dom., Commonwealth*, III (1651), 410. If this is the same Dr. Sclater, he may at this date have been still an unconverted Royalist. Thurloe, incidentally, at the time of this note was chief of secret service in charge of the interception of mail—a post that would have put the two future Cambridge burgesses in sharp opposition to each other, quite in contrast to the harmony of thought they seemed to display in 1658/9.

55. *Mercurius Politicus*, 29 December 1658, p. 135. For Palmer as a "Rumper", see quotation in Foster, III, 1109. For Petty, see *D.N.B.*. Petty's biographer, Lord Edmund Fitzmaurice (*Sir William Petty*, London, 1895), makes no mention of Petty's candidacy.

56. The only record of the election is in the *O.R.*, p. 509. No mention of it is found in the Oxford University Archives, or in any of Wood's works.

57. Mills's name often appears as "Mill" or "Mylles". The only connected accounts of his career that have come to light are in *Fasti*, II, 112; Foster, III, 1015; Williams, *Oxfordshire*, p. 152. Scattered references are fairly frequent in the *C.S.P.*, the volumes of the Historical Manuscripts Commission, the *Commons' Journal*, Rait, Burrows, and Wood's *Annals* and *Life and Times*. See especially *C.J.*, IV, 34–5; *Cromwelliana*, p. 176; Rait, I, 842, 925; Wood, Gutch, II, pt. i, 483; pt. ii, 124, 398, and note.

58. For Matthew Hale's career, see *D.N.B.*; *A.O.*, III, 1090–6; Gilbert Burnet, *Life and Death of Sir Matthew Hale* in *Works*, ed. Thos. Thirlwall, pp. 7–84; Lord Campbell, *Chief Justices of England*, II, Ch. xv–xviii; Foss, VII, 6–111; Foster, II, 626; J. B. Williams, *Life of Sir Matthew Hale*, including Appendix, 142–3; Holdsworth, *English Law*, VI, 574–95. *B.B.*, IV, 2475–6, draws largely on Burnet's work.

59. Ludlow, II, 48.

60. *Th. S.P.*, VII, 562, 575, 588.

61. *Ibid.*, p. 605; Burton, III, 25–6.

62. For Thurloe's speeches, see Burton, III, 314–15, 376–84, 481–9, and *Th. S.P.*, VII, 619.

63. Burton, IV, 68–70, 128, 243; *C.J.*, VII, 616, 619, 621, 627.

64. Burton, III, 308–9. One of the incidents following this debate was described in a letter to Sir Edward Hyde, telling how Sir Harry Vane pointed to where Thurloe sat, and said, "Formerly a little mushroom Secretary sat there who used to molest Parliament" by reading letters of intelligence. The allusions here were to former Secretary Windebanke, while member for Oxford in 1640, and to Thurloe, who had read a letter from the Protector Richard and defended it. *Cal. Clar. S.P.*, IV, 152.

65. See Hyde's instructions in the Clarendon Papers, *Cal. Clar. S.P.*, IV, 137, 149, 154, 159, 164–5; *Clar. S.P.*, III, 428, 435–6, 448–9, 453.

66. *The Clarke Papers*, ed. Firth, IV, 186. Burton's account of the incident is in IV, 257–8, 260–1, 301–2, 305–6. See also *Clar. S.P.*, III, 447–8; and *Cal. Clar. S.P.*, IV, 174, 179, 187.

67. *Th. S.P.*, IV, 562; Burton, IV, 301–3. See also *supra*, pp. 192, 195, and n. 45.

68. One of the royalist letters in the Clarendon Papers noted that this Parliament was a particularly uncertain quantity, because it was evenly balanced by country gentlemen and by young lawyers not yet affiliated with any party. *Clar. S.P.*, III, 441.

69. Burton, IV, 407, 410; *C.J.*, VII, 637.

70. *Th. S.P.*, IV, 655.

71. *Ibid.*, p. 636. See also *Clar. S.P.*, III, 456–7.

72. Burton, IV, 438; *C.J.*, VII, 640.

73. Some differences exist in the sources as to whether Thurloe stood with Richard in opposing dissolution. C. H. Firth in his biographical sketch of Thurloe in the *D.N.B.*; Noble, II, 459–60; and Thos. Birch, in his introduction to the *Thurloe State Papers*, I, xvii, all agree on Thurloe's opposition. Whitelocke, IV, 343, states that he himself opposed dissolution, but does not note how Thurloe stood.

74. For Thurloe's career, see references cited in n. 73, *supra*, and Evans, pp. 110–20; *Th. S.P.*, I, xi–xix; Venn, IV, 239.

75. *C.J.*, VII, 544, 608, 622, 641, 872.

76. Burton, IV, 326.

77. *C.J.*, VII, 622; Firth, *Cromwell*, pp. 355–6; Oxford University Archives, T26, p. 3839, ff. 339–42; Cambridge University Registry: Grace Book (1645–68), p. 240.

78. *Th. S.P.*, VII, 602.

79. The only list of members of the restored Rump seems to be in Prynne's pamphlet, *A true and full Narrative*, pp. 34–5, which states that on 7 and 9 May only forty-two were sitting of the original 500 and more members, although 300 members were still living. Lucas, having been among the "secluded" members in 1648, would not have been eligible for a seat at this date, so the absence of his name from the list of the forty-two is not surprising. But Bacon had been a "Rumper", and as such, should have returned with the first contingent. Indeed, according to one source, it is stated that he did so, but apparently not as Cambridge's representative, but rather as parliament man from Ipswich, the constituency that he had represented continuously all through the Protectorate.

80. Cooper, III, 477.

81. For Monck's candidacy, see: *Notes and Queries*, 1st ser., VII, 427; *H.M.C.*, *App. 2nd Rep.*, pp. 115–16; *C.J.*, VIII, 40. Cambridge's letter to Monck announcing his election was perhaps delivered by the messenger mentioned as paid £4 10s. 0d. "to wait on ye Lord Generall about ye Burgessship", Cooper, III, 477.

82. *Loc. cit.*

83. The only accounts of Crouch's career are in Foster, I, 358, and Venn, II, 427. Scattered references to him elsewhere are few and far between, except in the pages of the *Journal*. See below, Ch. IX, pp. 237, 239–41, 251–2.

84. He was restored to his fellowship in July 1660. *H.M.C.*, *App. 1st Rep.*, p. 67.

85. Palmer, p. 125.
86. Pepys, Wheatley, I, 110.
87. The full text of this letter is given below in Appendix VI. The young Mr. Gore mentioned is probably William, a fellow of Queens' College, and a grandson of Sir John Gore, Mayor of London. Venn, II, 241.
88. *O.R.*, p. 512.
89. Little information is available about William Montague, except what is in the *D.N.B.* See also Bailey, *Thos. Fuller*, pp 137–8; G. M. Edwards, *Sidney Sussex College*, pp. 57–8; John Hutchinson, *Middle Templars*, p. 167; Venn, III, 202. A calendar of Montague's correspondence, 1638–89, is in *H.M.C., Montagu*, I, 218, but there seems to be nothing there in relation to his Cambridge burgess-ship.
90. *Life and Times*, I, 311–13. The nephew (or grandnephew) of Lenthall sent by Monck was also one of Monck's kinsmen, Edmund Warcup. Keith Feiling and F. D. R. Needham, "The Journals of Edmund Warcup," *E.H.R.*, XL (1925), 236–7.
91. Lenthall had been on the parliamentary Committee of Appeal from the decisions of the Board of Visitors (Shadwell, IV, 273), and defended the university's interests there as well as on the floor of the House. See Mullinger, III, 336; Mallet, II, 394; Henry Cary, *Memorials*, II, 49–50. He may also have exerted himself on behalf of the civil law. *Supra*, p. 190.
92. The letter from Lenthall and the two letters of recommendation from Monck from the Oxford University Archives are printed in White Kennet, *Register and Chronicle*, pp. 100, 111, 112. See also Madan, III, 132, item 2509.
93. *Cal. Clar. S.P.*, IV, 643. The result was announced in another letter six days later. *Ibid.*, p. 664. There is no mention of this election in the *O.R.*, p. 515, but it is recorded in the Oxford University Archives, Ta27, p. 3839, f. 12, and in the *Old P.H.*, XXII, 218. It is possible that some dissension prevented the delivery of the return. For Henry Stubbs, see *D.N.B.*
94. For Wood's remarks about Clayton, see *A.O.*, IV, 215, 707; Wood, Gutch, II, pt. ii, 699, 700, 861, 883–4; *Life and Times*, I, 312 and n., 320, 361, 366, 379, 383, 385, 390–8. Merton College was Wood's own college, and therefore Clayton's wardenship there was all the more resented by him. For the warden-ship, see below, Ch. IX, 254, n. 2. There are many scattered references to Clayton in contemporary records, public and private, but almost no connected accounts of his career. In addition to Wood, see Foster, I, 288. Sir Wm. Musgrove, *Obituaries*, ed. G. J. Armytage, II, 14, seems to have confused Clayton with his father, the Master of Pembroke College.
95. The correspondence on the subject of Hale's candidacy is in Williams, *Hale*, pp. 44–7.
96. *Ibid.*, pp. 46–7.
97. *C.J.*, VIII, 117, 180, 192. The other Montague was George, member for Sand-wich and son of the first Earl of Manchester. He was also a lawyer, and could well have served on the same kind of committees that Oxford's William Mon-tague would have served on. Venn, III, 201.
98. *C.J.*, VIII, 2, 114, 146, 156, 202.
99. For the university members' action on ecclesiastical matters, especially for Crouch and Clayton, see *ibid.*, pp. 66, 81, 105, 106, 110, 177, 180, 202, and especially 185.
100. *P.H.*, IV, 79, 82.
101. *C.J.*, VIII, 217, 218; *Old P.H.*, XXIII, 60–1.
102. *C.J.*, VIII, 74, and Salway MS., f. 9, p. 3430, f. 25. (An opportunity to consult a photostatic copy of the privately owned Salway MS. was kindly provided by Professor Caroline Robbins of Bryn Mawr College.)
103. *C.J.*, VIII, 27, 136, 161, 180, 182.

104. *C.J.*, VIII, 177.
105. *Ibid.*, p. 2.
106. Two earlier university members were likewise to lose their places as a result of this Visitation—Dr. John Owen, Dean of Christ Church, and Dr. Jonathan Goddard, Warden of Merton. Goddard's place, in fact, went to Clayton himself. *Supra*, p. 201, and below, Ch. IX, 254, n. 2. Clayton was an active member of the Board of Visitors, to judge by the records in Varley, "The Restoration Visitation of the University of Oxford", *Camden Miscellany*, Vol. 18, C.S., 3rd ser., no. 79.

CHAPTER VIII

RETROSPECT, 1640–1660

The dissolution of the Convention Parliament presents a convenient point from which to look back and take stock of the history of university representation as it ran its course in the middle years of the seventeenth century. Some of the trends observable in this period were new, but most of them were not very different from the general developments of the earlier years. Through all the crises and all the changes of this period the function of university representation remained what it had been since the time of James I's original grant—partly a means whereby university interests could find expression in the assembly of the nation; but, partly, also—and indeed more often, except for the heyday of the Long Parliament—a means by which the hand of the ruling executive, now Protector rather than King, could be strengthened in his dealings with the Commons.

The opportunities for action in Parliament on behalf of university interests were greater in the period 1640 to 1660 than ever before, for with the Puritan party so bent on reforming and regulating, some defence of the universities was actually needed. Nevertheless, in the face of this challenge, the university members were for the most part silent. Only in the case of Selden, and possibly of Henry Lucas, and in the Convention of 1660, can we get an occasional glimpse of a university member on the floor of the House at work on behalf of his constituents. But even this is considerably more than was possible with regard to the burgesses of the period before 1640.

Then, too, over and beyond service on the floor of the House, there was other work to be done for their constituencies by the university members of this period—influence to be exerted and undercurrents to be resisted in various circles and areas outside of Parliament itself. Such action was most marked in the case of Eden, Owen, and Selden, and in general it was probably more extensive than similar services rendered by the burgesses of the earlier period. From one point of view, these activities of the university members might properly be disregarded here, since, strictly speaking, such action was not a direct result of the institution of university representation, except insofar as membership on the Committee of Appeal from the Board of Visitors stemmed from being a member of Parliament. But from another point of view, it seems proper to give some attention to these services, since they do show concern for the university community, and a closeness of relationship to it.

In general, the relationship of the burgesses to their universities in the middle of the century bore much the same character as in the preceding period. Eleven of the eighteen members[1] held degrees of some sort, either by "creation", "incorporation", or by actual achievement. Five of the remaining seven were without degrees, but had been at some time students in residence. Six had been fellows, and seven were college Heads or officials of some sort. Seven were later benefactors of the university, or of the particular college with which they had been associated.[2]

The question of degrees is always an interesting one, especially as it tends to throw light upon the extent to which the qualifications of the original grant regarding the choice of burgesses were still observed. The *de se ipsis* clause continued to be circumvented and at times openly disregarded, but it was still recognized as binding in a general way. Coke's original warning against the election of a clergyman was now strengthened by the law of 1642 forbidding the clergy to hold civil office, and by the precedent of the disqualification of Dr. John Owen. And Coke's advice in favour of choosing doctors of the civil law was not out of date, although the civil law, as a field of study, was steadily going out of favour—all the more so in this period, perhaps, because of its previous association with the authority of the Crown. It is striking that only two of the eighteen burgesses of the revolutionary Parliaments came from this faculty: Dr. Thomas Eden, who was held over from the 1620's, and Dr. John Mills, who bridged the gap between Richard the Protector and the Restoration. This is in sharp contrast to the period from 1604 to 1640, when nine out of twenty-two members were "civilians", and to the period after 1661, when there were seven out of eighteen.

The common law, on the contrary—well represented since the first exercise of the university franchise—still held its own. Eight of the eighteen members—Selden, Bacon, Sadler, the two Cromwells, Hale, Thurloe, Montague (and possibly Roe, as well)—all came from the Inns of Court, although in the case of the Cromwells this connection was perhaps merely nominal. In place of the civil law, as has been noted before, a new field of learning was beginning to furnish burgesses for the universities—the field of science—in particular medical science, as represented by Doctors Goddard, Sclater, and Clayton. This period is also distinguished by the fact that it provides the only case in all university history of a doctor of divinity's standing for Parliament.

Not all the higher degrees mentioned above were indeed earned degrees, for, although their lesser degrees were won in the normal way, the doctor's degrees granted to Eden, Owen, Sclater, and Mills, were all "created", and obtained quite as likely because of influence as through recognition of achievement.[3] There were also two "incorporated" degrees in this period, those of Goddard and Sclater. Each of these men reversed the pattern of the other's career. Goddard, having started his education at Oxford, took his medical degree at Cambridge, and was later "incorporated" and made a fellow at Oxford; while Sclater began work at Cambridge, transferred to Oxford for his first M.D., and then was finally "incorporated" in medicine at Cambridge.[4] Thus both of them would have relied upon their incorporated degrees to qualify according to charter as *bona-fide* members of the university they were to serve as burgesses—although, of course, in the case of Goddard, such qualification was not legally necessary, since he was nominated, and not elected, and not officially a true university member.

As to the lesser degrees, there was one member, Nathaniel Bacon, who held only a B.A., and four—Lucas, Sadler, Crouch, and Henry Cromwell—who only held master's degrees. Two of these master's degrees were "created"—those of Lucas and Cromwell. Five of the eighteen burgesses of this period had no degrees at all, although they had once been students. Among these were such notable figures as Selden, Fiennes, Hale, and Roe. This is in sharp contrast with the situation in the preceding period, for only Sir John Danvers of the earlier group would have belonged to this category.

In addition, there were two members during the Interregnum who had no university connections at all—that is, if the university records are correct. One was Richard Cromwell and the other John Thurloe. As in the case of Sir Thomas Edmondes in 1625, no attempt seems to have been made to confer courtesy degrees upon these members, although such a proceeding would have at least satisfied legal require- ments. For Thurloe, however, such a step was contemplated, since in the correspondence that preceded his nomination, it may be remembered that Dr. Whichcot wrote to Chancellor St. John:

> We do think to naturalize Mr. Secretary to us, and to make him of our body, by admitting him by proxy to the degree of master of arts, as by our university-statute we are enabled to doe, where persons are upon any account stiled honourable, which proceeding, he is *pulchre eligibilis*.[5]

It would seem that this plan of Whichcot's was not carried out, for Thurloe's name is missing from Venn's lists. As for Richard Cromwell, there is no evidence that such an arrangement was ever considered.[6]

The question of current residence as a qualification for candidacy had early entered the area of controversy, in the disputed election of

1614.[7] Although two outsiders, Bacon and Sandys, won their seats at that time, the issue had not been completely forgotten. The compromise that came to be accepted—without, apparently, anything official having ever been done in the matter—was that the patron of the university or the Crown was allowed to name one candidate, while the university reserved the other seat for a candidate of its own choice. In borough politics, such a division of seats had long been a custom.[8] In the universities, the arrangement frequently resulted in the nomination of a gremial by the university, and of a non-resident by the Crown. In the earlier period, for example, there were Coke and Eden, Marten and Danvers, and Windebanke and Danvers. During most of the Interregnum, when the universities had only one seat each, there had been no opportunity to continue the practice of this compromise, but with the re-establishment of the two seats in Richard's Parliament of 1658/9, Cambridge hastened to revert to the former system. In writing his first letter about Thurloe's candidacy, Whichcot thus explained the desire for a gremial. Later, Cudworth also, in writing to Thurloe in notification of his election, explained who Thurloe's colleague would be: Dr. Sclater, a stranger to him—one who lived "upon the place", who was selected because it was "the opinion of divers of the heads and others" that a "gremial" should be chosen, because such a one, "living amongst us was well acquainted with the state of things here, and one that would be vacant to attend our concernements".[9]

Perhaps this last reason should be given considerable weight, for it is possible that the universities had previously experienced neglect when their parliamentary interests were entrusted, as they were so often, to men of great affairs who may have had no time, and little inclination, to waste their efforts on the small concerns of their constituents. As it happened, during the period under consideration there were altogether more non-resident members than gremials—eleven as compared to eight. Cambridge, in fact, had had no resident member since the death of Dr. Eden, except for the brief term of John Sadler. This may account for the university's eagerness to insist upon its right to choose one of its own body in 1658/9, now that it was about to conduct its first comparatively free election since 1640. In any case, in thus asserting its legal claims, the university was setting a precedent that became more and more emphasized in later years.[10]

On the other hand, there was a certain advantage for a university to have as one of its representatives a man of large affairs, who could act not only as an elected representative but also as something of a patron in the traditional style, because of his wide influence. Therefore the division of the seats between resident and non-resident burgesses was not looked on with disfavour, and at times was even actually sought after. One such occasion was in 1660 at Cambridge, when much of the enthusiasm for Edward Montague's candidacy stemmed from the opinion that it would be best to have "one eminent person joined with Crouch and not two gremialls".[11]

The universities had not lacked "eminent persons" as representatives in the period from 1640 to 1660. Quite as much as in the previous period, the university burgesses of the mid-century had been men of affairs or distinction. Even some of those whose names are less well known have been subjects of articles in the *Dictionary of National Biography*—Eden, Lucas, Sadler, Nathaniel Bacon, and Montague—and two of those who might be classified as relatively obscure—Clayton and Mills—have their names spread widely over the pages of Anthony Wood as of considerable importance in university affairs, while both of them, as parliament member and Judge Advocate of the army, respectively—were not restricted in their activities to university circles alone. This leaves only Sclater and Crouch in the category of those whose celebrity was purely local.

The remaining university burgesses of this period ranked as high in the government and affairs of their time as any of the parliament men from the universities in the 1620's. There was Goddard, Cromwell's army surgeon, a member of the Council of State, and one of the foremost medical men of his day; Hale—"Immortal Hale!"—as Cowper called him—Justice of the Common Pleas and a recognized leader in the law; the two Cromwell brothers, one destined to be "the titmouse Prince",[12] and both members of the Council of State; John Owen, chaplain of the army, and universally recognized as one of the leading divines and religious writers of the age; Thurloe, Secretary of State; Fiennes, Commissioner of the Great Seal; to say nothing of those earlier celebrities, Sir Thomas Roe, Privy Councillor and ambassador *par excellence*,[13] and the great Selden, who crowns the assemblage with untimate distinction. Even among the lesser lights, there was Eden who was an Admiralty Judge and Navy Commissioner, and Sadler, Master of Requests, an Admiralty Judge, and a member of the Council of State.

In considering this array of celebrities and near celebrities, there seems to be no particular difference in calibre between those who were elected by the relatively free choice of the universities and those who gained their seats primarily through political favour. Selden and Hale represent parliament men of the first category; Goddard, Sadler, Owen, and Thurloe, of the second; while men of comparatively mediocre capacity are found in each group. Likewise, there seems to be no great difference between those chosen by the favour of the Cromwellian Court and those chosen by the favour of the Stuart Kings in the earlier years of the century, so far as diligence in their masters' business is concerned. Nevertheless, as individuals, the opinion might be ventured that the best of the Cromwellian appointees—Thurloe, Goddard, or Owen—taken in the fullness of their characters as statesmen, thinkers, men of action, and persons of integrity, would rank on the whole higher than the most prominent of the royal favourites of the 1620's —Sir George Calvert, Sir Thomas Edmondes, Sir John Coke; while the worst of the Cromwellians—perhaps Richard Cromwell himself—was of considerably better stuff than Sir Francis Windebanke or Sir John Bennett, the worst of the Stuart following. It is to be noted in this period, as earlier, that the knowledge and talents of the university members were generally recognized and put to use in carrying on the business of the House. For example, Sir Thomas Roe was set to work on the problem of the treaty with the Scots; Dr. Eden, on maritime questions and international law; John Sadler, on the reform of the law and on tithes; Nathaniel Bacon, likewise on law and religion, and Selden, on almost everything, from the value of the records in the Tower of London to the most obscure details of ecclesiastical and constitutional history. In this way, a large part of what the university members had to offer was made available for public use, and the institution of university representation was to some degree justified by the record of the members it provided. The only important exception to this practice seems to have been the cases of Matthew Hale and John Mills, whose legal abilities seem to have found little scope in their terms as university representatives.

As might be expected in a revolutionary period, some change is to be observed in the social status of the university burgesses who were elected between 1640 and 1660. As compared with the earlier years, fewer knights and representatives of the country gentry are to be found upon the university returns. Indeed, of all the eighteen members of this period, only Sir Thomas Roe bore this title at the time of his election. Younger men rising to prominence had less chance of being knighted in the Interregnum. The only Cromwellian knighthood that appears among the university representatives or candidates of this period is that of Sir Anthony Morgan, who was suggested as an alternative to Thurloe for the Cambridge burgess-ship in 1658/9. Sclater, Clayton, Montague, and Hale were all made knights or baronets immediately after the Restoration. The gentry were still well represented, with Eden, Crouch, Mills, Nathaniel Bacon, Sadler, and the two Cromwells, while Selden's mother had knightly connections, although his father was a yeoman. Sir Thomas Roe, though the son of a knight, drew his tradition from the City of London, where his grandfather had been Lord Mayor.

With Roe, an urban background was introduced, and this background figured also in the case of some of the members who came from the professional classes. The prominence of professional classes in the background of the burgesses was something relatively new in university representation. In the previous period, out of a total of twenty-two, Eden and Gooch, and perhaps Bennett and Wake, would fit into this group; whereas now there were seven members who might be thus classified out of a total of eighteen—Thurloe, Sadler, and Owen, who were the sons of clergymen; Sclater and Hale, the sons of lawyers (though in Hale's case some landed property also suggests other connections); Clayton, whose father was also a doctor, the Regius Professor of Physic at Oxford, and Eden, again, whose father was a schoolmaster, once tutor and secretary to Henry VIII. Of these, Hale, Eden, and Owen also had rural connections; the others may have been urban, although the evidence is inconclusive.

In the matter of descent and family connections, another new trend of this period was the appearance of two noblemen's sons, Nathaniel Fiennes, the son of Lord Say and Sele, and William Montague, the son of the second Baron Montague. On the whole, the number of other representatives with noble or especially distinguished relatives is notably few. The two Cromwells and Nathaniel Bacon, the nephew of Sir Francis Bacon, and possibly Sir Thomas Roe and John Sadler—whose wife was a descendant of the Seymours—appear to be the only names that belong in this group. Among all these eighteen university burgesses between 1640 and 1660 there is one man whom it is impossible to place socially—that is, Henry Lucas, whose origin is obscure, and who seems to have risen in the world through his own efforts, the only real *novus homo* of the group. But even here there is a rumour of a respectable and well-to-do background, and a fortune which Lucas was deprived of through the dishonest conduct of a faithless guardian.[14]

In age, as in social class, the university burgesses of the mid-century reflect to some degree the revolutionary time they lived in. Their average age is much lower than that of the period before the Long Parliament. All but four of the fourteen whose age it is possible to ascertain were below fifty at the time of their election, and three out of the four whose age is uncertain were probably also in the younger group. Four, and probably five, of the eighteen were under forty, while the youngest, Henry Cromwell, was only twenty-six. Roe and Selden, in their later fifties, and Eden—probably somewhat older, were the oldest of this group—all three the survivors of an earlier era.

With the general age-level thus reduced, it is not surprising to note that while twelve of the eighteen members were already distinguished in some way at the time of their election, only six of them had ever had previous experience in Parliament. This is in direct contrast to the university members who served in the period before 1640, when, out of twenty-three, at least twelve had already served for a term or more for other constituencies before they came to represent the universities.

Another fact to be noted in regard to parliamentary service in this period is that university members seldom succeeded themselves. There were only three who occupied their seats for a second term—Lucas and Eden, who had been carried over from the Short Parliament, and Mills in 1658/9 and 1660. This is also in direct contrast to the prolonged tenure of more stable periods, not only before the Civil War, but also in the Restoration and even more noticeably in the eighteenth and nineteenth centuries, when a university member was often continued in his seat almost for life. Like the lower age-level, the rapid succession of university members during the middle of the seventeenth century is clearly another manifestation of the revolutionary nature of the period.

The political significance of the careers of these university representatives has been already commented on in detail in the course of the past two chapters, but a general retrospect at this stage brings out some interesting conclusions. The most obvious of these is the fact that the political coloration of the various members follows the main trends of the time, from constitutional reform (Selden, 1640) through revolutionary Puritanism (Fiennes, 1656), back again to traditional monarchism (Crouch, 1660). Only one prominent phase of political thought is missing here—the militant army republicanism of Fleetwood and Ludlow. Possibly Nathaniel Bacon comes the nearest to representing this line of thinking.

The second rather obvious conclusion is that the most characteristic political attitude of the university members of this revolutionary period is their spirit of moderation. Whether Royalist or Parliamentarian, Anglican or Puritan, extremes seldom prevailed. On the Puritan side, Bacon and Fiennes were the most partisan, and possibly Sadler, while the two most completely royalist members were probably those whose election heralded the Restoration—Crouch and Montague. The other university burgesses with royalist leanings—Roe, Sclater, and Hale—apparently accommodated themselves without too much compromise to the régimes they found themselves in; Roe, because he felt the need for reform, and Hale, because his sympathies were with the Presbyterians. A good summary of Roe's position, written about a hundred years after his death, is in Arthur Collins, *Letters and Memorials of State*:

> As he was a strenuous Adviser of healing and moderate Measures, he met the usual Fate of cool and impartial Men in Times of publick Distraction, and became less personally acceptable to those who directed the Councils at Oxford and Westminster, and met with some Neglects from the King, and Hardships from the Parliament.[15]

About Sclater, as we have noted before, little is known, and that little surrounded by contradiction. Ejected from his fellowship as a Royalist in the 1640's, he reappears ten years later, certifying to the "godliness' of the local clergy, and standing for a seat in the House as a colleague acceptable to Thurloe. Then again, two years after this, we find him made a baronet by the King, only to fall under suspicion ten or fifteen years later for showing too much favour to Dissenters. Whether this alternation of loyalties indicates mere opportunism or indecision or whether it was the result of trying to cleave to the middle road, is impossible to say, with the little evidence at hand.

If any of the university burgesses of this period was an opportunist pure and simple, it was certainly Sir Thomas Clayton, an active Royalist after the Restoration, who had formerly, according to Anthony Wood, "cringed to the men of the interval", and kept his Regius Professorship when better men were ejected. Some allowance, however, must be made for any estimate of Clayton by Wood, for Clayton was the Head of Wood's college, and a particular object of his animosity.[16]

The men of the middle road on the parliamentarian side were happier than Clayton in their biographers. Even royalist writers acknowledge the willingness of Selden, Eden, Goddard, and Owen to recognize worth of mind and character in men of opposing views. Of Selden, David Lloyd wrote that he was a "large soul, finding that as swaddling clothes made children short breathed, so narrow systems and methods made them narrowly learned". Though this comment refers particularly to Selden's attitude on education, it was apparently also applicable to his attitude in general. Clarendon, also, among the Royalists, praised Selden for his "wonderful and prodigious abilities and excellences", not only his "stupendous learning", but his "humanity, courtesy and affability" which were so great that he

> would have been thought to have been bred in the best Courts, but that his good nature, charity, and delight in doing good, and in communicating all he knew, exceeded that Breeding.

Indeed, Clarendon noted, he himself had looked on Selden "with so much affection and reverence that he always thought himself best when he was with him". And even Anthony Wood, whose High Tory sentiments coloured all his judgments, said of Selden that "his mind was as great as his learning, full of generosity, and harbouring nothing that seemed base".[17]

We have already noted how David Lloyd commended Dr. Eden for his stand in relation to the fellows of his college, and how Seth Ward and the *Biographia Britannica* both paid tribute to Jonathan Goddard's "prudence", "integrity", and largeness of mind. John Owen, too, deserves an important place among men of this type, for, as several of his biographers point out, Owen was the first man in England to be a practical advocate of religious toleration, not because he was a member of a minority group, as is usually the case, but at a time when his party was in full control—a degree of magnanimity seldom encountered in the history of religious dissent. His conduct while Vice-Chancellor of Oxford during the régime of the Visitors was quite in keeping with these views, and won him the grudging admiration of Anthony Wood, while later, in the persecuting days of the Restoration, he had the respect and recognition of Clarendon, the Duke of York, and the King himself. As for Lucas—according to his biographer, Isaac Barrow—he also was not "immersed in Factions of State", and thus belongs in the same tradition of moderation, if on a less distinguished level. John Mills, likewise, although a Presbyterian and an early Cromwellian, was not an extremist, for he tempered the wind of the Visitation as much as he could, and later refused the Engagement—for which he suffered the loss of his canonry at Christ Church. Even such consistent supporters of the Protectorate as Henry Cromwell and John Thurloe were not fanatical or illiberal in their attitudes.[18]

Enough has been said to show that moderation was a characteristic of most of the university burgesses of this period, regardless of their political affiliations. In classifying these affiliations, however, it must never be forgotten that in many cases the views of the university members were changing as the years moved on, and that their thinking was affected by all three of the major allegiances of the period—to King, to Parliament, and to Protector—in varying proportions at various stages. The resulting fluidity of political thought is well illustrated by the fact that, in the end, those who had worked with the Protectorate—Hale, Sclater, Owen, Mills, and even Thurloe—welcomed the Restoration along with the true Royalists—or at least became reconciled to it—just as, earlier, the moderate Royalists and the constitutionalists, like Roe and Selden, had gone along with the revolutionary programme of the Long Parliament. These changing positions, of course, were not characteristic of the university representatives alone, but of the whole country during this period.

In intellectual interests, the parliament men of the universities in the mid-century measured up to a high standard. At least four of them ranked among the first of their professions. Chief of them all, of course, was Selden, as linguist, Orientalist, legal and ecclesiastical historian, authority on international law. Next, perhaps, comes Jonathan Goddard, one of the founders of the Royal Society, a writer on medical and scientific subjects, the inventor of a then popular medicine known as Goddard's Drops, and reputedly the first man in England to own a telescope. Matthew Hale, likewise, was one of the great legal figures of the century, whose writings and analyses of the English law are still classics in their field. In an age famous for its divines, John Owen stands forth as one of the three or four most eminent Independent preachers and theologians, the vigorous author of a long list of works, highly esteemed in their time, and still important for any study of seventeenth-century religious thought.

Of these four, three were versatile in their interests and capacities— only Owen confined his interests to one field. Goddard's interest in science went beyond the subject of medicine, while Hale was a man of the most diverse knowledge, his mind ranging eagerly outside his own province of law into the fields of theology, astronomy, and other sciences. Selden, again, in breadth as well as in thoroughness of learning, excelled them all—"the chief of learned men reputed in this land", as Milton wrote in *Areopagetica*, "the glory of the English nation", as Grotius styled him. Thomas Fuller—though none too tolerant of Selden's religious views—credited him with the broadest scholarship. "His learning", said Fuller, quaintly, "did not live in a lane, but traced all the latitude of the arts and languages."[19] Wilbur K. Jordan, writing in the twentieth century, points out that Selden's reputation is all the more impressive, since it was gained "during a century renowned for its learning". An unknown writer of the nineteenth century, quoted by Singer in his introduction to the *Table Talk*, presents the best summary of Selden's unique position as the scholar in public life, the beau-ideal of the university representative, as follows:

He appears to have been regarded [so the comment runs] somewhat in the light of a valuable piece of national property like a museum, or great public library, resorted to as a matter of course, and a matter of right, in all the numerous cases in which assistance was wanted from any part of the whole corpus of legal and historical learning. He appeared in the national council not so much the representative of the contemporary inhabitants of a particular city [or university, one might add], as of all the people and of all past ages; concerning whom, and whose institutions, he was deemed to know whatever, within so vast a retrospect, was of a nature to give light and authority in the decision of questions arising in a doubtful and hazardous state of the national affairs.[20]

To be such a representative was to be the university representative *par excellence*, an ideal that was realized only once in the seventeenth century, and perhaps never again in the history of university representation.

To turn from a figure of such stature to the lesser university burgesses of this period is to lose for a moment all sense of proportion. Compared to Selden, the scholarly interests and enterprises of the rest fall into the shade. But nevertheless, on this lower level, there were some men whose intellectual concerns must not be ignored in any general estimate of the quality of the university members of this time—for example, the two Nathaniels, Bacon and Fiennes, each the author of a political work; Bacon, reputedly the author of *Historical Discourses*, one of the classic political treatises of the century, and Fiennes, the author of *Monarchy Reasserted*, a defence of Cromwell as the "Single Person". Then there was John Sadler, a Hebrew and Oriental scholar, with writings on those subjects, and Sir Thomas Sclater, the size of whose private library was an object of wonder to his contemporaries. Sadler is also the probable author of another political work, *Rights of the Kingdom*, one of the numerous historical analyses of the origins and working of the English constitution so characteristic of the age. Although Sir Thomas Roe was described as a scholar in Wood's tribute—"There was nothing wanting in him . . . [as scholar], gentleman, and courtier"—he had led too active a life to engage seriously in scholarly pursuits, although his interest in collecting manuscripts abroad shows that he shared in the general intellectual concerns of his time. In Langbaine's words, "As he was learned, so was he also a great encourager and promoter of learning and learned men."[21] For the other university members, there is no special evidence of strong literary or scientific interests, although Henry Cromwell is claimed as a patron of learning, and Henry Lucas actually was one, as the founder of the Lucasian Chair at Cambridge which was later occupied by another university member, Isaac Newton—who, like Selden, stands in the first rank of university representatives, both as regards his service to his constituency and his intellectual eminence. Other university members of this period besides Lucas and Roe were also benefactors to their universities and colleges, in gifts made during lifetime or by bequest—Eden, Selden, Sclater, Hale, and Crouch; while the university interests of Nathaniel Bacon and John Owen extended even across the sea to the new Puritan college in Cambridge, Massachusetts.[22]

Such services and such interests—in addition to those rendered in a strictly political role as members of the House or of the Board of Visitors—show that a good number of the university burgesses of this period were men of intellectual interest and scholarly appreciation, who had the concern of the universities and the cause of higher learning close at heart, and were, in the larger as well as in the more limited sense, good representatives of the university communities. All things considered, inside Parliament and out, the calibre of the university members of this period reached a more satisfactory level than that of the burgesses of the opening years of the century.

In seeking for differences between the parliament men of the two universities during these middle years, we do not come upon anything very significant. The most striking fact is that the two burgesses who never attended any university at all were both elected by Cambridge—Richard Cromwell and John Thurloe. At Cambridge, also, an interesting reversal of social rating shows up, when the country gentry, perhaps for the only time in university history, tend to outnumber those in Oxford's delegation, six to a dubious three, the Oxford members being well distributed among various origins—urban, yeoman, noble, and professional. This is probably explained by the fact that the gentry of the eastern counties surrounding Cambridge, like Bacon and the Cromwells, were so largely Puritan in this period. There is only one other respect in which the Oxford statistics vary from those of Cambridge—that is, in intellectual distinction, where the pre-eminent intellects of the group all belong to Oxford—Selden, Goddard, Owen, and Hale. Beyond this, in such matters as age-level, service in Parliament, experience in public affairs, residence, degree-holding, and political views, the members from the two universities are in this period remarkably similar.

In looking back over the period 1640–60, some other points of importance in the history of university representation come to light besides those that bear on the character of the burgesses. These are mostly matters of procedure, which are discussed here as an addition to the observations on the subject set forth in Chapter III. One of these matters is the problem of university freedom. While there is no evidence of any open interference on the part of Cromwell with the university vote, it would be natural to surmise that, openly or tacitly, the universities were given to understand what candidates the Lord General wanted—or else that they forestalled such requests by settling beforehand on someone who would be agreeable to his wishes. At least, it seems significant that—except in the case of John Owen—there is no sign of electioneering or of election uncertainty from 1640 until 1658/9 and 1660, when the breakdown of the Protectorate set a great stir afoot in both the universities. The opportunity for a free choice, was, as always, none too much to the liking of the Heads, and Dr. Whichcot at Cambridge fretted a little at the prospect. This fretting, incidentally, shows that a really free election was under way again, in spite of the ruling of the Heads in 1614 and of King James again in 1621 that the election of burgesses should be carried on according to the procedure used for the choosing of the Vice-Chancellors.[23] It was Thurloe's seat that was at stake. The Heads were not completely sure that they could guarantee his election. They hoped the body of the university would agree with them in supporting him, but, so Dr. Whichcot wrote—perhaps with some surprise upon discovering the situation: "the uncertainty lies in this, that every master of arts hath as much to doe in this election as any doctor"—which was, after all, quite as the grant *De Burgensibus* seems to have intended it. Ten days later, on the same subject, the good doctor wrote again somewhat uneasily: "I am never confident of ought that is in the hands of a multitude." But in this case, he need not have been anxious, for the multitude supported Thurloe heartily in the poll.[24]

In the following election—that of 1660—the situation at Oxford shows further evidence of electoral freedom. It will be remembered that it was in this election that Oxford had wanted to choose General Monck but that the General had forestalled them by writing letters in behalf of William Lenthall. The Vice-Chancellor did his best to forward Lenthall's candidacy by calling a special Convocation to read Monck's letters, but in spite of all pressure from high places, the vote was swung against Lenthall by a last-minute rumour. This proves that the vote in this period was not always rigged beforehand by outside powers, and that from time to time the rank and file of the electors could regain their legal rights.

The Lenthall incident also calls attention to some special aspects of election campaigning. Lenthall, a non-resident, did not come to canvass for himself—whether because it was illegal to do so, or for some other reason is not clear. Lenthall wrote a letter announcing his readiness to serve, and his nephew and later his son—both Oxford men—came to the university to canvass and to treat. This is the first mention of "treating" as part of the election customs of the universities, though it was later a common practice. The two gremials, Mills and Clayton, Lenthall's successful rivals, also treated moderately, but *after* the election.[25]

By this time it seems clear that the promising of votes before the poll had become an accepted procedure in both universities. This is directly referred to in Whichcot's letter to Thurloe where he remarked that "Mr. Bacon" would have been undoubtedly given the second seat by Cambridge, had not most of the university been already "pre-engaged" by the time Bacon's name was brought forward. Another example is the campaign carried on at Cambridge in 1640 where some of the electorate were inclined to "reserve their suffrages" for Sir Henry Spelman even though Dr. Eden and his supporters "visited" vigorously to secure votes. Again in 1660, in the proposition made to Edward Montague that he stand for the seat at Cambridge in General Monck's place, it was stated that three-quarters of Thomas Crouch's following and all of Chancellor St. John's party were ready to support Montague, and were only waiting word from him before declaring themselves.[26]

Both of these latter campaigns involve a step in electoral procedure that has not yet been touched upon—the question of the candidate's consent to having his name put forward. At Cambridge there seems to have been no recognized policy in regard to this. There are instances of two divergent practices. In the case of Sir Henry Spelman, it may be remembered, Spelman had known nothing about the election until he was informed by his friend Wheelocke that he had failed to win the seat. On the other hand, in the letter to Edward Montague in 1660, Montague's correspondent appeared to be trying to persuade Montague to stand, going even so far as to promise him an almost unanimous poll. But in the previous election of General Monck, as we may infer from the letter in which the Vice-Chancellor reported the fact of Monck's election, the General's consent had not been obtained beforehand. At Oxford, on the contrary, it seems to have been the custom to have the candidate declare his willingness to serve before the campaign was launched. This was made particularly clear in the case of Matthew Hale in 1660, when Hale refused to take a clear-cut stand at the time of nomination, and appears to have lost the Oxford seat which he most likely would have gained if he had been more willing to take a risk. Monck however knew his own mind when he was approached, and quite firmly declined, after which Oxford went no further in entering his name in the poll. Still another example may be cited later from the Oxford election of 1661, when the desire was expressed that the court candidate, whose popularity was somewhat dubious, would declare his intention to serve if he succeeded in winning the seat.[27]

A repudiation of a university seat such as Monck's was indeed rare in the history of university representation. Sir Robert Naunton in 1620/1, to be sure, had hesitated about accepting the honour when he was elected, but merely because he feared the King's displeasure. It was only Sir Albertus Morton in the earlier period who had really seemed to prefer the seat of his native county to that of a university. Sir Francis Bacon, Sir Miles Sandys, Barnaby Gooch, Sir Francis Stewart—all had chosen to represent universities, when the opportunity was presented, just as Richard Cromwell and John Thurloe did, in the Protectorate. Matthew Hale, too, as noted above, had obviously yearned to serve again for Oxford, rather than for Gloucestershire. Of Selden, David Lloyd said that he regarded being Oxford's burgess as one of "the greatest honors of his life", although, if this were true, it is somewhat surprising that he made no special mention of it in the epitaph that he wrote for himself. Here all he said of his parliamentary service was that he had served in several Parliaments, "both in those which had a King, and which had none". But for the most part, throughout the whole century, the university seats seem to have been highly prized.[28]

In the discussion above concerning the question of obtaining the candidate's consent before nominating him, it may have been noted that there was a good deal of stress put upon unanimity. Both Thurloe's and Monck's elections were said to have been unanimous, when as a matter of strict fact, a count of "not ten dissenters" seems rather to have been the exact return in Monck's case. Selden's election also was said to have been unanimous, although, as noted in Chapter VI, there are reasons to doubt the statement. Likewise Edward Montague's correspondent tried to assure Montague that he would have a unanimous or near unanimous vote, if he consented to stand. Closely akin to this idea, is the notion that once a candidate's name was up he must not fail. It was this consideration that troubled Matthew Hale in 1660 when he hesitated over offering himself as Oxford's burgess, and it was on this assumption that Edward Montague's correspondent declared: "neither shall your name be once named *unless I am sure to carry it out of all question*".[29] This emphasis upon a foregone and unanimous conclusion was somewhat at variance with the tendency to vigorous and hard-fought contests that often characterized university parliamentary elections and was their chief distinction in contrast to the passivity of the closed boroughs.

Two more points in connection with electoral procedures may be noted in the history of this period. One is the size of the electorate. There are no recorded returns at either university for the years before 1640—except for a partial poll at Cambridge in 1614—and only a few figures for the middle years of the century, also at Cambridge. Therefore no comparisons are possible as to the size of the electorate in the middle period and in the early period. Between 1640 and 1660, however, it is clear that a considerable increase took place in the number of the voters at Cambridge, in spite of the disordered state of university education during the years of revolution. In 1640 the total number of votes for the Long Parliament was 493. Assuming that each man voted once for each of two candidates, and one man voted for one of the candidates only, this makes 247 electors. In 1660, there were 709 votes, making 355 electors, with one man again voting for only one of the candidates. The uneven numbers in these polls suggest that an elector was free to withhold his vote, if he wished to vote only for one candidate. This seems to have been generally permissible, except for one case—Oxford in 1678/9—when the Vice-Chancellor, according to Wood, forced the electors to cast all their suffrages. In the elections of 1656 at Cambridge and 1661 at Oxford, the great majority of the voters must have refused to vote, for the resultant figures—33 for Richard Cromwell and 20 for Sir Heneage Finch—are absurdly small. In the poll for John Thurloe in 1658/9, Thurloe's top score of 120 also makes the electorate far smaller than average. The question of the attendance of non-resident voters may account for some of the differences in numbers from election to election. This is touched upon in the letter to Edward Montague, where it is reported that "about 80 strangers" came to cast their votes for Chancellor St. John in 1660.[30] This may have been unusual during the Civil War and Interregnum, but it is probable that in normal times a considerable number of non-regents were also on hand for the university parliamentary elections, especially those men who lived in the local counties around each university.

It was in this same election of 1660 that an innovation seems to have been introduced in the reading of the results of the poll. According to a manuscript note quoted by Cooper:

> The Vice Chancellor & some of the Heads would have the loosers votes read first, & so it was done contrary to the antient Custom of the House in those Elections quia suffragia pauciora non sunt publienda sed supprimenda.

The writer of this note seems to be in error, for as early as 1614, in the second election ever held for parliamentary burgesses, the losing votes of Dr. Gooch and Dr. Corbet were revealed, and the trick that the presiding Vice-Chancellor tried to play upon the electorate lay exactly in the fact that he read the votes in the unofficial order, with Sir Francis Bacon and Sir Miles Sandys first, as if they were the defeated candidates.[31] Moreover, in the recorded polls, from 1640 on throughout the century, the votes are all recorded, losing and winning as well, and generally given in the order of "loosers votes" first. The same practice appears in the Oxford Archives. Whether the figures of the losers' votes were actually read aloud in the Senate, even though they were recorded in the Archives, may, of course, be a different matter. Then, too, it is possible that the practice of suppressing the losing votes was introduced during the Civil War and Interregnum because of the delicate political situation of the university. It is not surprising, if this is so, that the earlier system was resorted to with the return of free elections, but it is perhaps a little curious that this was done at a time when it would cast a certain reflection upon the university's own Chancellor, Chief Justice St. John, who was thus revealed as standing at the foot of the poll, with only half as many votes as those given for General Monck.

The fact that the university Chancellor should be a candidate for one of the university's seats is also an unusual feature of this election. One of the original principles of university representation laid down by Sir Edward Coke had been that the same man should never be at one time both Vice-Chancellor of the university and a university burgess. This rule had been generally adhered to throughout the fifty odd years since the grant of *De Burgensibus*, with the exception of the case of John Owen in 1654 and Clement Corbet, unsuccessful candidate in 1614. It would seem that the rule should apply with even more force against the candidacy of the university Chancellor, and indeed, except in this case of St. John, no suggestion appears ever to have been made that a Chancellor should stand.[32] Richard Cromwell, to be sure, was both Chancellor and university member in 1656/7, but not in relation to the same university, since he was elected Oxford's Chancellor while still parliamentary burgess for Cambridge. In normal times, of course, the university Chancellor was generally a great nobleman or archbishop who would not be eligible for or interested in a university seat.

NOTES FOR CHAPTER VIII

1. Any analysis of the characteristics of the university members of this period is rendered difficult by the confusion that exists as to who were really *bona-fide* university burgesses. This is not only because of the dubious position of Goddard and Sadler, as nominated members, but also because of the uncertain status of three other members-elect, Sir John Glanville, General Monck, and John Owen. From one point of view, Monck and Glanville might be included in the list on just as good grounds as Owen, since they were actually elected—at least there is clear evidence that Monck was. On the other hand, Monck, unlike Owen, declined the seat both before and after the election, and never tried to claim it after Parliament had opened; while Glanville's election is merely an unsubstantiated rumour, with no date attached to it, and therefore extremely dubious. For these reasons, Monck and Glanville are not counted in collecting material for the purposes of this chapter, but Goddard, Sadler, and Owen are included, even if somewhat arbitrarily.

    Another somewhat confusing point is the question of Lucas and Eden. When the Short Parliament is treated, as it is in this study, as the closing phase of the period of royal influence, since it was the last Parliament to have a major crown officer (Windebanke) in a university seat, this places Eden and Lucas both in the royal period and in the revolutionary period, and permits the facts of their careers to be used twice over, as material for analysis in retrospect of both periods. In the case of Eden this is certainly legitimate, for he had a respectable length of service in both periods, but it might be argued that for Lucas, a study of his career should be reserved for this later period only.

2. The material used in making the statistics for this chapter is chiefly drawn from the biographical references for the different burgesses as cited in Ch. VI and VII, and from the parliamentary records in the *Commons' Journal*, Burton's *Diary*, etc.

3. Cromwell's influence, of course, operated in the cases of Owen and Mills. Wood says that Sclater obtained his M.D. at Oxford in 1649 through the influence of Sir Thomas Widdrington, *Fasti*, II, 156.

4. Goddard's migration from university to university cannot be explained by the political situation, for his first move had been made before the Civil War. Sclater's migration, however, was probably caused by his ejection from his fellowship at Cambridge by the first parliamentary Visitors. He obtained his M.D., however, in 1649, when the Visitors were in control of Oxford, but for this, as indicated above, he had influential backing.

5. Cooper, III, 471.

6. If Richard Cromwell's candidacy as a burgess was not welcome at Cambridge in 1656, as the absence of the return and the small number of votes (33) would suggest, perhaps a created degree might have been granted with some difficulty. *Supra*, Ch. VII, p. 189. Oxford, however, the next year, was more regular in its proceedings, in making him a master of arts before electing him Chancellor.

7. *Supra*, Ch. III, pp. 63–5.

8. *Interim Report of the Commission on the House of Commons Personnel*, p. 33. See also Willson, *Privy Councillors*, p. 201 n.

9. Cooper, III, 470–2.

10. See below, Ch. XI, pp. 278, 280.

11. Appendix VI, below.

12. The phrase is Anthony Wood's. *A.O.*, III, 1135.

13. For Sir Thomas as the perfect ambassador—as Langbaine wrote in his epitaph, "the envoy of two Kings [James and Charles] to five Emperors and three Kings" —see Arthur Collins, *Letters and Memorials of State*, II, 640. For Langbaine's epitaph, see *A.O.*, III, 114–15.

14. As to Lucas, "he received some Splendour from his Family and reflected much more upon it", according to his biographer, Isaac Barrow. But this suggestion may be somewhat suspect as it appears only in Barrow's laudatory oration, delivered at the time of the latter's appointment to the Lucasian Professorship, where Barrow might be inclined to portray the founder's origins in the best light possible. On the other hand, Barrow, as a student and fellow at Cambridge, could have himself known Lucas, or at least have known persons who were well acquainted with him, so that the information after all may be quite authentic. In Lucas's will, Lucas is referred to as *armiger*. Barrow, p. xi; All Souls College Library MS., 208.

15. Collins, II, 542.

16. For the political positions of Roe, Hale, and Sclater, see *supra*, Ch. VI, pp. 158–63; Ch. VII, pp. 194–5, 197. For Wood on Clayton, see *Life and Times*, I, 366, and *supra*, Ch. VII, 201, 209, n. 94.

17. For estimates of Selden, see Lloyd, *Memoires*, p. 519; Clarendon, *Life* (1827), I, 35–6, 41; Whitelocke, IV, 156–7; Wood, *A.O.*, III, 366. For some modern writers' views of Selden, see W. K. Jordan, *Religious Toleration*, II, 480–2; Johnson, pp. 226, 342–3; Holdsworth, *English Law*, V, 407–12. Of Selden's contemporaries, some resented his liberal views on religion. See D'Ewes, *Autobiography*, I, 404–6; Fuller, *Worthies*, pt. 2, 110–11, representing criticism from the Puritan and the Anglican directions, respectively.

18. For earlier remarks on Eden and Goddard, see *supra*, Ch. VI, pp. 158, 168, and Ch. VII, pp. 186–7. For Mills, see Wood's account of the "dislike and detestation" Mills had of the extreme measures of the Visitors. Wood, Gutch, II, pt. ii, 612. For Owen, see Calamy, p. 157; Orme, p. 76; *A.O.*, IV, 102; Twells, I, 174, 223. For Lucas, see Barrow, p. x, and *supra*, Ch. VI, pp. 158, 169.

19. Fuller, *Worthies*, pt. 2, 110.
20. Jordan, II, 480–2; Singer, p. lxxvi. A contemporary verse paid tribute to Selden's ecclesiastical lore when a member of the Westminster Assembly: "There's more Divines in him then in all this, their Jewish Sanhedrim." (Quoted in *B.B.*, VI, pt. i, 3619n). It was characteristic of Selden that he was editing the *Fleta* in 1648, in the midst of the revolutionary crisis.
21. *A.O.*, III, 114–15. For Roe's MSS., see Wood, Gutch, II, pt. ii, 930; Lloyd, *State Worthies*, p. 1037. Roe was also interested in the selection of the Arundel Marbles, according to Collins, II, 541–2.
22. For some benefactions, see *supra*, pp. 134, 143, 174, and below, p. 262; Barratt, "The Library of John Selden", *Bodleian Library Record*, III (1951), 128–48, 208–13; Francis Blomefield, *Collectanea*, pp. 107, 110, 135; R. Willis and J. W. Clark, *Architectural History of Cambridge*, vols. I, II, *passim*. For the Harvard College connections of Bacon and Owen, see Samuel Eliot Morison, *Harvard College in the Seventeenth Century* (Cambridge, Mass., 1936), II, 367, 391 and n.
23. *Supra*, Ch. III, pp. 58–60; Ch. IV, p. 99; Appendix III, below.
24. Cooper, III, 470–2.
25. For Lenthall's campaign, see *supra*, Ch. VII, pp. 200–1. For treating, see below, Ch. XIII, p. 344.
26. For Whichcot's letter, see Cooper, III, 471. For the campaign of 1640, see above, Ch. VI, pp. 146–8. For Montague, see Appendix VI, below.
27. See references in n. 26, and *supra*, Ch. VII, pp. 198, 199–200, 201–2. For the election of 1661, see *C.S.P., Dom., Chas. II*, I (1660–1), 527. Naunton also may have been elected in 1620/1 without his consent and knowledge. *Supra*, Ch. IV, p. 97–8. See also below, Ch. XIII, p. 345.
28. For Selden, see Aiken, pp. 153–4; Lloyd, *Memoires*, p. 520. See also Lloyd's comment on Glanville's reputed election: "it was his honour that he was then chosen to represent an University in Parliament" (p. 585); and examples below, Ch. IX, p. 235, and Ch. XIII, pp. 344–5.
29. Appendix VI, below, and *supra*, Ch. VI, p. 174, n. 10; Ch. VII, pp. 193, 198, 199–200. For the number of contested elections in the period 1604–40, see *supra*, Ch. V, p. 142, n. 28.
30. Appendix VI. The Cambridge polls for 1640 and 1660 are printed in Cooper, III, 304, 477. For the Oxford polls of 1661 and 1678/9, see below, Ch. IX, p. 234, and Ch. X, pp. 269, 274, n. 27. For Richard Cromwell and Thurloe, see above, Ch. VII, pp. 189, 207, n. 49.
31. Cooper, III, 477; *supra*, Ch. III, p. 81.
32. Coke's statement is in Appendix I, item 5.

CHAPTER IX

THE UNIVERSITY MEMBERS IN THE CAVALIER PARLIAMENT

With the re-establishment of the monarchy, the universities took on once more their old political colouring, and became once again the fountain springs of Royalism and Anglicanism. All the university burgesses who served in the first Parliament summoned by Charles II, with one possible exception, came from strong royalist backgrounds. There were six of these burgesses in all, since the abnormally long duration of this Parliament—1660–78—allowed of two university by-elections. At Cambridge, there was Sir Richard Fanshawe, and his successor elected in 1666/7, Sir Charles Wheler, who had both served with the King in the Civil War, and Thomas Crouch, the Cambridge member re-elected from the Convention, who, during the parliamentary Visitations, had been ejected from his fellowship at King's. Oxford's three burgesses, surprisingly enough, had made a less spectacular show of royalist convictions, for both Lawrence Hyde and Thomas Thynne (the latter chosen in a by-election in 1673/4) had been too young to take part in the politics of the mid-century, while Sir Heneage Finch, Thynne's predecessor as burgess, had accepted the new dispensation of Cromwell, however reluctantly, and "minded his own business", as Wood put it, practising his profession peacefully and successfully in the law courts of the Commonwealth and Protectorate. All of these Oxford burgesses, however, like those of Cambridge, came from families of royalist sympathies, and one of them—the one who in the Interregnum had been the least attached to the monarchy of all, Sir Heneage Finch—was to become, from the moment of the Restoration, the chief spokesman of the Court in the House of Commons.

Finch's election at Oxford in 1660/1 was surrounded by some controversy, for he was not the university's first choice, and never seems to have been heartily liked there—at least to judge by the scathing comments of Anthony Wood. A series of letters to Joseph Williamson, a former member of Queen's College, now high in the royal administration, reveals the political undercurrents that were in operation at this election. As early as the preceding September (1660), Lord Clarendon, now both Chancellor of the Realm and Chancellor of the university, had recommended his own son, Lawrence Hyde—often known as "Lory"—and Sir Heneage Finch to be members of the new Parliament.

This double recommendation threw the university into some dismay, for other candidates were being considered. One of them was Dr. Thomas Clayton, Oxford's member then sitting in the Convention; the other, a certain Mr. Nicholas, who appears to have been John, the son of Sir Edward Nicholas, the Secretary of State.[1]

This campaign opened in September and lasted throughout the winter. In February, Dr. Clayton was still expecting to run, placing his hopes, perhaps, in the influence exerted by his brother-in-law, Sir Charles Cotterell, then secretary to the Duke of Gloucester.[2] Clayton also declared himself willing to support Nicholas as a colleague.[3] But Clayton's chances were slim in the face of the Chancellor's recommendations. Nathaniel Chyles of Magdalen College had written as much to Williamson when the Chancellor's letter had been first released in September: "This makes a greater rub than Dr. Clayton."[4] And so it did. Nevertheless, Clayton refused to retire until within a month of the poll.

At first the university had hoped that the Chancellor would not contest the choice of Nicholas or Clayton, but withdraw his nomination of Sir Heneage Finch, and rest content with the choice of his son Lawrence, then only twenty, and as yet no great advantage to the university—as Wood said, merely "a coxcomb" and "accounted then nobody in the House", and chosen only "to please the father".[5] But the Chancellor showed no sign of reconsidering, although it was thought that Sir Heneage need not be returned by Oxford, since he had a good chance of being elected by two other constituencies.

Finch had, however, so it seemed, support at the university apart from that offered by the Chancellor. Indeed, according to Daniel Escott of Wadham College, another of Williamson's correspondents, Finch owed his very nomination to certain Heads who wished to oppose Nicholas, and for this reason had put the Chancellor up to nominating Finch, "though", wrote Escott, "his [the Chancellor's] desire was to have some eminent person to assist his son, who is young and ignorant".[6] The implication of this remark shows an unfair prejudice against Finch, for Escott must have known that Finch had already gained eminence both as a member of the Convention and as a lawyer. Indeed, as Solicitor-General he was just about to enter upon the trial of the Regicides. But Escott was perhaps too strenuous a supporter of Nicholas to want to do Finch justice.

The Nicholas campaign gathered strength throughout February, despite the competition of Finch and Clayton. Promises of support were gathered in, and Dr. Thomas Lamplugh, Williamson's old tutor and another Queen's man, reported that Nicholas's own college, Queen's,

would be "zealous for him".[7] Another letter from Nathaniel Chyles a
few days later also engaged to pursue Nicholas's interest, "but with as
little animosity as may be".[8] Pressure from outside, it seems, was
getting stronger; the next day Chyles wrote:

> The Heads of houses have resolved to suspend their engagements about
> the election . . . till they know the mind of the Bishops of London and
> Winchester. The President called the college together, and advised them to
> no party-making for one or another, till they knew who stood, so that the
> University may avoid friction, and go unanimously together in choosing
> the fittest person.

Unlike Dr. Lamplugh, who had not wanted Nicholas's candidacy to be
announced until he was sure of votes, Chyles was eager to have it
"publicly known that Mr. Nicholas stands".[9] Another correspondent
wrote Williamson the following day that one of Nicholas's supporters
had been "engaged all week in canvassing", but that letters had come
from the Chancellor "wishing none to engage their votes, as persons of
quality would soon appear".[10] The old conflict between court influence
and the free will of the university had begun once more.

The next letters made this clearer. First a rumour suddenly arose
that Nicholas had withdrawn. A letter was circulated with the comment
that "Mr. Nicholas is so modest a man that he will never oppose Sir
Hen. F.". This was intended doubtless as a strong hint to Nicholas and
his party that their cause was hopeless, but Nicholas's supporters did
not agree, for one of them wrote, "If it comes to a canvass there will be
a notable struggling."[11] Daniel Escott, seemingly unaware of some of
the checks being placed on Nicholas's party, wondered why "they"—
probably meaning Nicholas's managers—were "so behind in engaging
the heads of colleges for Mr. Nicholas". This writer went on to say,
however, that he realized "how great a part" of the university were
"enslaved to their governors", and boldly proposed a meeting of
Nicholas's supporters, "each to report on the votes secured, so as to
know their strength". Escott also informed Williamson that he had
also "stayed a report spread by design that Nicholas had desisted".[12]

Two days later, however, 4 March, the Vice-Chancellor confirmed
this report by announcing that both Dr. Clayton and Mr. Nicholas
had renounced their pretensions to the burgess-ship. This was a bitter
disappointment to Nicholas's followers for they had been confident of
his success, in spite of the enthusiasm of the Heads for Finch. Daniel
Escott expressed the opinion of his colleagues when he said that the
Heads of houses had outwitted them,"the request for suspending engagements being to take off Mr. Nicholas whose election they [i.e. the Heads]
were not able to prevent". There had even been some attempts to

intimidate, through letters to the Chancellor, complaining of those who canvassed against Finch after he had been recommended, but the Nicholas supporters had tried to free themselves of this accusation by asking their friends not to commit themselves *against* Finch, but simply to withhold promises for the second place until it was certain that Nicholas had withdrawn.[13]

One of the factors that accounts for the vigour of the university's opposition to Finch in the face of all this pressure was a matter of privilege. As Escott had written, the university, "though willing to gratify the chancellor in the choice of his son, ... think they should have been left free to choose the other burgess".[14] This was the time-honoured understanding, often referred to in earlier pages, the compromise which never had been infringed upon, it would seem, except when Pembroke tried to force his secretary, Michael Oldisworth, along with Sir Henry Marten, upon Oxford University back in 1628.[15]

But in 1661 the Chancellor's wishes carried more weight. A second letter in favour of Finch arrived about a week after the announcement of Nicholas's withdrawal. In this letter Clarendon protested his wish to do the university service, and to increase the number of their friends and lessen the "power of those whoe by ye folly and wickednesses of ye late ill times, have contracted a Prejudice to learning, and learned Men". For burgesses they should have persons "of great and eminent Ability as well as of great affection and zeale", and therefore he considered it his duty to name his good friend Sir Heneage Finch, as one who had "had his education among you", and who had since "upon all occasions deserved soe well of ye Commonwealthe of learning". Finch would, the Chancellor predicted, discharge this trust "with great fruit and advantage to you"—a prediction that was not fulfilled, at least in the judgment of Anthony Wood, as will appear later in this chapter.[16]

This letter of Clarendon's was read at the Convocation held 1 April, and if there were any still hoping to place Nicholas's name in nomination this must have silenced them, for "the Chancellor's son and the Knight Solicitor", as Escott called them, were promptly chosen burgesses without competitors. Escott, however, noted that the greater part of the body refused to vote, only twenty votes in Finch's favour being given, with some even daring to give *non-placets*.[17]

Thus Oxford's first parliamentary election under the Restoration saw outside influence firmly re-established, and the old struggle between free choice and arbitrary nomination once more revived. Considering that the whole nation was at this moment in the throes of a reaction in favour of authority and tradition, it is probably remarkable that the opposition was as vigorous as it was.

At Cambridge there was no such furore, so far as the records reveal. The candidates there were elected promptly and without controversy —indeed the Cambridge University members were the first in all England to be elected and returned for the new Parliament.[18] Here the burgesses were Thomas Crouch, the university's representative in the previous House, and Sir Richard Fanshawe, the King's Latin Secretary and Master of Requests, soon to be named ambassador to Portugal and Spain. Of this election, Sir Richard's wife gave a considerable account:

> They chose him of their unanimous desire, without my husband's knowledge until the Vice Chancellor sent him in a letter by an officer of theirs to his house in Lincoln's Inn Fields, to acquaint him with it.
>
> He had fortune to be the first chosen and the first returned Member of the Commons House of Parliament in England, after the King came home; and this cost him no more than a letter of thanks, and two braces of bucks, and twenty broad pieces of gold to buy them wine.

Lady Fanshawe also recorded with dismay the fact that she had forgotten to make note of this distinction among the signal achievements of her husband's life as listed on his tombstone, "which fault", she wrote, "I do mean to repair by adding this inscription at the bottom of the tombstone, if God permit". Her design was carried out, for as the monument now stands, the notation, *Pro Academia Cantabrigiensi Burgensis* stands forth as the final line of the inscription.[19]

However grateful Sir Richard may have been for his Cambridge seat, he occupied it very little, and he had very little opportunity to do his constituents or the nation any service as a member of Parliament. He was made a member of the powerful Committee of Election and Privilege upon the opening of the session, 8 May 1661, and again in 1662/3, but during most of the sessions of the early 1660's, Fanshawe was abroad as the King's ambassador to Spain and Portugal, arranging the marriage with Catherine of Braganza and concluding Cromwell's war with Spain. His record in the House is almost a blank, since he served on only three committees other than the Committee of Privilege, all in the early weeks of the opening session of 1661.[20] What contribution he made to justify Cambridge's choice of him consisted only of the prestige he had gained through his literary work as poet and his brilliant reputation as a diplomat.[21]

Of the four university members elected in 1661, only Sir Heneage Finch could approach Fanshawe in distinction. His legal career from the time he had first entered the Inner Temple, both as legal scholar and as practising lawyer, was notable, and in the Convention Parliament he had come forward as the chief advocate of the prerogative and the

Established Church—one of the more solid favourites of the Court, early honoured with a knighthood and a baronetcy, as well as with the office of King's Solicitor. Later he became Attorney-General, and finally Lord Chancellor and Earl of Nottingham.[22] Sir William Holdsworth calls him "the one really great chancellor of the later seventeenth century", "a lawyer who mastered the technical learning of the law without being mastered by it", and "almost the only politician of the period who retained throughout his career the confidence of both king and Parliament".[23]

The other two university burgesses of 1661, as we have seen, were of no such stature. Lawrence Hyde was only twenty, "young and ignorant", though, as Anthony Wood wrote, "he later became wise"—which meant, in Wood's view, that he became one of the leaders of the Tory reaction and, as Earl of Rochester, in the last two decades of the century, a peer to be reckoned with.[24] Thomas Crouch was always of modest repute—so modest indeed that little attention has been paid to his career by the biographers, and a true impression of his importance can only be gained by paging through the *Journal* of the House. He had been, however, Cambridge's member in the previous Parliament, so he was not without parliamentary experience and the confidence of his constituency.

As zealous Royalists, the university members did not escape the attention of the pamphleteers and satirists of the period who pilloried those parliament men who belonged to the Court's sphere of influence. There are at least four different attacks of this sort which include reference to one or more of the university burgesses—three in pamphlet form and one in manuscript. These attacks consist of lists of names accompanied by jotted notes calling attention to the scandals or supposed scandals associated with each man. In the face of this barrage, Sir Heneage Finch, strangely enough, got off very lightly. He was named on only one of the lists, and was simply listed there without derogatory comment. If he fared so well, it is probably a tribute to his financial integrity and his just conduct as a Chancellor, rather than a failure on the part of the satirist to recognize the reactionary quality of his politics.[25] In the case of Lawrence Hyde, on the contrary, the attacks were made on the grounds that Hyde was a royal parasite. The pamphlet, "A Seasonable Argument . . . to petition for a New Parliament: or a List of the Principal Labourers in the Great Design of Popery and Arbitrary Power", put him down as "Master of the Robes to the King, has had in Boons 20,000l.",[26] while the *Flagellum Parliamentarium* noted that Hyde was Master of the Robes and had had given him crown lands to the value of £1000 per year.[27] All Hyde's biographers agree that he was notoriously mercenary, but excuse is made for him on the grounds that Clarendon's sons had had little financial aid from their father, and were in real need of money.[28]

Thomas Crouch was not mentioned on any of the printed lists, but in a manuscript in the British Museum entitled, "A List of those Members in Parliament who are by Pencion or Place, obliged to vote according to the Court's Desire or Interest", he is described somewhat theatrically as "Mr. of Arts, the Priests' mad Jade, who rides without Fear or Will, preferred by the Court, unto his Interest hee hath long since beene matriculated."[29] Crouch's first colleague, Sir Richard Fanshawe, escaped notice entirely—perhaps because of his early death—but his successor, Sir Charles Wheler, as will be seen later, received distinctly unfavourable treatment. Finch's successor at Oxford, Thomas Thynne, like Fanshawe, seems to have gone unnoticed.[30]

Such university members as these, most of them with ardent Anglican and ultra-royalist opinions, were doubtless more at home in the Cavalier Parliament than any university member had been in any House for a long time, except perhaps Nathaniel Fiennes in the Protectorate. Of them all, Sir Heneage Finch was the most prominent politically. His prominence, indeed, among all the members of the House was very great. As Solicitor-General, recent prosecutor of the Regicides, chief spokesman of the Court, eloquent and learned in the law, he soon became the leader of the Cavalier forces. His voice was seldom lacking in an important debate, his name seldom missing from a committee list of major consequence. He was a chief manager of many conferences with the Lords, a chief reporter from such conferences, and a reporter from various committees of the House. Unfortunately, perhaps, the full measure of his worth cannot be taken, because of the scantiness of the records during the early years of the Cavalier Parliament.[31]

Always a staunch supporter of the Established Church, Finch was especially zealous during the reaction against Catholicism that arose in 1662/3 after Charles's first Declaration of Indulgence, and in the steps leading up to the various bills that comprised the Clarendon Code, as well as the Quaker Bill and the act regulating the press.[32] His name is found on all kinds of committees, but especially those dealing with finance—he was eager to get the King supply, interested in the excise taxes and foreign trade—and of course, because of his great learning, was often called upon for committee service on bills involving legal questions. In debate, too, his ability to clear up legal points, and his lawyer's precision of thought, were probably useful contributions to the proceedings of the House.

In all this parliamentary activity, Finch seems to have taken on little or no business that was directly related to the universities. However, the strong Anglican position that he took in enacting the Clarendon Code was no doubt especially pleasing to most of his constituents. Lord Campbell, indeed, says that Oxford's satisfaction with the Five Mile Act—which would tend to eliminate all the dissenting clergy from the neighbourhood of the university—was so great that it led to Finch's being granted the degree of D.C.L. while Parliament was meeting at Oxford in 1665.[33] Finch was also on some of the committees that worked at different times on the hearth tax,[34] but here his concern may have been rather the securing of a good yield for the Crown rather than serving the wishes of his constituency. At least, as will be seen later, on this point his action was not pleasing to the university, and he came far from fulfilling the promises made in his behalf by the Earl of Clarendon's letter of recommendation. His interest in the printing bill, however, may have been more to their liking.

To the Earl himself, however, Finch's record must have been on the whole satisfactory, as in harmony with old Cavalier principles. Moreover, when the crisis of Clarendon's impeachment came, Sir Heneage seems to have done what he could to check the Commons' violence.[35] Nevertheless, he was probably relieved to have the question settled, for his exclamation seems to indicate as much, when he heard that Clarendon had fled: "If Clarendon is gone, fare him well."[36]

It was chiefly in defence of the King's interests that Finch exerted himself, but he also tried to protect the bishops from having to pay a poll tax, and the House of Commons from the encroachment of the House of Lords. "If we have no Liberties but what the Lords will allow," he protested in the Skinner case, "surely they are but small."[37] And when the Lords tried to interfere in the rates of customs duties, Finch stood firm and declared, "We must never depart from our power of raising or lowering." For his vigorous part in this controversy with the Lords, Sir Heneage presently received a vote of thanks from the Commons for having defended their rights so successfully. But it seems obvious from an examination of all of Finch's speeches on this subject that his real interest in the controversy stemmed from a fear that allowing the Lords a share in setting rates might lead, at least for the moment, to a reduction in the royal revenue.[38]

It was characteristic of Finch's conduct in Parliament that he should examine every issue from the angle of the King's interest. Even during the heated debates over the King's Declaration of Indulgence in 1672/3, Finch's respect for the prerogative tempered his rigid Anglicanism enough to allow him to make some defence of the dispensing power and to protest against the wording of the Commons' Address to the Crown, as well as to object to some of the more stringent provisions proposed in the Test Act.[39] Certainly, the Crown lost a faithful adherent in a body where every year it had fewer and fewer supporters, when Sir Heneage Finch gave up his university seat to become Lord Keeper in 1673.

There were no other university members in this Long Parliament who could be compared with Finch, in industry and attention to duty, except Thomas Crouch, and perhaps Sir Charles Wheler. As to Crouch, no one who carefully examines the *Journal* of the House during this period can fail to be impressed with his parliamentary activity. His name appears on all the committees, important and unimportant, and though he did not speak so often nor with such prestige as Finch, there is scarcely a page of the report or a daily entry in which he is not mentioned. Whether this means that he was really a man of ability and energy, whose qualities were recognized by his colleagues in the House, or whether he was just one of those hard-working busybodies who like to have a finger in every pie and who manage to get themselves noticed by their busyness, it would perhaps be impossible to say. But certainly if Thomas Crouch did half of the work assigned to him in committees, Cambridge did not elect him in vain, so far as the general affairs of the country were concerned. And one is inclined to conclude, as year after year saw him serving on more and more committees, that he must have been not only a man of energy and widespread interests, but also one with something above the average in speaking ability and leadership. This conclusion is based upon the fact that he early became the spokesman of committees in reporting bills to the House and in taking part in the preparation and conduct of conferences with the Lords. His first reports began in the opening session of the Parliament, quite characteristically on the bill for suppressing the Quakers.[40] In the opening session, too, he was first assigned to carry a bill to the Lords—the Quaker bill—and in the session ending May 1662 he made six reports, carried one bill to the Lords, and acted in connection with the conference with the Lords on the printing bill.[41] These activities continued throughout the life of the Parliament.

Foremost among his interests, as was proper for a university member, was the security of the Established Church. He was on the committees for all the more important church bills, such as the Act of Uniformity, the bill for restoring the clergy to civil office, the Quaker bill, the Conventicle Acts, the bill for regulating the press, the Corporation Act, the bill for the "Ease of Protestant Dissenters", and so on; not to speak of innumerable minor bills on advowsons, pluralities, "the better observation of the Lord's Day, etc.[42] Some of these issues may have had a university angle, as when advowsons or endowments were the property of various colleges, but this is not apparent from the *Journal's* records, except in the case of the printing bill, where the rights of the university presses were involved.

Thomas Crouch's speeches were by no means so notable as his committee service. At least they did not impress his contemporaries sufficiently to result in very satisfactory reports in the various parliamentary diaries. In Grey, Milward, and Dering, they survive for the most part in disjointed scraps, the bearing of which is not always clear. Generally they are found in debates pertaining to religion, especially to the Conventicle Act. The only period where they seem to have any sort of continuity is during the discussion of the Declaration of Indulgence in 1672/3. Crouch was especially concerned with the bill for the ease of Protestant Dissenters that was to be offered to the King as a kind of substitute for the Indulgence. Crouch, as became "the Priests' mad Jade", was not entirely happy over such a concession. He was particularly concerned, among other things, over where Dissenters should be allowed to meet. Certainly they were not wanted at Cambridge, he protested, while Sir William Coventry, possibly in a teasing humour, replied that he thought that would be a good idea, since the university would have the opportunity to convert them. Crouch stubbornly held to his point. "They [the Dissenters?] will be disturbed by the youths there with disputing", he maintained somewhat confusedly, and ended with his original declaration, that he would not want to have them at the university.[43] Strangely enough—though not so strange if he was a true courtier—Crouch was silent on the Test Act, though appointed to the committee to prepare the bill and plan the conference on it with the Lords.[44] Likewise during the Popish Plot, he made no speech, but contented himself with committee service connected with the investigation of the murder of Sir Edmundbury Godfrey, and with the laying of further disabilities upon Catholics.[45] The most curious assignment he received at this time was "to inquire into the Causes of the late Noises of Knocking that have been heard in the Night in the Old Palace Yard . . . and as to Papists living nearby".[46] But none of these alarms was sufficient to inspire him to a speech.

Church issues were not Crouch's only concern, for he also served on many committees on economic matters. Indeed a mere listing of these committees reflects very plainly the commercial and industrial trends of the day, from the law forbidding the importing of "fat live cattle" and the exportation of wool and wool fells, to the one proposed for the regulation of hackney coaches in Westminster; not to speak of bills concerning highways, bridges, enclosures, the "better regulation" of the goldsmiths' trade, the prevention of fraud in the making of gold and silver lace, the reforming of abuses in the packing and weighing of butter, the draining of the Fens, the preservation of fisheries, the sowing and planting of flax, the decline of the clothiers' trade, and the wearing of woollens for burial.

Private bills, also—reflecting the shifts in land ownership resulting from the upheavals of the Civil War—took up a good deal of Crouch's time; and he served on a surprising number of legal committees, for a man without formal legal training. He served on fewer revenue committees, and the absence of his name from committees having to do with foreign affairs is most conspicuous. On matters affecting the general procedure of the House, on the contrary, he was fairly active, being assigned on various and repeated occasions the duty of acting as teller, surveying the *Journal*, and taking stock of outstanding bills in order to assign them a place on the parliamentary calendar. Thus it can be seen that Thomas Crouch, if not a brilliant member of Parliament, was nevertheless an earnest and hard-working one, not entirely unworthy of his constituency, and understandably in harmony with its reactionary views on politics and religion.

In contrast to the activity of Thomas Crouch, and Sir Heneage Finch, Lawrence Hyde presents a more disappointing picture. "Young and ignorant", when elected, Hyde had little or nothing to offer the House besides the prestige of his father's name. He was accounted studious as a youth, and by temperament worthy of his honorary M.A. Wood, perhaps too generously, rated him as "equal to the first employments in the State".[47] But his talents took some time to ripen, and, according to Burnet, they never included the ability to speak gracefully.[48] Out of courtesy to his father—or more probably to the university—he was named to the Committee of Privilege at the opening of Parliament in 1661, and to fifteen committees during the first session. This record was continued, with Hyde's name appearing on a respectable number of committees each session throughout the 1660's No special subject seems to have engaged his efforts—the usual university and church interests, the usual private bills and trade bills, made up the matter to which he was invited to give his attention. Curiously enough in view of his later concern with foreign affairs, he never served on any committee dealing with foreign relations. He seems to have been a faithful attendant in the House and twice served as teller for a division,[49] but up to 1667 he made no speeches, reported no bills, entered upon no conferences, so far as the *Journal* reveals.[50]

It was the impeachment of his father that at last introduced Lawrence Hyde to more active participation in the proceedings of the House.

The speech he made on this occasion is commented upon both by the *Biographia Britannica* and by Hyde's latest biographer, Margaret Yates, but the appraisals put upon Hyde's stand by the two authors differ. To the editor of the *Biographia Britannica*, Hyde's defence of his father was conducted "with great modesty and resolution"; to Miss Yates, it was lukewarm and time serving.[51] It is possible that Miss Yates is a little too severe. Despite the heat of hasty debate, such an appeal as this to reason and to evidence might have proved effective:

> I shall endeavour to shew myself not so much a son of the earl of Claren-don as a Member of this House; and I assure you that if he shall be found guilty, no man shall appear more against him than I; if not, I hope everyone will be for him as much as I; let every man upon his conscience think what of this charge is true, for I believe that if one Article be proved, he will own himself guilty of all.[52]

Coming from Lawrence Hyde, a man later known for the hotness of his temper and the violence of his language, such restraint and com-posure is surprising, to say the least.[53] Nevertheless, as Miss Yates does not fail to point out, Hyde's contemporaries do not seem to have blamed him in any way for his conduct. Indeed, they even admired the stand he took a few days later, when he declared that, rather than let the question of the Earl's impeachment divide the two Houses, he would be in favour of having Clarendon brought to trial. Burnet, however, noted—though he elsewhere remarked that Hyde passed "for a sincere man" and seemed "to have too much heat to be false"—that Hyde was also thought "the smoothest man in the court", and that "during all the disputes concerning his father, he made his court so dextrously that no resentment ever appeared on that head".[54]

After this momentary prominence in the House, Lawrence Hyde subsided again into silence, and his name is missing from the pages of Grey for volume after volume, and in the *Commons' Journal* appears only intermittently. His interests perhaps became more and more involved in foreign affairs, as he was absent on diplomatic missions much of the time from June 1676 until September 1678, and it is curious to note that in his correspondence with his brother during the years 1677–8, he never once alluded to his constituency of Oxford or to his activities as a parliament man in that relation.[55] Miss Yates also points out that when he resumed his seat in the intervals between his foreign service, he never volunteered any information or expressed any opinion based upon his experience, as he might have been expected to do, coming fresh from the areas of controversy. This, she implies, may have been owing quite as much to "the discretion of the courtier" as to the "modesty of the mediocre orator", for by this time Hyde had begun to have some footing at Court, and was well on the way to becoming a "Young Chit" and later, Earl of Rochester.[56]

Hyde's last speech as Oxford's representative was in line with this new turn of his fortunes. It was to defend the Duke of York, his brother-in-law, who had always been his patron, and was now under attack by the Exclusionists. This time, however, Hyde's efforts had a great semblance of sincerity, and subjected his career to a greater risk— that is, if the Exclusionists had triumphed—than had been the case with his defence of his father eleven years before. He spoke with firmness, and with the kind of indignation that his reputation for hot language warranted, though he was, of course, quite mistaken in his grasp of the situation. He started out by stating that he could assure the House— "I think I have grounds to say"—that the Duke would not interfere with any measures they might take to secure the Protestant religion, and urged them to have the patience to wait and see; he declared that it was not true that the Duke favoured France; and ended with a flourishing appeal to sentiment: "the two sons of the martyred King, the only surviving sons, now to be torn from one another by such a Parliament as this! I speak for the King and not for the Duke." Thus he ended his service as Oxford's burgess on a strong High Tory note that should have been not at all unsatisfactory to the university.[57]

Two university by-elections were held during Charles II's long Parliament—one, 8 March 1666/7 to replace Sir Richard Fanshawe, Cambridge's member who died in Spain; the other, in January 1673/4 to replace Sir Heneage Finch, who had become Lord Keeper.[58] The Cambridge election was contested, but no details are available about the campaign. One of the candidates was Sir Charles Wheler, a Royalist in the Civil War, who had recently distinguished himself by his public spirit in assisting the people of London during the Plague and the Fire.[59] His opponent was Christopher Wren, the famous architect, Savilian Professor of Astronomy at Oxford, but also LL.D. from Cambridge, who was then entering upon his programme of rebuilding the churches of London. The poll was very close, Wheler winning over Wren, 118 to 112.[60]

Encouraged perhaps by his near success at Cambridge, Wren (now Sir Christopher), ran again in 1673/4 at his own University of Oxford in the by-election that was ordered to fill the seat of Sir Heneage Finch. Anthony Wood has one of his characteristically lively accounts of this campaign. The other candidates besides Wren were Dr. John Edisbury of Brasenose, D.C.L.; Dr. Thomas Boucher of All Souls, Regius Professor of Civil Law; and Mr. Thomas Thynne, a "pretty gentleman" of good family who had been envoy to Sweden in 1666-7. There was also a fourth candidate, Sir George Croke, whose candidacy was not pushed vigorously enough to make any impression.[61]

Anthony Wood's venom on this occasion was directed equally at Dr. Edisbury and Mr. Thynne. Edisbury, said Wood scornfully, stood for the election "like an impudent fellow; he stood to be king of Poland", meaning perhaps that his chances of election by the Oxford Convocation were no better than they would have been by the Polish Diet. In another place also Wood referred to Edisbury's pretensions with the same scorn: "being soundly jeered and laughed at for an impudent fellow (he) desisted".[62]

The withdrawal of Edisbury left the field to Sir Christopher Wren, Dr. Boucher, and Thomas Thynne. Wren was Wood's candidate, but Wren's solid qualities could not compete with the high-powered campaign put on by Mr. Thynne, which was calculated to win the votes of those whom Wood called the "pot-men". Wood wrote bitterly of Wren's difficulties:

> [his] paines about the Theater and his admirable skill in mathematick the pot-men slighted, and preferred Mr. Thyn before him because he kept . . . an open table for the M(aste)rs for a week or ten dayes and went to the coffee houses to court stinking breaths and to the common chambers. Sir Christopher Wren was not so expert this way.

The result was that Thynne won easily, with 203 votes to Wren's 125, while Boucher had only 20, and Sir George Croke, "very few votes, so few that the generality of M(aste)rs did not know that he stood".[63]

Thynne's contribution to the activities of Parliament was very slight. In his first session he served on five committees. In later sessions he acted as a teller three times, and continued to serve on scattered committees, including one on chimney money, the universities' perennial concern at this period.[64] It was not until his fourth session, however, in February 1676/7, that he gained a place on the powerful Committee of Privilege, usually given a university member from the very beginning.[65] Throughout his whole term of office, he never made a speech so far as the records go, and the only reference to him to be found in Grey is a somewhat uncertain one, when there was a stormy dispute over a division that lasted for half an hour and grew especially dangerous when some "young gallants, as Mr. Thynne, and others", leaped over the seats to join forces with two quarrelling members. The dubious quality of this reference, as in all the references to Thynne in the *Journal*, lies in the fact that there is always the possibility that the Thynne cited is not Oxford's Thynne at all, but instead his cousin, "Tom of Ten Thousand", who was serving at the same time for Wiltshire.[66]

Even if the possibility of such a confusion did not exist it would still be difficult to tell much about Thynne's political views merely from the division lists when he served as teller. His own letters written to Lord Halifax in 1679 after he had ceased to be Oxford's burgess provide a better clue. He was distinctly not a High Tory of the usual Oxford cast.

> I have sate in two Parlts. [he wrote] and have had ye hard fortune in ye first to displease the Court, in ye second ye Country. Whereby I perceive those who act by principle are not fit for Parlts., and therefore resolve to be quiet now.[67]

Just what he had done to displease the Court is not clear, but he seems to have been one of those more moderate Tories who joined the Country party in opposition to Danby, and yet were opposed to Shaftesbury and the Exclusionists. The kind of men Thynne hoped to see elected in 1679 were such as he predicted for Warwickshire—"not one unreasonable man—not Danbyites—nor fanaticks".[68] Moreover, in another letter written in May 1677 when he was still member for Oxford, Thynne wrote, in connection with the debate over naming Holland as an ally, in terms that showed he was not of the Court party.[69] It may be that what Thynne had done to displease the Court was connected with his parliamentary service during the agitation over the Popish Plot—although activity of this sort, if clearly in favour of the Exclusionists, would have been characteristic of his cousin Thomas Thynne, rather than of himself.[70]

But whatever the stand of Oxford's Thomas Thynne, it is clear at least that, despite his silence as a debater, he had considerable serious interest in political matters. Indeed, Lord Halifax's brother, Henry Savile, in a letter to Thynne's brother in June 1679, spoke of Thynne as something of a political authority:

> I wish I had known some of your brother Tho's politick reflections before hee left the towne, for they would have given me some light into ye present matters which are now grown so terrible obscure to my poor capacity that I can fathom noe thing you doe.[71]

Oxford's burgess was therefore not entirely unworthy of his seat, as far as interest and leadership go, even though he was silent in the debates, and somewhat less rigidly Tory than his constituency probably desired.[72]

If Thynne had been unusually silent while he was a university member, Sir Charles Wheler, the other burgess chosen at a university by-election, was quite otherwise. He was active and talkative, and was called to order more than once for his hasty words.[73] His name is spread widely through the records of the period, both as speaker and as committee member. He stood stoutly for the rights of the King as against Parliament, for the rights of the Commons against the Lords, for the Church of England as against Dissenters and Papists. His words often have a plausible and common-sense sound that suggests he may have played a useful part in the House in defining issues and calming passions, but at other times the suspicion arises that his plausibility was only a cover for advancing the most reactionary interests of Church and Crown. This suspicion is given weight by Wheler's record as a pensioner.[74]

He was an old-time Royalist of the Civil War—it was he who had carried the university plate from Cambridge to the King in 1642—and he still held a commission in the Foot Guards.[75] His election to the House in 1667 was his first appearance in Parliament. He arrived just in time to take part in the impeachment of Clarendon, and he immediately took sides and joined battle with all the vigour proper for a Captain of Foot. Nothing unfavourable that was said of the Lord Chancellor at this time was too much for Wheler to believe, and after a series of fiery speeches, he finished off triumphantly as teller for the Yeas in the vote on impeachment.[76] Later he worked on the bill for Clarendon's banishment.[77]

From that time on, he was chiefly prominent in connection with the debates and committee work involved in the Conventicle Act, and with proposals for the grant of supply.[78] His attitude in regard to the Dissenters is not always clear. As a strict High Churchman, he might be expected to take a stronger stand than he sometimes seems to have taken. For example, in the debates of February and March 1667/8 he professed "a great kindness for the Presbyterians" because of their part in the Restoration. This attitude caused Sir John Milward to express considerable surprise, especially when Wheler went on to criticize the church courts. "Such an invective speech was not expected . . ." wrote Milward, "he [Wheler] being accounted by some good men a severe son of the church." Other descriptive terms used by Milward for Wheler's speeches were "unexpected and unnecessary", "unpleasing", and "impertinent" (that is, off the subject).[79] Wheler's stand may possibly be explained by some temporary inclination of the Court to support plans for a "comprehension". At least, he was much against the Presbyterians only two years later. Likewise, his subsequent moments of charity towards the Catholics were probably also the result of the Court's current policy.[80]

Nothing striking occurred in Wheler's career for several years, except his appointment in 1671 as Governor of St. Kitts in the Leeward Islands, which led ultimately to his being brought into the King's bad graces. Sir Charles, in the beginning, was apparently not particularly well pleased with this appointment, and regarded it with some mis-giving.[81] As it turned out, he was right. Although he seems to have done well enough in carrying out the diplomatic part of his assignment, his governorship as a whole was not successful. He was recalled the follow-ing February 1671/2, and the royal displeasure was so great that he lost his prized position as Captain of the Foot Guards.[82]

Parliament had been prorogued during this entire interval and for a year thereafter, so Cambridge lost nothing by Wheler's stay in the West Indies. When the new session opened in February 1672/3 he took up his duties on the Committee of Privilege,[83] but he remained strangely subdued throughout the whole term—which lasted, however, only about eight weeks. He served on only two committees besides the Committee of Privilege, and took no noticeable part in the drawing up of the Test Act. It was not until the Parliament was resumed in October 1673 that he began to be his usual jaunty self. For a parliament man who was supposed to belong to the Court party, the subject upon which he chose to re-enter the lists is a somewhat surprising one. Perhaps he was still smarting under the rebuffs he had received, or, as seems more likely, the Declaration of Indulgence had aroused his inveterate Anglicanism. At any rate, when the Duke of York's marriage with Mary of Modena was made into an issue, Wheler seems to have taken the side of the opposition in insisting that the marriage was a legitimate concern of Parliament, since it involved the question of Popery.[84]

Again, when the Cabal was under fire in 1673/4, although he defended Buckingham and Lauderdale, it was a different matter in the case of Arlington. Once convinced that Arlington leaned towards Rome, Wheler was one of his fiercest prosecutors, and this, too, though he had reasons for personal gratitude to Arlington, which he readily acknow-ledged. Nevertheless, so he went on to declare, though he "must speak tenderly of Lord Arlington", he could not let private considerations silence him.[85] And here Sir Charles apparently mentioned his con-stituency for the first and only time in all his eleven years of representa-tion. He pointed out that, serving for one of the universities as he did, he was more than ordinarily obliged to speak out on such a subject as the danger of Popery.[86] And speak out he did, over and over again, driving the charges home[87] and most emphatically pointing out that when Arlington defended himself against the accusation of Popery, he had merely disclaimed being a "frequenter of Mass". This was not enough, cried Wheler. "He should say he abhors and detests the Church of Rome."[88] Indeed, it was entirely owing to a motion made by Sir Charles Wheler—"your old religious friend", so one of Sir

Joseph Williamson's correspondents wrote—that Arlington's speech in his own defence failed to satisfy the House.[89] As it was Wheler who made the first motion for further consideration of the case, so also it was he who made the final motion for Arlington's removal from the King's presence.[90] Indeed, as Heneage Finch the younger, the son of the former member for Oxford, complained, Wheler did move "Heavy Things", heavier, in fact, in this session of the Parliament, than the House was willing to agree to.[91]

By the time of the next session, however, Sir Charles had once more resumed close relations with the Court party, and was never found again among the ranks of the opposition. The change may probably be explained by the rise of Lord Danby and the pro-Anglican faction. Wheler became a Danby man for the rest of his political career. He had apparently already been a pensioner for some time, to judge by the attacks on him made by some of the pamphleteers. For both the *Flagellum* and the British Museum list of "those Members who are, by Pencion or Place, obliged to vote according to the Court's Desire or Interest", were written when Wheler was still a Foot Captain and Governor of Nevis. In both documents the charges against him were the same—that he held these two posts, and that he was once flattered with hopes of being Master of the Rolls. The *Flagellum* also adds: "Privy Chamber man", in reference to a place Sir Charles had been given at the time of the Restoration.[92]

Wheler's position as a pensioner, however, was probably strengthened still further during the Danby régime. Andrew Marvell's lampoons against him date from this period. By Marvell, Wheler was even credited with having been responsible for the prorogation of two sessions of Parliament, though just what Wheler's part was supposed to have been in this is not explained either by Marvell or by his editor.[93] That Marvell considered Wheler a paid agent of the Court is made clear in the satire, "The Chequer Inn" ("The Exchequer"), where Wheler is pictured as seated at the board close by the lady (possibly one of the King's mistresses).[94] Two other satirical publications of this later period also include Wheler in their black lists.[95]

Even more telling, however, is a short series of letters between Wheler, Danby, and Williamson written in the latter part of 1678. Here Wheler's position as a pensioner seems to be made quite clear. The subject of the letters was a request for the appointment of Wheler's second son to a post in the Guards. Sir Charles asked both Danby and Williamson to obtain the royal commission. Danby wrote favourably to Williamson upon this matter, pointing out that the King would not wish to discourage anyone like Sir Charles who served him "so heartily in the House" and who would "stick to him so firmly in all places". Wheler's third letter reveals still more plainly how closely he was tied to the Court. He referred to the disfavour he had suffered in the past, when the King had been "misinformed" about his services in the West Indies, and how he had lost his own command in the Foot as a result, "and all the credit I had been labouring for all my life". He acknowledged that this loss had been made up to him since—"something has been done for me in place of it"—but this "benefit", whatever it was, was "very private", and he wanted some public recognition—some "mark of his Majesty's grace"—so that it would "be known that the King thinks my poor family still worthy of the honour of his service".[96] For our present purposes, the important part of this correspondence is, of course, the recognition by Danby of Sir Charles's service in the House, and Sir Charles's own admission of having received a "benefit" that was "very private", even though it may have only been a just recompense for genuine injuries he had received from the Court in the past. Perhaps, indeed, this "benefit" was that very £400 a year that was revealed as paid to him from the secret service fund when Sir Stephen Fox was forced to make public his list of pensioners in the spring of 1679, six months after this series of letters.[97]

Whether Sir Charles's faithful service in the House was owing only to conviction, or to his pension—or to a combination of both, as is more likely—it is apparent that from 1675 on his activities in Parliament ran increasingly parallel to court policy, even on minor issues. He had always been concerned with supply, and he continued to press for it. He also objected to the Commons' attempt to define expenditures, or to investigate the Treasurer's accounts.[98] He resisted the Place bill and all such attempts to check royal control of the House, arguing that it was a restriction on the King's power and an injustice to his faithful subjects, making it impossible for a man to serve his prince and his country at the same time. And here he did not hesitate to speak of himself, as one who would be "highly tempted" to take an office, "after all the inconveniences of these thirty years" in the King's service.[99] He defended Lauderdale and his own patron Danby, when they were threatened with impeachment.[100] In the stormy debates of May 1678, when the Commons were trying to make the King declare a Dutch Alliance, Wheler repudiated their pretensions as he had once before in 1675, asking how could it be that the people were "entitled to the consideration of War and Peace? It never belonged to the Commons of England."[101] A year later he was still protesting on this point.

Even on the subject of Popery, despite his genuine antipathy to Rome, and despite his duty as a university member to defend the supremacy of the Church of England, Wheler was less violent than formerly. His only positive move at this time was his insistence that the King be addressed to recall from their posts officers in the colonies who were Catholics. Wheler's interest in this action was entirely personal—and was so recognized by his contemporaries. To him the motion offered an opportunity to discomfit his successor at St. Kitts, whom he was still "pecking at"—to use the words of a contemporary writer.[102] Except for this, Wheler's actions were surprisingly moderate. He took a position against the bill that forbade Catholic Lords to sit in Parliament, and during the furore over the Popish Plot, like the other university members, he stood by the Duke of York, and failed to show alarm at the revelations of Titus Oates.[103] Indeed, he reserved his utmost expressions of horror—not for the "horrid" plot itself or any danger anticipated from Rome—but rather for the suggestion made in debate that the people should be armed against the Papists.

> That the people should rise—I know not the meaning of that. I am as much against Papists being in arms as any man; but that the people should have swords in their hands, and muskets! I know not the meaning of that.[104]

With this speech, very characteristic of him, both in style and in sentiment, Sir Charles Wheler's term as Cambridge's representative drew to a close. There remained for him only a word or two in defence of Danby, and then the session ended, and the Cavalier Parliament was at last dissolved.

Looking back over the Cavalier Parliament and the careers of the university members who sat in it, we may note that the career of Sir Charles Wheler, from the impeachment of Clarendon, through the Cabal and the supremacy of Danby, down to the beginning of the Exclusionist agitation, reflects the political trends of the time more completely and continuously than the career of any other university member, even though two of those members, Crouch and Hyde, sat for a longer span than Wheler. Likewise, Wheler's career illustrates in its most extreme form the dependence of the university members upon the Court, and the full extent to which the old alliance between the universities and the Crown had been restored.

From another point of view, however, perhaps this alliance is demonstrated even more convincingly in the cases of other royalist members, such as Thynne and Crouch, who were not so closely tied to the Court by place or pension, but rather by conviction. Nevertheless, from whatever angle this relationship is viewed, it is clear that it was the King's business during all these years that chiefly occupied the university members' attention. University affairs in themselves seldom claimed their time. Sir Charles Wheler, as has been already noted, mentioned his constituency only once, and served on only three committees that concerned university matters—two on the hearth tax and one on a Magdalene College bill. An interesting sidelight on his status as a university member, however, is found in a letter in the *Calendar of State Papers* regarding his plan for supplying the West Indies with clergymen. He regarded this need, he said, as coming properly under his attention as a university burgess, and his plan involved the co-operation of the universities, and the establishment of a bishopric in the Islands, with a Cambridge Head, Dr. Francis Turner of St. John's, as bishop and Head of a college to be founded there.[105] Most of the other university members were even more inconspicuous as representatives of the universities than Wheler. Sir Richard Fanshawe and Thomas Thynne were as silent on university issues as on other topics, while Sir Heneage Finch and Lory Hyde were openly criticized at Oxford for having neglected the university's interests in the matter of the hearth tax.

This leaves only Thomas Crouch as the sole university member who seems to have assumed responsibility for university interests. The only one of the six members who was still resident in a college, it is perhaps not surprising that he was the most active in this respect. Along with his service on innumerable other committees, his name is found on the lists of those set to study such subjects as the confirmation of college leases, a petition from Magdalene College, and the building of pest houses in the town of Cambridge.[106] He made one speech on the revenues of Trinity College, and, as was noted in discussing his interest in the Anglican Church, in another he protested against any bill that would permit Dissenters to hold conventicles in Cambridge. It was Crouch, also, who asserted the university's claims when, in connection with a bill on the plague, the usual question arose as to priority in naming the mayor of the town before the Vice-Chancellor of the university. Crouch acted as teller for the Noes, and the Noes won.[107] A similar familiar controversy about the wording of a bill came up in a debate upon "the precedency of the University of Oxford before Cambridge", and this also must certainly have engaged Crouch's attention, as well as that of the other university members, if they were present, but there is no record of any of them having taken any part in this debate.[108]

Likewise, there is no record in the *Commons' Journal* of Crouch's aid to the Cambridge Press against the printers of London in 1674, but this is cited by the editor of Lady Fanshawe's *Memoirs* as one of his signal services to the university.[109] Moreover, in a letter from the Vice-Chancellor in 1667, Crouch was recommended as a person who could be consulted with profit about the complicated relations of the university and the town, a subject with which he was said to be well acquainted.[110] All of which suggests that he was thoroughly informed and alert on all matters that could affect the welfare of his constituency.

An especially interesting incident in connection with Crouch's activity as a university member is his public waiver of any right to "parliamentary wages". Something, apparently, had caused a bill for the abolition of such payments to be introduced in the House of 1676/7. Crouch spoke on the question, opposing the bill as an encroachment on property rights, but noting that he himself had never received any such wages, and expected none. Nine months later—possibly to reassure his constituents on the point—he signed a legal waiver releasing the university of all claims that might later be raised by himself or his executors.[111] In this move, as in others, Crouch showed himself eager to safeguard the interests of his constituency.

This seems also to have been true of his action on the hearth tax. Of all the measures that may have concerned the universities during the Cavalier Parliament, this tax seems to have been considered the most important, and the greatest grievance—at least, to judge by Anthony Wood's account. Wood reported Oxford's bitter disappointment when the tax was first passed in February 1661/2:

> Had the burgesses for the Universitie (esp. Sir Heneage Finch) stood up to save our Universities from paying, 'tis thought the colleges and halls therein would have been freed from that tribute, but not one word did either speak. Every chimney in every college and hall pays 2 sh. per annum which was never known before—no, scarce that they were before taxed.

Here Wood referred to the customary proviso exempting the universities from payment that was formerly included in all tax bills, but left out of the law taxing chimneys. Wood continued to blame the Oxford members further for not trying to get the chimney tax repealed.[112]

Lawrence Hyde, in fact, seems to have acted quite contrary to the university's wishes, if he indeed is the "Mr. Hide" named as a teller for a division in 1664. In this division, Hyde was standing for the Noes, in regard to a clause providing for punishment of officers who misbehaved in collecting the hearth tax.[113] Such action must have certainly seemed strange to the complaining university. Sir Heneage Finch did serve on two hearth tax committees, but apparently to no avail so far as the university's wishes were concerned.[114] Wood, indeed, seems to have been correct in stating that neither of the Oxford members exerted himself over the matter.[115] This is a distinct contrast to the record of Thomas Crouch, who served on committee after committee considering the hearth tax and how it might be improved, moved for a bill to correct abuses, twice acted as reporter to the House on the question, and once was teller to keep a bill from being recommitted.[116] His colleague, Wheler, on the contrary, showed no more concern than the Oxford burgesses.

When Parliament met at Oxford in the fall of 1665 because of the plague, the Commons were impressed with the courtesy they had received from the university, and it was proposed that they should "take off the payment of chimney money from the colleges because they had bin so civil to receive them and to afford them their scooles for session places", but, as Wood went on, "our burgesses Sir Heneage Finch and Laurence Hide . . . did not at all to forward it or promote the Universitie their exemption from taxes, etc.: and soe it came to nought". The time speedily came, however—and before the session closed—when the university found an opportunity to deliver a mild reproof to its representatives for their stand. In fact, it was only a week after this debate when the Commons delegated the two Oxford members and some other gentlemen to present the thanks of the House to the university for its loyalty to the King and its stand against the Solemn League and Covenant back in 1647. Lawrence Hyde made the formal presentation of thanks.[117] According to Wood's account, "he plucked out a paper containing the thanks of the parliament to the University for the 'reasons' given 1647" . . . ("timorously", says a marginal note on this item) . . . "together with the names of those that were appointed . . . to deliver the message". Then the university orator made a speech in reply, in which he took occasion to twit the university's burgesses a little for their failure to defend their constituents on the matter of the hearth tax. "The University", said the orator, "'wished that they had more Colledges to entertaine the parliament men, and more chambers, but by noe means noe more chymneys'."[118] At which, Sir Heneage Finch, according to another version of Wood's, showed visible embarrassment.[119] But the university did not carry its resentment farther. On the other hand, it proceeded to finish off the ceremony by creating Sir Heneage and one of the other delegates doctors of the civil law—to Wood's great disgust[120]—and the King's agents continued to collect chimney money as before.

The Long Parliament of Charles II, then, was little concerned with university matters, and the university members of this period, so far as they were active in the House, were, like the members of the first decades of the century, chiefly significant as consistent supporters of the Court and the Established Church in a period when both these institutions were at the core of the political life of the day. This situation continued into the three Parliaments that followed.

NOTES FOR CHAPTER IX

1. *C.S.P., Dom., Chas. II,* I (1660–1), 275. Joseph Williamson was then attached to the Secretary's office, and perhaps for this reason was concerning himself in the election of the Secretary's son, or else from a natural interest in the advancement of another Queen's man—for the two Nicholases were also former students of Queen's College. There was also another factor that may have given impetus to Williamson's activity. The elder Nicholas at this time was the leader of a faction that was opposing the influence of Clarendon, and, as part of this movement, it would have been good policy to thwart the Chancellor's efforts to place two members in Parliament, by setting up a rival to Finch. See *D.N.B.* for Nicholas and Williamson. For the younger Nicholas, see Foster, III, 1068.

2. Cotterell's influence was being used successfully at that very moment to get Clayton the Wardenship of Merton College. *Life and Times,* I, 361, 383–5; *C.S.P., Dom., Chas. II,* I (1660–1), 625.

3. *C.S.P., Dom., Chas. II,* I (1660–1), 512, 514.

4. *Ibid.,* p. 275.

5. *Life and Times,* I, 398.

6. *C.S.P., Dom., Chas. II,* I (1660–1), 275.

7. *Ibid.,* p. 512.

8. *Ibid.,* p. 514.

9. *Loc. cit.*

10. *Loc. cit.*

11. *Op. cit.,* p. 517.

12. *Ibid.,* p. 525.

13. *Ibid.,* pp. 526, 527, 530.

14. *Ibid.,* p. 527. This complaint is also voiced by A. Wood, but it is rather curious that the usual gossipy Wood has nothing further to say regarding so controversial and involved a campaign. On the contrary, he simply records the fact of the election, his dissatisfaction with the result being only shown later by some uncomplimentary remarks about the subsequent parliamentary record of the two new burgesses. *A.O.,* III, 66; *Life and Times,* I, 398, and see below, pp. 252–3.

15. *Supra,* Ch. IV, pp. 114–16. See also *supra,* Ch. VIII, p. 214.

16. Clarendon's letter is in the Oxford University Archives, Ta27, p. 3839, f. 100. For Wood's estimate of Finch, see below, pp. 252, 253, and n. 120.

17. *O.R.,* p. 526; *C.S.P., Dom., Chas. II,* I (1660–1), 562. There is no indication of anything but unanimity in the entry in the Oxford University Archives.

18. 9 March 1660/1. *O.R.,* p. 519; Lady Fanshawe, *Memoirs,* p. 211.

19. Lady Fanshawe, *Memoirs,* pp. 211, 587. A photograph of the inscription is opposite p. 208.

20. For Fanshawe on the Committee of Privilege, see *C.J.,* VIII, 246, 436. He was apparently out of the kingdom at the time of this second appointment. For his other committees, see *ibid.,* pp. 249, 258, 265.

21. For Fanshawe's diplomatic career, see *Fasti,* II, 75–7; for his career in general, Lady Fanshawe's *Memoirs; D.N.B.; B.B.,* III, 1885–7; Foster, II, 482; Venn, II, 120; G.E.C., *Baronetage,* III, 12. According to the chronology of the events of Fanshawe's life in the introduction to the *Memoirs,* p. xxix, he was only in England for about sixteen months out of three years, before he left on his last mission in January 1663/4.

22. For Finch's career, see *D.N.B.;* Foss, *Judges,* VII, 87–96; Campbell, *Lord Chancellors,* II, 307–43; *A.O.,* IV, 66–70; Foster, II, 497; Holdsworth, *English Law,* VI, 539–48; William A. Aiken, *The Conduct of the Earl of Nottingham,* p. 40 and n.; G.E.C. *Baronetage,* III, 30; *Peerage,* IX (1936), 790–2.

23. Holdsworth, VI, 539, 540–1.

24. For Hyde's career, see Margaret V. Yates, "The Political Career of Lawrence Hyde, Earl of Rochester"; *D.N.B.*; *Fasti*, II, 229–30; *B.B.*, IV, 2738–40; Foster, II, 782; G.E.C., *Peerage*, XI (1949), 49–50.

25. *Flagellum Parliamentarium*, p. 17. Tributes to Finch's honesty are numerous, but he did not escape the lampoons of Andrew Marvell, where he appears in various uncomplimentary connections, called in one place, "false Finch"; in another, described as "leading the lawyers' sordid band"; and in still another— this time, apparently as Chancellor—as "a talking fool—A minister able only in his tongue To make harsh empty speeches two hours long." See "Britannia and Raleigh", "Last Instructions", and "Nostradamus' Prophecy", in *Satires*, ed. G. A. Aitken, pp. 27, 86, 96.

26. *P.H.*, IV, Appendix III, xxix. The pamphlet was supposedly written by Marvell in 1677.

27. *Flagellum*, p. 17. A list of pensioners in the *Commons' Journal* substantiates these charges by saying that Hyde received in 1676 a grant of £500 for thirteen years, and £4000 out of post office money to go to himself and his son for a period of ninety-nine years. *C.J.*, X, 108. Strangely enough, he does not appear in Sir Stephen Fox's famous list of pensioners. *Ibid.*, IX, 629. References to other money payments to Hyde are found in *C.S.P., Dom., Chas. II*, XVII (1675–6), 481, and in *H.M.C., Ormonde*, IV, 115 (February 1677/8). Hyde's name is also found among those disapprovingly listed as High Tories in *A List of One Unanimous Club of Voters . . . very fit to be thought on at the Next Choice*, p. 2 (Pamphlet in the Library of Congress [1678], n.p.), but no charge of receiving payment is implied here.

28. Yates, p. 18.

29. Add. MSS., 3813, p. 4053, f. 246.

30. The reference in the *Flagellum*, p. 24, is to Thynne's cousin, Thomas Thynne of Longleat, member for Wiltshire. See n. 61. For Wheler, see below, pp. 248–9.

31. Up to 1667 the *Commons' Journal* is the only real source of information about Finch's activities, for the *Parliamentary History* has no record of individual debates in this period. The Reymes Diary (Egerton MS., 2043, p. 4648) covers the sessions of 1661–1661/2. It shows both Finch and Crouch characteristically active. For Finch, see ff. 6, 12a, 12b, 13b, 30a–b, 31, 39a. For Crouch, ff. 39b, 40c, 46a. (A photostat of the Reymes Diary was made available to me by the kindness of Professor Caroline Robbins.) After 1666, *The Diary of Sir John Milward*, ed. Caroline Robbins, and Anchitell Grey's *Debates* have detailed notes. Milward especially admired Finch. See Milward, *Diary*, p. lxi and comments throughout.

32. No attempt can be made to cite more than sample references to Finch's numerous appearances in the parliamentary records. For the Act of Uniformity, see *C.J.*, VIII, 288, 415, 617. For the Corporation Act, *ibid.*, pp. 313, 554. For the Conventicle Act, *ibid.*, p. 542; IX, 104. For the Quaker Bill, *ibid.*, VIII, 367, 376, 429. For the Press Act, *ibid.*, pp. 312, 313, 315, 316, 618.

33. Campbell, *Lord Chancellors*, II, 311; *Fasti*, II, 286. For Finch's part in bringing up legal points in the debates on the Five Mile Act, see Gilbert Burnet, *History of My Own Times*, ed. Osmond Airy, I, 225.

34. *C.J.*, VIII, 539, 637; Milward, *Diary*, p. 27.

35. *D.N.B.*; Grey, I, 11.

36. *C.J.*, IX, 21, 30, 40; Milward, pp. 86, 123; Grey, I, 53, 54, 56–7.

37. For the bishops, see Milward, p. 23. A variation of Finch's speech on this occasion was later used as part of the campaign arguments at Oxford in 1678/9 when Finch's son Heneage was standing for the university seat. See below, Ch. X, p. 269. For the rights of the Commons, see Grey, I, 205, and Finch's later speeches, 210–11. See also Milward, pp. 289–90, 292, 302.

38. Grey, I, 438–44, *passim*, 463.

39. Grey, I, 34, 58, 62–3, 80, 83, 86, 87, 88; Sir Edward Dering, *Parliamentary Diary*, ed. Basil Duke Henning, pp. 115–16. Grey says that the courtiers received word from the Court as to their line of action in the debate on the Declaration. *Debates*, II, 67.

40. *C.J.*, VIII, 303, 311, 313.

41. *Ibid.*, pp. 305, 356, 396, 401, 415, 428, 436.

42. References to Crouch's committee service are so numerous that no attempt will be made to cite them except in special cases. Almost any page in the *Commons' Journal* will discover him acting in some capacity.

43. Grey, II, 70.

44. *C.J.*, IX, 259, 263.

45. *Ibid.*, pp. 518, 519, 554.

46. *Ibid.*, p. 530.

47. Quoted in *B.B.*, IV, 27–58.

48. Burnet, Airy, I, 473–4.

49. *C.J.*, VIII, 598, 681. But see below, p. 252, and n. 113, on Hyde as teller.

50. For Hyde's parliamentary career, see Yates, pp. vi, 69. The presence of another Lawrence Hyde in the House (M.P. for Winchester) makes it impossible to follow "Lory" Hyde's activities with complete accuracy. See also n. 113.

51. *B.B.*, IV, 2738; Yates, pp. 10–14.

52. Grey, I, 10–11. Burnet says that Clarendon had told his sons to use this last argument. Burnet, Airy, I, 456.

53. Burnet, Airy, I, 463, 464, and notes; Feiling, p. 191.

54. Grey, I, 41; Pepys, Wheatley, VIII, 469–70. Burnet, Airy, I, 463–4. Hyde's own defence of his conduct, written eight years later in his *Meditations* is in Earl of Clarendon, *Correspondence*, ed. S. W. Singer, I, Appendix IV, 649.

55. *Ibid.*, passim.

56. Yates, p. 47. The "Young Chits" were the group of younger men who became chief ministers in 1680. See below, Ch. XI, pp. 287, 293, n. 46. It may also be noted in this connection that it was after 1676, if not before, that Hyde was clearly enrolled as a pensioner. *Supra*, n. 27.

57. Grey, VI, 140. Before the session closed, he made two other speeches in opposition to the Exclusionists, and acted as a teller and as a member of a conference committee, thus closing his career with more show of activity than he had displayed for many a year. *Ibid.*, pp. 195, 253; *C.J.*, IX, 543.

58. *O.R.*, pp. 519, 526.

59. Information supplied by Miss Marjory Hollings of Charlbury, Oxon. For Wheler's career, see below, n. 75.

60. Cambridge University Registry, 50. For Wren's university connections and career, see *D.N.B.*

61. For Edisbury and Boucher, see Foster, II, 445, and *Fasti*, II, 266. For Croke, see Foster, I, 352; *Fasti*, II, 169. For Thynne, see *D.N.B.* and Pepys, Wheatley, VII, 258. Thynne was related to Halifax, Shaftesbury, and the Coventrys. See H. C. Foxcroft, *Life and Letters of Sir George Savile, First Marquis of Halifax*, I, 8, and n. Thynne is not to be confused with his notorious cousin, Thomas Thynne of Longleat, member for Wiltshire, who was murdered in 1682 (see D.N.B.), and whose estate Oxford's Thomas Thynne inherited. For the latter, strangely enough, there is no proper entry in any of the university registers. Wood has only two incidental notes, *A.O.*, III, 440; IV, 766.

62. *Life and Times*, II, 279, 441. Edisbury, however, later had his innings, and won the Oxford seat in 1678/9, as will be seen below. Ch. X, pp. 267–70.

63. *Life and Times*, II, 279. The taking of the poll is fully described in the Oxford University Archives, but Croke's name does not appear. See below, Appendix VII. Thynne's victory had been predicted two months before by a correspondent of Sir Joseph Williamson's. W. E. Christie, ed., *Letters Addressed to Sir Joseph Williamson*, II, 62.

64. *C.J.*, IX, 298, 301, 303, 305, 313, 315, 369, 372, 397.

65. *Ibid.*, p. 384.

66. Grey, III, 129; *O.R.*, 530. For the political views of the other Thomas Thynne, see *D.N.B.*; p. 245, below, and nn. 69 and 70.

67. Foxcroft, I, 175. Thynne reconsidered this resolution, however, for he sat a second time for Tamworth in 1679–81.

68. *Ibid.*, p. 179.

69. *Ibid.*, p. 129. Anthony Wood's unfavourable view of Thynne seems to bear out this interpretation. According to Wood, Thynne had been "turned from his service (as a gentleman of the bedchamber to the Duke of York) for baseness and ingratitude" and was "a person now much against the king's interests in parliament—a hot head". *Life and Times*, II, 279. Were it not that this comment was made directly in connection with Wood's description of Thynne's election at Oxford, it might be thought that Wood, also, confused the two cousins, and was speaking of the other Thomas Thynne, who had first been an adherent of the Duke of York, and then gone over to Monmouth. See n. 70, below.

70. For example, it is more likely that it was the second Mr. Thynne who took part in a conference with the Lords on the subject of removing the Queen from the Court and was the reporter of this conference, and also a few days later carried up the impeachment of Lord Bellasis. *C.J.*, IX, 549, 550, 553. For the change in position of Thomas Thynne, M.P. for Wiltshire, cf. the list compiled by E. D. de Beer, "Members of the Court Party in the House of Commons, 1670–78", *Bulletin of the Institute of Historical Research*, XI (1933–4), 23, and that printed by Andrew Browning and Doreen J. Milne. "An Exclusion Bill Division List", *ibid.*, XXIII (1949–50), 221. The name of Thomas Thynne of Oxford, on the other hand, is conspicuously absent from the Court party list of de Beer, although among those opposing the Exclusion Bill, as a member for Tamworth in 1679. In fact, he was a teller for the Noes when the Bill was voted on. *Ibid.*, p. 219; *C.J.*, IX, 626. For his cousin, see also *supra*, n. 30.

71. Foxcroft, I, 188. Thynne's concern with politics is further shown by the series of newsletters that he received from his brother Henry and from John Rushworth during the years 1675–82, and by his interest in the compilation of documents relating to the Long Parliament of 1640 that Rushworth was then collecting. These newsletters are printed in part in *H.M.C., App. 5th Rep.*, pp. 317–18, now Add. MS., 32,095, p. 4053.

72. Thynne's lapse from extreme Toryism seems to have been only temporary, for as Viscount Weymouth, Thynne became later associated with Lawrence Hyde, Earl of Rochester, and Daniel Finch, second Earl of Nottingham—the one, his former colleague, the other, the son of the burgess whom he succeeded in 1673/4. This association puts Thynne among the group of noblemen who were the core of the Tory opposition of the 1690's, and re-establishes him once more in the old university political tradition.

73. *C.J.*, IX, 106; Grey, I, 84–5, 167; III, 158; VI, 256; Milward, p. 191.

74. See below, pp. 248–9.

75. Strangely enough, in view of Wheler's relative prominence, there is very little in the way of connected biographical material written about him. The only connected accounts are in Carter, *Cambridge*, pp. 343, 465 (where he is miscalled "Sir Christopher"); G.E.C., *Baronetage*, III, 107; Venn, IV, 380. Chas. S. S. Higham, *The Development of the Leeward Islands under the Restoration, 1660–1688* (Cambridge, 1921), pp. 76–8, discusses Wheler as a colonial governor, and also gives a brief sketch of his life in a note, p. 76. Wheler's military career is touched on in Sir Frederick William Hamilton, *The Origin and History of the First or Grenadier Guards* (London, 1874), I, 9, 133, 144, 146, and *passim*. There are many scattered references to him in the *C.S.P., C.J.*, and Grey. He

is not to be confused with another Wheler of the same name from Charing, Kent, mentioned in *A.O.*, IV, 370, and Foster, IV, 1608. The family connections of Cambridge's Wheler are given in the sketch of his son, Admiral Sir Francis Wheler, in the *D.N.B.*

76. Grey, I, 22, 33; *Proceedings . . . touching the Impeachment*, etc., pp. 22, 23; Milward, pp. 100, 101, 113, 115, 124, 335. Curiously enough, Wheler's speeches are omitted in *P.H.*, IV, 374–6. But see *ibid.*, p. 382.

77. *C.J.*, IX, 18, 41.

78. *Ibid.*, pp. 109, 130, 150, 168, 180; Grey, I, 84, 85, 179.

79. Grey, I, 111; Milward, pp. 191, 218.

80. Grey, I, 221, and see below, pp. 249–50.

81. A letter written from St. Christopher in July 1671 to Sir Thomas Osborne, later Lord Danby, then Treasurer of the Navy, complained in doleful terms of his exile. "It was a sort of death when I undertooke this voyage and the leave of you and of my friends, was very like dying." He feared that they would be like strangers at their next meeting, begged Osborne to assure him that at so great a distance he would not be forgotten, and ended by presenting his most humble service to the Duke of Buckingham. Add. MS., 28,053, p. 4653, f. 34. It seems possible that Wheler's distress here could have been quite as much owing to the thwarted ambition of a pensioner as to the nostalgia of an exile. Higham, p. 211, however, regards Wheler's appointment to the governorship as a mark of royal favour. This is also the implication of the entries where Wheler is mentioned in the various political black lists. See below, p. 248.

82. *C.S.P.*, *Dom.*, *Chas. II*, XII (1671–2), 171, 243. Sir Frederick Hamilton and C. S. S. Higham (especially p. 213) do not always agree on Wheler's conduct as governor. As late as 1675 the Privy Council was still investigating Wheler's case, and calling him before it to explain matters, even though by this time his friendly rapport with the Court was re-established. *C.S.P.*, *America*, IX (1675–6), 245, 250, 253, 255–6, 271–4, etc.

83. *C.J.*, IX, 254.

84. Grey, II, 194.

85. *Ibid.*, p. 281. Arlington had received him kindly upon his arrival after the debacle in the West Indies, and conducted him to the King. See *ibid.*, p. 271–3, and *C.S.P.*, *Dom.*, *Chas. II*, XIII (1672), 213–14, 333, 440.

86. Grey, II, 271–2.

87. *Ibid.*, pp. 281, 283, 289, 291–3, 294, 295, 302, 303, 305, 309.

88. *Ibid.*, p. 294.

89. *C.S.P.*, *Dom.*, *Chas. II*, XVI (1673–5), 108.

90. Grey, II, 305. Wheler is also credited with having seconded the first motion for Arlington's impeachment. *C.S.P.*, *Dom.*, *Chas. II*, XVI (1673–5), 106–7. See also Christie, II, 62, 115–16, 126, 135.

91. Grey, II, 309.

92. *Flagellum*, p. 3; Add. MS., 5813, p. 4053. E. D. Beer, p. 21, dates Wheler's place as Gentleman of the Privy Chamber from 1676.

93. See "The Statue at Charing Cross" in the *Satires* with Aitken's note, p. 98. Aitken identifies the prorogations as those of November 1674 (the date on which Parliament was scheduled to meet after being prorogued the previous February), and again in June at the end of the first session of 1675. This interpretation of the prorogations does not agree with the statements by Ogg, II, 529, 533, where the reason given for the first prorogation is Charles II's promise to the French Ambassador, and for the second, Shaftesbury's desire to postpone the bill for a non-residence test. Ogg says that Shaftesbury used the Fagg-Shirley controversy for this purpose. Wheler was very active in this debate (Grey, III, 112–13, 154, 196, 245, 251, 255, 270–2, 274), but with his current connections, could have scarcely been playing Shaftesbury's game.

94. Marvell, *Satires*, ed. Aitken, p. 207.

95. *One Unanimous Club of Voters* [1678], p. 1; "A Seasonable Argument", 1677, *P.H.*, IV, App. III, xxiii. In the light of all these reports, it is probably significant that Sir Charles's daughter was made a lady in waiting to the Princess of Orange in 1677 (*H.M.C.*, *Bath*, II, 159), and his eldest son, a major in the Guards, and that Wheler's own name is on a list of M.P.s called in for the King's service at special meetings at Secretary Coventry's. Wheler also seems to have been restored to his military post. *H.M.C.*, *Ormonde*, IV, 517; *C.S.P.*, *Dom.*, *Chas. II*, XVI (1673–5), 382.

96. *C.S.P.*, *Dom.*, *Chas. II*, XX (1678), 449, 451–4, 455, 574, 594.

97. Grey, VII, 323; Wheler's "yearly bounty" was noted by Southwell in writing to Ormonde, *H.M.C.*, *Ormonde*, IV, 518. The fact that some of the items on Fox's list were later explained as legitimate, does not necessarily clear Wheler of the charge of being a pensioner, in view of the rest of the evidence.

98. Grey, III, 46, 53, 56, 86, 317.

99. *Ibid.*, pp. 53–4; IV, 16.

100. For Lauderdale, see *ibid.*, III, 107, 213; V, 363, 370, 384; *C.S.P.*, *Dom.*, *Chas. II*, XX (1678), 160. For Danby, see Grey, III, 46, 53, 54, 86, 92, 94; VI, 361, 365, 368, 374.

101. Grey, III, 317; IV, 378–9; V, 307–8; VI, 82.

102. *H.M.C.*, *Ormonde*, IV, 477. Wheler was on the committee for this address. *C.J.*, IX, 542.

103. Grey, V, 86, 241.

104. *Ibid.*, VI, 329.

105. *C.J.*, IX, 58, 98, 372; *C.S.P.*, *America*, VII (1669–74), 242–3, 289.

106. *C.J.*, VIII, 458; IX, 19, 102.

107. Grey, I, 310; II, 70; *C.J.*, VIII, 653.

108. *C.J.*, VIII, 333.

109. Fanshawe, footnote to note, p. 589. Crouch's action may have been connected with the times when the university members as a group served on committees concerned with printing issues. For example, *C.J.*, VIII, 418, 618.

110. *C.S.P.*, *Dom.*, *Chas. II*, VIII (1667–8), 4.

111. Grey, IV, 237–8; Cambridge University Registry, 50: 22. Crouch's diligence in representing his constituents is alluded to in the waiver: "at all and every the sessions of Parliament since holden I have constantly attended". W. C. Townsend, *History of the House of Commons*, I, 243–4, mentions this debate on wages and attributes the introduction of the bill to a later Cambridge burgess, Sir Robert Sawyer. For a discussion of parliamentary wages, see *supra*, Ch. III, pp. 88–9; Thomson, *Constitutional History*, p. 80.

112. *Life and Times*, I, 431, 433. A bit of doggerel attributed to the year 1675 confirms Wood's report of the university attitude on the hearth tax: "W'are censuring the Chimney Parliament. Poor colleges do pray they may repent." *C.S.P.*, *Dom.*, *Chas. II*, XVII (1675–6), 338.

113. *C.J.*, VIII, 550. This "Mr. Hide", however, may be, not Lawrence, but his brother Edward, M.P. for Wiltshire, or the other Lawrence Hyde from Winchester.

114. *Ibid.*, pp. 539, 637; Milward, p. 27.

115. Likewise, later, Thomas Thynne served on only one committee on chimney money (*C.J.*, IX, 372), but in proportion to his committee service as a whole, this suggests more interest than shown by either Hyde or Finch.

116. For the committees, see *C.J.*, VIII, 539, 637; IX, 33–4, 35, 58, 102, 368, 387, 403, 408. As reporter, see *ibid.*, IX, 66, 70. Milward also has a record of Crouch's activities, pp. 157–8, 225, 235–6.

117. Hyde's name does not appear upon the list of delegates with Finch in *C.J.*, VIII, 623, but a newsletter in the *C.S.P.*, *Dom.*, *Chas. II*, V (1665–6), 35, and Wood's account of the ceremony both cite Hyde as a member of the delegation.

118. *Life and Times*, II, 49, 61–2.

119. *A.O.*, IV, 66–7; *Fasti*, II, 286.

120. Wood was especially disgusted at the flattery bestowed upon Sir Heneage Finch in his citation: "encomiums as if he had bin the greatest scholar, lawyer, etc. that the world ever produced". *Life and Times*, II, 61–2. Hyde was modestly satisfied with the M.A. he had been given in 1660/1. For Finch as D.C.L., see also *supra*, p. 238.

CHAPTER X

THE FIRST EXCLUSION PARLIAMENT

When Charles II dissolved the Long Parliament of 1661–78/9, he had hoped to obtain a more tractable House of Commons in the new election. But he was disappointed in this hope; the new House was far less manageable than the old one had been. The excitement into which the Popish Plot had plunged the country was reflected even in the university elections, where the contests were unusually lively, and the prerogative cause met an enemy, in the appearance of James Vernon, successful member from Cambridge—secretary, to be sure, to the university's Chancellor, but nevertheless a potential agent of Exclusion, when the Chancellor happened to be the Whig's favourite Protestant candidate, the Duke of Monmouth.

The election campaign opened late in January, with a spate of letters from the Duke recommending his secretary—to the Vice-Chancellor, to the Archbishop of Canterbury, to two other persons whose influence with the university was worth having; and at the end of the month, 27 January, to the Vice-Chancellor again, reminding the university that this was their Chancellor's first request since becoming their head, and perhaps the only occasion when they would have an opportunity to "express their affection and respect".[1] The same—or a very similar letter—is given in Cooper's *Annals* under a date four days later, 31 January. This second letter closes on a complimentary, but nevertheless rather demanding, note:

> But I know I have to doe with persons of an Ingennuous Education which gives me a confidence in you & a firm beleefe that there is that right understanding between us that as you will finde me always ready to receive your Addresses & procure your satisfaction upon them to the utmost of my power, Soe on your side I shall meet with that cheerfull mutual compliance in what I have to desire of you which may yet further engage me ever to continue Your most Affectionate Friend to serve you.[2]

Besides this matter of his own personal wishes, the Duke's arguments for the choice of his secretary rested upon the latter's devotion "to the Church & the Protestant religion", and the alleged fact that he had always been found "faithfull" to the university's interests, though what particular service Vernon had performed is not stated in either reference. To further his candidacy, the Duke was to send Vernon down to Cambridge "to solicit there his own business in person".[3]

This time, however, the university was not waiting passively for their Chancellor to name his man. The first general election for eighteen years was something to rouse men's interests and passions, and a great stir was running through the colleges and halls.[4] Candidates were coming forward from all sides. Besides Mr. Vernon, the Duke's nominee, there were the two recent incumbents, Thomas Crouch and Sir Charles Wheler, both loath to retire from the seats they had held so long. There was also the former burgess, Dr. Thomas Sclater, member in the Parliament of 1658/9, and in addition, a new figure—Sir Thomas Exton, LL.D., Master of Trinity Hall, chancellor of London, and Advocate-General of the army. The intrigues and manœuvres that surrounded the campaigns of these five aspirants are described in some detail in a series of letters in the Tanner Collection written by Dr. Francis Turner, Master of St. John's, Vice-Chancellor of the university, and later Bishop of Ely.[5]

These letters were addressed to the Archbishop of Canterbury, William Sancroft. Among the first items of information revealed is the fact that the Archbishop had not heeded the Duke of Monmouth's plea that he "owne" James Vernon as a candidate, and by this recognition "further his pretensions".[6] Instead, his Grace seems to have written promptly to Dr. Turner that it would be wise to re-elect the old burgesses. Perhaps this recommendation of the Archbishop's was a churchman's natural reaction to the danger of placing a probable Whig, such as Vernon, in one of the university seats. Whatever the reason, his suggestion could not be followed. "*The Thing*", wrote Dr. Turner on 1 February, had "by this time advanct so far" that the old burgesses had no chance. Indeed, they had not been really considered by the Heads at all, "because the Body had made it long agoe unpracticable by laying other designes".[7] Instead, the most immediate probability was thought to be the candidacy of Dr. Sclater, who, according to Turner, was "ready to muster his forces" at the merest intimation of success, and had long laid a foundation for popularity among the rank and file by the generosity of his loans and gifts to the colleges. Moreover, according to Turner, Sclater "practised also by another powerful Attractive that is Entertainment", himself being an "Eater & Drinker, time out of mind". Turner also went on to marvel that a "man of Ease", "vastly rich", and "in his old Age", should "putt himselfe into the new World and Sea of Business which he understands not at all", and lose the favour of the Duke of Monmouth and make clear to "all his Adherents how his Benefactions were all Hookes only to catch their votes". And still more Turner marvelled that the electors should be willing to "send upp such a Dumb Burgess".

But Sclater and his followers had begun agitation from the very moment that the news of the dissolution of the last Parliament reached Cambridge, and though Turner had tried to get Sclater to stand for the borough of Cambridge instead—"promising to clapp on all our strength for him, engage all the Tutors with the Tradesmen"—it was of no avail. Sclater continued to lay claim to the university seat, and it was felt quite likely he could win. Indeed, he would not even join forces with Mr. Vernon in making a united stand, though Dr. Turner had finally made this suggestion as a last resort. In fact, Turner suspected that quite another pooling of forces had taken place, and that it had perhaps existed for some time. This was an alliance between "the two Sir Thomas's, Sclater & Exton, and their Intimates". Sir Thomas Exton had already visited around the university and called upon the Vice-Chancellor with a letter of recommendation from his ecclesiastical superior, the Bishop of London (Henry Compton), but had not pressed his cause further.

There remained Sir Charles Wheler. He was also on his way to Cambridge, though Turner had tried to prevent his coming. Apparently he was not popular in the university, despite his record of activity in Parliament and the fact that he had the support of the present Bishop of Ely (Peter Gunning). In an attempt to regain prestige for this election, Wheler had obtained a statement of approval from the King four days after the date of Turner's first letter to Sancroft. The King, so the statement read, "is fully satisfied with Sir Charles Wheler's constant services and particularly with his faithful discharge of the trust the University reposed in him, being informed by him that he is under a great discouragement as if that university thought him to be less in the King's good opinion and favour".[8] But this declaration was likely to serve no purpose, for—if Turner's estimate of Wheler's chances was at all accurate—Wheler was already out of the running: "'Tis not imaginable", wrote Turner, "that he should make an Impression unless to serve some people's turns that will vote for Mr. Vernon only for fear of adding to the numbers of the other two and should fling away their other vote on Sir Charles Wheler and laugh in their Sleeves."[9]

James Vernon, as the officially designated candidate, should have had the best chance to win of all, but his nomination introduced a larger issue into university politics. This was, of course, the fact that the Chancellor of the university was the instrument by which the opposition party in Parliament was preparing to break the tradition of hereditary succession and overthrow the royal prerogative—and with it the exclusive privileges of the Established Church. The strong prerogative views of the Heads were thus brought into conflict with their accustomed submission to their Chancellor's orders, and Dr. Turner and other officials were put into a real quandary. Moreover, in addition to the fact that Vernon was probably suspect to the university because of its High Tory views, there was the fact that he was not a true son of Cambridge at all, but an Oxford man (M.A., 1669), and only incorporated at Cambridge in 1676 in compliment to his master, and thus not to be preferred over the other candidates, all of whom had *bona-fide* Cambridge connections.[10]

The Heads, as a whole, however, decided to accept the Chancellor's nominee, despite whatever doubts they may have had about his politics. They declared for him, "and that vigorously", so Turner reported. As for any other candidates, the Heads let it be known that they would not support anyone until the Duke's will should be thoroughly known. It was perhaps hoped that Vernon would withdraw—indeed Turner stated that Vernon himself had said that he wanted to retire, and had begged the Duke's permission to do so—and it was expected by some that Dr. Turner would be able to prevail upon the Duke to retract his nomination. But the Duke persisted, despite all persuasion, and ordered Mr. Vernon down to Cambridge where Dr. Turner was going to receive him in his own lodgings to vindicate himself from the charge that he, Turner, was not sufficiently warm in supporting the Chancellor's choice. "Some say", he wrote, "*I am not hearty for him* because I am not Eager (if I were, I should hurt him as some do with their Eagerness)." This sounds, indeed, as if Turner was actually a little lukewarm, although by others—anti-Vernon men—Turner was accused of being too partial to Vernon, because he and Vernon were both originally from Oxford.

We have already seen that the Archbishop of Canterbury had also tried to escape the unwelcome burden of sponsoring Monmouth's secretary, by suggesting that the university retain its former members. It seems that his first letter to Turner must have gone further in expressing his dissatisfaction with Vernon's candidacy, for he had given Turner leave to read in Vernon's favour only "those three Lines and not a syllable more"—thus Turner described the section of the Archbishop's letter where it was suggested that it was "by no means Advisable to Disoblige our Chancellor". Even this lukewarm recommendation was revealed by Turner only under pressure from Vernon's adherents, whom Turner had been forced to agree to meet in the vestry after his sermon on 30 January for the express purpose of reading them the Archbishop's letter. At first, this word from his Grace satisfied them, but on the next day "some foolish prating Knave" remembered that Turner had not read the whole letter, nor allowed them to peruse it themselves. Then it began to be said that Turner had changed the

Archbishop's message to suit his own views. This charge Turner met by saying that "he would not gratify their Insolence" and his own vanity by letting them read the letter and see the kind things that the Archbishop had written about himself. This reason—so Turner admitted in his reply to Sancroft—although true, was not the whole truth. What the Archbishop had written we may only surmise, but, from this attitude of Turner's we may judge that Sancroft must have spoken plainly, and probably not in Vernon's favour. This at least was the judgment placed upon his reticence by the university, for indeed it had already been rumoured about, so Turner reported, that the Archbishop would never write to the Vice-Chancellor on Vernon's behalf, and that, on the contrary, some other person had already received a "very cold Leter" in favour of Mr. Vernon, to the effect that "how unreasonable however his pretenses were, if they [the university] could part with their Sentiments, they would do well, &.,"—presumably meaning that they would do well not to disoblige their Chancellor, the same advice quoted from the Archbishop's later communication to Turner. In view of all these rumours of coolness and all the pressure for Vernon, Turner was forced to ask Sancroft for some further expression of support, and begged him to write to Dr. Holbeach, Master of Emmanuel, "such a letter . . . that Mr. S [?] may by your Grace's order lette fly as many Leters as he pleases among all his young Acquaintance. I needs must beg this of yr Grace", Turner went on distractedly, "for I could almost kneele to them that they would returne to some Sobriety" —"they" being apparently the rank and file of the university, eager for Vernon. Again, in a postscript which he added to beg the Archbishop to burn his letter—a request that Sancroft seems happily to have ignored—Turner asked once again for an additional recommendation: "Good my Ld. write to Emmanuel[11] for yr Leter to me did us right"— the rest is illegible, and the purport is thus not completely clear, but that the Master of St. John's was uncomfortably anxious about the whole affair there is no doubt.

What went on between the time of this letter, 1 February, and the day of the election, 22 February, is not known, but the final outcome of all the manœuvres was the triumph of the Duke's secretary. This was the first election in England in which the Whigs were recognized as a political group, and Vernon thus was the first Whig ever elected as a university representative—indeed one of the very few Whigs ever chosen by a university constituency at any time in the seventeenth century. His colleague was a Tory, Sir Thomas Exton.[12] As for Sir Thomas Sclater, that gentleman apparently failed to pursue his alternative interests in the town, for he was not elected by either town or university, although

—as Turner had scornfully remarked, when trying to divert him from the university contest—Sclater was assured of the borough seat because of his leniency with Dissenters, when acting as justice of the peace— "his shameful conniving at the Conventicles", as Turner put it. The other two candidates, Crouch and Wheler, both retired after the campaign, and Crouch died a few months later.

In this election, Oxford, no less than Cambridge, experienced the full force of the political agitations of the period. And for Oxford, also, there exists a series of electioneering letters that present a full picture of backstage manœuvres similar to those described in the Turner-Sancroft correspondence. The first of these is a formal letter of recommendation from the Duke of Ormonde, Oxford's Chancellor, on behalf of Secretary of State Coventry. This antedates by a whole month another letter of Ormonde's referring to the same subject, and both letters raise some unanswered questions in regard to Coventry's eagerness for a university seat.[13] But Coventry was not among the candidates whose names were first brought forward in the gossip of university circles. There it was another Secretary of State, Sir Joseph Williamson —always close to Oxford affairs—and Dr. John Lamphire (M.D.), Principal of Hart Hall and Camden Professor of History, who were the principal figures.[14]

But outside influence again came into play, as it had in the election of 1661. And again this influence was exerted on behalf of a Heneage Finch and a Solicitor-General, this time the candidate being the son of the first Heneage, recently appointed to his father's old post, and now applying for his father's old university seat. And this time, again, his cause was urged by the Lord Chancellor of the Realm, as Clarendon had urged the first Finch's cause in 1661—only now the Lord Chancellor was also the candidate's own father, the first Heneage himself. He opened the campaign by writing on 28 January to the Duke of Ormonde, asking for his Grace's support. He realized, wrote the Lord Chancellor, that his request might come too late, and that the university might already be engaged, but since he understood that the two Secretaries of State had found seats elsewhere, and that Mr. Hyde, the recent burgess, had bought himself a place at Wootton-Bassett, he was applying for a recommendation for his son. Since the latter had just been appointed Solicitor-General, he, the Chancellor, was anxious to "make him as serviceable to His Majesty as is possible for him to be", and thus secure him the Oxford seat.[15] No action seems to have been taken on this application immediately. Perhaps Ormonde was still concerned for the Secretaries. At least, it would seem this might have been the case, for four days after the Lord Chancellor's letter, there came an appeal from Coventry, not referring to any earlier recommendation made by Ormonde, but asking for a letter—apparently a second one—in case he should decide to accept the invitation he had received to stand for Oxford.[16] Likewise, another letter written on 3 February telling inside news from Queen's College (this time probably reflecting the rank-and-file point of view), noted that Sir Joseph Williamson was being considered, and that Queen's, of course, would do all it could to support him. This letter reported other candidates who had come into sight, also. Altogether four university figures were being proposed, including Dr. Lamphire—two of them college Heads, and all four, "either civilians or physicians"; Doctors Lamphire, Edisbury, Yerbury, and Boucher.[17] John Edisbury and Thomas Boucher were not new in the field—they had both been considered in the last by-election in 1673/4, but at that time, it will be remembered, both had lost out in the face of the redoubtable Thomas Thynne's lavish entertainment. Now, however, it would seem that a reaction had set in, for Mr. Thynne himself, as likewise Lawrence Hyde, was set aside for members more directly representative of the university body. At least the writer of 3 February states as much, though with studied quietness: "I think we shall chuse neither of the former—Mr. Laurence Hyde or Mr. Thin—if they should appear."

They did not appear—nor did in the end the two Secretaries, Coventry and Williamson. News came to Ormonde (through his son, Lord Ossory) on 4 February that Williamson had obtained the Borough of Thetford and on 15 February he heard from Coventry direct that the latter was still acceptable in his former constituency and would yield his claims to the Oxford seat in favour of the son of the Lord Chancellor.[18] Ormonde had already (8 February) written to the university on Finch's behalf,[19] and from now on outside influence concerned itself solely with Finch and his chances of success. Ormonde's letter had diplomatically noted that it might by now be too late for the university to consider their Chancellor's recommendation, but that he would in any case nominate Mr. Solicitor Finch as "a person whose parts & Abilities are very eminently known", and added that he did not doubt "of his Endeavours to serve the University on any occasion they may have for them". [20]

From this point on, the story is told from inside the university rather than by observers writing from without. The popular candidate here was Dr. John Edisbury, an advocate of Doctors' Commons. Indeed, according to Anthony Wood, who, with his usual intensity of feeling, disliked Edisbury extremely, it was on purpose to cut off Edisbury's pretensions that Finch was put up as a candidate.[21] This, however, may be one of Wood's exaggerations, as it is likely that a safe Tory seat, such as Oxford, would have seemed a good place for the Chancellor's son and Solicitor-General to campaign for, in an election where the Court party was uncertain of its popularity in other constituencies. Hence, also, probably, the interest of Coventry and Williamson. But Tory politics or no, Oxford proved to be no easy seat for Heneage Finch to capture, despite the enthusiastic support of Humphrey Prideaux of Christ Church, Dr. John Fell, Bishop of Oxford, and others of the High Tories who admired Finch's father, the Lord Chancellor.

Prideaux's concern with the campaign is expressed in one of his letters to John Ellis, dated 23 February. Here we learn that it was because of strong opposition[22] that Sir Joseph Williamson had withdrawn his name, and that the field was now divided between Finch, Lamphire, and Edisbury. Yerbury and Boucher, among the original candidates, were likewise eliminated. Yerbury, according to Anthony Wood, gave his votes to Finch "for fear Edisbury should carry it", while Boucher, for some reason soon ceased to be a serious contestant, perhaps because he was more interested in the prospect of becoming Principal of St. Alban Hall.[23] Between Edisbury and Lamphire for second place, Prideaux thought it was not a "half-penny to chuse", and added, of the election, "a great deal of bussle and noise hath been made about it".

Further information about the "bussle" is gleaned from other letters of Sir Robert Southwell, Clerk of the Privy Council and friend of Ormonde, from his young nephew, John Perceval, a student at Christ Church. Christ Church was a campaign centre for the Finch interests, for it was Heneage Finch's own college, and its Dean, Bishop John Fell —the Dr. Fell of the famous ditty—was among Finch's most ardent supporters. Perceval reported that, even before Finch had entered the lists, there was a tendency to "talk very hot" over the election, and later, after the Chancellor's letter for Finch had been read, Perceval predicted that although the university as a whole would not like to disoblige its Chancellor, Ormonde (and Lord Chancellor Finch as well), the younger Finch was nevertheless going to find it a drawback that he had selected as his agents some of the most unpopular men in the university.

> namely, Dr. Prideaux of our house and Mr. Bernard of Merton, who, though they be both very honest gentlemen, yet . . . unfit persons . . . as too hot and violent. The former [Perceval went on] out of an unhappy failing, spends more time and words in abusing those who are against Mr. Finch than he himself doth in his behalf, and hath proceeded so far that he [Finch] is threatened to be beaten.

Finch's other agent, Mr. Bernard, erred in the opposite direction. According to Perceval, Bernard was "a man who . . . observes no decorum in his recommendation", praising the Lord Chancellor as one who "had more honesty and credited the church more than all the bishops since the Reformation". This, as Perceval sagely pointed out, no matter how just an opinion, was calculated to injure the feelings of many worthy churchmen, and "the speaking this openly in a coffee house and to the masters, most of whom are themselves in orders, and the scandalizing those who give not an immediate assent . . . hath rendered many indifferent persons his enemies and many zealous persons indifferent".[24]

A similar estimate of Finch's position was given by the same young observer five days later. In the interim, the Solicitor himself had visited the university, but without much success.

> Even Mr. Finch's friends say it had been better had he stayed away, and the others said nothing in his behalf, for then they say Mr. Finch would have carried it by an unanimous election . . . they all, even his adversaries, say his greatest fault is to be recommended by such persons. . . . I am heartily sorry that Mr. Finch's interest is upheld by such persons whose silence would have benefited him more, and have permitted all to have been swayed by their reason, and to vote for Mr. Finch as they all naturally inclined before the appearance of these persons.

The writer goes on to add, however,

> but the graver sort of persons are still for Mr. Finch. Our bishop [Dr. John Fell] spoke for him to the masters of our college, and the vice-chancellor, perceiving the animosities and heats of the masters, deferred the election . . . that people might have time to cool and think seriously upon what they were about.[25]

The "animosities and heats", however, had not dissipated by the time the election came on 27 February. Wood's account of the proceedings shows that feeling still ran high. The election was not orderly, and it lasted for about five hours:

> After the writts had been read, was a strange noise made in Convocation house; some cried out *Hennage Finch*, others *Lamphire*, another *Edisbury*; and being like to prove troublesome, the vice-chancellor, with consent of the house, appointed two Masters for each person that was a candidate to take votes. . . . These stood at and within the dore leading from the Convocation to the Divinity Schole, who took all votes and those they mistrusted or doubted of they marked with an *. But some, especially those of the Edisbury party, gave but one vote, so that the papers being brought to the vice-chancellor all reckoned, it was found that Dr. Boucher had 7; Lamphire 209, besides one that was doubted, Finch 243, of which two were doubted; and Edisbury 245, besides one doubted.

Wood, an eye-witness, wrote two accounts of this crisis, the first of which is none too clear.[26] In both, however, he accused the Vice-Chancellor of juggling the votes to make Finch come in second instead of Lamphire, by forcing those who had each given but one vote—i.e. for Edisbury—to give their second vote for Finch, so that the Chancellor's nominee and the Lord Chancellor's son might not miss the election. When this was done, the Vice-Chancellor "proposed to the Convocation whether the indentures of election should be sealed, but the *non*-partie being most, the bishop (Dr. Fel) was sent for, who though he pleaded hard for his owne man (Finch sometime of his house), yet the *non's* prevailed still, and Dr. Lamphire again protested against the unlawfulness of it. So about one of the clock the Convocation was dissolved." The other of Wood's entries ends: "The vice-chancellor shewd himself fals to Dr. Lamphire at that time, though a pretended friend to him. We were poled by two writers, without swearing, in the Divinity School." But Wood also reported that it was later found out that the calculations had been all wrong anyway, and that Finch in the first count had had four votes more than Lamphire after all.[27] This was accepted by the opponents, "whereupon the vice-chancellor, avouching it tru to Dr. Lamphire, he rests quiet", and so Finch's election in the second place, next to Edisbury, stood as final.[28]

Wood's dislike of Edisbury led him to note further, commenting on the latter's victory, that "Edisbury carried it by the juniors and potmen, he being one himself", and that Edisbury and his party had canvassed up till the night before the election, and got all the Magdalen and Christ Church votes, for Dr. Lamphire only got eighteen votes at Magdalen and none at Christ Church.

Wood's report of the disorderly character of the election is confirmed by two other letters from Oxford written after the Convocation—one from Thomas Dixon, M.A. of Queen's, to "D. F." (Daniel Finch, brother of Heneage?), and one from the Vice-Chancellor, Dr. Nicholas, to the Duke of Ormonde. The Vice-Chancellor in his letter lamented that there had been some disputes "that required a better management than his who is now in your Grace's service". Dr. Fell, on the other hand, reported that the university had done its duty in accepting the Chancellor's nominee, but gave Ormonde no hint that the election had been at all dubious. Ormonde in due time thanked both gentlemen, and the campaign closed, with outside influence again supreme and Oxford represented by two burgesses, one of whom was chosen by the Court, and the other by the "pot men", a combination that was to prove popular for three Parliaments to come.[29]

Of the two new members, only Heneage Finch had had anything of a public career, being already Solicitor-General appointed in 1678,[30] while Dr. John Edisbury was a mere advocate of Doctor's Commons, and not even a college Head.[31] In the short Parliament of 1678/9 neither had much opportunity to advance either himself or the university. Edisbury was placed on the Committee of Privilege at the opening of the session, probably in deference to his university seat, but his name is mentioned very infrequently among the later records of the House. He was assigned to the harmless task of inviting a preacher to preach a parliamentary sermon, and would have been automatically included along with the other university members who were asked as a group to thank the preacher afterwards.[32] In the case of Dr. John Nalson, whose writings were suspected of Popery, Edisbury was on the committee that inspected some pamphlets,[33] and when the bill from the Lords regarding the disenabling of persons from sitting in the House of Convocation without passing a Test was put to a committee, Edisbury acted as spokesman for the committee.[34] These activities were all in line with the usual interests of university representatives, as champions of the Established Church. There is only one other trace of Edisbury's presence in the House. On a list of members who opposed the Exclusion Bill in May 1679 is found the name of "Dr. Edgbury", along with that of Heneage Finch and Sir Thomas Exton of Cambridge.[35]

Unlike Edisbury, Finch made a number of speeches, and engaged himself chiefly on behalf of the King's interest, making himself "serviceable to His Majesty" according to his father's plan, as laid down when the latter applied to Ormonde for an Oxford seat. The session opened with an immediate opportunity for such service. The King had refused to accept the House's first choice of Speaker, the House insisted, and Finch sprang to the defence of the prerogative, urging the House to make a new choice, and not to stand firm upon their right of election after the King had twice denied them. "The King's negative power", he maintained, "is as much as chusing a Speaker." In this he was supported by one of Cambridge's new members, Sir Thomas Exton, who hastened to add that giving up the right of free choice at this time did not mean giving it up for ever, though other members of the House feared for this very reason to make it a precedent, and asked, in characteristic cryptic phrase, "What if a Popish ruler, and no choice of a Speaker?" The court spokesmen were unable to convince the Commons, and after a long altercation, the King finally accepted another Speaker who was equally acceptable to the House.[36]

The next prerogative crisis in which Heneage Finch took part was the pardon of Danby. In this case, Finch was more engaged on his father's behalf than on the King's, for the question was raised as to what part the Lord Chancellor had had in permitting the pardon. Finch rose. He had knowledge of this point. "Nature bids me speak", he said, alluding to his father. Against the Chancellor no blame could be laid. "I cannot say who advised this pardon, or who was for it, but who was against it, I know." He then told the story of the King's ordering the Chancellor to wait upon him with the seal, and of his taking the seal into his own hands and placing it upon the pardon, before returning it again to the custody of the Chancellor. "Pardon me", then continued Finch, "if my relation to this Lord constrains me so early to give you an account of this." The result was that a committee of investigation cleared the Lord Chancellor of any share in the pardon of which the House so strongly disapproved.[37]

Finch spoke twice more in this session, once to dissuade the Commons from voting dissatisfaction with the sale of Tangier—though his efforts were in vain—and again to urge forward the prosecution of the trial of the four Lords accused of complicity in the Popish Plot, even though the case should be tried without the presence of the fifth, Lord Bellasis, who was ill.[38] Curiously enough, the *True Copy* of the proceedings of this Parliament has no trace whatsoever of these speeches by Finch. Likewise the *Commons' Journal* does not have Finch listed on a single committee during the session. This is indeed incredible—that the "silver-tongued Finch", the King's Solicitor, should remain so passive a member, or that he should not have received the accepted honour of being named to the Committee of Privilege, along with other university burgesses, or that he should not have served on at least one, if not on several, of the committees of the House.[39] Even the Whiggish temper of this first Exclusion Parliament can hardly account for such omissions. But if it was indeed true that he was so neglected at this time, it must have been all the more a satisfaction to him to be recognized by his constituency in later years, as he was by being elected to four other Parliaments, from 1688/9 on into the eighteenth century—being honoured in this way more times by the university than was any other Oxford burgess thus far in the history of university representation, with the sole exception of Sir John Danvers.

Of the two Cambridge representatives in this Parliament, James Vernon was the less conspicuous—at least in the records. He was placed on the Committee of Privilege[40] and on four committees of inspection—one for army accounts, another for the post office, and two that were to examine evidence against accused persons (one being the same Nalson case for which Edisbury served).[41] He was probably also included with the other university members on the committee for the Convocation Test.[42] The only speeches by Vernon recorded by Grey are on the subject of the quartering of the army.[43] He was qualified to speak on army matters as the Duke's secretary, for Monmouth had been in charge of the armed forces since 1670. None of these activities, except for the Nalson case and the Convocation issue, were particularly the business of a university burgess, nor do they, on the other hand, reflect any particular Whiggishness of policy or give any indication of Vernon's future prominence as Secretary of State under William III. It is on the whole rather remarkable that one so close to the storm centre of the Exclusion movement should have cut so modest a figure in this Parliament—unless, indeed, it was a calculated matter of policy for the Duke's secretary to keep himself discreetly aloof.

James Vernon's colleague, Sir Thomas Exton, as we have seen, began his parliamentary career with a speech in favour of waiving the right of the House to select a Speaker. His committee work was mostly upon economic matters,[44] but he served on the committee on the bill for securing the King and kingdom against Popery, and he also must have been on the committee regarding the Test for Convocation.[45] Like Dr. Edisbury and Mr. Vernon, Sir Thomas was assigned to the committee who were to pass judgment on the writings of Nalson. On this question he made his second speech—in Nalson's defence—and gave the final report, exonerating Nalson from the charge of Popery.[46]

The session of 1678/9 was brought to an end 27 May by a sudden prorogation upon the passing of the first Exclusion Bill—the bill that we have already noted as opposed by all the university representatives except, significantly enough, James Vernon[47]—and the Parliament was dissolved later in the summer, throwing the country and the universities again—twice within six months—into the turmoil of another election campaign.

NOTES FOR CHAPTER X

1. *C.S.P., Dom., Chas. II*, xxi (1679–80), 53, 55, 59.
2. Cooper, iii, 577.
3. *C.S.P., Dom., Chas. II*, xxi (1679–80), 55, 59.
4. Ogg, ii, 476, 479, notes the intensity of interest aroused by the election of 1678/9, and points out that there was an increased demand for seats, which was making the cost of election much greater. This would render the university seats all the more valuable, since the expenditure involved in a university election would be, even at the most, considerably less than in any kind of a pocket borough.
5. For Turner, see *D.N.B.* For the letters on the election, see Tanner MS., 39.
6. *C.S.P., Dom., Chas. II*, xxi (1679–80), 55.
7. Tanner MS., 39: 171.
8. *C.S.P., Dom. Chas. II*, xxi (1679–80), 70. E. Lipson, in his article, "The Elections to the Exclusion Parliaments", *E.H.R.*, xxviii (1913), 80, mistakes this letter of the King's for an outright order for Wheler's re-election. This error in interpretation is noted by M. Dorothy George, in her "Elections and Electioneering, 1679–81", *ibid.*, xlv (1930), 553–4.
9. Tanner MS., 39: 171. Wheler's unpopularity seems to have stemmed from his close association with Danby. Sir John Reresby mentioned various members,

including Sir Charles Wheler, who had all been "put into good places at Court by the means of his lordship, but were now all displaced". Sir John Reresby, *Memoirs*, ed. A. Browning, p. 175.

10. For Vernon's career, see *D.N.B.*; Venn, IV, 299; Foster, IV, 1543.

11. Emmanuel College had the reputation of being tinged with Puritan and libertarian views. It would therefore be likely to favour Vernon's cause.

12. *O.R.*, p. 534. Exton won 244 votes, Vernon, 158, and Wheler, 85. Camb Univ. Registry, 50: Voting Papers. For Exton's career, see *D.N.B.* and *Errata*, p. 119; Venn, II, 113; *C.S.P., Dom., Chas. II*, XVII (1675–6), 401.

13. *H.M.C., Ormonde*, IV, 618. Is it possible that this first letter is incorrectly dated 8 January instead of 8 February? If so, Ormonde would have written only one letter for Coventry, and that at Coventry's request. See below, pp. 266–7, n. 19.

14. *H.M.C., Egmont*, II, 79. For Williamson's interest in Oxford elections, see above, Ch. IX, pp. 231–8, 254, n. 1.

15. *H.M.C., Ormonde*, IV, 310.

16. *Ibid.*, p. 314.

17. *H.M.C., Le Fleming*, p. 161. The writer makes a vague reference to other aspirants besides these—"and a great many more"—but no other names besides Coventry and Finch have been so far discovered. For Edisbury and Boucher, see Ch. IX, pp. 243–4, 256, n. 61. For Lamphire and Yerbury, see *Fasti*, II, 217, 235; Foster, IV, 1702.

18. *H.M.C., Ormonde*, IV, 317, 325.

19. Ormonde seems to have written his second letter for Coventry on the same date as that on which he recommended Finch (8 February)—at least to judge from Coventry's letter of 15 February acknowledging a communication and recommendation from Ormonde as of 9 February. *Ibid.*, p. 325.

20. *Ibid.*, p. 618. Oxford University Archives, Tb28, p. 3839, f. 225. An error in the *Ormonde* entry describes Ormonde's recommendation as for "Mr. Solicitor Finch's son" instead of "Mr. Solicitor Finch. Sonne of my Ld. Chancellor" as it appears in the Archives manuscript.

21. *Life and Times*, II, 440.

22. Humphrey Prideaux, *Letters to John Ellis*, C.S., n.s., no 15, pp. 65–6.

23. *Life and Times*, II, 441; *H.M.C., Ormonde*, IV, 338, 354, 618.

24. *H.M.C., Egmont*, II, 78–9. The remark comparing the Lord Chancellor and the bishops was a variation of the elder Finch's own comment in the Commons some years before. *Supra*, Ch. IX, 255, n. 37. Prideaux's zeal for the Finch cause is explained in part by the fact that Prideaux himself was a protégé of the Lord Chancellor. For Prideaux and Fell, see *D.N.B.* For Mr. Bernard of Merton, see Foster, I, 115. Another of Finch's agents was his own old tutor, Dr. Benjamin Woodrof, *A.O.*, IV, 652–3; *H.M.C., Egmont*, II, 80.

25. *H.M.C., Egmont*, II, 80.

26. *Life and Times*, II, 440–1, 442–4.

27. Another set of figures cited by Wood comes closer to this count, but whether they are figures for the first or second poll is not clear; Finch, 201; Lamphire, 209; Edisbury, 245. *Ibid.*, p. 443.

28. *O.R.*, p. 537.

29. *H.M.C., Le Fleming*, p. 158; *H.M.C., Ormonde*, IV, 334, 336, 358, 359.

30. There is comparatively little information available about the second Heneage Finch. Professor William Aiken of Lehigh University, who has made the history of the Finch family his special province, reports that the papers of Heneage Finch the younger were destroyed by fire in the nineteenth century. For brief biographical sketches, see *A.O.* IV, 652–3; G.E.C., *Peerage*, I (1910), 364–6; Foster, II, 497; Roger North, *Lives of the Norths*, II, 185; Townsend, *House of Commons*, II, 72–80.

31. For Edisbury, see Foster, II, 445—the only biographical sketch so far found. except for a scanty note in *Fasti*, II, 331–2.

32. *A True Copy of the Journal Book of the Last Parliament*, pp. 15, 28, 67.
33. This was the same Nalson who was the author of the famous *Collections of the Proceedings of the Long Parliament*. See *D.N.B.* For Edisbury on the Nalson Committee, see *True Copy*, p. 126. Curiously enough, his name is not listed for this committee with those of Vernon and Exton in *C.J.*, IX, 592.
34. *True Copy*, p. 163; *C.J.*, IX, 600.
35. Feiling, *Tory Party*, App. I, pp. 494, 495. But according to the list published by Andrew Browning and Doreen Milne in the *Bulletin of the Institute of Historical Research*, XXIII (1949–50), 217, Edisbury was listed as absent at the time of this vote. Finch and Exton, however, were listed as present and voting against the bill, while James Vernon was present and voted for it. *Ibid.*, pp. 208, 217.
36. Grey, VI, 432, 436, 437. There is no record at all of these opening days in *C.J.*, IX, 567.
37. Grey, VI, 53–4.
38. *Ibid.*, VII, 98, 124.
39. He would, in any case, have been entitled to serve on the Committee for the Convocation Test along with the other members for the universities who were appointed as a group, but his name was not cited separately, as was Edisbury's. *C.J.*, IX, 588.
40. *True Copy*, p. 14; *C.J.*, IX, 568.
41. *True Copy*, pp. 77, 126, 129, 235; *C.J.*, IX, 581, 592, 618.
42. *C.J.*, IX, 588; *True Copy*, p. 249.
43. Grey, VII, 64, 65.
44. *True Copy*, pp. 124, 170, 191; *C.J.*, IX, 601.
45. *True Copy*, p. 149; *C.J.*, IX, 597.
46. *C.J.*, IX, 592, 608; Grey, VII, 103, 104, 164.
47. *Supra*, n. 35.

32. A Vindication of the Journal Book of the Last Parliament, pp. 15, 25, 67.

33. This was the same Watson who was the author of the famous Collection of the Proceedings of the Late Parliament . . . For Fairbury on the Watson Committee, see T. case copy, p. 135. Curiously enough, his name is not listed for the committee on that very page, though it appears on p. 133.

34. C.J., IX, 585; T. case copy, p. 244.

35. Finally, Fag says Apr. 1, according to the list published by Andrew Browning and Doreen Milne in the Bulletin of the Institute of Historical Research, XXXII (1959-60), 217. Shaftesbury was listed as absent at this time of this

CHAPTER XI

THE LATER EXCLUSION PARLIAMENTS
1679–1681

The dissolution of 12 July 1679, caused Dr. Francis Turner, Vice-Chancellor of Cambridge, to take to writing again to Archbishop Sancroft about candidates for the university seats. This time, however, it was not the Chancellor's secretary who presented a problem, but the nominee of the King himself, Sir William Temple, the first candidate directly supported by the Crown since before the Civil War. Dr. Turner, however, did not seem to find the royal interference in any way irregular or displeasing, except that it involved rather more trouble than usual in the matter of electioneering, since Sir William Temple was not personally well known in the university.

His career had been spent largely abroad, and he was but just returned from his labours in concluding the war between France and Holland.[1] The King had asked him some months earlier to become Secretary of State, but he refused because he had failed to secure a seat in the last two Parliaments,[2] and he had come to believe that the ministry could function satisfactorily only when some of the ministers were members of the Commons as well as of the Lords. He had, however, consented to become a member of the new Privy Council, constituted in the spring of 1679 according to a plan of his own, whereby the King was to rule, not with the advice of a small inner clique, but by the aid of a greatly enlarged, coalition-like ministry, including representatives of the most divergent views.[3] The new Council proved to be a dubious experiment, and in the light of its breakdown, Temple's biographer, Thomas Courtenay, expressed wonder that Sir William still wanted to enter Parliament in the summer of 1679.[4] Why he did so, and, still more, why he settled upon a university constituency does not appear.

As for Cambridge, he had no particular bonds that attached him to the place, beyond the fact that he had been a student at Emmanuel College back in 1644. The usual attractions of a university seat may have influenced him, as they must have influenced many a prospective candidate—the small financial outlay required for campaigning and the generous amount of prestige obtained, if elected—but nothing of this is mentioned in his own account of his decision to run, although indeed, some years before, in 1666, he had expressed an interest in entering the House of Commons if he could find a seat "from such a part where a sheet of paper does the business".[5] The University of Cambridge was "such a part", but, as will be seen, more than one sheet of paper was needed to "do the business".

Some account of his efforts here is found in his *Memoirs*.[6] "I had resolved to stand for the University of Cambridge", he wrote—explaining that he had asked the King to speak for him to the Duke of Monmouth, so that the Duke, as Chancellor of the university, might write letters on his behalf. Here Sir William met with his first rebuff, though it was not a serious one, or one that could have been entirely unexpected, in view of the fact that Temple had been associated with the party of the Earl of Danby and was opposed to the Duke's interests. The Duke demurred. "He excused himself first, upon engagements", said Temple. Then the King pressed him further, and declared that it was impossible that he, the Duke, could have been engaged for any candidate, since he did not know that the Parliament would be dissolved—for it had been dissolved suddenly on the King's own initiative, and without the advice of the Council. But all such arguments were in vain—neither the King nor Temple could gain the Duke's open support for Temple's cause. All that the Duke would say was that he would not interfere in the election at all, and this promise he seems to have faithfully kept, beginning with a letter of 17 July sent by Vernon to the Vice-Chancellor, doctors, and masters of Cambridge, disclaiming the report that the Duke had recommended anyone as burgess for the university. Vernon, on the contrary, assured the university in the Duke's name that they were left "their entire freedom of choice".[7] This letter confirms Temple's own later belief that the Duke had kept his hands off and that no opposition was offered on the Duke's account, although at the time of the campaign, Temple's friend, Henry Sidney, writing in his diary 19 July, expressed doubt in regard to one of the other candidates, Sir Robert Sawyer, who, Sidney claimed, was "a creature of his"—that is, of Monmouth's.[8] However, if the Duke did favour Sir Robert's candidacy, his support seems to have remained unofficial, and there is even some doubt as to whether Sidney may not have been misinformed on this point.[9] Openly, at least, the Duke was not untrue to the declaration of non-interference that he had made to Sir William Temple at the beginning of the campaign.

By this stand, James Vernon was removed from the field—perhaps to Vernon's own relief, if it is true that he had wished to withdraw during the spring election. But there still remained Vernon's old colleague, Sir Thomas Exton, who had a good chance of re-election—according to Dr. Henry Paman, one of Archbishop Sancroft's correspondents at Cambridge. There was also the irrepressible Sir Charles

Wheler, who had not ceased to hanker after his old seat.[10] Wheler's strength, Paman reported, was in Trinity College, a clerical stronghold, and in the support of his usual patron, the Bishop of Ely—who was opposing Sir William Temple, so Temple said in his *Memoirs*, because of what Temple had written in favour of toleration as practised in the Netherlands.[11]

On the same day that Dr. Turner received the letter from James Vernon for the Duke, he must also have received a letter from Archbishop Sancroft, revealing His Majesty's desire that Sir William Temple be elected by the university.[12] Turner's reply, written some four or five days later, explained the plans of the campaign, and this, along with a later letter from Turner and the report of Dr. Paman—all in the Tanner Manuscripts—provide the rest of the election picture, so far as it can be placed together. Neither Turner nor Paman made any objections to Sir William's candidacy. Paman readily agreed to "visit & goe of Sir William's errand", while Turner thanked God "wee are yet so well affected in ye University, yt no body yt I heare of expresses himselfe Dissatisfied at his Majy's Interposing on this occasion".[13]

Nevertheless there were some doubts as to the results of the campaign. Besides Exton and Wheler, a new star had risen on the university's parliamentary horizon—Dr. Robert Brady, Master of Caius College, Regius Professor of Physic, and a writer of some distinction on historical subjects.[14] Paman believed that Brady would stand next to Exton in university popularity, and that Exton, being first, would no doubt "to the second . . . play his game under his interest", which may be taken to mean that Exton and Brady would each agree to further the other's cause. Brady's claim as against Temple's was all the stronger because he was a *bona-fide* resident of the university, while Sir William was a "foreigner". To offset this argument, Dr. Paman suggested that Sir William be entered on the rolls of his former college, Emmanuel, just as James Vernon had been previously admitted to St. John's, so as to comply with the words of "K. James his patent".[15]

The day after Paman's letter to Sancroft—22 July—Vice-Chancellor Turner further reported that Dr. Brady was prepared to make a stand on the matter of residence, even to petitioning Parliament on the illegality of any outsider's election in preference to a "gremial", but Turner begged the Archbishop not to mention this, as Dr. Brady was one of his "worthy friends"—a caution that suggests the degree of intrigue that was involved in these election manœuvres. One of Sancroft's letters, too, must have included sections that contained some private comment, since, when Turner reported that he had communicated the Archbishop's recommendation of Temple to the university, Turner hastened to add, somewhat apologetically, that he had passed on only the parts that "might safely be divulged". However, the fact that he had such a letter of recommendation for Temple, he explained, must of necessity be revealed to some extent, "it being the only Foundation for him who is unacquainted among us to build upon".[16]

At this stage in the campaign a fifth candidate appeared—Monmouth's supposed "creature", Sir Robert Sawyer, a former fellow of Magdalene College, temporary Speaker in the last House and soon hereafter to be appointed Attorney-General. Dr. Turner made no reference to any relationship between Sawyer and Monmouth in his letter of 22 July, when he told Sancroft that he regretted that Sawyer had come forward so late, "for though Sir W. T. be my noble friend, yet the other would have found more friends here had he been ye foremost man". But the matter being as it was, the Vice-Chancellor advised Sir Robert through one of his friends that it was too late for Sawyer to push his claims, and likewise warned the Archbishop that if it were true that the Court was trying to favour both candidates, that "the most immediate Consequence will be this infallibly: that neither of them will be accepted heere, & our young Princes of the Senate will unite uppon the two Masters of Trinity Hall & Caius College", that is, Exton and Brady.[17]

Sir William was also concerned over this possibility, and on 26 July he himself wrote to Sancroft, asking him very urgently to deny that the King's support was divided, and to have the Archbishop's own chaplain vote for Sir William, lest otherwise it would be said that the Archbishop himself was also for Sawyer, and divided in his support.[18] Dr. Turner had already advised Sir William from Cambridge not to depend solely upon the Archbishop and the Vice-Chancellor, but to get others to come out in his behalf, such as some powerful personage at Court, like Henry Coventry, Secretary of State, who might write, Turner suggested, especially to Sir Thomas Page, Provost of King's, one of Temple's chief supporters.[19] No record of such a letter has been found, but there is another recommendation of Temple, written by Dr. Tillotson, Dean of Canterbury, to the Master of Clare, which is probably the result of this letter-writing campaign.[20] Temple himself told Sancroft that he planned to write to his own friends, and that the King had asked other persons to write, and that in addition, he himself, Temple, would go down to make an appearance at the university.[21]

This letter-writing campaign must have had some effect, for by 1 August Temple's chances looked better. One of his supporters wrote to Henry Sidney, "I have done Sir W. Temple all the good I can at

Cambridge and I do not doubt that he will be chosen there, also."[22] Ten days earlier Dr. Turner had not taken so optimistic a view. He told Sancroft that he had advised Temple not to neglect his interests elsewhere, "nor to raise any great expectation of succeeding heere; for both those Heads [Brady and Exton] are strongly affected by the Body, and the best we can hope is but a Controverted Election", in which case, as noted above, Dr. Brady was likely to petition Parliament on the grounds of preference as a gremial.[23]

What deterred the doctor from this plan is not known, but for some reason the tide began to turn in Temple's favour. By 8 August, Lord Sunderland, one of Temple's close associates in the new Privy Council, wrote to Sidney that Sir William would certainly be chosen at Cambridge;[24] and Temple himself later, in describing his candidacy, made light of the difficulties he had experienced, although then, perhaps, he was thinking only of the influence that might have been wielded against him by the Duke of Monmouth when he wrote:

> I think his Grace kept his word with me in this point better than I expected for my election in the University proceeded with the most general concurrence that could be there, and without any difficulties I could observe from that side.[25]

Such difficulties as there were, he observed, came from the Bishop of Ely, who, it will be remembered, was supporting Sir Charles Wheler and opposing Temple on religious grounds. Again, in another place, Temple noted the ease with which he was elected. Writing to his friend Sidney, he reported:

> For my own part, I have been taken up of late with a journey to Cambridge, but not so pleasantly as you have been with that to Amsterdam. All that was good in mine is, that I had what I proposed to myself by it, and in the best manner that could be, without a voice against me, and with all the honour and compliments that could be upon it, from the university.[26]

It would seem that in the end all the opposing candidates retired before the day of the election, leaving Sir William to be returned 22 August along with Sir Thomas Exton. Dr. Brady was thus forced aside, to wait for a later victory in 1680/1.[27]

At Oxford, no less than at Cambridge, a great electioneering bustle was going on. Humphrey Prideaux, in writing to John Ellis on 29 July, mentioned a new aspirant for the university seat, "Coll. Vernon", perhaps Col. Edward Vernon (D.C.L., 1677). Whoever he was, he had, so Prideaux wrote:

> come hither to stand to be Parliament man, under the title of my Ld. of Ossory's friend; but that will not doe his businesse. We laugh at him for a

fool, and soe he will come off. He is a person we never heard of or knew before his appearing here, and since, on examination, we find yt his wife and all his children are papists, and therefor we much admire ye presumption of the man yt he should thinke he must be regarded here.[28]

Up to this time no other serious candidates were in line. Lord Ossory, however, was not the only one of the Chancellor's sons who had been appealed to. Ormonde's eldest son, the Earl of Arran, had also been asked to use his influence on behalf of one Robert Spencer, D.C.L., a canon of Christ Church.[29] But the Duke seems to have sponsored neither Vernon nor Spencer. The university had persons of much greater consequence in mind. Prideaux continued his remarks:

> I know not whom we shall choose, no one as yet appearing worthy of our choice. Secretary Coventry and Sr. Lionel Jenkins may be, if they will appear for it, but yt is left to their own discretion.

Coventry's interest in an Oxford seat, however, had apparently subsided, for he never appeared in the campaign. Sir Lionel (or Leoline) Jenkins, on the contrary, stood and was chosen burgess. Always a devoted Oxford man, Principal of Jesus College, 1661–73, Judge of the Admiralty and of the Prerogative Court of Canterbury, long member of Parliament from Hythe, now just returned from Nimwegen after four and a half years of arduous diplomatic service, Jenkins was indeed a likely candidate.[30] But when the election was held on 19 August, he did not stand without competitors. There were four contestants in all. The first—and the only one provided with Chancellor's letters—was Mr. James Lane, the son of Viscount Lanesborough, Ormonde's Secretary of State in Ireland.[31] On 23 July, Ormonde wrote to Dr. Fell, Bishop of Oxford and Head of Lane's former college, Christ Church, in regard to the coming election:

> If Parliaments continue to be so short lived and I to be Chancellor of Oxford, the University is like to have frequent recommendations from me. That which I have now given Mr. Lane . . . is with much assurance that he will discharge the trust with zeal for the Church and the University. . . . If I did not think thus of him, I should not desire your lordship's furtherance to his pretensions as now I do.[32]

Dr. Fell's reply assured his Grace that his "commands" would be obeyed, by himself and by the new Vice-Chancellor, Dr. Timothy Halton, who also hastened in a separate letter to assure the Duke of his readiness to further Mr. Lane's interests.[33]

But all this influence was of no avail. The university was beginning to assert itself, and this time it was successful in maintaining its freedom of choice. Anthony Wood's account of the election dismissed Lane's claims as of little weight: "He, being a young, conceited person and absent, was layd aside." However, since there were so many others in the field, and the election seemed "like to prove troublesome", tellers were appointed for each of the candidates, Lane being included. The other aspirants beside Sir Leoline Jenkins, were two college worthies, both "civilians", Dr. Charles Parrott (or Perrott) of St. John's, and Dr. William Oldys (or Oldish) of New College. Neither of these men were Heads of colleges, and Parrott in particular seems to have been quite undistinguished, to judge from the scantiness of the information that there is to be found about him.[34]

Notwithstanding Parrott's obscurity, in the election he led the poll, even ahead of the celebrated Sir Leoline Jenkins. According to Anthony Wood, this was because Parrott had the support of "the black pot men", as he was himself a "pot-companion" and a "thorough-paced soaker". Parrott's poll was 224, Jenkins's, 204, Oldys's, 104, and young Mr. Lane's, only 45.[35] From these results, it is clear that outside influence carried no weight in this campaign, and that internal factions were in full play.

Unlike Dr. Parrott, Sir Leoline Jenkins had very solid qualities that must have recommended him impressively to the voters, even perhaps to some of the "black pot men". His connections with Oxford, as fellow and Head of Jesus College, and patron of the university press, were close and genuine, and his early years had been spent in scholarly and academic pursuits. He was an ardent adherent of the Established Church—to the point of bigotry and superstition, according to Burnet[36]—and his devotion to the royalist cause during the Civil War, and to the maintenance of the prerogative since the Restoration, was well attested. A person less likely to work in harmony with the House of Commons in its present excited state would have been hard to choose. Yet Oxford sent him as its only active burgess—for Parrott's contribution to the work of the House was negligible—and before the Parliament was out, the King had made Jenkins Secretary of State and chief spokesman for the Court. The discomfort of his position was similar to that of Sir John Coke back in the 1620's when the latter was trying to stem the tide of criticism then rising against Charles I. Indeed, Jenkins's position was even worse, since by now the Commons distinctly had the upper hand and were well aware of their power, and were bent, not merely upon opposing him, but upon humiliating him as well. His very prominence was thus his weakness.[37]

Parliament opened 7 October 1679, but it was quickly prorogued until 30 October, and ultimately until the next year, 21 October 1680. At that time, Sir Leoline immediately became prominent in the debates that arose over the revived Exclusion Bill. It was his business to turn the Commons from an Exclusion Bill pure and simple to some substitute in the shape of what he called "expedients", that is, legislation placing restrictions upon the Duke of York when he should become King, but stopping short of Exclusion itself.[38] This was the King's favourite proposal, often repeated through Sir Leoline's lips throughout the session. Jenkins's fullest speech was delivered 4 November against the second reading of the bill. The arguments of this speech and the following have often been summarized and quoted.[39] He protested first against the Duke's being condemned unheard, and then attacked the Bill as an innovation which would make the monarchy elective, instead of hereditary, and run counter to the oath of allegiance taken to the King and his successors by all members of Parliament. In the course of this speech, Jenkins assumed the full divine-right Tory position, long cherished in the universities, even after 1689. "When God gives us a King in his wrath it is not in our power to change him; we cannot require any qualification; we must take him as he is."[40] Nevertheless, in stating this view, Jenkins was also quick to conciliate Parliament: "I will be cautious how I dispute the Power of Parliaments. I know the legislative Power is very great, and it ought to be so." But even so, "a government cannot alter the species it is of, for 'tis not the People that make this a successive monarchy".[41] And again he repeated this argument on the third reading, 11 November:

> By the fundamentals of the Government, how can you make a King by Parliament, I have always taken it that the Government had its original not from the People but from God. . . . it will be much less, when we see it from the people, and not from God immediately.[42]

Thus Oxford's chief member gave explicit expression to the divine-right doctrine that undoubtedly underlay the political thinking of most of the university and that proved later to be something of an embarrassment in 1689 and far into the eighteenth century.

Both at the beginning of the session and at the end, Jenkins was prominent in these debates on the Exclusion Bill. But also almost daily throughout the session he appeared constantly as the King's messenger and mouthpiece. Made Secretary of State in the preceding January 1680, his presence in the House necessarily provided the normal channel of communication between the Sovereign and the Commons. Item after item in the *Commons' Journal* begins with the phrase, "Mr. Secretary Jenkins acquaints the House . . ." and it was Jenkins's misfortune that many of these messages proved to be storm centres of argument. There was, for example, the question of Tangier—whether it should be kept and fortified, or whether it was not worth the expense involved.[43]

Jenkins spoke for the Court in urging the support of Tangier, and in characteristically mild phrase, put forth an argument that to the opposition must have sounded both subservient and evasive:

> The giving of Money for the support of Tangier, being his Majesty doth so earnestly desire it, is, I think, the only way for this House to gain a good Opinion with his Majesty, and to obtain what they desire.[44]

In the debates on Tangier and against the proposals for the removal of Lord Halifax from the King's presence and the impeachment of Chief Justice North, Sir Leoline was joined by Sir William Temple, who, like Jenkins, was both a university member and a Privy Councillor. But although Temple ultimately made an effort to enter the debates on the King's behalf, his position was none too happy, for soon after his triumphant election in August 1679, he had begun to harbour doubts about the success of the new Parliament. As early as 1 November 1679, and again later in the month, his friend Sidney noted in his diary that Sir William was discontented and talked of giving up all part in public affairs.[45] The cause of this discontent was the change in the Court's attitude since the brave hopes of the early spring when Temple's new Privy Council was installed. The truth was, Charles was no longer willing to play the game of conciliation, and Temple, therefore, was no longer a man to his hand. So it came about that, though a Privy Councillor, Temple no longer had a share in the royal decisions, and the continued prorogation of Parliament filled him with dismay. By 23 January 1679/80, his old ally and colleague, Lord Sunderland, could write to Sidney that Sir William now knew "not a word of anything . . . but when it is in the Gazette".[46] Nevertheless Temple lingered on, attending Council meetings at rare intervals, and finally accepted an appointment as ambassador to Spain. By this time, however, Parliament was again actually about to meet, and so the King asked Temple to stay on for the opening, in order to help with the business of keeping the House to some degree pacified.

Sir William was a courtier, but he was not, like Jenkins, a convinced divine-right enthusiast. He was a "Trimmer"—a moderate Tory—opposed to Exclusion, though inclined to look hopefully in the direction of the Prince of Orange; one whose life career as diplomat had accustomed him to look to the Crown rather than to Parliament for authority, and yet one whose concept of the English constitution did not comfortably accept the Crown as the sole fountainhead of power. His position resembles somewhat that of that other ambassador-burgess, Sir Thomas Roe of Oxford, who found himself torn between his customary concern for the King's interest and that King's failure to accommodate himself to the new claims of Parliament. And like

Sir Thomas, Temple also ultimately found himself forced to abandon the role of mediator and to retire from a scene in which he could not fully align himself with either side.

In this session of 1680/1, however, Sir William made one last attempt to bring the Commons and the King together. He described his own disinterestedness in his *Memoirs*: "During the whole proceedings", he wrote, he had "played a part very impertinent [that is, inappropriate] for a man that had any designs or ambitions about him."[47] He gave up opposing the Exclusion Bill when he saw how bent the House was upon it, and he told the King to wait and let it be defeated by the Lords.[48] He even prevented a call for a division, when the Bill was passed with only a few Noes against it: "We were not a dozen that durst cry out", wrote Thomas Bruce, later Earl of Ailesbury, in his *Memoirs*, "and as a young inexperienced member, out of zeal, I insisted that the House should divide . . . but by Sir William Temple's entreaty, I desisted."[49]

Temple went but seldom to Parliament or to the Privy Council during these months, though everywhere he tried, as he said, to "allay the heats on either side"; and he told the King that, as a result, he expected to be turned out of the House in the morning and out of the Council in the afternoon.[50] He seems to have served on remarkably few committees for a man of his experience. The *Journal* has his name listed only once—on the committee for uniting His Majesty's Protestant subjects to the Church of England[51]—which must have been a congenial objective for the admirer of Dutch toleration. He did not speak often, but in the pages of Grey there are several speeches on Tangier, and on the impeachment of North and Halifax.[52] In almost every case, Temple seized upon the opportunity to urge moderation, and the adoption of a conciliatory attitude towards the King. But in contrast to Sir Leoline Jenkins's complete and placid acceptance of the Court's whole position, Temple's speeches breathe a sincerely reasonable spirit, and some real comprehension of the House's point of view. The House seems to have recognized this, for though Temple was called to order once—and Grey in a special note observed that Temple's misdemeanour had been committed on purpose "to give time to the Attorney" to answer the House's question[53]—in general, the House allowed Temple to say his say without accusing him of partiality, and even went so far as to accept two of his suggestions in the wording of controversial statements in the address on the granting of pardons to informers.[54] To his pleas against condemning Halifax on the grounds of "common fame", on the other hand, his moderate defence of Chief Justice North, and his remarks on the address on Tangier, they turned a deaf ear.[55]

Another example of the esteem in which Temple was held by the Commons, was when he announced that Lord Stafford, then a prisoner in the Tower for alleged complicity in the Popish Plot, had asked to see him, and "humbly desired" that some of the members should go with him, presumably as witnesses to the innocence of the visit. The House, Grey reported, "out of respect to Sir William Temple, all cried out, 'No! No!' and he had leave to go". Even with this endorsement, how ever, Sir William was wary enough not to go alone.[56]

The theme of all Temple's speeches was that the fate of Christendom depended upon the outcome of this Parliament; that the cause of Protestantism in Europe and even the welfare of some Catholic countries depended upon the English King and his Parliament's coming to a good understanding, since only a strong England could turn the tide against the ambitions of France.[57] This was not the view of Sir William's royal master, nor of the Exclusionists, who "laughed at" all allusions to the seriousness of foreign affairs as "court tricks" and "too stale to pass any more".[58] So Temple's efforts were of no avail, and his last act in the session (4 January 1680/1) was to assume the unwelcome task deemed impossible for the unpopular Secretary Jenkins—on whom it would have normally fallen—of delivering the King's final rejection of all schemes for Exclusion. The House, Sir William wrote, received this just as he had expected, with outspoken distaste; but apparently it was Temple alone, of all the Court party, who could risk his standing with the Commons by being the bearer of such an unwelcome message.[59]

Certainly it was clear that Sir Leoline Jenkins could afford no such risk. For he had received no such tributes as Temple had been given by the House. On the contrary, open attacks were made upon him as Secretary for his procedure in handling some incidents of the Popish Plot, and the Commons finally resolved that his action had been "illegal, and arbitrary, and an Obstruction to the Evidence for the Discovery of the horrid Popish Plot". Nothing came of this move at the time, but in the Parliament that followed, even more pointed efforts were taken to make Jenkins feel the House's displeasure.[60] Through it all, however, he persisted stubbornly and meekly in stating the King's case.

Thus, of the four university members, two—Jenkins and Temple—played prominent parts in the stormy debates of Charles II's "Tangier Parliament". The other two university members passed through the session almost unnoticed. As to Sir Thomas Exton—fairly vocal in the previous Parliament—the only indication that he was ever present at all consists of a grant of leave for him to be absent to go into the country.[61] Similarly, Dr. Charles Parrott of Oxford is mentioned in action only twice: once as a committee member to study the bill for uniting all Protestants to the Church of England, and again in defence of the university on the subject of a Popishly inclined sermon given at Oxford.[62] This, incidentally, was the only piece of university business that came up during the session. On this question Sir Leoline Jenkins also spoke in the university's behalf, while Sir William Temple's share in the debate was to turn the subject away from Oxford's unfortunate sermon back into the main channel of discussion—the problem of Tangier.[63] From the university point of view, as from all other points of view, the Parliament was a failure.

Soon after Sir William Temple had presented the King's ultimatum upon the Exclusion Bill, the Parliament was prorogued, but not before Sir Leoline Jenkins had delivered one more speech, patiently urging "Expediences" to secure the Protestant religion,[64] and not before the House had begun an attack upon Oxford's former burgess, Lawrence Hyde, now high in the royal favour. Hyde's defence, in which he broke off weeping, and showed, it was thought, much too much passion, brought the session to its close.[65] Not long after its prorogation, on 20 January, the Parliament was formally dissolved, "for acting high and doing little", so Wood wrote.[66] A new Parliament was summoned to meet at Oxford, 24 March 1680/1.

Such a prorogation—if not a dissolution—had long since been threatened by Temple, as far back as his November speech about Tangier,[67] and this outcome of a Parliament on which he had counted so much discouraged him still further with his part in public affairs. At first, however, he seems to have entertained some fond hope that he might still be of value to the King's cause as an agent of reconciliation. But the time for that was past. There was no place at Court now for a mere moderate.[68] This Temple found out when he considered the question of whether he should stand again at Cambridge. "The Heads of the University . . . sent to me", he wrote, "to know whether I intended to stand again for that election"; after which he spoke to the King, who

> seemed at first indifferent, and bid me do what I would: but when I said I was very indifferent, too, and would do in it what his Majesty liked best; he said, in a manner kind and familiar, that considering how things stood at this time, he doubted my coming into the House would not [sic] be able to do much good; and therefore he thought it was well for me to let it alone; which I said I would do.[69]

This left the field clear at last for Dr. Robert Brady, who was accordingly returned with Sir Thomas Exton in the Cambridge election held on the first of March 1680/1.[70] Except for a letter from Dean Tillotson at Canterbury, written very early in the campaign (27 January) to

Dr. Blithe of Clare recommending Sir Robert Sawyer to be burgess,[71] nothing is known about the details of this election. The results, however, were an entire victory for the Court party. Dr. Brady was a real addition to the Tory cause, for his avocation of historian was just bringing to light some significant facts about the origins of Parliament. He had discovered what is now taken to be the proper view—that the House of Commons did not date from time immemorial and the dawn of Anglo-Saxon history, but, on the contrary, was a product of revolution, rising in a comparatively modern age, out of the rebellions against Henry III; and thus was essentially more of a real innovation than any of the innovations upon parliamentary power complained of by the "anti-monarchical antiquaryes" of the seventeenth century.[72] As the discoverer of this new doctrine, Dr. Brady was indeed a find, and he remained comfortable in his university seat for two Parliaments.[73]

Oxford also made no ado about its election, but promptly returned its previous burgesses, Sir Leoline Jenkins and Dr. Parrott, within two weeks after the dissolution of the preceding House. "Nobody else stood: so there was not controversie", was Wood's comment.[74] In fact, the university was so set upon re-electing Jenkins that on the very day of the dissolution, the Vice-Chancellor wrote to Sir Leoline to express the hope that he would be their burgess again, since, so Dr. Halton reported, the university had "on all occasions found you both ready and able to give them assistance".[75]

When the actual day of the election came, however, an incident occurred that may have only been a youthful prank on the part of some of the newer masters, or may, on the contrary, have had some greater political significance in view of the turbulence that had been manifested before at the last three Oxford elections. "Nobody stood . . ." said Wood; but then went on to describe how "a hot head" called for a poll "ad capitationem". "Whereupon the vice-chancellor being amazed at it, bid the company those that were for Sir Leoline Jenkins goe on one side, and those for another on the other, Whereupon all went on one side, and left Grimes (?), Adams, New, and others of Exeter"—the hot heads and "their gang", as Wood called them—"on the other; but they being ashamed went there too." And Jenkins and Parrott were declared burgesses.[76]

The new Parliament met at Oxford and only lasted a week. There was little time for the university members to distinguish themselves. Even so, Sir Leoline was still in the forefront of the royal forces, and the butt of the Whigs more than ever. Early in the session he opposed the publishing of the votes taken in Parliament, with his usual ineffectiveness.

He took the ground that no great assembly did such a thing, and vainly tried to win the members by an appeal to their parliamentary pride. "It is against the gravity of this Assembly", he argued, "and it is a sort of Appeal to the People. It is against your Gravity, and I am against it." But the Whigs were not to be so easily cajoled, and asked bluntly, "Pray, who sent us hither?", and went on with the resolution to print the votes.[77]

The Exclusion Bill was then reintroduced, and Jenkins moved against it. "The King has given his vote against it and therefore I must do so, too",[78] he said. The next day there was a concerted plan to humiliate Jenkins, carried out with "Indecency and Ridicule"—to use the words of Wynne, Jenkins's biographer.[79] We have already noted that this idea had first taken shape in the previous Parliament, where it had been planned to censure Jenkins and make him kneel at the bar—apparently in connection with his alleged obstruction of the discovery of the Popish Plot—although North, who recounted the incident, did not say exactly what the offence was. But at that time, North said, if Sir Leoline had "squeaked, as they call it, that is recanted, and whined for an excuse, then he had been lost in every respect; for a sneaking man is despised . . . on all sides". An attempt was made to sound him out and see whether he stood firm. In this case, the conspirators would still have some satisfaction, for this would be contempt of Parliament, and, as North noted, "a secretary of state is no slight person to send to the Tower". Some "half-faced friends" told him that he would have to kneel at the bar of the House and apologize for his offence. To this he answered, "in his formal way" that he was "a poor creature, not worth the resentment of the House; he should always be submissive to such great men as they were, in everything that concerned himself", but when the King was concerned, "by the grace of the living God, he would kneel to and ask pardon of no mortal upon earth, but to the king he served".[80] Perhaps his simplicity and firmness disarmed his persecutors. At least nothing of the sort was actually attempted until the next Parliament in 1680/1.

But here, when the impeachment of Fitzharris, the informer, was ordered to be taken up to the House of Lords, Jenkins was designated as the Commons' messenger. The account of this incident, as given in Grey and other contemporary sources shows very well the atmosphere of unfriendliness in which Jenkins had had to conduct himself as Oxford's burgess. At first he refused to be the bearer of the impeachment, for he viewed it as being a reflection upon the King to have the King's Secretary appointed for this purpose. This caused an uproar indeed. There was "a great cry, 'To the Bar, To the Bar'". Sir Thomas

Lee protested that the very being of Parliament was at stake. "Jenkins had no ground to bring the King's name in question, nor was there any reflection upon his Majesty, or Jenkins, in sending him with the impeachment. But for Jenkins to say . . . 'I will not go . . .'." Others joined in, saying that they had never heard of such a thing in Parliament before, and there were more outcries of "to the Bar". Jenkins finally got the floor again, and denied that he had said that the House "reflected on the King", only that he himself had taken it as such a reflection. "This message had not been put upon me but for the character I bear—I value not my life or liberty; do what you will with me, I will not go." This was repeated in a second speech which precipitated still more indignation.

> "If he be too big to carry your Message," said another member, "he is too big to be your Member, and not fit to be chosen one. Thus, to scorn the commands of the House, and to be too big for a Messenger of the House of Commons. Secretaries are sent on Messages every day, and is he too big for this, to accuse a person of the Popish Plot?"

This speaker also finished by suggesting that Jenkins's attitude boded ill to Parliament's very existence: "He may be privy to things hid from us possibly by this extraordinary carriage." Sir Leoline then disclaimed any intention to set himself above the authority of the House, but still insisted that he would not take the message, since what he objected to was, that the motion was made in ridicule. Two other speakers denied this, or at least said that even if moved in ridicule, a member should never refuse any command of the House. By this time, however, the game had spent itself somewhat. Jenkins was induced by some of the more friendly members to express regret that he had offended the House by his having attributed their act to an intention to cast reflections upon the King, and although some of the fiercer spirits were still insisting that he ask the House's pardon upon his knees, others admitted that "the thing was a little smilingly moved", and were willing to accept Sir Leoline's explanation as it stood. And Jenkins, "after all his huffing and striving", as North noted, "found it best" to take the impeachment to the Lords. "And so the thing passed over", said Grey, and the incident was brought to a close.[81]

One more episode of the Oxford Parliament brings out the uncomfortable character of Jenkins's position. He spoke again when the Exclusion Bill was taken up the second time, but to no effect. Grey rather scornfully notes that he gave only the same old arguments, and so his speech "passed off without notice".[82] Jenkins realized that his words were useless. "Possibly I am too tedious and not willing heard," he said somewhat helplessly at one point. Then, when he proposed that the Bill be thrown out, he was met with jeers. "Nobody seconds him", cried a member, rudely. "Let him second himself."[83]

On this unhappy note Sir Leoline Jenkins's parliamentary career for Oxford ends, for although he was elected again to the first and only Parliament of James II, he never lived to take his seat.

Of the other university burgesses, almost no trace of their presence in the House remains. Not one of them was honoured with a place on the Committee of Privilege. The only committee to which any of them was assigned was that where the representatives for Oxford as a group were joined with other members of Parliament to seek a better meeting-place for the Commons than the Schools.[84] Besides this, there was one specific reference to Cambridge's new burgess, Dr. Brady, and in this he figured as the author of the book on the succession to the throne rather than as a member of Parliament. If the session had lasted longer, Brady, too, might have been called to the bar of the House, for such a move was indeed proposed in the speech of one irate member, who urged that Brady's book be investigated, since he saw both in Brady's theories and in Jenkins's defiance, a plain "design" to "depress the Honour of this House".[85] Thus, of the four university representatives sent to the Oxford Parliament, two were under direct attack for their High Toryism, and two others, probably just as reactionary in their views, were silent and obscure.

NOTES FOR CHAPTER XI

1. For Sir William Temple's career, the first source is his own *Memoirs*, published in his *Collected Works*, ed. 1814, II, 245–569. There is also a life by his sister, Lady Giffard, in G. C. Moore Smith, ed., *The Early Essays and Romances of Sir William Temple*, pp. 3–31, and an early biography by Abel Boyer (1714). The studies by Thomas P. Courtenay, *Memoirs . . . of Sir William Temple* (1836), and Homer E. Woodbridge, *Sir William Temple* (1940), represent later research. Chapter XIV in the latter work especially takes up Temple's political career. Short sketches are in the *D.N.B.*; *B.B.*, VI, pt. i, 3915–23; Venn, IV, 213.

2. Temple himself in one case stated that he "ordered my pretensions so they came to fail". Does this mean that he wanted them to fail, or merely that the business was badly managed? *Works*, II, 506. Temple's biographer, Courtenay, takes the first view (*Memoirs*, II, 52), but other writers appear to differ. The seat involved seems to have been that of Northampton, where Temple's election was declared illegal when the dispute was brought to the House in November 1678. *H.M.C.*, *Egmont*, II, 76; *C.J.*, IX, 537, 546; *H.M.C.*, *Ormonde*, IV, 448, 471; Feiling, p. 173 n. Boyer, *Memoirs*, p. 352, seems to refer to this disputed election, but he has placed it in 1680 instead of in 1678. Temple himself also referred to other failures to secure a seat—at Windsor, in particular—but this seems to have been in 1678/9. *Works*, II, 506.

3. For Temple's Privy Council, see E. R. Turner, *The Privy Council of England, 1603–1784* (Baltimore, 1927), II, 439–50. Foxcroft, I, 145, discussing the Privy Council plan, thinks that the plan was Monmouth's and Sunderland's, rather than Temple's. See also Woodbridge, pp. 194–5, and n.

4. Courtenay, II, 62 n.
5. *Ibid.*, I, 244.
6. *Works*, II, 527–8.
7. *C.S.P., Dom., Chas. II*, XXI (1679–80), 197.
8. *Works*, II, 527–8; Henry Sidney, *Diary and Correspondence*, I, 33.
9. It seems incredible that Sawyer should have been considered Monmouth's "creature" at any point in his career, for he was anything but a Whig during most of his political life. But see below, Ch. XII, p. 323, n. 67.
10. Tanner MS., 38: 54, 62.
11. *Works*, II, 528.
12. Temple himself had also addressed the Archbishop about the same time, asking that the latter write in his behalf to the Vice-Chancellor and other friends at Cambridge, and reminding the Archbishop that the King had already spoken to him, and that the Duke had agreed to remain neutral. Tanner MS., 38: 57.
13. *Ibid.*, 62, 64.
14. For further details about Dr. Brady, see below, p. 288, and nn. 72, 73.
15. This is the first time since 1658 that such stress was laid in an election campaign on the matter of residence. From this time on, the issue was repeatedly revived. See Ch. XIII, pp. 328–9. It is curious to note, however, that the words from "King James his patent", that were quoted by Paman did not include the *de se ipsis* phrase that places the emphasis on residence, but only the section, *duos et magis sufficientibus viris.*
16. Tanner MS., 38: 64.
17. *Loc. cit.*
18. *Ibid.*, 65.
19. *Ibid.*, 64
20. Tillotson's letter to Dr. Samuel Blithe, Master of Clare College, pressed Temple's claims as one "not only a friend to learning, but a learned man himself", and noted that "the King is concerned for him, and I believe my Lord of Canterbury will heartily engage in his behalf". *H.M.C., App. 2nd Rep.*, p. 114. There is no date given here for this letter. It may have been written before the rumour of the Archbishop's coolness had been noised about, or perhaps, on the contrary, on purpose to counteract the rumour.
21. Tanner MS., 38: 57, 65. Sidney, I, 105. Earlier, Dr. Turner had also suggested that Sir William's secretary come down to Trinity Hall, where he was a fellow and canvass for his patron.
22. Sidney, I, 79.
23. Tanner MS., 38: 64.
24. Sidney, I, 105
25. *Works*, II, 527.
26. Sidney, I, 105
27. *O.R.*, p. 540. For Brady, see below, pp. 288.
28. Prideaux, *Letters*, p. 70 and n. For Col. Edward Vernon, see Foster, IV, 1542. He had been created D.C.L. 6 August 1677, probably through the indulgence of the Duke of Ormonde. He was a friend of the Duke's son, Lord Ossory, and was constantly taking advantage of this connection to ask for places and promotions. As early as 1677/8 he had expressed a desire to be parliament man in one of the Duke's towns, but there is no evidence that the Duke ever recommended him as a university burgess. *Calendar of Treasury Papers*, I, 151, 398, 428; *H.M.C., Ormonde*, IV, 111, 114; V, 217, 523, 525; *C.S.P., Dom., Chas. II*, XXVI (1684–5), 328, 373.
29. *H.M.C., Ormonde*, V, 154–5. This Spencer may possibly be the Robert Spencer mentioned in Venn, IV, 133; Foster, IV, 1395; *Fasti*, II, 317.
30. For Jenkins's career, see *D.N.B.*; *B.B.*, IV, 2748–58; William Wynne, *Life of Sir Leoline Jenkins*; Aubrey, II, 7–8.

31. For James Lane, see Foster, III, 874; G.E.C., *Peerage*, VII (1929), 422–3; and *D.N.B.* under Sir Edward Nicholas. Young Mr. Lane was no more successful in obtaining an Oxford seat in 1679 than his uncle, John Nicholas, had been in 1661, although this time the weight of the Chancellor's recommendation was in his favour, instead of in his opponent's.

32. *H.M.C., Ormonde*, IV, 619; V, 160–1.

33. *Ibid.*, pp. 173, 174. Halton, indeed, could scarcely refuse, since the Duke had recommended him, Halton, to the vice-chancellorship only three weeks before. *Ibid.*, IV, 617.

34. For Oldys, see *D.N.B.* under his nephew (or son), William. As for Parrott, no notice is taken of him even in the usual university registers, except for what is found in *Fasti*, II, 309; *Life and Times*, III, 188–9, and Williams, *Oxfordshire*, p. 156. He is to be distinguished from Charles Parrott, of Oriel, Sir Joseph Williamson's editor of newsletters. See *A.O.*, III, 1185; *Fasti*, II, 120, 176; Venn, III, 349; Foster, III, 1148. (Williams, *loc. cit.*, confuses the two Parrotts.)

35. *Life and Times*, III, 460–1.

36. Burnet, Airy, II, 257.

37. B. Behrens, "The Whig Theory of the Constitution", in the *Cambridge Historical Journal*, VII (1941), 48, 58, points out the disadvantages that the Tories seemed to have in this Parliament, despite their real numerical superiority. See below, n. 49.

38. Grey, VII, 403.

39. *P.H.*, IV, 1190–1, 1193, 1205–6, 1289; Grey, VII, 418–20; *An Exact Collection of the Most Considerable Debates*, pp. 51–3; Wynne, pp. xciv–cii.

40. Grey, VII, 420.

41. Wynne, p. xciv.

42. Grey, VII, 446.

43. *Ibid.*, p. 471; *C.J.*, IX, 654.

44. *Exact Coll.*, pp. 122–3.

45. Sidney, I, 176–7, 179, 186.

46. *Ibid.*, pp. 248–9. This was the period when the "Young Chits", Sunderland, Godolphin, and Oxford's former member, Lawrence Hyde, were at the height of their power.

47. *Works*, II, 549–50.

48. *Ibid.*, p. 551.

49. Thomas, Earl of Ailesbury, *Memoirs*, I, 48–9. Behrens, *Camb. Hist. Journal*, VII, 58, notes the timidity with which the Tories behaved in this session—as also Ailesbury elsewhere in his *Memoirs* (I, 34)—in spite of their having a numerical superiority in the House. Behrens attributes this to their fear of being listed on the black lists that were then being circulated about, such as the one mentioned in the *C.S.P., Dom., Chas. II*, XXII (1680–1), 675. Behrens places this list, incidentally, in the autumn of 1679 rather than in January 1680/1, as dated by the *C.S.P.* On this list only one of the current university burgesses is cited—Sir Thomas Exton—although two former university members, Thomas Thynne of Tamworth and Heneage Finch are both named. Public Record Office: S.P., Dom., Chas II, 29/417/232 (1). Jenkins had already been unfavourably mentioned in the "Seasonable Argument", *P.H.*, IV, App. III, p. xxxiii, but his name was not on Sir Stephen Fox's list of pensioners. Grey, VI, 323.

50. *Works*, II, 552.

51. *C.J.*, IX, 687.

52. See below, especially n. 55. Temple, *Works*, II, 552, mentions another speech in connection with the first address on general grievances.

53. Grey, VIII, 64.

54. *Ibid.*, pp. 37–8.

55. *P.H.*, IV, 1219–21; Grey, VII, 374; VIII, 19–20, 23, 47–8, 51, 68, 101–2. The chief speech on Tangier is also in *Works*, II, App., 583–6.

56. Grey, viii, 176, 182. Ailesbury in his *Memoirs*, i, 34, also noted how Temple retained the respect of the House through all this period.
57. *Exact Coll.*, pp. 123–6; Grey, vii, 374; *P.H.*, iv, 1219–21.
58. *Works*, ii, 549.
59. Grey, viii, 234; *C.J.*, ix, 699; *Works*, ii, 553. Woodbridge, p. 203, thinks that Temple lost popularity both with Parliament and with the King by his share in this affair. The reason that the King took offence was because Temple demurred at taking a message that he had had no part in formulating.
60. Grey, viii, 115–18, 122–7; *C.J.*, ix, 676; *H.M.C.*, *Ormonde*, v, 514, 519, 525–6; North, *Lives*, ii, 64–5. For the details of the action against Jenkins, see below, pp. 289–90.
61. *C.J.*, ix, 679.
62. *Ibid.*, 687; Grey, viii, 17–18.
63. For Jenkins's and Temple's remarks, see Grey, viii, 18. Reference to this incident is found in a letter to the Vice-Chancellor of Oxford, where Jenkins, predicting that the Exclusion Bill would pass, spoke of the sermon, about which his "brother Parrott" had given him some papers, and added—like a good university burgess—"I will have all the care I can to do you right." *C.S.P.*, *Dom.*, *Chas. II*, xxii (1680–1), 7–9.
64. *Exact Coll.*, pp. 257–8; Grey, viii, 277–8.
65. *H.M.C.*, *Ormonde*, v, 561; Grey, viii, 281–3; *C.J.*, ix, 703; Burnet, Airy, ii, 262.
66. *Life and Times*, ii, 513.
67. *Exact Coll.*, pp. 125–6.
68. See Sunderland's view in Courtenay, ii, 71.
69. *Works*, ii, 555.
70. *O.R.*, p. 546. In the Cambridge University Registry, 50, there are 107 ballots for Exton. Dr. Brady's ballots are seemingly missing.
71. *H.M.C.*, *App.*, *2nd Rep.*, p. 114.
72. Prideaux, *Letters*, pp. 137–8. Brady's works are listed under various titles, the chief of which are: *Reply to Wm. Petit* (on the rights of the Commons); *The Great Point of Succession* (both 1681); *A Complete History of England*, 1685 (sometimes entitled *An Introduction to the Old English History*, 1684); *A Historical Treatise of Cities and Burghs*, 1690. Brady was Keeper of the Records of the Tower from possibly as early as 1670 until he was displaced after the Glorious Revolution in March 1688/9. *C.S.P.*, *Dom.*, *Wm. III*, i (1689–90), 22.
73. For Brady's career, see *D.N.B.*; *B.B.*, ii, 960–1; David C. Douglas, *English Scholars*, pp. 155–9; Munk, *Roll of the Royal College*, i, 418; Venn, i, 203. An autobiographical account of part of Brady's earlier life is in *C.S.P.*, *Dom.*, *Chas. II*, xi (1671), 78. The most thorough study of Brady is J. G. A. Pocock, "Robert Brady", *Cambridge Historical Journal*, x (1951), 186–204.
74. *Life and Times*, ii, 515.
75. *C.S.P.*, *Dom.*, *Chas. II*, xxii (1680–1), 139. This suggests that Jenkins had rendered more service in the term of office just closed than that noted above in connection with the Popishly inclined sermon, but what it was, has not yet been brought to light. Later expressions of gratitude show that his care continued in 1684. *Ibid.*, xxvi (1684–5) 218, 303, 316, 364; Prideaux, *Letters*, p. 135.
76. *Life and Times*, ii, 515–16, 522; *O.R.*, p. 549.
77. Grey, vii, 293–4; *Debates in the House Assembled at Oxford, 1680*, pp. 4–5.
78. Grey, viii, 295–6.
79. Wynne, p. xliii.
80. North, ii, 64–5.
81. *Loc. cit.*; *Debates in the House, 1680*, pp. 12–16; Grey, viii, 304–5. Other contemporary accounts of the affair are found in *H.M.C.*, *Ormonde*, vi, 6, 7, 20–2, and Ailesbury, ii, 55; *C.S.P.*, *Dom.*, *Chas. II*, xxii (1680–1), 225. Jenkins himself found some "ingredients of refined malice" in the incident, "some evil spirit behind the curtain that is not seen", as he put it. *H.M.C.*, *Ormonde*, v, 20.

The *Historical Collections*, p. 241, characteristically Tory, has no reference to the affair.

82. Grey, VIII, 339.
83. *P.H.*, IV, 1337-8. In Grey's account as in the *Debates, 1680*, pp. 238-9, the speech appears less offensive: "Nobody, it seems seconds him; therefore pray let him go on and second himself." Grey, VIII, 339.
84. *C.J.*, IX, 706, 708.
85. Grey, VIII, 306.

CHAPTER XII

UNIVERSITY REPRESENTATION THROUGH ABSOLUTISM AND REVOLUTION, 1685–1690

The death of Charles II in February 1684/5 made necessary the calling of a new Parliament. In the four years that had intervened since the short session at Oxford in 1681 the opposition had been broken and scattered. The Whig leaders were prosecuted and suppressed; the town governments were rendered safe for the Court through *Quo Warranto* proceedings; and the Rye House Plot had given rise to a strong Tory reaction throughout the whole country. Even without manipulation, James II could count on a Parliament after his own heart when he caused the writs of summons to be issued for a meeting in May 1685. But to make sure that things would go even better, the elections everywhere were rigged by the Court party—so thoroughly indeed that, as the King himself said, there were not more than forty members in the House, "but such as he himself wished for".[1] Needless to say, among these forty unwelcome members there were no university burgesses.

On the contrary, the staunch Tories of the previous Parliament were re-elected to a man. Oxford quickly returned Sir Leoline Jenkins and Dr. Parrott without, as Wood said, "any competition or controllment".[2] Indeed, no "controllment" by the King or Chancellor was necessary at Oxford to insure the highest kind of a Tory slate, for the university after the Rye House Plot had issued an official repudiation of all doctrines that in any way resembled the principles of the Whig Party, which placed the university on record—to its later embarrassment—as maintaining the most extreme form of the divine-right theory.[3]

At Cambridge, on the contrary, certain "controllments" were attempted, though unsuccessful. These were not of a political nature, however, but rather represented the personal interests of the new Chancellor, Christopher Monck, Duke of Albemarle, son of the famous general.[4] The Duke was determined that the university should name his cousin, Colonel Arthur Fairwell, to one of its seats, and wrote a long complaining letter to the Vice-Chancellor on the subject.[5] The tenor of the letter seems to indicate that Albemarle had some reason to suspect that his wishes might not be obeyed. He expressed his doubt and displeasure that some of the colleges should have presumed to engage themselves for the election, or that any member of the university should have presumed to ask them to engage themselves, before their Chancellor's permission was granted. If he had the honour of being their head, the Duke said, he must also have the privileges that went with this honour. Even in the towns where he only held the office of Recorder, he was accustomed to such privileges, and certainly in a university, he argued, in "a Society of Men which is expected to be the Pattern of Wisdom", there should be as much "decency and duty" as in a town. "Except", he added, "you think the Wisest Members may well be suited with the most insignificant Head", and be served by their Chancellor without return on their part. Such a position he could not accept. "When my Honour is concerned, I am in too high a Sphear to recede", he declared loftily.

But indeed the Chancellor could scarcely believe that Cambridge would be so unaccommodating as to deny to his "nearest Relation" the post that they had previously bestowed upon the "Ordinary Servant" of his predecessor (James Vernon, Monmouth's secretary). Moreover, he reminded them that his cousin, Colonel Fairwell, was a nephew of the great General Monck who had made possible the Restoration— this was an appeal that Tories should respond to—and that the late King Charles had favoured Fairwell with a mandate degree at Cambridge for the express purpose of making him eligible for a university seat. It was true, the Duke admitted, that Fairwell had once been a fellow-commoner at Oxford, but he had never been matriculated there, held no degree, and belonged there no more than at Paris or Padua, whereas at Cambridge he was now actually a master of arts, a member of the university[6]—and also, as cousin to the Chancellor, one who stood "near the Court", and therefore suitable for the university's first burgess. Indeed it was a compliment to the university for the Duke's cousin to accept the seat, "otherwise far below him", but this honour was offered as a testimony of their Chancellor's esteem. The second seat, Albemarle generously declared, should be left to the university's own free choice.

This long tirade seems to have had no effect upon the university whatsoever, for about a month later they re-elected their previous burgesses, Sir Thomas Exton and Dr. Robert Brady, without any contest. Both Exton and Brady were good Tories and supporters of the Court, but as we have already seen, stubborn campaigners, well entrenched, and *bona-fide* residents of the university, quite able to maintain themselves even against Chancellor's orders. Thus, even in a time of royal supremacy when outside influence was elsewhere at its height, Cambridge vindicated the right of the university to a free choice of representatives.[7]

The Parliament that met on 19 May 1685 was the most docile of all the Restoration Parliaments. Even without the stimulus of Monmouth's Rebellion, it was ready to do the King's will as no Parliament had been since the Parliament of 1661.[8] Its sessions were short, and there is not much information available about its proceedings. It would seem that Sir Leoline Jenkins was not present at all, for his name is found on none of the committee lists in the *Commons' Journals*. By this time he was no longer Secretary of State, and ill health probably kept him in the country, since he died shortly after the first session ended. Dr. Brady was the most active of the university members, being assigned to six committees, the most interesting of which was perhaps the committee to inspect the *Journals* and consider what proceedings of the Exclusion Parliaments should be expunged.[9] Dr. Parrott and Sir Thomas Exton each served on three committees,[10] and, in addition, all three worthies, as members for the two universities were among those set to study an ecclesiastical matter, the repairs needed in the diocese of Bangor.[11] There was in this Parliament no business that concerned the universities directly.

When the second—and last—session of this Parliament met on 9 November, a new writ was ordered to fill the seat at Oxford left vacant by the death of Sir Leoline Jenkins in July,[12] and on 23 November the by-election took place. Chancellor's letters had been read on 26 October in favour of Mr. George Clarke, Judge Advocate of the army and fellow of All Souls.[13] But Clarke was not chosen without a contest, for Dr. William Oldys, candidate in 1679,[14] once more tried for the place, and lost by about eighty votes. A letter from Dr. Fell to Chancellor Ormonde, dated 14 September, had opposed Oldys's candidacy, and pointed out that, despite the recommendation in his behalf sent to Ormonde by the Bishop of Winchester, Oldys had offended the university by suing another university resident in the Court of Common Pleas, which was contrary to the university oath on privileges which he had previously taken. "This affront", declared Fell, "the University will not easily forget, and much less will they reward it."[15] His prediction was borne out by the results of the election. Wood, however, had nothing to say of Oldys, either for good or ill, but for Clarke's success, had his usual ready explanation. Clarke was "a junior and a good fellow" (he was about twenty-eight at this time), and "the pot men and juniors carry all before them".[16]

But Clarke had no opportunity in this House to prove his worth one way or the other, for Parliament was prorogued three days before his election and continuously thereafter until July 1687, when it was dissolved.[17] In later years he was returned again—and more than once

—as Oxford's representative, but this part of his career belongs to the history of the eighteenth century.[18]

In the time between the prorogation of November 1685 and the final dissolution, things were rapidly shaping to a climax. James II's increasing absolutism began to touch the university members individually, to their advantage or disadvantage, as the case might be—with the exception of Parrott who died in 1686 before the crisis had sharpened. Even Sir Thomas Exton, Court party man as he had always been—Advocate-General and recently Dean of the Arches—now found himself called before the Commission of Ecclesiastical Causes without a charge— "for what, he is to know when he appeares", reported Sir John Bramston—and soon thereafter he was dismissed from his post in the Admiralty.[19] George Clarke, on the other hand, though threatened by Obadiah Walker, James's Catholic protégé at Oxford, managed to keep his place as Judge Advocate of the army by visiting around the country out of reach of the Court.[20] He did not escape, however, at least one uncomfortable encounter, when James II visited Oxford in 1687 and asked Clarke if it were not illegal for the fellows of All Souls to have ceased offering prayers for the dead. "No, sir," replied Clarke (according to Wood's version), "not that I know of", and went on to explain the technicalities of the college charter in a way that did not much suit the King. "I was told afterwards", Clarke wrote, "that I was but an ill courtier in going so far."[21] Dr. Robert Brady, however, the fourth of the university M.P.s seems to have been completely at home with the new order of things, and it was as one of the Court physicians to certify to the birth of the Prince that he made his last public appearance in the world of great affairs, 22 October 1688, shortly before the landing of William of Orange.

By this time sentiment in the universities was beginning to change. Dismay and alarm over King James's course of action were undermining the High Tory position. At Oxford the King had forced the election of one Papist as Head of Madgalen College, and at Cambridge had insisted upon the granting of a degree to another—both illegal proceedings according to college and university statutes. Moreover, the King's whole policy of favour to Roman Catholics ran completely counter to the strong Anglican loyalties of the university tradition. This feeling is shown in the reports returned by the King's agents who were sent out to gauge the sentiment of the country early in 1688, for the purpose of trying to secure a Parliament that would agree with the King's policy on the Test Act. Questions were asked of voters and officials in every county and borough as to their views on repeal. On the basis of this information, steps were taken to remove

unco-operative officials from posts of influence, and otherwise overawe
the voters.

But what the King's agents reported on the universities was most
unpromising for this purpose. The replies made by a list of individuals
at Oxford in February 1687/8 were respectful but evasive, and the
general conclusion of the reporters was that the elections of members of
Parliament there were to be free, with no pre-engagement in favour of
the King's candidates or policies.[22] At Cambridge in March 1687/8 the
Vice-Chancellor was named on a list of J.P.s labelled the "Right ones"
—that is, the ones deemed favourable to the Court—but by April the
King's agents wrote dubiously of their efforts. "We cannot undertake
for them", they complained of the university. Worse still, the borough
was also uncertain, for the magistrates were "wholey under the Influence
of the University, and such as cannot influence the Electors, nor are the
University wanting to improve their Interest".[23] For the moment it
would seem the old rivalry between university and town had been
resolved in the university's favour. But the situation was probably
only the result of a common fear of the King and the Catholics that
had driven the two enemies together. Such harmony of sentiment did
not prevail. Soon after the King's inquiry, the town underwent a
royal purge. But the university persisted. By September the outlook
was still not reassuring to the Court. "We can say nothing to it," the
royal reporters wrote. Here again, as from time to time throughout the
century, the fundamental freedom of university elections was again
being successfully asserted.

But King James never had the opportunity of pressing his claims
upon the universities further. When the next Parliament finally met, it
was a Convention, called to meet with William of Orange, and the
elections to this Convention were quite free and undicted. It would be
of absorbing interest to know what were the cross-currents flowing
beneath the surface at this time, but little has survived regarding the
universities' activities in this election. Even Wood disappoints us in his
brief account of the Convocation at Oxford, merely noting that there
were two elections—one 10 December, apparently in response to James's
desperate last-minute summons; and another 7 January (not in the
Convocation records in the Archives), to choose representatives for the
Convention. In both elections the same members were chosen, Sir
Thomas Clarges and the Honourable Heneage Finch, late Solicitor-
General. No other contestants appear to have stood.[25] Finch, it will
be recalled, had been member for Oxford in 1678/9.[26] His choice at
this time may have been owing to his family's known devotion to the
Church of England, and his own recent defence of the Seven Bishops.

Sir Thomas Clarges was an old-time political figure who had first come to prominence in helping General Monck to usher in the Restoration, and who had served almost continuously in all the Parliaments since 1656. He had in the course of time acquired something of a reputation for opposing undue use of the prerogative, and had been connected with the passing of the Habeas Corpus Act. Hence his election may reflect something of the revolutionary temper of the times, as much of it at least, as Tory Oxford could tolerate.[27]

At Cambridge there is more evidence of conflicting cross-currents in the election of 1688/9, though not enough evidence to make the situation clear. Sir Robert Sawyer, who had twice before looked longingly at a Cambridge seat, made now another attempt to win it. He began in September 1688 by writing to Archbishop Sancroft. In this letter he reported that he had received an invitation to stand for the university's seat, but that he was unwilling to do so without the approval of the Archbishop—perhaps remembering how without this support his efforts against Sir William Temple in 1679 had been unavailing.[28] He declared that his "affection to serve the University and in them the establisht church" was as great "as any persons in my Sphiare", but said that he was "loath to raise disputes between Gremials at a time when the greatest Unity and concordance in Elections ought to be throughout the nation". For nothing, he went on, could so dismay "the enemies of our religion" as "an unanimous choice of members to serve in Parliament", and if his Grace deemed it proper for him to stand, he would render faithful service.[29] From this letter, it appears that Sir Thomas Exton, Cambridge's old burgess of three Parliaments past, was seriously ill—he died before the election[30]—and this may have encouraged Sawyer in his readiness to stand for the seat. His reference to Exton's illness, however, was in connection with an appeal for a post for a brother-in-law, rather than because it had any bearing on his own case.

As things turned out, however, instead of the Parliament summoned by King James that Sawyer expected, it was for the Convention that he was to offer himself, and at a time when the spirit of the country was far from unanimous in supporting one who, like Sawyer, had had unsavoury connections with some of the more high-handed actions of the late régimes. At least for some reason the poll was very close. Sawyer stood at the head, but it was only by three and eight votes respectively over his two competitors. Nine days before the election his chances had been dubious. He wrote in alarm—perhaps to the Archbishop's secretary—an unpromising account of the state of his affairs in the university.

> I have met with, from some, farre other usage than I could have expected from the nursury of Ingenuity, for after they had raised upon mee many

false calumnyes and those wiped off, some of them now attempt tricks [circumventing?] a considerable majority of the University—about two parts in three are for mee [the poll showed he was too optimistic]—by Endeavouring to presse Mr. Vice-Chancellor against all law and right either to omit mee out of the returne upon pretense I am no resient . . . or otherwise to make a double returne by returning three whereby the University would be deprived any representation this convention.

In this last remark, Sir Robert was implying that the Convention would be of such short duration that there would not be time enough for a disputed election to be settled. He could not, of course, foresee that the Convention would be turned into a Parliament by its own decree and continued for a whole year. His argument on the university's behalf was therefore a telling one. Although he admitted that he could scarcely believe that the Vice-Chancellor would have any part in such unjust proceedings, he insisted that he had recently heard "by a good accompt" that the Vice-Chancellor had let fall some words indicating that such was his intention. For this reason, Sir Robert had hastened to write this letter to make an appeal to the university's Chancellor, that the latter might forestall such practices by a note to the Vice-Chancellor.[31]

Sawyer's remarks on the subject of gremials recall the fact that at Cambridge the question of the eligibility of a non-resident had been raised in Temple's campaign of 1679.[32] Since that time the claims of the gremials had been strengthened by the fact that the two previous burgesses for two elections past (1680/1 and 1685) had both been gremials. Neither of these, Sir Thomas Exton and Dr. Brady, was now a candidate in 1688/9, but others were being pushed to the fore. One was Edward Finch, fellow of Christ's College, and brother of the Honourable Heneage Finch of Oxford and of Daniel Finch, second Earl of Nottingham.[33] The other was Cambridge's master-mind, Isaac Newton, Lucasian Professor of Mathematics. Finch's claims probably rested upon his close relation to the Earl—he was secretary as well as brother—and his family's traditional Anglicanism, while Newton's popularity was grounded, not alone upon his intellectual distinction—the *Principia* had just been published the year before—but upon his service to the university in its resistance to the encroachments of James II.

Newton, in fact, according to his biographer, Brewster,[34] had been the first to protest seriously against the granting of a mandate degree to the Benedictine, Father Alban Francis. His protest was made in a university meeting in which the majority were about to follow their former Vice-Chancellor, Francis Turner, now the Bishop of Ely, in yielding to the King's wishes. It was largely because of Newton's suggestion that the legal aspects of the matter be explored, that the university finally sent a delegation to present its case before the

Ecclesiastical Commission.[35] Newton was sent as a member of this delegation,[36] and endured along with the others the violent attacks of Lord Chancellor Jeffreys, who presided. Nevertheless, he ultimately had the satisfaction of seeing the King drop the issue, as a result of the delegation's arguments. That this was no light service to the university is shown by the fact that the Vice-Chancellor, as a result of his share in the resistance, was deprived of his post. Newton himself, however, does not seem to have suffered.[37]

The absence of further evidence about the manœuvres of the election of January 1688/9, involving as it did the greatest university figure of the century, is unfortunate, especially since Sawyer's letter suggests that there was a good deal of intrigue and electioneering on foot. It is not even clear whether or not there was an earlier election, as there was at Oxford, in response to the summons of King James. All that is known is that the election was held in the afternoon, and that the poll was very close, and that the disputed result that Sawyer had feared was very near to coming into being, Sawyer having only 125 votes to Newton's 122 and Finch's 117. Newton's popularity was shown by the complimentary titles that his electors wrote on their voting papers— "integerrimus vir", "clarissimus vir", "doctissimus", venerabilis", "reverendus"—which may perhaps indicate that, in naming him, more honour was intended than was usually bestowed upon parliamentary candidates.[38]

Once elected, Newton continued to serve his university with an honesty and seriousness completely worthy of the scientific mind in politics. He seems never to have made a speech in the House,[39] and his name is found on only three committee lists, including one for the relief of French Protestant ministers, and another for indulgence to Protestant Dissenters.[40] Both of these might reflect Newton's own interest in religion, as well as university concern with church matters. But the public records give no real picture of Newton's actual service in the Convention Parliament. This must be sought elsewhere, in a series of letters written by Newton to Dr. John Covell, Vice-Chancellor of Cambridge, Master of Christ's College, and formerly chaplain to Queen Mary when she was Princess of Orange. Here the great mathematician is seen constantly and earnestly preoccupied with the problems of the university created by this time of crisis.[41]

The first letter dates from 12 February, before William and Mary were recognized and proclaimed King and Queen. Newton informed Covell that a proclamation ceremony would have to be carried out at the university, and expressed the wish that it could be performed "with a reasonable decorum", because he felt that it was to the university's interest "to set the best face upon things they can", just as the London divines had done.[42] The proclamation, apparently, was a somewhat delicate subject in a community where many were still doubtful of the Revolution's legality. All passed off well, however, for in another letter, nine days later, Newton was rejoicing that the ceremony had been carried through "with so much decence" by the "wiser & more considerable part of ye University", and urged that congratulatory verses, according to custom, be offered the new Sovereigns at once.[43] The verses referred to seem to have caused some dismay. Covell wrote to the Archbishop immediately for advice,[44] but a month later no verses had yet been presented. Edward Finch consulted Nottingham and told the Vice-Chancellor they must be forthcoming.[45] They were finally produced, one of the authors being Dr. George Oxenden, later a university burgess.

The matter of the new oaths was Newton's next concern. As a result of the Revolution, oaths of allegiance and supremacy recognizing the new Sovereigns were to be required of all office-holders, clerical and secular, on pain of loss of office. This was to apply to those who occupied university posts as well as to members of Parliament. Moreover the wording of the oaths themselves was to be somewhat altered from the original Tudor form. Such a measure was likely to cause great dismay in university circles, where the purest divine-right doctrines had recently been so ardently asserted. Newton was well aware of how this proposal would appear to his constituents. Many persons "of less understanding than Dr. Covell"—so he wrote earnestly—would be apt to "scruple at" the new oaths, and, realizing that this would be a great cause of disturbance among "ye dissatisfied part of ye University", he particularly set himself to try to remove the scruples of "as many as have sense enough to be convinced with reason". He then laid down his thoughts on this matter in a series of propositions. They were the usual arguments used at this time to support the transfer of the Crown to the new King, emphasizing that the duty of subjects was to obey the law, not the individual monarch, and stressing the legality of allegiance to a *de facto* King. "Fidelity & Allegiance sworn to ye King is only such a Fidelity and Obedience as is due to him by ye Law of ye Land." If it were otherwise, "we should swear ourselves slaves & ye King absolute, whereas by the law we are free men notwithstanding those Oaths". "Allegiance & protection are always mutual and therefore when King James ceased to protect us we ceased to owe him Allegiance by ye law of ye Land. And when K. W. began to protect us we began to owe Allegiance to him."[46]

In these propositions, Newton had become quite a lawyer, quoting

Justice Hale and the relevant statutes of Edward III and Henry VII along with the best of them. But this was not an entirely new role for the great mathematician. More shows that he had been concerned with the relative position of the King and the law long before he was elected parliament man, and that he had shown a preference for Whig principles from the start.[47] The Alban Francis episode had already given him some experience in legal matters. Now after his entrance into Parliament, acquaintance with John Locke, John Somers, and Charles Montague, later Earl of Halifax, sharpened his interest in public affairs and political philosophy.

Newton's dexterity in political dialectic is shown in the use he made of the once popular doctrine of passive obedience, where, in the same letter, in a final attempt to persuade the dissatisfied, he gave the doctrine a new parliamentary twist: "If ye dissatisfied party accuse the Convention for making ye P. of Orange King; tis not my duty to judge those above me. . . . And those at Cambridge ought not to judge & censure their superiors but to obey & honour them according to the Law and the doctrine of passive obedience"—a sentiment that seems to replace the absolutism of Kings by the absolutism of Parliaments, and from one point of view, scarcely a reasonable way for a representative to address his constituents.[48]

A week later Newton was still concerned with the oaths, particularly as the new law regarding them was not likely to be ready in time for "commencers" to comply, in which case they might be in danger of losing credit for the time they had spent in the university. Newton had spoken to the gentleman in charge of the bill, to urge that it might be brought in as soon as possible, and was contemplating having a clause added to allow for the university's difficulty, in case the bill was delayed too long. In this same letter to Covell, Newton also gave advice about the validity of proceedings in the university courts, and reported on the bills "we voted" the day before—on France, Ireland, and taxes—for the information of his constituents.[49]

By 2 March, Newton was more hopeful that the bill on the new oaths would be ready, and gave further advice upon the status of the university courts. At the end of the letter he was able to report the glad tidings that the King of his own volition had offered to forego the hated hearth tax, so bitterly resented by the colleges with their many chimneys ever since the first Heneage Finch had failed to oppose it on Oxford's behalf back in the early years of the Restoration. The letter closed with news of more legislation, and the fact that the Lords and Commons had taken the new oaths, this last no doubt intended as an encouragement to the faint-hearted of Cambridge.[50]

One lord, at least, had not taken the new oaths—William Sancroft, Archbishop of Canterbury, the university's own Chancellor. This presented Cambridge with an additional problem—to elect a new Chancellor—for Sancroft's determination to refuse the oaths was followed by the resignation of all his posts of honour, including the university chancellorship. Newton's next letter made reference to this problem, noting that the names of both the Earl of Danby and the Earl of Dorset were mentioned for the place. He told Dr. Covell that Cambridge friends in London were much inclined to Dorset, and he went on to say that if no other candidate had been determined on, he believed that the university would "do a grateful Act to those above in favouring ye Election of that Honourable person".[51] Newton took up the question of the oaths again, and noted that he had given up the idea of adding a special clause safeguarding the interests of those about to take degrees, recommending instead that the Vice-Chancellor find a way to adjust the time allowed for the taking of the oaths by means of a grace of the Senate or by Letters Patent from the King.[52]

The next letter, written one day later, 6 March, shows Newton hard at work on the matter of the university charters, which it was thought were in need of renewal in view of changes introduced by the Revolution. The renewal gave occasion for alteration of some of the terms of the charters as well, and this entailed some search of the records, and several exchanges between the university and its representative. For the present Newton was concentrating on the problem of the charters of the colleges, rather than those pertaining to the university as a whole. At the same time, a new candidate for Chancellor appeared, the Duke of Somerset, and Newton notified Dr. Covell of the Duke's interest in the honour.[53]

But the question of the new oaths was much more on his mind, for he referred to decisions made 5 March and 6 March where "they outvoted us by about 50 votes" in the Grand Committee. The 16 March saw the whole bill finished in the Commons, but Newton gave no details. He would, he said, prefer that Dr. Covell have the whole matter "from another hand"—perhaps from Sir Robert Sawyer, Cambridge's other member. Why Newton took this position, it is impossible to say. He had obviously been exerting himself over the provisions of the bill for a considerable time.

I perused it a week before it was brought into the House (that is, three weeks ago) & found nothing in it for imposing the new oaths on all persons in preferments, but only on those who take new preferments. Being acquainted with ye Gentleman who drew it up, I discoursed him about ye designe of it before he drew it up . . . & after . . . he shewed me ye draught to satisfy me it was not for imposing ye new oaths on all. . . . This I acquaint you particularly because I would have ye University satisfied that these new oaths are not designed to be imposed on them all as I am told they still believe, tho' I wrote formerly to remove this their prejudice.[54]

Newton, however, was over-optimistic on this point, for despite his efforts, when the bill reached its final form, more severe amendments were added, making the oaths compulsory on all clergy and laity.[55]

Newton now devoted himself to the confirmation of the charters, both those of the colleges and of the university. On 29 March he wrote for copies of the originals, with any comments that might be attached, and reminded the university carefully that such matters as the press and the university preachers and professorships, as well as the wine licences, might be included, and in such case it would be well "to have all in readiness & for that End".[56]

A month later Newton, together with Sir Thomas Clarges of Oxford, introduced a motion for a bill to settle the charters of the two universities, and leave to bring in such a bill was granted by the House.[57] Oxford, Newton reminded his constituents, had already sent up instructions as to what the university wanted in the bill, but Cambridge had so far left him without advice. "If you at Cambridge neglect your advantage as you seem to do", he wrote, "I will take ye best care I can of it. But I think that it may deserve a little of your care." He went on to suggest that if it was too difficult to communicate their wishes in writing, they might send up "one or two intelligent persons . . . for us to consult with . . . But", he added, "if you send up anybody, pray let him be moderate as well as intelligent, and let him be sent as soon as may be."[58]

On 5 May, Newton wrote again, still complaining of having received no instructions.[59] It seemed, however, that the university had not been so negligent as he believed, for letters with the information he wanted had been lost *en route*. Newton's reply to the one communication that had been received contained a copy of the Oaths Act and a summary of the bill recommended by Oxford, with a note on additional items that he considered worthy of inclusion. Interestingly enough, these additional items are the suggestions of a scholar, covering such matters as limitation of degrees granted by mandate, and the publishing of books, rather than ecclesiastical or political interests. That they appear to have been Newton's own suggestions is indicated by the fact that he had passed them on to Sir Robert Sawyer for the latter's consideration.[60]

Newton's next letter returned to the subject of the oaths and the declaration, explaining how they should be handled, and cautioning the university to obey the law.[61] Five days later, 15 May, he gave further advice, jointly this time with Sawyer, and urged care in keeping a record of the oaths sworn. In addition, he acknowledged the information in regard to the charters which he had at last received, and explained why he and Sir Robert did not think it wise to act upon some of the suggestions given. One point especially Newton found, upon private inquiry, would not be acceptable, but would engage the House "in hazzardous debate". He went on, in closing, to deplore the circulation of a petition regarding a definition of allegiance, which he was told was going "up and down amongst you for hands". This he considered dangerous.

> I can neither perswade nor diswade any man from subscribing it but yet I think it my duty to acquaint you that I have endeavoured much to feel ye puls of ye house about such an explication of allegiance & find such an aversness from it that I am of opinion ye petition can do no good, but may do much hurt if ill resented by ye Houses.

Enclosed with this letter was a joint statement signed by both burgesses giving full instructions about the tendering of the new oaths.[62]

With this communication, the letters of Isaac Newton to Dr. John Covell come to an end, and the best picture to be found of a university representative in action in any period is completed. It is certainly of much interest that the greatest figure to act as university burgess in the whole century should have left the most complete account of his services, and the most perfect record of attention to duty and disinterested exertion.

Throughout Newton's letters, there is frequent mention of his colleague, Sir Robert Sawyer, with whom he seems to have conferred from time to time, and from whom he very likely obtained much legal information. But Newton—as became a resident burgess, with closer ties to the university—appears to have been the chief mediator and correspondent regarding the university's interests. Sawyer, however, is known to have communicated his opinions more than once to his constituents, for, in addition to the document referred to above, enclosed in Newton's final letter, another manuscript exists, dated 19 February, addressed to Dr. William Cook, fellow of Jesus College, and later chancellor of the Diocese of Ely.[63]

In this letter, Sawyer endeavoured to allay the doctor's doubts on the subject of abdication, just as Newton had tried to allay those of Dr. Covell at about the same time. The arguments are the usual ones, very similar to those cited by Newton—the matter of the allegiance's being dissolved by the late King's entering into what Sawyer called "Civill Death"; the validity of a *de facto* monarchy; and the responsibility for the decision to forsake the legitimate heir as resting not upon individual subjects but only upon those who actually had the power of naming the next heir. Sawyer, interestingly enough, admitted that he shared in some of the scruples mentioned by Dr. Cook, though he did not specify which ones. It would seem, however, that they were the scruples that were raised about the giving of the Crown in full right to William as joint Sovereign with Mary, for on this point Sawyer noted that the majority of the Lords and 152 of the Commons[64] were in favour of regarding Mary as the "only visible & unsuspected Heir", and that this was the opinion "of which . . . my Brother [i.e. Newton] & I were", though the majority of the House voted against it, "out of affection to ye Prince".[65] If Newton did take this stand, he seems to have recovered more readily from his misgivings than Sawyer, for Newton's letter to Dr. Covell about the same date as Sawyer's to Cook sounded a much more confident note. Indeed, it is hardly likely that the man who was later recognized by Macaulay as "the glory of the Whigs" would have had very much difficulty in adjusting himself to the change in the monarchy.

With Sawyer, however, the case was different. To be sure, his first appearance on the university stage was as a reputed favourite of the Duke of Monmouth,[66] and it is said that he had a hand in the drafting of the Exclusion Bill,[67] but his career since that time had been completely tied up with the absolutist policies of the Crown.[68] Made Attorney-General in 1681, he had assisted first in the prosecution of Shaftesbury, and then of Russell, Sidney, and others who had fallen under suspicion in connection with the Rye House Plot, and he had been active in carrying through the campaign against the independence of the towns under the writs of *Quo Warranto*. He and Heneage Finch together—Finch being Solicitor-General at the time—had been particularly active both against the City of London, and against Lord Russell. But with the accession of James and the increasing evidence of the King's intent, as it seemed, to foist Catholicism upon the nation, Sawyer, like Finch, began to experience doubts. But, where Finch made his position clear as early as April 1686, when asked to co-operate in regard to the dispensing power—"he refused plumb", as Roger North put it,[69] and was discharged from his post—Sawyer lingered on as Attorney-General until December 1687, protesting in the meanwhile and asking for dismissal—perhaps half-heartedly.[70] North, a contemporary and a Tory, put Sawyer's action in a somewhat better light than later writers, and spoke well of his conduct in the trial of Russell and others; and in relation to the dispensing power pointed out that one of the cases which Sawyer did not hesitate to repudiate was that of Obadiah Walker's election to be Head of University College at Oxford.[71] This stand brought Sawyer forward as something of a champion of university rights, and may have contributed to his election as burgess at

Cambridge. When the King finally saw that Sawyer was unwilling to go further with the policy of dispensing, he was "soon off the hooks" in North's phrase, and now, freed from his crown office, in a few months became counsel for the defence of the Seven Bishops, once again in alliance with Finch. This put him well on the way to redeeming himself in the eyes of all good Anglicans, including his future constituency at Cambridge. And the same may probably also be said for Finch's reputation at Oxford.

In Sawyer's case at least, no shadow was cast on his career for some time after his election. In his first months as university representative, he took a leading part in the proceedings of the House. His legal knowledge naturally placed him in a prominent position, especially at a time when the whole foundation of English law and government was under examination. He spoke early in favour of abdication, and criticized the late King's reign in the strongest language.[72] About the legality of bestowing the Crown upon the Prince of Orange, as we know from the letter to Dr. Cook, Sawyer was not clear, and so it is not surprising to find him silent during the debates that led up to this decision.[73] Once the new monarchs had been proclaimed, however, Sawyer's legal mind busied itself with the question of the Convention's legitimacy, and this led him to take a stand among those cautious members who urged the necessity of a new election to make their acts valid. Macaulay and Feiling point out that this was only a Tory manœuvre resorted to in the hopes of getting a more thoroughly Tory House by taking advantage of the reaction of doubt that was spreading over the country, now that the Revolution had actually been carried through.[74] In general, however, Sir Robert's activities seem to have been such as would have supported the new régime, so far as can be gathered from the limited evidence available in the *Commons' Journals* and Grey's *Debates*. He served on eighteen committees during the first session, including the Committee of Privilege and such committees as were suitable for a university burgess—on the repeal of the Corporation Act, the relief of French Protestant ministers, the new oaths, the right of presentation to benefices.[75] These last two bills directly concerned the universities, and the question of the new oaths, as we have seen from Newton's letters, was occupying a major place in the thoughts and efforts both of Newton and Sawyer during the early months of the session; while the bill regarding benefices—a provision for the further endowment of the universities by granting them rights of presentment formerly controlled by dispossessed Papists—would also have been of special interest. For this committee, Sawyer acted as reporter, and was later sent to the Lords with the bill to ask their concurrence.[76]

He also seems to have spoken in his special character of university burgess three different times. Once this was in answer to a slur cast on the loyalty of the clergy to the new régime. Sir Robert was quick to take exception to this charge. "I speak of the clergy of Cambridge. I had a letter from Cambridge yesterday (the place I serve for) which gives me notice that they are very well satisfied with what you have done."[77] The date of this remark, 20 February, makes it very likely that the letter referred to was the one from Dr. Cook to which Sawyer had written the reply described some paragraphs above. Sir Robert must have made some observation on the oaths also, for although there is no record of such words in Grey or the *Parliamentary History*, a remark in another member's speech in relation to the oaths indicates that Sawyer had been "asserting a thing" on a matter of law.[78] His third appearance on behalf of his university was to allay the alarm of the House on a report that whole boxes of the Jacobite pamphlet, "The Declaration of King James", had been sent to Cambridge to the Masters of Queens' and St. John's. This report was true, Sawyer announced, except that all the boxes had been taken to the Vice-Chancellor and remained there in his custody.[79] We know from Newton's letters, and the frequent mention he made there as to his consultations with Sir Robert, that the latter was much more occupied with university concerns than these meagre references in the debates and the *Journal* indicate, and we also know from Newton's letter on 7 May that one of these concerns was the confirmation of the university charters, although no mention is made of Sawyer in this connection in the public records.

Besides his university concerns, Sir Robert Sawyer was a speaker on a number of other occasions during this first session, and was twice listed among the managers of a bill to be sent to conference with the Lords.[80] His parliamentary career indeed seemed at first to be going along smoothly and successfully. But by the month of May rumbles began to be heard, and the danger to which he was ultimately to succumb began to show itself.

In the meantime, his old colleague the Honourable Heneage Finch, now representative for the sister university, was already having difficulties. At the outset of the session, like most High Tories, he spoke strongly in favour of a regency, and thereby laid himself open to the charge that he was intending to provide a loophole for the return of the King.[81] Against this accusation, he defended himself by saying somewhat obscurely: "I am so far from that, that I think there can be no safety in the King's return [even?] by unanimous consent of the nation. I think the government not safe by his administration."[82] His unpopular stand did not keep him from being appointed to thirty-one committees. Some of them apparently were such as would make use of his legal knowledge; others were on various subjects of general concern. None of them were related to any special university interests, except the committees on the hated chimney tax, the new oaths and church matters such as those mentioned above in connection with Newton and Sawyer.[83] Finch was also employed on four other committees concerned with conferences with the Lords, and for two of these conferences he was listed among the managers.[84] Besides his committee work, he was also moderately active as a speaker, more particularly on the subject of the coronation oaths and the new oaths of allegiance.[85] With these topics he could well be concerned, both as a lawyer and as university representative.

Nevertheless, all through his parliamentary career in the Convention, despite his apparent success, Finch must have felt ill at ease, for the same resentment was directed against him that ultimately brought the House's displeasure down upon the head of Sir Robert Sawyer—the feeling that both men in the past had been much too closely associated with Stuart absolutism to be tolerated as members of the present Parliament.

This resentment was borne in upon Finch early in the session when the bill for the reversal of Lord Russell's attainder was speeding through the House. Finch had been Solicitor-General at the time of Lord Russell's trial, and although he was conceded to have acted less outrageously than the unspeakable Jeffreys, nevertheless he had handled the evidence—to use Burnet's words—with a "vicious eloquence and ingenious malice" that was felt to have hastened Russell's conviction.[86] Likewise, the address that he had delivered in Sidney's case was complained of by Sidney in his remarks on the scaffold, where Sidney declared that it was the Solicitor-General's "long painted speech" that had misled the jury at his trial.[87] Finch had also replied to Lady Russell's paper containing her husband's last declaration with a pamphlet entitled "An Antidote against Poison", thus carrying his prosecution beyond the walls of the court-room.[88]

All this was in the minds of the legislators as they went about to annul Russell's attainder, and Finch was well aware of it. He tried to speak: "I see many gentlemen's eyes are upon me: therefore I stand up to give my reason for the part I acted in that unfortunate business." He would have gone on, but he was immediately called to order, as not speaking directly to the bill. But he tried again: "Give me leave to vindicate myself; what I shall offer will be very short . . . if law-books have led me in the wrong I am ready to rectify my opinion." He went on to discuss the question of whether conspiring without levying war was in itself treason or whether actual war was a necessary factor in such a case. During these remarks, although he kept assuring the House that he was in favour of reversing the attainder, he was again called to order two separate times; the last time by a member who commented bitterly: "It is strange to me to hear this learned gentleman vindicate himself when nobody accuses him, and therby to arraign the justice of the Bill. . . . This is not to be suffered." The Speaker then reproved Finch, who apologized and said he did not intend to arraign "this noble person"—that is, Russell—and then himself hastened to second the motion for the second reading of the bill. After some further angry murmurs against "the learned person", and some doubts expressed as to whether so speedy a second reading was legal, it was finally moved to read the bill again, and solely on Finch's account, for, so it was argued, "This Bill declares that the Law-Books the learned gentleman has quoted were wrong; and if he doubts it, the reading of it a second time will set that part right".[89]

After this episode, Heneage Finch's position in the House was never secure, and in all the controversy that later revolved around Sir Robert Sawyer, it was felt that the accusations levelled against Sawyer might with equal justice be levelled against Finch.[90] Townsend, in his *History of the House of Commons*, however, appears to exaggerate the effect of the Russell incident, when he says that Finch was silenced by it, for we have just seen above that his committee service, speeches in the House, and activity in conference were all very considerable throughout the whole first session of the Parliament. Even in the second session, Townsend's statement can scarcely be accepted when he says that "after some abortive struggles, the eloquent representative of Oxford, the best fitted by nature and art among all his competitors at the Bar to sway that deliberative assembly, was reduced to the condition of a mute", and that as time went on, Finch attended Parliament more and more infrequently.[91] It is true that in the second session Finch was much less prominent than in the first, but notwithstanding, he was named to six committees and made six speeches. One of the committees was that on the university charters, and one of the speeches was a vigorous plea against the Sacheverell clause in the act to restore the town charters. This provision would have deprived all those who had co-operated in the *Quo Warranto* proceedings of any capacity to participate in borough government. Finch's part in regard to both these issues shows that he was still in action at the very end of the Parliament's existence.[92] It was not in the Convention Parliament, then, that Finch became a mute, whatever may have been his parliamentary conduct in later years.

There remains Sir Thomas Clarges, the fourth of the university burgesses to sit in the Convention Parliament. Clarges is distinguished by the fact that opposite his name in the index to speakers in the *Parliamentary History* there are more page references than for any other member of the Convention. There was scarcely an issue raised to which he did not rise to say his say. An old Parliament man, his service beginning under the Protectorate, he had a long memory and a ready tongue which he could call upon for any occasion. His political position was somewhat mixed. As brother-in-law to General Monck he had been one of the chief instruments in bringing about the Restoration, and for this reason was long looked upon as a friend of the Court, and indeed in many matters his policies did run clearly along Tory lines. But he had not hesitated at times to oppose the Court, particularly in money matters—where he prided himself upon his advocacy of strict economy —or upon issues where the Established Church seemed threatened by Popish encroachments, or when the rights of Parliament were endangered by arbitrary prorogations.[93] He had also been one of the promoters of the Habeas Corpus Act, and one of his proudest boasts in the Convention was that he had been the member who had introduced that Act into the House.[94] On the whole, in the light of all this evidence, although it is true that Clarges's name is found on the list of those who voted against making William and Mary actually King and Queen, the note in the 1850 edition of Burnet to the effect that Clarges was inimical to the Revolution is probably exaggerated.[95]

On the contrary, he was the only one of all the university members then living who is known to have taken a positive part in favour of the Revolution in the early days before the calling of the Convention. He was among those who answered the summons of the Prince of Orange in December 1688, when all former members of Parliament were asked to meet with His Highness in London to prepare for the meeting of a Convention.[96] Moreover, Clarges's name appears upon the committee appointed by this irregular assembly to prepare an address to the Prince urging him to proceed with the assumption of executive power and the summoning of a Parliament.[97] It was not until six weeks later, when it came to pronouncing the throne vacant, and proclaiming new Sovereigns, that Sir Thomas began to demur,[98] and from this point on, he is to be found more often on the side of the High Tories, along with Finch and Sawyer.[99] Like the Tories, he avowed scruples that impelled him to urge a new election in order to make the Convention a true Parliament, and out of his own experience made many comparisons between the Convention of 1660 and the present Convention.[100]

Tory also was his interest in the Established Church. Like Sawyer, he defended the clergy against aspersions cast upon them, and referred especially to his constituency, Oxford, and its resistance to King James: "They stood like Apostles in the Magdalen College case, which is remarkable", he declared; thus causing his opponent, although only partly convinced, to modify his statement slightly, adding, "Clarges speaks honestly, as I believe he thinks." In discussing the repeal of the Corporation Act, Clarges was unqualifiedly in favour of keeping the sacramental test, and when the question of the wording of the new coronation oath was brought up, he insisted on inserting "as by law established" to make it quite clear that it was no other religion but that of the Church of England to which the Sovereign should be committed.[101]

As a committee member also, Sir Thomas Clarges was prominent, being especially interested in financial and ecclesiastical matters. He served with the other university burgesses on various bills on religious subjects,[102] and was active in connection with proposals for indulgence and comprehension in various capacities—as debater, committee member, or manager of a conference.[103]

To university matters he was also attentive. When the King offered to relinquish the hated hearth tax, it was Clarges who moved that the House present his Majesty with an address of thanks. He served on the committee to prepare the address, and later to prepare the bill of repeal.[104] This action must have been very welcome to his constituents, exasperated as they had been over this tax since the days of Lawrence Hyde and the first Heneage Finch. We know also from Isaac Newton's letters that Clarges was much occupied with the confirmation of the university charters and that he, with Newton, asked for leave to bring in a bill for this purpose.[105] Clarges continued to work on this subject, and at the very end of the session, presented the finished bill.[106] In regard to other university questions, such as the oaths and presentation to benefices, there is no evidence that Clarges concerned himself especially, although he was on the committee to consider the Lords' bill on the oaths, and was dissatisfied with the outcome of this issue, as bearing too hard on the clergy in general.[107] It is surprising indeed that Sir Thomas had any time whatever for university matters, in view of his general activity, for his name is scattered so broadly over page after page of the *Parliamentary History* and the *Journal*, that to note the frequency of these entries is to feel that the House could hardly have done business without the assistance of the senior burgess for Oxford. At different times, he was reporter, teller, manager, committee member for the famous Painted Chamber conference on the status of the throne, and champion of the House's right to control the purse. In the latter character, he was equally on guard against both King and Upper House —in the one case, he was not for "letting the Lords into raising money";

in the other, he did not hesitate to protest, when a bad report of the
Irish campaign was coupled with a request for supply, "To have a sad
tale told us, and Money at the end, it is very extraordinary", and went
on to declare that the Crown should instead present a statement of
revenue, not a request "by surprise"; and in another connection
declared, "I hope it will never be admitted that we should take instructions from the King to pass bills here."[108] He was also strongly against
any kind of suspension of Habeas Corpus,[109] and in favour of reversing
Lord Russell's attainder,[110] but he was equally fearful of allowing the
Kingdom to "fall into a Commonwealth", in the event of a lapse in the
succession.[111]

In spite of his occasional Whiggish sentiments,[112] Sir Thomas found
himself from time to time attacked as an extreme Tory, and viewed
by the more radical members of the House with the same kind of
suspicion that was attached to Finch and Sawyer.[113] It was on these
occasions that Clarges, in defending himself, asserted the right of members of Parliament to have their own opinions and to state them, and
thus he became a kind of champion of parliamentary freedom of speech.
Two of the attacks were made in reference to Clarges's stand for a
regency at the beginning of the session, and this led him to object to
the persistence of a distinction between those who had wanted a regency
and those who had opposed it. "To be pointed at in Westminster Hall
as one of 150 against the throne vacant; to have printed papers of men
on one side or other"—this, he thought outrageous. Three months later
he still encountered aspersions of this nature, and again asserted, "I am
arraigned for debates. We ought to be free here."[114]

Likewise, when impeachment proceedings were being instituted
against Justice Blair for having aided in James II's dispensations,
Clarges pleaded for a less severe interpretation of treason, with the
sensible argument that "Parliament may be oversevere as Judges have been
under James II." When he was making his second speech to this effect,
he was interrupted by cries of "Agree, agree", and a member remarked
that he hoped the House would not connive at treason. To which Sir
Thomas rejoined, again with indignation: "This is an extraordinary
thing for a gentleman to say. That when a man speaks his mind here,
he connives at treason." On another occasion, when he proposed that
his beloved Habeas Corpus be discussed before the question of the new
oaths, a member implied that Clarges was using this as an excuse to
postpone the unwelcome issue of the oaths. Here again Sir Thomas
repudiated the insinuation, though in terms of fact, rather than in terms
of parliamentary freedom of speech. "I stand up to vindicate myself.
I am as free as anybody to take these oaths. I desire to justify myself."[115]

But these little irritating barbs let fly from time to time at Clarges were as nothing to the final attack upon Sir Robert Sawyer, or to what might also have happened to the Honourable Heneage Finch. Sawyer's discomfiture began to be prepared in May, three months after the session had been under way.[116] Some vague allusions to charges against Sawyer appeared in a debate on the suspension of Habeas Corpus.[117] Then, in an investigation of the "Authors of Grievances", Sawyer's share in the *Quo Warranto* proceedings was referred to, though Sawyer himself was not named among the "Authors". By 17 June, the attack had begun, occasion being offered by mention of Sawyer's failure to prevent the granting of a writ of dispensation in the case of Sir Edward Hales, a Catholic appointed to be governor of Dover. Sawyer gave his version of the affair—that he had protested against the action as illegal, and even begged the King to dismiss him for his stand—"Nobody then about the King, but knows I stood stiffly upon it"—but that the King had bade him go by the opinions of the Judges, not by his own opinion—"I submit whether any officer must not do as I did." This defence did not satisfy his enemies. They pointed out that nonetheless he did grant the patent, and that, as far as results were concerned, "all are post horses alike", the first and the last; while one member called him "the greatest criminal", and another declared with indignation in favour of excepting Sawyer from the bill of indemnity, exclaiming, "Those who were the great darlings of King James, not to turn them out. Those are the persons to be excepted. I mean Sawyer." In the meantime, other members were blaming Sir Robert with the imposition of chimney money, and one declared, "If you fall not upon them that did this, you are defective in justice." Then followed a reference to the fatal Armstrong case, not yet brought out into the open, but ultimately to be Sir Robert's nemesis.[118]

For the present, the crisis was resolved by Sir Robert Howard, who urged the House to withhold judgment until some papers Sawyer had offered to show in his defence were brought in, and Sawyer was ordered to bring them in the following day. Nothing more is recorded in regard to this incident, but about a month later another issue was raised. This issue dragged on throughout the rest of the session, with frequent orders set down in the *Journal* for Sir Robert to appear and report, and plans made for him to be able to summon witnesses before the bar.[119] But all this came to naught with the adjournment of Parliament on 20 August.

The next session opened on 19 October. Sir Thomas Clarges was busy with his usual excess of committees, and especially with the matter of the university charters.[120] Isaac Newton appeared on one committee, a financial one,[121] and the Honourable Heneage Finch, on several, including that on the university charters.[122]

The two Oxford burgesses, as usual, made speeches—Clarges, on his favourite themes of economy and efficiency in the management of the armed forces, and the security of the Established Church.[123] In the latter connection he was one of the first speakers of the session at the opening, when he was the only member to take exception to the King's speech for having omitted the classic phrase, "as by law established", after mention of the Church. This exception, Ralph says in his *Continuation*, was not taken up by the House, but instead "met with little countenance".[124] Clarges also felt later called upon to defend the Church against those who were disposed to attribute the Revolution to the Dissenters, and to express their doubts of the High Churchmen's loyalty to the new régime. On the contrary, Sir Thomas asserted, the present King "came in by the Church of England, their pens, sermons, and sufferings"—a view not in opposition to that of some modern historians who emphasize the importance of James II's alienation of the High Tories as a decisive factor in a movement formerly characterized as largely Whig.[125] Clarges also made a spirited defence of the Test Act and Penal Laws, with the implication that those who were against these laws were also likely to be against monarchy itself, thus introducing one of his favourite minor themes—opposition to anything that savoured of Commonwealth or republican notions.[126]

Through this session Finch joined with Clarges in urging a special grant for the Princess Anne—a measure favoured by all the High Tories—and, as has been mentioned before, made a strong stand against the Sacheverell clause regarding the town charters on the ground that this provision would put the corporations in the hands of men "of little or no fortune" who had "given no testimony of their affection to the Government" and who were called by some "the *Mobile*".[127]

All this time, Sir Robert Sawyer remained silent, although his name appears upon five committees throughout the session.[128] Finally the moment came for which his enemies had been waiting. The bill for the reversal of the attainder of Sir Thomas Armstrong had been introduced in the House in November. Sawyer had even been placed on the committee to which it was entrusted at its second reading. On 13 January 1689/90, the committee was ordered to find out who were the "Prosecutors and Advisers" of Armstrong's execution".[129] By the 18th, Sawyer was named, as one who had been responsible for Armstrong's execution because of having failed, as Attorney-General, to issue a writ of error at the trial, when Armstrong's plea was not being given due consideration. A demand for money reparation for

Armstrong's family arose. The House showed great indignation. In the debate that followed, there was some attempt to shield Sawyer as being a member of the House and therefore beyond a mere committee's power of accusation. In this case, he could only be properly accused by the whole House. But his enemies were not so easily sidetracked. "How scandalous it is", exclaimed one, "when a man guilty of the murder of Sir Thomas Armstrong should be protected within these walls"; while another protested, "Did I think I sat in the house with a murderer, I would not sit till I had thrown him out." Still another, Sir William Williams, whom Sawyer had once prosecuted on the King's behalf, proclaimed Sir Robert to be a "betrayer of the law", while another, along similar lines, declared, "If the profession of the law gives a man authority to murder a man at this rate, it is the interest of all men to rise and exterminate that profession", and added that he would like to hear what Sawyer could say.

By this time the issue had resolved itself into two propositions—to hear Sawyer immediately, or to recommit the bill with instructions to the committee to conduct an investigation about Sawyer in particular. The second procedure was followed, and on 20 January the committee made its report, this time on Sawyer alone, without reference to the other persons involved in the Armstrong case. This circumstance was again seized upon as an excuse for further delay,[130] but Sawyer's enemies prevailed, and the case proceeded on the spot. An important witness was Sir Thomas Armstrong's daughter who testified against Sawyer, after which the latter gave his defence. He claimed that he had only done his duty as Attorney-General, that he did not ask for execution until the court had declared Armstrong guilty, and that there was serious evidence against Armstrong which the King was unwilling to condone. After this, Sawyer retired and the House went on with the debate. Some pleaded for the Commons not to create a precedent that would make it hard for those who served in the courts, but others pressed the case against Sawyer relentlessly. "We have a new sort of monster in the world," cried the grandson of John Hampden, "haranguing a man to death; these I call bloodhounds that make speeches so long as my stick. Sawyer is very criminal, and guilty of this murder." Others chimed in, and a transcript of the trial was read. The hesitant members seem to have been convinced. A last attempt in Sawyer's behalf was made in a motion to adjourn, but it was defeated, and the question of his expulsion was brought to a vote. The count was against him, by a good majority, 131–71. He was duly expelled, and a few days later ordered to pay a money indemnity to Sir Thomas Armstrong's family.[131]

The Convention Parliament was nearing its end. Prorogation came on 27 January, but not before Clarges had made one last speech.[132] This was the final word from any of the university representatives in this Parliament. At least three of them, Finch, Clarges, and Sawyer, had been rather more active and prominent than generally had been the case with other university members in the earlier Parliaments of the century, and they had all three had a good share in the making of the Revolution Settlement, both as debaters, and as members of committees working on the Declaration of Rights, the Toleration Act, the Mutiny Act, and other pieces of significant legislation. Even the fourth member, Isaac Newton, if not prominent, had been at least active as a representative of his own constituency at a critical time in its history. The record of these members as to capability and energy is notable; as to vision and glory, less distinguished, if the shadows cast upon Finch and Sawyer are to be given any weight. Sawyer's constituents, to be sure, did not take his disgrace too seriously—on the contrary, they were even moved to champion him—for they promptly re-elected him for the next Parliament a month after his expulsion, and Newton himself voted for him.[133] In Cambridge's eyes, at least, he appeared to have cleared himself—or perhaps rather to have redeemed himself by his later actions. As far as the cold record goes, however, Sir Robert Sawyer remains as the second of the two university burgesses of the century to be expelled for misconduct in appointive office,[134] and this circumstance in itself adds to the interest and importance of the Convention as a landmark in the history of university representation.

NOTES FOR CHAPTER XII

1. Grey, VIII, 343.
2. O.R., p. 554; Life and Times, III, 135.
3. H.M.C., Kenyon, pp. 163–6; H.M.C., Ormonde, VII, 79.
4. Monmouth, the former Chancellor, had been deposed by Charles II after the Rye House Plot, and Cambridge had ordered his portrait burned and his name erased from the records. G. N. Clark, The Later Stuarts, p. 101.
5. Albemarle's letter is in Cooper, III, 608–10, and also in H.M.C., App., 4th Rep., p. 419.
6. For Fairwell, see A.O., IV, 816; Foster, II, 482; Venn, II, 124. He was a grand-nephew, not a nephew, of General Monck.
7. O.R., p. 552. Albemarle was greatly offended at the university, and nourished such a grudge against them that when Cambridge presented some verses to the King a week after the election, the Duke would not act on their behalf in assisting in the presentation. Life and Times, III, 136.
8. Clark, p. 113.
9. C.J., IX, 719. See also ibid., pp. 723, 733, 740, 750, 753.
10. Ibid., pp. 727, 739, 740, 744, 753.
11. Ibid., p. 751.
12. Ibid., p. 756.

13. *Life and Times*, III, 168. There is no record of such a letter in the Oxford University Archives or among the letters addressed to Oxford in *H.M.C., Ormonde*, VII.

14. *Supra*, Ch. XI, p. 282.

15. *H.M.C., Ormonde*, VII, 359.

16. *Life and Times*, III, 171. A footnote here from a Bodleian MS. gives the exact poll: Oldys, 130, Clarke, 209. This figure is confirmed by Clarke's autobiography, which notes that the seat was won by "79 voices to the best of my remembrance". *H.M.C., Popham*, p. 263. There is no indication of a contest in the Oxford University Archives. No figures are recorded, and Oldys's name does not appear. Oxford University Archives, Bb29, p. 3239, f. 110.

17. Clarke's election is not entered in the *Official Return*, possibly because he never took his seat.

18. For Clarke's career, see *D.N.B.*; Foster, I, 280; Montague Burrows, *The Worthies of All Souls*, pp. 314–18; and Clarke's autobiography in *H.M.C., Popham*, pp. 259–89.

19. Sir John Bramston, *Autobiography*, C.S., o.s., no. 32, pp. 247, 248, 251; Narcissus Luttrell, *Historical Relation*, I, 387; Roger Morrice, *Entring Book*, II, f. 30. (Reference provided by Professor D. R. Lacey of the United States Naval Academy.)

20. One of his retreats was at Longleat, with Oxford University's former M.P., Thomas Thynne, now Viscount Weymouth. *H.M.C., Popham*, p. 264.

21. *Life and Times*, III, 232; *H.M.C., Popham*, pp. 265–6.

22. Sir George Duckett, *Penal Laws and Test Act, 1687–1688*, pp. 329–33.

23. *Ibid.*, pp. 321–3.

24. *Ibid.*, p. 323. For the town, see Foster, *Alderman Newton*, pp. 91–2.

25. *Life and Times*, III, 287, 296; *O.R.*, p. 560.

26. *Supra*, Ch. X, pp. 266–70, 271–2. At the time of Finch's election, 18 December 1688, it was rumoured that he was being considered for Lord Chancellor. This would suggest that he was not yet entirely alienated from the Court. *H.M.C., Kenyon*, p. 212.

27. For accounts of Clarges, see *D.N.B.*; Foster, I, 278; Aubrey, II, 73; Burnet (ed. 1850), I, 67, and n.; G.E.C., *Baronetage*, IV, 65. For his stand in the House against the encroachments of the King, Clarges was once praised heartily by the Whig leader, Sir Robert Howard: "I shall never forget a worthy Member holding two speeches of King James in his hand and declaring them contradictory to each other. I shall ever honour him for it." *P.H.*, V, 295. Probably the occasion referred to was that described in *ibid.*, IV, 1393. Clarges, however, was once rated as a pensioner. Burnet, *loc. cit.*; *C.J.*, X, 108–9. See below, n. 112.

28. *Supra*, Ch. XI, pp. 277, 279.

29. Tanner MS., 28, p. 178R.

30. Exton died on 5 November, the very date of William of Orange's landing. Luttrell, I, 473.

31. Tanner MS., 28, p. 316R. Sancroft was now Chancellor of the university, elected 15 December.

32. *Supra*, Ch. XI, pp. 278, 280.

33. For Edward Finch, see *D.N.B.*; Venn, II, 138; and Luttrell, I, 81, 529.

34. For Newton's career, see *D.N.B.*; *B.B.*, V, 3210–44, especially 3230; Venn, III, 252. Of full-length biographies, the only ones that treat of his political career are Sir David Brewster, *Life of Sir Isaac Newton* (one vol., 1832), and *Memoirs . . . of Sir Isaac Newton* (two vols., 1855), and Louis T. More, *Isaac Newton*, Ch. X, especially.

35. Brewster, II, 107. Edward Finch supported Newton's view, and, through him and his brother Nottingham, legal advice was obtained. More, p. 342. Newton's stand on this issue, interestingly enough, included a reference to the university's parliamentary franchise, so soon to be used in his own honour: "If one priest

be a Master you may have a hundred and they must choose a Burgess to Parliament." (Letter quoted in More, p. 343.)

36. *B.B.*, v, 3230.

37. More, pp. 337–42; Brewster, II, 107–10; Cooper, III, 618–32.

38. Cooper, IV, 1; Brewster, II, 112 n. Foster, *Alderman Newton*, p. 97.

39. More, p. 346, refers to a sarcastic source, not identified, that reported Newton's sole speech as having to do with ordering an usher to close a window.

40. *C.J.*, x, 93, 133, 281.

41. Some of these letters are in Brewster and More, but the whole series is published in a pamphlet by Dawson Turner (*Thirteen Letters from Sir Isaac Newton*, Norwich, 1848). The original manuscripts are in Trinity College Library at Cambridge, with copies in the Cambridge University Library (Mm 6.50), and in the British Museum with Covell's correspondence (Add. MSS., 22910–14).

42. Brewster, II, 114; More, p. 347.

43. Cambridge University Library MS., Mm 6.50, pp. 95–8. Quoted in Brewster, II, App. VIII, 459, and More, pp. 348–50. The delay in the proclamation was owing, not to the university's reluctance, according to Alderman Newton, but to the absence of the Sheriff and the under Sheriff. Foster, *Alderman Newton*, pp. 99–101.

44. George D'Oyly, *William Sancroft*, I, 407.

45. Camb. Univ. MS., Mm 6.50, p. 111; Rawlinson MS., D 1232; Cooper, IV, 3.

46. Camb. Univ. MS., Mm 6.50, p. 96.

47. More, pp. 337–8, 342–3.

48. More, p. 350, also notes the twisting of the doctrine of passive obedience, the better to appeal to the university mentality.

49. Camb. Univ. MS., Mm 6.50, pp. 101–2. The university's concern for its "commencers" is further expressed in a letter from the Vice-Chancellor to the Earl of Nottingham. *Ibid.*, p. 123.

50. *Ibid.*, p. 104.

51. *Ibid.*, p. 105. In this Newton seems to have been in error, for a letter in the correspondence of Bishop Turner, dated 25 March, states that because no letters "from above" came on behalf of either Dorset or Danby, the Duke of Somerset was elected instead.

52. *Ibid.*, pp. 106–7.

53. *Ibid.*, pp. 107–8.

54. *Ibid.*, pp. 109–10.

55. For the question of the oaths, see Feiling, pp. 263–6; Thomas B. Macaulay, *History of England*, ed. C. H. Firth, III, 1400–11; Griffiths, *Enactments*, pp. 47–8.

56. Camb. Univ. MS., Mm 6.50, pp. 115–16. On the date of this letter a warrant was issued for delivery of the statutes of the university from the public records to Newton. *C.S.P., Dom., Wm. III*, I (1689–90), 46.

57. Camb. Univ. MS., Mm 6.50, pp. 106–7, 117. There is no record of this in any of the debates in *P.H.*, or Grey. *C.J.*, x, 112, mentions the leave, but gives no names connected with the motion.

58. Camb. Univ. MS., Mm 6.50, pp. 117–18.

59. *Ibid.*, p. 127.

60. *Ibid.*, pp. 123–4.

61. *Ibid.*, pp. 127–8.

62. *Ibid.*, pp. 131, 132, 133, 134. The letter is referred to by More, p. 351.

63. Rawlinson MS., D 1232, 7R–8R. For Dr. Cook, see Venn, I, 388. Dr. Cook had taken a leading part in the Alban Francis case. Cooper, III, 620, 625, 626, 629, 632.

64. Clark, p. 139, says the vote in favour of a regency was only a majority of two in the Lords.

65. For Sawyer's stand on this issue, see below, p. 310; Macaulay, Firth, III, 1266–8, 1274. According to Macaulay, this had been Sawyer's original position

when among those present at the pre-Convention meeting of members of Parliament called by the Prince of Orange in December 1688. There he had been active in suggesting that the Prince be given a limited title such as Regent or Administrator. *Ibid.*, p. 1244 and n.; Feiling, p. 248.

66. *Supra*, Ch. XI, pp. 277, 279.

67. The question of Sawyer's early Whiggery is somewhat uncertain. According to a letter of John Locke's mentioned in an entry in Thomas More's diary, 19 December 1823 (*Memoirs, Journal and Correspondence*, ed. Lord John Russell, London, 1853, IV, 153), Sawyer took an active part in introducing the Exclusion Bill. This rather elusive reference, however, is the only evidence for such action on his part. Almost all the other information available about him points in the opposite direction. North, a contemporary, writing in Sawyer's interest, stated that "his bias was toward loyalty which had been the character of his family". (*Lives*, I, 376.) He was rated a pensioner in the "Seasonable Argument"—"a lawyer of ill repute", paid £1,000 for his attendance, and promised the places of Speaker and Attorney-General. (*P.H.*, IV, App. III, p. xxiii.) In 1678 he was the court candidate for Speaker against strong opposition (Sir Robert Southwell to Ormonde, *H.M.C., Ormonde*, IV, 421), and at that time was named with Finch and Wheler on the list of those who were accustomed to meet at Secretary Coventry's in the King's interest—which would make him a Danbyite. *C.S.P., Dom., Chas. II*, XX (1678, with Addenda 1674–9), 194, 537. But More, in writing of Newton (*Isaac Newton*, pp. 345, 356, 422), classifies Sawyer as a Whig, and finds it a matter of surprise to discover in 1690 that he was a Tory. Feiling (p. 252 n.) makes no mention of any past Whig connections, but finds it difficult to determine which of the various Tory factions Sawyer belonged to. Macaulay, Firth, III, 1266, places him among the more moderate Tories. See below, p. 310 and n. 73.

68. For Sawyer's career, see *D.N.B.*; Foster, IV, 1320; Venn, IV, 24; *Fasti*, II, 189; Townsend, *House of Commons*, I, 397–408; North, I, 376–9; III, 125–6; Burnet, Airy, II, 344.

69. North, I, 378.

70. Macaulay, Firth, II, 736–8, 987–8, however, takes Sawyer's part in saying that as Attorney-General he showed "no want of honesty or of resolution", and that the reason he was kept on in the office was because the Crown could find no other man of his ability to take the place.

71. North, *loc. cit.* See also Reresby, *Memoirs*, p. 422.

72. 28 January and 2 February. *P.H.*, V, 47, 62.

73. Grey, IX, 55–6, 58. Feiling, p. 252 n., finds Sawyer's role in the Convention obscure. He disagrees with Macaulay's view that Sawyer was of the Danby faction (Firth, III, 1266), and finds his permanent association to be with the High Church party and even with the more extreme bishops. Sawyer, but not Newton, is listed in Feiling's App. II, p. 496, among those who voted against making William and Mary King and Queen, 5 February.

74. *P.H.*, V, 119–20; Macaulay, Firth, III, 1337; Feiling, pp. 252–3.

75. *C.J.*, X, 10, 74, 93, 202, 204.

76. *Ibid.*, p. 202.

77. *P.H.*, V, 130.

78. *Ibid.*, p. 221.

79. *C.J.*, X, 190. These boxes may be the ones referred to in Covell's letter to Nottingham, Camb. Univ. MS., Mm 6.50, p. 123.

80. Camb. Univ. MS., Mm 6.50, p. 242.

81. *P.H.*, V, 39, 40, 45, 49, 61–2. Feiling, p. 249, notes that Finch and his colleague Clarges were the leaders in the House in favour of a regency. In view of Finch's stand on this subject, it is somewhat surprising not to find Finch's name along with Clarges on the list of those that were against making the Prince and Princess of Orange King and Queen. *Ibid.*, App. II, p. 497.

82. *P.H.*, v, 49. Macaulay, Firth, III, 1274–6, regards this as a retraction of Finch's real intent.

83. *C.J.*, x, 53, 77, 84, 88, 93, 133, 138. Mention of Finch in the *Journal* is too frequent to cite except in special cases.

84. *Ibid.*, pp. 143, 155.

85. *P.H.*, v, 174, 187, 202–4, 209, 220.

86. Burnet, Airy, II, 376.

87. Townsend, II, 73–5.

88. *A.O.*, IV, 652–3.

89. *P.H.*, v, 169–71. Macaulay describes the incident (ed. Firth, IV, 1650–2).

90. Grey, IX, 527, notes, in recording the arguments in defence of Sawyer, that it was said privately, "that all this fencing was not to save Sawyer but Finch". See below, pp. 316, 318–19, n. 130.

91. Townsend, II, 79–80.

92. *C.J.*, x, 273, 277, 297, 312, 338, 343; *P.H.*, v, 514–15.

93. For Clarges, and his political position, see *supra*, p. 301 and n. 27; also below, nn. 96, 112, 113.

94. Grey, IX, 87.

95. Feiling, App. II, p. 497; Burnet (ed. 1850), I, 67n.

96. See Clarges's own statement: "I have contributed to this Revolution, have suffered for it." Grey, IX, 549. His action in the pre-Convention meeting in December was certainly more positive than that of Sawyer, if Macaulay is correct. See *supra*, n. 65.

97. *C.J.*, x, 5.

98. *P.H.*, v, 61; Feiling, pp. 249, 253.

99. Feiling, p. 263. See below, nn. 112, 113.

100. *P.H.*, v, 121–3, 130.

101. *Ibid.*, pp. 130, 138, 200, 205.

102. *C.J.*, x, 84, 88, 138.

103. *P.H.*, v, 264, 265; *C.J.*, x, 74, 143. No attempt is made here to cite all the committees that Clarges served on.

104. *C.J.*, x, 38, 42, 153.

105. *Supra*, p. 307.

106. This is Wood's account. See *Life and Times*, III, 317, 322. *C.J.*, x, 343, mentions this bill, but Clarges's name appears only among the members of the committee to which the bill was ultimately assigned, not as a special sponsor.

107. *C.J.*, x, 69; Feiling, p. 266.

108. *P.H.*, v, 331, 343, 493–4.

109. *Ibid.*, pp. 152, 155, 271, 273.

110. *Ibid.*, p. 171.

111. *Ibid.*, p. 251.

112. Clarges's occasional Whiggish sentiments were noted by Oswald B. Miller, in his *Life of Robert Harley* (Stanhope Prize Essay, Oxford, 1925), p. 3, as of the date December 1691. By Foxcroft, however (*Halifax*, II, 258), Clarges was described, not as a Whig, but rather as a man of old Country party principles, which seems a more accurate estimate of his political position. This is Feiling's view of Clarges also (Feiling, p. 179).

113. Clarges's close personal association with the Hydes and the Finches as a group gave some grounds for these suspicions. He is constantly mentioned as a dinner companion in Clarendon's diary, especially *Correspondence*, II, 252–3, for 1688 and 1689. See also Ailesbury, p. 106, and Feiling, p. 265.

114. *P.H.*, v, 123, 272.

115. *Ibid.*, pp. 152, 352–3.

116. Feiling, p. 266, explains why the Whigs grew impatient at this time.

117. *P.H.*, v, 268–9; *C.J.*, x, 158.

118. *P.H.*, v, 326–7. Sawyer's last recorded speech in the session was in connection with this allusion to the Armstrong case. *Ibid.*, p. 329.

119. *Ibid.*, pp. 215, 217–18, 231, 236, 240.

120. As stated before, his name appears in this connection only once, but mention of action on the bill itself is encountered several times in the *Journal* of this session, especially since it aroused some opposition on the part of the City of Oxford. *C.J.*, x, 274, 300, 301, 308, 342.

121. *Ibid.*, p. 281.

122. *Ibid.*, pp. 273, 277, 297, 312, 338, 343. It seems strange that Newton with all his interest in the subject of the charters, did not get a place on this committee along with Clarges and Finch.

123. *P.H.*, v, 407, 408, 409, 417, 418, 426, 429, 436, 444–5, 451, 454.

124. Ralph, *Continuation* of Rapin's *History*, quoted in *P.H.*, v, 404n.

125. See J. H. Plumb, "Elections to the Convention Parliament, 1689", *Cambridge Historical Journal*, v (1935–7), 240.

126. *P.H.*, v, 474–6.

127. *Ibid.*, pp. 493–4, 496–7, 499, 502n, 514–15.

128. *C.J.*, x, 275, 296, 297, 300, 321.

129. *Ibid.*, p. 331.

130. As stated above in n. 90, an entry in Grey notes that all this "fencing" was resorted to, not to save Sawyer, but Finch, who might be equally subject to such charges. Why the House was so much tenderer of Finch than of Sawyer is not clear, unless it was because of the prestige of his brother, the Earl of Nottingham, or because it was felt that Sawyer had not repudiated Stuart tyranny so promptly as Finch.

131. *P.H.*, v, 516–27; *C.J.*, x, 337, 344. Macaulay, Firth, IV, 1786–9, has an account of Sawyer's expulsion.

132. *P.H.*, v, 534.

133. *O.R.*, p. 564; More, p. 356; Macaulay, Firth, IV, 1794–5, and n. Newton, surprisingly enough, was not re-elected in 1689/90. Whether he chose not to run, because of growing ill health, as Brewster surmised (II, 116–17, 208–9), or whether his Whiggish notions had made him unpopular with the university at a time of Tory reaction, as More has suggested (p. 356), is not clear. So far as can be determined, Newton did not try to run, nor was he put forward at the by-election after Sawyer's death, two years later. He had, however, acquired a taste for public business, which was later gratified by his appointment as Warden of the Mint, and in the early eighteenth century he again ran for Parliament and resumed once more his old university seat.

134. Sir John Bennett's offences in 1621 were, however, less excusable than Sawyer's, since they sprang from greed alone, and not from finding himself in an anomalous position.

CHAPTER XIII

RETROSPECT, 1660–1690

In surveying the thirty years of university representation that followed the Restoration, it becomes apparent that university politics were affected by the same trends that characterized the parliamentary history of the period. To be sure, the tendency towards Whiggism, so important during the Exclusion Parliaments, reached the universities in an extremely mild form. But with this significant exception, there was the same lively interest in contests for seats, the same general ebb and flow of court sentiment, the same countenancing of pensioners and "court cullies" that obtained in other constituencies. The Tory sentiments of the time were, of course, particularly well exemplified. From the very first, not one of the six university burgesses who served in the Cavalier Parliament at one time or another could be counted as anything but a vigorous and enthusiastic Tory, unless perhaps it was the moderate, Thomas Thynne, and in his case it is probably significant that he came into possession of his university seat in the later years of the Parliament when the King's popularity was already waning.[1]

By the time of the elections of 1678/9 this trend away from the Court had become dominant. The great uproar that had spread over the nation and filled the Exclusion Parliaments with Whigs could scarcely have been expected to affect the Tory strongholds at Oxford and Cambridge very markedly, but nevertheless some faint reflection of the political state of the country may be observed in the appearance of James Vernon, the first Whig to be chosen for a university seat, and of Sir William Temple, one of the few university representatives under the Monarchy to be consistently lukewarm towards the more extreme claims of Church and prerogative. The fact that both these members were traditionally eligible because of their recommendations—coming from university Chancellor and King respectively—should not entirely obliterate their significance as symbols of the tide of opposition that had at last reached even into Cambridge.

On the other hand, the opposing sentiment—the firm resistance of the Abhorrers—is well typified by Sir Leoline Jenkins, Heneage Finch the younger, and the university gremials, Exton, Edisbury, Parrott, and Brady. It is interesting to note that at this time it was Cambridge, and not Oxford, that allowed the Whiggish inroads, whereas, in the early years of the century, it was Oxford that was the most restive under royal dictation.[2] But now, in the later Restoration, while Oxford never wavered, Cambridge three times foreshadowed its Whiggish future, with the election of Vernon, of Temple, and—in 1688/9—of Isaac Newton, "the glory of the Whigs". This political trend, however, was far from being established. In most of its elections, Cambridge showed itself as Royalist as Oxford.

At Oxford the Exclusion controversy from the beginning aroused the strongest sentiments of loyalty. Always Tory, in the second election of 1679, its choice of the ultra-Tory, Sir Leoline Jenkins, as a complement to Temple, Cambridge's "Trimmer", was a forecast of the Tory reaction that was to come in all constituencies in the 1680's. This reaction reached Cambridge by 1680/1 in the last of the Exclusion Parliaments, when Cambridge—anticipating the national trend by a few months—reverted to the Tory fold with the election of Dr. Robert Brady to fill Sir William Temple's seat. In 1685 the re-election by both universities of their two completely Tory slates was in keeping with the strongly royalist sentiment of the whole country.

Similarly, when the tide turned again, with the Glorious Revolution, the universities moved with it, but it was not so easy for them to fall in with the spirit of 1688. Their devotion to the prerogative and to the doctrine of non-resistance found itself in conflict with their Anglicanism, and it was Anglicanism that in the end triumphed. But the conflict is evident in their choice of representatives. Isaac Newton and Sir Thomas Clarges, as Whig and old school Country party respectively, represent the Revolution, one for each university: while, on the other hand, the choice of Heneage Finch the younger and Sir Robert Sawyer, show that the universities had not completely deserted their old favourites, high prerogative men and holders of crown appointments. This division of opinion became characteristic of university politics during the rest of King William's reign and on into the eighteenth century, until political alignments shook down into a more permanent form, Oxford then remaining unqualifiedly Tory—even to the point of Jacobitism; and Cambridge—so far as its parliamentary representation went—becoming the particular province of the Duke of Newcastle and the predominant Whigs.

Electoral campaigns in the universities, throughout the whole Restoration period and up to 1690, were carried on with great vigour, as we have seen. There were fewer uncontested elections than in the period during and before the Civil War, much evidence of electioneering behind the scenes, and fewer occasions of direct outside control. The King supported only one candidate openly, Sir William Temple; Sir Charles Wheler's interests he advanced in only a lukewarm and indirect fashion.[3] Thus the return of the monarchy had not meant the return of much royal dictation at the polls, despite the increasing prevalence of mandate degrees and the repeated verbal protests of loyalty and submission on the part of the two universities.

Neither did the Chancellors dictate as formerly. We have only to recall the doubtful reception accorded at Oxford in 1661 to the double nomination of Sir Heneage Finch and the Chancellor's own son, Lawrence Hyde—even by the ardent Royalist, Anthony Wood—as well as the unenthusiastic moves made by the Heads on behalf of Monmouth's secretary, Vernon, in 1678/9; the reluctant support of the younger Finch at Oxford in the same year; and the outright omission of any attempt to support Albemarle's much-recommended cousin, Colonel Fairwell, in 1685. Likewise, the Duke of Ormonde's words on behalf of the too-young Mr. James Lane in 1679 were ignored, while— even more significant—his suggestion that the university make choice of Dr. Oldys in 1685 was boldly repudiated.[4] The impression conveyed by all this, as also by the universities' increasing insistence upon gremials, is that there was during this period a good deal of freedom of choice in the university elections and that the pocket-borough system, already making its appearance elsewhere, was clearly not being fixed upon the "nurseries of learning" in this period.

The insistence upon gremials is interesting, as being a conscious return to the original intention of the charter of enfranchisement. The most notable example of this insistence was the action threatened by Dr. Brady in 1679 to assert his claims to a Cambridge seat as against those of Sir William Temple, who was neither a resident nor the holder of a degree. To counteract such a move, it will be remembered, Dr. Turner had recommended that Temple be "naturalized" as a member of some college, as had been previously done in the case of James Vernon. A similar eagerness to prove a candidate eligible as *de se ipsis* was shown by the Duke of Albemarle in 1685 when he reminded the university that the King had ordered Colonel Fairwell to be given a mandate degree some years before so that he might be made legally acceptable for a university seat. Sir Robert Sawyer, also, though a degree-holder and a former fellow, complained in 1688 that he was at a disadvantage (as against Edward Finch and Isaac Newton), because of his being a nonresident. And the letter from Robert Spencer to the Duke of Ormonde, asking for the Duke's support, was careful to add in a postscript: "I am one of their body, being a Doctor and Canon of Christ Church."[5] It was indeed towards the end of the period under consideration that the success of the gremials as against outsiders—even outsiders who were *bona-fide* degree-holders—appears most strikingly. By this time,

Cambridge was able to go so far as to elect a complete set of gremials in two successive elections—Exton and Brady in 1680/1 and again in 1685. In earlier periods, the closest parallel to this situation had been the election at Oxford in 1660 of Sir Thomas Clayton and Dr. John Mills, one of whom had been the university's burgess in the preceding Parliament. But now in 1679 and 1680/1 Oxford matched Cambridge's double gremial record, and in 1685 would have again succeeded in presenting another set of gremials, had the Parliament lasted long enough for George Clarke to join Dr. Parrott after the death of Sir Leoline Jenkins. Indeed, as for Jenkins, were it not that he was so distinctly the Court's spokesman, the Jenkins-Parrott combination might also be regarded as a double gremial slate, for Sir Leoline, as Principal of Jesus College, had so long been a resident of Oxford that he might very well be accounted a gremial. If this view were taken, then Oxford would score over Cambridge in maintaining its double gremial slate for three successive elections, rather than for two—1679, 1680/1, and 1685.

Other sets of gremials from both universities might also have been sent up in 1678 and 1679, had the polls gone in their favour. Such combinations at Cambridge would have been Exton and Sclater (for the latter seems to have been accounted a gremial according to Benjamin Whichcot's letter of 1658),[6] or Exton and Brady; and at Oxford, Lamphire and Edisbury, Oldys and Parrott. Furthermore, in 1688/9 at Cambridge, the two gremials, Newton and Finch, came close to taking the poll from Sir Robert Sawyer. As it turned out, however, in all these cases, only one gremial at a time was actually chosen. Each of these gremials, according to the long-established compromise, was paired with a candidate pleasing to the Court or to the university Chancellor. Such were the combinations of Parrott and Jenkins, Exton and Vernon, Exton and Temple. In the case of Temple, there had been a tendency for the Court to encroach upon the university's privilege of naming at least one candidate—or so Temple suspected when he protested that Sir Robert Sawyer's claims were being pushed forward as well as his own. He and Dr. Turner both warned Archbishop Sancroft that this policy would never do, and would result in failure for both outsiders. The "body"—"our young Princes of the Senate"—as Turner called the university electors—would no longer permit dictation of this sort.[7] This was indeed a far cry from the 1620's, when the King could fill the two university seats with crown officers at his pleasure—most conspicuously with Calvert and Wake in 1623/4 and Naunton and Morton in 1625.[8] In the latter part of the century, on the contrary, it was only in the election of 1661, when the first flush of

Restoration enthusiasm was at its height, that the Earl of Clarendon, as Chancellor of Oxford, could push through the nomination of two candidates of his own choice—Hyde and the first Finch. And this, as previously noted, was done only with considerable difficulty. However, it must not be forgotten that Oxford had been successful in resisting a similar move, in the case of the Earl of Pembroke and his secretary, Oldisworth, even in the years of royal supremacy.[9]

Re-elections in this period, as we have observed, were fairly common. Oxford chose two parliament men, Jenkins and Parrott, each three times, and one—Heneage Finch the younger—twice; while Cambridge elected Sir Thomas Exton three times, and Dr. Brady, twice. It is interesting to note that the re-elections took place when the candidates were the highest kind of High Tories—especially Jenkins, Brady, and Finch—a fact that recalls the frequent re-elections of the early Stuart period, rather than the changing days of the Interregnum. A similar tendency to re-elections was characteristic of the static Whig régime of the eighteenth century, when political conformity of another variety was in vogue.

The natural result of the growing interest in gremials was that one-third of all the eighteen parliament men of this period were current university residents, although some of the gremials, like Eden and Mills in the mid-century, had outside occupations, such as Sir Thomas Exton, with his Admiralty post and his chancellorship of the Diocese of London, and George Clarke, with his place as Judge Advocate of the army. In addition, three of the non-residents had formerly been gremials—Wheler, fellow of Trinity; Jenkins, Principal of Jesus; and Sawyer, fellow of Magdalene—making nine burgesses in all, or fifty per cent of the total number, who had close university connections. This proportion of gremials is in striking contrast to the situation in the early days of university representation, when non-resident Masters of Request, Ambassadors, Judges, and Secretaries of State far outnumbered the three gremials, Mountlowe, Gooch, and Eden—although, to be sure, men who had once been gremials were fairly numerous.[10] During the Long Parliament and Interregnum, however, the proportion of true gremials—eight out of eleven—was even greater than in the thirty years of the Restoration. So although in the Restoration there was much more to-do made of residence as a qualification for office—at least there is much more in the available records on the subject—there was in practice no greater observance of the *de se ipsis* clause than there had been in the twenty years preceding, although there was certainly much greater freedom of election than ever before.

In regard to the matter of degrees—another possible way of fulfilling

the *de se ipsis* requirement—the situation had, however, become somewhat more regular. Whereas only ten of the eighteen parliament men
of the Civil War period were degree-holders, in the Restoration fifteen
out of eighteen held degrees of some sort.[11] And even though in general
this was a great period for "created" degrees, issued by the King's
mandate, only six of the degrees held by the university burgesses of
this time were created degrees—Hyde's M.A.; the two M.D.s, Clarges
and Brady; and the D.C.L.s of Fanshawe, Finch the elder, and Jenkins.
And even among these holders of created degrees, there was one, Brady,
who had already received an earned degree. Moreover, only two of the
eighteen members, Sir Thomas Clarges and Lawrence Hyde, were utter
strangers to any university whatsoever—that is, were without either a
previous degree or some temporary attendance at one university or the
other. This practice of allowing men with no university connections
to be chosen burgesses had first appeared in the Interregnum with
John Thurloe and Richard Cromwell—and possibly earlier with Sir
Thomas Edmondes. For Thurloe, Cromwell, and Edmondes, so far as
appears, nothing was done to regularize their status. With Hyde and
Clarges, however, steps were promptly taken before their elections to
comply with tradition. Hyde was created M.A. early in February
1660/1, and Clarges was enrolled in Wadham College six days before
the poll of January 1688/9.[12] Likewise, as noted above, at Cambridge
the pretensions of James Vernon, who had obtained his M.A. at
Oxford, were looked at somewhat askance until he was "naturalized"
by "incorporation", and enrolled as a member of St. John's College.
Such action properly should have been taken for Cambridge's other
Oxford degree-holder, Sir Richard Fanshawe, but nothing seems to have
been done in this case, perhaps because of the confusion of the Restoration adjustments, perhaps because Fanshawe had been a Cambridge
man in the beginning, though not a degree-holder. As it happened, the
record of his degree at Oxford was none too certain, and even if clearly
established, the degree would have been only a created one.[13]

With the return of the Monarchy, the civil law regained some of its
pre-eminence. Seven out of the eighteen burgesses of this period were
"civilians". The degree in law, indeed, was only rivalled by the master's
degree—six or seven out of the eighteen members qualified in one way
or another as masters, and had no other status. Others, of course, held
master's degrees as well as doctorates. Medicine was holding its own,
with two representatives, Clarges and Brady, as the symbols of the new
age of science, while the common law still had its practitioners—seven
out of eighteen, about the same proportion as before. Three of the
eighteen members held no degrees at all—Temple, Finch the younger,

and Thomas Thynne—but all of them had spent some time in residence at their respective colleges, and one was a Bencher of the Inner Temple.

As to social class, one innovation, begun in the Interregnum with the election of Nathaniel Fiennes, was continued—that is, the appearance of noblemen's sons as university members. In the Restoration there were only two of these—Lawrence Hyde, the son of Clarendon, and the second Heneage Finch, the son of Nottingham. In the eighteenth century this practice became well established. A related trend pointing towards the aristocratic rule of the eighteenth century was the ennoblement of four men who had once been university members—the two Finches, who became Earl of Nottingham and Earl of Aylesford, respectively; Lawrence Hyde, who became the Earl of Rochester; and Thomas Thynne, later Viscount Weymouth. None of the Interregnum burgesses, naturally, enjoyed this honour, and in the first part of the century, only Sir George Calvert and Sir Francis Bacon. Thus a close connection began to be established between the new aristocracy and the institution of university representation.

The gentry, however, still predominated in the period of the Restoration, claiming twelve out of the whole eighteen members, with knights and baronets often to be found either in family backgrounds or in immediate personal titles. Sixteen were the sons of knights or baronets, four were baronets themselves, four were knights, and two bore both titles.[14] Not all of the current knights or baronets, however, were of knightly origin. Two of the group—Clarges and Jenkins—were even of lowly birth—one rumoured the son of a blacksmith, the other the son of a tailor[15]—while two others were descended respectively from a goldsmith and a town official. Among the burgesses who were not knights, there were also some of urban and trading origins—notably Vernon and Brady. In all, there were nine names out of the eighteen that came from backgrounds of trade, officialdom, or the legal profession.[16] In the case of most of the urban burgesses, however, glimpses of country forebears and associations with the older type of gentry can often be detected in their family histories and connections. All of which suggests that the university representatives, like the rest of Restoration England, were in process of becoming part of the modern world and growing farther away from England's rural past.

In the case of Newton this shift is all the more obvious. For he was rising to be a "new man", not from an urban background, as was the case with the other "new men" among the university burgesses, but, like Selden, his compeer, directly out of a modest agricultural beginning. Newton was, in fact, so sensitive on this point that he always stressed the fact that the small country property of his family was of manorial rather than of yeoman status, whatever this may mean. Further detailed information about some of the more obscure burgesses might reveal other examples of an upward shift in social standing, but enough has been said to show that, even though the traditional country gentleman still dominated the university seats, he was being pressed upon from both sides, on the one hand, by the townsmen; on the other, by the scions of the nobility.

Connected with this trend is the emergence of a professional class, separate to some degree in interest from the landed gentry, though often at this time closely related to it. It is interesting to note that in this period, for the first time, university representation becomes really representative of this class—a class in modern times so closely associated with the idea of a university. Twelve of the eighteen members elected between 1661 and 1690 were either lawyers, doctors of medicine, or university fellows or Heads, while only five—Hyde, Thynne, Wheler, Fanshawe, and Temple—belonged to the group that might be considered purely "leisure class", or high government officials. This is in contrast to the statistics of the earlier periods, where the professional and non-professional groups were equally divided in the years 1604–40, and from the Long Parliament on were in the proportion of ten to eighteen, with the professional group increasing in its representation, but not yet arrived at the two-thirds majority that it reached in the Restoration.

Despite the large proportion of obscure or humble origins to be found among the university members of this period (six to eight out of eighteen), seven of the eighteen burgesses inherited family backgrounds containing men of distinction—Chancellors, Speakers, Lord Keepers, Secretaries of State, Judges. Moreover, as a whole, the burgesses of this period themselves maintained the level of their forebears, or—in the case of the "new men"—established similar records of their own.[17] Like the notable burgesses of the previous periods, the university parliament men of the Restoration included many who had made their marks in Parliament or outside, before being chosen for the university seats. Among those who held high office before or during their terms as burgess were the two Finches and Sir Robert Sawyer, as Solicitors- and Attorneys-General; Sir Leoline Jenkins as ambassador and Secretary of State; Lawrence Hyde, Thomas Thynne, Sir Richard Fanshawe, and Sir William Temple, as ambassadors and members of the Privy Council. Others became prominent—but after they had ceased to be university members—such as James Vernon, Secretary of State, and George Clarke, Secretary at War and a Lord of the Admiralty.

To these must be added those whose attainments were outside the field of political life. Here perhaps there were not so many men of the highest order as there had been in the Long Parliament and the Interregnum, but the record on the whole, as it stands, if not brilliant, is not undistinguished, and probably considerably better than that made by the university members of the eighteenth century. The presence of Newton alone raises the score fairly high in estimating real achievement, while the figure of Sir Richard Fanshawe, poet and translator of Greek poetry, and Sir William Temple, the first English writer to experiment with the familiar essay as a form of literature, give university representation some place in the literary history of the age. Then, too, Dr. Brady's discovery of the true facts about the origins of Parliament should win him some recognition as a historian of energy and originality (though of admitted prejudice); while in their day both the Finches, father and son, were admired for their great legal learning and their eloquence.[18]

The intellectual interests and achievements of the remaining university representatives were on a considerably lower level, but still worthy of those honoured by the name of university burgess. George Clarke, who really belongs to a later age, owned a large library and became a collector of pictures and sculpture, and made a notable contribution to architecture by planning and executing the reconstruction of All Souls College. Sir Leoline Jenkins was a great patron of the university press, and Sir Thomas Clarges was reported to have written part of Baker's *Chronicles*, attributed to General Monck, his brother-in-law.[19] Thomas Thynne, like Sir Heneage Finch, Earl of Nottingham,[20] was regarded as a great patron of learning and learned men, and may be especially mentioned for his interest in John Rushworth's famous *Collections* of source materials concerning the Long Parliament. Thynne was also himself a collector of manuscripts and coins, and, as Viscount Weymouth, was credited with having introduced the larch tree into English landscaping at his celebrated estate at Longleat, whence it became known as the Weymouth pine. Lawrence Hyde was regarded by his contemporaries as a man of studious nature, not unworthy of his honorary M.A., and for a nobleman, rather more addicted to intellectual pursuits than might be expected, but nothing concrete remains to justify his reputation.[21]

When it comes to surveying the relative value of the eighteen burgesses in their capacity as parliamentary representatives, the situation is much the same as in earlier periods. In the Restoration only five of the members had seen previous service as M.P.s before being chosen for the university seats—Jenkins, Temple, Sawyer, Hyde, and Clarges. Jenkins and Clarges were really old hands of long standing, Clarges's service indeed having gone back to the time of the Protectorate. Sawyer, also, had been in the Cavalier Parliament in its later years, and had been elected Speaker in 1678. Temple, on the other hand, had served merely in the Irish Parliament, and that, many years before in the early days of the Restoration; while Hyde had sat—for a few months only—in the second session of the Convention Parliament of 1660. The rest of the university members of this period entered the House for the first time when they took their university seats. This deficiency in parliamentary experience may be accounted for partly by the presence of a large number of gremials who had never left their colleges before, and partly by the fact that most men of strong royalist views would have had no opportunity in the Protectorate to enter Parliament in their earlier years, while the long duration of the Cavalier Parliament continued to limit such opportunity as time went on. After their terms as university members, however, a considerable number of these burgesses later served for other constituencies, for example, Vernon, Hyde, Thynne, Finch the younger, and George Clarke.

The comparative youth of the burgesses of this period also helps to account for their lack of parliamentary experience. Eight of those whose ages are known were under forty, or bordering it, at the time of their election. This includes two members who were still in their twenties— George Clarke being twenty-four and Lory Hyde only twenty. Three other members were in their forties, and four more in their fifties. So far as is known there were no university representatives in this period older than fifty-seven at the time of election (Sir Leoline Jenkins), except Sir Thomas Clarges, spoken of in 1685 by young Thomas Bruce, later Earl of Ailesbury, as a "reverend old gentleman", and about seventy-four years old at the time of the Glorious Revolution.[22]

The question remains, what kind of members did the university burgesses of this period make, regardless of their youth or previous experience? Their record on the whole is not unlike that of the burgesses of earlier periods. Six of them made little or no contribution to the conduct of parliamentary business—at least so far as the records go. Four of these were gremials—Brady, Edisbury, Exton, and Parrott— while a fifth, Sir Richard Fanshawe, was almost never present because of his ambassadorial missions. James Vernon, though neither a gremial nor an ambassador, was the sixth of the relatively inactive members. Besides these six there was a seventh of whom nothing can be said at this time, since he never took his seat—George Clarke, also a gremial. Among the remaining eleven representatives, on the other hand, there were two court spokesmen who spoke long and often, and on the major subjects of the day—Sir Heneage Finch in the 1660's and Sir Leoline Jenkins in the 1680's—and two other members who were always active on their own initiative on all sorts of subjects, large and small—Thomas Crouch and Sir Thomas Clarges[23]—while Sir Charles Wheler, Sir William Temple, and Sir Robert Sawyer were also all three moderately prominent. Heneage Finch the younger, although busy with committees, figured only modestly in the debates, despite all his great reputation for oratory, while Isaac Newton, as we know, paid close attention to business, but did not speak at all. Two other burgesses who were seldom heard from were Lory Hyde and Thomas Thynne, partly perhaps from choice and temperament—at least in Hyde's case, for he wrote better than he spoke, according to all accounts[24]—and partly because of long absences abroad. When present, however, their names are found on a respectable number of committee lists, so they were far from being ignored by their fellow legislators. As far as attendance goes, except for Hyde and Thynne, the burgesses of this period were much more faithful in their duty than their predecessors in the first part of the century.[25]

One of the most curious aspects of this matter of parliamentary service, as noted before, is the case of Thomas Crouch. No one of all the eighteen university names appears with more regularity upon the committee lists of the *Journal* over a period of eighteen years than that of Crouch. Indeed, it would seem that the name of no other M.P. whatsoever, from county, university, or borough, could possibly appear more often than his. Business of almost every sort engaged his attention—private bills, the law, the Church, commerce and manufacturing, everything indeed except diplomacy. To be named to so many committees, and to serve as spokesman for several, argues some degree of prominence in the House—some recognized ability and versatility, in addition to an undoubted willingness to undertake hard work—that is curiously at odds with the silence of other contemporary records on the subject of Thomas Crouch's career. Certainly it would seem at least that in Crouch the University of Cambridge made one of its most consistently useful contributions to the House of Commons during this whole period—a contribution of a sort that would help to justify the institution of university representation, not, as might have been expected, by the brilliance of its achievement or its wisdom and foresight, but rather by virtue of the steady application of capacity to the business of each moment as it came along.

In the midst of this preoccupation with public matters, Crouch was also one of the members most attentive to university concerns. Although fairly numerous, these were less pressing and serious than those that occupied the university burgesses of the Civil War and the Interregnum, for, once the Restoration had taken place, there were no major changes to be debated concerning the universities until the Revolution of 1688. There were, instead, the usual vested interest of press and church livings, and the ever-present question of the defence of the Established Church.[26] This last was probably regarded as the chief university concern of the period, the Church being menaced as it was by the twin dangers of Dissent and Popery. A good many of the university members, even the silent ones, put in their words—perhaps their best and only words—on this subject. But, of course, as in previous Parliaments, not all the university interests of the period were advanced by the university members. It was still true, as a note in the introductory section of Burton's *Diary* in the Interregnum had pointed out, that the universities had many friends in Parliament besides those who sat for them, and accordingly, members from other constituencies still continued to take the lead in university matters.[27] Of the university members of the Restoration, perhaps the ones who best represented their constituents in defending university interests were—in addition to Crouch— Wheler (that is, so far as he was concerned with church matters), and possibly Jenkins, in the earlier Parliaments, and Newton, Clarges, and Sawyer in the crisis of 1689. The fullest picture of a university member acting solely in his capacity of university member is that obtained from Newton's letters, but it may be that this is so perfect a picture of the active university burgess only because it was at a time of crisis, and that no such close attention to university business would have been necessary on the part of burgesses in more normal times. However that may be, this period of university history is unique in having such a record surviving.

In contrast to the six members who are known to have made some effort to serve their constituencies, Anthony Wood would certainly have insisted on naming Sir Heneage Finch and Lawrence Hyde among those who failed to do so, because of their inertia in resisting the hearth tax. The other passive members, however, throughout the whole period, went without personal reproach from any quarter—although, to judge from the *Journal* and the debates recorded by Grey and the *Parliamentary History*, fully one-third of these eighteen burgesses did nothing in particular in the House to justify their special function as university members. To be sure, this situation was not peculiar to the Restoration, but characteristic of university representation as a whole, in earlier and in later periods, though the lack of evidence in public records on this point perhaps should not be taken as wholly conclusive, especially in the light of what is known from other sources about the service of Newton.

Nevertheless, in this connection it is interesting to note that John

22

Ayliffe, writing in 1714, and Anthony Wood, writing in the 1690's, both complained of the neglect their university had received from its burgesses, and deprecated the value of the institution of university representation as a whole for the reason that the presence of specially elected members tended to make the other university men in Parliament less active in defending university causes. It is not clear that university representation actually had this effect, for there are numerous instances of university matters still being handled by representatives from other constituencies. It is also not obvious from a study of the seventeenth century that Ayliffe was entirely justified in his charges against the university members, when he wrote:

> . . . how well these have acquitted themselves, we may learn from the frequent Loss of Privileges in Parliament, either thro' their Neglect, Interest, or Want of sufficient Knowledge of our Customs and Charters.[28]

In particular, the allusion here to loss of privileges is not easy to explain. We know, of course, as far as Wood was concerned, that what he had in mind was the failure of Parliament to exempt the universities from the chimney tax, but from passing reference in the parliamentary records, it would seem that otherwise the universities had maintained their supremacy over the borough corporations, their printing rights, their charters all substantially intact.[29] Moreover, in the early years of the eighteenth century at least one other special concession was made to the universities when their burgesses were exempted from the Property Qualification Act of 1711. The full bearing of Ayliffe's accusation, therefore, can probably not be assessed without further exploration of the history of university representation in the years between 1690 and 1714.

Apart from the question of specific service to the universities, it must be conceded, in looking back over the whole list of university members from 1660 to 1690, that the calibre of the representation is fairly high, if achievements outside of Parliament and careers after serving as university members are taken into account. Some of these men, to be sure, might be regarded as narrow-minded and without vision, but this must not be held seriously against them, considering the time in which they lived. For if such a man as Thomas Crouch was narrow-minded, he at the same time possessed energy and versatility within his limitations; and if it is the qualities of tolerance and moderation that are sought, they were not entirely lacking in a group which included Sir William Temple, Isaac Newton, and, from some points of view, Sir Thomas Clarges. Newton, of course, was the only member of the period who could be awarded a place in the first rank of celebrity, but there were many others of second and third rank, from Sir William Temple,

Dr. Brady, Sir Thomas Clarges, and the two Finches, down to Lory Hyde and Sir Charles Wheler. Altogether, perhaps fourteen of the eighteen burgesses of this period belong to this secondary level. The other three, Exton, Edisbury, and Parrott, were of lesser stature, but only Parrott seems to have been a complete nonentity. The record, on the whole, is about as good as for any period preceding it, and probably better than for some following. To the historian of university representation, however, it is somewhat disappointing to be forced to note that the gremials—who might be supposed to be the truest embodiments of the university mind—do not in general come off very well in this analysis, in spite of having Newton, Brady, Crouch, and Clarke[30] to redeem their record.

The question of differences and likenesses between the two universities is always a matter of interest. We have already noted that their political opinions, as indicated by the parliamentary elections, seldom differed in any significant way in this period, except for the faint indications of future Whiggery that were shown by Cambridge in 1679 and 1689. In the light of this latter circumstance, and in view of Oxford's steadfast royalism, it might be expected that Oxford would have a preponderance of the highest kind of High Tories. As it happens, however, Cambridge seems to have had just as many ultra-Tories as Oxford, although perhaps not such vocal ones as Jenkins and Finch, while its Whigs and "Trimmer"—Vernon, Newton, and Temple—are balanced by Oxford's moderates, Thynne, Clarges, and Clarke. There was also an equal number of royal pensioners. The Oxford pensioners named were Hyde, Jenkins, Clarges, and Finch the elder, while those from Cambridge were Crouch, Wheler, Brady, and Sawyer. It must be remembered, of course, that sometimes these royal payments were made for good reason and also that the accusation of pensioner was very loosely levelled.[31]

In making these estimates of the political leanings of the university representatives, some difficulty arises from the silence and obscurity of some of the members. It is probably fairly safe to conclude in the absence of detailed evidence that most or all of them were High Tories and ultra-Anglicans, but the fact that party alignments shifted throughout the period must also be taken into account, for persons who were High Tories in the 1660's might well become active Anglican rebels by 1688. Another angle of party affiliation, not so far considered, is the pre-Restoration attitudes of the burgesses or their families. Exton, Clarke, Temple, and even the first Heneage Finch, either of themselves or because of family connections, were on the side of the Parliament, or came to some kind of terms with it. Others, such as Hyde, Fanshawe,

Jenkins, Crouch, Wheler, and Thynne had always belonged among the Cavaliers. Viewed in this light, Oxford again does not seem to come out much more traditionally Royalist than Cambridge.

While considering this question of political affiliation, an opportunity is offered to make some comparisons between the positions in Parliament assumed by these burgesses and the stands taken by the university burgesses of earlier periods. Some interesting parallels may be discovered. In each period, certain university members served conspicuously as spokesmen for the Court—Bacon, Calvert, and Sir John Coke in the early years of university representation; Nathaniel Fiennes and John Thurloe during the Protectorate; Sir Heneage Finch and Sir Leoline Jenkins in the Restoration. And among these advocates of court policy, three members at least—Coke, Thurloe, and Jenkins, and to some degree, Bacon, also—were each in their turn fighting a losing battle with the Commons. Likewise, in each period, there were other university parliament men who were not major spokesmen for the Court, but who were crown officers or pensioners, and therefore bound to speak favourably—or at least vote favourably—on most prerogative issues. Such men were almost all of the early university members, beginning with Sir Daniel Dunne, and including others like Bennett, Morton, Wake, and the two Edmondes. Such also were the Cromwellians, Goddard and Sadler—and probably Owen, if he had been permitted to take his seat. And in the Restoration, Sir Charles Wheler, Lawrence Hyde, Sir Richard Fanshawe, Dr. Brady, and the royal legal officers, Exton and Edisbury, also belong in this category. There was in addition a third group. These were the university members who were comparatively free agents. Such were Sir Miles Sandys, Barnaby Gooch, and Sir Francis Stewart in the earlier period; Selden and Lucas in the Long Parliament; Hale, Mills, and Sclater at the end of the Interregnum; and in the Restoration, Crouch, Thynne, Parrott, Newton, and Clarges. The fact that these members had no obvious ties to bind them to the Court did not mean of course that they were all men of the opposition. On the contrary, many of them were genuine and convinced Royalists and High Churchmen. But their political position in the House of Commons seems to have been the result of pure conviction rather than of official duty. Likewise, among the free agents may also be listed occasional office-holders who found themselves sometimes unable to support the prerogative cause, as Sir Henry Marten in the 1620's, Dr. Eden and Sir Thomas Roe in the Long Parliament, and in the later period, Sir William Temple. Thus there appears to be some general similarity in the overall pattern of political behaviour among university members throughout the whole century.

In analysing the political views of the university members of the Restoration and the Glorious Revolution in a previous paragraph, we found little difference to be observed between the positions taken by the parliament men of the two universities. In the matter of social classes, however, there is greater divergence. Oxford, for example, had all three of the noblemen, and Cambridge more of the burgesses with urban backgrounds, and fewer country gentlemen—only Crouch and Wheler whose fathers had estates in Hertfordshire and Worcestershire, and Fanshawe and Temple, who occasionally retreated to the country between bouts of diplomacy. Oxford also had more parliament men who could be classed as professional rather than purely "leisure class" —seven to Cambridge's five. This preponderance had also existed in the period 1640 to 1660. As to ages, Oxford's representatives were the younger, all being below forty except for Sir Leoline Jenkins and Sir Thomas Clarges. For the rest, the same proportion of knights and baronets, the same proportion of distinguished and obscure origins, seem to prevail.

It now becomes convenient to inquire what further light, if any, is cast on the mechanical procedures of university parliamentary elections by the events and circumstances of the years between the Restoration and the Glorious Revolution. The prevalence of gremials in this period, as members and as candidates, has already been commented upon, and the renewed and intentional insistence that gremials alone could satisfy the requirements of the original Letters Patent. Likewise, the comparative freedom of election that prevailed in this period has been noted. Several other tendencies may be observed, some new, some merely continuing practices established before.

The number of voters who actually exercised the franchise is more easily estimated than in earlier periods, as there were fewer elections with no contests, and more polls recorded. The electorate at Oxford was somewhat larger than at Cambridge, rising as high as 348 and 353 (or 328) in 1673/4 and 1678/9, and dropping to 289 in 1679. At Cambridge the highest number of voters in this period was 244—in 1678/9, an election that aroused great public interest. In the by-election of 1666/7 the count was as low as 118, while in various polls between 1679 and 1688/9, it ranged between 176 and 186. In no election did it reach its high for the century—355 for the Convention Parliament of 1660.[32]

Another point that arouses interest is the possibility of the universities exerting some influence over parliamentary elections in the towns. There is no evidence for this in the case of Oxford, and only two examples of it at Cambridge have come to light. But the subject is worthy of mention

since, in so far as such influence existed, it would tend toward a kind
of indirect university representation in addition to the official allowance
granted by King James's Letters Patent. Such influence would be all
the more remarkable in view of the long-established jealousies that
had existed between the municipal corporations and the universities.
But it is a fact that during the Exclusion controversy the town and the
university of Cambridge were to be found on the same side in politics,
at a time when at Oxford the city was staunchly Whig, and the
university Tory. This situation at Cambridge is probably to be
explained, not by the influence of the university, but by the influence
of the county, made effective through the practice of admitting
honorary freemen to the privileges of the corporation.[33] The same
courtesy may have been granted to some of the members of the Senate,
as indeed was done in the case of Sir Thomas Sclater, but there were
probably not enough such persons to affect the corporation's vote.
However, even without any legal concessions of this sort, the university
had its own peculiar ways of interfering in borough politics. An
example is the announcement of Dr. Francis Turner in 1678/9 that he
had tried to dissuade Sir Thomas Sclater from running for the university's seat by promising to "clapp on all our strength for him, &
engage all the Tutors with the Tradesmen". This suggests that other
candidates (not necessarily only those with university connections like
Sclater) might likewise receive similar support from the university.
There is also further evidence in the report made by the King's agents
on Cambridge in 1688, where it was stated that the town officials were
not amenable to royal control, but "wholey under the influence of the
University".[34] How this came to be, is not entirely clear, and indeed
from all angles this whole matter of borough and university political
relationship still remains extremely obscure.

Mention of loss of the town charters, however, brings up the question
of the universities' own charters. Some apprehension was expressed
that there might be *Quo Warranto* proceedings entered into also against
the universities.[35] Indeed, in view of James II's willingness to override
university statutes and opinion in the cases of Father Francis and
Magdalen College, Oxford, such a move would not have been out of
character. As it happened, the universities escaped without further
interference, but the danger must have still been vivid in their minds.
In view of this, it is not surprising that the university representatives
hastened to secure a renewal of the charters by a grant of Parliament as
part of the Revolution Settlement. What is to be wondered at, however,
is that at this time nothing was done to make certain of the additional right of parliamentary representation. With all his assiduity and

foresight, Newton, for example, never seems to have thought of having this royal grant confirmed by parliamentary authority, now that Parliament was on the point of becoming the supreme power in the realm. But the full bearing of this aspect of the Revolution was probably not apparent at that time, and the universities may still have felt more confidence in royal benevolence than in a mere legislative statute, subject to repeal on partisan grounds. In any case, if doubts arose, they were probably satisfied by the belief that the statute of confirmation was inclusive enough to safeguard the parliamentary franchise along with various other valuable but unspecified privileges, and, as it happened, nothing was done to put the franchise upon a full parliamentary basis until the Reform Bill of 1867, although representation was recognized from time to time by implication in such bills as the Property Qualification Act of 1711 and the Reform Bill of 1832.[36]

Reference has already been made to several unusual circumstances that distinguished the history of university representation in this period. One of these was the official relinquishment of any claim to parliamentary wages on the part of Thomas Crouch, Cambridge's burgess, in 1677. Another was the alliance between the Chancellor of the university and the rank and file of the voters in opposition to the plans of the Heads in the parliamentary election of 1678/9. This situation in regard to Monmouth and James Vernon is only comparable to what seems to have happened at Cambridge in the case of Sir Miles Sandys in 1614, although in the Sandys case, the evidence is less clear. A third remarkable event in the history of university representation in the Restoration period was the expulsion of a university burgess from the House of Commons for misconduct in a public office, something that had not happened in university history since Sir John Bennett was similarly disgraced in 1621. All of these incidents have a special interest because of their novelty or uniqueness.[37]

The problem of disorders in election, however, was no new one, and in this period Wood's account of the Vice-Chancellor's misconduct and the subsequent counting of votes in the Oxford election of 1678/9, as well as the prank played by the younger masters in the election of 1680/1, awaken memories of similar Convocations in earlier years.[38] The fact that the Duke of Ormonde wrote to Oxford in 1682 reproving the university for its disorder in Convocation and that a royal letter directed to Cambridge in 1669 endeavoured to hold the university to the strict letter of its statutory code in the election of esquire bedell are both further indications of the prevalence of disorder in public meetings.[39]

With the increase in freedom of election in the universities came a corresponding increase in electioneering. The busy campaigners of the period, as we have seen, were occupied for weeks before a general election with "visiting" for their favourite candidates, with letter-writing, and even, as the election day approached, with "treating" on their behalf. "Treating" as an election procedure was becoming more common all over the country, and measures were introduced in Parliament, with small success, to minimize the evils of this custom.[40] Wood stressed again and again the influence in university elections of those he called "the black pot men", notably in the case of Thomas Thynne, Dr. Edisbury, Dr. Parrott, and George Clarke. Thynne, in particular, it will be remembered, he accused of such reckless expenditure as to amount to outright bribery—"an open table for the M(aster)s for a week or ten days", etc.[41]

At Cambridge, on the other hand, both Fanshawe and Temple found their elections without cost to themselves. Temple's desire had been to stand for a place where "a sheet of paper does the business", and Lady Fanshawe marvelled that her husband gained his seat for "no more than a letter of thanks, and two braces of bucks, and twenty broad pieces of gold to buy them wine", presented, we judge, after the election, and not, as in Thynne's case, for ten days before. Dr. Sclater, on the contrary, according to Dr. Francis Turner, was a lavish entertainer, "an Eater & Drinker, time out of mind", as well as a generous provider of financial backing in the way of loans and gifts to the colleges.[42]

In describing Thynne's campaign, Wood implies that Thynne appeared in person to canvass before the election. Heneage Finch the younger also visited the university in 1678/9, though there is no evidence that his father and Lawrence Hyde had done so in 1660/1. However, in 1679, the unknown Colonel Edward Vernon arrived at Oxford quite on his own initiative, and young Mr. James Lane seems rather to have been blamed by Anthony Wood for not putting in an appearance.[43] All this would seem to indicate that whatever rules Oxford had in the eighteenth century about forbidding candidates to canvass within a ten-mile radius, such a limitation did not exist in the Restoration period. The case of the gremials, of course, presented no such problem, since they were already on the spot. At Cambridge, there seems never to have been any objection to a personal canvass—indeed a candidate was not only not forbidden, but on the contrary even expected to put in a personal appearance. As evidence of this, observe the pressure put upon James Vernon and Sir William Temple to show themselves before the election.[44]

In this period there is still some evidence that a degree of honour was thought to be attached to a university seat, though the two best examples are to be found at the very opening of the period, in the case of Sir Heneage Finch and Sir Richard Fanshawe. Finch had the choice of a seat for Oxford or for another constituency, and he chose Oxford,[45] while Fanshawe's wife reproached herself greatly for having forgotten to have Sir Richard's Cambridge burgess-ship mentioned on his tombstone, and took the pains to have an inscription added later, because of her sense of its importance.

Mention of Fanshawe also brings to mind another matter of interest regarding the subject of electoral procedure—the question of a candidate's personal efforts exerted on his own behalf during an election campaign. In the case of Fanshawe, no exertions whatsoever were made to secure a seat. Sir Richard, in fact—if we are to credit Lady Fanshawe's *Memoirs*—was voted into the House without having even been consulted in advance. This was quite unusual, but it had possibly happened before in the case of General Monck in 1660 and of Sir Robert Naunton in 1620/1.[46] The only other similar instance was in 1640, when Sir Henry Spelman was entered as a candidate without his knowledge but failed to win the seat. In all other elections for which information is available, it appears that candidates were invited to stand by some group within the university, were recommended by "those above", or else boldly announced their own willingness to serve, and pushed their claims strenuously by dint of letters, visits, treating, etc.

This latter procedure was widely practised in the Restoration. Examples of it seem to be Sir Robert Sawyer's persevering efforts to gain a Cambridge seat; the insistence of Sir Thomas Sclater and Sir Charles Wheler on trying for re-election; the repeated attempts of Sir Christopher Wren, Dr. Edisbury, Dr. Oldys, and Dr. Brady to gain recognition;[47] the unexpected appearance of Colonel Vernon at Oxford in 1679; and the generally unpublicized candidacy of Sir George Croke in 1673/4, who seemed to be standing without any general support at all.

As has been noted, the elections were seldom uncontested in this period, and it is clear that even in some of the apparently uncontested elections, there had been earlier candidates who withdrew before the poll. For example, at Oxford, 1660/1; and at Cambridge in 1678/9, 1679, 1680/1, and 1685. Counting these as contested elections, and comparing the total number to the number of elections known to be contested in the period between 1640 and 1660, the result amounts to ten contested elections out of fifteen in the Restoration (that is, two-thirds) as compared to six (or possibly seven), out of eleven elections held from the time of the Long Parliament through the Convention of 1660 (one-half), and a possible eight out of nineteen for the period 1604 to 1640 (less than one-half). Along with this increase in competition for seats naturally went less emphasis on the necessity for unanimity. A show of unanimity was still a desideratum, but seldom really obtained—unless at Oxford in 1680/1 and 1685; and possibly at Cambridge in 1660/1 and at Oxford in 1688/9. For these latter three elections, however, insufficient detail is available to determine whether or not other aspirants were in the field at some earlier stage of the campaign. Indeed, if the elections cited for Oxford were completely unanimous from the very first, it is difficult to understand what Wood meant, in commenting on the re-election of Clarges and Finch in 1689/90. Here, after noting that the Vice-Chancellor asked the Convocation whom they wished to elect as burgesses and they all shouted, "Finch and Clarges" and no other names, he added that this was a "rare thing and not before known".[48]

But with this incident we have stepped beyond the bounds of this particular study and into its next stage, the history of university representation in the eighteenth century, that is, from 1690 to 1832.

NOTES FOR CHAPTER XIII

1. The statistics on which this section is based are taken as before from the biographical references given previously for each university representative. Insufficient information about some of the members, such as Crouch, Edisbury, Parrott, etc., makes it impossible for the conclusions drawn to be anything but tentative. Moreover, the addition of Sir Richard Fanshawe and George Clarke to the list of the eighteen representatives may in some cases distort the truth, since in actuality neither member counted for much in the history of university representation, Fanshawe being almost never present, and Clarke never having taken his seat. However, they are included here, since their names do belong officially upon the lists, and in so far as qualifications for candidacy and methods of election are concerned, the facts connected with them both are of as much significance as those connected with any other burgesses.
2. *Supra*, Ch. V, p. 149
3. *Supra*, Ch. X, p. 263; Ch. XI, pp. 276–9.
4. *Supra*, Ch. IX, pp. 231–4; Ch. X, pp. 263–5, 267–70; Ch. XI, pp. 281–2; Ch. XII, p. 297.
5. *H.M.C., Ormonde*, v, 155; *supra*, Ch. XI, p. 281. For the data about James Vernon, Temple, and Brady, see *supra*, Ch. X, p. 264; Ch. XI, p. 278. For Fairwell and Sawyer, see Ch. XII, pp. 297, 302. See also mention of the degrees of Clarges and Hyde below, p. 331.
6. *Supra*, Ch. VII, p. 192.
7. *Supra*, Ch. XI, p. 279.
8. There were also lesser crown officers in both university seats when Dunne and Bennett, and Bennett and Sir Clement Edmondes were serving for Oxford in 1614 and in 1620/1.
9. *Supra*, Ch. IX, pp. 231–4; Ch. IV, pp. 114–16.
10. *Supra*, Ch. V, pp. 134–5.
11. In this discussion of degrees, statistics have been cited on the basis of degrees held at the time of election, not considering degrees that may have been granted later.

12. "In Conventione delegatus Univ. futurus in matriculam ejuisdem ascriptus est", as quoted by Foster from an unspecified source (I, 278). But neither Foster nor Wood in their registers give any exact data about Clarges's reputed degree in medicine (either as to date or university), which leaves his status after all almost as uncertain as that of Thurloe and Cromwell. For Hyde, see *Fasti*, II, 229–86.

13. *Fasti*, II, 75.

14. Again, as in the case of degrees, these statistics are based only upon knighthoods and baronetcies possessed at the time of election.

15. These origins were only ascribed to Clarges and Jenkins by their enemies or in such documents as the *Flagellum*, etc., and are therefore perhaps not to be taken seriously. The absence, however, of any other information gives the rumours some presumability of truth.

16. Of the knights and baronets, Wheler and Sawyer were the sons of a goldsmith and an auditor of London, respectively. Of the burgesses who were not knights, Brady was the son of an attorney, and Vernon, the grandson of a goldsmith.

17. Of the eighteen members, only four are not included in the *D.N.B.*

18. For a modern estimate of Brady's work, see Douglas, *English Scholars*, pp. 155–9; E. Evans, "Of the Antiquity of Parliaments", *History*, n.s., XXIII (1938–9), 206; Pocock, pp. 191–204. As for the elder Finch, Dryden's phrase describing him—"so just, and with such claims to eloquence"—is frequently quoted. Of his literary style, Burnet—perhaps not an unprejudiced critic—said that it was "much laboured and affected", and out of date. Finch was so eloquent, Burnet concluded, "that eloquence in him became ridiculous". (Burnet, Airy, II, 42–3). To North, however, Finch appeared to have "a natural felicity of speech", that was characteristic of the whole Finch family. Quoted in Campbell, *Chancellors*, II, 343. So also Roger Coke, quoted in *A.O.*, IV, 68–70. Anthony Wood had a poor opinion of Finch as a scholar (*supra*, Ch. IX, p. 260, n. 120), but to Sir William Holdsworth in modern times he seemed "a lawyer who mastered the technical learning of the law without being mastered by it". Holdsworth, VI, 540–1.

19. *A.O.*, III, 148.

20. Foss, VII, 96.

21. *B.B.*, IV, 2738. For Hyde's interest in his brother's education, see Clarendon, *Correspondence*, II, *passim*.

22. Ailesbury, p. 106; Luttrell, III, 334.

23. It was pointed out in the previous chapter that the page references to Clarges's speeches in the *Parliamentary History*, V, take up more space in the index of speakers than those for any other member of the Convention Parliament.

24. E.g., Burnet, Airy, I, 243.

25. *Supra*, Ch. V, pp. 132–3.

26. According to the list in Shadwell, I, xviii, there were twenty-three pieces of legislation affecting the universities passed between 1660 and 1690, most of them relating to questions of religious conformity.

27. Burton, *Diary*, I, cx.

28. Ayliffe, I, 203; *supra*, Ch. I, p. 36.

29. For Wood and the hearth tax, see *supra*, Ch. IX, pp. 252–3. For the legislation actually passed in this period, see list referred to in n. 26, above.

30. Clarke is included here by virtue of his later distinction, rather than for his achievement as of 1685.

31. *Supra*, Ch. IX, pp. 236–7, 248–9, 255, n. 27; Ch. XII, p. 321, n. 27, p. 323, n. 67 See also John Yonge Akerman, "Moneys Received and Paid for Secret Services of Charles II and James II", *Camden Miscellany*, C.S., o.s., No. 52, pp. 61, 87.

32. In comparison with these figures, Browne Willis's estimates of the eighteenth-century electorate are of interest. In the *Notitia*, I (1715), 153, App., p. 9, two figures are given for Cambridge—200, then 340. In III, 40, it is stated that there were 455 voters at Oxford in 1722. This last was a highly contested election that

would have drawn out the maximum number of votes. The proportion between the two universities has changed greatly over the centuries. In the general election of 1945, only about fifty per cent of the potential university vote was cast, but the total number of electors at Oxford was about 29,000 in comparison with Cambridge's approximate 43,000.

33. Arthur Gray, *The Town of Cambridge*, pp. 130–1; *The Victoria County History of Cambridgeshire*, II, 410.
34. *Supra*, Ch. X, p. 263; Ch. XII, p. 300.
35. *Life and Times*, III, 269.
36. Sir W. E. Anson, *The Law and Custom of the Constitution*, I, 127.
37. *Supra*, Ch. IX, p. 252; Ch. X, pp. 261–5; Ch. XII, pp. 318–19.
38. *Supra*, Ch. X, pp. 269–70; Ch. XI, p. 288.
39. *H.M.C.*, *Ormonde*, IV, 620; *supra*, Ch. III, pp. 84, 85.
40. For "treating" as a form of bribery—a "lay simony", see Lipson, *E.H.R.*, XXIX (1913), 80–1, and Ogg, II, 609, who quotes a contemporary verse entitled "The Pot Companions", wherein the Tories drink beer "sotting", and the Whigs, coffee, "plotting".
41. *Supra*, Ch. IX, p. 244.
42. *Supra*, Ch. IX, p. 235; Ch. X, p. 262; Ch. XI, pp. 276–7.
43. *Supra*, Ch. X, p. 269; Ch. XI, pp. 280–1, 282.
44. *Supra*, Ch. X, pp. 261, 264; Ch. XI, pp. 279, 280.
45. *C.J.*, VIII, 247. The university, however, was a little fearful that Finch would not choose the Oxford seat, if elected elsewhere. *C.S.P.*, *Dom.*, *Chas. II*, I (1660–1), 527.
46. *Supra*, Ch. IV, pp. 97–8; Ch. VII, p. 198; Ch. IX, p. 235.
47. Dr. Oldys tried a third time for an Oxford seat in 1708. *D.N.B.*
48. *Life and Times*, III, 325–6. Wood might perhaps have been alluding here to the Vice-Chancellor's manner of putting the question, but if he intended his remark to emphasize an unusual unanimity of opinion—and his memory was not at fault—then there must have been other potential candidates in the two previous elections, of whom no trace so far has been discovered. If this was so, the contests of this period were even livelier than they now appear.

CHAPTER XIV

CONCLUSION

With the completion of the first eighty-six years of the history of university representation, what can be said for the institution as a whole in this, the first cycle of its existence? Certainly not that the universities were extremely well served, or that the cause of pure learning was much advanced through the presence of these champions in the councils of the nation. The ideal representative only presented himself once in the century—if we are to venture to bestow that distinction upon John Selden, the one member of all the fifty-six who seems to be most worthy of it. But perhaps this is as much as can be expected in the ordinary run of political affairs. Perhaps, indeed, to have one such member is really an exceptional stroke of luck, when the obstacles to ideal university representation are considered—obstacles such as the prevalence of dictation by King or Protector, the overweighted concern of the universities with the interests of the Established Church, and the changing conditions of formal university education in this period.

From the point of view of that time, when defence of the Church was one of the major interests of higher education, the university burgesses must have been considered on the whole to have done their work well; and certainly the average level of their ability and achievement—given the conditions of the age as regards public office—both in and out of Parliament, was not inconsiderable. Nevertheless, when one surveys the university lists of the century, it is made clear that the universities did not use their franchise to accomplish the one thing that might be expected of them, in any period—that is, except in the choice of Newton, they did not discover of their own penetration any unknown genius whose claims to a share in the government of the State were worthy of recognition. Instead, they generally chose to honour men who had already been discovered by King or Protector, county or borough. And when they selected new men out of their own numbers, these often proved to be persons of minor calibre, if not mere nonentities. Thomas Crouch and Thomas Eden—and perhaps one or two others whose energy and diligence may justify their status—are among the few who might be accounted above this level. In making this disparaging estimate of the new men chosen by the universities, it must, of course, be kept in mind that judgment in Newton's case would be equally unfavourable, were it not for the survival of evidence other than the public records, and for this reason we must remember that for some of the other minor figures a different judgment might be forthcoming if further information were available.

Yet the right to send even nonentities to the House of Commons has a certain justification when used in free elections at a time when the electoral system of the country was coming more and more under the influence of the pocket borough. Therefore university representation has this one claim to attention and respect, if no other: that even under the pressure of four absolutist Kings and two revolutions, it never was permanently permitted to degenerate into a mere form and fiction. Recurrently it gathered together enough life to assert itself in its true shape again and again—1614, 1625/6, 1627/8, 1640, 1658/9, 1660, 1678/9, 1688/9—so that the idea of a free and untrammelled election was never lost for ever. How far this essential vigour was maintained as the years went on will remain for a study of the eighteenth and nineteenth centuries to reveal, but at least by the end of the seventeenth century stagnation and inertia had not yet triumphed.

APPENDIX I

SIR EDWARD COKE'S LETTER TO THE UNIVERSITY OF CAMBRIDGE[1]

To the Right Worshipfull etc. Vicechancellor of the Universitie of Cambridge:

Having found by experience, (and specially when I was Speaker) how necessary it were for our University to have Burgesses of the Parliament, First for that the Colledges and Houses of learning being founded partly by the King's progenitors and partly by the nobles and other godly and devout men have locall statutes and ordinances prescribed to them by their Founders as well for the disposing and preserving of your possessions as for the good government and vertuous Educacion of students and schollers within the same. (2) For that to the dewe observance of those Statutes and Ordinances they are bounden by Oath. And lastly for that it is not possible for any one generall Lawe to fitt every particular Colledge especially when your private Statutes and Ordynaunces be not knowne; and finding, especially now of later time, that many Bills are preferred in Parliament, and some have passed, which concerne our university, I thought good out of the great duty and service I owe to our University (being one of the famous eyes of the Commonwealth) to confer with Mr. Dr. Nevill Deane of Canterbury and Sir Edward Stanhope (two worthy members thereof) that a sute were made at this time (when his Majestie, exceeding all his progenitors in learning and knowledge, so favoureth and respecteth the Universities, when our most worthie and affectionate Chancellor my Lord Cecill his Majesties principall Secretary is so propense to further anything that may honour or profitt our University) for the obteyning of two Burgesses of Parliament that may informe (as occasion shall be offered) that High Court of the state of the University and of every particular Colledge: which with all alacrity the good Deane and Sir Edward Stanhope apprehended, our Chancellor was moved, who instantly and effectually moved his Majestie, who most Princely and graciously graunted and signed yt. The Booke being ready drawne and provided I know your wisedomes have little neede of myne advise yet out of my affectionate love unto you I have thought good to remember you of some things that are comely and necessary to be doune.

First, as sone as you can that you acknowledge humble thanks to his Majestie for that he hath conferred so great an honour and benefit to our University.

(2) To acknowledge your thankfulness to our Noble Chancellor and also to the Lord Chancellor of England, who have most honorably geven furtherance to yt.

(3) That you thanke the good Deane and Sir Edward Stanhope for their inward and harty sollicitations.

(4) That at the first Eleccion you make choice of some that are not of the Convocation House, for I have known the like to have bredd a Question. And it is good, that the begynning and first season be cleere and without

---

[1] Baker MS., xxix, 385. Copied into Cambridge University Registry, 50: Book of Representatives, p. 1. Printed in Seward, *Anecdotes*, pp. 258–61; Humberstone, *University Representation*, pp. 28–9.

scruple. In respect whereof if you elect for this tyme some Professor of the Civil Lawe or any other that is not of the Convocacion House yt is the surest way.

(5) The Vice-Chancellor, for that he is Governour of the University where the choice is to be made, is not eligible.

(6) There is also a new wrytt provided for this present Eleccion. When you have made Eleccion of your two Burgesses you must certifie the same to the sheriffe and he shall retorne them. Or if you send your Eleccion to me under your Seale I will see them retorned. And thus ever resting to do you service with all willing readyness I commytt you to the blessed protection of the Almighty.

From the Inner Temple this 12th of March 1603.

Your verie loving Freind

Edward Coke.

You shall receive the Letters Patent under the greate [Seal] to you and your Successors forever and likewise a writt for this present Election.

(Note: The postscript is in his own hand and his seale affixt to the Letter.)

APPENDIX II

Cum in Collegiis Academiae nostrae Cantabrigiensis multa sunt Statuta localia, Constitutiones, Ordinationes, Jura et Instituta,—quae Virtute Juramenti sunt observanda et manutenenda,—cumq. Temporibus retroactis, praecipueq. nuperis multa Statuta et Actus Parliamenti facta fuerent haec eadem concernentia:—Idcirco Operae Pretium et necessarium videtur, quod dicta Universitas—habeant Burgenses Parliamenti de se ipsis, qui de Tempore in Tempus supremae illae Curiae Parliamenti notum facient verum Statum ejusdem Universitatis, et cujuslibet Collegii, Aulae, et Hospitii ibidem ita ut nullum Statutum aut Actus generalis illis aut eorum alicui privatim sine justa et debita Notitia et Informatione in ea Parte habita praejudicet aut noceat— Sciatis igitur quid nos—de Gratia nostra speciali—per praesentes pro nobis Haeredibus et Successoribus nostris volumus et concedimus Cancellario, Magistris, et Scholaribus Universitatis Cantebrigiae et Successoribus suis,— quod sint et erint in dicta Universitate nostra Cantebrigiae, duo Burgenses Parliamenti;—quodq. praedicti Cancellarius, Magistri et Scholares Universitatis Cantebrigiae, et Successores sui, Virtute Praecepti, Mandati, seu Processus super Breve nostri, Haeredum, et Successorum nostrorum in ea Parte debite directi, habeant et habebunt Potestatem, Authoritatem, et Facultatem eligendi et nominandi duos de discretioribus et magis sufficientibus viris de praedicta Universitate pro tempore existentibus fore Burgenses Parliamenti:—eosdemq. Burgenses sic electos ad Onera et Custagia dictorum Cancellarii, Magistrorum, et Scholarium Universitatis Cantebrigiae et Successorum suorum pro Tempore existentium mittere in Parliamentum, eisdem Modo et Forma prout in aliis Locis, Civitatibus, Burgis sive Villis Regni nostri Angliae usitatum et consuetum est. Quos quidem Burgenses sic electos et nominatos volumus interesse et Moram facere ad Parliamentum,—prout alii Burgenses, Parliamenti faciant, seu facere consueverunt. Et qui quidem Burgenses in huijusmodi Parliamento—habebunt voces suas tam affirmativas quam negativas, caeteraq. omnia et singula ibidem facient et exequantur, ut allii Burgenses quicunq. habeant, facient, et exequantur, aut habere, facere, et exequi valeant.

Translation

WHEREAS, in the colleges of our University of Cambridge there are many local statutes, constitutions, laws and foundations, which by virtue of oaths are bound to be observed and maintained, and since in times long past and especially of recent date many Statutes and Acts of Parliament have been enacted concerning these same matters;

THEREFORE, it seems worth while and necessary that the said University should have parliamentary Burgesses of their own body who from time to

---

[1] Printed in Dyer, I, 135–6. A fuller version is in Heywood and Wright, II, 207–11.

time shall make known to that supreme High Court of Parliament the true state of the same University and of each college, hall, and hospice there, so that no Statute or Act may prejudice or injure them generally or any one of them separately, without fair and due notice and information there;

THEREFORE, be it known that we, of our special grace by these presents for our heirs and successors, will and grant to the Chancellor, Masters, and Scholars of the University of Cambridge and their successors, whoever are or will be in our said University of Cambridge, two parliamentary burgesses;

THAT the aforesaid Chancellor, Masters and Scholars of the University of Cambridge and their successors, by virtue of our precept, mandate, or process upon our writ, or that of our heirs and successors, duly directed there, shall have the power, authority and faculty of electing and nominating two of the more discreet and more sufficient men of the aforesaid University as parliamentary Burgesses for the time being, to send these same Burgesses thus elected to Parliament at the expense and charge of the said Chancellor, Masters and Scholars of the University of Cambridge and their successors for the time being, according to the same form and manner as is usual and customary in other places, cities, boroughs and towns of our Realm of England.

AND it is our will that these Burgesses so elected and nominated should be present and remain in Parliament, just as other parliamentary Burgesses do or are accustomed to do;

AND these same Burgesses in such a Parliament shall have their own votes both affirmative and negative, and shall do and carry out all other business there, just as other Burgesses have votes, do and carry out business, or are able to have votes, and do and carry out business.

APPENDIX III

No. 1. Ratification of Method of Election of Burgesses by James I.

Whereas by our letters patent sealed at Westminster the xii day of March in the first years of our Reigne of England France and Ireland, and of Scotland the xxxvii we have given and graunted power and authoritie to our Chancellor, masters and Schollers of our University of Cambridge to nominate and chos duos de discretioribus et magis et sufficientibus viris de predicta Universitate pro tempore existentibus Burgienses [sic] Parliamenti nostri heredum et successorum nostrorum pro eadem Academia sive Universitate, As by the sayd letters patents appears. And whereas we are given to understand that some question hath heretofor been made about the manner of your election of the said Burgesses; And that our Vice-chancellor and heads of Colledges (for prevention of such faction and disorder as have heretofor happened herein) have setled a course so that election [be] ordered and [directed] that it should be made juxta formam et electionis Procancelarii infra 14 dies post tradicionem brevis nostri a Vicecomite Procancellario Universitatis factam which order we doe hereby notifie and confirme requiring all whom it doth or may concerne dewly to observe the same at all times hereafter [for] validity of election. 28 February 1620/21.

No. 2. Letter from the Registrary to One of the Burgesses[2] about the Election.

Sir,

My dutie and service remembered, the occasion of my writing at this present is a rumor cast abroad (for ought I can learne originally from Mr. Lukis[3] further I cannot send it) that our Burgesses are questioned in the Parliament for the manner of their election. I am sure you have said that election was peaceable without tumult or any opposition; all men present had a free voyce and you were chosen by suffrages, many of them mentioninge that they did liber et secundum tenencium brevis Regis. All the suffrages are in my custody but 7 or 8 that Redinge slyly stole away as they were reeding.[4] Cambridge election is farre worse be[ing] they were chosen only by 6 the bodye never gave voyce. In ours every man was at liberty to chose or denye I hope it is but a Towne hubbub yet many [a Burgess] is very [descouraged] to serve whether there be any such matter either moved or intended.

I praye be carefull you lose none of my papers. Be [by] the sewars we feare the drayninge is again expounded; yf I had of the particulars of the bill I dout not but I could acquaint you with some materiall poynts to be stood upon for us. . . .

Soe I take my leave this last day of February A.D. 1620.

Yours in all dutye   James Tabor

[1] Cambridge University Registry, 50: Book of Petitions, no. 1, 2.
[2] Probably Barnaby Gooch, as Naunton was in seclusion. See Appendix V.
[3] Could this be Henry Lucas, later M.P. for the university, 1640–9?
[4] Redinge is possibly Joseph Reding (mat. King's 1619, B.A., 1622/3) or more likely Richard Ridding (esquire bedell, 1596–1626). Venn, III, 457.

APPENDIX IV

AN ACCOUNT OF THE ELECTION AT OXFORD, 1625/6[1]

The 17 of Jan. [over 6 of Feb., crossed out] 1625/6 there was an Election
of Burgesses for ye university of Oxon. to sit in parliament,
6 Feb. following one of wch. viz. Sr Thom. Edmonds
Kt being chose in a tumult, there was a
petition drawne & put [sent?] up by
sevall of ye university against it.
The tenor of wh runs thus with
ye answer.

To ye right honorable ye kts citizens & Burgesses of ye comons house of parliament: this humble petition of ye (1) Bachelours of Divinitie & (2) Mrs of Arts of ye University of Oxford.

The Answer

(1) Most Bachelours of Divinitie are against it & disavow it.

(2) Some only through ye importunity of Mr. Vauze & Mr. Lancaster, who have been noted for their scandalous misdemeanors a long time in ye university, wch shall be great?

Humbly show yt by ye charters & antient customes & privileges of ye said university, all (3) elections as well of Burgesses, as other officers of ye sd university, ought to be by scrutiny for avoiding many inconveniences, Mr. Dr. Prideaux, now Vicechanc. of ye said University having recd a warrant from ye sherif to chose ye Burgesses for ye said University, did for ye purpose call a convocation, & after reading of said warrant, did read ye letters of two noble personages wch had recommended unto them sr Thomas Edmonds to be elected Burgess for ye said University if it might be lawfully & fairly effected. After ye reading of these letters, ye said Vicechanc. did in his speech concerning ye said election use these words.

(4) Facilius est irritare magnates quam reconciliare, & having gotten the consent of (5) some of ye Doctors, ye (6) greater part of ye convocation required a scrutiny wch he denyed,

(3) Absolutely false, the election of Burgesses hath ever been viva voce sithence ye first grant of yt prvilege by K. James except once in Dr. Pierce's vicechancellorship & in ye same manner as they were now chosen.

(4) no such words were used, but these Facilius est multos amicos irritare, quam unum reconciliare.

(5) Of every one of ye Doctors distinctly not by any getting of ye Vicechan. but of their free concurrence.

(6) Not ye greater part nor ye half & yt onlie after ye election of both Burgesses was past & registered as appears by ye Acts.

[1] Bodleian MS., 594, ff. 133R–135R.

(7) & being by him demanded, whome else they would name answered

(8) generally

Sr. Francis Steward, but still required a scrutiny; the said Vicechancellor demanding whome they would have for ye 2d place, agreed all with one consent sr. John Danvers. (9) Then ye Vicechan. told them they had chosen sr. Tho. Edmonds for ye first place, & major part denied, & said they had chose

(10) Sr. Francis Stuart. The Vicechancellor (11) bade them divide themselves, & a greater part by much went on Sr. Franc. Stuart's part or side, & thereupon ye Vicechanc. dissolved yt convocation & having dispatched some ordinary businesses, the

(12) whole convocation called for a scrutiny yt Sr. Franc. Stuart's (13) election might be confirmed, wch ye Vicechanc. denied & presently dissolved ye convocation. Some few days after ye Vicechanc. in a third convocation would have read an Act made by (14) himself without ye consent of

(7) Because it was to no purpose both Burgesses being before chosen, without any man being named not either of them, vid. Act.

(8) Most false for they generally cried Edmonds & *placet* Not above 5 or 6 then crying *Non*, others held their peace & being willed by ye Vicechancellour to name anyone whom they pleased against Sr. Tho. Edmonds, & to divide themselves yt their number might appeare, they would not, neither did; coming indeed as some have since confessed, to oppose Sr. Tho. Edmonds but having not agreed wn ye Election was first proposed whom to name.

(9) That was after ye election of both Burgesses was past, not demanded, but then took up of themselves to make [illegible]

(10) This was all done before Sr. Franc. Stewart was observed to be named.

(11) all this is false; the Vicechanc. willed them to name one in ye first place wth Sr. Tho. Edmonds, & divide themselves, but then they would not, as having not agreed whome to name, yt wch they pretend to be done afterwards was in a tumult, & not of so many as disliked it.

(12) No such matter, but only one spake ut haberetur ratio nobilissmi Stuarti, & yt. after ye Vicechanc. was departing, to whome he answered in his passing away, yt yt matter for Burgesses was concluded already & could not be recalled.

convocation; wherin was suggested yt
Sr. Tho. Edmonds was chosen Burgess
for ye said University, wch was denied
(15) by almost ye (16) whole convoca-
cation.   The Vicechancellour (17)
libere eligunt et eligent. But ye convocation (18) replyed *Libere non pos-
sunt eligere, sed suffragio.* The Vicechanc. observing (19) yt ye major part
were against him & yt he could (20)
not have ye university seal wch was
[in] ye Custody of ye Proctors, hath of
his (21) owne hand made indentures
importing an election of Sr. Tho.
Edmonds & hath (22) not ye university
seale therto & sent ye said indentures
up. And hath since picked unjust and
causeless quarrells against (23) someone of the Masters of ye said university
wherof he imprisoned for not (24)
yeilding to his will in ye said election.

Most humbly beseech this majestic
[*sic*] honorable assembly out of their
pious care to justice & religion, this
fountaine wherof by this oppression
is much troubled, to take into their
consideration those oppressions & injuries & apply such (25) speedy remedy
as in their wisdome they shall find
right cause. And ye petit

(13) Wch never was intended by them
at first wch now stand for it, as
it should seem having agreed of
no man.

(14) Intollerable calumny! It may be
done by ye Regester fide publica
& was only declaratory how
things had passed wch ye Vicechanc. commanded the Regts to
read to give satisfaction of his
legall proceedings, but it would
not be heard.

(15) Strange! How denied they yt,
wn they would not heare wt it
was?

(16) The whole signifieth with these petitioners some few [disorderly?] men
who keepe a greater noise than ye rest.

(17) The Vicechanc. remembreth no such words; protesteth against any such
thought, distinctly told them after ye reading of the Noblemen's letters in
these words Viz. illi honoratissimi contantum vobis et suadent, nil praecipiunt,
vos habetis libera suffragia; And told them in ye Beginning after ye reading of
ye sheriff's warrant nobis omnibus sunt seque libera suffragia & in ye letter
end of his speech me quod a [   ] nihil cuiquam praescribo sed pro ratione
loci video et nomine D. Thom. Edmonds.

(18) alwaies a few vocall men without Vicechanc. Drs., Servitors, or head of
college or Hall are termed by these petitioners the convocation.

(19) For yt ye election was past & there was nothing to be observed but a few
men keeping up a stirre for they knew not wt.

(20) He never demanded it of ye Masters they never denied it, it is in his

Custody as well as ye proctors. He was well informed yt a legall certificate might be given without ye seal.

(21) The Register did it, whose office it is, according to ye antient forme of ye Universitie. Is it lawfull to abuse the honorable assembly of parliament with such gross [untruths?]

(22) The university hath 2 seales. It was certified under ye manuall seals, with wh wee send all our letters to his Majestie, or others from ye convocation house & hath ye university arms upon it. This is alwaies in ye Vicechancellours keeping & this was held sufficient.

(23) The Vicechanc. acknowledgeth yt he met with two, one a Mr. of Arts & a Minister between 10 & 11 of ye clock at night [illegible] ye Streets with certaine Bachelours of Arts, contrary to ye Statute of Noctivagation, who besides his fault gave him very ill termes, & Proctors there present. The other Bachelour of Divinity, was taken by himself by ye Proctors in a Taverne drinking sack at sermon time on Sunday, wn others were at St. Marie's. The same man also was proved to have stricken a Mr. of Arts of good esteeme & heartily villified him. such are ye petitioners, Bachelours of Divinity, & Mrs. Others ye Vicechanc. knows not yt he had dealt with since ye election, & desires they may be named.

(24) Wt was done agst him was in open court, ye records wherof will show there were other matters agst him.

(25) No remedy so speedy for ye cleering ye fountaine of religion here among us, as by sharpe censuring, or taking away such, idle, drunken, swearing & irreligious companions wch drew into it & corrupt others by their examples such (as some of ye cheif sticklers in this petition) are notoriously to be.

APPENDIX V

SIR ROBERT NAUNTON'S ABSENCE FROM PARLIAMENT

The length of Sir Robert Naunton's "seclusion" is not treated very clearly in any of the references that discuss it. All agree that it began in January 1620/1, and that Naunton was not present in the Parliament of that winter. Both the *D.N.B.* and Willson, *Privy Councillors*, are somewhat evasive on the question of whether or not he was released in time to serve in the Parliament of 1623/4. The *D.N.B.* does not mention his re-election at all. Willson says that he was re-elected, but probably did not serve (p. 65) although in another part of the book (p. 93) the statement is made that he "spoke occasionally for the government in 1624". This statement seems to be an error, as will be seen below.

It is clear from Naunton's own letter to Buckingham (*supra*, Ch. IV, p. 193) that he was still in confinement at the opening of the session in 1623/4. The facts that are in question are whether this situation had continued ever since January 1620/1, or whether it was the result of a new order. Both Willson and the *D.N.B.* imply that Naunton was released sometime between the two Parliaments, and then recommitted. The entries in the *Calendars of State Papers* do not entirely support this view. In the Venetian papers the statement is made that Naunton was released in August 1621, not permanently, as Willson and Evans seem to think, but only for the purpose of visiting the palace to revise the archives; and to make a trip to the country. In September 1622, Naunton is still mentioned by the Venetian agent as under a "severe punishment for innocence and honour", and in May 1623, it is noted that he was requested not to leave his house until the Prince of Wales was safely back from Spain. Whether this last was an entirely new order, the Venetian agent does not say. The *D.N.B.* refers to a second order for seclusion dating from October 1623 rather than May, but gives no specific source for the statement. Willson merely says Naunton had "once more incurred the displeasure of the court, and probably was not wanted in parliament by the government", but the inference here is that the year was 1627/8, and not 1623/4 (p. 62).

It would seem that special weight might be attached to the remarks of the Venetian agent, since he was particularly interested in Naunton as a friend of Venice. If Naunton had been entirely freed from seclusion during this period, it would seem that the ambassador must certainly have reported it. Moreover, the fact that Naunton's name never appears on any of the committee lists in either the Parliament of 1620/1 or the Parliament of 1623/4 seems to indicate that he was never permitted to attend, since it is unlikely that a Secretary of State—or an ex-Secretary—would have been so neglected as to escape all committee assignments. The conclusion therefore seems to be that Naunton remained under the ban of seclusion throughout the whole period, and that he therefore was prevented from taking his seat in either Parliament. In any case, his final release did not come until Buckingham interceded with the King in August 1624, well after the second Parliament was over.

For the references to this subject, see:

Naunton in *D.N.B.*

Evans, *Principal Secretary*, p. 78.

Willson, *Privy Councillors*, pp. 61–2, 64, 65, 75, 92–3.

C.S.P., *Ven.*, xvi (1619–21), 402, 432, 552; xvii (1621–3), 64, 68, 108, 443, 557; xviii (1623–5), 9.

C.S.P., *Dom.*, *Edw. VI–Jas. I*, xi (1623–5, with Addenda, 1603–5), 319.

APPENDIX VI

LETTER CONCERNING THE CANDIDACY OF EDWARD MONTAGUE[1]

My lord,
  There are all the heads and many other persons desirous to name your
Lordship for the University in General Monkes roome, so he does intend to
reject it, only they are not satisfied that your Lordship would accept it and doe
not question the carrying it against any man unless it be Mr. Sr. John Gore's
son make a dimission who is a young man of 7 years master of Art but able
to foile my Lord St. John and be one, but I have that interest in him that if
your Lordship be named I know he will lay it down to your Lordship rather
than any man, and I find his interest will not carry him of now nor wilbe so
many eminent men named but I know the University will suspend their
resolutions except Gore's party which I beleeve will not be the fourth part till
I heare from your Lordship. I have all my Lord St. John's party and at lest
two parts of three of Mr. Crouch's party together with Mr. Crouch himself
that will not give for Mr. Gore, because they would have one eminent person
ioined with Crouch and not two gremialls, neither shall your name be onse
named unless I am sure to carry it out of question which if Mr. Gore lay down
willbe as [many] as Generall Monkes who had 340 voices not ten dissenters.
Mr. Crouch had 211 and my Lord St. John 157 whereof about 80 strangers,
soe that though you are not named my Lord St. John will not be named for if
they should they would not have 40 voices, both parties are desirous to have
you, my Lord St. John's party that they may have a moderate sober man and
the other that they may have an honest man and one eminent and [our ?]
neere neibour and one that they would have a greater honour for hereafter.
I am in hast your humble servent

Cambridge April   '59[2]   Will Hetley[3]
Address: For the right honourable Lord Generall Mountague
Indorsed: Mr. Hetley from Cambridge.

[1] Carte MS. 73, p. 400.
[2] The date must be an error for '60.
[3] See Venn, II, 349.

APPENDIX VII

THE METHOD OF VOTING IN THE OXFORD ELECTION OF 1673/4[1]

Each candidate designated three others who should inspect as censors and diligently take care that everything should be transacted fairly and legitimately. The censors along with the official tellers, having been located one on each side at the door which leads from the Convocation House to the School of Theology, took the names of those passing through one by one and recorded them on separate pages in three columns according to the number of the candidates, in the meantime noting with an obelisk [(†) *obelisco*], if the right of anyone voting should be called in doubt, so that afterwards if it should be necessary, it could be recalled for examination. When the business was finished, and the lists had been brought to the Vice-Chancellor, after each was counted, he announced openly how many votes each one received, viz.,

> Dr. Boucher obtained 20
> Dr. Christopher Wren 125
> Dominus Thynne 203

Accordingly, he pronounced the same Mr. Thynne duly and legitimately elected as parliamentary burgess for this university.

Then at the order of Mr. Vice-Chancellor the indenture was read by the Registrar, and to it the seal of the university was affixed with the common consent of the House. The provisions of the indenture follow, and read: [The indenture is given in full].

When the Convocation was concluded, the Vice-Chancellor and others, about 6 doctors and as many masters, with both proctors, went to the Apodyterium, and one by one subscribed their names to the said indenture, and they fastened their own private seals on one side and the other by a weight with coloured ribbons. Then the Registrar sent the indenture to the Sheriff along with the writ to be delivered to Parliament.

[1] Oxford University Archives, Tb28, p. 3839, ff. 54–5r. (Translation).

APPENDIX VIII

Oxford University

1603/4 *Sir Daniel Dunne*
(?–1617)

B.C.L., D.C.L.
Fellow, All Souls
Principal of New Inn Hall,
1580, 1598
Dean of the Arches
Master of Requests
M.P., 1601
D.N.B.

Cambridge University

1603/4 *Henry Mountlowe*
(1555–1634)

B.A., M.A., LL.D.
Fellow, King's.
Law Professor, Gresham
College, 1596–1607

Sir Thomas Crompton
(1558–1608)

B.A., M.A., B.C.L., D.C.L.
Fellow, Merton
Advocate-General for
Ecclesiastical Causes
Advocate-General for
Foreign Causes
M.P., 1597, 1601

Nicholas Steward
(?—1634)

LL.B., LL.D.
Chancellor of Norwich,
1570
Queen's Counsellor, 1599

1608 *(Sir) William Byrd*
(c. 1561–1624)

B.C.L., D.C.L.
Fellow, All Souls
Dean of the Arches, 1617

1614 *Sir John Bennett*
(?–1627)

B.S., M.A., B.C.L., D.C.L.
Council of North, 1599
Judge of Prerogative Court
of Canterbury, 1620
M.P., 1597, 1601, 1503
Expelled, 1621

D.N.B.

1614 *Sir Francis Bacon*
(1561–1626)

M.A. (cr.), 1577
Solicitor-General, 1607
Attorney-General, 1613
Lord Chancellor, 1618
(Impeached, 1621)
Viscount St. Albans, 1621
M.P., 1584, 1586, 1589,
1593, 1597, 1604
D.N.B.

Oxford University	Cambridge University
Sir Daniel Dunne (re-elected)	

*Sir Miles Sandys, Kt. &
Bart.* (1563–1645)

B.A., M.A.
Fellow, Queens'
Sheriff of Cambs. & Hunts.,
1615–16
M.P., 1597, 1621, 1628

1620/1 *Sir John Bennett*
(re-elected)

Expelled, 1621

Sir Clement Edmondes
(1576–1622)

B.A., M.A.
Fellow, All Souls
Remembrancer of London,
1605
Clerk of Privy Council, 1609
Muster-Master General, 1611
Master of Requests
Appointed Secretary of State,
1622
D.N.B.

1620/1 *Sir Robert Naunton*
(1563–1635)

B.A., M.A.
Fellow, Trinity Hall
Master of Requests, 1616
Secretary of State, 1616–23
Master of the Wards,
1623–5
M.P., 1606, 1614, 1626

D.N.B.

1621 *Sir John Danvers*
(1588–1655)

Replaced Sir John Bennett,
expelled.
Attended Brasenose. No
degree
M.P., 1610, 1614, 1624,
1645
Regicide, 1649
D.N.B.

Barnaby Gooch
(?–1626)

B.A., M.A., LL.D.
Master of Magdalene,
1604–26
V.C., 1611
Chancellor of Exeter and
Worcester.

1623/4 *Sir George Calvert*
(1580?–1632)

B.A., M.A. (cr.)
Clerk of the Council, 1608
Secretary of State, 1618–25
Baron Baltimore, 1625
M.P., 1609, 1621
D.N.B.

1623/4 *Sir Robert Naunton*
(re-elected)

Barnaby Gooch
(re-elected)

Oxford University	Cambridge University
Sir Isaac Wake (1580?–1632) B.A., M.A. Fellow, Merton Ambassador to Savoy, 1615–30 D.N.B.	

1625	Sir Thomas Edmondes (1563?–1639) No university connections Clerk of Council Treasurer of King's House- hold, 1618 M.P., 1601, 1604, 1621, 1624, 1628 D.N.B. Sir John Danvers (re-elected)	1625	Sir Robert Naunton (re-elected) Sir Albertus Morton (1584?–1625) B.A., M.A. (?) Fellow, King's Minister to Savoy, 1612 Clerk of Council, 1614–23 Ambassador to France, 1624 Secretary of State, 1625 D.N.B.
1625/6	Sir Thomas Edmondes (re-elected and disquali- fied to sit, 1626) Sir John Danvers (re-elected)	1625/6	Sir John Coke (1563–1644) B.A., M.A. Fellow, Trinity College Navy Commissioner, 1618 Master of Requests, 1622 Secretary of State, 1625–39 M.P., 1621, 1624, 1625 D.N.B.
1626	Sir Francis Stewart (? – ?) (replacing Edmondes 1626) B.A., M.A. (cr.) Vice-Admiral, 1625 M.P., 1628		Thomas Eden (?–1645) LL.B., LL.D. (cr.) Fellow, Trinity Hall Master, Trinity Hall, 1626– 45 Professor of Law, Gresham College, 1613–40 Chancellor of Ely, 1630 Commissioner of the Ad- miralty, 1645 D.N.B.

Oxford University

1627/8   *Sir Henry Marten*
          (1562?–1641)

B.C.L., D.C.L.
Fellow, New College
Judge of Admiralty, 1617–41
Court of High Commission,
  1620–41
Dean of the Arches
Judge of Prerogative Court
  of Canterbury, 1624–33
M.P., 1625, 1626, 1640
      D.N.B.
Sir John Danvers (re-elected)

1640, Apr. (S.P.) *Sir John Danvers*
              (re-elected)

Sir Francis Windebanke
  (1582–1646)
B.A.
Secretary of State, 1632–40
M.P., 1640 (L.P.)
      D.N.B.

1640, Nov. (L.P.) *Sir Thomas Roe*
              (1581–1644)

Attended Magdalen College
No degree
Ambassador to India, 1614–
  18
Ambassador to Turkey,
  1621–9
Ambassador to Sweden, etc.,
  1629
Ambassador to Germany,
  1638–42
Privy Councillor, 1640
M.P., 1614, 1621
      D.N.B.

John Selden
  (1584–1654)

Attended Hart Hall
No degree
M.P., 1624, 1626, 1628
Imprisoned, 1629–35
      D.N.B.

Cambridge University

1627/8   *Sir John Coke* (re-elected)

Thomas Eden (re-elected)

1640, Apr. (S.P.) *Thomas Eden*
             (re-elected)

Henry Lucas
  (?–1663)
M.A. (cr.)
Founded Lucasian Pro-
  fessorship.
Secretary to Earl of Holland
      D.N.B.

1640, Nov. (L.P.) *Thomas Eden*
             (re-elected)
             (d. 1645)

Henry Lucas (re-elected)

Oxford University	Cambridge University
	1645 *Nathaniel Bacon* (1593–1660)
	B.A. Recorder of Ipswich, 1640 Judge of Admiralty, 1657 Master of Requests Council of State M.P., 1654, 1659, 1660. *D.N.B.*
1653 (Nominated Parliament) *Jonathan Goddard* (1617–75)	1653 (Nominated Parliament) *John Sadler* (1615–74)
M.B., M.D. (Cambridge) M.D., Inc. Oxford Warden of Merton, 1651–60 Chief Physician to Army, 1649–51 Council of State, 1653 Professor of Physics, Gresham College, 1655 *D.N.B.*	B.A., M.A. Fellow, Emmanuel Master of Magdalene, 1650–60. Master in Chancery, 1644–56 Master of Requests Town Clerk of London, 1649–60 Council of State, 1653 M.P., 1659 *D.N.B.*
1654 *John Owen* (1616–83)	1654 *Henry Cromwell* (1628–74)
B.A., M.A., D.D. (cr.) V.C., 1652–8 Dean, Christ Church, 1651–60 Cromwell's Chaplain, 1649–50 *D.N.B.*	M.A. (cr.) Parliamentary Army, 1647–50 Lord-Lt. Ireland, 1658 M.P., 1653 *D.N.B.*
1656 *Hon. Nathaniel Fiennes* (1608–69)	1656 *Richard Cromwell* (1626–1711)
Attended New College, 1624 No degree Parliamentary Army, 1642–3 Long Parliament Committees, 1641–2, 1647–8 Commissioner of Great Seal, 1654–9 Council of State, 1654 Member of Upper House, 1658 M.P., 1640 (S.P., L.P.). *D.N.B.*	No university connections Later M.A. (cr.), Oxford Chancellor of Oxford, 1657–60 Council of State, 1657 Member of Upper House, 1658 Protector, 1658–9 M.P., 1654 *D.N.B.*

Oxford University

1658/9 (Sir) *Matthew Hale*
(1609–76)

Attended Magdalen Hall
No degree
Serjeant-at-Law, 1654–60
Justice of Common Pleas,
1654–8
Council of State, 1655
Ld. Chief Baron of Exchequer,
1660–71
Chief Justice of King's Bench,
1671–6
M.P., 1654, 1660
D.N.B.

John Mills
(1604–76)

B.A., M.A., B.C.L., D.C.L.
(cr.)
Canon, Christ Church, 1648–51
(ejected, 1651; restored, 1659;
ejected, 1660)
Judge Advocate of Army
Chancellor of Norwich,
1661–73

1660 (Sir) *Thomas Clayton*
(1612–93)

B.A., M.A., B.M., M.D.
Fellow, Pembroke
Regius Professor of Medicine,
1647–65
Warden of Merton, 1661–93

John Mills (re-elected)

Cambridge University

1658/9 *John Thurloe*
(1616–68)

No university connections
Secretary to Council, 1651
Secretary to Oliver St. John,
1652
Chief Secretary of State,
1653–9
Secret Service, 1655
Council of State, 1657
M.P., 1654, 1656
D.N.B.

(Sir) *Thomas Sclater*
(1615–84)

B.A., M.A.
M.D., Oxford, 1649
M.D., Inc., Cambridge,
1649
Fellow, Trinity College,
1631
(ejected, 1649)
Sheriff, 1680–1

1660 (Sir) *William Montague*
(*c.* 1616–1706)

Attended Sidney Sussex
No degree
Attorney-General to Queen,
1662–76
Serjeant-at-Law, 1676
Ld. Chief Baron of the
Exchequer, 1676–86
M.P., 1640 (S.P.), 1661.

Thomas Crouch
(1620–79)

B.A., M.A.
Fellow, King's College
(ejected, 1650; migrated
to Trinity Hall; restored
to King's, 1660)
Proctor, 1643, 1649, 1650

Oxford University

1661   Hon. *Lawrence Hyde*
        (1641–1711)
        M.A. (cr.), later D.C.L. (cr.)
        Ambassador Extraordinary
            to Poland, 1676
        Ambassador to Nimwegen,
            1677–8
        Privy Council, 1679–88, 1692
        1st Ld. of Treasury, 1681
        Ld. President of Council,
            1684–5, 1710
        Ld. Treasurer, 1685–7
        Ld.-Lt. of Ireland, 1684,
            1700–3
        Earl of Rochester, 1682
        M.P., 1660, 1679, 1681
                D.N.B.

        Sir Heneage Finch, Kt. & Bart.
        (1621–82)
        D.C.L. (cr.)
        Solicitor-General, 1660–70
        Attorney-General, 1670–3
        Ld. Keeper, 1673–4
        Ld. Chancellor, 1675–82
        Earl of Nottingham, 1681
        M.P., 1660
                D.N.B.

1673/4   (Sir) *Thomas Thynne*
        (1640–1714)
        Attended Christ Church
        No degree
        Envoy to Sweden, 1666–8
        Viscount Weymouth, 1682
        M.P., 1678/9
                D.N.B.

1678/9   Hon. *Heneage Finch*
        (1649–1719)
        Attended Christ Church
        No degree
        Solicitor-General, 1667–86
        Privy Council, 1703–6, 1714
        Baron Guernsey, 1703
        Earl of Aylesford, 1714
        M.P., 1685 (and for Oxford
            Univ. 1689, 1690, 1695,
            1701)
                D.N.B.

Cambridge University

1661   Sir *Richard Fanshawe, Kt.
        & Bart.* (1628–66)
        Attended Jesus College
        No degree
        D.C.L. (cr.), Oxford, 1644 (?)
        Missions to Spain, 1636–8
        Sec. of War to Prince
            Charles
        Royalist Army, 1644–9
        Mission to Poland, 1662
        Privy Council, 1663
        Mission to Spain, 1664–6
                D.N.B.

        Thomas Crouch (re-elected)

1666/7   Sir *Charles Wheler*
        (c. 1620–83)
        B.A., M.A.
        Fellow, Trinity College
            (ejected, 1644)
        Royalist Army, 1644
        Colonel, Grenadier Guards
        Governor, St. Kitts, 1671–2

1678/9   Sir *Thomas Exton*
        (1631–88)
        LL.B., LL.D.
        Fellow, Trinity Hall
        Master of Trinity Hall,
            1676–88
        Chancellor of London,
            1663–85
        Advocate-General, 1675,
            1681, 1685
        Judge of Admiralty, 1686
        Dean of Arches
                D.N.B.

Oxford University

John Edisbury
(1646–?)

B.A., M.A., B.C.L., D.C.L.
Master in Chancery, 1684–1709
Chancellor of Exeter, 1692

Cambridge University

James Vernon
(1646–1727)

B.A., M.A., Oxford
Incorporated Cambridge, 1676
Secretary to Duke of Monmouth
Clerk in Sec. of State's Office
Sec. to Duke of Shrewsbury, 1693–7
Sec. of State, 1697–1702
M.P., 1695, 1698, 1705, 1708
D.N.B.

1679   *Sir Leoline Jenkins*
(1623–85)

D.C.L. (cr.)
Fellow, Jesus College
Principal, Jesus College, 1661–73
Judge of Admiralty, 1668–73
Judge of Prerogative Court of Canterbury, 1668–85
Envoy to Germany, 1673, 1675
Privy Council, 1679/80–84
Secretary of State, 1680–4
M.P., 1673
D.N.B.

Charles Parrott

D.C.L.
Fellow, St. John

1679   *Sir Thomas Exton*
(re-elected)

Sir William Temple
(1628–99)

Attended Emmanuel College
No degree
Envoy, Holland, 1667–8
Privy Council, 1679–81
Envoy to Spain, 1680
M.P., 1660
D.N.B.

1680/1   *Sir Leoline Jenkins*
(re-elected)
Charles Parrott
(re-elected)

1680/1   *Sir Thomas Exton*
(re-elected)

Robert Brady
(1643–1700)

B.M., M.D. (cr.)
Master of Caius College, 1660–1700
Regius Professor of Medicine, 1677–1700
Keeper of Records in the Tower, 1670 (?)
Physician to Charles II and James II, 1680–8
D.N.B.

	Oxford University		Cambridge University
1685	Sir Leoline Jenkins (re-elected, died)	1685	Sir Thomas Exton (re-elected)
	Charles Parrott (re-elected)		Robert Brady (re-elected)

	Oxford University		Cambridge University
	George Clarke (1661–1736), replacing Jenkins, deceased B.A., M.A., B.C.L., D.C.L. Fellow, All Souls Judge Advocate-General, 1681–1705 Secretary at War in Ireland, 1690–2 Secretary at War in England, 1692–3, 1704 Secretary to Prince George of Denmark Secretary of Admiralty, 1702–5 Lord of Admiralty, 1710–14 M.P., 1702–5, 1705, 1711–13 (for Oxford Univ., 1717–36) D.N.B.		
1688/9	Sir Thomas Clarges (?–1695) Enrolled at Wadham M.D. (no date, no University cited) M.P., 1654, 1656, 1659, 1660, 1666, 1679, 1685 D.N.B.	1688/9	Sir Robert Sawyer (1633–92) B.A., M.A., M.A., Inc. Oxford Fellow, Magdalene Speaker, 1678 Attorney-General, 1681–7 M.P., 1661, 1673–9 Expelled, 1690; re-elected Cambridge Univ. 1690 D.N.B.
	Hon. Heneage Finch (re-elected)		(Sir) Isaac Newton (1642–1727) B.A., M.A. Fellow, Trinity College Lucasian Professor of Mathematics, 1669–1702 Warden of Mint, 1696 Master of Mint, 1698 President, Royal Society, 1703–27 M.P., Camb. Univ., 1701 D.N.B.

GLOSSARY

Baron of the Exchequer: judge in the Court of Exchequer.

Bedell: university official attending upon the Vice-Chancellor.

Chancellor of a diocese; the chief judicial officer of an episcopal court.

Civilian: holder of a degree in the civil law.

Dean of the Arches: judge in ecclesiastical cases in the appellate court of the Archbishop of Canterbury.

Ex officio oath: used in the Court of High Commission: required defendant to answer all questions, even if of an incriminating nature.

Gremial: a resident graduate of a university, non-regent as well as regent.

Head: head of a college or hall; called variously Dean, Warden, Principal, Master, etc.; a member of the Caput or Council.

Master of Requests: judge of a prerogative court for "poor men's causes"; handled some admiralty cases.

Master of the Rolls: chief of the Masters in Chancery; originally custodian of governmental records.

Prerogative Court of Canterbury: probate court over all cases where property involved in wills was located in more than one diocese.

Proctor: university official with general regulatory powers over discipline, fees, etc.

Public Orator: a master of arts especially appointed to make addresses on public occasions and write formal letters on behalf of the university.

Remembrancer: an official of the Court of Exchequer; or of the courts of town governments.

Recorder: a town official who acted as judge in lesser criminal cases.

Register or Registrary: keeper of university records.

Taxor: university official in charge of markets, the assize of bread and wine.

Treasurer of the King's Household: royal official with judicial powers over crimes committed in the royal residence.

Scrutator: university election official.

NOTE ON SOURCES

The materials for a history of university representation are widely scattered. As noted in the Foreword, scarcely any notice has been taken of university representation in secondary works, either in special studies of the seventeenth century or in constitutional histories in general. Such information as is available must be gathered from a wide variety of sources, some in printed form, some in manuscript. As a whole, whether in print or in manuscript, the material divides itself into five main categories.

(1) The first class consists of the university archives. These are not very full at the best, and are occasionally entirely lacking; but they often provide essential information on important points.

(2) The second group contains parliamentary and administrative records, both official and unofficial, such as the *Journal of the House of Commons*, Burton's *Diary*, Grey's *Debates*, the State Papers, and the *Calendar of State Papers*. Information in these sources is only found by extensive search, and the entries are often obscure and fragmentary. Except in the *Calendar of State Papers*, the indexes are inadequate or non-existent, and in any case, with such a vast mass of material, it is only too easy for a significant item to escape notice.

(3) The third class consists of personal records—diaries, letters, recollections, etc., of which there are a great number, beginning with the immortal Pepys (who is of very little use on this subject), and including a long series of minor chroniclers and letter writers, such as Henry Sidney, Sir John Reresby, Humphrey Prideaux, Joseph Mead, and John Chamberlain. Private records of this sort have proved to be one of the most fruitful sources of information about university representation. Most valuable of all is the *Life and Times* of Anthony Wood, and the Bliss edition of this work makes its information readily available. However, a large part of the private papers for this period have been poorly edited and poorly indexed—or not indexed at all—and often present considerable difficulty to the research worker. From this point of view, the reports of the Historical Manuscripts Commission, which furnish a good deal of such material, are the most usable, especially the more recent volumes. Several valuable files of personal correspondence may also be found in the *Calendar of State Papers*, which are likewise provided with more or less satisfactory indexes and cross references.

(4) The fourth class of works used in this study is the biographical—both the full biographies of university members where such works exist, and the sketches in the various biographical dictionaries. Some of the biographical collections, fortunately, are contemporary or near-contemporary, like Fuller's *Worthies*, Lloyd's *"Sufferers"*, North's *Lives*, and the *Biographica Britannica*. Others are modern, such as the *Dictionary of National Biography*, Foss's *Judges*, Shaw's *Knights*, and above all, the biographical registers of the two universities, by Andrew Clark, Joseph Foster, and John and J. A. Venn. In this group, Anthony Wood again figures prominently with his seventeenth-century collection of Oxford celebrities, *Athenae Oxonienses*. One disadvantage encountered by the historian of university representation in connection with many of these biographies and biographical sketches is that there is very often no mention whatever made of the subject's term of service as university

representative. And even when the fact of election is noted, additional information that might cast light on the matter is frequently lacking.

(5) Among works that may be classified as background and supplementary reading, the standard histories of the universities, by J. Bass Mullinger and Sir Charles Mallet have a conspicuous place. Here, also, C. H. Cooper's *Annals of Cambridge* and Anthony Wood's *History and Antiquities of the University of Oxford* (also known as the *Annals*), with their abundant extracts from contemporary records, are important, not only for the general university history they provide, but for specific items contributing directly to the history of university representation. Another kind of supplementary reference which appears very little in the notes of this study, but which is none the less essential for an understanding of the milieu in which university representation functioned in the seventeenth century, is the special constitutional study or general history, such as the writings of Gardiner, Firth, and Macaulay, and the more recent work of W. C. Abbott, Wallace Notestein, David Harris Willson, Florence Evans, Mark Thomson, David Ogg, G. N. Clark, Godfrey Davies, G. M. Trevelyan and others. Above all, the Porritts' *Unreformed House of Commons* must be mentioned, since that work contains the first study ever made of university representation.

In the formal bibliography below, the works are classified more or less according to the categories just described. But in order for the reader to understand the nature of the sources for each period, as the history of university representation develops stage by stage, some further discussion of the matter follows. Here the chief references for each chapter or chronological unit will be taken up in separate sections.

1. CHAPTER I (ORIGINS).

The material on the subject of the origins of university representation is scantier than for any other period. Among the really significant items discovered are the petitions to Parliament in the reign of Elizabeth (mostly to be found in the *Calendar of State Papers*, Cooper's *Annals*, and Gilbert Burnet's *History of the Reformation*), and Sir Edward Coke's letters to the two universities informing them of their new privilege and his "demurre" citing arguments in favour of it. There are, in addition, the royal grants themselves —*De Burgensibus*—a note in Wood's *Annals*, and a manuscript letter of Lord Ellesmere, written some years after the grants. Most of this material has been gathered together and printed in T. Lloyd Humberstone's book and articles on university representation. This is about all the evidence there seems to be on the subject. All the vast calendar of the *Salisbury Papers* (eighteen volumes in the Historical Manuscripts Commission series), all the writings of James I, the parliamentary journals of Elizabeth's reign, the biographies of Whitgift and Parker, have nothing to contribute. As a result, there is very little to be found in any secondary source on the subject of the origins of university representation. Humberstone's work is the most complete; the Porritts, Mullinger, and V. A. Huber (*The English Universities*) take the subject under consideration, but they do not have much to say.

Lists of the university members from 1604, when they first appeared in Parliament, are to be found in several places. The *Official Return*, issued as a parliamentary paper in 1878, is the usual source for information regarding membership in the House of Commons, although it is not always complete.

Names of university members are also recorded in the archives of the two universities, although here again the lists are sometimes incomplete, and in the record of the election of 1614 at Cambridge one name is incorrect. The official *Historical Registers* of the universities also print lists of former members of Parliament taken from the archives, along with other data on university officers. For Oxford, a brief survey of the university's representation and a biographical list of members was published in 1899, by W. R. Williams in his *Parliamentary History of Oxfordshire*. A seventeenth-century list of university dignitaries, *Notitiae Oxonienses*, lists all the other personages of the university, but curiously enough neglects its representatives in Parliament.

2. CHAPTERS II–V (1604–40).

For information about the parliamentary activity of the university members during the reigns of the first two Stuarts, the *Commons' Journal* is reinforced by the various private diaries of proceedings in the House of Commons, edited by S. R. Gardiner and others, especially the seven volumes of *Commons Debates in 1621* edited by Notestein, Relf, and Simpson, and the one-volume collection for 1629 edited by Notestein and Relf. The seven-volume work includes a series of scattered private diaries, never before available in print. For the period before 1621, the lack of such diaries (with two or three exceptions, unimportant for this study) is felt less keenly than otherwise would be the case, because of the custom followed at this time of recording in the *Journal* some fragments of the debates in addition to the bare notices of bills and committees, as was the later practice. But in all records of parliamentary proceedings of this period, the part played by the university members is exceedingly hard to discover, because of the obscurity of the allusions and the infrequency of the entries.

Supplementary light as to what went on in the House of Commons is sometimes furnished by random references in contemporary letters. Such material for the period of James I and Charles I is provided by those busy correspondents, John Chamberlain and Sir Dudley Carleton, envoy to the Netherlands. Another important file of letters for this period is the correspondence of the Reverend Joseph Mead, a fellow of Christ's College at Cambridge. Neither of these sets of correspondence has ever been published in any collected form. Separate items from each may be found scattered through the *Calendar of State Papers* and the collections of Thomas Birch and Godfrey Goodman, and—in the case of the Mead letters—in Heywood and Wright's *Cambridge University Transactions*.

One of the most valuable first-hand sources for the history of university representation dates from this era—the account of the election of 1614 held at Cambridge, printed in Cooper's *Annals*, Volume V. The archives of both universities, though brief, have some helpful items not met with elsewhere. Neither university recorded the figures of the election returns at this time.

Biographical information is particularly scanty for the early part of this period, and has to be sought in isolated items here and there, or in the bare facts of the university directories. Spedding's great work on Sir Francis Bacon, Volume XI, pt. v, is the only thorough study of any university member of this period. Most of the members, however, appear in the *D.N.B.*, and for a number of them, seventeenth-century biographers like Lloyd, Fuller, Aubrey, and Wood supply interesting details. The special studies of the royal administration by David Harris Willson and Florence M. Grier Evans provide estimates of some of the university members when they acted as royal spokesmen and managers. Evans is good for this purpose for almost the entire century. As background for this early period, Gardiner's *History* in its ten volumes is essential, although there is little or nothing in it that bears directly on university representation or the individual careers of the university members.

3. CHAPTER III (PROCEDURES).

For information about the procedures and machinery of university elections, no one source is sufficient. Bits may be gleaned from Wood's narratives or Cooper's extracts; from the official archives; from accounts of elections in print or in manuscript (notably the 1614 account in Cooper, Volume V, mentioned above, and the manuscripts printed in the Appendices of this present study); and from correspondence written during the campaigns, for or against various candidates, or letters reporting the activities and results of the elections. Some of these letters are transcribed or calendared in the *Calendar of State Papers* and the reports of the Historical Manuscripts Commission, or printed in various collections such as the correspondence of Joseph Mead noted above. Others are in manuscript, like the letters of Dr. Francis Turner describing the manœuvres of 1678/9 and 1679, quoted at length from the Tanner MSS. in Chapters X and XI of this study.

Valuable hints may also be obtained from writers who have studied the general subject of university government, such as, for Oxford, Strickland Gibson and Andrew Clark (*Register of Oxford*); and for Cambridge, Heywood and Wright, Dyer, Peacock, and Walsh. These works are valuable for their general information and the documents they contain, but the matter of procedures in university parliamentary elections is not touched on anywhere except for a brief section in Wall's *Ceremonies of the University of Cambridge*, and a passing note in the Oxford Statutes of 1636 (ed. John Griffiths).

4. CHAPTERS VI–VIII (1640–60).

Anyone who works in the period of the Long Parliament must remain greatly indebted to Wallace Notestein and Willson Coates for their well-edited versions of Sir Simonds D'Ewes's parliamentary *Journal* for the years 1640–2. Although there is surprisingly little in the *Journal* that illuminates the history of university representation, the works as a whole add much to a comprehension of the period, and provide some scraps of information that would otherwise be unavailable. These two books also include notes on the debates from some other diaries, less useful and less voluminous, but comparable to those two other well-known records of the period, the *Notebook* of Sir John Northcote and *The Verney Papers*. After 1641, the dearth of parliamentary information is striking. For information as to what went on in the House during the later years of the Civil War and the first years of the Interregnum, the historian must depend upon the *Commons' Journal* until Burton's *Diary* (and the brief note on the Parliament of 1653 in its introduction) is at hand to supply the material for a somewhat fuller narrative. The lack of other sources for the intervening period is made all the more serious by the act that the *Commons' Journal* after 1640 ceases to record debates and incidental business as it did before, and becomes instead a mere schedule of bills and committees. Scobell's *Severall Proceedings* does not fill this lack, as it is equally sketchy in its entries, nor does the *Old Parliamentary History*.

From the university point of view there is also a break in continuity. Oxford, in the Civil War, was for four years the royalist headquarters, and thus out of touch with its parliamentary representatives at Westminster. The most important sources for Oxford at this period are Wood's *Life and Times* and *Annals*, and *The Register of Visitors* (ably edited by Montagu Burrows). This last contains the proceedings of the committee appointed by Parliament to regulate and inspect the university after the capture of the city. The records for Cambridge are much more defective. Some useful extracts are printed in Cooper's *Annals* and in Heywood and Wright's *Transactions*, but the reports of the parliamentary Visitors of Cambridge have been lost since the eighteenth century, and the university archives have little or no information in regard to university representation.

Some information is to be obtained from private letters, but not so much as in earlier or later periods. The confusion of the times perhaps prevented the writing of as many letters and diaries as the seventeenth century otherwise produced—at least it seems significant that the only considerable quantity of this kind of material is found in the beginning and at the end of the period. In particular, there are some useful pieces of electioneering correspondence in 1640 and in 1658/9 and 1660—in the *Calendar of State Papers* and in the Additional Manuscripts in the British Museum, in Cooper's *Annals*, in the *Thurloe State Papers*, and in *Notes and Queries*—not to speak of the personal comments of Anthony Wood. One or two letters to Selden on university matters in the middle period are to be found in Leland's *De Rebus Britannicis* and in the new Selden papers recently acquired by the Bodleian Library. And for Sir Thomas Roe's relation to Parliament and his political views, there is an extremely valuable file of his correspondence in the Harleian Collection (MS. 1901). Many of these letters are calendared with considerable fullness in the printed *Catalogue of the Harleian Manuscripts*. But as a whole, there is less evidence in the form of private letters and journals in this period than is usual in the history of university representation.

Full biographical studies of individual members, on the other hand, are more numerous than in the first part of the century. Besides the ordinary biographical dictionaries and anecdotal collections, there are separate works on John Selden, John Owen, Henry and Richard Cromwell, and Matthew Hale. In four of these accounts, more or less adequate mention is made of university representation as it affected the career of the personage described. Towards the end of the Interregnum, however, it becomes more difficult to discover biographical information about some of the more obscure members, and scattered facts have to be gathered together from Wood's *Annals*, the *Calendar of State Papers*, etc.

The works of Gardiner and Firth furnish the indispensable background of events and ideas for this period, but they provide nothing specific for the history of university representation. The same may be said of the writings of the standard diarists, such as Evelyn, Whitelocke, and Ludlow, and also Clarendon's *Life* and *History*. *The Clarendon State Papers*, however, both in the Scrope and Monkhouse edition, and in the *Calendar*, have something to add to the question of elections and university business as transacted by the representatives. There appears to be little in the files of the rising newspapers of the period, although these have not been searched exhaustively. A few items regarding university elections in the 1650's are to be found in the *Mercurius Politicus*.

5. CHAPTERS IX–XIII (1661–90).

For the Restoration, the material for a history of university representation is markedly more plentiful than in the previous period. Both the public and private records are fuller and less restrained in expression. Wood's *Life and Times*; personal letters in the *Calendar of State Papers* and the reports of the Historical Manuscripts Commission; Henry Sidney's *Diary and Correspondence*; Sir William Temple's and Lady Fanshawe's *Memoirs*; the letters of Humphrey Prideaux; the correspondence of the Duke of Ormonde as published by the Historical Manuscripts Commission—all these have valuable specific contributions to make to the history of university representation. Less of value is found in Bishop Burnet's *Own Times*, and North's *Lives*, and almost nothing in Luttrell, Pepys, and Evelyn. One of the most important sources in the whole history of university representation in the seventeenth century belongs in this period—the letters of Isaac Newton, written while member for Cambridge in the Convention Parliament, and printed in pamphlet form by Dawson Turner in 1848. This printed collection is somewhat scarce, but the letters themselves, or copies of them, are to be found in manuscript in several repositories. There are also other manuscript materials for this period—especially the letters of Dr. Francis Turner on the Cambridge election campaigns of 1678/9 and 1679 (Tanner MS., 38, 39)—that provide valuable information. The university archives, likewise become more useful, particularly since they now begin to record the complete figures of the election returns.

The parliamentary history of the time is fairly well covered, except for the period before 1667, where there is little more than the *Commons' Journal* and the fragment of the Reymes Diary in 1661–2 (Egerton MS. 2043). Grey's *Debates*, beginning in 1667, are supplemented by the parliamentary diaries of Sir Edward Dering and Sir John Milward, recently edited by Duke Basil Henning and Caroline Robbins, respectively. A new, and probably very important, register and newsletter, now being examined in manuscript by Douglas R. Lacey of the Naval Academy at Annapolis, is *The Entring Book* of Roger Morrice, covering the years 1677–91, but this document has not been used in connection with the present study. Better known are the numerous pamphlets, published illegally during the controversy over the Exclusion Bill—the *Exact Collection*, the *Historical Collections*, the *True Copy*, etc. Some of these are partisan and inaccurate, but occasionally a speech or a motion is set down that does not appear in Grey. The famous blacklists of the period, such as the *Seasonable Argument*, the *Flagellum Parliamentarium*, and the *Satires* of Andrew Marvell, also are of some assistance in discovering the political positions of the university members.

Modern scholarship has been at work on the Restoration for some years. To Macaulay have been added David Ogg's *England in the Reign of Charles II*, Keith Feiling's *The Tory Party*, G. N. Clark's *The Later Stuarts*, and the articles by Wilbur C. Abbott in the *English Historical Review* on "The Long Parliament of Charles II". There are other useful constitutional studies in the form of articles in periodicals, as well as some full-length biographies. Of these last, the most helpful for the history of university representation are the lives of Isaac Newton and Sir William Temple, by Louis Trenchard More and Homer E. Woodbridge respectively. Some of the university burgesses of this period, such as Thomas Crouch and Sir Charles Wheler, deserve more attention than they have received from the *D.N.B.* and biographers in general. Information about them is available in scattered sources, but the facts needed for this present study have had to be gathered together for the first time. The same situation would prevail in the case of Lawrence Hyde, if it were not for the existence of an unpublished doctoral dissertation by Margaret Yates in the possession of the University of London.

Another aspect of this period that is not very well covered is university history in general. Mullinger's *History of Cambridge* comes to an end in the midst of the reign of Charles II, and it is not until the books of Denys Winstanley take up the story again in the eighteenth century that there is any solid and continuous reference to consult on this subject. For Cambridge during the interval between Mullinger and Winstanley we have only Cooper's *Annals,* with its isolated extracts. The University of Oxford fares somewhat better, since Mallet's *History* goes on to the nineteenth century, but the great fundamental source of information about early Oxford—Anthony Wood's *History and Antiquities* (the *"Annals"*)—does not continue into the Restoration. The disconnected items of the *Life and Times* do not provide the same kind of long-range picture, but they are nevertheless immensely useful for all phases of university history.

BIBLIOGRAPHY

I

GENERAL HISTORIES

Bogue, David, and Bennett, James. *A History of Dissenters*. London, 1833. Vol. I.

Clark, George N. *The Later Stuarts, 1660–1714*. Oxford, 1934.

Davies, Godfrey. *The Early Stuarts, 1603–1660*. Oxford, 1937.

Feiling, Keith. *A History of the Tory Party, 1640–1714*. Oxford, 1924.

Firth, Sir Charles Harding. *The House of Lords during the Civil War*. London, 1910.

——. *Oliver Cromwell and the Rule of the Puritans*. ("Heroes of the Nation Series".) London and New York, 1900.

——. *The Last Years of the Protectorate, 1658–1659*. London, 1909. Vols. I–II.

Gardiner, Samuel Rawson. *The History of England from the Accession of James I to the Outbreak of the Civil War, 1603–1642*. London, 1894–6. [1896–1901.] Vols. I–X.

——. *The History of the Great Civil War*. London, 1891. Vols. I–II.

——. *The History of the Commonwealth and Protectorate, 1649–1660*. London, 1894–1903. Vols. I–IV.

Holdsworth, Sir William. *The History of English Law*. London, Vol. IV (1937); Vol. V (1937); Vol. VI (1924).

Jordan, Wilbur Kitchener. *The Development of Religious Toleration in England from the Convention of the Long Parliament*. London, 1938. Vol. II.

Keir, D. L. *The Constitutional History of Modern Britain, 1485–1937*. London, 1938.

Macaulay, Thomas Babington. *History of England from the Accession of James II*. Ed. C. H. Firth. London, 1913–14. Vols. I–IV.

Ogg, David. *England in the Reign of Charles II*. Oxford, 1934. Vols. I–II.

Tanner, J. R. *English Constitutional Conflicts of the Seventeenth Century, 1603–1689*. Cambridge, 1948.

Thomson, Mark A. *A Constitutional History of England, 1642–1801*. London, 1938.

Traill, H. D. (ed.). *Social England*. New York, 1904. Vol. IV.

Trevelyan, George M. *England under the Stuarts*. London, 1933.

II

SPECIAL CONSTITUTIONAL STUDIES

Abbott, Wilbur Cortez. "The Long Parliament of Charles II." *English Historical Review*, XXI (1906), pp. 21–56, 254–82.

Anson, Sir William R. *The Law and Custom of the Constitution*. 5th ed. Oxford, 1922. Vol. I (ed. Sir Maurice Gwyer).

Behrens, B. "The Whig Theory of the Constitution." *Cambridge Historical Journal*, VII (1941), pp. 46–71.

Duckett, Sir George. *Penal Laws and Test Act, 1687–88*. London, 1882.

Evans, Florence M. Grier. *The Principal Secretary of State, 1558–1680*. Manchester and New York, 1923.

George, M. Dorothy. "Elections and Electioneering, 1679–81." *English Historical Review*, XLV (1930), pp. 552–78.

[Glanville, Sir John]. *Laws concerning the Election of Members of Parliament*. London, 1768.

Glass, Henry A. *The Barebone Parliament*. London, 1899.

Gwynn, Stephen. *Ireland*. London and New York, 1925. Appendix.

Hatsell, John. *Precedents of Proceedings in the House of Commons*. London, 1796. Vol. II.

Hulme, Harold. *A Study of the Personnel of the House of Commons, 1604–29*. Abstract of Thesis, Cornell University, Ithaca, New York, 1930.

Humberstone, Thomas Lloyd. *University Representation*, London, 1951.

——. *Parliamentary Affairs*, I (1947–8), no. 1, 67–82; no. 2, 78–93; no. 4, 78–88,

Interim Report of the Commission on the House of Commons Personnel and Politics, 1264–1832. London, 1932.

J. C. *The Candidates' Guide, or the Election Rights Decided . . . 1624–1730*. London, 1735.

Kershaw, R. N. "The Recruiting of the Long Parliament, 1645–47." *History*, n.s., VIII (1923–4), pp. 169–72.

——. "The Elections for the Long Parliament, 1640." *English Historical Review*, XXXVIII (1923), pp. 496–508.

Kohn, Leo. *The Constitution of the Irish Free State*. London, 1932, pp. 186–96.

Lipson, E. "The Elections to the Exclusion Parliaments." *English Historical Review*, XXVIII (1913), pp. 59–85.

E. Lousse. *La Société d'Ancien Régime. Organisation et représentation corporatives*. Vol. I of *University of Louvain, Recueil de Travaux d'Histoire et de Philologie*, 3ᵉ série, 16ᵉ fasc. Bruges-Louvain-Paris, 1943.

McCallum, R. B., and Readman, Alison. *The British General Election of 1945*. London, 1947. Chap. XII.

Maclagan, Michael. "The University Franchise." *Oxford*. Special no. (1949), pp. 13–38.

Neale, J. E. *The Elizabethan House of Commons*. London and New Haven, 1950.

Notestein, Wallace. "The Winning of the Initiative by the House of Commons." The Raleigh Lecture, 1924. *British Academy Proceedings*, 1924–5, pp. 125–75.

Oldfield, Thomas H. B. *An Entire and Complete History, Political and Personal, of the Boroughs of Great Britain*. London, 1792. Vols. I–II.

Plumb, J. H. "Elections to the Convention Parliament, 1689." *Cambridge Historical Journal*, V (1935–7), pp. 235–54.

Porritt, Edward and Annie G. *The Unreformed House of Commons*. Cambridge, 1903. Vol. I, Ch. 5; Vol. II, Ch. 49.

Rex, M. "The University Constituencies in the Recent British Election." *Journal of Politics* (Durham, N.C.), VIII (1946), pp. 201–11.

Robson, R. J. *The Oxfordshire Election of 1754*. London, 1949.

Sanford, John Langton. *Studies and Illustrations of the Great Rebellion.* London, 1858.

Townsend, William Charles. *The History of the House of Commons.* London, 1843. Vols. I–II.

Usher, Roland G. *The Institutional History of the House of Commons 1547–1641. Washington University Studies* (St. Louis), Vol. II, pt. ii, Humanistic Series, no. 2 (April 1923), pp. 187–254.

Whitelocke, Sir Bulstrode. *Notes upon the King's Writt for choosing members of Parlement.* Ed. Charles Morton. London, 1766. Vols. I–II.

Willson, David Harris. "The Earl of Salisbury and the 'Court' Party in Parliament, 1604–10." *American Historical Review,* XXXVI (1931), pp. 274–94.

———. *The Privy Councillors in the House of Commons, 1604–29.* Minneapolis, 1940.

III

LISTS OF MEMBERS OF PARLIAMENT

Browning, Andrew, and Milne, Doreen J. "An Exclusion Bill Division." *Bulletin of the Institute of Historical Research,* XXIII (1949–50), pp. 205–25.

de Beer, E. D. "Members of the Court Party in the House of Commons, 1670–78." *Bulletin of the Institute of Historical Research,* XI (1933–4), pp. 1–23.

Flagellum Parliamentarium: Sarcastic Notices of nearly Two Hundred Members of Parliament, 1661–78. Reprint. London, 1827.

Hulme, Harold. "Corrections and Additions to the Official Return of Members of Parliament, 1603/4." *Bulletin of the Institute of Historical Research,* I (1927–8), pp. 96–105.

The Official Return of Members of Parliament (*Accounts and Papers,* v. 17). London, 1878. Vol. I, pts. 1–2. ("*O.R.*").

One Unanimous Club of Voters . . . very fit to be thought on at the Next Choice. Pamphlet, n.p., n.d. [1678] (Library of Congress).

Williams, William R. *The Parliamentary History of the County of Oxford, 1213–1899.* Breaknock, 1899. ("*Oxfordshire*".)

Willis, Browne. *Notitia Parliamentaria.* London, 1715–50. Vols. I–III.

IV

PARLIAMENTARY DEBATES AND RECORDS

A

Bruce, John (ed.). *The Verney Papers: Notes and Proceedings of the Long Parliament.* London: Camden Society, o.s., no. 31 (1845).

Burton, Thomas. *Diary, 1656–59.* Ed. John T. Rutt. London, 1828. Vols. I–IV.

Cobbett, William (ed.). *The Parliamentary History of England from the Normans . . . to the Year 1802.* London, 1806–9. Vols. I–V. ("*P.H.*")

Dering, Sir Edward. *Parliamentary Diary, 1670–1673.* Ed. Basil Duke Henning. New Haven, 1940.

D'Ewes, Sir Simonds. *The Journal of All the Parliaments during the Reign of Queen Elizabeth.* London, 1682.

D'Ewes, Sir Simonds. *Journal* (November 3, 1641—March 1641). Ed. Wallace Notestein. New Haven, 1923.

——. *Journal*, (October 1641—January 1641–2). Ed. Willson H. Coates. New Haven, 1942.

Gardiner, Samuel R. (ed.). *Commons' Debates, 1625.* London, Camden Society, n.s., no. 6 (1873).

——. *Notes of the Debates in the House of Lords, 1621.* London, Camden Society, o.s., no. 103 (1870).

Grey, Anchitell. *Debates in the House of Commons, 1667–1694.* London, 1759. Vols. I–IX.

Milward, Sir John. *Diary, 1666–1668.* Ed. Caroline Robbins. Cambridge, 1938.

Nalson, John. *An Impartial Collection of the Great Affairs of State.* London, 1682–3. Vols. I–II.

Northcote, Sir John. *Notebook.* Ed. A. H. A. Hamilton. London, 1877.

Notestein, Wallace, Relf, Frances Helen, and Simpson, Hartley (ed.). *Commons' Debates, 1621.* Oxford and New Haven, 1935. Vols. I–VII.

Notestein, Wallace, and Relf, Frances Helen (ed.). *Commons' Debates for 1629.* Minneapolis, 1921.

Relf, Frances Helen (ed.). *Debates in the Lords, 1621, 1625, 1628.* London, Camden Society, 3rd ser., no. 42 (1929).

Rushworth, John. *Historical Collections of Private Passages of State, 1618–48.* London, 1680–92. Vols. I–IV.

Scobell, Henry. *Severall Proceedings in Parliament.* Vol. IV. London, 1652–4.

Townshend, Hayward. *Historical Collections.* London, 1680.

B

Debates in the House Assembled at Oxford, 1680.

An Exact Collection of the Most Considerable Debates in the House of Commons.

Historical Collections . . . of the Two Last Parliaments . . . at Westminster and Oxford, 2nd ed., London, 1685.

The Journal of the House of Commons. N.p., n.d. [1742]. Vols. I–X. ("*C.J.*")

The Journal of the House of Lords. N.p., n.d. Vol. III. ("*L.J.*")

The Parliamentary or Constitutional History of England. 2nd ed. London, 1762–3. Vols. XI, XVIII–XXIII. ("*Old P.H.*")

Proceedings in the House of Commons touching the Impeachment of Edward, late Earl of Clarendon, 1667. N.p., 1700.

A True Copy of the Journal Book of the Last Parliament. London, 1680.

V

UNIVERSITY HISTORIES, REGISTERS, ETC.

Ayliffe, John. *The Antient and Present State of the University of Oxford.* London, 1714. Vols. I, II.

Atkinson, Thomas D. *Cambridge Described and Illustrated.* London, 1897.

Blomefield, Francis. *Collectanea Cantabrigiensis.* Norwich, 1751.

Brodrick, George C. *Memorials of Merton*. Oxford, 1885.

Burrows, Montagu. *The Register of the Visitors of the University of Oxford, 1647–1658*. London, Camden Society, n.s., no. 29 (1881).

——. *The Worthies of All Souls*. London, 1874.

Buxton, L. H. Dudley and Gibson, Strickland. *Oxford University Ceremonies*. Oxford, 1935.

Carter, Edmund. *The History of the University of Cambridge . . . to the year 1753*. London, [1753].

Clark, Andrew. *The Register of the University of Oxford, 1571–1622*. Oxford, 1887–9. (Oxford Historical Series, Vols. X–XIV.) Vol. II, pts. i–iii; Vols. III–IV.

Cooper, Charles Henry. *The Annals of Cambridge*. Cambridge. Vols. I–III (1843); Vol. V (ed. John William Cooper, 1908).

Cooper, Charles Henry, and Cooper, Thompson. *Athenae Cantabrigienses, 1586–1609*. Cambridge, 1858–1913. Vol. II (1861).

Dyer, George. *The Privileges of the University of Cambridge*. London, 1824. Vol. I.

Edwards, Gerald M. *Sidney Sussex College*. London, 1899.

Foster, Joseph. *Alumni Oxonienses, 1500–1714*. Oxford, 1891–2. Vols. I–IV.

Fuller, Thomas. *A History of Cambridge*. Ed. M. Pritchett and Thomas Wright. Cambridge, 1840.

Gibson, Strickland. *Statuta Antiqua Universitatis Oxonienses*. Oxford, 1931.

Gray, Arthur. *Cambridge: An Episodical History*. Cambridge, 1926.

——. *The Town of Cambridge*. Cambridge, 1925.

Griffiths, John. *Enactments in Parliament specially concerning the Universities of Oxford and Cambridge*. Oxford, 1869.

——. *The Statutes of the University of Oxford Codified in the Year 1636*. Oxford, 1888.

Heron, Denis C. *The Constitutional History of the University of Dublin*. Dublin, 1847.

Heywood, James, and Wright, Thomas. *Cambridge University Transactions*. London, 1864. Vols. I–II.

The Historical Register of the University of Oxford. Oxford, 1900, pp. 39–40.

Hobhouse, Christopher. *Oxford as it Was and as it Is Today*. London and New York, 1939.

Huber, V. A. *The English Universities*. Tr. Francis W. Newman. London, 1843. Vols. I–II.

Madan, Falconer B. *Oxford Books*. Oxford, 1895–1931. Vol. I (*The Early Oxford Press*, 1895); Vol. II (1912); Vol. III (1931).

Malden, Henry Elliot. *Trinity Hall*. London, 1902.

Mallet, Sir Charles Edward. *The History of the University of Oxford*. London, 1924. Vols. I–II.

Mullinger, James Bass. *The History of the University of Cambridge*. Cambridge, 1873–1911. Vols. I–III.

——. *A History of the University of Cambridge*. London, 1888. (One vol.)

Peacock, George. *Observations on the Statutes of the University of Cambridge*. London, 1841.

Poole, Reginald Lane. *A Lecture on the History of the University Archives*. Oxford, 1912.

Rashdall, Hastings. *The Universities of Europe in the Middle Ages.* Oxford, 1895. Vol. II, pt. 2.

Shadwell, Lionel Lancelot. *Enactments in Parliament specially concerning the Universities.* Oxford, 1912. Vols. I, IV.

Smith, John James. *A Cambridge Portfolio.* London, 1840.

Tanner, J. R. (ed.). *The Historical Register of the University of Cambridge to 1910.* Cambridge, 1917, pp. 30–33.

Varley, Frederick John. *Cambridge during the Civil War.* Cambridge, [1935].

——. "The Restoration Visitation of the University of Oxford." *The Camden Miscellany,* Vol. 18. London, Camden Society, 3rd ser. no. 79, 1948.

——. *The Siege of Oxford.* London, 1932.

The Victoria County History of Cambridgeshire and the Isle of Ely. London, 1948. Vol. II.

Venn, John and J. A. *Alumni Cantabrigienses, Part I to 1751.* Cambridge, 1922–7. Vols. I–IV.

——. *Matriculations and Degrees, 1544–1659.* Cambridge, 1913.

Wall, Adam. *An Account of the Different Ceremonies in the Senate House of the University of Cambridge.* Cambridge, 1798.

Walsh, Benjamin Dann. *A Historical Account of the University of Cambridge and its Colleges.* London, 1837.

Willis, Robert, and Clark, J. W. *An Architectural History of the University of Cambridge.* Cambridge, 1886. Vol. I, pts. ii, iii; II, pt. iii.

Wood, Anthony, *Athenae Oxonienses.* Ed. Philip Bliss. London, 1813–20. Vols. I–V. ("*A.O.*")

——. *Fasti.* Vols. I–II. (Vol. V of *Athenae Oxonienses*). ("*Fasti.*")

——. *The History and Antiquities of the University of Oxford.* Ed. John Gutch. Oxford, 1796. Vol. II, pts. i, ii. ("*Annals*".)

VI

BIOGRAPHICAL COLLECTIONS

Aubrey, John. *Brief Lives.* Ed. Andrew Clark. Oxford, 1898. Vols. I–II.

Bayle, [Pierre]. *A General Dictionary: Historical and Critical.* Ed. John Bernard, *et al.* London, 1739. Vol. IX.

Biographia Britannica. London, 1747–66. Vols. I–VI. ("*B.B.*")

Burke, John and J. B. *The Extinct and Dormant Baronetage of England.* London, 1838.

Calamy, Edmund. *The Non-Conformists' Memorial.* London, 1778. Vol. I.

Campbell, John, Lord. *The Lives of the Chief Justices of England.* Northport, Long Island, N.Y., 1894. Vol. II.

——. *The Lives of the Lord Chancellors.* Philadelphia, 1851. Vol. II.

Cokayne, G. E. (G.E.C.). *The Complete Baronetage.* Exeter. Vol. I (1900); III (1904); IV (1909).

——. *The Complete Peerage.* Ed. Vicary Gibbs, *et al.* London. Vol. I (1910); IV (1916); VII (1929); XI (1949).

The Dictionary of National Biography. Ed. Sir Leslie Stephen and Sir Sidney Lee. London, 1932–9. 24 vols. ("*D.N.B.*")

D.N.B., Errata. New York, 1904.

Foss, Edward. *The Judges of England.* London, 1857–64. Vols. VI, VII.

Fuller, Thomas. *The History of the Worthies of England.* London, 1662.

Hutchinson, John. *A Catalogue of Notable Middle Templars.* London, 1902.

Lloyd, David. *State Worthies, or The States-men and Favourites of England.* London, 1665.

——. *Memoires of the Lives, Actions, Sufferings, Deaths, etc. of those . . . Excellent Personages that suffered . . . for the Protestant Religion and Allegiance to the Sovereign.* London, 1668.

Munk, William. *The Roll of the Royal College of Physicians.* London, 1878. Vols. I–II.

Musgrove, Sir William. *Obituaries prior to 1800.* Ed. G. J. Armytage. London, 1899. Vols. I–II.

Noble, Mark. *The Lives of the English Regicides.* London, 1789. Vol. I.

North, Roger. *The Lives of the Norths.* Ed. Augustus Jessopp. London, 1890. Vols. I–III.

Seward, William. *Anecdotes of Distinguished Persons.* London, 1798.

Shaw, William A. *The Knights of England.* London, 1906. Vols. I–II.

Ward, John. *The Lives of the Gresham Professors.* London, 1740.

VII

BIOGRAPHIES

Aiken, John. *The Lives of John Selden and Archbishop Ussher.* London, 1812.

Aiken, Wm. A. *The Conduct of the Earl of Nottingham.* New Haven, 1941.

Bailey, John E. *The Life of Thomas Fuller.* London, 1874.

Barratt, D. H. "The Library of John Selden and its Later History." *Bodleian Library Record,* III (1951), pp. 128–48, 208–13.

Barrow, Isaac. *Oratorical Preface spoken before the University on his being elected Lucasian Professor of the Mathematics.* London, 1734.

Boyer, Abel. *Memoirs of Sir William Temple.* London, 1714.

Brewster, Sir David. *The Life of Sir Isaac Newton.* New York, 1832. (One vol.).

——. *Memoirs of the Life, Writings and Discoveries of Sir Isaac Newton.* Edinburgh, 1855. Vol. II.

Brown, P. Hume (ed.). *The Vernacular Writings of George Buchanan.* Edinburgh, The Scottish Text Society, 1892.

Burnet, Gilbert. *The Life and Death of Sir Matthew Hale.* (*Works of Sir Matthew Hale.* Ed. Thomas Thirlwall.) London, 1805.

Courtenay, Thomas Peregrine. *Memoirs of the Life, Works, and Correspondence of Sir William Temple, Bart.* London, 1836. Vols. I–II.

Cromwell, Oliver. *Memoirs of the Protector, Oliver Cromwell.* London, 1821. Vol. II.

D'Oyly, George. *The Life of William Sancroft.* London, 1821. Vol. I.

Forster, John. *Sir John Eliot.* London, 1864. Vols. I–II.

Foster, William. *The Embassy of Sir Thomas Roe, 1615–1619.* London, Hakluyt Society, 2nd ser., no. 1–2 (1899).

Foxcroft, H. C. *The Life and Letters of Sir George Savile, Bart., First Marquis of Halifax.* London, 1898. Vols. I–II.

Johnson, George W. *Memoirs of John Selden.* London, 1835.

Memoirs of the Life of Dr. Robert South. Oxford, 1842. Vol. I.

More, Louis Trenchard. *Isaac Newton.* London and New York, 1934.

Mowat, R. B. "The Mission of Sir Thomas Roe to Vienna, 1641–42." *English Historical Review,* XXV (1910), pp. 264–75.

Noble, Mark. *Memoirs . . . of the Protectorate House of Cromwell.* Birmingham, 1784. Vols. I–II.

Orme, William. *Memoirs of the Life and Writings of John Owen. (Works of John Owen.* Ed. Thomas Russell.) London, 1826. Vol. I.

Palmer, W. M. "Sir Thomas Sclater." *Proceedings of the Cambridge Antiquarian Society,* XVII, n.s., XI (1912–13), pp. 124–7.

Pocock, J. G. A. "Robert Brady, 1627–1700. A Cambridge Historian of the Restoration." *Cambridge Historical Journal,* X (1951), pp. 186–204.

Ramsey, Robert W. *Henry Cromwell.* London, 1933.

——. *Richard Cromwell.* London, 1935.

Schuyler, Robert L. "The Antiquaries and Sir Henry Spelman." *Proceedings of the American Philosophical Society,* XL (1946), pp. 91–103.

Singer, S. W. (ed.). *Table Talk of John Selden.* London, 1897.

Smith, G. C. Moore. *The Early Essays and Romances of Sir William Temple, Bart.* Oxford, 1930.

Spedding, James. *The Letters and Life of Francis Bacon.* London, 1869. Vol. IX, pts. iv, v.

Strype, John. *The Life of Matthew Parker, Archbishop of Canterbury.* Oxford, 1821. Vols. I–II.

——. *The Life and Acts of John Whitgift.* Oxford, 1822. Vols. I–IV.

Thomson, Andrew. *The Life of John Owen, D.D.* Edinburgh, 1853.

Twells, Leonard. *The Lives of Dr. Edward Pocock, etc.* London, 1819. Vol. I.

Waters, Robert. *John Selden and his Table Talk.* New York, 1899.

Wilhelm, Lewis W. *Sir George Calvert, Baron of Baltimore.* Baltimore, Maryland Historical Society, no. 20 (1884).

Wilkins, David. *Vita Seldenis. (Opera Omnia Johannis Seldenis.)* London, 1725–6. Vol. I.

Williams, J. B. *The Life of Sir Matthew Hale.* London, 1835.

Woodbridge, Homer E. *Sir William Temple: The Man and his Work.* New York, 1940.

Wynne, William. *The Life of Sir Leoline Jenkins.* London, 1724.

Yates, Margaret F. "The Political Career of Lawrence Hyde, Earl of Rochester." Unpublished doctoral dissertation, University of London, 1934.

VIII

CONTEMPORARY LETTERS, DIARIES, ETC.

Abbott, Wilbur Cortez. *The Writings and Speeches of Oliver Cromwell.* Cambridge, Massachusetts, 1937–47. Vols. I–IV.

Ailesbury, Thomas, Earl of. *Memoirs.* Westminster, The Roxburghe Club, 1890.

Barlow, William. "The Sum and Substance of the Conference." *The Phoenix* (London), I (1707), pp. 139–80.

Birch, Thomas. *The Court and Times of Charles I.* Ed. R. F. Williams. London, 1848. Vols. I–II.

Birch, Thomas. *The Court and Times of James I.* Ed. R. F. Williams. London, 1849. Vols. I–II.

———. (ed.). *Thurloe State Papers.* London, 1742. Vol. VII. (*"Th. S.P."*)

Bramston, Sir John. *Autobiography.* London, Camden Society, o.s., no. 32 (1845).

Burnet, Gilbert. *The History of My Own Times.* Ed. Osmund Airy. Oxford, 1897–1900. Vols. I–II.

———. *The History of My Own Times.* London, 1850. Vols. I–II.

———. *The History of the Reformation of the Church of England.* Ed. Nicholas Pocock. Oxford, 1865. Vols. II, V.

Calendar of the Clarendon State Papers. Vol. I (ed. O. Ogle and W. H. Bliss. Oxford, 1872); Vol. IV (ed. C. H. Firth. Oxford, 1938). (*"Cal. Clar. S.P."*)

The Camden Miscellany. Vol. 2. London, Camden Society, o.s., no. 52 (1851); no. 55 (1853).

Cary, Henry (ed.). *Memorials of the Great Civil War.* London, 1842. Vol. II.

Christie, W. D. (ed.). *Letters Addressed to Sir Joseph Williamson.* Vols. I–II. London, Camden Society, n.s., nos. 8–9 (1874).

Clarendon, Edward Hyde, Earl of. *Life.* Oxford, 1827. Vols. I–III.

———. *The History of the Rebellion and Civil War in England.* Ed. W. Dunn Macray. Oxford, 1888. Vols. I–VI.

Clarendon, Henry Hyde, Earl of. *Correspondence.* Ed. S. W. Singer. London, 1828. Vols. I–II.

Clarendon State Papers. Ed. Richard Scrope and Thomas Monkhouse. Oxford, 1767–86. Vols. II, III. (*"Clar. S.P."*)

Clarke, Sir William. *The Clarke Papers.* Vol. IV. Ed. C. H. Firth. London: Camden Society, n.s., no. 62 (1901).

Collins, Arthur (ed.). *The Sidney Papers: Letters and Memorials of State.* London, 1746. Vols. I–II.

Cromwelliana. London, 1810.

Crossfield, Thomas. *Diary.* Ed. Frederick Boas. London, 1935.

D'Ewes, Sir Simonds. *Autobiography.* Ed. James Orchard Halewell. London, 1845. Vol. I.

Ellis, Sir Henry (ed.). *Original Letters of Eminent Literary Men.* London, Camden Society, o.s., no. 23 (1843).

Evelyn, John. *Diary.* Ed. William Bray. London, 1872. Vol. I.

Fanshawe, Anne, Lady. *Memoirs.* Ed. Herbert Charles Fanshawe. London, 1907.

Feiling, Keith, and Needham, F. D. R. "The Journals of Edmund Warcup, 1676–84." *English Historical Review,* XL (1925), pp. 236–7.

Foster, J. E. (ed.). *The Diary of Alderman Newton, 1662–1717.* Cambridge Antiquarian Society, no. 23. Cambridge, 1890.

Fuller, Thomas. *The Church History of Great Britain.* London, 1655.

Goodman, Godfrey. *The Court of King James the First.* Ed. John S. Brewer. London, 1839. Vols. I–II.

The Harleian Miscellany. London. Vol. VI (1810).

Jonson, Ben. *Epigrams, The Forest, Underwoods.* New York; Facsimile Text Society, 1936.

Kennet, White. *A Register and Chronicle, Ecclesiastical and Civil.* London, 1728.

Laud, William. *Works.* Ed. James Bliss. Oxford, 1847–57. Vols. III–VII.

Leland, John. *De Rebus Britannicis.* Ed. Thomas Hearne. London, 1770. Vol. V.

Ludlow, Edmund. *Memoirs, 1625–72.* Ed. C. H. Firth. Oxford, 1894. Vols. I–II.

Luttrell, Narcissus. *A Brief Historical Relation of State Affairs, 1678–1714.* Oxford, 1857. Vols. I–II.

Marvell, Andrew. *Satires.* Ed. G. A. Aitken. New York, 1892.

Mercurius Politicus. [Ed. Marchmont Needham.] London, 1653–60.

Nichols, John B. (ed.). *The Progresses of King James the First.* London, 1828. Vols. I–IV.

Pepys, Samuel. *Diary.* Ed. Henry B. Wheatley. New York, 1942. Vols. II, III, VII, VIII.

Prideaux, Humphrey. *Letters to John Ellis.* London, Camden Society, n.s., no. 15 (1875).

[Prynne, William]. *A Vindication of the Imprisoned and Secluded Members.* London, 1649.

——. *A true and full Narrative.* N.p., 1659.

Reresby, Sir John. *Memoirs.* Ed. Andrew Browning. Glasgow, 1936.

Selden, John. *Table Talk.* Ed. Sir Frederick Pollock. London, Selden Society, 1927.

Sidney, Henry (Earl of Romney). *Diary and Correspondence.* Ed. R. W. Bledsoe. London, 1843. Vols. I–II.

The Somers Tracts. Ed. Sir Walter Scott. London, 1809. Vol. II.

Temple, Sir William. *Memoirs* in his *Collected Works.* London, 1814. Vol. II.

Turner, Dawson (ed.). *Thirteen Letters from Sir Isaac Newton . . . to John Covell, D.D.* Norwich, 1848.

Whitelock, Sir Bulstrode. *Memorials of the English Affairs.* New ed. Oxford, 1853. Vols. I–IV.

Wood, Anthony. *Life and Times.* Ed. Philip Bliss. Oxford, 1891–1900. (Oxford Historical Series, Vols. XIX, XXI, XXVI, XXX, XL.) Vols. I–V. (*"Life and Times".*)

Worthington, John. *Diary and Correspondence.* Vols. I, II. Manchester: Chetham Society, XIII (1847); CXIV (1886).

Yonge, Walter. *Diary.* Ed. George Roberts. London, Camden Society, o.s., no. 41 (1848).

IX

DOCUMENTS

Calendar of State Papers. ("*C.S.P.*")

    Domestic: *Edward VI–James I.* Vols. VI–XII. London, 1856–72.

        Charles I. Vols. I–XXIII. London, 1858–97.

        The Commonwealth. Vols. I–XIII. London, 1875–86.

        Charles II. Vols. I–XXVIII. London, 1860–1947.

        William III. Vol. I. London, 1896.

    America and the West Indies. Vols. VII, IX, X. London, 1894–6.

    Venetian. Vols. IX–XXXVIII. London, 1898–1947.

Calendar of Treasury Papers. Vol. I. London, 1868.

Gardiner, S. R. (ed.). *Constitutional Documents of the Puritan Revolution, 1625–1660.* Oxford, 1899.

Rait, Sir Robert Sangster, and Firth, Sir Charles Harding. *Acts and Ordinances of the Interregnum, 1642–1660.* London, 1911. Vols. I–II.

X

HISTORICAL MANUSCRIPTS COMMISSION REPORTS ("*H.M.C.*")

Historical Manuscripts Commission. *Appendix to 1st Report.* London, 1870.

——. *Appendix to 2nd Report.* London, 1872.

——. *Appendix to 4th Report,* Part 1. London, 1874.

——. *Appendix to 5th Report,* Part 1. London, 1876.

——. *Appendix to 6th Report,* Part 1. London, 1877.

Bath MSS. Vol. II (Historical Manuscripts Commission Report, XV, App. X. London, 1907).

Buccleugh MSS. (Montagu House.) Vol. I (Historical Manuscripts Commission Report XV, App. VIII. London, 1899).

Cowper MSS. Vols. I, II (Historical Manuscripts Commission Report, XII, App. I. London, 1888).

Egmont MSS. Vol. II (Historical Manuscripts Commission Report, XV, App. X. London, 1905).

Kenyon MSS. (Historical Manuscripts Commission Report, XIV, App. IV. London, 1894).

Le Fleming MSS. (Historical Manuscripts Commission Report, XII, App. VII. London, 1890).

Lonsdale MSS. (Historical Manuscripts Commission Report, XIII, App. VII. London, 1893).

Montagu MSS. Vol. I (Historical Manuscripts Commission Report, XV, App. X. London, 1900).

Ormonde MSS., n.s., Vols. IV, V, VI, VII (Historical Manuscripts Commission Report, XIV, App. VII. London, 1906–11).

Popham MSS. (Historical Manuscripts Commission Report, XV, App. X. London, 1899).

Salisbury MSS. (Cecil), Vols. IX, X, XIV, XV, XVI, XVIII (Historical Manuscripts Commission Report, IX, App. IX–XVIII. London, 1902, 1904, 1923, 1930, 1933, 1942).

XI

MANUSCRIPTS

A. British Museum.

Additional Manuscripts: 3813; 5813; 28,053; 32,095; 34,179; 34,601.

Cottonian Manuscript: Faustina C, VII.

Egerton Manuscript: 2043.

Harleian Manuscripts: 1901: 74; 81; 87; 6799; 7046.

The Catalogue of the Harleian Manuscripts in the British Museum. Ed. Humphrey Wanley. London, 1802–12. Vols. I–II. (Letters of Sir Thomas Roe, II, 328–44.)

Stowe Manuscripts: 176; 743.

B. University of Cambridge.

> Cambridge University Registry: Grace Book; Book of Representatives; Book of Petitions; Voting Papers.
>
> Manuscripts in the University Library: Mm 6.50; Mm 457; Add. MS., 22.
>
> *Index to Catalogue of Manuscripts in the Library of the University of Cambridge*. Ed. Henry Richards Luard. Cambridge, 1667. Vols. I–V.

C. University of Oxford.

> University Archives: Convocation Registers: K22; N23; R24; Sb25; T25; Ta27; Tb28; Bb29; Victorian Papers relating to Parliamentary Elections
>
> Bodleian Library: Bodleian Manuscript, 594.
> > Carte Manuscript, 73.
> > Rawlinson Manuscript, D 1232.
> > Tanner Manuscript, 28, 38, 39, 65, 72, 74.
> > Wood Manuscript, F 27.
>
> All Souls College Library Manuscript: 208.

D. Public Record Office: S.P., Dom., Chas. II, 29/417/232 (1).

E. Salway Manuscript. (Privately owned.)

XII

MISCELLANEOUS

The Gentleman's Magazine and Historical Chronicle. London, LXVIII, pt. i (1798); LXXIV, pt. ii (1804); XCVI, pt. i (1826). ("*G.M.*")

Notes and Queries.
> 1st ser., VII (1853); 4th ser., X (1872).

INDEX

A

Abbot, George, Archbishop of Canterbury, 76, 107
Acclamation, election by, 73, 80, 269, 346, 357; see also Voice Vote
Agreement of the People, the, 205 (n. 19)
All Souls College, Oxford, 137, 299, 334
Anglicanism, 21, 23, 27, 188, 231, 247, 299, 327; see also Church of England
Anglicans, 131, 159, 167, 170, 205 (n. 24), 218, 229 (n. 17), 237, 238, 248, 251, 302, 310, 339
Anti-Parliament, of 1643–4, 93 (n. 37), 162, 163, 179 (n. 83), 90
Arminianism, 112
Armstrong, Sir Thomas, 317, 318–19, 325 (n. 118)
Ayliffe, John, 16, 36, 337–8

B

Bachelors, as electors, 61–2, 84, 91 (n. 17), 188, 205 (n. 24), 356, 359; see also Electors
Bacon, Sir Francis, later Viscount St. Albans, 100, 133, 135, 136, 137, 140, 142 (n. 24), 164, 217, 225, 332, 364; election of, 63, 64–5, 66–7, 74, 81, 214, 227; political position of, 49–51, 52, 131, 132, 340, 364
Bacon, Nathaniel, 179 (n. 73), 180 (n. 96, 98, 99), 193, 198, 208 (n. 79), 212, 215, 216, 217, 222, 223, 368; election of, 164; political position of, 165, 166, 174, 218
Bacon, unidentified, 165, 179 (n. 95), 193, 224
Ballots, 74–5, 78, 79, 303; secrecy of, 73–4, 78–80, 94 (n. 51); stolen or missing, 74, 78, 85, 294 (n. 70), App. III, No. 2; see also Votes, Voting papers
Baronets, burgesses or former burgesses as, 137, 197, 216, 219, 236, 332, 341, 347 (n. 14, 16)
Barrow, Isaac, 169, 220, 229 (n. 14)
Bell, Sir Robert, 26, 31, 32
Bennett, Sir John, 51, 136, 138, 216, 340, 346 (n. 8), 364; election of, 48–9, 97, 365; expelled from House, 99, 100–2, 325 (n. 134), 343
Bishops, attack on, 151, 153–4, 157; as electors, 62; influence of, in elections, 147, 233, 263, 268, 269, 270, 278, 280, 281, 298; the Seven, 300, 310

Blacklists, 255 (n. 27), 258 (n. 81), 293 (n. 49), 379; see also Lampoons, Pensioners
Blackpot men, 83, 282, 344; see also Pot Companions, Treating
Blithe, Dr. Samuel, Master of Clare, 279, 292 (n. 20)
Boroughs, 26, 32, 36, 49, 63, 66, 68, 87, 214, 265–6, 300, 349; their relations with the universities, 22–3, 24, 25, 28, 31, 33–5, 114, 251–2, 300, 338, App. III, No. 2; university influence in their elections, 87, 96 (n. 77, 79), 263, 300, 341–2; see also Cambridge, Charter, Oxford, Pocket boroughs
Boucher, Dr. Thomas, 243, 244, 267, 268, 269, 363
Boyd-Orr, Sir John, 141 (n. 8)
Brady, Dr. Robert, Master of Caius, 204 (n. 5), 294 (n. 72), 298, 302, 331, 332, 334, 335, 338–9, 347 (n. 16, 18), 371; election of, 278, 279, 280, 287, 294 (n. 70), 297, 328, 329, 330, 345, 372; political views of, 288, 291, 297, 299, 326, 327, 330, 339, 340
Brent, Sir Nathaniel, Warden of Merton, 146, 149
Bromley, Sir Thomas, Lord Chancellor, 27
Buchanan, George, 22
Buckhurst, Thomas Sackville, Lord, Chancellor of Oxford, 29, 30
Buckingham, George Villiers, Duke of, 75, 97, 99, 102, 103, 104, 105, 106, 110–11, 116, 117, 118, 119, 124 (n. 41), 125 (n. 46), 126 (n. 62), 127 (n. 100), 131, 156, 360; as Chancellor of Cambridge, 71–2, 99, 111–12, 113–14, 126 (n. 79), 175 (n. 13); impeachment of, 107, 111–13, 118, 132, 140
Burgesses, University, their absences from Parliament, 98, 99, 102, 103, 106, 124 (n. 28), 132–3, 141 (n. 8), 148–9, 150, 161, 163, 184, 190, 191, 235, 242, 254 (n. 21), 275 (n. 35), 298, 335, 336, App. V; age of, 138, 139, 217–18, 335, 341; their attendance at universities, 65, 66, 135, 212, 213, 223, 331–2; appointed, not elected, 14, 37 (n. 6), 70, 185, 213, 228 (n. 1); as benefactors, 89, 100, 134, 135, 143, 174, 212, 222, 262; calibre of, 16, 131–3, 135, 143–4, 164, 215–16, 221–3, 333–4, 338–9, 347 (n. 17), 349–50; degrees held by, 42–3, 65, 66–7, 136, 142 (n. 24), 212–13, 229 (n. 4, 6), 330–2, 346 (n. 11); lacking degrees, 65, 66, 135, 136, 212,

Burgesses—*continued*
213, 328, 331, 347 (n. 12); of distinguished family, 137, 217, 332-3;
expenses of, 89; see also Election campaigns, Parliamentary wages; as free
agents, 50, 52, 103, 158, 340; geographical distribution of, 137; ideal,
49, 144, 221-2, 349; inactivity of, 44,
51, 100, 106-7, 118, 122, 183-4, 197,
211, 242, 244, 271, 282, 286-7, 291,
335, 336, 337; intellectual interests of,
133-4, 139, 221-3, 333-4; their
moderation in politics, 143-4, 152,
167, 218-25, 338; political views of,
46-8, 97-8, 130-2, 143-4, 191-2, 218-
20, 231, 236, 237, 296, 326-7, 338,
339-40; previous parliamentary
experience of, 43, 138, 139, 218, 334-5;
qualifications of, 62-7; their relation
to university, 43, 65, 135, 136, 139,
143, 212-13, 276, 282, 330-2; resident,
251; see also Gremials; social status
of, 137-8, 139, 216-17, 223, 332-3,
341; see also Baronets, Gentry,
Knights, Peers; as statesmen, 16, 49-
50, 51, 52, 131-2, 135, 136, 143-4, 215-
16, 218-20, 221-2, 333, 335-6, 338-9,
349-50; of the two universities, compared, 136-7, 138, 223, 327, 339-40,
341; useful public service of, 16, 43-4,
148, 149, 151, 175 (n. 17), 216, 221-3,
237, 239, 240-1, 336, 340; without
university connections, 66, 135, 213,
223, 331
Burleigh, William Cecil, Lord, Chancellor of Cambridge, 26-7, 28, 33, 83,
84, 137
Byrd, Dr. William, 42, 43, 47, 53 (n. 13),
127 (n. 99), 134, 135, 136, 142 (n. 25),
364; election of, 42, 48, 49, 53 (n. 11)
By-elections, 42, 78, 92 (n. 26), 100, 109,
139, 164, 179 (n. 89, 90, 91), 189, 198,
199-200, 205 (n. 27), 231, 243-4, 267,
298, 325 (n. 133), App. VII

C

Calvert, Sir George, later Baron Baltimore, 101, 103, 104, 116, 124 (n. 28),
130, 131, 135, 136, 137, 142 (n. 24),
216, 329, 332, 340, 365
Calvinism, 21, 23, 27, 83, 146
Cambridge, Borough of, 22, 25, 28, 31,
33, 54 (n. 22), 96 (n. 79), 193, 194, 199,
251, 263, 265-6, 300, 342, App. III,
No. 2; see also Boroughs
Cambridgeshire, 64, 86, 96 (n. 76, 79,
80), 137, 184, 185; see also Counties
Cambridge University, see Senate, Universities
Campaign Letters, 88, 224, 261-6, 268-9,
344, 378; see also Recommendation

Candidates, advanced on own initiative,
262, 263, 280-1, 345; name of, on
ballot, 74; qualifications of, 62-7;
unsuccessful, 79, 81, 227; see also
Boucher, Brent, Croke, Edisbury,
Edmondes (Sir Thomas), Finch
(Edward), Hopkins, Lambe, Lamphire, Lane, Lenthall, Nicholas (John),
Oldys, Palmer, Petty, St. John, Spelman, Vernon (Edward), Wren; see also
Court candidates, Nomination, Recommendation
Canvassing, in person, 73, 147, 224, 244,
261, 263, 264, 269, 270, 279, 280-1,
344; by supporters, 71, 147, 200, 201,
224, 233, 278, 292 (n. 21), 344; see also
Electioneering
Carleton, Sir Dudley, 132; his corre-
spondence, 51, 54 (n. 31), 55 (n. 42),
104, 125 (n. 44), 126 (n. 58), 140
Cartwright, Thomas, 24, 26
Catholicism, 237, 309; see also Popery
Catholics, 26, 27, 122, 240, 246, 250, 299,
317; see also Papists, Recusants
Cavaliers, 160, 162, 163, 171, 182 (n.
138), 237, 238, 340; see also Royalists
Cecil, Sir Robert, later Earl of Salisbury,
Chancellor of Cambridge, 29, 30, 34,
38 (n. 26), 40, 46, 132, 351
Chamberlain-Carleton letters, 55 (n. 31),
123 (n. 20), 374, 376; see also Carleton
Chancellor of the Realm, see Lord
Chancellor
Chancellor, Masters, and Scholars, as
legal phrase, 57, 61, 88, 91 (n. 14, 17),
277, 353, 354, 355
Chancellors, of universities, 24, 32, 65,
85, 130, 204, 225; of Cambridge, see
Burleigh, Buckingham, Holland,
Monck, Monmouth, Northampton,
Sancroft; as candidates, 199, 225,
227-8; in Convocation, 69, 80, 114;
election of, at Cambridge, 58-9, 67,
71-2, 74, 80, 81, 99, 111-12, 175 (n.
13), 306, 322 (n. 51); election of, at
Oxford, 68, 71, 73, 99, 229 (n. 6);
their influence over elections, 57, 70,
71, 90, 91 (n. 9), 98, 130, 301, 328,
329-30; see also Recommendation;
of Oxford, see Clarendon, Laud,
Ormonde, Pembroke (3rd Earl), Pembroke (4th Earl); secretaries of, 98;
see also Lucas, Oldisworth, Vernon;
their part in obtaining university
representation, 26, 27-8, 29, 30, 351;
on side of electors, 59, 91 (n. 9), 140,
343
Charles I, 57, 71, 82, 105, 107, 110, 111,
112, 119, 120, 128 (n. 111), 137, 151,
152, 154, 155, 156, 158, 162, 165, 166,
168, 171, 179 (n. 90), 183, 187, 195,
231, 243, 246, 253, 282; as Prince of
Wales, 100, 104; his relations with Sir

Thomas Roe, 143,1 44–5, 159–64, 179 (n. 83)

Charles II, 71, 84, 85, 197, 219, 220, 231, 235, 237, 238, 243, 246, 248, 249, 250, 257 (n. 69), 258 (n. 93), 259 (n. 95), 261, 272, 273, 276, 284, 294 (n. 59), 296, 320 (n. 4)

Charters, of Boroughs, 313, 318, 321 (n. 24), 342; see also *Quo Warranto*; of universities, 24, 25, 112, 126 (n. 78), 306, 307, 311, 313, 315, 317, 318, 325 (n. 122), 328, 338, 342–3, 356; see also Incorporation, *De Burgensibus*

Chimney Money, see Hearth Tax

Church of England, 119, 261, 269, 282, 285, 287, 300, 336; and Crown, 21, 46, 48, 63, 156, 158, 246, 253; defence of, 21, 46, 47, 48, 147–8, 203, 236, 237, 239–40, 246, 250, 253, 271, 281, 301, 314–15, 318, 337, 349; establishment of, 42, 47, 153; lukewarm attitude of university member to, 326; opposition to, 156, 263; its petition for representation, 28; and the universities, 22, 28, 166, 169; see also Anglicanism, High Church

Chyles, Nathaniel, 232, 233

Civil Law, status of, 40, 190, 209 (n. 91), 212, 331

Civil lawyers, "civilians", as burgesses, 40, 41, 43, 108, 134, 136, 203, 212, 331

Clarendon, Edward Hyde, Earl of, 208 (n. 64), 237, 254 (n. 1); as Chancellor of Oxford, 231–4, 238, 328, 330; impeachment of, 238, 241–2, 246, 250, 254 (n. 1), 256 (n. 52); quoted, 116, 122, 135, 155, 157, 176 (n. 47), 219, 220

Clarges, Sir Thomas, 195, 196, 307, 317, 320, 331, 332, 334, 335, 336, 337, 338, 341, 347 (n. 12, 15, 23), 372; election of, 300–1, 346; political views of, 301, 313–16, 318, 321 (n. 27), 323 (n. 81), 324 (n. 96), 112, 113, 327, 338, 339, 340

Clarke, Dr. George, 298–9, 321 (n. 20), 329, 330, 333, 334, 335, 339, 346 (n. 1), 347 (n. 30), 372; election of, 298, 321 (n. 16, 17), 344

Clayton, (Sir) Thomas, 202–4, 209 (n. 94), 212, 215, 216, 217, 254 (n. 2), 369; election of, 201, 224, 232, 233, 329; political views of, 201, 203, 210 (n. 107), 219

Clergymen, as burgesses, 32, 40–1, 53 (n. 7), 67, 134, 188–9, 212, 351–2; as electors, 62, 92 (n. 21), 192, 279

Clerical Disabilities Act, 41, 67, 168, 188, 212, 239

Coke, Sir Edward, 42, 49, 101, 135, 136; his advice on candidates, 40–1, 67, 134, 212, 228, 351–2; his Demurre, 34,

375; as founder of university representation, 29–34, 35, 36; his instructions on writs, 68, 352; his interest in universities, 31, 37 (n. 3), 124 (n. 31); his letters, to universities, 29–30, 40, 63, App. I, 375

Coke, Sir John, 119, 120, 122, 131, 132–3, 135, 136, 154, 174 (n. 2), 216, 366, 367; election of, 108, 114, 127 (n. 82), 130, 142 (n. 28), 214; political views of, 107, 111, 112–13, 116–18, 121, 131–2, 132–3, 195, 282, 340

Colleges, of burgesses, 137; candidates enrolled in, 278, 347 (n. 12); in election lists, 79; their influence in elections, 73, 78, 96 (n. 79), 147, 231–3, 254 (n. 1), 265, 267, 268–70, 274 (n. 11), 278, 281, 292 (n. 21); interests of, 44, 45, 102, 119, 191, 240, 250; see also Heads of Colleges

Committee of Privilege, 51, 65, 108–9, 110, 122, 188, 204, 235, 241, 244, 247, 271, 272, 291, 310

Common Law lawyers, as burgesses, 41, 136, 182 (n. 138), 212, 221, 235–6, 331

Convocation, of the Church, 40, 47, 153, 154, 271, 272, 273, 275 (n. 39), 351

Convocation, of Oxford University, 57; composition of, 60–2, 84, 87, 114; discussion in, 81–2; minutes of, 56, 75, 79, 94 (n. 58), App. VII; parliamentary elections by, 69, 70, 73, 75, 76, 77, 78, 80, 89, 93 (n. 36), 121, 224, 234, 244, 269, 270, 343, 346, App. IV, VII; place of meeting of, 69; seating arrangements of, 69; see also Electors, Regents

Cook, Dr. William, 308, 309, 310, 311, 322 (n. 63)

Corbet, Dr. Clement, Vice-Chancellor of Cambridge, 63, 67, 81, 227, 228

Cosin, Dr. John, Vice-Chancellor of Cambridge, 147, 152, 167, 181 (n. 119)

Cotterell, Sir Charles, 232, 254 (n. 2)

Council, see Privy Council

Council of State, 186, 187, 195, 196, 207 (n. 54), 215

Counties, influence of, in borough and university elections, 87–8, 96 (n. 80), 100, 135, 137, 187, 192, 342, 349

Country party, 52, 115, 127 (n. 87), 132, 245, 324 (n. 112), 327

Court, 32, 103, 143, 144, 159, 160, 161, 163, 178 (n. 71, 73, 79, 80), 219, 242, 245, 257 (n. 70), 258 (n. 82), 279, 284, 287, 296, 297, 299, 300, 321 (n. 26), 326; opposition to, by university burgesses, 52, 109, 115, 118–19, 121, 132, 143, 147, 156, 162, 165, 245, 263, 273, 301, 302–3, 314, 321 (n. 27); support of, by university burgesses, 46–8, 50, 51, 99–100, 106, 108, 112–13, 114, 120–1, 122, 123 (n. 3), 125 (n. 46),

Court—*continued*
  131–2, 156, 158, 159, 168, 231, 236,
  237–9, 243, 245–6, 248–9, 250, 253,
  256 (n. 39), 271, 274 (n. 9), 282–7, 296,
  297, 314, 323 (n. 67), 329, 335, 340,
  377; see also Crown, King
Court candidates, 79, 114, 118, 121, 133,
  139, 146, 225, 233, 270, 276, 278, 279,
  323 (n. 67), 329; see also Recommendation
Court, Cromwellian, 192, 195, 215–16
Court Cullies, 326; see also Pensioners
Court party, 97, 103, 109, 119, 127
  (n. 90), 245, 247, 248, 257 (n. 70), 268,
  286, 288, 296; see also Tory Party
Covell, Dr. John, Vice-Chancellor of
  Cambridge, 303–6, 308, 309; his
  correspondence, 322 (n. 41), 323 (n. 77)
Covenant, Solemn League and, 132, 155,
  158, 163, 164, 166, 168, 170, 171, 172,
  177 (n. 48, 62), 253
Coventry, Henry, Secretary of State,
  257 (n. 95), 266, 267, 268, 274 (n. 13,
  17, 19), 279, 281, 323 (n. 67)
Croke, Sir George, 244, 256 (n. 63), 345
Crompton, Sir Thomas, 40–4, 46, 47,
  48, 52 (n. 1), 53 (n. 13), 54 (n. 15),
  134, 136, 137, 141 (n. 14), 364
Cromwell, Henry, 88, 184, 187–8, 190,
  192, 195, 196, 205 (n. 21), 206 (n. 46),
  212, 213, 215, 216, 217, 220, 222,
  368
Cromwell, Oliver, 88, 96 (n. 79), 156,
  184, 185, 186, 187, 188, 189, 190, 191,
  194, 195, 197, 199, 204, 215, 222, 223,
  229 (n. 3), 231, 235; as Chancellor of
  Oxford, 186, 188; his influence over
  university elections, 88, 90, 183–4, 185,
  191–2, 223, 349
Cromwell, Richard, 88, 184, 187, 189–90,
  191, 206 (n. 33), 207 (n. 49), 212, 213,
  215, 216, 217, 223, 225, 227, 228, 229
  (n. 6), 331, 347 (n. 12), 368; as Chancellor of Oxford, 190, 228, 229 (n. 6);
  as Protector, 191, 194, 195, 196, 197,
  198, 208 (n. 64, 73), 212, 214
Cromwellians, 174, 184, 189, 191, 192,
  197, 200, 202, 216, 220, 340
Crouch, Thomas, 89, 203, 204, 208
  (n. 83, 84), 213, 215, 216, 222, 236,
  239, 240–1, 251, 256 (n. 42), 259 (n.
  109, 111), 266, 336, 337, 338, 339, 341,
  343, 346 (n. 1), 349, 369; election of,
  92 (n. 20), 198–200, 204, 225, 231, 235,
  262, 266, 362, 370; political views of,
  203, 218, 237, 239–40, 250, 339, 340
Crown, 14, 104, 190, 191, 197, 212, 246,
  284, 304, 309, 316, 323 (n. 73), 342;
  advantage of university representation
  to, 15, 16, 21, 22, 35, 97, 130, 133, 211,
  266, 271; its relations with universities,
  22, 32–3, 88, 112, 166, 250, 342; see
  also Court, King

Crown officers, as university burgesses
  and candidates, 40, 41–2, 46, 48, 50,
  51, 97, 103, 108, 118, 121, 127 (n. 99),
  130–2, 136, 149, 157, 215, 228 (n. 1),
  236, 242, 262, 266, 268, 281, 282, 284,
  289–90, 298, 299, 300, 309–10, 321
  (n. 26), 323 (n. 70), 327, 329, 330, 333,
  340, 346 (n. 8); see also Cromwellians,
  Privy Councillors
Cudworth, Dr. Ralph, 193, 194, 207
  (n. 49), 214
Curzon, Lord, 14, 36

D

Danby, Thomas Osborne, Earl of, 245,
  248, 249, 250, 258 (n. 81), 271–2, 273
  (n. 9), 277, 306, 322 (n. 51), 323 (n. 67,
  73)
Danvers, Sir John, 106, 108–9, 111, 122,
  128 (n. 111), 133, 135, 136, 137, 138,
  181 (n. 128), 201, 213, 365; election of,
  100, 101, 105, 107, 115, 121, 128 (n.
  113), 130, 142 (n. 28), 214, 272, 357,
  366, 367; political position of, 100,
  118, 120, 132
Dartmouth College, New Hampshire,
  15
De Burgensibus, 30–2, 56–7, 60, 62, 63,
  224, 228, App. I, II; see also James I,
  Letters Patent
Degrees, by creation, 66, 67, 136, 142
  (n. 24), 158, 189, 194, 213, 229 (n. 3,
  6), 238, 292 (n. 28), 331; held by
  university burgesses, 66–7, 136, 212–
  13, 330–2; held by M.P.s in general,
  129–30; honorary, 65, 66, 241; by incorporation, 66, 136, 213, 264, 331;
  by mandate, 66, 113, 127 (n. 81), 136,
  142 (n. 24), 158, 297, 299, 307, 328,
  331; by naturalization, 66, 213, 278,
  328, 331; as qualification for burgesses, 66–7; as qualification for
  electors, 61–2, 66, 321 (n. 35); see also
  Bachelors, Doctors, Masters; in Tudor
  era, 24
De modo eligendi, 58–60, 67, 99, 224,
  App. III, No. 1
Demurre, of Sir Edward Coke, 34, 375
De se ipsis, 63, 66, 212, 292 (n. 15), 328,
  330, 331; see also Residence
Desisting before the poll, 71, 146, 147,
  193, 199, 232, 233, 234, 244, 264, 267,
  268, 280, 345
Dissenters, 219, 238, 239, 240, 246, 251,
  266, 303, 318, 337; see also Calvinism,
  Covenant, Puritans
Divine Right, 133, 143, 283, 284, 296,
  304; see also Tory Party
Division, as method of election, 76, 77–8;
  see also Scrutiny
Dixon, Thomas, 270

Doctors, D.D., D.C.L., LL.D., M.D., as Burgesses, 41, 134, 136, 212–13, 331; see also Civil lawyers, Owen (John), Physicians; as electors, 62, 69, 80, 92 (n. 18), 130, 188, 205 (n. 24), 224, 277, 356, 358; as witnesses of elections, 68, 363

Duport, Dr. John, Deputy Vice-Chancellor of Cambridge, 63; his account of election of 1614, 56, 64, 65, 68, 74, 80, 81, 82, 83, 84, 92 (n. 24), 95 (n. 62)

Dunne, Sir Daniel, 30, 41–8, 53 (n. 13), 127 (n. 99), 134, 136, 137, 340, 346 (n. 8), 364; election of, 40, 48–9, 142 (n. 28), 365; political views of, 46–8

Durham, proposed university at, 197–8

E

Eden, Charles (?), 147, 175 (n. 13)

Eden, Dr. Thomas, Master of Trinity Hall, 122, 126 (n. 75), 127 (n. 97), 134, 136, 142 (n. 24), 150, 164, 198, 212, 213, 215, 216, 217, 228 (n. 1), 330, 349; his defence of university, 111–12, 120, 149, 166, 167–8, 173, 180 (n. 109), 211; election of, 65, 108, 114, 121, 127 (n. 82), 130, 142 (n. 28), 146–7, 148, 214, 218, 225, 366, 367; political position of, 118, 132, 143, 144, 149, 157–8, 159, 167, 175 (n. 22), 177 (n. 62), 219, 220, 340

Edisbury, Dr. John, 272, 273, 274 (n. 31), 329, 335, 339, 346 (n. 1), 371; election of, 70, 243–4, 256 (n. 62), 267–70, 274 (n. 27), 344, 345; political views of, 271, 326, 340

Edmondes, Sir Clement, 97, 99, 123 (n. 3), 130, 132, 133–4, 135, 136, 138, 340, 346 (n. 8), 365

Edmondes, Sir Thomas, 106, 116, 120, 125 (n. 46), 130, 132, 135, 136, 138, 141 (n. 7), 142 (n. 22), 213, 216, 331, 340, 366; election of, 75–7, 105, 107, 108, 109, 115, 126 (n. 62), 140, 142 (n. 28), App. IV, 366

Election campaigns, cost of, 125 (n. 44), 140–1, 235, 273 (n. 4), 276–7; see also Campaign Letters

Election Day, see Poll

Electioneering, 48–9, 71–3, 85, 113–14, 147, 188, 192–3, 198, 199–201, 205 (n. 24), 224–5, 232–4, 261–70, 277–82, 287–8, 296–7, 300, 301–2, 303, 327–8, 344, 345; see also Canvassing, Recommendation

Election officials, 73, 78, 80, 94 (n. 51); see also Chancellor, Proctor, Vice-Chancellor

Election records, 49, 53 (n. 11), 74, 77–9, 81, 226, 227–8, App. VII, 374, 375–6, 377, 379; deficient, 64, 78, 164, 179

(n. 89, 90), 189, 205 (n. 27), 207 (n. 56), 226, 254 (n. 17), 294 (n. 70), 300, 321 (n. 16, 17), 374, 376, 377, 378

Election returns, certification of, 63–4, 68–9, 359, 375; defaced, 187, 189; disposed of, 78–9; double, 302; dubious, 92 (n. 26); see also Elections, disputed; first returned, 235; missing, 53 (n. 11, 34), 108, 164, 189, 209 (n. 93), 321 (n. 17), 375; reporting of, 81, 227–8; see also Ballots, Indentures, Votes

Elections, by Acclamation, see Voice Vote; date of first, 58, 90 (n. 5); descriptions of, 56, 74, 75, 84–5, 243–4, 269–70, 288, App. III, No. 2, App. IV, App. VII, 376, 377; see also Duport, Prideaux; disorders in, 58, 60, 63–4, 70, 74, 75–7, 82–6, 269–70, 288, App. III, Nos. 1–2, App. IV; disputed, 48–9, 58, 63–5, 66–9, 70, 72–7, 81, 83, 86, 92 (n. 26), 99, 107, 108–9, 111, 139–40, 184, 188–9, 227, App. I, No. 2, App. IV; dispute predicted, 108, 280, 302; freedom of, 57, 60, 77, 80, 86, 90, 98, 106, 130, 139–40, 143, 183–5, 191, 198, 202, 214, 215, 223–4, 234, 277, 281, 297, 300, 328, 329–30, 341, 350, 355; influence in, interference in, see Bishops, Chancellor, Colleges, Heads of Colleges, King, Vice-Chancellor; intimidation in, 76, 201, 233–4, 358, 359; right to vote in, easily determined, 86; success in assured, 121, 199–200, 225, 226, 233, 362; success in, not assured, 108, 193, 201–2, 224; success in, notified, 103, 105, 193, 198, 214, 235; uncontested, 70, 139, 142 (n. 28), 183–4, 327, 345–6, 348 (n. 48); examples of uncontested, 49, 103, 105, 106, 114, 121, 200, 235, 288, 296, 300, 329 (n. 16); see also Voting, unanimity of; without notice to candidates, 97–8, 103, 189, 198, 235, 345; see also De modo eligendi, Petitions

Elections, 1603/4: 40, 49; C.U., 58, 63, 68; 1614: C.U., 48–9, 63–5, 66–8, 72, 74, 81, 83, 86, 92 (n. 26), 227; O.U., 48–9; 1620/1: C.U., 97–8, App. III; O.U., 75; 1623/4: 103; 1625: C.U., 105–6; O.U., 105; 1625/6: C.U., 107–8; O.U., 68–9, 70, 72, 73, 75–7, 83, 86, 107, 108–9, 111, App. IV; 1627/8: C.U., 113–14; O.U., 114–16; 1640: S.P., 121; L.P., C.U., 146–8; L.P., O.U., 144–6; 1653: N.P., 184, 185; 1654: 184; C.U., 187; O.U., 67, 188–9; 1656: 184; C.U., 189, 227; 1658/9: 191–2; C.U., 192–4, 224; O.U., 194; 1660: C.U., 198–200, 227–8, 341; O.U., 72, 200–2, 224, 329; 1661: 231; C.U., 235; O.U., 231–4; 1678/9: C.U., 83, 261–6; O.U., 266–70; 1679: C.U.,

Elections—*continued*
 276–80; O.U., 280–2; *1680/1*: C.U., 287–8; O.U., 288; *1685*: 296; C.U., 296–7; O.U., 296; *1688/9*: 299–300; C.U., 301–3; O.U., 300–1; see also By-elections

Electoral procedure, 77; lack of information about, 56, 60, 75, 374, 376, 377, 378; in Laudian Statutes, 77–8; no statutes for, 58, 60; suggested by *De Burgensibus*, 56–7; unknown in first election, 58; see also Chancellor (election of), Convocation (minutes of), Elections (descriptions of), Vice-Chancellor (election of), Votes, Voting

Electors, 262; age of, 62, 84; forced to vote, 227, 270; list of, 78–9, 86; number of, 226–7, 341, 347 (n. 32); see also Votes (number of); qualifications of, 60–2, 66, 86, 89; refusal to vote of, 227, 234; see also Bachelors, etc.

Eliot, Sir John, 106, 108, 115, 116, 118, 119, 120, 125 (n. 46), 132, 135, 138

Ellesmere, Thomas Edgerton, Lord, Lord Chancellor, Chancellor of Oxford, 30, 49, 375

Engagement, the, 178 (n. 65), 194, 220

Escott, Daniel, 232–4

Establishment, see Church of England

Exclusion Bill, 243, 245, 250, 257 (n. 70), 261, 271, 273, 283, 284, 285, 286, 287, 289, 290, 291, 294 (n. 63), 309, 323 (n. 67), 327, 342; see also Whig Party

Exton, Sir Thomas, Master of Trinity Hall, 273, 286, 298, 299, 301, 321 (n. 30), 330, 335, 370; election of, 262, 263, 265, 274 (n.12), 277, 278, 279, 280, 287, 294 (n. 70), 302, 329, 330, 371, 372; political views of, 265, 271, 275 (n. 35), 293 (n. 49), 297, 326, 339, 340

F

Fairclough, old Mr., 192, 206 (n. 46)

Fairwell, Col. Arthur, 296–7, 320 (n. 6), 328

Falkland, Lucius Cary, Lord, 155, 160, 161, 162

Fanshawe, Sir Richard, 243, 251, 331, 333, 334, 335, 341, 345, 346 (n. 1), 370; election of, 231, 235, 344; political views of, 231, 237, 339–40

Fell, Fel, Dr. John, Bishop of Oxford, Dean of Christ Church, 268, 269, 270, 281, 298

Fiennes, Hon. Nathaniel, 88, 181 (n. 128), 184, 206 (n. 33, 39, 40), 213, 215, 217, 332, 368; political views of, 189, 190–1, 218, 222, 237, 340

Finch, Daniel, 2nd Earl of Nottingham, 257 (n. 72), 270 ("D. F."), 302, 304, 321 (n. 35), 322 (n. 49), 323 (n. 79), 324 (n. 113), 325 (n. 130)

Finch, Hon. Edward, 302, 303, 304, 321 (n. 35), 328, 329

Finch, Sir Heneage, later Earl of Nottingham, 231, 235, 237, 243, 251, 252, 253, 255, (n. 31, 33), 305, 315, 331, 332, 333, 334, 337, 339, 345, 347 (n. 18), 370; election of, 182 (n. 138), 231–4, 254 (n. 1), 328, 330, 344, 348 (n. 45); political views of, 235–6, 236, 237–9, 255 (n. 25), 260 (n. 120), 266, 274 (n. 24), 339, 340; see also Lord Chancellor

Finch, Hon. Heneage, later Earl of Aylesford, 248, 274 (n. 30), 302, 320, 324 (n. 83, 113), 325 (n. 122), 331, 332, 333, 334, 335, 336, 339, 347 (n. 18), 370; election of, 95 (n. 59), 255 (n. 37), 266–70, 274 (n. 17, 19, 20, 24, 27), 300, 328, 344; political views of, 271–2, 275 (n. 35), 293 (n. 49), 309, 310, 311–13, 314, 316, 317, 318, 321 (n. 26), 323 (n. 67, 81), 324 (n. 82, 90), 325 (n. 130), 326, 327

Francis, Father Alban, 66, 302, 305, 322 (n. 63), 342

G

Gentry, burgesses belonging to, 40, 137–8, 216–17, 223, 332–3

Glanville, Serjeant Sir John, 34–5, 130, 164, 179 (n. 90), 205 (n. 27), 228 (n. 1), 230 (n. 28)

Goddard, Dr. Jonathan, 184, 185–6, 188, 210 (n. 107), 212, 213, 215, 216, 221, 223, 228 (n. 1), 229 (n. 4), 368; political views of, 186–7, 219, 220, 340

Gooch, Dr. Barnaby, Master of Magdalene, 102–4, 134, 136, 225, 330, 340, 365; election of, 63–4, 65, 92 (n. 26), 97, 140, 142 (n. 28), 227

Gore, William, 199, 200, 209 (n. 87), App. VI

Gremials, as burgesses, 63, 72, 198, 199, 213–15, 326, 335, 373; two not wanted, 215, 362; paucity of, 134; preferred, 65, 193, 214, 278, 280, 302, 328–30, 341; lack of distinguished, 339; see also Residence

H

Hale, (Sir) Serjeant Matthew, 172, 198, 212, 213, 215, 216, 217, 221, 222, 223, 305, 369; election of, 194, 201–2, 225; political views of, 194–5, 197, 215, 218, 220, 340

Halifax, George Savile, Marquis of, 245, 256 (n. 61), 284, 285

Halton, Dr. Timothy, Vice-Chancellor of Oxford, 281, 288, 293 (n. 33)

Harvard University, Mass., 15, 222

Heads of Colleges, as burgesses, 43, 63, 64, 65, 108, 136, 143, 185, 187, 188–9, 212, 262, 281, 282, 287, 329, 333; as candidates, 63, 140, 146, 194, 232–3, 243–4, 254 (n. 2), 266, 267–8, 278, 279, 280; as governors of universities, 24, 57, 58, 68 (Caput), 69, 83, 84, 85, 203, 233, 373; influence of, in elections, 58–60, 63, 64, 65, 67, 70, 81, 91 (n. 9), 99, 106, 146, 223–4, 227, 263–4, 268, 287, 355; see also Blithe, Fell, Holbeach, Turner, Whichcot; nomination by, 58, 71, 147–8, 232, 233, 362

Hearth Tax, Chimney Money, 238, 244, 251, 252–3, 259 (n. 112), 300, 305, 312, 315, 317, 337, 338

Hide, unidentified, 252, 256 (n. 50), 259 (n. 113)

High Church, 106, 117, 152, 167, 246, 318, 323 (n. 73), 340; see also Laudian Church

Holbeach, Dr. Thomas, Master of Emmanuel, 265, 274 (n. 11)

Holland, Henry Rich, Earl of, Chancellor of Cambridge, 121, 136, 147, 150, 158, 181 (n. 115)

Honorary Freemen, university electors as, 87, 342

Hood, Dr. Paul, Vice-Chancellor of Oxford, 146, 200

Hopkins, Henry, 147, 148

Humphrey, Dr. Lawrence, Vice-Chancellor of Oxford, 27

Hyde, Edward, 259

Hyde, Hon. Lawrence, later Earl of Rochester, 236, 241–2, 250, 252, 253, 256 (n. 50, 54), 259 (n. 113, 117), 260 (n. 120), 266, 315, 324 (n. 113), 331, 332, 333, 334, 335, 336, 337, 339, 347 (n. 21), 370; election of, 70, 231–4, 267, 328, 330, 344; political views of, 236, 242–3, 255 (n. 27), 256 (n. 56), 257 (n. 72), 287, 293 (n. 46), 324 (n. 113), 339, 340

Hyde, Lawrence, 252, 256, 259

I

Impeachment, 100, 249, 257 (n. 70), 258 (n. 90), 271–2, 284, 289–90; see also Bennett, Buckingham, Clarendon, Danby, Eden, Laud, Strafford

Incorporation, statutes of, 25, 26, 32, 61, 120, 322 (n. 56); see also Charters

Indentures, 57, 68–9, 70, 81, 93 (n. 36), 270, 358, 363

Independents, 167, 171, 184, 194, 221; see also Puritans

Indulgence, Declaration of, 237, 238, 240, 247, 256 (n. 39)

Instrument of Government, 184, 188

J

James I, 46, 47, 50, 51, 55 (n. 40), 101, 104, 105, 107, 109, 110, 129, 133, 137, 156, 175 (n. 16), 229 (n. 13); advowsons granted by, 21, 37 (n. 3), 91 (n. 14); his confirmation of De modo eligendi, 60, 99, 224, App. III, No. 1; his grant of university representation, 13, 16, 21, 29, 30, 32, 34, 35, 36, 38 (n. 26), 58, 59, 88, 97, 99, 211, 278, 292 (n. 15), 351, App. II, 356; his influence in elections, 65, 90, 97–8, 99, 103; not the inititator of university representation, 21–2, 30, 35, 36; his interest in universities, 21, 29, 37 (n. 2), 105, App. I; his relations with Sir Robert Naunton, 65, 97–8, 102, 103, 104–5, 123 (n. 4), 225, 360; and religious conformity, 21, 23, 38 (n. 27)

James II, 66, 296, 298, 299, 300, 301, 302, 303, 304, 308, 309, 310, 311, 315, 316, 317, 318, 319, 320 (n. 7), 321 (n. 24), 342; see also York

Jenkins, Sir Leoline, Lionel, 282, 287, 294 (n. 63), 298, 329, 331, 332, 333, 334, 335, 337, 341, 373; election of, 95 (n. 59), 281–2, 288, 296, 329, 330, 371; political views of, 282–4, 286, 288–91, 293 (n. 49), 294 (n. 81), 296, 326, 327, 330, 335, 339, 340

Juniors, 83, 84, 85, 91 (n. 13), 270, 298; see also Masters, Regents

K

King, 21, 22, 24, 33, 46, 48, 57, 70, 77, 88, 90, 98, 101, 119, 157, 176 (n. 38), 211, 216, 220, 226, 229 (n. 13), 283, 304, 305, 315; his influence in elections, 57, 130, 214, 276, 296, 329, 349, 350, (Chas. I), 106, 113, 121, (Chas. II), 263, 276–9, 287, 292 (n. 12, 20), 297, 326, 327–8, 329, (Jas. II), 300; see also Court candidates, Recommendation; see also Court, Crown

King's Ministers, 98, 174 (n. 6); see also Crown officers, Privy Councillors

Knights, burgesses as, 40, 109, 137–8, 142 (n. 25), 197, 216–17, 236, 332, 341, 347 (n. 14, 16)

Knollys, Sir Francis, 27

L

Lambe, Sir John, 121, 142 (n. 28)

Lamphire, Dr. John, Principal of Hart Hall, 70, 204 (n. 5), 266–7, 268, 269, 270, 274 (n. 27), 329

Lamplugh, Dr. Thomas, 232–3

Lampoons, 236–7, 248, 255 (n. 25, 26), 258 (n. 93), 347 (n. 15); see also Blacklists, Pensioners

Lane, James, 281–2, 293 (n. 31), 328, 344

Langbaine, Dr. Gerald, Provost of Queen's, 170, 172–3, 229 (n. 13)

Laud, William, Archbishop of Canterbury, Chancellor of Oxford, 149, 151, 152, 154, 156, 170, 174 (n. 2), 176 (n. 43), 195; as Chancellor of Oxford, 57, 69, 83, 84, 85, 95 (n. 71), 120, 154; election of, 73, 99; his interference in elections, 60, 121, 128 (n. 115), 144–6, 174 (n. 1)

Laudian, Church, 149, 152, 154, 157, 159, 167; see also High Church; Code, 60, 78, 92 (n. 17), Statutes, 57, 67, 69, 77, 80, 84, 96 (n. 77), 120; see also Statutes (Oxford)

Lawyers, see Civil lawyers, Common Law lawyers

Leicester, Robert Dudley, Earl of, Chancellor of Oxford, 21, 24, 27

Lenthall, Sir John, 201

Lenthall, William, 72, 73, 88, 181 (n. 128), 190, 200–1, 209 (n. 90, 91), 224

Letters Patent, 16, 21, 33, 58, 59, 61, 67, 68, 88, 278, 292 (n. 15), 341, 342, 352, App. I, II; see also De Burgensibus

Lord Chancellor, 27, 30, 49, 231, 236, 255 (n. 25), 266–70, 271–2, 274 (n. 20, 24), 303, 321 (n. 26), 351

Lucas, Henry, 122, 132, 136, 137, 142 (n. 24), 144, 166, 167, 168–9, 174, 176 (n. 31), 180 (n. 112), 198, 211, 213, 215, 217, 222, 228 (n. 1), 229 (n. 14), 355 (n. 2), 367; election of, 121, 142 (n. 28), 143, 146–8, 218; political views of, 121, 150–1, 158, 167, 169, 178 (n. 65), 208 (n. 79), 220, 340

Lucasian Chair of Mathematics, 134, 151, 169, 222, 229 (n. 14), 302

M

Magdalen College, Oxford, 315, 342

Manchester Commission, 170, 180 (n. 101), 181 (n. 112)

Marten, Sir Henry, 120, 121, 127 (n. 99), 134, 136, 137–8, 149, 367; election of, 89, 114–15, 130, 214, 234; political views of, 118–19, 127 (n. 100), 132, 340

Marvell, Andrew, 255 (n. 25, 26)

Mason, Robert, 113–14, 127 (n. 81), 142 (n. 28)

Masters of Arts, as burgesses, 114, 136, 213, 331; considered residents, 64–5; definition of, 61, 62, 91 (n. 13, 15, 17); as electors, 57, 61, 62, 69, 72, 77, 80, 82, 84, 85, 92 (n. 20), 121, 130, 188, 201, 205 (n. 24), 224, 244, 269, 321 (n. 35), 356, 358, 359; as witnesses of elections, 68, 363; see also Juniors, Regents

Mead, Joseph, 71–2, 99, 106, 107, 109, 110, 111, 112, 113, 123 (n. 20), 126 (n. 53), 140, 183, 374, 376, 377

Middle Ages, universities in, 15, 22, 24, 37 (n. 6), 61, 62, 73, 82, 84

Mills, Dr. John, 203, 204, 207 (n. 57), 212, 213, 215, 216, 229 (n. 3), 330, 368; election of, 194, 201, 224, 329; political views of, 184, 192, 194, 197, 220, 229 (n. 18), 340

Monck, Christopher, Duke of Albemarle, Chancellor of Cambridge, 296–7, 320 (n. 7), 328

Monck, Gen. George, later Duke of Albemarle, 209 (n. 90), 296, 297, 301, 314, 320 (n. 6), 334; election of, 198–200, 208 (n. 81), 224, 225, 228, 228 (n. 1), 345, 362

Monmouth, James Scott, Duke of, 257 (n. 69), 272, 279, 291 (n. 3), 292 (n. 9), 297, 298, 309, 320 (n. 4); as Chancellor of Cambridge, 261–5, 276, 277, 280, 292 (n. 12), 326, 328, 343

Montague, Edward, later 1st Earl of Sandwich, 88, 199–200, 215, 225, 227, App. VI

Montague, George, 209 (n. 98)

Montague, Sir William, 200, 202–3, 204, 209 (n. 89, 98), 212, 215, 216, 217, 218, 369

Montague, unidentified, 202, 203, 204

More Burgensium, 58, 59, 60, 90 (n. 6); see also Elections (freedom of)

Morgan, Sir Anthony, 192–3, 206 (n. 46), 216

Morton, Sir Albertus, 130, 136, 137, 329, 340, 366; absence of, 132, 141 (n. 8); choice of seats by, 106, 125 (n. 44), 140, 225; election of, 105, 106, 124 (n. 41), 142 (n. 28)

Mountlowe, Dr. Henry, 40–4, 46, 47, 53 (n. 13), 88, 94 (n. 44), 134, 136, 141 (n. 16), 142 (n. 24), 330, 364

N

Nalson, Dr. John, 271, 272, 273, 275 (n. 33)

Naunton, Sir Robert, 116, 124 (n. 35), 125 (n. 46), 126 (n. 75), 130, 131, 134, 135, 136, 140, 142 (n. 19), 365; absence of, 98, 99, 102, 103, 104–5, 123 (n. 5), 132, 141 (n. 8), App. V; election of, 65, 97–8, 99, 103, 104–5, 106, 107–8, 126 (n. 51, 53), 329, 345, 360, 365, 366

Neville, Dr. Thomas, Dean of Canterbury, 29, 30, 38 (n. 26), 351

Newton, (Sir) Isaac, 66, 144, 222, 308, 309, 312, 320, 321 (n. 35), 322 (n. 39), 332–3, 334, 336, 337, 338, 339, 340, 349, 372; election of, 302, 303, 325 (n. 133), 328, 329; his letters to Covell, 303–8, 309, 310, 311, 315, 337, 379; political views of, 302–3, 323 (n. 73), 327, 339

Nicholas, Sir Edward, Secretary of State, 113, 162, 163, 178 (n. 80), 232, 254 (n. 1), 293 (n. 31)

Nicholas, Dr. John, Vice-Chancellor of Oxford, 270

Nicholas, John (?), 232–4, 254 (n. 1), 293 (n. 31)

Nominated Parliament, 184, 185–7, 188; universities threatened by, 186, 204 (n. 10)

Nomination, of candidates, 57, 60, 70–1, 73, 82, 213, 214, 345; by Chancellor, see Chancellor (influence of); declined, 147, 200, 201–2, 225, 228 (n. 1), 287; double, 232, 328, 329–30; by electorate, 70–1; by Heads of Colleges, 58, 71, 147–8, 232, 233, 362; by King, see Recommendation; in Letters Patent, App. II, III; meaning of word, 93 (n. 41); offered, 199–200, 201–2, 225, 267, 287, 288, 301, 345, 362, App. VI; withdrawn, see Desisting; without notice, 147, 189, 225, 235, 345; see also Elections; by Vice-Chancellor, see Vice-Chancellor (influence of); see also candidates, court candidates, Recommendation

Northampton, Henry Howard, Earl of, Chancellor of Cambridge, 59, 64, 65, 82, 140

O

Oaths, of allegiance and supremacy, 304–9, 310, 311, 312, 315, 316

Oldisworth, Michael, 115–16, 127 (n. 87), 142 (n. 28), 182 (n. 136), 234, 330

Oldys, Oldish, Dr. William, 282, 298, 321 (n. 16), 328, 329, 345, 348 (n. 47)

Opposition Party, 106, 115, 118, 119, 132, 133, 139, 156, 263, 340; see also Country party, Court, Parliamentarian party, Whig Party

Orange, Princess Mary of, 259 (n. 95), 303; as Queen, 303, 309, 314, 323 (n. 73, 81)

Orange, Prince William of, 284, 299, 300, 305, 309, 310, 314, 322 (n. 65); see also William III

Ormonde, James Butler, Duke of, Chancellor of Oxford, 266, 267, 268, 270, 271, 274 (n. 13, 19, 20), 281, 292

(n. 28), 293 (n. 31, 33), 298, 328, 343, 379

Owen, Dr. John, Vice-Chancellor of Oxford, 194, 210 (n. 107), 211, 213, 215, 216, 217, 221, 222, 223, 228 (n. 1), 229 (n. 3), 368; elected and disabled to sit, 67, 184, 188–9, 205 (n. 23, 24, 26), 212, 223; political views of, 186–7, 219, 220, 340

Oxenden, Dr. George, 304

Oxford, City of, 22, 25, 96 (n. 77), 160, 161, 162, 163, 179 (n. 90), 181 (n. 112), 219, 238, 325 (n. 120), 342, 378; see also Boroughs

Oxfordshire, 96 (n. 80), 100, 135, 137, 184, 185, 204 (n. 4)

Oxford University, see Convocation, Universities

P

Page, Sir Thomas, Provost of King's, 279

Palmer, Dr. John, Warden of All Souls, 194

Paman, Dr. Henry, 277, 278, 292 (n. 15)

Papists, 149, 240, 246, 250, 281, 298; see also Catholics

Parkins, Sir Christopher, Dean of Carlisle, 41

Parliament, absences from 98, 99, 102, 103, 106, 124 (n. 28), 132–3, 141 (n. 8), 148–9, 150, 161, 163, 184, 190, 191, 235, 242, 254 (n. 21), 275 (n. 35), 298, 335, 336, App. V; burgesses' previous experience of, 43, 138, 139, 218, 334–5; burgesses disabled to sit in, 50, 184, 205 (n. 27), 212; burgesses excluded from, 190; see also Naunton, Pride's Purge; burgesses expelled from, 99, 100–2, 150, 156, 174, 208 (n. 79), 318–19, 320, 343; members' attendance at universities, 54 (n. 21), 129–30; and regulation of universities, 31, 166–7, 168, 170–3, 180 (n. 101, 102, 107), 181 (n. 112, 126, 128), 191, 209 (n. 91), 211, 378; relations with universities, 22, 23, 31–3, 111–12, 166; and university franchise, 32–3, 342–3; university interests in, see University interests; see also Nominated Parliament, Statutes

Parliamentarian party, 35, 100, 132, 149, 152, 158, 159, 163, 165, 166, 167, 201, 218, 219; see also Opposition Party, Puritans

Parliamentary wages, 88–9, 114–15, 252, 342

Parrott, Dr. Charles, 286–7, 293 (n. 34), 294 (n. 63), 298, 335, 339, 346 (n. 1), 371; election of, 282, 288, 296, 329,

26

Parrott—*continued*
330, 344, 371, 372; political views of,
326, 329, 340
Peers, once university burgesses, 137,
332; sons of, as burgesses, 217, 332,
341; as voters, 62, 80, 92 (n. 19)
Pembroke, William Herbert, 3rd Earl
of, Chancellor of Oxford, 76, 88, 105,
107, 111, 114–16, 126 (n. 62), 127
(n. 87), 182 (n. 136), 234, 330
Pembroke, Philip Herbert, 4th Earl of,
Chancellor of Oxford, 115, 145–6, 172,
174 (n. 6), 182 (n. 136)
Pensioners, 246, 248–9, 255 (n. 27),
256 (n. 56), 258 (n. 81), 259 (n. 95, 97),
273 (n. 9), 293 (n. 49), 321 (n. 27),
323 (n. 67), 326, 339, 340; see also
Blacklists, Lampoons
Pepys, Samuel, 88, 92 (n. 20), 199, 374,
379
Perceval, John, 268–9
Perrott, see Parrott
Petition of Right, 117, 118, 133
Petitions, of universities, 26, 88, 167,
168, 170, 175 (n. 19), 180 (n. 125),
187, 190, 191, 198, 203, 308; regarding elections, 75, 76–7, 82, 83, 108,
188–9, 278, 280, App. IV; for university representation, 24–9, 32, 33,
36, 63
Petty, Sir William, 194, 204 (n. 5), 207
(n. 55)
Physicians, as burgesses, 185, 193–4, 201,
204 (n. 5), 212, 213, 267, 331
Placet, and *non-placet*, 73, 76, 83, 95
(n. 62), 357
Plural votes, 86–8, 96 (n. 76, 77, 80);
see also Boroughs (university influence in)
Pocket boroughs, 57, 90, 141, 226, 266,
273 (n. 4), 328, 350
Pocock, Dr. Edward, 170, 171, 181
(n. 130)
Poll, university, day of, 67–8, App. III,
No 1; hour of, 80–1, 95 (n. 63), 121,
189, 269, 303; postponement of, 95
(n. 66), 269; see also Elections
Popery, 44, 171, 236, 247–8, 249–50, 271,
273, 287, 294 (n. 75), 314, 337; see also
Catholicism
Popish Plot, 240, 245, 250, 261, 272, 286,
287, 290
Pot Companions, Potmen, 94 (n. 45),
244, 270, 282, 298, 348 (n. 40); see also
Blackpot men, Treating
Precedence, Oxford before Cambridge,
45, 55 (n. 41), 102, 105, 129, 180
(n. 103), 251; university before town,
251
Presbyterians, 156, 167, 171, 194, 200,
218, 220, 246; see also Puritans
Prideaux, Humphrey, 268, 274 (n. 24),
280–1, 374

Prideaux, Dr. John, Vice-Chancellor of
Oxford, 108–9, 146; his account of
election of 1625/6, 62, 75–7, 83, 92
(n. 18), App. IV
Pride's Purge, 150, 155, 156, 158, 165
Privy Council, 75, 116, 118, 120, 122,
140, 159, 258 (n. 82), 276, 277, 280,
284, 285, 291 (n. 3); clerk of, 97, 99;
see also Council of State
Privy Councillors, university burgesses
as, 46, 51, 52, 75, 97, 99, 100, 103, 104,
105, 107, 116–18, 118–19, 120–1, 122,
123 (n. 3), 125 (n. 51), 136, 140, 148,
215, 282, 284–5, 289–90, 330, 333,
340; see also Crown Officers
Proctors, 24, 43, 62, 68, 69, 70, 71, 73,
74, 77, 78, 80, 81, 82, 85, 89, 92 (n. 20),
95 (n. 64), 96 (n. 72), 358, 359, 363,
373
Property Qualification, exemption from,
of burgesses, 89–90, 338, 343; of
electors, 89
Protector, 90, 157, 189, 199, 220, 349; see
also Cromwell, Oliver and Richard
Puritanism, 23, 27, 44, 170, 173, 218
Puritans, Puritan party, 26, 27, 131, 145,
146, 153, 155, 158, 165, 167, 169, 171,
174, 175 (n. 22), 211, 218, 222, 223,
229 (n. 17); see also Covenant, Cromwellians, Dissenters, Independents,
Parliamentarians, Presbyterians

Q

Quo Warranto, 296, 309, 313, 317, 321
(n. 24), 342

R

Read, Dr. Thomas, 145
Recommendation, of candidates, 70,
345; by Chancellor, 70, 76, 82, 105,
107, 114, 115, 145, 231–2, 234, 238,
261, 265, 266–7, 274 (n. 13, 19, 20),
277, 278–9, 281, 292 (n. 28), 293 (n. 31,
33), 296–7, 298, 321 (n. 13), 326, 355,
358; double, 114–16, 231–2; by King,
59, 70, 199, 263, 276, 277–9, 300, 326,
329; by others, 196, 200, 201, 224, 263,
264, 266, 287–8, 292 (n. 12, 20), 356,
358; see also Candidates, Nomination
Recruiters, 179 (n. 91), 193
Recusants, 21, 100, 116, 117, 119; see also
Catholics
Redinge, Ridding, Richard (?), App. III,
No. 2 (n. 3)
Re-election, 218, 330; examples of, 75,
97, 103, 108, 109, 114, 121, 143, 147,
201, 204, 262, 272, 273 (n. 8), 277, 288,
291, 296, 297, 298–9, 320, 325 (n. 133),
327, 329, 345, 346, 365–7, 369–72

Regents, House of, 84, 91 (n. 12); see also Senate

Regents, and non-Regents, 61, 69, 81, 83, 84, 91 (n. 12, 13), 94 (n. 51), 227, 373; see also Juniors, Masters

Register, Registrary, 74, 81, 91 (n. 10), App. III, No. 2, 358, 359, 363

Religious Conformity, 21, 23, 25, 27, 38 (n. 27), 42–3, 112, 119–20, 238, 240, 251, 266, 347 (n. 26); see also Covenant

Religious Toleration, 220, 240, 278, 285

Rescripts, 57, 67, 70, 81

Residence, as qualification, for burgesses, 62–6, 70, 82, 134–5, 213–15, 278, 280, 292 (n. 15), 302, 328–30; for electors, 62, 92 (n. 20, 21), 227, 362; see also Gremials

Roe, Sir Thomas, 122, 143, 144, 148–9, 150, 158–64, 174 (n. 2), 175 (n. 17, 19, 20), 191, 198, 212, 213, 215, 216, 217, 222, 230 (n. 21), 367; election of, 143, 144–6, 174 (n. 6, 10); his letters, 144, 159–63, 378; political views of, 143, 144, 145, 146, 158–63, 165, 166, 218–19, 220, 284–5, 340

Roundheads, 157; see also Parliamentarians, Puritans

Royalists, 35, 121, 131, 148, 155, 158, 159, 160, 161, 163, 164, 166, 169, 194, 195, 196, 200, 201, 207 (n. 54), 218, 219, 220, 231, 236, 243, 246, 328, 340; see also Cavaliers, Court, Tory Party

Rump, the, 151, 157, 165, 174, 177 (n. 55), 198, 208 (n. 79)

Rushworth, John, 257 (n. 71)

Russell, Lord, 309, 312, 316

Russell, Sir Francis, 192, 206 (n. 46)

S

Sadler, John, Master of Magdalene, 185, 187, 188, 204 (n. 4), 212, 213, 214, 215, 216, 217, 218, 222, 228 (n. 1), 340, 368

St. John, Oliver, Chief Justice, Chancellor of Cambridge, 192, 193, 199, 206 (n. 47), 213, 225, 227, 228, App. VI

St. Mary's Church, Oxford, 69, 93 (n. 37), 359

Sancroft, William, Archbishop of Canterbury, 261–5, 276–80, 329; as Chancellor of Cambridge, 301, 304, 306, 321 (n. 31)

Sandys, Sir Miles, 51–2, 55 (n. 47), 88, 134, 136, 137, 140, 225, 365; election of, 49, 52, 63, 64, 65, 67, 68, 70, 72, 74, 75, 81, 82, 83, 97, 142 (n. 28), 214, 227, 343; political position of, 52, 340

Savile, Henry, 245

Sawyer, Sir Robert, 259 (n. 111), 306, 307, 311, 312, 320, 325 (n. 133), 333, 334–5, 336, 337, 347 (n. 16), 372; election of, 277, 279, 288, 301–2, 303, 320, 328, 329, 345; expulsion of, 313, 317, 318–19, 320, 324 (n. 90), 325 (n. 130, 134), 343; political views of, 292 (n. 9), 308–10, 314, 316, 317, 323 (n. 65, 67, 70, 73), 324 (n. 96), 327, 339

Scholars, 65, 82, 86–7; as electors, 57, 61–2, 90 (n. 16); see also Electors

Sclater, Dr. (Sir) Thomas, 87, 197, 198, 199, 212, 213, 215, 216, 217, 222, 229 (n. 3), 329, 342, 369; election of, 193–4, 207 (n. 49), 214, 262–3, 265–6, 344, 345; political views of, 194, 197, 207 (n. 54), 218, 219, 220, 229 (n. 4), 266, 340

Scrutiny, 73, 74, 75, 76–8, 80, 86, 94 (n. 51), 115, 269–70, 282, 288, 357, App. VII; see also Division, Voting

Seal, used in elections, 68, 69, 77, 81, 270, 358, 359, 363

Secret Ballot, see Ballots

Selden, John, 119, 132, 140, 141, 143, 144, 148, 164, 174, 177 (n. 55, 56), 180 (n. 99), 194, 198, 212, 213, 215, 216–17, 221–2, 223, 230 (n. 20), 349, 367; election of, 143, 144–6, 176 (n. 1, 6, 10), 215, 226; political views of, 118, 119, 132, 151–7, 159, 163, 165, 167, 177 (n. 59), 179 (n. 90), 187, 218, 219–20, 340; his services to university, 144, 157, 166, 168, 169–74, 181 (n. 126, 130), 182 (n. 137, 138), 211, 378

Senate, of Cambridge University, 57, 58, 84, 85, 306, 342; composition of, 60–2, 87; elections in, 69, 71, 81, 87, 89, 147, 189, 227, 279, 329; its place of meeting, 69; time of meeting of, 80; see also Electors, Regents

Seven Bishops, the, 300, 310

Shaftesbury, Anthony Ashley-Cooper, Earl of, 245, 256 (n. 61), 258 (n. 93), 309

Sheriff, 57, 64, 67, 68, 70, 81, 89, 101, 164, 322 (n. 43), 352, 353, 355, 356

Sidney, Algernon, 309, 312

Sidney, Henry, 277, 279, 280, 284, 374, 379

South, Dr. Robert, 205 (n. 23, 24, 26)

Southwell, Sir Robert, 259 (n. 97), 268

Spelman, Sir Henry, 128 (n. 116), 147–8, 225, 345

Spencer, Dr. Robert, 281, 292 (n. 29), 328

Stanhope, Sir Edward, 29, 30, 38 (n. 26), 351

Statutes, Parliamentary, regarding general elections, 41, 60, 68, 70, 93 (n. 40); regarding universities, 24, 31–3, 107, 129, 351; regarding university representation, 14, 15, 32–3, 342–3; see also Incorporation, Parliament, University interests

Statutes, of the universities, 24, 25, 31, 34, 57, 58, 59, 60, 67, 73, 74, 80, 83, 84, 95(n. 62), 166, 213; Oxford Statutes, of 1636, 90 (n.1), 120; see also Laudian Statutes,

Steward, Dr. Nicholas, 40, 41, 42, 43, 44, 47, 53 (n. 13), 88, 106, 136, 364

Steward, Sir Simeon, 106, 142 (n. 28)

Stewart, Sir Francis, 126 (n. 64), 133, 134, 135, 137, 142 (n. 24), 225, 366; election of, 70, 72, 73, 75–7, 107, 108–9, 126 (n. 62), 140, 142 (n. 28), 146, 357–8; political views of, 109–11, 132, 340

Strafford, Thomas Wentworth, Earl of, 132, 151, 152, 158, 176 (n. 36, 38), 177 (n. 62), 195

Stubbs, Henry, 201

Suffrages, 74, 76, 83, 225, App. III, No. 2; see also Ballots, Votes

T

Taxation, universities' exemption from, 48, 102, 166, 169, 191, 252, 253

Tellers, in elections, 75, 78, 269, 270, 282, App. VII

Temple, Sir William, 51, 284–7, 291 (n. 3), 331, 333, 334, 335, 336, 338, 341, 371; election of, 276–80, 287, 291 (n. 2), 292 (n. 12, 20, 21), 301, 302, 327, 328, 329, 339, 340; political views of, 284–5, 326, 327

Ten mile limit, for candidates, 73, 344

Test Act, 239, 240, 247, 299

Thurloe, John, 184, 194, 198, 207 (n. 54), 212, 213, 215, 216, 217, 219, 223, 225, 331, 347 (n. 12), 369; election of, 192–3, 206 (n. 47), 207 (n. 49, 50), 214, 215, 216, 224, 227; political views of, 195–7, 208 (n. 64, 73), 220, 340

Thynne, Thomas, later Viscount Weymouth, 251, 256 (n. 61), 257 (n. 67), 259 (n. 115), 321 (n. 20), 332, 333, 334, 335, 336, 370; election of, 72, 78, 243–4, 256 (n. 63), 267, 344, 363; political views of, 231, 237, 244–5, 257 (n. 69, 70, 71, 72), 293 (n. 49), 326, 339, 340

Thynne, Thomas, M.P. for Wiltshire, 244, 256 (n. 61), 257 (n. 66, 69, 70)

Tillotson, Dr. John, Dean of Canterbury, 279, 287, 292 (n. 20)

Tory Party, 219, 236, 243, 245, 255 (n. 27), 257 (n. 72), 265, 284, 291, 293 (n. 37, 49), 295 (n. 81), 297, 299, 309, 310, 311, 314, 316, 318, 323 (n. 67), 325 (n. 133), 326, 327, 330, 339, 342, 348 (n. 40); see also Cavaliers, Court, Royalists, Trimmers

Tory sentiment, in universities, 73, 243, 245, 257 (n. 72), 264, 267–8, 283, 296

Treating, as election practice, 72, 201, 224, 244, 262, 344, 348 (n. 40)

Trimmers, 284, 327, 339

Trinity College, Dublin, 13–14, 30

Trinity Hall, Cambridge, 158, 168, 173, 180 (n. 109), 220

Tudor era, universities in, 24

Turner, Dr. Francis, Vice-Chancellor of Cambridge, 251, 302; his correspondence, 262, 276, 322 (n. 51), 344, 377, 379; his influence in elections, 262–5, 278–80, 292 (n. 12, 21), 329, 342

U

Universities, attendance at, of M.P.s as a whole, 129–30; burgesses' attendance at, 65, 66, 135, 212, 213, 223, 331–2; and the boroughs, 22–3, 24, 25, 28, 31, 33–5, 114, 251–2, 300, 338, App. III, No. 2; Charters of, see Charters, Incorporation; and the Crown, 22, 32–3, 88, 112, 166, 342; ejections in, 24, 26, 166, 168, 171–2, 180 (n. 109), 194, 199, 203, 204, 210 (n. 107), 219, 220, 229 (n. 4), 231; finances of, 24, 168–9, 170, 181 (n. 115), 203; general government of, 56–7; men from, in Parliament, not university burgesses, 16, 45, 54 (n. 21), 129–30, 338; officials of, 85, 112, 135; see also Chancellor, etc.; and Parliament, 22, 23, 31–3, 111–12, 166; political sentiments of, 21, 98–9, 139, 140, 143, 146–7, 166, 183–4, 199, 200, 234, 238, 253, 263–4, 274 (n. 11), 278, 296–7, 299–300, 303–4, 315, 326–7, 339–40; exemption of, from Property Qualification Act, 89–90, 338, 343; reform of, 36, 107, 167; regulation of, 31, 166–7, 168, 170–3, 180 (n. 101, 102, 107), 181 (n. 112, 126, 128), 191, 209 (n. 91), 211, 378; see also Statutes; exemption of, from taxation, 48, 102, 166, 169, 191, 252, 253; in Tudor era, 24

University College, Oxford, 309

University interests, in Parliament, 16, 44–5, 50, 104–5, 106, 107, 108–9, 111–12, 119–20, 122, 129–30, 166–73, 186–7, 187–8, 190, 191, 197–8, 203, 211, 238, 239–40, 247, 250–3, 287, 294 (n. 63, 75), 298, 303–9, 310–11, 312, 315, 336–8, 347 (n. 26), 349, 355; defended by other than university burgesses, 16, 36, 45, 48, 129–30, 167, 180 (n. 103), 202, 209 (n. 91), 337, 338; neglected by university burgesses, 16, 36, 107, 113, 188, 197, 211, 214, 234, 237–8, 242, 250–1, 252–3, 337–8

University Press, 113, 119, 126 (n. 78), 240, 251, 259 (n. 109), 282, 307, 334, 338

University Representation, abolition of, 13, 15, 17; conditions leading to desire for, 22–4; granting of, see *De Burgensibus*, Letters Patent; ignored by historians, 13, 36, 56, 374, 375, 377; in the Middle Ages, 15, 22; outside England, 13–15; recent interest in, 13; sought for self-protection, 24, 32, 33–5, 36; see also Petitions; as useful to Crown, 15, 16, 21, 22, 35, 97, 130, 133, 211 266, 271; the two universities compared, 136–7, 138, 140, 223, 327, 339–40, 341, 347 (n. 32); value of, 16, 36, 39 (n. 40); 129–31, 211–12, 222–3, 239, 336–8, 349–50; see also Burgesses

University seats, compromise in filling of, 108, 115, 121, 130, 191–2, 214–15, 234, 297, 329–30; number of, 14, 25, 26, 28, 29, 184, 185, 188, 191, 205 (n. 19), 206 (n. 43); prized, 49, 64, 106, 123 (n. 1), 125 (n. 44), 140–1, 147, 189, 193, 199, 200, 202, 225–6, 230 (n. 28), 344–5, 348 (n. 45); rejected, 65–6, 97–8, 106, 147, 198, 200, 225, 297; see also Elections

V

Venetian agents, reports of, 108, 126 (n. 79), 159, 160, 186, 196, 360

Vernon, Col., Edward (?), 280–1, 292 (n. 28), 344

Vernon, James, 272–3, 332, 333, 335, 347 (n. 16), 371; election of, 261–5, 274 (n. 11, 12), 277, 278, 297, 328, 329, 331, 343, 344; political views of, 261, 272–3, 275 (n. 35), 326, 327, 339

Vice-Chancellors, acting or deputy, 43, 63, 65, 66, 68; as candidates, 63, 67, 188, 205 (n. 24), 228, 352; charges against, 68–9, 108–9, 152, 167, App. IV; correspondence of, 170, 198, 202, 225, 235, 261, 262, 265, 276, 277, 278, 279, 281, 288, 292 (n. 12), 296, 302, App. I; see also Covell, Turner; court rights of, 27, 28, 103, 166, 168, 180 (n. 119), 359; election of, 57, 58–60, 91 (n. 10), 224, App. III, No. 1; financial accounts of, 87, 88, 89; as governors of university, 57, 61, 63, 65, 83, 85, 171, 187, 192, 220, 251, 294 (n. 63), 303, 304, 306, 311, 322 (n. 49), 335; their influence over elections, 57, 74, at Cambridge, 58–9, 147, 300, 355, at Oxford, 83, 86, 108–9, 121, 200 224, 227, 233, 264, 269–70, 279, 302, 343; as presiding officers, 69–71, 80–6, 269, 346, 348 (n. 49), App. IV, VII; as returning officers, 64–5, 68–9, 81, 358, 359, 363; as voters, 61, 80

Visitors, university, 26, 127 (n. 87), 128 (n. 110), 166, 168, 170, 173, 180 (n. 101), 185, 186, 187, 188, 191, 194, 204, 210 (n. 107), 211, 220, 222, 229 (n. 4, 18), 378

Voice Vote, 73, 75, 76, 77, 86, 357; see also Acclamation

Voters, see Electors

Votes, counting of, 78–80; see also Division, Scrutiny, Tellers; recording of, 78–80, App. VII; see also Election (records), (returns); reporting of, 81, 227–8; number of, 79, 81, 189, 198, 207 (n. 49), 234, 243, 244, 269, 270, 274 (n. 27), 282, 294 (n. 70), 303, 321 (n. 16), 363; plural, 86–8, 96 (n. 76, 77, 80); see also Ballots

Voting, order of, 62, 80, 95 (n. 62); secrecy of, 73–4, 78–80, 94 (n. 51); unanimity of, 71, 146, 174 (n. 10), 192, 198, 199–200, 207 (n. 49), 225, 226, 233, 235, 254 (n. 17), 269, 280, 301, 346; see also Elections (uncontested)

Voting papers, 79, 92 (n. 21), 303; see also Ballots

W

Wake, Sir Isaac, 103, 104, 116, 130, 132, 133, 134, 136, 329, 340, 366

Walker, Obadiah, 299, 309

Westminster Assembly, 155, 173, 176 (n. 41), 177 (n. 48), 182 (n. 141), 230 (n. 20)

Wheelocke, Abraham, 147, 148, 225

Wheler, Sir Charles, 239, 253, 257 (n. 75), 258 (n. 82), 330, 333, 336, 337, 339, 341, 347 (n. 16), 370; election of, 231, 243, 262, 263, 266, 273 (n. 8), 274 (n. 12), 277–8, 280, 327–8, 345; political views of, 237, 245–51, 258 (n. 81, 90, 92, 93), 259 (n. 95, 97), 273 (n. 9), 339, 340

Whichcot, Dr. Benjamin, Provost of King's, his election correspondence, 192–3, 206 (n. 47), 213, 214, 223–4, 329

Whig Party, 261, 262, 265, 272, 273, 288, 289, 292 (n. 9), 296, 305, 309, 316, 318, 321 (n. 27), 323 (n. 67), 324 (n. 112, 116), 325 (n. 135), 326, 327, 330, 339, 342, 348 (n. 40); see also Exclusion Bill

Whitelocke, Sir Bulstrode, 35, 107, 197, 208 (n. 73)

Whitgift, John, Vice-Chancellor of Cambridge, Archbishop of Canterbury, 27, 33, 44, 74, 83, 84, 375

Widdrington, Sir Thomas, 194, 229 (n. 3)

William III, 273, 304, 305, 315, 318, 327; see also Orange

William and Mary, joint sovereigns, 303, 309, 314, 323 (n. 73, 81)

William and Mary College, Virginia, 14–15

Williams, John, Lord Keeper (later Bishop of Lincoln and subsequently Archbishop of York), 103, 125 (n. 46)

Williamson, Joseph, later Sir, 254 (n. 1), 266, 267, 268, 293 (n. 34); his election correspondence, 231–4, 248, 249, 256 (n. 63)

Windebanke, Sir Francis, 121–2, 132, 135, 136, 137, 148, 174 (n. 2, 6), 208 (n. 64), 367; election of, 120–1, 128 (n. 113, 115), 130, 144–6, 214; political views of, 122, 132, 145, 146, 228 (n. 1)

Wood, Anthony, his view of university representation, 16, 36, 338; his opinions cited, 83, 132, 163–4, 167, 172, 186, 194, 201, 205 (n. 4), 219–20,

222, 231, 232, 234, 236, 241, 244, 252, 253, 254 (n. 14), 257 (n. 69), 260 (n. 120), 267, 270, 281–2, 287, 298

Worthington, Dr. John, 121

Wray, Sir Christopher, 26

Wren, Sir Christopher, 243–4, 345, 363

Writs, for university elections, 35, 58, 59, 63, 64, 68, 70, 77, 90 (n. 3), 101, 106, 125 (n. 44), 164, 179 (n. 91), 189, 205 (n. 27), 269, 296, 298, 352, 363

Y

Yerbury, Will, 267, 268

York, James, Duke of, 220, 243, 247, 250, 257 (n. 69), 283; see also James II

STUDIES PRESENTED TO THE INTERNATIONAL
COMMISSION FOR THE HISTORY OF
REPRESENTATIVE AND PARLIAMENTARY
INSTITUTIONS

(*Études présentées à la Commission internationale
pour l'histoire des Assemblées d'états*)

I. *Histoire des Assemblées d'états*, with preface by A. Coville, in *Bulletin of the International Committee of Historical Sciences*, Vol. IX, fasc. IV, no. 37, 1937, pp. 409–73.

II. *L'Organisation corporative du Moyen Age à la fin de l'Ancien Régime*, with preface by A. Coville, in *University of Louvain. Recueil de Travaux publiés par les Membres des Conférences d'Histoire et de Philologie*, 2e série, 44e fasc. Louvain, 1937. In-8º, XVI–98 pp.

III. *L'Organisation corporative du Moyen Age à la fin de l'Ancien Régime*, with preface by A. Coville, in *University of Louvain. Recueil de publiés par les Membres des Conférences d'Histoire et de Philologie*, 2e série, 50e fasc. Louvain, 1939. In-8º, XII–265 pp.

IV. J. Verhavert, *Het ambachtswezen te Leuven* [Les Corporations de métiers à Louvain sous l'ancien régime], with summary in French, in *University of Louvain. Recueil de Travaux d'Histoire et de Philologie*, 3e série, 2e fasc. Louvain, 1940. In-8º, IV–210 pp.

V. C. J. Joset, *Les Villes au Pays de Luxembourg (1196–1383)*, in *University of Louvain. Recueil de Travaux d'Histoire et de Philologie*, 3e série, 5e fasc. Louvain, 1940. In-8º, 236 pp., with one map.

VI. E. Lousse, *La Société d'Ancien Régime. Organisation et représentation corporatives*. Vol. I of *University of Louvain. Recueil de Travaux d'Histoire et de Philologie*, 3e série, 16e fasc. Bruges-Louvain-Paris, 1943. In-8º, VIII–376 pp.

VII. *L'Organisation corporative du Moyen Age à la fin de l'Ancien Régime*, with preface by E. Lousse, in *University of Louvain. Recueil de Travaux d'Histoire et de Philologie*, 3e série, 18e fasc. Louvain, 1943. In-8º, XVI–296 pp.

VIII. A. Darquennes, *De juridische structuur van de Kerk volgens Sint Thomas van Aquino* [La Structure juridique de l'Église d'après saint Thomas d'Aquin], with preface by E. Lousse and a summary in French, in *University of Louvain. Recueil de Travaux d'Histoire et de Philologie*, 3e série, 32e fasc. Louvain, 1949. In-8º, XVI–228 pp.

IX. A. Marongiu, *L'Istituto parlamentare in Italia dalle origini al 1500. Senato della Repubblica, nel centenario del parlamento italiano (1848–1948)*, with a preface by S. E. Iv. Bonomi, President of the Senate of the Italian Republic. Milan or Rome, A Guiffrè, 1949, In-8º, XVI–328 pp.

X. H. G. Richardson and G. O. Sayles, *The Irish Parliament in the Middle Ages*, University of Pennsylvania Press, Philadelphia, Penna. 1952. 400 pages.

XI. *IXe Congrès International des Sciences Historiques*, Paris, 1950, *University of Louvain. Recueil de Travaux d'Histoire et de Philologie.* 3e série, 45e fasc. Louvain, 1952. In-8º, 279 pp.

XII. J. van der Straeten, *Het Charter en de Raad van Kortenberg* [La Charte et le conseil de Kortenberg], Vol. I, in *University of Louvain. Recueil de Travaux d'Histoire et de Philologie*, 3e série, 46e fasc. Louvain, 1952. In-8º, L–300 pp.

XIII. J. van der Straeten, *Het Charter en de Raad van Kortenberg* [La Charte et le conseil de Kortenberg], Vol. II, appendices (sources) and summary in French, in *University of Louvain. Recueil de Travaux d'Histoire et de Philologie*, 3e série, 47e fasc. Louvain, 1952. In-8º, 266 pp.

XIV. J. S. Roskell, *The Commons in the Parliament of 1422: English Society and Parliamentary Representation under the Lancastrians.* Manchester, 1953.

XV. Millicent Barton Rex.

XVI. Catherine Sims. Edition of *Expedicio Billarum Antiquitus*, Louvain.

XVII. *Medieval Representative Theory and Practice: Essays by American Members of the Commission.* Medieval Academy of America, Cambridge, Mass., U.S.A.

DATE